DATE DUE

SECOND EDITION

Psychological Intervention and Cultural Diversity

Edited by

Joseph F. Aponte
University of Louisville

Julian Wohl
Professor Emeritus of Psychology, University of Toledo

Allyn and Bacon

Boston ■ London ■ Toronto ■ Sydney ■ Tokyo ■ Singapore

Executive Editor: Becky Pascal
Series Editorial Assistant: Susan Hutchinson
Manufacturing Buyer: Megan Cochran

Copyright © 2000, 1995 by Allyn & Bacon
A Pearson Education Company
Needham Heights, MA 02494

Internet: www.abacon.com

Library of Congress Cataloging-in-Publication Data

Psychological intervention and cultural diversity / edited by Joseph
  F. Aponte, Julian Wohl. — 2nd ed.
     p. cm.
   Includes bibliographical references and index.
   ISBN 0-205-29474-X (alk. paper)
   1. Minorities—Mental health services—United States.   2. Cultural
psychiatry—United States.   3. Psychiatry, Transcultural—United
States.   4. Cross-cultural counseling—United States.   I. Aponte,
Joseph F.   II. Wohl, Julian.   III. Psychological interventions and
cultural diversity.
   [DNLM: 1. Mental Health Services—United States.   2. Minority
Groups—psychology—United States.   3. Ethnic Groups—United States.
4. Psychotherapy—methods—United States.   WA 305 P9738 2000]
RC451.5.A2P79   2000
362.2'086'930973—dc21
DNLM/DLC
for Library of Congress   99-37811
                                              CIP

Printed in the United States of America

10   9   8   7   6   5   4   3   2   1   03   02   01   00   99

CONTENTS

PREFACE

In prefacing the first edition of *Psychological Intervention and Cultural Diversity,* we noted a dramatic change in the conception of America as a melting pot that would produce a common American product out of the national, ethnic, and cultural differences among immigrants and other culturally varied people. We asserted that, in the closing decades of the twentieth century, a decidedly different condition prevailed: Cultural pluralism was recognized as a fact and celebrated as a value. Furthermore, we observed that mental health professionals, increasingly encountering "nontraditional" clients, were forced to examine and critique the assumption that their theories and methods of intervention were universally applicable. The conduct of clients or patients who seemed different, who did not seem to grasp what therapists were attempting to do with them, who seemed unappreciative of their sincere efforts to be useful, and whose inability or reluctance to "play by our rules" befuddled and exasperated the best therapists, could no longer be dismissed as "psychopathology." It became incumbent upon mental health service providers to adapt to the huge increase in members of minority groups who needed our services and could benefit from them, were we to deliver them appropriately.

The mental health professions are coming to recognize their obligation to prepare students to work with a far more culturally diverse population. Academic and clinical programs, although still not yet near the level that will be required in the twenty-first century, have begun the effort. Concurrently, a body of literature is being developed to accompany it. This book is another of several that have appeared in the last quarter of the twentieth century that attempt to provide students and practitioners with theoretical understanding and practical suggestions for dealing with a clientele whose lifestyles, ways of conducting themselves, communication modes, and manifestations of psychological disorder may be different from what they have previously encountered. That a second edition now appears not only attests to the continuing need for materials, but also suggests the rapidity of change in this expanding professional domain.

Although a number of changes are introduced in this edition, what have not changed are the minority groups comprising its subject matter. They are the groups, among many minorities in this country, that have been the most neglected and ill-served both by society at large and by the mental health professions: African Americans (Blacks), Asian Americans, Hispanics (Latinos/Latinas), and Native Americans (American Indians and Alaskan Natives). We recognize that preferences for the labels designating these groups vary geographically and even within the groups in any one area. The terms of reference in these chapters are those in common use and most generally understood. We reiterate also the point made in the first edition—that, although the term *minority* for some people has a pejorative connotation, such should not be taken here. We use the term in a statistical sense only. In the United States, each ethnic group is a minority in that no ethnic group comprises more than 50 percent of the national population.

As with the first edition, the chapters in this volume are not reprinted journal articles. All were prepared specifically for this book. Several chapters from the first edition were not included in order to make room for topics that seemed to us more germane to the interests and needs of practitioners and students. The subject of psychopathology and ethnicity is presented in a new chapter (3) by Draguns. New in this edition also is a consideration of the issues and problems presented by refugees and immigrants, increasingly noteworthy populations, discussed in Chapter 12 by Bemak and Chung. In another new chapter (16), Aponte and Johnson consider, as a special aspect of training, supervision problems in work with ethnic minorities. In addition to these completely new contributions, all the authors whose chapters appeared in the first edition have revised and updated their contributions to reflect more recent research and clinical thinking. Our intent is to be as close to the cutting edge of knowledge and theory as any text can be. In this way we hope, as we said in the earlier edition, to help students and practitioners develop and refine skills required to address the needs and problems of these clients and to further the progress of service delivery in this burgeoning domain.

ACKNOWLEDGMENTS

The coeditors would like to express their appreciation to Margaret L. Biegert and Laura R. Johnson for their contributions to various aspects of this book. In addition, the ideas and editorial comments of Catherine E. Aponte and Katherine Todd were particularly helpful on a number of chapters. Finally, we would like to thank our students, who have stimulated our thinking on the topic of diversity and who will find themselves working with diverse populations in one capacity or another.

ABOUT THE EDITORS
AND CONTRIBUTORS

Joseph F. Aponte is Professor of Psychology at the University of Louisville. He served as director of clinical psychology training at the University of Louisville for ten years, and chair of the department for three years. He is Puerto Rican and has been active in the Minority Post-Doctoral Fellows Program, National Research Council; he has chaired or served as a member of American Psychological Association committees focusing on the education, training, and delivery of mental health services to ethnic populations. He has presented and published a number of papers on the education and training of ethnic persons and on the education and training of majority students and service providers to work with ethnic populations.

Julian Wohl is Professor Emeritus of Psychology at the University of Toledo, where he served at different times as chair of the Psychology Department and director of the Clinical Psychology Training Program. For many years he taught a variety of graduate and undergraduate courses, and supervised clinical psychology graduate students in psychotherapy. He is a Diplomate in Clinical Psychology of the American Board of Professional Psychology. His intercultural experience includes Fulbright Lectureships in Burma (Myanmar) and Thailand. Dr. Wohl has taught in Hong Kong and participated in the founding of the Association of Psychological and Educational Counselors in Asia (APECA). He has lectured, written, and published on intercultural psychology.

About the Contributors

Catherine E. Aponte received her M.A. in clinical psychology from Duke University and her Psy.D. from Spalding University. She maintains an active private practice and is an adjunct clinical professor and coordinator of the Clinical Faculty at Spalding University, Louisville, Kentucky.

Fred Bemak, D.Ed., is an Associate Professor in Counselor Education at The Ohio State University. He has done extensive clinical supervision, research, writing, presentations, and consultation in the area of refugee and immigrant mental health. His work has focused on cross-cultural mental health and at-risk populations throughout the United States and in over 25 countries.

Howard F. Bracco received his Ph.D. in clinical psychology from the University of Kentucky. He has been involved in community mental health services since the mid 1960s and is in his twentieth year as president and CEO of Seven Counties Services, Inc., the largest community mental health center in Kentucky.

Julie Chen received her Ph.D. in industrial/organizational psychology from Colorado State University. She is a research associate at the Tri-Ethnic Center for Prevention Research in the Department of Psychology at Colorado State. Her research focuses on substance use among ethnic adolescents.

Rita Chi-Ying Chung, Ph.D., is an Assistant Professor in Counselor Education at The Ohio State University. Previously she was the Project Director for the National Research Center on Asian American Mental Health at UCLA and a consultant for the World Bank. She has written and done research extensively on immigrant and refugee adjustment, interethnic group relations, and cross-cultural mental health.

Chi-Ah Chun, Ph.D., is a postdoctoral fellow at the VA Palo Alto Health Care System and Stanford University School of Medicine. Dr. Chun received her Ph.D. in Clinical Psychology from the University of California in Los Angeles. Her research is on the role of culture in human adaptation and expressions of psychological distress, with a special focus on Asian Americans.

Ronald T. Crouch received his M.A. in sociology and M.S.S.W. from the University of Louisville, and his M.B.A. from Bellarmine College. He is currently Director, Kentucky State Data Center, University of Louisville, the official clearinghouse for the Census Bureau for the State of Kentucky.

Richard H. Dana, Ph.D., is University Professor Emeritus, University of Arkansas, Fayetteville. Earlier, he served in state and private universities as faculty member, Director of Clinical Training, departmental chair, and dean, publishing nine books on clinical psychology, personality assessment, and training as well as nearly 150 book chapters, monographs, articles, and reviews from 1953 to 1988. Since taking early retirement he has devoted his professional time to cross-cultural/multicultural mental health research, training, and consultation. In Oregon he was principal investigator (1989–1991), Minority Cultural Initiative Project, Research and Training Center, Regional Research Institute, Portland State University, and, since 1991, Research Professor (Honorary). He has also taught various courses and held seminars on multicultural mental health in Oregon and Lisbon.

Juris D. Draguns, Ph.D., is Professor Emeritus of Clinical Psychology at Pennsylvania State University. His focal interests in cross-cultural psychology are personality, psychopathology, psychotherapy, and counseling. He has coauthored and coedited several books on psychopathology and cross-cultural psychology including four editions of *Counseling Across Cultures,* and *Volume 6: Psychopathology* in the six-volume *Handbook of Cross-Cultural Psychology.* In addition to these publications, he has contributed many chapters to edited books, and has written numerous articles that have appeared in psychological, psychiatric, and anthropological journals.

Ruth W. Edwards, Ph.D., is a research scientist and Associate Director of the Tri-Ethnic Center for Prevention Research at Colorado State University. She is currently Principal

Investigator of both a grant from the National Institute on Drug Abuse addressing community-level factors and substance use among rural adolescents and a grant from the Centers for Disease Control concerned with prevention of intimate partner violence in rural and ethnic populations. Dr. Edwards was the principal investigator of a grant from the National Institute on Drug Abuse to develop The American Drug and Alcohol Survey, now used by over 200 school systems each year to assess drug and alcohol use among their students.

Kenneth K. Gee, M.D., is Unit Chief of the Asian Focus Inpatient Unit at San Francisco General Hospital and Assistant Clinical Professor at the University of California, San Francisco, School of Medicine. He received his B.A. in Chemistry from Brown University and completed medical school and psychiatric residency training at UCSF. He specializes in cross-cultural psychiatry, in particular, the inpatient care of the severely mentally ill Asian patients.

Ay Ling Han, Ph.D., works at Smith College's Counseling Service and School for Social Work (SCSSW). She provides training in group work, the clinician of color's professional challenges, and clinical work with diverse populations. She received awards from SCSSW Bertha Reynolds Summer Fellowship, Okura Mental Health Leadership Foundation, and APA Minority Fellowship Program.

Laura R. Johnson received her B.A. from the University of Mississippi, and her M.A. from the University of Louisville majoring in anthropology and psychology. She attended Kenyatta University in Nairobi and was a Peace Corps volunteer in Papija, New Guinea. Ms. Johnson is a graduate student in clinical psychology at the University of Louisville.

Laura P. Kohn, Ph.D., is currently an NRSA-funded Primary Care Research Fellow working in the Clinical Economics Research Unit and the Department of Psychiatry at Georgetown University Medical Center. Dr. Kohn received a Ph.D. in clinical psychology from the University of Virginia in 1996. Dr. Kohn's research has centered on determining the relationship between psychosocial issues, culture and ethnicity, family factors, and psychological outcomes including the development of psychiatric disorders in normative and non-normative populations.

Joan D. Koss-Chioino, Ph.D., is a Professor of Anthropology and an affiliate of the Women's Studies Department at Arizona State University. She is also Visiting Professor of Psychiatry and Neurology at Tulane Medical Center in New Orleans and a member of the Public Health Program faculty through the University of Arizona at which she directs the Program in Medical Anthropology. As a medical anthropologist Dr. Koss-Chioino works at the interface between anthropology, psychiatry, and psychology. Her primary interest is the treatment of illness and emotional problems, whether traditional, alternative, or psychotherapeutic in Latino cultures in the United States, Latin America, Spain, and Thailand. Currently she is completing treatment research with Mexican American youths and families in Arizona and is initiating a study of mood change and depression among older women in Andalucia, Spain.

Karen S. Kurasaki, Ph.D., is Associate Director of the National Research Center on Asian American Mental Health, University of California, Davis. She received her B.A. in psychology from the University of California, Berkeley, and M.A. and Ph.D. in clinical-community psychology from DePaul University, Chicago. Her research includes ethnic and racial identity, cross-cultural mental health, and community-based primary preventive youth and family interventions.

Trinda Lee, B.A., is a doctoral candidate in the Clinical Psychology program at the University of Virginia. She received her bachelor's degree from Amherst College in Amherst, Massachusetts. Her current research interests include parent involvement in children's education and single fathers' relationships with their children.

Barbara Plested is a research associate with the Tri-Ethnic Center and has worked extensively in provision of direct services to special populations. She has fifteen years of administrative and therapeutic services in both mental health and substance abuse. In this capacity, a primary role has been the development of policy and procedure as well as quality assurance issues. She has also been involved in the evaluation of treatment and prevention programs for the past six years.

Robin Young Porter, Ph.D., is a licenced clinical psychologist whose interests include child and adolescent psychotherapy, mental health issues of ethnic minority women and children, multicultural awareness and cultural diversity training, and stress management training for African American professionals. She currently engages in consultation and a full-time private practice in Louisville, Kentucky.

Stanley Sue, Ph.D., is Professor of Psychology and Psychiatry, Director of Asian American Studies and of the National Research Center on Asian American Mental Health, University of California, Davis. He received his bachelor's degree from the University of Oregon and his doctorate degree in psychology from the University of California, Los Angeles. Dr. Sue's research has been devoted to the adjustment of and delivery of mental health services to culturally diverse groups.

Randall C. Swaim received his Ph.D. in counseling psychology from Colorado State University in 1987. He is a research scientist at the Tri-Ethnic Center for Prevention Research in the Department of Psychology at Colorado State. His research focuses on cross-cultural epidemiology and etiology of adolescent substance use. He is currently supported by the National Institute on Alcohol Abuse and Alcoholism, examining alcohol use and related problems among Mexican American Youth.

Pamela Jumper Thurman, Ph.D., is a research associate with the Tri-Ethnic Center for Prevention Research and has conducted research in the areas of cultural issues related to ATOD, violence and victimization, rural women's concerns, and solvent abuse among youth. She currently serves as principal investigator for one component of the Center's NIDA grant to examine the factors related to solvent use among youth. She is also coprincipal investigator of a NIDA-funded grant that charts the trends in the epidemiology of drug use among American Indian youth who live on reservations. This project examines the rates for violence, victimization, and other related behaviors.

Melba J. T. Vasquez, Ph.D., is a psychologist in independent practice in Austin, Texas. She is a Fellow of the American Psychological Association, and holds the Diplomate from the American Board of Professional Psychology. She is the 1998–1999 President of Division 35, Psychology of Women, of the APA, and serves on the APA Policy and Planning Board. She is coauthor, with Ken S. Pope, Ph.D., of *Ethics in Psychotherapy and Counseling: A Practical Guide,* 2nd ed. (1998).

Melvin N. Wilson, Ph.D., is Professor of Psychology at the University of Virginia, Charlottesville. His research has focused on various aspects of family process and functioning in diverse African American families, and he has authored numerous papers on their extended-family structure. He is the principal investigator on the project titled "Cultural and Family Functioning Studies."

CHAPTER

1

The Changing Ethnic Profile of the United States in the Twenty-First Century

JOSEPH F. APONTE

RONALD T. CROUCH

Over the last several decades, census data have revealed significant changes in the number and distribution of culturally diverse populations, changes in immigration and migration patterns, and changes in ethnic group population characteristics (Aponte & Crouch, 1995; O'Hare, 1989; O'Hare & Felt, 1991; O'Hare, Pollard, Mann, & Kent, 1991). This chapter will identify and describe these changes among African Americans, Hispanics, Asian Americans, and American Indians, and within each of these groups. From this discussion will emerge a portrait of cultural diversity that will provide a context for assessment of the current mental health status and needs of these groups, and for the organization and delivery of mental health services and treatment of ethnic groups in this country as we move into the twenty-first century.

While it can be argued that American "racial" categories are too constrictive, illogical, confusing, and inconsistent, and may have adverse effects on ethnic group members (Betancourt & López, 1993; Phinney, 1996; Spickard, 1992; Yee, Fairchild, Weizmann, & Wyatt, 1993), others have argued for their usefulness (Helms & Talleyrand, 1997). Several standard categories for classifying ethnic groups will be used in this chapter. These categories are limited to those used by the U.S. Bureau of the Census and include Blacks, Hispanics, Asian Americans and Pacific Islanders, and American Indians, Eskimos, and Aleuts. Use of these categories is meant to communicate that these individuals have similar histories, traditions, and personal experiences. However, the rich diversity in individual differences that exist within each of these groups, as well as across these groups, must be recognized.

For purposes of this chapter, African Americans (this term will be used interchangeably with Blacks) are considered to be those individuals who identify their heritage as being of African descent (O'Hare, 1992). Non-Hispanic White and White also will be used interchangeably for brevity. Hispanics refer to those individuals who trace their cultural heritage

1

to Spanish-speaking countries in Latin America and the Caribbean, to Spain or Mexico, or to the southwest region of the United States, once under Spanish or Mexican control (del Pinal & Singer, 1997). Asian Americans include those individuals who identify their ancestry or country of origin as Asian (e.g., China, Japan, Korea, Vietnam, Thailand, Cambodia) or are from the Pacific Island region (e.g., Philippines, Samoa, Guam) (O'Hare & Felt, 1991). The last U.S. Bureau of the Census category includes those individuals who can trace their ancestry to American Indian, Eskimo, or Aleutian backgrounds.

Over the years the racial and ethnic categories used in the decennial census have been refined, reflecting the changing social climate and demographic profile of this country (O'Hare, 1992). The year 2000 census will usher in new changes in the type of multiracial/ethnic data collected (O'Hare, 1998). Gone are five previous categories. The new categories incorporate new labels (e.g., Black/African American, Spanish/Hispanic/Latino); and the single category Asian/Pacific Islander will be made into eleven. Respondents will also have the choice of checking off more than one category. The changes are an improvement over the 1990 census categories; however, they do not satisfy all groups and present problems with researchers who will have to grapple with unwieldy data tables and reduced comparability over time (O'Hare, 1998).

The following sections of this chapter, based on mid-decade census data, will provide information on the changing population base, background variations, place of residence, demographic characteristics, family structure and living arrangements, and socioeconomic status of the ethnic groups that are the focus of this book. It is important to recognize and understand the diversity that exists across and within these groups. Such diversity will be present regardless of the projections into the twenty-first century and will provide the context for providing mental health services to these populations.

Changes in the Number of Ethnic Persons in U.S.

According to the mid-decade census data there are 33,947,084 Blacks, 29,347,865 persons of Hispanic origin (of any race), 10,032,885 Asian and Pacific Islanders, and 2,322,044 American Indians, Eskimos, and Aleuts (U.S. Bureau of Census, 1996). Of the total U.S. population of 267,636,061, 27.3 percent (73,064,664) currently fall into the major ethnic categories identified above. Analysis by specific groups yields the following percentages of the total population: African Americans—12.6 percent, Hispanics—10.2 percent, Asian/Pacific Islanders—3.6 percent, and Indians/Eskimos/Aleuts—0.9 percent. Reference to Figure 1.1 indicates that these percentages represent only slight changes from the 1990 census data.

Rapid increases in the number and percentage of these ethnic persons over the last several decades, however, have been noted by a number of scholars and researchers (De Vita, 1996; Neighbors, 1989; O'Hare, 1989; O'Hare & Felt, 1991; O'Hare et al., 1991). These changes have served as a precursor for the dramatic changes that are anticipated by the year 2050 (see Figure 1.1). It is projected that the non-Hispanic White population will slowly grow until the year 2030, then slowly decline by the year 2050. The non-Hispanic White share of the population will steadily fall from 72 percent in the year 2000 to 60 percent in 2030, then to 53 percent in the year 2050 (U.S. Bureau of Census, 1996).

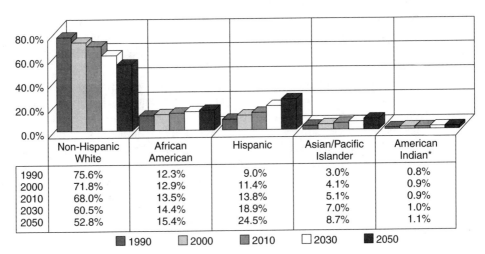

	Non-Hispanic White	African American	Hispanic	Asian/Pacific Islander	American Indian*
1990	75.6%	12.3%	9.0%	3.0%	0.8%
2000	71.8%	12.9%	11.4%	4.1%	0.9%
2010	68.0%	13.5%	13.8%	5.1%	0.9%
2030	60.5%	14.4%	18.9%	7.0%	1.0%
2050	52.8%	15.4%	24.5%	8.7%	1.1%

■ 1990   □ 2000   ■ 2010   □ 2030   ■ 2050

* Includes Eskimo and Aleutian Islanders.

FIGURE 1.1   Percent Distribution of the United States Population by Race for Selected Time Periods.

Of particular significance are the changes that are projected in the next century for the different ethnic groups. By the year 2030 it is projected that 14.4 percent of the population will be African American, 18.9 percent Hispanics, and 7.0 percent Asian/Pacific Islanders, and 1.0 percent will consist of American-Indians/Eskimos/Aleuts (U.S. Bureau of Census, 1996). By 2050, African Americans, Hispanics, Asian Americans/Pacific Islanders, and American Indians/Eskimos/Aleuts will comprise 15.4, 24.5, 8.7, and 1.1 percent of the population, respectively. The largest percent change in population will be in the Hispanic and Asian/Pacific Islander groups. By 2050, it is projected that there will be 62 million Hispanics, accounting for approximately 24 percent of the population (del Pinal & Singer, 1997).

Immigration accounted for most of the ethnic population growth during the last several decades (De Vita, 1996; O'Hare, 1992; Passel & Edmonston, 1992). Nearly 1 in 11 Americans is foreign born (U.S. Bureau of Census, 1997). Almost 3,000 immigrants arrive each day in the United States, and legal (immigrants, refugees, and nonimmigrants) and illegal (unauthorized) immigration adds approximately 1 million people per year to the U.S. population (Martin & Midgley, 1994). Some immigrants maintain dual citizenships, traveling regularly between their country of origin and the United States. Changing immigration laws and policies, unstable economic and political conditions, interethnic marriages, and wars have accounted for the increased immigration (Martin & Midgley, 1994; Thornton, 1992) and will continue to play an important role in the decades to come.

Recent immigration data indicate that from 1991 to 1993 there were 3,705,400 immigrants to this country (U.S. Department of Commerce, 1997). Most of these immigrants were from North America (51.2 percent) and Asia (30.0 percent), followed by Europe (11.8 percent), South America (5.1 percent), and Africa (2.5 percent). Most of the

North American immigrants were from Mexico (1,286,500), the Caribbean (337,000), and Central America (226,800); and most of the Asian immigrants were from Vietnam (192,700), Philippines (188,100), China (137,500), and India (121,900). The same immigration patterns will probably continue into the next decade.

These recent immigration patterns are reflected in the current racial and ethnic makeup of the U.S. foreign-born population. For example, 40 percent of the foreign-born population were Hispanic, while 6 percent of the native-born were Hispanic. Asians made up approximately 23 percent of the foreign-born, compared with only 1 percent of the native-born population (Martin & Midgley, 1994). The large number of foreign-born Hispanics helps keep fertility high among them since they tend to be younger than Whites. In addition, these immigration patterns—while ensuring diversity in communities—mean that oftentimes these foreign-born immigrants may not speak English fluently.

Variations within Ethnic Groups

Many view African Americans as being very similar, overlooking differences in cultural heritage (Baker, 1988), ethnic identity (Dana, 1993; McGoldrick, Pearce, & Giordano, 1982), family structure (Boyd-Franklin, 1990; Fullilove, 1985; Hardy, 1990), religious affiliation and spirituality (Dana, 1993; Gary, 1987), socioeconomic status (Bass, 1982), and geographical residence (O'Hare et al., 1991). There are a number of variables on which African Americans, as well as other ethnic groups, can vary (Aponte & Barnes, 1995; see Chapter 2 in this book). African Americans, however, are bound together by ancestral heritage and by their experiences with slavery, racism, discrimination, and oppression in this country (Atkinson, Morten, & Sue, 1998; Fleming, 1992; Howard & Scott, 1981).

Hispanics come from different countries and reflect a variety of migratory waves. Hispanics of Mexican ancestry account for 61.2 percent of Hispanic Americans, followed by Puerto Ricans (12.1 percent), Central and South Americans (10.7 percent), and Cubans (4.8 percent). Six percent of Hispanics are from Central American countries and 4.7 percent are from South America (del Pinal & Singer, 1997). Some Hispanics of Mexican ancestry can trace their origins prior to the settlement of the Southwest and the establishment of this country. Puerto Ricans have a special status because the Island is a commonwealth of the United States and this group is free to travel back and forth between Puerto Rico and the mainland United States.

Asian Americans are among the most diverse and one of the fastest growing of the ethnic groups in the United States. There were more than 29 Asian Ethnic groups enumerated in the 1990 Census (Lee, 1998). Some segments of this population have been in this country for many generations, whereas others are recent arrivals. The largest percentage of Asian Americans are Chinese (24 percent), followed by Filipinos (21 percent), Asian Indian (13 percent), Vietnamese (11 percent), Japanese (10 percent), and Korean (10 percent) (Lee, 1998). These groups, as well as more recent arrivals such as the Cambodians and Laotians, vary in age and have different cultural backgrounds, languages, religions, and socioeconomic status. The forces that have led many of these individuals to migrate to this country also vary from seeking economic opportunities to fleeing political oppression. It is projected that by the year 2050 the Asian American population is likely to exceed 32 million (Lee, 1998).

The American Indian population is also markedly diverse. There are more than 200 tribes in the United States alone, speaking one or more 200 different tribal languages (LaFromboise, 1988). According to Manson and Trimble (1982), there are 511 federally recognized native entities and an additional 365 state-recognized American Indian tribes. Despite these differences there is a common ethnic background tying American Indians together that is a product of historical experiences, legacy of conquest, and political ideology more than racial and cultural similarities (Deloria, 1992). Eskimos and Aleutians are more homogenous groups residing primarily in distinct geographical regions—the Alaskan Peninsula and the Aleutian Islands. These groups have closely related languages, race, and culture.

Where Ethnic Groups Live

At the beginning of the twentieth century approximately 90 percent of African Americans lived in the South (O'Hare, 1992; O'Hare et al., 1991). Difficult economic times in this region led to an exodus of African Americans to the Northeast and Midwest in the 1930s and 1940s. From 1970 to 1990 this trend reversed itself and continued into the late 1990s, with African Americans moving back to the South. The most recent data indicate that approximately 53.4 percent of African Americans reside in the South, 9.5 percent are in the West, and the remaining 37.0 percent are evenly split between the Midwest and Northeast (U.S. Department of Commerce, 1997) (see Figure 1.2).

Most African Americans continue to live in metropolitan areas and tend to be concentrated in the central parts of cities. According to the 1990 Census, 31 cities have Black

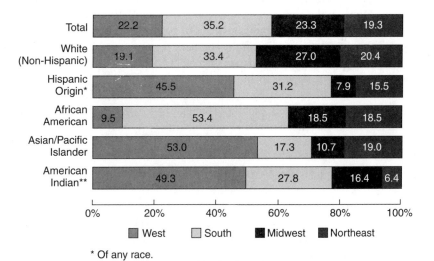

* Of any race.
** Includes Eskimo and Aleutian Islanders.

FIGURE 1.2 Percent Distribution of Race by Region in the United States for 1997.

populations of 100,000 or greater (O'Hare et al., 1991). Eight cities (Atlanta, Baltimore, Birmingham, Detroit, Memphis, New Orleans, Newark, and Washington) have populations that are greater than 50 percent African American. African Americans tend to reside in segregated neighborhoods within cities and suburbs (O'Hare et al., 1991). Although they have experienced a decline in residential segregation over the last two decades, they still remain more segregated than Hispanics and Asian Americans (Massey & Denton, 1987).

The various Hispanic groups' geographical distribution has been determined primarily by their historical origins and point of entry into the United States. Hispanics are concentrated in nine states: California, Texas, New York, Florida, Illinois, New Jersey, Arizona, New Mexico, and Colorado. Approximately 85 percent of Hispanics reside in these states (del Pinal & Singer, 1997). California has 9,900,000 persons of Hispanic origin and Texas has 5,700,000 (U.S. Bureau of Census, 1997). Most of the Hispanics in these two states are Mexican American. Puerto Ricans, the second largest Hispanic group, are concentrated primarily in the Northeast, particularly in the New York metropolitan area. Central and South Americans, although entering the United States typically through California, are found primarily in the Northeast, while Cubans are concentrated primarily in southern Florida.

Asian Americans historically, and at the present, are concentrated in the western region of the United States (see Figure 1.2). According to Lee (1998) and O'Hare and Felt (1991), 53 percent of the Asian population resided in the West. The largest concentration of Asian Americans can be found in California (3,800,000), followed by New York (952,736), Hawaii (748,748), Texas (532,972), and New Jersey (423,738). Most Asian Americans are concentrated in metropolitan areas; in 1996, this was the case for 94 percent of the Asian population. However, Asians tend to live in less segregated neighborhoods than Blacks and Hispanics (Lee, 1998).

American Indians, Eskimos, and Aleuts are found primarily in the southern and western regions of the United States (O'Hare, 1992; U.S. Bureau of Census, 1991; 1992b; 1992c). The most recent data indicate that 49.3 percent of this group is located in the western region and 27.8 percent live in the southern region (see Figure 1.2). Within the southern region most American Indians are located in Oklahoma (12.9 percent), and within the western region most American Indians are located in California (12.4 percent), Arizona (10.4 percent), and New Mexico (6.8 percent). Although most Eskimos and Aleuts reside in the Alaska Peninsula and Aleutian Islands, the groups can also be found in the sub-Arctic regions of Canada, Greenland, and Siberia.

Characteristics of the Ethnic Population

African Americans are younger than the United States population as a whole and younger than Whites in particular. According to recent census data the median age of Blacks was 29.2 years whereas Whites had a median age of 36.6 years (U.S. Bureau of Census, 1996). It is anticipated that these differences will continue to increase in the future. By the year 2030, it is projected that the median ages of Blacks and Whites will be 32.4 and 43.3 years, respectively. By the year 2050, the median age of Blacks and Whites will be 32.7 and 44.0 years, respectively (U.S. Bureau of Census, 1996). As the populations age however, the White population will age at a faster rate than the Black.

Compared with the total United States population, the Hispanic population is younger. The median age of Hispanics in 1995 was 26.3 years, which is less than both the Black and White median ages (U.S. Bureau of Census, 1996). Future population projections indicate that differences between Hispanics and Blacks will diminish. It is projected that by the year 2030 the median age of Hispanics will be 29.8 years in comparison to the 32.4 and 43.3 years of Blacks and Whites, respectively. By the year 2050 it is projected that the median age of Hispanics will be 31.0 years but that of Blacks and Whites will be 32.7 and 44.0 years, respectively (U.S. Bureau of Census, 1996). Thus, as the Hispanic population ages it will begin to look like the Black population, but will still be much younger than the White population.

Asian/Pacific Islanders fall in between Blacks and Whites in age. According to recent census data the median age of this group was 30.6 years in comparison to that of Blacks and Whites, which was 29.2 and 35.6 years, respectively (U.S. Bureau of Census, 1996). However, it must be remembered that recent immigrants from Southeast Asia are considerably younger than the more established groups such as Japanese and Philippines. Asian/Pacific Islanders will age at a more rapid rate than Blacks and Whites, so that by the year 2050 the median age for Asian/Pacific Islanders is projected to be 34.8 years in comparison to 32.7 and 44.0 years for Blacks and Whites, respectively (U.S. Bureau of Census, 1996).

American Indians/Eskimos/Aleuts also tend to be younger than Whites. Their median age in 1995 was 26.8 years and as such is almost identical to that of Hispanics (U.S. Bureau of Census, 1996). Future projections for American Indians/Eskimos/Aleuts are also similar to those of Hispanics. According to U.S. Census population projections, by the year 2030 the median age of these groups will be 30.4 years. By the year 2050 these groups will have a median age of 31.3, which is almost identical to the Hispanic median age of 31.0 years (U.S. Bureau of Census, 1996). Few changes in age between American Indians/Eskimos/Aleuts are projected for the years 2000, 2030, and 2050.

To obtain a better understanding of the age characteristics of the various ethnic groups, the 1990 Census data was clustered into eight categories (Aponte & Crouch, 1995). These categories consist of the following: (1) 0–4 years (preschool); (2) 5–13 years (childhood); (3) 14–17 years (adolescence); (4) 18–24 years (young adulthood); (5) 25–44 years (young families); (6) 45–64 (older families); (7) 65 years and above; and (8) 85 years and above. These categories correspond to well-established age categories and are reflective of periods during which specific major life changes, milestones, and a variety of stressful life events and experiences occur.

Reference to Table 1.1 indicates that all of the ethnic groups are younger than Whites. American Indians/Eskimos/Aleuts are the youngest with 34.3 percent 17 years of age or younger (preschool, childhood, and adolescence categories), followed by Hispanics (35.1 percent), Blacks (31.8 percent) and Asian/Pacific Islanders (29.3 percent). At the other end of the continuum, Whites are clearly older than the other ethnic groups, with 14.8 percent of this population at 65 years of age or older. Of particular note is the large White cohort (24.1 percent) that is in the 45–64 years-of-age group that will be moving into the elderly category. Recent projections of census data to the year 2050 indicate that the major ethnic groups will continue to age significantly, with Whites aging at higher rates than these groups.

TABLE 1.1   Percentage of Total, Age by Race for the United States in 1997.

Age Category (yrs)	Non-Hispanic White	African American	Hispanic	Asian/Pacific Islander	American Indian*
0–4	6.0%	8.8%	10.2%	8.2%	8.7%
5–13	11.7%	16.2%	18.0%	14.6%	17.4%
14–17	5.3%	6.8%	6.9%	6.5%	8.2%
18–24	8.9%	11.2%	11.7%	10.3%	11.8%
25–44	29.2%	30.5%	31.9%	33.4%	29.8%
45–64	24.1%	18.4%	15.2%	19.7%	17.3%
65+	14.8%	8.1%	6.0%	7.3%	6.9%
85+	1.9%	0.9%	0.6%	0.5%	0.9%

*Includes Eskimos and Aleutian Islanders.

Ethnic Group Birth Rates

Although birth rates (number of live births per 1,000 population) for both Blacks and Whites have declined significantly over the last several decades, the birth rate for Blacks is still higher than that for Whites (Ahlburg & De Vita, 1992; U.S. Bureau of Census, 1996). Differences in birth rates between African Americans and Whites can be accounted for primarily by socioeconomic status. Comparison of the same socioeconomic status cohorts reveals few differences between the groups (O'Hare, 1989; O'Hare et al., 1991). The most recent census data indicate that the birth rate for married Black couples has fallen nearly 50 percent since 1970. The percent of single Black women who have given birth has also been declining since 1989 and reached a yearly low of 40 percent in 1996 (U.S. Bureau of Census, 1996).

Hispanics currently have the highest birth rate of all ethnic groups (U.S. Bureau of Census, 1996). It is projected that this group's rate will remain stable until the year 2050 despite a declining birth rate since 1990 (U.S. Bureau of Census, 1996). This stability will in all likelihood be accounted for by the continuous flow of young female immigrants into this country being balanced by the aging of those Hispanic women of child-bearing age already here. Differences in birth rate also exist within Hispanic groups, with Cubans having the lowest fertility rates and Puerto Ricans and Mexican Americans having relatively higher rates (U.S. Bureau of Census, 1996).

The birth rates for Asian Americans/Pacific Islanders is the lowest of all the ethnic minority groups, although it is slightly higher than that of Whites. As previously mentioned, the rapid population growth that will continue in the future for this group is due primarily to immigration into this country from Asia and the Pacific Islands (De Vita, 1996; Lee, 1998; O'Hare & Felt, 1991). Asian Americans tend to wait longer to have children and to have fewer children than other ethnic groups. Within the Asian groups there is some variation, with the Vietnamese, Laotians, and Cambodians having higher birth rates than the other groups such as Chinese and Japanese. Most Asian American children are second-generation Americans, with more than 80 percent of them having a foreign-born mother (Lee, 1998).

American Indians/Eskimos/Aleuts have the highest birth rates of all the ethnic groups. The birth rates by 2050 are projected to be very similar to current figures (U.S. Bureau of Census, 1992a; 1992b; 1996). Thus, the differences in birth rates between this group and those of Whites and the other ethnic groups will continue to increase as we move into the twenty-first century as the birth rates for these other groups level off. Few differences in birth rates exist between American Indian, Eskimos, and Aleuts. There are insufficient data to predict whether these similarities will continue in the future.

Ethnic Group Mortality Rates

Life expectancy for African Americans and Whites has increased over the last several decades, and the gap in life expectancy between these two groups also has decreased during the same period (O'Hare et al., 1991; Soldo & Agree, 1988; Treas, 1995). Whites, however, continue to have a longer life expectancy at birth than Blacks (76.8 vs. 69.7 years) (U.S. Bureau of Census, 1996). Closer inspection of the available health statistics data yield important gender differences. The differences between Whites and Blacks become even more striking when male and female comparisons are made. White males have a life expectancy of 73.6 years, while Black males have a life expectancy of 64.8 years, a difference of 8.8 years. White females have a life expectancy of 80.1 years, whereas Black females have a life expectancy of 74.5 years, a difference of 5.6 years.

What accounts for these sharp differences in Black and White life expectancy rates? One major factor is the high infant mortality rate for Blacks (14.1 infant deaths per 1000 live births) in comparison to Whites (6.0) (National Center for Health Statistics, 1990). Additionally, Blacks have higher death rates for a number of illnesses. They are 3.4 times more likely than Whites to die of AIDS, 2.8 times more likely to die of kidney diseases, and 2.4 times more likely to die of diabetes than Whites. Another important contributor to the differences in life expectancy rates is homicides—the leading cause of death for young Black males. They are 7.6 times more likely to die by homicide than their White counterparts (Hammond & Yung, 1993; MacKellar & Yanagishita, 1995).

Family Structure and Living Arrangements

Household size varies among the ethnic groups. African American households are larger than White households but not as large as Hispanic households. The average Black household contained 2.9 persons in 1990 in comparison to 2.5 persons for Whites and 3.6 persons for Hispanics (O'Hare, 1992). Asian/Pacific Islanders households contained an average of 3.4 persons, whereas American Indian/Eskimo/Aleutian households contained 3.1 persons. The households of all of the ethnic groups were more likely to include other adults in addition to a married couple. However, Asian families in particular are more than twice as likely as Whites to live in extended families (Lee, 1998; O'Hare & Felt, 1991).

Marriage patterns for these ethnic groups are significantly different than those of Whites (Ahlburg & De Vita, 1992). Although divorce rates for ethnic groups and Whites has increased since the 1960s, the percentage of ethnic women who had never married increased dramatically in comparison to the figure for White women (O'Hare et al., 1991). Recent data indicate that 19.0 percent of White females, 42.0 percent of Black females, and 31.0 percent of Hispanic females had never married (U.S. Department of Commerce, 1997). Current data are not available for Asian/Pacific Islanders and American Indian/ Eskimo/Aleuts. These patterns are also reflected in households with children that were headed by females with no husband present (Bianchi, 1990; del Pinal & Singer, 1997). The percentages were 14.0, 47.0, 22.2, 10.1, and 28.7, respectively, for Whites, Blacks, Hispanics, Asian/Pacific Islanders, and American Indian/Eskimos/Aleuts (U.S. Bureau of Census, 1990).

Socioeconomic Status of Ethnic Groups

The socioeconomic status (SES) of ethnic groups has a direct impact on the goods, services, opportunities, and power that are available to individuals from these groups. Although the SES of most ethnic groups has improved over the last several decades, there still remains a significant gap between these groups and Whites (O'Hare et al., 1991). It is also important to recognize the differences in socioeconomic status that exists both across and within ethnic groups (De Vita, 1996; O'Hare & Felt, 1991; O'Hare et al., 1991). For example, although some groups—such as Asian Americans—have prospered, there are subgroups such as Laotians and Vietnamese that have not and who have remained at the low end of SES.

Several key variables can be viewed as constituting socioeconomic status: These include occupational status, income, and education (Adler et al., 1994). Each of these variables can be viewed as important in its own right. Gains have been made by almost all of the ethnic groups in each of these areas, yet many African Americans, Hispanics, Asian Americans, and American Indians still lag behind Whites in the types of jobs they have, the income they earn, and the educational levels they have achieved (De Vita, 1996; O'Hare & Felt, 1991; O'Hare et al., 1991). In addition, some of the gains experienced by these groups in such areas in the 1970s appear either to have leveled off or, in some cases, to have been reversed in the 1980s and 1990s.

Occupational Status and Opportunities

Although African Americans are one of the groups that made occupational strides in the 1970s, a comparison between this group and Whites indicates that clear disparities still remain (O'Hare et al., 1991). According to the 1990 census, whereas 27.1 percent of Whites were in managerial and professional positions, only 16.5 percent of Blacks were in the same positions (U.S. Bureau of Census, 1990; 1992b). At the other end of the continuum, 22.9 percent of Blacks were in semiskilled labor positions in comparison to 14.2 percent of Whites. Occupational patterns for Black women were similar to that for men, although the disparities were not as pronounced.

The labor market experience of Hispanic groups reflects the migration history of each group as well as the education, training, and English language skills of each group.

Hispanics tend to cluster in jobs that are lower-paying, less stable, and more hazardous occupations with little or no fringe benefits than for non-Hispanics (del Pinal & Singer, 1997). Occupational differences, however, exist within the Hispanic subgroups. For example, Cubans and U.S.-born Hispanics are much more likely than other Hispanics to have managerial, professional, technical, and administrative positions (del Pinal & Singer, 1997).

The overall distribution of occupations for Asian/Pacific Islanders is similar to that of Whites (O'Hare & Felt, 1991). About one-third of Asian Americans had high-level managerial and professional jobs, about the same as Whites, and well above the share for Blacks, Hispanics, and American Indians (Lee, 1998). These occupational data, however, mask striking differences within this group. Asian Indians, Japanese, and Chinese Americans have a high rate of managerial and professional positions (44, 37, and 36 percent, respectively), while more than 20 percent of Vietnamese and 37 percent of Southeast Asian Americans worked in low-skilled or unskilled jobs (Lee, 1998).

American Indian/Eskimos/Aleuts resemble African Americans at the higher occupational levels and Hispanics at the lower levels (O'Hare, 1992). Of particular importance is their concentration in the semiskilled and service positions, with 38.7 percent having occupations in these categories. Almost 4 percent of this group are engaged in farming and related occupations, which is reflective of the rural backgrounds of many members of this group. The high concentration of ethnic group members in these lower-level occupations has a direct bearing on the quality of career opportunities available to them and on individual and family income.

Levels of Income

Income levels were up and poverty down across all ages, races, and regions as a by-product of the improved economy of the mid-1990s in the United States. Striking disparities, however, can still be found across and within ethnic groups. According to recent census data, Asian/Pacific Islanders had the highest median household income ($45,249), followed by Whites ($38,972), Hispanics ($26,628), and Blacks ($25,050) (U.S. Bureau of Census, 1998). Such figures are misleading since Asian/Pacific Islanders and Hispanics tend to have more persons per household than other groups (O'Hare & Felt, 1991). The most dramatic changes came from Black families, with their median income jumping by 4.3 percent from 1996 to 1997.

The relative economic well-being of Asians/Pacific Islanders taken as a group does not reflect the subgroup differences within this broad ethnic category. For example, according to O'Hare and Felt (1991), the median family income of Chinese Americans was four times that of Laotians. Income levels for Asian Americans appear to be driven by residence and immigration status. Those Asian Americans living in high-cost areas—for example, Los Angeles, San Francisco, and Honolulu—may have higher salaries compared to other Asian Americans, but their living expenses would also be very high. Recent immigrants from China, Laos, Thailand, and Cambodia would tend to earn lower incomes than those Asian Americans who were born in the United States (Lee, 1998).

Reference to Figure 1.3 indicates that the poverty rates reflect the previously noted income differences. All ethnic groups had higher poverty rates than Whites (Bianchi,

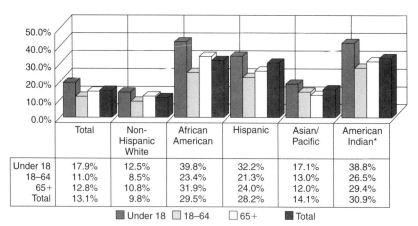

	Total	Non-Hispanic White	African American	Hispanic	Asian/Pacific	American Indian*
Under 18	17.9%	12.5%	39.8%	32.2%	17.1%	38.8%
18–64	11.0%	8.5%	23.4%	21.3%	13.0%	26.5%
65+	12.8%	10.8%	31.9%	24.0%	12.0%	29.4%
Total	13.1%	9.8%	29.5%	28.2%	14.1%	30.9%

■ Under 18   ▨ 18–64   □ 65+   ■ Total

* Includes Eskimo and Aleutian Islanders.

FIGURE 1.3   Percent Distribution of Poverty by Age for the United States by Race for 1997.

1990; O'Hare, 1992; U.S. Bureau of Census, 1990). These differences become even more dramatic when one focuses on those persons under 18 years of age. Whites in this age group had a poverty rate of 12.5, whereas Blacks, Hispanics, Asian/Pacific Islanders, and American Indian/Eskimo/Aleutian Islanders had rates of 39.8, 32.2, 17.1, and 38.8, respectively. The Asian/Pacific Islander group was the only ethnic group that came close to the Whites. High poverty rates tended to occur outside the West region, particularly the Northeast and Midwest, for Blacks and in the Northeast for Hispanics (Massey & Eggers, 1990).

Educational Status

Educational levels can serve as another indicator of socioeconomic status, because education provides access to income and economic opportunity in this country. Inspection of recent census data indicates that Blacks and Hispanics have experienced gains in educational attainment, whereas, as a group, Blacks, Hispanics, and American Indian/Eskimos/Aleuts are still more likely than Whites to have less than a high school education (see Figure 1.4). Young Black adults (25–29 years) who have completed high school have for the first time reached graduation rates of young White adults. Hispanics are the least likely to have a high school education while Asian/Pacific Islanders are almost identical to Whites (O'Hare, 1992), although striking differences exist within Asian groups and recent immigrants of the same group (Lee, 1998). At the other end of the continuum, Blacks, Hispanics, and American Indian/Eskimos/Aleuts are less likely to have a bachelor's degree or graduate and professional work. The highest percentage of college graduates are Asian/Pacific Islanders.

Ethnic youth present a number of problems in the occupational, economic, and educational domains. African American, Hispanic, and American Indian youth tend to be unemployed or underemployed. Since individuals from these groups tend to drop out of school early, they find themselves in the job market with limited skills. The positions they

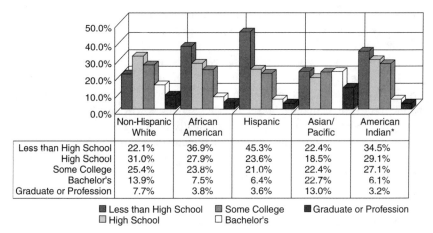

	Non-Hispanic White	African American	Hispanic	Asian/ Pacific	American Indian*
Less than High School	22.1%	36.9%	45.3%	22.4%	34.5%
High School	31.0%	27.9%	23.6%	18.5%	29.1%
Some College	25.4%	23.8%	21.0%	22.4%	27.1%
Bachelor's	13.9%	7.5%	6.4%	22.7%	6.1%
Graduate or Profession	7.7%	3.8%	3.6%	13.0%	3.2%

■ Less than High School ■ Some College ■ Graduate or Profession
□ High School □ Bachelor's

* Includes Eskimo and Aleutian Islanders.

FIGURE 1.4 **Percent Distribution in the United States Educational Levels by Race in 1997.**

do find tend to be in the service sector at or close to minimum wage. African American youth are particularly at risk, with unemployment rates over twice that of their White counterparts (U.S. Bureau of Census, 1992d). Patterns are thus in place at a very early age that prevent these individuals from obtaining an education and skills that will allow them to escape from poverty.

Implications for Mental Health Status and Delivery of Services to Ethnic Groups

What are the mental health status and service delivery implications in light of the changing ethnic group profile in this country? It is clear that the absolute number of African Americans, Hispanics, Asian Americans/Pacific Islanders, and American Indian/Eskimos/Aleuts continues to increase and that they will represent a larger percentage of the total population in the twenty-first century. Although the mental health service utilization patterns vary by ethnic group, there have been increased demands for these services by various ethnic groups (Cheung & Snowden, 1990). The increased numbers of ethnically diverse individuals will further tax the mental health system in this country, which many believe is underfunded, as members of these ethnic groups find their way into the mental health care delivery system.

These population changes and the resulting pressures on the mental health care delivery system will force mental health planners, administrators, and frontline workers to look more closely at how individuals from various ethnic groups present for treatment and are misdiagnosed (see Chapter 3). Standard types of psychological assessment devices will also need to be critically evaluated for their appropriateness and adequacy for use with ethnic individuals (see Chapter 4). Finally, the premature termination and unsuccessful treatment outcomes that ethnic persons experience in the mental health system will need to be closely examined in order for the system to be more responsive and effective with those persons (see Chapter 14).

Although ethnic groups are not evenly distributed throughout the United States, the sheer increase in their numbers means that, as time goes by, mental health service providers will be more and more likely to come into contact with ethnic clients in either the public or private mental health sector. These contacts will increase as the number of ethnic group members continues to grow dramatically after the year 2000. Therefore, it will be incumbent upon graduate and professional mental health training programs to incorporate ethnic content and training experiences into their programs in order to train service providers who are competent to work with these groups (American Psychological Association, 1993; Aponte & Clifford, 1995; see Chapter 15).

The increasing number of recent immigrants will also tax mental health services in a number of ways. Some of the issues for this group are generic to all ethnic groups, others are unique to recent immigrants (see Chapter 12). Those immigrants who come from impoverished, politically volatile, and war-torn countries present with a number of economic, social, and psychological issues that are difficult challenges for mental health service providers (see Root, 1992 and Takaki, 1994 for more detailed discussions). Recent changes in public attitudes and policies will exacerbate such difficulties as attempts are made to slow immigration and limit access to social services, health care, and education.

Changing ethnic population characteristics (age, fertility rates, and mortality rates) will also have a profound impact on the need for mental health services as well as on the types of services to be provided to these groups. Ethnic persons tend to be young and will experience problems that are common to all young populations, as well as other issues that are unique to them such as struggles around their ethnic identity, discrimination, oppression, and experiences with war (see Chapters 2 and 10). Members of these groups are also aging and will begin to experience more frequently some of the same problems faced by the White elderly and some problems that are unique to the ethnic elderly (Grant, 1995).

There are a number of social, health, and psychological problems that have a greater impact on ethnic group members than on Whites (National Center for Health Statistics, 1991a, 1991b). Members of these groups are more likely to experience acts of violence directed against them. High rates of alcohol and drug abuse are also found within African American, Hispanic, and American Indians, and high rates of AIDs are found in both African American and Hispanic men and women (Cummings & DeHart, 1995; see Chapter 13). Specialized services may be needed to address these problems. The importance of addressing these issues will increase as the ethnic population grows, particularly within the younger age cohorts, which are more susceptible to these problems (see Chapter 10).

Family structure and marriage patterns for these groups are significantly different than those of Whites (see Chapter 6). Ethnic households tend to be larger than White households. African Americans, Hispanics, and American Indian households are also more likely than White households to be headed by females, a high percentage of whom have never married (see Chapter 11). Although extended families and flexibility of roles within ethnic groups can provide social support and serve as a rich resource, the pressures faced and limited resources available to group members can take their toll, leading to the development of a variety of social and psychological problems.

Socioeconomic status and those components that are subsumed under this rubric (occupational status, income, and education) have a direct impact on a number of issues faced by ethnic groups. The relationship between SES and health and mental health functioning is well established (Adler et al., 1994; Dohrenwend & Dohrenwend, 1969; Lorion & Felner, 1986). Ethnic groups, particularly African Americans, Hispanics, and American Indians tend to be overrepresented in the lower SES strata. Socioeconomic status is also linked to the availability and utilization of mental health services, with low SES persons having fewer services available to them, having less-experienced clinicians assigned to treat them, being placed on medication more frequently, and finding themselves in the least desirable service setting.

In addition, the existence of barriers to desirable occupations, the high rates of poverty, and the limited educational opportunities and early dropout rates of ethnic students all have a demoralizing and debilitating effect on ethnic group members. Such forces, which limit upward mobility and keep ethnic groups oppressed, can be viewed as "economic trauma" leading to stress (Herzberg, 1990). Ethnic children (especially when they grow up in single-parent households without the support of extended families) are particularly at risk to perform poorly in school and also to develop psychological problems. Moreover, the economic forces and limited opportunities experienced by ethnic persons can also lead to the persons' families becoming homeless (Milburn & Curry, 1995).

The increasing need for mental health services resulting from the changing ethnic profile in the United States is obvious. Such a statement was made over two decades ago by the President's Commission on Mental Health (1978). These services need to target high-risk ethnic populations such as children, adolescents, single-parent females, and the elderly. In addition to individual therapeutic intervention strategies, other intervention strategies such as family approaches, group treatments, and community interventions are called for (see Chapters 5, 6, 7, and 8). These approaches will need to be altered, when appropriate, and new intervention approaches and strategies developed in order to ensure their effectiveness with ethnic clients.

REFERENCES

Adler, N. E., Boyce, T., Chesney, M. A., Cohen, S., Folkman, S., Kahn, R. L., & Syme, S. L. (1994). Socioeconomic status and health: The challenge of the gradient. *American Psychologist, 49,* 15–24.

Ahlburg, D. A., & De Vita, C. J. (1992). New realities of the American family. *Population Bulletin, 47* (2), 1–44.

American Psychological Association (1993). Guidelines for providers of psychological services to ethnic, linguistic, and culturally diverse populations. *American Psychologist, 48,* 45–48.

Aponte, J. F., & Barnes, J. M. (1995). Impact of acculturation and moderator variables on the intervention and treatment of ethnic groups. In J. F. Aponte, R. Young Rivers, & J. Wohl (Eds.), *Psychological interven-*tions and cultural diversity (pp. 19–39). Boston: Allyn and Bacon.

Aponte, J. F., & Clifford, J. (1995). Education and training issues for intervention with ethnic groups. In J. F. Aponte, R. Young Rivers, & J. Wohl (Eds.), *Psychological interventions and cultural diversity* (pp. 283–300). Boston: Allyn and Bacon.

Aponte, J. F., & Crouch, R. T. (1995). The changing ethnic profile of the United States. In J. F. Aponte, R. Young Rivers, & J. Wohl (Eds.), *Psychological interventions and cultural diversity* (pp. 1–18). Boston: Allyn and Bacon.

Atkinson, D. R., Morten, G., & Sue, D. W. (Eds.). (1998). *Counseling American minorities* (5th ed.). Boston: McGraw-Hill.

Baker, F. M. (1988). Afro-Americans. In L. Comas-Díaz & E. E. H. Griffith (Eds.), *Clinical guidelines in cross-cultural mental health* (pp. 151–181). New York: Wiley.

Bass, B. A. (1982). The validity of socioeconomic factors in the assessment and treatment of Afro-Americans. In B. A. Bass, G. E. Wyatt, & G. J. Powell (Eds.), *The Afro-American family: Assessment, treatment, and research issues* (pp. 69–83). New York: Grune & Stratton.

Betancourt, H., & López, S. R. (1993). The study of culture, ethnicity, and race in American psychology. *American Psychologist, 48,* 629–637.

Bianchi, S. M. (1990). America's children: Mixed prospects. *Population Bulletin, 45,* 1–43.

Boyd-Franklin, N. (1990). Five key factors in the treatment of Black families. In G. W. Saba, B. M. Karrer, & K. V. Hardy (Eds.), *Minorities and family therapy* (pp. 53–69). New York: Haworth.

Cheung, F. K., & Snowden, L. R. (1990). Community mental health and ethnic minority populations. *Community Mental Health Journal, 26,* 277–291.

Cummings, C. M., & DeHart, D. D. (1995). Ethnic minority physical health: Issues and interventions. In J. F. Aponte, R. Young Rivers, & J. Wohl (Eds.), *Psychological interventions and cultural diversity* (pp. 234–249). Boston: Allyn and Bacon.

Dana, R. H. (1993). *Multicultural assessment perspectives for professional psychology.* Boston: Allyn and Bacon.

Deloria, V., Jr. (1992). American Indians. In J. D. Buenker & L. A. Ratner (Eds.), *Multiculturalism in the United States: A comparative guide to acculturation and ethnicity* (pp. 31–52). New York: Greenwood.

del Pinal, J., & Singer, A. (1997). Generations of diversity: Latinos in the United States. *Population Bulletin, 52* (3), 1–48.

De Vita, C. J. (1996). The United States at mid-decade. *Population Bulletin, 50* (4), 1–48.

Dohrenwend, B. P., & Dohrenwend, B. S. (1969). *Social status and psychological disorder: A casual inquiry.* New York: Wiley.

Fleming, C. G. (1992). African-Americans. In J. D. Buenker & L. A. Ratner (Eds.), *Multiculturalism in the United States: A comparative guide to acculturation and ethnicity* (pp. 9–29). New York: Greenwood.

Fullilove, M. T. (Ed.). (1985). *The Black family: Mental health perspectives.* San Francisco: Rosenberg Foundation.

Gary, L. E. (1987). Religion and mental health in an urban Black community. *Urban Research Review, 7,* 5–7.

Grant, R. W. (1995). Inventions with ethnic minority elderly. In J. F. Aponte, R. Young Rivers, & J. Wohl (Eds.), *Psychological interventions and cultural diversity* (pp. 199–214). Boston: Allyn and Bacon.

Hammond, W. R., & Yung, B. (1993). Psychology's role in the public health response to assaultive violence among young African-American men. *American Psychologist, 48,* 142–154.

Hardy, K. V. (1990). The theoretical myth of sameness: A critical issue in family therapy training and treatment. In G. W. Saba, B. M. Karrer, & K. V. Hardy (Eds.), *Minorities and family therapy* (pp. 17–33). New York: Haworth.

Helms, J. E., & Talleyrand, R. M. (1997). Race is not ethnicity. *American Psychologist, 52,* 1246–1247.

Herzberg, J. H. (1990). Economic trauma: A public health problem. In J. D. Noshpitz & R. D. Coddington (Eds.), *Stressors and the adjustment disorders* (pp. 447–454). New York: Wiley.

Howard, A., & Scott, R. A. (1981). The study of minority groups in complex societies. In R. H. Munroe, & B. B. Whiting (Eds.), *Handbook of cross-cultural development* (pp. 113–152). New York: Garland Stem.

LaFromboise, T. D. (1988). American Indian mental health policy. *American Psychologist, 43,* 388–397.

Lee, S. M. (1998). Asian Americans: Diverse and growing. *Population Bulletin, 53* (2), 1–40.

Lorion, R. P., & Felner, R. D. (1986). Research on psychotherapy with the disadvantaged. In S. L. Garfield & A. E. Bergin (Eds.), *Handbook of psychotherapy and behavior change* (3rd ed., pp. 739–775). New York: Wiley.

MacKellar, F. L., & Yanagishita, M. (1995). *Homicide in the United States: Who's at Risk?* Washington, DC: Population Reference Bureau.

Manson, S. M., & Trimble, J. E. (1982). American Indian and Alaska Native communities: Past efforts, future inquiries. In R. L. Snowden (Ed.), *Reaching the underserved: Mental health needs of neglected populations* (pp. 143–163). Beverly Hills, CA: Sage.

Martin, P., & Midgley, E. (1994). Immigrants to the United States: Journey to an uncertain destination. *Population Bulletin, 49* (2), 1–47.

Massey, D., & Denton, N. (1987). Trends in the residential segregation of Blacks, Hispanics, and Asians: 1970–1980. *American Sociological Review, 52,* 802–825.

Massey, D., & Eggers, M. L. (1990). The ecology of inequality: Minorities and the concentration of poverty, 1970–1980. *American Journal of Sociology, 95,* 1153–1188.

McGoldrick, M., Pearce, J. K., & Giordano, J. (Eds.). (1982). *Ethnicity and family therapy.* New York: Guilford.

Milburn, N. G., & Curry, T. L. (1995). Intervention and treatment for ethnic minority homeless adults. In J. F. Aponte, R. Young Rivers, & J. Wohl (Eds.), *Psychological interventions and cultural diversity* (pp. 250–265). Boston: Allyn and Bacon.

National Center for Health Statistics. (1990). *Monthly vital statistics report 39, No. 7. Supplement.* Washington, DC: Government Printing Office.

National Center for Health Statistics. (1991a). *Life tables, Volume 2 of vital health statistics of the United States, 1988.* Washington, DC: U.S. Government Printing Office.

National Center for Health Statistics. (1991b). *Vital and health statistics. Family structure and children's health: United States, 1988.* Washington, DC: U.S. Government Printing Office.

Neighbors, H. W. (1989). Improving the mental health of Black Americans: Lessons from the community mental health movement. In D. P. Willis (Ed.), *Health policies and Black Americans* (pp. 348–380). New Brunswick, NJ: Transaction.

O'Hare, W. P. (1989). Black demographic trends in the 1980s. In D. P. Willis (Ed.), *Health policies and Black Americans* (pp. 37–55). New Brunswick, NJ: Transaction.

O'Hare, W. P. (1992). America's minorities—The demographics of diversity. *Population Bulletin, 47* (4), 1–47.

O'Hare, W. (1998). Managing multiple-race data. *American Demographics,* 42–44.

O'Hare, W. P., & Felt, J. C. (1991). *Asian Americans: America's fastest growing minority group.* Washington, DC: Population Reference Bureau.

O'Hare, W. P., Pollard, K. M., Mann, T. L., & Kent, K. M. (1991). African Americans in the 1990s. *Population Bulletin, 46,* 1–40.

Passel, J. S., & Edmonston, B. (1992). *Immigration and race: Trends in immigration to the United States.* Washington, DC: Urban Institute.

Phinney, J. S. (1996). When we talk about American ethnic groups, what do we mean? *American Psychologist, 51,* 918–927.

President's Commission on Mental Health (1978). *Volume 2: Task panel reports: The nature and scope of the problem.* Washington, DC: U.S. Government Printing Office.

Root, M. P. P. (Ed.). (1992). *Racially mixed people in America.* Newbury Park, CA: Sage.

Soldo, B. J., & Agree, E. M. (1988). America's elderly. *Population Bulletin, 43,* 1–51.

Spickard, P. R. (1992). The illogic of American racial categories. In M. P. P. Root (Ed.), *Racially mixed people in America* (pp. 12–23). Newbury Park, CA: Sage.

Takaki, R. (Ed.). (1994). *From different shores: Perspectives on race and ethnicity in America.* New York: Oxford University Press.

Thornton, M. C. (1992). The quient immigration: Foreign spouses of U.S. citizens, 1945–1985. In M. P. P. Root (Ed.), *Racially mixed people in America* (pp. 64–76). Newbury Park, CA: Sage.

Treas, J. (1995). Older Americans in the 1990s and beyond. *Population Bulletin, 50* (2), 1–48.

U.S. Bureau of Census. (1990). *1990 Census of population and housing—Summary tape file 3. Summary social, economic, and housing characteristics.* Washington, DC.

U.S. Bureau of Census. (1991). Race and Hispanic origin. *1990 Census Profile,* No. 2, 1–8.

U.S. Bureau of Census. (1992a), *Current population reports, P25-1092, Population projections of the United States by age, sex, race, and Hispanic origin: 1992–2050.* Washington, DC: U.S. Government Printing Office.

U.S. Bureau of Census. (1992b), *1990 Census of population, 1990 CP-1-4, General population characteristics.* Washington, DC: U.S. Government Printing Office.

U.S. Bureau of Census. (1992c), *1990 Census of population and housing, 1990 CPH-1-1, Summary population and housing characteristics.* Washington, DC: U.S. Government Printing Office.

U.S. Bureau of Census. (1992d). *Statistical abstract of the United States: The national data book.* (112th Ed.). Washington, DC: U.S. Government Printing Office.

U.S. Bureau of Census. (1996). *Current population reports: Population projections of the United States by age, race, and Hispanic origin: 1995 to 2050.* pp. 25–1130. Washington, DC: U.S. Government Printing Office.

U.S. Bureau of Census. (1997). *Current population reports: Special studies,* P23–193. Washington, DC: U.S. Government Printing Office.

U.S. Bureau of Census. (1998). *United States Department of Commerce news,* CB98-175. Washington, DC.

U.S. Department of Commerce. (1997). *Statistical abstract of the United States: 1997.* Washington, DC: U.S. Government Printing Office.

Yee, A. H., Fairchild, H. H., Weizmann, F., & Wyatt, G. E. (1993). Addressing psychology's problems with race. *American Psychologist, 48,* 1132–1140.

2

The Impact of Culture on the Intervention and Treatment of Ethnic Populations

JOSEPH F. APONTE

LAURA R. JOHNSON

The beliefs, values, attitudes, feelings, and behavior of ethnic group members have a direct impact on their psychological functioning, concept of illness, and expression of symptoms. These factors also affect their entry into the mental health system, the types of services utilized, the processes involved in working with them, and the outcomes of the interventions or treatments given. These factors are influenced by unique individual characteristics, those experiences occurring within their culture, and experiences occurring within the majority or dominant culture (Aponte & Barnes, 1995; Dana, 1993).

The overall approach taken in this chapter is that one's cultural background and experiences within the majority culture provide a framework through which current experiences and information are processed and behavior is produced (Hughes, 1993). A variety of factors will be identified and discussed that have a direct impact on four major ethnic groups (African Americans, Hispanics, Asian Americans, and American Indians). These factors will be subsumed under two major headings: (1) enculturation, acculturation, and racial/ethnic identity; and (2) moderator variables. Understanding these factors can lead to the enhancement of existing mental health services and/or the creation of new and effective services for the ethnic populations that are the focus of this book.

This chapter is organized around the theoretical framework that is depicted in Figure 2.1. Enculturation, acculturation, and racial/ethnic identity are viewed as constructs with overlapping commonalities and reciprocal interactions that result from dominant and nondominant cultural influences. A number of moderator variables are also seen as being byproducts of dominant and nondominant cultural influences. These moderator variables can directly affect the acculturation process, ethnic/racial identity development, psychological functioning, symptom presentation, service utilization, and treatment process and outcomes for ethnic group members (Aponte & Barnes, 1995).

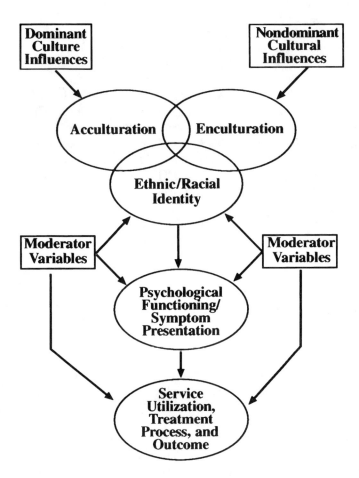

FIGURE 2.1   Relationship between Culture, Moderator Variables, and Treatment.

Enculturation, Acculturation, and Racial/Ethnic Identity

African Americans, Hispanics, Asian Americans, and American Indians have a number of cultural characteristics that distinguish them from the dominant European culture. Within each of these broad ethnic groupings are also cultural differences that need to be acknowledged and understood (Atkinson, Morton, & Sue, 1998; Sue, Chun, & Gee, 1995). Enculturation, acculturation, and racial/ethnic identity development are processes that account for many of these across and within group differences. The nature of these constructs, including how they are different and where they overlap, will be reviewed.

Enculturation

It is important to make a distinction between enculturation and acculturation. Whereas acculturation occurs as an individual responds to the influence of a dominant or second culture, enculturation occurs as an individual is socialized into his or her own cultural group. The transmission of cultural knowledge, awareness, and skills that occurs during enculturation can be a result of formal instruction or informal tacit learning from a variety of sources including parents, peers, or other adults and "own group" institutions (Berry, 1993; Casas & Pytluk, 1995). These within-group influences or nondominant group experiences are often in conflict with the second or dominant culture influences (see Figure 2.1).

If the enculturation process is "successful," then an individual will have the competencies needed to function effectively in his or her cultural group of origin. One of these "competencies" is the development of a strong, "achieved" racial/ethnic identity. The degree to which one is enculturated and the relative strength of one's racial/ethnic identity will likely affect the manner in which the individual responds to acculturation. For example, if one maintains a strong sense of racial/ethnic identity, he or she may be less likely to assimilate and instead maintain a sense of groundedness in his or her culture of origin, or in both the culture of origin and in the second culture. On the other hand, the pressures of acculturation may reverse, undo, or inhibit processes of enculturation (Casas & Pytluk, 1995).

Acculturation

Acculturation is a process that includes psychosocial changes occurring as a result of interaction with a second culture (Casas & Pytluk, 1995). As a by-product of contact with a second culture, either willingly or unwillingly, an ethnic person's values, attitudes, and behaviors change. According to Marín (1992), these changes can occur at three levels: *superficial* level (e.g., minimal changes in one's cultural beliefs and practices); *intermediate* level (e.g., moderate changes in behavior, such as relinquishing the use of one's native language that is part of the person's life); and *significant* level (e.g., changes in beliefs, values, and norms that are central to the person's worldviews, behavior, and interaction patterns in his or her culture of origin).

Acculturation has been historically viewed as a unidirectional process of assimilation by which a person relinquishes his or her ethnic values, beliefs, customs, and practices for that of the majority culture. More recently, others have argued that acculturation is a bidirectional and dynamic process in which the nondominant culture is influenced and changes as a by-product of interacting with the dominant or second culture (Aponte & Barnes, 1995; Casas & Pytluk, 1995). The majority culture can also be affected and changed by the ethnic person or group. Both the assimilated and retained cultural components need to be assessed in order to obtain an accurate picture of the person's level of acculturation (Berry, 1993; Sodowsky, Lai, & Plake, 1991).

According to Berry and his associates (Berry & Kim, 1988), acculturation can be broken down into a series of phases occurring at the individual and group level, which include: (1) *precontact phase,* during which each independent cultural group has its own characteristics; (2) *contact phase,* in which the groups interact with each other; (3) *conflict phase,* in which pressure is exerted on the nondominant group to change in order to fit with the majority group; (4) *crisis phase,* during which the conflict comes to a head; and (5) *adaptation phase,* in which relations between the two groups are stabilized into one of several outcomes or modes of acculturation. The psychological functioning and amount of stress experienced by individuals going through these phases will vary according to the acculturation phase (Berry & Kim, 1988; Berry, Kim, Minde, & Mok, 1987).

Different modes of acculturation can emerge at each of the above phases or at the final adaptation phase. Which mode is assumed will depend upon how an individual deals with two fundamental questions: How much of one's cultural identity is valued and is to be retained? and, To what degree are positive relations with the majority (dominant) culture sought? (Berry & Kim, 1988). The four modes of acculturation are *assimilation, separation, marginalization,* and *integration.* Each mode is differentially associated with acculturative stress, social competence and support, and overall psychological adjustment (Berry, 1998).

The *assimilation mode* consists of a shift toward the dominant culture coupled with a rejection of one's culture of origin. The goal is complete acceptance by, and absorption into, mainstream American culture via disengagement from one's ethnic culture and the formation of a new, majority group identity (LaFromboise, Coleman, & Gerton, 1993). These individuals run the risk of being rejected by both their families/communities and the majority culture (Phinney, Chavira, & Williamson, 1992) and may thus be prone to experience high levels of stress and anxiety, low self esteem, and susceptibility to social problems (LaFromboise et al., 1993).

In contrast to the assimilation mode, the *separation mode* describes individuals who retain their cultural identity, values, and behaviors while rejecting those of the majority culture (Berry, 1998). These individuals will be socially effective within their cultures of origin, but may not have the facility to negotiate or derive full benefit from the core institutions of American society such as government, education, economic, and health/mental health care systems (LaFromboise et al., 1993). Individuals operating from this mode are more likely to turn to indigenous social supports and ethnomedical systems for care (see Chapter 9).

The *marginalization mode* involves a simultaneous rejection of both ethnic and majority group cultures (Berry, 1998). These individuals are not socially effective nor accepted in any culture, and they will lack a sense of cultural identity, groundedness, and self efficacy (LaFromboise et al., 1993). As such, they are the most apt to experience high levels of acculturative stress and psychological maladjustment (Berry & Kim, 1988; Phinney et al., 1992).

According to Berry (1998) the *integration mode* (sometimes referred to as biculturalism) involves the adoption of some majority culture attitudes and practices coupled with the retention of ethnic group cultural practices and identity. These individuals demonstrate psychological flexibility and have a wide behavioral repertoire that allows them to be effective across varying cultural contexts. Furthermore, they will feel a sense of belonging to both cultures, maintain an integrated cultural identity, and have positive attitudes toward both groups (LaFromboise et al., 1993).

Over the past two decades, attempts have been made by a number of scholars and researchers to conceptualize and measure the extent and nature of acculturation of individuals from different ethnic groups (Atkinson et al., 1998; Ruiz, 1990). These efforts have sometimes employed the terms *cultural* or *racial/ethnic identity,* and *acculturation* inter-changeably. However, acculturation and racial/ethnic identity should not be viewed as synonymous, but as separate conceptual constructs or elements (Casas & Pytluk, 1995; Kitano, 1989; Phinney, 1998). While acculturation can be viewed as focusing on the values, beliefs, and behaviors of the person, racial/ethnic identity can be seen as the process and outcome of integrating racial/ethnic aspects into his or her overall self-concept and identity (Helms, 1990a).

Racial, Cultural, and Ethnic Identity

Theory and research on racial, cultural, and ethnic identity has been called "one of the most promising contributions to the field of multicultural counseling..." and it has been increasingly recognized as an important variable in treatment processes and outcomes (Atkinson et al., 1998, p. 31). Racial, cultural, and ethnic identity refers to an individual's awareness and sense of self as a racial, ethnic, or cultural being. Identity development in these respects refers to a psychological process in which individuals become aware of, and ascribe meaning to, racial or cultural "material" and integrate this information into their overall self-concept. Although the terms *racial, ethnic,* and *cultural identity* are often used interchangeably, it is important to note their conceptual differences (Helms, 1995; Helms & Talleyrand, 1997; Phinney, 1996).

Racial identity refers to an individual's awareness of himself or herself as a member of a particular, socially defined racial group, e.g., Black, Asian, White, or Indigenous people. Cultural identity, on the other hand, refers to one's identification with a particular reference group defined by geographical location, national origin, religious affiliation, or language. As noted by Carter and Qureshi (1995), more recent approaches have expanded the reaches of cultural identity to include any factor that may account for "differential" patterns of learned or shared behavior. This inclusive definition of cultural identity would include sexual orientation, gender identification, physical disability, age cohort, and socio-economic status. The term *ethnic* or *ethnic identity* is a broader category that may refer to racial classification and/or cultural factors.

Use of the term *race* as a biological construct is quite controversial and no longer considered valid or useful (Jackson & Sellers, 1997), however, Helms and her associates (Helms, 1995; Helms & Talleyrand, 1997) argue that it is premature to abandon the construct of race, which continues to be the predominant measure of social inclusion or exclusion, determining the allocation of goods, services, and opportunities for "people of color." As such, racial rather than cultural identity may be an extremely salient part of the overall self-concept and identity of ethnic persons in the United States (Cook, 1994), and thus define and structure social interactions (Helms, 1990b, 1995; see Chapter 16).

Atkinson et al. (1998) note the existence of an array of identity models. Historically, racial identity models described the transformation that Blacks went through in becoming aware of themselves as racial beings (Cross, 1972; Jackson, 1975). Many of the African American experiences identified in the early models of Black racial identity development (Cross, 1972; Jackson, 1975) have been similarly noted among other ethnic groups, and more recent models have been updated and expanded to include Latinos/Latinas (Bernal &

Knight, 1993; Ruiz, 1990), Whites (Helms, 1995), and biracial groups (Kerwin, Ponterotto, Jackson, & Harris, 1993; Poston, 1990). Other models, such as the Minority Identity Development Model (MID) (Atkinson et al., 1998) and the People of Color Racial Identity Model (PCRI) (Helms, 1995) are more broadly applicable across ethnic group members.

Helms's PCRI model, for example, describes five stages that all "people of color" may go through in their struggles to understand themselves as ethnic persons in relation to their own ethnic group, other ethnic groups, and the majority culture. Although a linear course of development is expected, the "stages" are not rigid but permeable and flexible (Cross, 1995; Helms, 1995). Individuals may not experience each stage over the course of their lives, and furthermore, individuals may have attitudes associated with more than one stage at any given time. Like the modes of acculturation, different stages of ethnic/racial identity development have differing implications for psychological functioning and service utilization.

The first stage or "status" of the PCRI model, *Conformity,* is associated with a devaluing of one's own ethnic/racial group and an emulation of White standards, values, and norms (Helms, 1995). Individuals with conformity attitudes may seek help from, and be influenced by, White counselors (Parham & Helms, 1981), have a belief in the effectiveness of counseling (Austin, Carter, & Vaux, 1990) and have positive attitudes toward seeking professional mental health services (Delphin & Rollock, 1995). However, attitudes reflective of this stage have also been positively linked to global psychological distress, anxiety, and alcohol concerns (Carter, 1991).

Dissonance, the next status, occurs when an individual becomes aware of his or her ethnic/racial identity and what it means to be a member of a particular socially defined racial or ethnic group. This status marks a transitional period and is associated with ambiguous feelings and conflict between self- and group-appreciating and depreciating attitudes. Individuals may become anxious in the face of racial or cultural material and thus attempt to ignore or repress this information (Helms, 1995).

Immersion/Emersion is the next status. This involves the person's moving to a positive commitment to his or her own ethnic/racial group (Helms, 1995). This includes an idealization and complete immersion in own-group beliefs and values coupled with a total rejection of White (or other) standards and values. Individuals in this stage may evidence hypervigilence toward racial material, blame all psychological problems on racism, and, consequently, may have negative attitudes toward seeking professional psychological help (Delphin & Rollock, 1995). Under these circumstances, ethnic/racial matching with a mental health worker can facilitate the therapeutic process.

The fourth status, *Internalization,* reflects a concern for the basis of self- and group-appreciation and a newly developed capacity to use internal standards to define oneself and respond objectively to majority individuals (Helms, 1995). The final stage, *Integrative Awareness,* reflects flexible and complex thinking as individuals come to value the many aspects of their identities. A sense of security in one's identity will emerge, and it has been suggested that these individuals will experience the least amount of anxiety. Ethnic/racial matching of client and therapist is less important at these later stages than in the earlier ones. (See Chapter 16 for a discussion of racial/ethnic identity interactions.)

A number of acculturation and racial/ethnic identity measures have recently been developed. Table 2.1 identifies and briefly describes a small sample of those measures that

TABLE 2.1   **Selected Acculturation and Ethnic/Racial Identity Measures.**

Acculturation and Ethnic/Racial Identity Measures

Measure	*Description*
African American Acculturation Scale (Landrine & Klonoff, 1994)	Unilinear measure of dimensions of African American culture including religious beliefs/practices, family structure, socialization, food, superstitions, interracial attitudes, health beliefs/practices, preferences
Africentrism Scale (Grills & Longshore, 1996)	Unilinear scale measuring degree to which one adheres to Nguzo Saba principles of African and African American culture
Bidimensional Acculturation Scale (Marín & Gamba, 1996)	Bidimensional measure of changes in language use, linguistic proficiency, electric media use for Hispanics
Acculturation Rating Scale for Mexican Americans II (Cuellar, Arnold, & Moldanado, 1995)	Measures 2 orthogonal behavioral bidirectional dimensions: Anglo Mexican and Mexican/Mexican American orientations
Suinn-Lew Asian Self Identity Acculturation Scale (Suinn, Richard-Figueroa, Lew, & Vigil, 1987)	Unilinear measure of language, identity, friendship choice, behaviors, generation/geographic history, attitudes
Rosebud Personal Opinion Surley (Hoffman, Dana, & Bolton, 1985)	Unilinear measure covering language, value orientation, cultural attitudes, social behavior, status, ancestry of American Indians
People of Color Identity Scale (Helms, 1995)	Extension of Black racial/minority development models assessing multiethnic information processing strategies associated with shared racial socialization experiences
Multi-Ethnic Identity Measure (Phinney, 1992)	Measures 3 domains (sense of belonging to one's group, ethnic identity achievement, behaviors/practices), other-group orientation, parent's ethnic background for different ethnic groups
Multi-Construct African American Identity Questionnaire (Smith & Brookins, 1997)	Measure of ethnic identity in African American youth including social orientation, appearance, attitudes toward own group, cooperative values
Multidimensional Measure of Cultural Identity (Felix-Ortiz, Newcomb, & Meyers, 1994)	Measures cultural identity in Latino/Latina adolescents, including language, behavior/familial, values/attitudes
Measure of Enculturation for Native American Youth (Zimmerman, Ramirez-Valles, Washienko, & Walter, 1996)	Measures cultural affinity, identity, family involvement, and traditional activities of Native American youth

are available. Some have been developed for specific groups, others are designed to measure the acculturation and racial/ethnic identity of more than one group. A clear distinction between acculturation and racial/ethnic identity is not made in all of these measures, and their psychometric properties have not been well established (see Dana, 1993; Helms, 1990b; Ponterotto, Casas, Suzuki, & Alexander, 1995; Zane, 1998 for more detailed descriptions). Nevertheless, these instruments provide important information on the ethnic person's background as well as the current level of acculturation and racial/ethnic identity.

Relationship between Acculturation and Racial/Ethnic Identity

Acculturation and racial/ethnic identity are increasingly recognized as central in understanding the mental health of ethnic populations. There is also an increasing need to gain a more complete understanding of these concepts and the relationship between them (Lee, 1997a). Both acculturation and racial/ethnic identity development are complex, multifaceted, multidimensional, and interacting processes that occur at the individual and group levels (Aponte & Barnes, 1995). Both can be situation driven in that a person may adopt different acculturation and racial/ethnic identity options in different interpersonal and social situations. Both acculturation and racial/ethnic identity are associated with varying degrees of psychological health and adjustment, as well as with different approaches to help seeking and treatment outcomes (Aponte & Barnes, 1995; Atkinson, et al., 1998; Sue et al., 1995).

Acculturation and racial/ethnic identity will also interact with, and be impacted by, a number of different variables, including but not limited to: socioeconomic status, residence (including years of residence in the United States and ethnic density of the person's neighborhood), racism and oppression, worldview, language usage fluency, religious/spiritual beliefs, gender, and familial and social network structure (Aponte & Barnes, 1995; Sodowsky & Carey, 1987). Furthermore, the impact of these factors will be affected by individual differences among ethnic group members (Lee, 1997a).

Carter, Sbrocco, and Carter (1996) developed a framework for examining anxiety disorders in African Americans that is useful for understanding the relationship between acculturation and ethnic identity. Ethnicity is conceptualized by the authors as a higher order construct comprised of two lower order factors, namely acculturation and racial/ethnic identity. The framework contains overlap between racial/ethnic identity and acculturation to reflect their shared meaning and reciprocal influence. The Carter et al. framework predicts that acculturation and racial/ethnic identity will interact to affect beliefs about mental illness, the actual symptoms or syndrome experienced, as well as treatment seeking, expectations, and outcomes.

Those with *High Acculturation/Weak Ethnic Identity* will be similar to the mainstream culture in terms of language and clothing and will have little sense of belonging to their ethnic group of origin (Kitano & Maki, 1997). This can be a conscious choice or can be motivated by overt/covert messages from the majority culture about their own ethnic group. For example, they may have learned that the key to success is rejecting an ethnic worldview (Lee, 1997b). These individuals may be most likely to exhibit the same symptoms as Whites and to seek out, remain in, and benefit from standard mental health treatment (Carter et al., 1996).

Individuals with *Low Acculturation/Strong Ethnic Identity* may include newly arrived immigrants, older individuals, or others who have limited contact with American society. These individuals are likely to have limited command of English as well as beliefs that are incongruent with those of the majority culture. They may be unfamiliar with the mental health system and have very different views about the etiology and treatment of symptoms. They may, in fact, exhibit dissimilar symptoms and/or communicate their symptomatology in different ways. Accordingly, they may be misdiagnosed, mistrustful of mental health providers, and less likely to seek out or benefit from standard mental health treatment. These individuals will most likely seek out traditional forms of treatment, and, as a last resort, enter the mental health system late and with more severe symptoms (Carter et al., 1996). Culture-specific treatments may be more acceptable and useful with these individuals, and they may prefer an ethnically similar counselor.

Those individuals exhibiting *Low Acculturation/Weak Ethnic Identity* may feel alienated from both their ethnic group and the dominant culture. With a limited sense of belonging to any specified group membership, they may be dysfunctional mentally, spiritually, and/or physically (Kitano & Maki, 1997; Lee, 1997b). These individuals may be at the highest risk for psychological maladjustment, yet be the least likely to seek treatment. In fact, they may only rarely encounter the mental health system (Carter et al., 1996). Approaches to treatment that include the development of ethnic identity may be useful.

Last, those with *High Acculturation/Strong Ethnic Identity* will be the closest to a "bicultural adaptation" and will thus move comfortably, physically and psychologically, between both the dominant and ethnic cultures and are likely to have friends and contacts from a variety of cultures (Kitano & Maki, 1997; LaFromboise et al., 1993; Lee, 1997b). One overt example of this bicultural competence would be bilingualism and a concomitant belief in the value and validity of both styles of communication (Lee, 1997b). Individuals with a strong racial identity and high acculturation will exhibit some similarities to Whites in symptomatology and some similarity in benefits from treatment (Carter et al., 1996). These individuals should be able to access and benefit from both traditional and "Western" mental health services, and they may prefer a combined, holistic approach that integrates spiritual or cultural forms of healing with standard techniques (see Chapter 9).

Role of Moderator Variables

Moderator variables are shaped by dominant and nondominant cultural influences. As previously noted, they can affect acculturation modes, ethnic/racial identity development, psychological functioning, symptom presentation, service utilization, and treatment process and outcome for ethnic group members. Among the moderator variables that will be reviewed in this chapter are the following: (1) type of acculturating group; (2) social characteristics; (3) oppression and legal constraints; (4) racism, prejudice, and discrimination; (5) cultural characteristics; (6) language usage and fluency; and (7) individual characteristics. For additional discussions of these and other moderator variables see Dana (1993) and Sodowsky et al. (1991).

Type of Acculturating Group

A critical factor affecting the process and outcome of acculturation is whether the accultur-ation is voluntary or forced (Berry & Kim, 1988). African Americans were forced through slavery to come to this country and suffered numerous hardships over four centuries. Some Hispanic and Asian groups departed their country because of political reasons, whereas others voluntarily came to the United States seeking educational and economic opportuni-ties or to join family members already present in this country. American Indians have had their tribal values, beliefs, practices, and traditions forcibly changed by the majority cul-ture, as well as being actively removed from their ancestral lands in the early history of the United States (LaFromboise, 1988).

These aspects of acculturation are reflected in the different types of acculturating groups described by Berry and Kim (1988), including the following: (1) *immigrants,* who are migratory and relatively voluntary; (2) *refugees,* who are migratory and relatively invol-untary; (3) *native people,* who are indigenous, nonmigratory, and involuntary; (4) *ethnic groups,* who are nonmigratory and who more or less willingly interact with the larger soci-ety of their own choosing; and (5) *sojourners,* who have temporary cultural contact with the society (e.g., foreign students, diplomats, international workers).

The five groups correspond to a number of ethnic populations found in this country, and each is at differential risk of developing psychological problems. High rates of anxiety, depression, and adjustment problems, for example, have been found among recent immi-grants and refugees (Mollica & Lavelle, 1988; Westermeyer, 1993; see Chapter 12). This can be attributed to the tumultuous circumstances with which some of the refugees left their country and to the lack of traditional resources and social supports that some immi-grants and refugees experience in this country. As native peoples, American Indians, have also experienced a great many social and psychological problems that can be traced to their earlier experiences with White culture and current status in this country (LaFromboise, 1988).

Social Characteristics

Social characteristics as moderator variables can be conceptualized as consisting of socio-economic status and family and social network structure. Although a substantive body of literature exists in each of these areas, this section will focus primarily on the relationship of ethnicity to these variables. Although these areas are necessarily interrelated, they will be discussed separately. Of particular interest is how these variables affect the encultura-tion and acculturation process, the psychological functioning and symptom presentation of ethnic persons, and mental health service utilization, process, and outcome.

Socioeconomic status (SES) lacks a clear operational definition in the mental health literature (Lorion & Felner, 1986). Classification into SES categories ranging from low SES to high SES is sometimes done on the basis of either education, occupation, or income (Adler et al., 1994). However, reliance on any single factor for classifying an ethnic per-son's SES is problematic since he or she may be well educated but earning little income, or may have limited education yet have a reasonable income through the pooling of familial financial resources. Any operational definition of SES needs to be multidimensional and involve consideration of the individual's economic resources, social prestige, and social influence (Lorion & Felner, 1986). The latter two factors are particularly important for ethnic groups.

Using any one factor, or a combination of the previously identified factors, to determine an ethnic person's SES would lead to the inescapable conclusion that, according to dominant culture standards, there is a disproportionately high number of ethnic persons—particularly African Americans, Hispanics, and American Indians—in the low SES stratum (O'Hare, 1996; see Chapter 1). Even among Asian Americans, who more closely approximate Whites in SES status, there is variability such that a number of groups (e.g., Vietnamese, Laotians, Cambodians) are disproportionately represented in the low-SES stratum, having recently arrived in this country and/or come from impoverished backgrounds in their countries of origin.

Research across a variety of community and clinical samples indicates that there is a strong relationship between SES and rates of psychopathology, the utilization of mental health services, and the effectiveness of these services (Atkinson et al., 1998; Comas-Díaz & Griffith, 1988; Gaw, 1993a; Wierzbicki & Pekarik, 1993). The general findings of such research are that persons from low-SES backgrounds exhibit more psychopathology, utilize mental health services less, and have less successful treatment outcomes than middle-class and upper-class persons. It becomes important, then, to identify the role that SES plays in each of these arenas. Does SES or ethnicity account for the differential outcomes between ethnic groups and Whites in psychological functioning and service effectiveness?

The research findings have been mixed. Some investigators have found that, when SES is controlled, differences in psychopathology, mental health service utilization, and treatment outcomes between ethnic groups and Whites continue to exist (Dohrenwend & Dohrenwend, 1981a). Other researchers have found that when SES is controlled, differences between ethnic groups and Whites on standard measures of psychological functioning disappear, mental health service utilization rates are similar, and few differences in treatment outcomes are found (Briones et al., 1990).

Despite these mixed results it can be argued that coming from a low-SES background can lead to more stresses than are found in middle- and upper-SES experiences. Low-SES ethnic persons can experience more *victimization* (stressful life experiences), be more *vulnerable* (have fewer personal resources and social supports), experience more *additive burdens* (additive effects of stressful events, limited personal resources, role strain, and limited social support), and be subject to more *chronic burdens* (long-term personal and situational stressors) than persons from other social classes (Dohrenwend & Dohrenwend, 1981b; Lorion & Felner, 1986). Despite these factors it is possible for low-SES ethnic persons to function well in society and be "resilient." The question then becomes: What accounts for this resiliency?

Familial and social network structures are other important moderator variables that account for some of the resiliency found in ethnic populations. This is reflected in the area of social support, which has been extensively researched and has been found to be linked to physical and psychological well-being in the general population (Sarason, Sarason, & Pierce, 1990; Schradle & Dougher, 1985). Although conflicting findings have emerged in the literature, it is apparent that, upon closer scrutiny, the source of the social support

(Dakoff & Taylor, 1990), the strength of the social ties (Lin, Woelfel, & Light, 1985), and the nature and severity of stressors (Cohen & Willis, 1985) have important effects on physical and psychological well being.

The use of immediate and extended families for social support among ethnic populations is well documented in the literature (Guarnaccia & Parra, 1996). African Americans may have complex networks that involve immediate kin, several generations of relatives, and close friends residing in the same household (Boyd-Franklin, 1990; Miller, 1992). Hispanics and Asian Americans also rely heavily on immediate and extended family members, particularly grandparents (Kitano, 1989; Martinez, 1988). Some groups have a formal system such as the *compadrazco* (godparents and coparents) of Puerto Ricans that is built into the extended network (Ramos-McKay, Comas-Díaz, & Rivera, 1988). American Indians utilize immediate family, extended family, tribal elders, and community for social support (Thompson, Walker, & Silk-Walker, 1993).

Supports that involve role flexibility and interdependence can have a moderating effect on the stress and difficulties experienced by ethnic persons. Several factors, however, can place ethnic persons at risk of having their social supports diminished or lost. Immigration policies that discourage the entrance of intact families into the United States have historically contributed to the fragmentation of African American and Asian families (see Chapter 12). Immigration and resettlement policies that encourage Hispanics and Asians to reside in parts of the country where there is a low density of these groups may also lead to isolation and feeling disconnected from one's group.

The extended support system of ethnic persons can also be put at risk through a variety of other factors. Requiring African American and Hispanic children to attend non-neighborhood schools for purposes of desegregation can strain neighborhood ties. Some American Indian children have also been sent to boarding schools away from their tribes. Because of harsh economic conditions on the reservations, some adults have been forced to seek economic opportunities in urban areas where community support may not be present.

Oppression and Legal Constraints

African American experiences with racism have taken the form of oppression during different periods in the history of the United States. First, Africans were forcibly removed from their homelands to be slaves. This era was followed by emancipation, Reconstruction, and Black Codes or Jim Crow during the nineteenth century (Dana, 1993). Terrorism in the form of physical violence, lynchings, and property damage has been part of the African American history in this country, and still continues today. African Americans continue to experience limited opportunities and difficulties as reflected in their levels of health, education, occupations, and poverty (see Chapter 1). More recently, they have experienced the effects of the resurgence of political conservatism as civil rights legislation and affirmative action gains have been reversed (Griffith & Baker, 1993).

The experience of Hispanics with the dominant culture has been quite varied. Oppression for Mexican Americans has taken the form of job discrimination, immigration restrictions, school segregation, and electoral disenfranchisement (Martinez, 1993; Montejano, 1987). Puerto Ricans have experienced job discrimination, but they arrive in this country as citizens and have easily accessible transportation back to their place of birth (Ramos & Morales, 1985). The Cuban experience has been primarily a politically linked migration, with services such as the Cuban Refugee Program in place for them (Bernal & Gutierrez, 1988), until the recent changes in 1994 by the Clinton administration. However, all Hispanic groups have experienced discrimination, as reflected in the national opposition to bilingualism in this country (Padilla et al., 1991).

Asian Americans consist of a variety of groups with different experiences of oppression in this country. The Chinese and Japanese have the longest history in this country. They migrated here in the nineteenth century seeking employment and economic opportunities. The Vietnamese, Cambodians, and Laotians are the most recent immigrants. The Chinese, Japanese, Koreans, and Filipinos were subjected to restrictive immigration laws, limited rights to own property, and segregated schooling. In addtition, during WW II, mainland Japanese were incarcerated in internment camps even though they were American citizens. The Exclusion Laws limiting immigration of Asians to this country were not repealed until 1965 (Gaw, 1993b; Fujii, Fukushima, & Yamamoto, 1993).

Like other ethnic groups, American Indians are not a homogenous group (LaFromboise, 1988; Thompson et al., 1993). The over 500 native entities that exist, however, share common experiences of oppression. These experiences have been that of a conquered people who have been displaced from their land, had children removed from their families, had the roles of males in their family and community undermined, and had their language eliminated (Dana, 1993; Trimble, 1987). Oppression has also been reflected in the contentious and distrusting relationships with federal government agencies such as the Bureau of Indian Affairs and the Indian Health Service.

Oppression can also take the form of limited economic opportunities. Individuals from different ethnic groups are more likely to be unemployed or underemployed (O'Hare, 1996; see Chapter 1). African Americans and Hispanics have significantly higher unemployment rates and poverty rates than Whites (De Vita, 1996). Refugees and immigrants tend to have higher unemployment rates upon their arrival in this country (Al-Issa & Tousignant, 1997). For many of these groups, unemployment and underemployment not only represent a loss of social status, but are also related to the loss of access to goods and services, and the subsequent failure to meet family obligations. As such, these conditions also increase the mental health risks of these groups and their access to mental health services (Al-Issa & Tousignant, 1997; Aponte & Barnes, 1995).

Racism, Prejudice, and Discrimination

Another important moderator variable is prejudice and discrimination. When directed at ethnic groups it is referred to as *racism,* and it has similar characteristics to the many "isms" encountered in our society—including sexism, classism, and ageism (Adams, 1990). Racism can take two forms—attitudinal (McConahay & Hough, 1976) and structural (Kluegl & Smith, 1983). It can be viewed as a psychosocial stressor that affects the daily lives of ethnic group members and subsequently interferes with the psychological functioning, adjustment, and social adaptation of ethnic groups in the larger society.

At the individual level, *attitudinal racism* refers to the dominant group behaving toward ethnic groups in the following manner: (1) teasing, belittling, ridiculing, and disparaging; (2) labeling, stereotyping, stigmatizing, and derogating; (3) scapegoating and dehumanizing; (4) ignoring, neglecting, and looking away; and (5) denying equal opportunity and equal rights (Adams, 1990). At the broader level, *institutional racism* refers to patterns of rules, regulations, and behaviors that are exclusionary and exploitive and are part of an organization, or social system. Such institutional racism typically has an ideology, set of procedures or practices, and physical apparatus supporting it (Adams, 1990).

Racism, prejudice, and discrimination have been viewed as affecting the ethnic person's work, self-regard, interpersonal relationships, and broader social environment. Impaired self-esteem is frequently cited as a psychological consequence of racism (Asamen & Berry, 1987; Brantley, 1983; Hughes & Demo, 1989). Racism has also been cited as a key contributor to psychological problems in ethnic groups, including substance abuse in African Americans, Hispanics, and American Indians (Harper, 1988; Lopez-Bushnell, Tyer, & Futrell, 1992; Oetting, Edwards, & Beauvais, 1988), child abuse and suicide among American Indians (Hurejsi, Craig, & Pablo, 1992; McIntosh, 1984), and domestic violence among Asian Americans (Ho, 1990).

In addition to contributing to the development of psychological distress, these forces have a negative impact on entry into the mental health system and subsequent treatment process. A "healthy cultural paranoia" engendered in African Americans as a consequence of experience with racism and prejudice has been identified (Jones, 1990; Ridley, 1995). This distrust of majority institutions, combined with the stigmatization associated with entering treatment, may prevent the seeking of services (Priest, 1991). Having overcome this initial barrier, the ethnic help-seekers may find themselves misdiagnosed, channeled away from needed services, assigned to inappropriate treatments, and serviced by the least experienced practitioners because of racist attitudes (Adams, 1990; Atkinson et al., 1998; Jones, 1990).

Ethnic group members may carry the hostility and suspicion resulting from discriminatory experiences into treatment. Barbarin (1984) held that many African Americans have "highly refined sensors capable of detecting racially based slurs in the most innocent of acts" (p. 14). When this "cultural paranoia" (Jones, 1990) combines with inadequate training, inexperience, and perhaps outright racism and prejudice on the therapist's part (thus confirming the client's suspicions), grossly impaired treatment process and outcomes are likely to result (Barbarin, 1984; Jones, 1990; Sook Wha Ahn Toupin, 1980).

Cultural Characteristics of Ethnic Groups

Worldview constitutes part of the cultural characteristics of ethnic groups as well as the dominant culture. It consists of those values, beliefs, and attitudes that serve to organize and shape perceptions, expectations, and behavior. It also consists of a number of components, including cultural heritage as reflected in values, beliefs, language, practices, and individual identity or self-concept (Dana, 1993; Landrine, 1992). The worldviews of members of ethnic groups in the United States are also, to some extent, necessarily shaped and modified by variables related to dealing with the dominant culture, such as experiences with racism, prejudice, discrimination, and oppression.

Culture-specific elements of worldview can impact upon entry into treatment and its subsequent course and outcome. A representative sample of ethnic culture-specific components of worldview might include the individual's beliefs about mental illness and emotional difficulties, beliefs about the appropriate expression of emotion, and attitudes toward authority figures. Once treatment has begun, any or all of these elements might prove to be significantly discrepant from the therapist's conceptualization and treatment of psychological distress (Kleinman, 1980). A therapist's failure to appreciate such discrepancies—how these elements may have differently shaped a client's approach to life in general and to therapy in particular—can result in early termination and impaired treatment effectiveness (Atkinson et al., 1998).

To identify this discrepancy between client and therapist, one must first have a context. Western psychotherapy is heavily influenced by language, class-bound values, and culture-bound values (Atkinson et al., 1998). The latter involves seeing therapy as: (1) centered on the individual; (2) encouraging verbal, emotional, and behavioral openness and intimacy between client and therapist; (3) employing an analytic, linear, and cause-and-effect approach to problem definition and solution; and (4) making a clear distinction between spiritual, physical, and mental functioning. Disparities between this Western model of the therapeutic enterprise and the worldviews of ethnic group members can be found in all of the above dimensions.

Western individualism is a value not shared by other cultures (Draguns, 1988). An emphasis on anonymity, humility, and submission of the self to the welfare of the tribe, for example, is characteristic of American Indian culture (Foster, 1988; Heinrich, Corbine, & Thomas, 1990). Among Asian Americans, the group (both family and community) is also valued above the individual (Bemak, 1989; Lee, 1988). The intense focus on the individual that is typical of Western therapy is alien to these worldviews, and a lack of sensitivity to the discomfort engendered in an ethnic client by such a focus can lead to ineffective treatment and early termination.

In Western treatment, a premium is placed on verbal communication and the overt expression of emotions. In contrast, verbal expression and communication may be lacking or take different forms, in other non-Western groups (see the section on language usage and fluency in this chapter). In addition, suppression, reserve, and caution in the display of emotions when dealing with Whites or people in authority and power who represent the majority culture occur among African Americans (Ridley, 1984), Hispanic (particularly with the male machismo norm) (Ghali, 1977), and Asians (Lee, 1988).

Western patterns of thinking involve linearity, analytical and deductive reasoning, and abstract verbal conceptualization. For most American Indians, however, a more holistic processing style, utilizing metaphor, intuition, and visual representation, is characteristic (Foster, 1988). Lee (1988) contrasts Western logic of the mind with traditional Asian logic of the heart. A linear cause-and-effect approach to the framing and solving of such clients' problems is likely to be conceptually quite alien, leading clients to perceive a lack of therapist understanding and thus prompting early termination from treatment.

Other worldview differences between Western and ethnic groups that have an impact on the therapeutic endeavor include: (1) the emphasis placed on traditional practices by African Americans (Wilson & Stith, 1991), Hispanics (Ramos-McKay et al., 1988), Asian Americans (Lee, 1988), and American Indians (Heinrich et al., 1990); (2) the perceived relationship of the person to nature and the attribution of causality to internal and external events, with groups such as Asian Americans and American Indians taking a more fatalistic approach than White majority persons to the experiencing of psychological problems (Atkinson et al., 1998); and (3) the emphasis placed upon spirituality in accounting for psychological problems (Atkinson et al., 1998; see Chapter 9).

Language Usage and Fluency

Language usage and fluency can be viewed as an outcome and as a component of the enculturation and acculturation process. Although language usage and fluency are critical factors in all human interactions, they take on added importance in the therapeutic process with members from ethnic groups. For example, African Americans may not use standard English and Hispanics and Asians may not be fluent in English (Preciado & Henry, 1997; Russell, 1988; Sciarra & Ponterotto, 1991). Russell (1988) argues that language not only communicates the content of the message, but also provides information on the context of the message and the background of the messenger. This background information can include the messengers' place of origin, group membership, status in the group, and relationship to the person with whom he or she is communicating.

According to the 1990 Census there were 17,405,064 persons five years of age or older who spoke Spanish (U.S. Bureau of Census, 1990). Of these individuals 26.2 percent are reported to speak English "not well" or "not at all." Another 4,471,621 individuals used an Asian or Pacific Island language, with 23.8 percent of this group having minimum or no ability to speak English. In both groups, those speaking little or no English were concentrated primarily in cohorts that would use the mental health system (i.e., 18–64 years). For these individuals, communication between the client and therapist would be hampered, affecting not only entry into the system but also the process and outcome of treatment (Flaskerud & Liu, 1991).

Bilingual clients enter into the treatment process at risk because most clinicians are White and use standard English (Preciado & Henry, 1997). Marcos (1976), for example, has found that clients who spoke primarily Spanish were rated as having more pathology, having less connection with the interviewer, and being more emotionally withdrawn when interviewed in English as compared to Spanish. These findings were attributed to the disruptive speech patterns and reduced expression of affect that emerge when a person is required to speak in a nondominant language (Marcos & Urcuyo, 1979). The disrupted speech and reduced affect can be interpreted as signs of psychological disturbance and pathology and have a negative impact on the interactions between the client and therapist.

It is imperative that practitioners identify the dominant language in their bilingual clients. This is easy to determine when the person does not speak English well or does not speak English at all, but is more difficult when the client is bilingual. Under these circumstances, it is necessary to determine the client's degree of acculturation. This is achieved by gathering information about the person's use of language with family and friends and on the ethnic moderator variables described in this chapter, such as the nature and extent of the person's social networks and the degree to which he or she embraces and practices ethnic rituals and customs.

Working with monolingual or bilingual clients may call for the use of translators during the assessment and treatment processes. Translators need to be aware of the verbal and nonverbal nuances within the language they are translating and should have a mental health background (Sabin, 1975; Westermeyer, 1990; 1993). It is also imperative that clinician be aware of the clinical and linguistic differences in expression of emotional and psychological experiences in various languages (Westermeyer, 1993), the differential importance assigned to psychological symptoms (Kinzie & Manson, 1987), and the connotations that may be present in expressing psychological symptoms.

Individual Characteristics

Scholars have attempted to sort out the relative importance of culture and personality in the development of psychopathology and its treatment (Marsella, Tharp, & Ciborowski, 1979; Odejide, 1979; Smither, 1982). Juris Draguns (1988) makes a persuasive argument for the importance of personality in the development and expression of psychopathology. Within any given culture, normal and abnormal persons share common personality characteristics; yet, people's values, cognitions, locus of control, ego identity, valued behavior within the culture, and sense of belongingness can vary as a by-product of their culture and socialization experiences. In addition, variations exist in the manner in which thoughts, feelings, and behaviors are expressed publicly. These variations need to be identified and addressed in treatment interventions directed at ethnic persons.

Ethnic groups in this country are faced with a number of stressors, including those centering around education, employment, housing, family life, marriage, child-rearing, security, safety, and health. They continually have to deal with racism, prejudice, and oppression. Many of these forces are external to the individual and beyond his or her control. Ethnic persons often have to turn to different internal coping strategies—particularly when difficult situations are externally caused and difficult to change. The specific types of coping strategies will vary, given that there is evidence from cross-cultural research that members of different cultures use different coping strategies when confronted with similar stressors (Marsella & Dash-Scheuer, 1988).

Summary

This chapter has reviewed experiences of ethnic populations within the United States. Identifying the level of enculturation and acculturation as well as the degree of racial/ethnic identity development is extremely important and provides a framework for understanding ethnic populations. However, these processes do not provide a complete picture of ethnic persons or groups. It is essential to consider a number of moderator variables in order to more fully understand the beliefs, values, feelings, and behaviors of African Americans, Hispanics, Asian Americans, and American Indians. It is by comprehending the interaction of these processes and variables that one can then more fully appreciate the psychological functioning, symptom presentations, service utilization, and treatment processes and outcomes for ethnic populations.

REFERENCES

Adams, P. L. (1990). Prejudice and exclusion as social traumata. In J. D. Noshpitz & R. D. Coddington (Eds.), *Stressors and the adjustment disorders* (pp. 362–391). New York: Wiley.

Adler, N. E., Boyce, T., Chesney, M. A., Cohen, S., Folkman, S., Kahn, R. L., & Syme, S. L. (1994). Socioeconomic status and health: The challenge of the gradient. *American Psychologist, 49,* 15–24.

Al-Issa, I., & Tousignant, M. (Eds.). (1997). *Ethnicity, immigration, and psychopathology.* New York: Plenum Press.

Aponte, J. F., & Barnes, J. M. (1995). Impact of acculturation and moderator variables on the intervention and treatment of ethnic groups. In J. F. Aponte, R. Young Rivers, & J. Wohl (Eds.), *Psychological interventions and cultural diversity* (pp. 19–39). Boston: Allyn and Bacon.

Asamen, J. K., & Berry, G. L. (1987). Self-concept, alienation, and perceived prejudice: Implications for counseling Asian Americans. *Journal of Multicultural Counseling and Development, 15,* 146–160.

Atkinson, D. R., Morton, G., & Sue, D. W. (1998). *Counseling American minorities: A cross-cultural perspective* (5th ed.). Boston: McGraw-Hill.

Austin, N. L., Carter, R. T., & Vaux, A. (1990). The role of racial identity in Black students' attitudes toward counseling and counseling centers. *Journal of College Student Development, 31,* 237–244.

Barbarin, O. A. (1984). Racial themes in psychotherapy with Blacks: Effects of training on the attitudes of Black and White psychiatrists. *American Journal of Social Psychiatry, 4,* 13–20.

Bemak, F. (1989). Cross-cultural family therapy with Southeast Asian refugees. *Journal of Strategic and Systemic Therapies, 8,* 22–27.

Bernal, G., & Gutierrez, M. (1988). Cubans. In I. Comas-Díaz & E. E. H. Griffith (Eds.), *Clinical guidelines in cross-cultural mental health* (pp. 233–361). New York: Wiley.

Bernal, M. E., & Knight, G. P. (Eds.). (1993). *Ethnic identity: Formation and transmission among Hispanics and other minorities.* Albany: State University of New York Press.

Berry, J. W. (1993). Ethnic identity in plural societies. In M. E. Bernal & G. P. Knights (Eds.), *Ethnic identity: Formation and transmission among Hispanics and other minorities* (pp. 271–296). Albany: State University of New York Press.

Berry, J. W. (1998). *Conceptual approaches to understanding acculturation.* Paper presented at the International Conference on Acculturation: Advances in

Theory, Measurement, and Applied Research, University of San Francisco.

Berry, J. W., & Kim, U. (1988). Acculturation and mental health. In P. R. Dasen, J. W. Berry, & N. Sartorius (Eds.), *Health and cross-cultural psychology: Toward applications* (pp. 207–236). Newbury Park, CA: Sage.

Berry, J. W., Kim, V., Minke, T., & Mok, D. (1987). Comparative studies of acculturative stress. *International Migration Review, 21,* 491–511.

Boyd-Franklin, N. (1990). Five key factors in the treatment of Black families. In G. W. Saba, B. M. Karrer, & K. V. Hardy (Eds.), *Minorities and family therapy* (pp. 53–69). New York: Haworth.

Brantley, T. (1983). Racism and its impact on psychotherapy. *American Journal of Psychiatry, 140,* 1605–1608.

Briones, D. F., Heller, P. L., Chalfant, H. P., Roberts, A. E., Aaguirre-Hauchbaum, S. F., & Farr, W. F., Jr. (1990). Socioeconomic status, ethnicity, psychological distress, and readiness to utilize a mental health facility. *American Journal of Psychiatry, 147,* 1333–1340.

Carter, R. T. (1991). Cultural values: A review of empirical research and implications for counseling. *Journal of Counseling and Development, 70,* 164–173.

Carter, R. T., & Qureshi, A. (1995). A typology of philosophical assumptions in multi-cultural counseling and training. In J. G. Ponterotto, J. M. Casas, L. A. Suzuki, & C. M. Alexander (Eds.), *Handbook of multicultural counseling* (pp. 239–262). Thousand Oaks, CA: Sage.

Carter, R. T., Sbrocco, C., & Carter, T. (1996). African Americans and anxiety disorders research: Development of a testable, theoretical framework. *Psychotherapy, 33,* 449–463.

Casas, J. M., & Pytluk, S. D. (1995). Hispanic identity development: Implications for research and practice. In J. G. Ponterotto, J. M. Casas, L. A. Suzuki, & C. M. Alexander (Eds.). *Handbook of multicultural counseling* (pp. 155–180). Thousand Oaks, CA: Sage.

Cohen, S., & Willis, T. A. (1985). Stress, social support, and the buffering hypothesis. *Psychological Bulletin, 98,* 310–357.

Comas-Díaz, L., & Griffith, E. E. H. (Eds.). (1988). *Clinical guidelines in cross-cultural mental health.* New York: Wiley.

Cook, D. A. (1994). Racial identity in supervision. *Counselor Education and Supervision, 34,* 132–141.

Cross, W. E. (1972). The Negro-to-Black conversion experience. *Black World, 20,* 13–27.

Cross, W. E., Jr. (1995). The psychology of Nigresence: Revising the Cross model. In J. G. Ponterotto, J. M. Casas, L. A. Suzuki, & C. M. Alexander (Eds.), *Handbook of multicultural counseling* (pp. 93–122). Thousand Oaks, CA: Sage.

Cuellar, I., Arnold, B., & Moldanado, R. (1995). Acculturation Rating Scale for Mexican Americans-II. A revision of the original ARSMA scale. *Hispanic Journal of Behavioral Sciences, 17,* 275–304.

Dakoff, G. A., & Taylor, S. E. (1990). Victim's perception of social support. What is helpful from whom? *Journal of Personality and Social Psychology, 58,* 80–89.

Dana, R. H. (1993). *Multicultural assessment perspectives for professional psychology.* Boston: Allyn and Bacon.

Delphin, M. E., & Rollock, D. (1995). University alienation and African American ethnic identity as predictors of attitudes toward, knowledge about, and likely use of psychological services. *Journal of College Student Development, 36,* 337–346.

De Vita, C. J. (1996). The United States at mid-decade. *Population Bulletin, 50* (4), 1–48.

Dohrenwend, B. P., & Dohrenwend, B. S. (1981a). Quasi-experimental evidence on the social-causation-social-selection issue posed by class differences. *American Journal of Community Psychology, 9,* 128–146.

Dohrenwend, B. S., & Dohrenwend, B. P. (1981b). Hypotheses about stress processes linking social class to various types of psychopathology. *American Journal of Community Psychology, 9,* 146–159.

Draguns, J. G. (1988). Personality and culture: Are they relevant for the enhancement of quality of mental life? In P. R. Dasen, J. W. Berry, & N. Sartorius (Eds.), *Health and cross-cultural psychology: Toward applications* (pp. 141–161). Newbury Park, CA: Sage.

Felix-Ortiz, M., Newcomb, M. D., & Myers, H. (1994). A multidimensional measure of cultural identity for Latin and Latina adolescents. *Hispanic Journal of Behavioral Sciences, 16,* 99–115.

Flaskerud, J. H., & Liu, P. Y. (1991). Effects of an Asian client-therapist language, ethnicity, and gender match on utilization and outcome of therapy. *Community Mental Health Journal, 27,* 31–42.

Foster, D. V. (1988). Consideration of treatment issues with American Indians detained in the Federal Bureau of Prisons. *Psychiatric Annals, 18,* 698–701.

Fujii, J. S., Fukushima, S. N., & Yamamoto, J. (1993). Psychiatric care of Japanese Americans. In A. C. Gaw (Ed.), *Culture, ethnicity, and mental illness* (pp. 305–345). Washington, DC: American Psychiatric Press.

Gaw, A. C. (Ed.). (1993a). *Culture, ethnicity, and mental illness.* Washington, DC: American Psychiatric Press.

Gaw, A. C. (1993b). Psychiatric care of Chinese Americans. In A. C. Gaw (Ed.), *Culture, ethnicity, and mental illness* (pp. 245–280). Washington, DC: American Psychiatric Press.

Ghali, S. B. (1977). Cultural sensitivity and the Puerto Rican client. *Social Casework, 58,* 459–468.

Griffith, E. E. H., & Baker, F. M. (1993). Psychiatric care of African Americans. In A. C. Gaw (Ed.), *Culture, ethnicity, and mental illness* (pp. 147–173). Washington, DC: American Psychiatric Press.

Grills, C., & Longshore, D. (1996). Africentrism: Psychometric analyses of a self-report measure. *Journal of Black Psychology, 22,* 86–106.

Guarnaccia, P. J., & Parra, P. (1996). Ethnicity, social status, and families' experiences of caring for a mentally ill family member. *Community Mental Health Journal, 32,* 243–260.

Harper, F. D. (1988). Alcohol and Black youth: An overview. *Journal of Drug Issues, 18,* 15–20.

Heinrich, R. K., Corbine, J. L., & Thomas, K. R. (1990). Counseling Native Americans. *Journal of Counseling & Development, 69,* 128–133.

Helms, J. E. (1985). Cultural identity in the treatment process. In P. Pederson (Ed.), *Handbook of cross-cultural counseling and therapy* (pp. 239–245). Westport, CT: Greenwood.

Helms, J. E. (1990a). Three perspectives on counseling and psychotherapy with visible racial/ethnic group clients. In F. C. Serafica, A. I. Schwebel, R. K. Russell, P. D. Isaac, & L. B. Myers (Eds.), *Mental health of ethnic minorities* (pp. 171–201). New York: Praeger.

Helms, J. E. (Ed.). (1990b). *Black and White racial identity: Theory, research and practice.* Westport, CT: Greenwood.

Helms, J. E. (1995). An update of Helms' White and people of color racial identity models. In J. G. Ponterotto, J. M. Casas, L. A. Suzuki, & C. M. Alexander (Eds.), *Handbook of multicultural counseling* (pp. 181–198). Thousand Oaks, CA: Sage.

Helms, J. E., & Talleyrand, R. M. (1997). Race is not ethnicity. *American Psychologist, 52,* 1246–1247.

Ho, C. K. (1990). An analysis of domestic violence in Asian American communities: A multicultural approach to counseling. *Women & Therapy, 9,* 129–150.

Hoffmann, T., Dana, R. H., & Bolton, B. (1985). Measured acculturation and MMPI-168 performance of native American adults. *Journal of Cross-Cultural Psychology, 16,* 243–256.

Hughes, C. C. (1993). Culture in clinical psychiatry. In A. C. Gaw (Ed.), *Culture, ethnicity, and mental illness* (pp. 3–41). Washington, DC: American Psychiatric Press.

Hughes, M., & Demo, D. H. (1989). Self-perceptions of Black Americans: Self-esteem and personal efficacy. *American Journal of Sociology, 95,* 132–159.

Hurejsi, C., Craig, B., & Pablo, J. (1992). Reactions by Native Americans to child protection agencies: Cultural and community factors. *Child Welfare, 71,* 329–342.

Jackson, B. (1975). Black identity development. *MEFORM: Journal of Educational Diversity & Innovation, 2,* 19–25.

Jackson, J. S., & Sellers, S. L. (1997). Psychological, social, and cultural perspectives on minority health in adolescence: A life-course framework. In D. K. Wilson, J. R. Rodrigue, & W. C. Taylor (Eds.), *Health-promoting and health-compromising behaviors among minority adolescents.* Washington, DC: American Psychological Association.

Jones, N. S. (1990). Black/White issues in psychotherapy: A framework for clinical practice. *Journal of Social Behavior and Personality, 5,* 305–322.

Kerwin, C., Ponterotto, J. G., Jackson, B. L., & Harris, A. (1993). Racial identity in biracial children: A qualitative investigation. *Journal of Counseling Psychology, 40,* 221–231.

Kinzie, J. D., & Manson, S. M. (1987). The use of self-rating scales in cross cultural psychiatry. *Hospital and Community Psychiatry, 38,* 190–196.

Kitano, H. H. L. (1989). A model for counseling Asian Americans. In P. B. Pedersen, J. G. Draguns, W. J. Lonner, & J. E. Trimble (Eds.), *Counseling across cultures* (3rd ed., pp. 139–151). Honolulu: University of Hawaii Press.

Kitano, H. H. L., & Maki, M. T. (1997). Continuity, change, and diversity: Counseling Asian Americans. In P. B. Pederson, J. G. Draguns, W. J. Lonner, & J. E. Trimble (Eds.), *Counseling across cultures* (4th ed., pp. 124–144). Honolulu: University of Hawaii Press.

Kleinman, A. (1980). *Patients and healers in the context of culture.* Berkeley, CA: University of California Press.

Kluegel, J. R., & Smith, E. R. (1983). Affirmative action attitudes: Effects of self-interest, racial affect, and stratification beliefs on Whites' views. *Social Forces, 61,* 797–824.

LaFromboise, T. D. (1988). American Indian mental health policy. *American Psychologist, 43,* 388–397.

LaFromboise, T., Coleman, H. L. K., & Gerton, J. (1993). Psychological impact of biculturalism: Evidence and Theory. *Psychological Bulletin, 114,* 395–412.

Landrine, H. (1992). Clinical implications of cultural differences: The referential versus the indexical self. *Clinical Psychology Review, 12,* 401–415.

Landrine, H., & Klonoff, E. A. (1994). The African American Acculturation Scale: Development, reliability, and validity. *Journal of Black Psychology, 20,* 104–127.

Lee, E. (1988). Cultural factors in working with Southeastern Asian refugee adolescents. *Journal of Adolescence, 11,* 167–179.

Lee, L. C. (1997a). The promise and pitfalls of multicultural counseling. In L. C. Lee (Ed.), *Multicultural issues in counseling: New approaches to diversity* (pp. 3–13). Alexandria, VA: American Counseling Association.

Lee, L. C. (1997b). Cultural dynamics: Their importance in culturally responsive counseling. In L. C. Lee (Ed.), *Multicultural issues in counseling: New approaches to diversity* (pp. 15–30). Alexandria, VA: American Counseling Association.

Lin, N., Woelfel, M. W., & Light, S. C. (1985). The buffering effect of social support subsequent to an important life event. *Journal of Social and Health Behavior, 26,* 247–263.

Lopez-Bushnell, F. K., Tyre, P., & Futrell, M. (1992). Alcoholism and the Hispanic older adult. *Clinical Gerontologist, 11,* 123–130.

Lorion, R. P., & Felner, R. D. (1986). Research on mental health interventions with the disadvantaged. In S. L. Garfield & A. E. Bergin (Eds.), *Handbook of psychotherapy and behavior change* (3rd ed., pp. 739–775). New York: Wiley.

Marcos, L. R. (1976). Bilinguals in psychotherapy: Language as an emotional barrier. *American Journal of Psychotherapy, 30,* 552–560.

Marcos, L. R., & Urcuyo, L. (1979). Dynamic psychotherapy with the bilingual patient *American Journal of Psychotherapy, 33,* 331–338.

Marín, G. (1992). Issues in the measurement of acculturation among Hispanics. In K. F. Geisinger (Ed.), *Psychological testing of Hispanics* (pp. 235–251). Washington, DC: American Psychological Association.

Marín, G., & Gamba, R. J. (1996). A new measurement of acculturation for Hispanics: The Bidimensional Acculturation Scale for Hispanics (BAS). *Hispanic Journal of Behavioral Sciences, 18,* 297–316.

Marsella, A. J., & Dash-Scheuer, A. (1988). Coping, culture, and healthy human development: A research and conceptual overview. In P. R. Dasen, J. W. Berry, & N. Sartorius (Eds.), *Health and cross-cultural psychology: Toward applications* (pp. 162–178). Newbury Park, CA: Sage.

Marsella, A. J., Tharp, R. G., & Ciborowski, T. J. (Eds.). (1979). *Perspectives on cross-cultural psychology.* New York: Academic Press.

Martinez, C., Jr. (1988). Mexican-Americans. In L. Comas-Díaz & E. E. H. Griffith (Eds.), *Clinical guidelines in cross-cultural mental health* (pp. 182–232). New York: Wiley.

Martinez, C., Jr. (1993). Psychiatric care of Mexican Americans. In A. C. Gaw (Ed.), *Culture, ethnicity, and mental illness* (pp. 431–466). Washington, DC: American Psychiatric Press.

McConahay, J. B., & Hough, J. C. (1976). Symbolic racism. *Journal of Social Issues, 32,* 23–45.

McIntosh, J. L. (1984). Suicide among Native Americans: Further tribal data and considerations. *Omega: The Journal of Death and Dying, 14,* 215–229.

Miller, F. S. (1992). Network structural support: Its relationship to the psychosocial development of Black females. In A. K. H. Burlew, W. C. Banks, H. P. McAdoo, & D. A. Azibo (Eds.), *African American psychology: Theory, research, and practice* (pp. 105–126). Newbury Park, CA: Sage.

Mollica, R. F., & Lavelle, J. (1988). Southeast Asia refugees. In L. Comas-Díaz & E. E. H. Griffith (Eds.), *Clinical guide lines in cross-cultural mental health* (pp. 262–293). New York: Wiley.

Montejano, D. (1987). *Anglos and Mexicans in the making of Texas, 1836–1986.* Austin, TX: University of Texas Press.

Odejide, A. O. (1979). Cross-cultural psychiatry: A myth or reality? *Comprehensive Psychiatry, 20,* 103–108.

Oetting, F. R., Edwards, R. W., & Beauvais, F. (1988). Drugs and Native American youth. *Drugs and Society, 3,* 1–34.

O'Hare, W. P. (1996). A new look at poverty in America. *Population Bulletin, 51,* (2), 1–48.

Padilla, A. M., Lindholm, K. J., Chen, A., Duran, R., Hakuta, K., Lambert, W., & Tucker, G. R. (1991). The English-only movement: Myths, reality, and implications for psychology. *American Psychologist, 46,* 120–130.

Parham, T. A., & Helms, J. E. (1981). The influence of Black students' racial identity attitudes on preference for counselor's race. *Journal of Counseling Psychology, 28,* 250–257.

Phinney, J. S. (1992). The Multi-Group ethnic identity measure: A new scale for use with diverse groups. *Journal of Adolescent Research, 7,* 156–176.

Phinney, J. S. (1996). When we talk about American ethnic groups, what do we mean? *American Psychologist, 51,* 918–927.

Phinney, J. S. (1998). *Ethnic identity and acculturation.* Paper presented at the International Conference on Acculturation: Advances in Theory, Measurement, and Applied Research, University of San Francisco.

Phinney, J. S., Chavira, V., & Williamson, L. (1992). Acculturation attitudes and self-esteem among high school and college students. *Youth and Society, 23,* 299–312.

Ponterotto, J. G., Casas, J. M., Suzuki, L. A., & Alexander, C. M. (Eds.). (1995). *Handbook of multicultural counseling.* Thousand Oaks, CA: Sage.

Poston, W. S. C. (1990). The biracial identity development model: A needed addition. *Journal of Counseling and Development, 69,* 152–155.

Preciado, J., & Henry, M. (1997). Linguistic barriers in health education and services. In J. G. García & M. C. Zea (Eds.), *Psychological interventions and research with Latino populations* (pp. 235–254). Boston: Allyn and Bacon.

Priest, R. (1991). Racism and prejudice as negative impacts on African American clients in therapy. *Journal of Counseling and Development, 70,* 213–215.

Ramos-McKay, J. M., Comas-Díaz, L., & Rivera, L. A. (1988). Puerto Ricans. In L. Comas-Díaz & E. E. H. Griffith (Eds.), *Clinical guidelines in cross-cultural mental health* (pp. 204–232). New York: Wiley.

Ramos, H. A., & Morales, M. M. (1985). U.S. immigration and the Hispanic community: A historical overview and sociological perspective. *Journal of Hispanic Politics, 1,* 1–17.

Ridley, C. R. (1984). Clinical treatment of the nondisclosing Black client: A therapeutic paradox. *American Psychologist, 39,* 1234–1244.

Ridley, C. R. (1995). *Overcoming unintentional racism in counseling and theory: A practitioner's guide to intentional intervention.* Thousand Oaks, CA: Sage.

Ruiz, A. S. (1990). Ethnic identity: Crisis and resolution. *Journal of Multicultural Counseling and Development, 18,* 29–40.

Russell, D. M. (1988). Language and psychotherapy: The influence of nonstandard English in clinical practice. In L. Comas-Díaz & E. E. H. Griffith (Eds.), *Clinical guidelines in cross-cultural mental health* (pp. 33–68). New York: Wiley.

Sabin, J. E. (1975). Translating despair. *American Journal of Psychiatry, 132,* 197–199.

Sarason, B. R., Sarason, I. G., & Pierce, G. R. (Eds.). (1990). *Social support: An interactional view.* New York: Wiley.

Schradle, S. B., & Dougher, M. J. (1985). Social support as a mediator of stress: Theoretical and empirical issues. *Clinical Psychology Review, 5,* 641–661.

Sciarra, D. T., & Ponterotto, J. G. (1991). Counseling the Hispanic bilingual family: Challenges to the therapeutic process. *Psychotherapy, 28,* 473–479.

Smith, E. P., & Brookins, C. C. (1997). Toward the development of an ethnic identity measure for African American youth. *Journal of Black Psychology, 23,* 358–377.

Smither, R. (1982). Human migration and the accultura-tion of minorities. *Human Relations, 35,* 57–68.

Sodowsky, G. R., & Carey, J. C. (1987). Asian Indian immigrants in America: Factors related to adjust-ment. *Journal of Multicultural Counseling and Development, 15,* 129–141.

Sodowsky, G. R., Lai, E. W., & Plake, B. S. (1991). Mod-erating effects of socio-cultural variables on accul-turation attitudes of Hispanics and Asian Americans. *Journal of Counseling & Development, 70,* 194–204.

Sook Wha Ahn Toupin, E. (1980). Counseling Asians: Psychotherapy in the context of racism and Asian-American history. *American Journal of Orthopsychi-atry, 50,* 76–86.

Sue, S., Chun, C., & Gee, K. (1995). Ethnic minority intervention and treatment research. In J. F. Aponte, R. Young Rivers, & J. Wohl (Eds.), *Psychological interventions and cultural diversity* (pp. 266–282). Boston: Allyn and Bacon.

Suinn, R. M., Richard-Figueroa, K., Lew, S., & Vigil, S. (1987). The Suinn-Lew Asian Self-Identity Accul-turation Scale: An initial report. *Educational and Psychological Measurement, 47,* 401–407.

Szapocznik, J., Kurtines, W., Santiesteban, D. A., Pantín, H., Scopetta, M., Mancilla, Y., Aisenberg, S., McIn-tosh, S., Pérez-Vidal, A., & Coatsworth, J. D. (1997). The evolution of a structural ecosystematic theory for working with Latino families. In J. G. García & M. C. Zea (Eds.), *Psychological interventions and research with Latino populations* (pp. 166–190). Boston: Allyn and Bacon.

Thompson, J. W., Walker, R. D., & Silk-Walker, P. (1993). Psychiatric care of American Indians and Alaska Natives. In A. C. Gaw (Ed.), *Culture, ethnicity, and mental illness* (pp. 189–243). Washington, DC: American Psychiatric Press.

Trimble, J. E. (1987). Self-perception and perceived alien-ation among American Indians. *Journal of Commu-nity Psychology, 15,* 316–333.

U.S. Bureau of Census (1990). *1990 census of population and housing Summary tape file: Summary popula-tion and housing characteristics.* Washington, DC.

Westermeyer, J. J. (1990). Working with an interpreter in psychiatric assessment and treatment. *Journal of Nervous and Mental Diseases, 178,* 745–749.

Westermeyer, J. J. (1993). Cross-cultural psychiatric assessment. In A. C. Gaw (Ed.), *Culture, ethnicity, and mental illness* (pp. 125–144). Washington, DC: American Psychiatric Press.

Wierzbicki, M., & Pekarik, G. (1993). A meta-analysis of psychotherapy dropout. *Professional Psychology: Research and Practice, 24,* 190–195.

Wilson, L. L., & Stith, S. M. (1991). Culturally sensitive therapy with Black clients. *Journal of Multicultural Counseling and Development, 19,* 32–43.

Zane, N. (1998). *Major approaches to the measurement of acculturation: A content analysis and empirical validation.* Paper presented at the International Con-ference on Acculturation: Advances in Theory, Measurement, and Applied Research, University of San Francisco.

Zimmerman, M. A., Ramirez-Valles, J., Washienko, K. M., & Walter, B. (1996). The development of a measure of enculturation for Native American youth. *American Journal of Community Psychology, 24,* 295–310.

3 Psychopathology and Ethnicity

JURIS G. DRAGUNS

"We treat mental illness, not Hawaiians"

(Higginbotham, 1987, p. 108)

*An area psychiatrist is alleged to have said: "I know the diagnosis
immediately, all our Amish patients are schizophrenic."*

(Egeland, Hofsteter, & Eshleman, 1983, p. 68)

The Scope and Purpose of This Chapter

The two quotations above set the stage and define the task for this chapter. The former quotation, by a director at a public psychiatric clinic in Hawaii, boldly proclaims the irrelevance of ethnocultural considerations in implementing mental health treatment programs. The latter assertion, by a private practitioner in Pennsylvania, highlights two dangers that have not yet been fully overcome. The first of these involves equating, all too readily, mental disorder with difference (Draguns, 1996a). The second exemplifies the distortion that results when judgments are hastily formed and stereotypically imposed upon phenomena observed across a cultural gulf.

Against this background, the principal objective of this chapter is to assess the role of ethnocultural influences upon the symptoms and manifestations of mental disorder. The scope of this undertaking is restricted to the patterns of distress and disability as defined by the American Psychiatric Association (1994) in the current, fourth edition of its Diagnostic and Statistical Manual (DSM-IV). Furthermore, the chapter will be focused upon the ethnic and cultural diversity of the United States and will concentrate upon the principal cultural and ethnic groupings in this country, as recognized in current public policy. Specifically, the following racial and/or ethnic groups will be considered: African Americans,

Hispanics, Asian Americans/Pacific Islanders, and American Indians. Occasionally, data pertaining to Canadians will be included, to the extent that this information is thought to overlap with information pertinent to one or several of the above ethnic groups. In reference to Puerto Ricans, efforts will be made to discuss the rich store of data pertaining to the members of this group in the continental United States. Because of space limitations, however, no attempt will be undertaken to do justice to the mental health problems of the population of Puerto Rico, a subject that deserves, and has received, systematic treatment elsewhere (e.g., Canino, Bird, & Shrout, 1987; Rivera Ramos, 1984).

Three Sources of Data

The interplay of cultural characteristics and psychological disturbance has been studied from a variety of vantage points for more than a century (Murphy, 1982). The enterprise of ethnic psychopathology is a multidisciplinary undertaking, pursued simultaneously by a variety of methods. In particular, three distinct approaches have evolved and attained prominence: clinical, comparative, and epidemiological. They now remain to be described.

Clinical Studies

The oldest of these approaches is based upon clinical inquiry. It has played a pivotal role in biomedicine in delineating disease entities, tracing them to their origin, and developing effective means for counteracting them. Quite often clinical observation and the insights derived from it constituted byproducts of diagnostic and treatment activity. Extended to psychological dysfunction, the clinical approach aims at a thorough factual description of its symptoms in the context of their occurrence. Clinical observation also encompasses recording changes in the patient's general state of well-being, as well as in specific symptoms and their patterns. These changes are then linked by the clinician to the conditions that have preceded or accompanied the onset of illness, and that may have brought it about.

To this day, the clinical method remains indispensable in the early stages of investigating a problem pertaining to mental health. Only by observing as factually and thoroughly as possible can the clinician capture the relevant information about the disorder so that it is recorded and eventually used, in both research and treatment. The richness and complexity of clinical data are, however, partially offset by major limitations. They are especially apparent when the multiple and interacting threads of potential influence upon a disorder must be traced and disentangled—for example, the political, economic, interpersonal, and subjective factors that often coalesce in impinging upon a person. Remote antecedents and causes are notoriously difficult to trace—for example, the possible effect of traumatic and other events in childhood upon the psychiatric symptoms of a middle-aged woman. Moreover, clinically gathered data are highly susceptible to the confounding of observation and inference or of description and explanation. Clinicians at their best strive to separate the information that comes through their senses from the constructions that they cognitively impose upon it.

Comparative Studies

Faced with the limitations of clinical data, some researchers have shifted to interethnic comparisons. There are numerous comparative studies of symptoms and related indicators in the ethnocultural literature (e.g., Enright & Jaeckle, 1963; Escobar, Randolph, & Hill, 1986; Fabrega, Swartz, & Wallace, 1968; Katz, Sanborn, Lowery, & Ching, 1978; Marsella, Sanborn, Kameoka, Shizuru, & Brennan, 1975). Interethnic comparisons provide quantitative data rather than qualitative impressions and rely upon statistical inference instead of subjective judgment. Of necessity, comparing patients of two or more ethnic groups is accomplished with samples based on availability rather than on explicit criteria of random or representative selection. Therefore, it is hazardous to generalize such findings to the entire ethnic group from which the samples were drawn. The more cautious and realistic procedure is to proceed piecemeal, by replicating and extending findings to a variety of other samples of the same ethnicities. Eventually, the findings so obtained have to be integrated with other relevant data, including clinical observations.

Another intractable issue concerns the equivalence of samples different not only in ethnic composition, but in a host of other social indicators as well—socioeconomic, educational, occupational, and so forth (see Chapters 1 and 2). The consensus in ethnic studies of mental health phenomena is that there are dangers involved in both overmatching and undermatching samples differing in ethnicity (Draguns, 1982, 1996b). In either case, only provisional conclusions can be drawn from either imperfectly matched or laboriously equated, but artificial, samples.

Finally, the yield of interethnic comparisons remains limited in its conclusiveness unless groups of normal subjects as well as psychiatric patients are included in the same research design (Draguns, 1982). Within the last decade, three such comparisons have been published in the international cross-cultural literature (Rader, Krampen, & Sultan, 1990; Radford, 1989; Tseng, et al., 1990). None of these reports, however, pertains to ethnicity in the United States. As yet, the potential of comparative studies for providing information on psychopathology and ethnicity is incompletely realized. By themselves, such comparisons provide an additional perspective, but not the definitive solution, for researchers in this field.

Epidemiological Studies

Epidemiology is an established branch of contemporary scientific medicine. Its principal task is to provide objective, quantitative data on the distribution of diseases in designated human populations and/or in specified geographic areas. Epidemiological research generates data that pertain to the number of cases of a given disease within a territory and to the percentage or proportion of such cases within the total population (Escobar, 1993). Epidemiologists also search for, and systematically study, those variables that increase or decrease the chances of the occurrence of a disease. Epidemiological data yield something akin to a psychiatric census as standardized biographic, demographic, and psychological information is compiled on a representative sample of a specified population. Epidemiological study of psychiatric syndromes goes back to the early decades of the twentieth century. In the Midtown Manhattan study (Srole, Langner, Michael, Opler, & Rennie, 1962) ratings of psychiatric impairment were investigated in relation to ethnocultural categories. More recently, the National Institute of Mental Health Epidemiologic Catchment Area Program (ECA) studied over 20,000 community respondents at five locations in different regions of the United States (Robins & Regier, 1991). Of interest in the present context, ECA provided a wealth of data on the characteristic disorders in three major ethnic groupings: African Americans, Hispanics, and Caucasians.

By now epidemiological psychiatric research has evolved into an operation of staggering scope and complexity. It has generated a rich set of objective, standardized data on the prevalence of many psychiatric disorders, their manifestations, antecedents, concomitants, and correlates. In several respects, epidemiological research stands in contrast to the clinical approach, even though in other respects it complements it. As a rule, clinicians tend to learn a lot about a specific person or a small number of individuals. Epidemiologists gather data about a multitude of persons. Of necessity, however, the amount of information collected about a specific research participant is restricted by the standardized and uniform research procedures. Thus, there is no opportunity to improvise, to pursue a promising point, or to follow an unanticipated lead. Epidemiological findings then resemble a bird's-eye view or an aerial photograph; a lot of objects are perceived from afar, but only a few features are detected for any one of them. By contrast, an intensive clinical study is similar to an artistic portrait; a great deal of insight is gained about the unique individual. In order to apply this wealth of knowledge to other persons, one must make a daring inferential leap.

Combination and Alternation of the Three Approaches: Stepping Stones toward Integration and Synthesis

All too often, the three research approaches have been applied in isolation or even in competition. Yet, it is clear that none of the three methods is ideal or optimal; each is useful, but imperfect. Thus, the future of ethnic research on psychopathology crucially demands blending and pooling of the three approaches. Initial clinical observations may provide the impetus for a systematic epidemiological investigation. Conversely, epidemiological findings may spark a clinical study in depth. Moreover, epidemiological projects at two or more sites and/or on several populations may be based on standardized procedures and instruments and may be coordinated so as to yield comparable results. Thus, Gaw (1993a) shifts smoothly from epidemiological evidence to illustrative case studies, and Tseng and Streltzer (1997) proceed from comparative to clinical data in a seamless fashion. In the present chapter, the same kind of alternation will be attempted, with the goal of contributing toward the eventual creation of a coherent and organized body of findings.

A Survey of Results

In this section, the empirical results will be presented that pertain to differences in psychopathology across ethnocultural groups. The question will be asked: What is known on the basis of systematic research of the three varieties described above about the modes of expression and experience of distress and disability in socioculturally and ethnically distinct groupings of the United States population? This portion of the chapter is for the most part organized on the basis of the categories in DSM-IV, with emphasis upon those varieties of disorder that have been intensively and continuously studied across ethnic lines.

Anxiety Disorders

Recent reviewers (Al-Issa & Ouidji, 1998; Draguns, 1997; Good & Kleinman, 1985; Kirmayer, Young, & Hayton, 1995; Tanaka-Matsumi & Draguns, 1996) are in agreement on two points: Anxiety disorders occur in a wide variety of cultures, yet their manifestations across cultures differ substantially in both rates of incidence and modes of expression. These conclusions apply to the multicultural microcosm of the United States.

Anxiety disorders in African Americans have been described and investigated rather intensively (Carter, Sbrocco, & Carter, 1996); Kirmayer et al., 1995; Neal & Turner, 1991). Early findings, based on clinical populations and/or somewhat unrepresentative community samples, had created the impression of generically increased rates of anxiety disorders in African Americans (cf. Carter et al., 1996). However, these conclusions were substantially revised upon the intensive analysis of the results of recent, large-scale and representative, community surveys. When sociodemographic disparities between African Americans and Caucasians were partialed out, raw differences between these two groups declined to nonsignificance (Eaton, Dryman, & Weissman, 1991), notably in the prevalence of panic disorder with agoraphobia, together with some of the key symptoms of these disorders (Horwath, Johnson, & Horing, 1993). On the basis of these findings, Horwath et al. concluded that panic disorder is essentially similar among African Americans and Caucasians. The only significant differences they found pertained to greater frequency of reported tingling in the extremities by African Americans and the higher mean number of symptoms in the same population. Rates of simple phobia, however, appear to be elevated among African Americans by comparison with Caucasians (Brown, Eaton, & Sussman, 1990). Even this finding failed to be confirmed in a more recent and very thorough epidemiological study, the National Comorbidity Survey (Kessler et al., 1994). Somewhat surprisingly, school phobia was found to be less prevalent among African American children than among their Caucasian counterparts (Neal, Lilly, & Zakis, 1993), and African American children's fears did not coalesce into a specific and recognizable school phobia factor.

Proceeding from these somewhat unexpected findings, Carter et al. (1996) proposed a theoretical framework that goes beyond ethnocultural differences and incorporates a number of demographic and other indicators such as the age of the patients, their socioeconomic status, the stress levels experienced, as well as their beliefs, expectations, and a number of variables pertaining to identity and acculturation. Carter et al. predicted that the most pronounced differences from Caucasians in symptoms and their antecedents would be found in African American samples characterized by high racial identity and low acculturation. Such patients would also pose the greatest challenge in responding to or benefiting from standard, noncultural modes of therapeutic intervention. This model was designed specifically for African Americans, but its potential relevance appears to extend to other ethnically distinctive populations.

With Hispanics, the results of epidemiological research are more fragmentary. In the Los Angeles component of ECA, the Mexican American segment of the community sample presented higher rates of generalized anxiety disorder, agoraphobia, and simple phobia compared with Caucasians (Karno, Golding, Sorenson, & Burnham, 1988). Remarkably, phobia was more prevalent among Mexican Americans who were born in the United States than among those who had immigrated (Karno et al., 1987).

Even less epidemiologically based information is available about the anxiety disorders in the various groups of Asian Americans. Lin and Endler (1993) reported that anxiety levels were elevated among Chinese immigrants. These authors attributed this elevation to the stress of adapting to a new environment and to the resulting sense of insecurity and inadequacy.

At the opposite end of the spectrum of investigations, clinical inquiry has focused on culture-bound syndromes (CBS), that is, patterns of symptoms that are unique to or characteristic of a culture, ethnic group, or region. Of the numerous CBSs described in recent literature (Simons & Hughes, 1993), *ataque de nervios* (literally, "an attack of nerves") is both relevant to anxiety and prevalent among Hispanics. It is frequency encountered among Puerto Rican patients, but has been known to occur among Mexican Americans and presumably other Hispanic populations. These attacks are "dramatic episodes in which the person trembles, begins to shout, sometimes becomes aggressive, and then falls to the floor" (Canino & Canino, 1993, p. 477). *Ataqe de nervios,* then, is a culturally patterned state of being flooded with anxiety and of reacting to stress in a global and undifferentiated way, with a gamut of psychophysiological reactions. Epidemiological studies of distribution and frequency of *ataque de nervios* apparently have not yet been conducted.

Posttraumatic Stress Syndrome (PTSD)

Although in DSM-IV PTSD is subsumed within the rubric of anxiety disorders, it shall be treated here under a separate heading. PTSD is a relatively "new" disorder that has generated a continuous and cumulative body of observations and findings only in the past two decades (see Chapter 1). In reference to ethnoculture, two foci of research have emerged. One of them pertains to the patterns of behavior exhibited by the waves of refugees that have been admitted to the United States in the past few decades. Many of these people have experienced intense suffering, physically and psychologically, that has left scars in the form of culturally patterned symptoms of PTSD. The other active area of research pertains to the role of ethnic factors in shaping stress-related manifestations in the much studied population of American Vietnam War veterans.

Boehnlein and Kinzie (1995) have provided an excellent summary and evaluation of relevant findings on refugees. Much of the available information is based on the authors' copious clinical experience with Cambodian survivors of brutal persecution by the Khmer Rouges (1975–1979). Many of them had lost all or most of their family and had witnessed murder and brutality on a mass scale, in some cases for as long as four years. Not surprisingly, a high proportion of these samples—in some cases well over 50 percent—satisfied the diagnostic criteria for PTSD and exhibited persistent and debilitating symptoms that, in many cases, resisted treatment. Psychophysiological symptoms were a prominent idiom of distress, combined with vegetative depressive manifestations. Therapy was effective in reducing depressive and somatic symptoms, but anxiety, distress, and hostility declined only slightly, if at all.

The major ethnocultural finding that emerged from a large-scale national study of PTSD in Vietnam War veterans pointed to significant differences of this disorder across ethnic lines (Schlenger & Fairbank, 1996). Specifically, PTSD was diagnosed for 27.9 percent of the Hispanics, 20.6 percent of African Americans, and 13.7 percent of Caucasians. When several important disparities—for example, in combat exposure—were eliminated, the difference between Caucasians and either of the other two groups retained its statistically significant status whereas the difference between Hispanics and African Americans become nonsignificant. A partial explanation of this finding emphasizes the experience of discrimination and disadvantage for many members of both groups. Such experiences increased their vulnerability and enhanced the risk of PTSD.

Depressive Spectrum

Depression has been intensively investigated across the major ethnocultural groupings. One of the major findings that has resulted from this research effort is the prominence of somatic or bodily distress in the presenting picture of depressive patients of several Asian and Hispanic groups by comparison with their Caucasian counterparts (Araneta, 1993; Canino & Canino, 1993; Fujii, Fukushima, & Yamamoto, 1993; Gaw, 1993b; Sue & Morishima, 1982; Tseng, 1975). Three caveats should be appended to the above statement. First, somatic symptoms are prominent in depression, but are by no means confined to it. Somatic symptoms also occur in the context of anxiety states, psychotic disorders, and other conditions. Second, somatic symptoms are rarely, if ever, the sole or exclusive mode of expression of depression or any other negative feeling states. Third, while a variety of Asian and Hispanic groups have differed from the Caucasian American majority by virtue of a greater number and/or prominence of somatization, it does not follow that the somatic symptoms of all of these groups are identical. However, the investigation of such differences, for example, between Japanese and Chinese Americans, or between Mexicans and Puerto Ricans in the United States, has been rarely attempted. The implementation of such objectives is a worthwhile task for future research.

There may, however, be generic influences operating in facilitating the communication of somatic distress and in inhibiting expressions of personal misery. The better known and more universal role of the physician as a healer of physical ailments may come into play here. Moreover, physical distress is widely recognized, in various cultures, to have an imperious sense of urgency. Whether psychological discomfort has a similarly pressing claim for professional attention and compassion may be an open question in a variety of sociocultural milieus. Finally, it has been suggested (Draguns, 1996b) that it is easier and less embarrassing to present impersonal physical symptoms, especially across a culture gulf, than it is to "bare one's soul" and "to pour one's heart out" to a stranger in an alien setting. For these reasons, it is not surprising that bodily discomfort should be an important medium of distress in an unfamiliar new environment. This is especially true when the encounter between a helper and a help seeker occurs with little or no prior orientation or preparation.

Another aspect of depression that may be ethnoculturally variable is the experience of guilt. Clinicians have observed that guilt is a less prominent component of depression in those cultural groups that emphasize social acceptance and solidarity over self-realization and individual responsibility. This notion has received substantial support in cross-national investigations (cf. Draguns, 1997), but has not been systematically tested across the ethnic groups in the United States. It retains considerable plausibility and is buttressed by clinical experience. However, the prospects of verifying this prediction are complicated by the multiple and conflictual social influences in the lives of those people who are both members of their respective ethnic communities and participants in the highly individual-istic North American culture. Therefore, there is, at this point, no realistic way of saying how important and central the sense of guilt is in the experience of depression by individuals is the several ethnoculturally distinct components of the population of the United States.

Epidemiological population surveys have, of course, included tallies of depression across ethnicity. Differences in prevalence rates for depression between Caucasians and African Americans were found to shrink, but not altogether disappear, in the preliminary assessment of results from ECA, once standardized and objective diagnostic scales were applied to both groups (Weissman, Bruce, Leaf, Florio, & Holzer, 1991). An important epidemiological finding from the National Comorbidity Study (NCS) (Blazer, Kessler, McGonagle, & Swartz, 1994) is consonant with these results; African Americans were found to have a substantially lower lifetime prevalence rate of depression by comparison with Caucasians. If these trends are further corroborated, they would suggest that spiritual and social supports that were observed to be effective in counteracting depression in African American communities in the early studies (e.g., Prange & Vitols, 1962) are still operating. In any case, the differences reported by Weissman et al. (1991) are a lot smaller than those found in earlier studies that were based on institutionalized patient samples and that allowed greater scope to diagnostician's discretion and judgment (e.g., Simon, Fleiss, Gurland & Sharpe, 1973). It has been suggested that the recognition of states of subjective mood and feeling is facilitated by empathy, distorted by preexisting stereotypes, and obstructed by the social distance between the participants in a social transaction (Draguns, 1996b). As stated elsewhere (Draguns, 1973, p. 13), "Across the cultural barrier, the observer tends to see the patients as though he were viewing them from afar. Consequently, he may selectively perceive conspicuous or dramatic symptoms and may miss some of the subtler expressions of disorder. Empirically, these effects have been demonstrated to occur even across subcultures, as in the case of a white psychiatrist interviewing a black patient in the United States (De Hoyos & De Hoyos, 1965; Singer, 1967). These findings suggest that the clinician's prized tools—his empathy and sensitivity—suffer impairment as they are applied outside his cultural domain. As a consequence, the record obtained runs the risk of being quantitatively and qualitatively impoverished."

Adebimpe (1997) independently applied the triad of empathy, stereotype, and cultural distance to explain why majority-group diagnosticians underdiagnose depression in African Americans and overdiagnose schizophrenia. Confronted with a mixture of cognitive and affective symptoms, such diagnosticians may opt for schizo-affective disorders in a Caucasian patient and may label an African American patient schizophrenic, even if he or she presents an identical symptom pattern. On the basis of the notion that social distance increases the risk of confounding difference with disturbance, the same distortion may be present in the diagnosis of other ethnic minorities, but so has it been episodically (see Sue, 1996), and not yet systematically, documented.

Despite this diagnostic bias, Asian American groups have the reputation of having low rates of depressive disorder. This belief rests on data pertaining to the distribution of depression in their respective countries of origin, rather than on solid epidemiological research in the United States (cf. Young, 1997). As far as Hispanics are concerned, there is more substantial evidence that points to lowered rates of depressive disorders among Mexican Americans (Frerichs, Aneshensel, & Clark, 1981; Roberts, 1980). It is unclear, however, to what extent these findings may have been affected by the culturally determined Hispanic emphasis upon self-presentation of distress through bodily and physical symptoms (Koss, 1990). There are, moreover, subgroups, specifically within the Asian American communities and possibly within Hispanic ones as well, that are selectively vulnerable to depressive experiences. In a major comparison of several Asian groups in Seattle, Kuo (1984) demonstrated a link between the prevalence of depression and recency of arrival. Thus, Koreans, with the highest percentage of recent immigrants, had the most elevated rates of depression. Another vulnerable segment of the population proved to be the elderly male Chinese, whose depression was probably exacerbated by loneliness, estrangement, and loss of status, together with separation from family and established reference groups.

In contrast with the epidemiological orientation of most of the studies reviewed in this section, Manson, Shore, and Bloom (1985) relied upon an exploratory, naturalistic methodology in investigating the experiences of depression among the Hopi Indians. They identified five clusters of depression, corresponding, in paraphrase, to worry, unhappiness, "broken heart," sullen disillusionment, and drunken craze, respectively. This study opens a glimpse to the subjective world of ethnically distinctive depression and thereby helps to offset the prevailing tendency of ethnocultural psychopathology research, which in recent decades has been tipped toward large-scale universalistic studies.

Schizophrenia

Over the past two decades, the biogenic conception of schizophrenia has pushed alternative formulations to the sidelines. Consequently, psychosocially oriented research has declined in both scope and prominence. However, tallies of schizophrenia across the three major ethnic groupings, Caucasian, African American, and Hispanic, were included among the findings of ECA and other major epidemiological projects (Kessler et al., 1994; Robins & Regier, 1991). These results fail to confirm the elevated rates of schizophrenia for African Americans that earlier studies, based on hospitalized patient samples, had reported (e.g., Simon et al., 1973). The disparities between these sets of results are probably traceable to diagnostic practices by majority-group professionals, who more liberally assign diagnoses of schizophrenia to African American patients. The higher rates of delusions and hallucinations that have been observed in African American patient groups (Vitols, Waters, & Keeler, 1963) may have contributed to this reported difference, especially before the advent of DSM-III and the application of more rigorous criteria for diagnosis of schizophrenia. At this point, the contextual and artifactual sources of these differences are more generally recognized, rather than being attributed exclusively or primarily to patient characteristics (Adebimpe, 1997). Hallucinations, in particular, have been found to differ across cultures in their thresholds of social acceptability (Al-Issa, 1995); they are no longer regarded as virtually pathognomonic indicators of schizophrenia.

In reference to Mexican Americans, the distinctive characteristics pertain to the course and outcome of schizophrenia rather than to its incidence. In particular, family members of Mexican American schizophrenics have been observed to exhibit lower levels of expressed emotion (EE) in light of norms based on Anglo-American families (Karno et al., 1987). EE refers to a cluster of negative and affectively charged attitudes, such as hostility, criticism, and intrusiveness, that was found to disrupt schizophrenic social functioning and predict their relapse (Kazarian, 1992). The more acceptant and compassionate social climate within Mexican American households is likely to promote a more benign outcome (Karno et al., 1987). This finding, of course, must be extended and replicated. It does, however, highlight the potential importance of the family context as one of the ethnoculturally distinctive features of schizophrenia.

Beyond that, there is a host of promising clinical leads pertaining to ethnically characteristic modes of expression of schizophrenia. The potential of investigating hallucinations and delusions across ethnic lines and within ethnic groupings has already been indicated. Potentially delusional beliefs must be carefully scrutinized for their generality and acceptability within the patient's community, so as to prevent overdiagnosis of delusions on the basis of culturally prevailing and socially accepted modes of expression. Flaskerud and Soldevilla (1986) reported that paranoid symptoms are both characteristic and frequent among Filipino American schizophrenics. Explosive and destructive behavior is also often observed. These and other trends deserve to be taken seriously in order to be more systematically investigated, by both comparative and clinical methods.

Personality Disorders

Personality disorders (PD) constitute crystallized patterns of behavior that are poorly tolerated by the society at large. Diagnosis of personality disorders is then of necessity value-driven, and as such shifting and variable across both space and time. Moreover, many of the PDs in DSM-IV have been named, defined, and described recently at a specific point in space and time, here in the United States. Cross-cultural study of personality disorders has only recently been inaugurated (Alarcon & Foulkes, 1995) and as yet has brought forth few definitive results. ECA investigations (Robins, Tipp, & Przybeck, 1991) have reported no significant differences in the prevalence of antisocial personality disorder between Caucasians, African Americans, and Hispanics, thereby dispelling stereotypic expectations based on incarceration rates and other indirect indicators. Buffenstein (1997) has hypothesized that avoidant personality disorder, as an exaggeration of culturally fostered shyness and modesty, may be over-represented among Asian Americans. Machismo, in Hispanic and other groups, may shade off into narcissistic personality disorder, especially among younger men. These hypotheses remain to be systematically and rigorously tested.

Alcohol Abuse

Ethnic and cultural variations in alcohol usage and its consequences have long been suspected on the basis of social impressions and unsystematic clinical data. Recent large-scale epidemiological data have produced more substantial results. Surprisingly, the overall rates of alcohol abuse have been found not to differ significantly between African Americans,

Hispanics, and Caucasians, upon the systematic application of rigorous and objective criteria (Helzer, Burnham, & McEvoy, 1991). This finding, however, masks an extremely complex pattern of ethnic differences by gender and age group that defies being succinctly described. Moreover, this intricate mosaic of differences needs to be extended and corroborated before it is definitively accepted. As expected, the available evidence, mostly of the clinical variety, points to low representation of problematic or abusive alcohol usage in the Japanese Americans (Fujii et al., 1993), Chinese Americans (Gaw, 1993b), and Filipino Americans (Araneta, 1993). Differences have been observed between the two principal Hispanic groupings. Apparently, immoderate drinking is more widespread among Puerto Ricans than among Mexicans (Canino & Canino, 1993; Martinez, 1993). It is also worth noting that the rates of alcohol abuse are lower among Mexican immigrants than among Mexican Americans born in the United States. Alcohol abuse is increased with the stresses of acculturation, and it has been claimed that the marginalized descendants of immigrants who have lost their traditions and values are especially prone to alcohol abuse as they become alienated in the new culture (Madsen, 1964). Gender ratios are lopsided among both Mexican Americans and Puerto Ricans; it is preponderantly men who develop alcohol-related problems.

Thompson, Walker, and Silk-Walker (1993) reviewed the clinical and research literature on American Indian alcohol abuse and concluded that "the stereotype of the 'drunken Indian' is just as inaccurate as the stereotype of the 'suicidal Indian,' although Indians themselves may believe these myths (May & Smith, 1988). Alcoholism rates are high in some communities, but prevalence rates vary by tribe and location" (p. 215). As yet, there is no definitive explanation for this variation. However, some Indian groups, such as the Chippewa, have been shown to have similar alcoholism rates to those of the majority Caucasian population. Exogenous influences, such as unemployment, play a significant role and loss of status as traditional roles become obsolete as well as alienation may be important contributory factors. However, endogenous beliefs, for example, ascribing magic power to alcohol, are also relevant. Moreover, the acceptance and tolerance of consumption of alcohol may be an important factor in promoting general and excessive alcohol abuse. By contrast, defining alcoholism as deviant and "bad" and struggling against it throughout the community may also reduce the prevalence of alcohol-related problems. (See Chapter 14 for a more detailed discussion of alcohol issues.) Other dimensions of cultural variation include the thresholds for acceptable behavior under the influence of alcohol. MacAndrew and Edgerton (1969) have described culturally shaped "drunken comportment," a composite of physiological effects of alcohol, socialized patterns of alcohol consumption, and the socially shared standards and expectations of behavior under the influence of alcohol.

Suicide

Although suicide is not a DSM-IV diagnostic category, it is a major concomitant of several mental disorders. Moreover, except for the—presumably infrequent—rational and serene instances, suicide constitutes the ultimate expression of human despair and distress. The current state of knowledge about suicide and ethnicity can be summarized under four headings. First, there is substantial evidence for lower suicide rate among African Americans by comparison with the entire population of the United States (Griffith & Bell, 1989). This conclusion, however, must be tempered with the recognition that certain segments of the African American population are relatively at risk for suicide. Such is the case with men in the age range between 25 and 34 and, in line with the national and worldwide trend, for adolescents as well (Gibbs, 1990). Second, in a similar manner, reports about Mexican Americans converge in documenting a substantially lowered suicide rate, perhaps by as much as 50 percent by comparison with national statistics (Hoppe & Martin, 1986). These conclusions are greatly strengthened by the results of ECA pertaining to Los Angeles (Sorenson & Golding, 1988), which substantiate parallel enthnocultural differences in both completed suicides and suicidal ideation. At the same time, some vulnerable portions of the Mexican American community have been identified; Hoppe and Martin (1986) reported that female suicide rates were rising and approaching the national average. Immigration status, however does not appear to be correlated with suicidal risk (Sorenson & Golding, 1988). Third, investigators of American Indians recognize suicide as a major public health problem in many American Indian groups and communities. However, they point out that the total number of suicides committed by Indians is small. Suicidal risk is concentrated upon specific demographic groups, especially young men, as well as tribes. There is as yet a paucity of factual comparative information on those milieus that are characterized by unusually high or remarkably low suicide rates. Fourth, there is as yet no firm empirical basis for general statements about Asian American suicides. Two reports, from Hawaii (Rogers & Izutsu, 1980) and Los Angeles (Yamamoto, 1976) respectively, describe Japanese American suicide rates as no different from those of the general population. A study in San Francisco (Bourne, 1973) identified some groups at risk for suicide in the Chinese American community, but provided no generalizable data across spacc or time on this ethnic group's suicide rate. Finally, it is worth noting that the bulk of the reviewed studies focused on completed suicide. Some suicidologists (e.g., Paris, 1991) have concluded that attempted suicide is much more affected by sociocultural variation. It would therefore appear to be an important topic to pursue in future ethnocultural research.

The Problem of Comorbidity

DSM-IV has allowed for a wider scope of recording two or more diagnoses simultaneously. Thus it has been recognized that experiencing anxiety and depression is the rule rather than an exception. This new provision in the current diagnostic manual has opened a new area of investigation; ethnic and cultural variations in the pattern of comorbidity (Good, 1993). Dinges and Duong-Tran (1993) reported a combination of substance abuse, depression, and suicidality among American Indian and Alaskan Native adolescents and thereby confirmed the impressions by Hippler (1975) based on ethnographic evidence. Independently, the co-occurrence of alcohol abuse and suicide has also been reported for a variety of American Indian groups outside of Alaska (Walker & La Due, 1986). In recent epidemiological surveys such as ECA and NCS, Klein (1994) detected a trend toward higher comorbidity for depression and substance abuse in Caucasian agoraphobic women than in African American female patients of the same diagnosis. He also noted lower incidence of separation anxiety in African American agoraphobics by comparison with Caucasians. At this point, these impressions are tentative: they deserve to be converted into hypotheses and to be systematically investigated. The configurations of comorbidity may vary across ethnocultural lines in degree and in kind; they constitute a fruitful subject of future research.

Pathways of Help-Seeking

Ethnic groups may differ in the ways in which they seek and find mental health services, which all to often are designed universalistically—presumably for everyone, yet without the awareness of the various cultural barriers that many of their ethnically distinctive users have to overcome in order to obtain services. Lin, Tardiff, Donetz, and Goresky (1978) have developed a typology of such pathways. In Type A, the family actively and persistently tries to intervene and find treatments for the mental health problems experienced by one or more of its members. If these efforts do not bear fruit, the family turns to a medical practitioner rather than a social agency. Hospitalization or outpatient treatment would then follow on the basis of the demands of the situation. This pattern was characteristic of Chinese families with members who presented psychotic or noncriminal antisocial problems. Type B was marked by early use of social and outpatient treatment agencies, with inpatient treatment deferred as a measure of last resort. It was typical of Anglo-Saxon and Central European families. Type C involved early social and legal agency intervention that was initiated outside the family and sometimes against its desires. This was the characteristic pathway for Native Indian families, which tended to present social problems, alcohol and drug abuse, and suicidal crises. The assumption of Lin et al.'s model is that families and programs vary, but agencies and problems remain constant. The culture accommodation model, developed by Higginbotham, West, and Forsyth (1988), provides an alternative conception for introducing mental health services into ethnically distinctive or diverse settings. Its cardinal feature is the involvement of community members in the assessment of needs, development of services, and their implementation.

Conclusions and Recommendations

The following trends have emerged on the basis of this rapid survey of the current state of knowledge on the interplay of ethnicity and psychological disorder in the United States:

1. Major progress has been achieved in the past decade, especially in acquiring substantial epidemiological information on the prevalence of mental disorders in the United States, including, to a limited degree, the three major ethnocultural components: Caucasian, African Americans, and Hispanics.

2. This achievement has raised new questions and has left many old ones unanswered. Above all, it must be recognized that the three named ethnic categories are broad, inclusive, and supraordinate. It is therefore not surprising that the simple effects of these three categories upon the rates of mental disorders and their modes of expression are relatively few in number. It is imperative to proceed from a more differentiated model that provides for the effect of three-way interaction of ethnicity × age group × gender. Moreover, it should not be overlooked that ethnically distinctive symptoms and syndromes occur in response to specific stresses.

3. To supplement and counterbalance epidemiological information, it is necessary to revitalize and reassert the application of clinical and comparative avenues of research. Investigations of patients with a uniform diagnosis and thoroughly documented case studies may help fill gaps in the present state of knowledge and help eventually formulate functional relationships between social antecedents, socioeconomic status, and psychopathological manifestations.

4. Hispanics, Caucasians, and, to a somewhat lesser extent, African Americans are highly abstract constructions. They do not correspond to the ways in which persons experience and designate themselves. In large-scale epidemiological projects it may be necessary to resort to such abstractions. In general, however, the principle that applies is: Proceed in research data collection from as specific and uniform a group as is possible. It is always preferable to design and implement a study on Japanese, Chinese, Korean, and Filipino Americans rather than to lump the four groups under the label of Asian Americans. Similarly, it is better to study, for example, the Chippewa rather than to refer generically to American Indians. Among Hispanic Americans, the prospective investigator would do well to start with Cubans, Puerto Ricans, Mexicans, Colombians and/or Dominicans rather than with a heterogeneous composite of Hispanics. Even among African Americans, there are distinctive groups of West Indian immigrants and their descendants from Jamaica, Haiti, and many other locations. Common threads among these several interrelated groups—for example, between Chinese and Japanese in somatic symptoms or between Puerto Ricans and Mexicans in alcohol abuse—are well worth pursuing.

5. Beyond ethnic categorization, information should be included and, if possible, incorporated into the research plan on the person's self-designation or identity and on his or her acculturation (see Chapter 2). Current conceptions of acculturation (e.g., Berry, 1998) not only differentiate the degree of acculturation, but also recognize several of its distinctive modes. According to Berry, marginalization, which leaves the person bereft of adaptive skills acquired in the original culture, yet without resources for functioning in the host culture, poses the greatest risk for maladaptive behaviors and symptom formation. Integration, in which the social learning from both cultures is utilized and fused into a whole, is posited as optimal for cross-cultural adaptation. Both assimilation and isolation are compatible with adequate mental health, even though they lack the flexibility of integration. Finally, in a multicultural society, the possibility of multiple cultural identities should be envisaged. The several strands of such identity may tend toward integration or conflict.

6. Symptoms, syndromes, and other related descriptors of disturbance should be regarded as the result of social transaction or negotiation (Kleinman, 1988). It is therefore necessary to incorporate the observer's, interviewer's, or diagnostician's contribution to the determination of psychopathology.

7. A number of formulations converge in suggesting that empathy is an important catalyst in enhancing self-disclosure, especially in relation to personal impairment and distress. Conversely, social and cultural distance interferes with both the spontaneous production and the veridical perception of personal information. Finally, stereotypes obtrude upon the recognition of a person's unique experience and outlook, especially as it relates to suffering and distress. These considerations carry special weight in the early stages of investigation with persons in new and different environments. In later stages of a study, standardized methods of data collection assume greater importance.

8. Avenues of establishing and promoting empathic contact and communication differ across cultures. It is useful to learn about such variations and to incorporate the resulting knowledge into clinical inquiry. The emic concept of *jeong* in Korea provides an example of such an indigenous version of empathy (Kim, 1993).

9. The specificity of findings about the links between ethnocultural and psychopathological characteristics should not be overlooked. Especially hazardous are *a priori* generalizations from men to women, from young to old, from children to adults (and *vice versa*), as well as concerning socioeconomic differences.

10. In a rapidly changing and interdependent world, findings become dated and obsolete at a rapid, yet unpredictable, rate. Social psychology is, at least in part, a historical discipline that records social phenomena and their interrelationships at specific points in space and time (Gergen, 1982). The findings reviewed here document such time-bound and location-specific social reality in especially complex, multicultural environments. They do not represent ageless discoveries of immutable truth.

11. A cautionary note is indicated for these readers who may want to apply the results reported in this chapter to clinic and everyday life: Do not confound trends with principles, remember that virtually all socially significant traits are distributed multimodally within any population, and, above all, do not equate statistically significant findings with absolute and categorical distinctions. As Cohen (1997, p. 153) has reminded us, "all members of a minority group are not the same." It would be unfortunate if stereotypes, which this chapter has endeavored to overcome, reappeared on the basis of information contained within it. To this end, information contained in this chapter should be brought to bear upon, but never allowed to overshadow, the understanding of the individual and his or her unique lifetime experience in a specific sociocultural environment. As Dinges and Cherry (1995, p. 51) put it, "reducing stereotyping and bias in understanding their impact on the treatment process involves awareness of the client's *individualized* linguistic and sociocultural background."

R E F E R E N C E S

Adebimpe, V. R. (1997). Mental illness among African Americans. In I. Al-Issa & M. Tousignant (Eds.) *Ethnicity, immigration and psychopathology* (pp. 95–120), New York: Plenum Press.

Alarcon, R., & Foulkes, E. (1995). Personality disorders and culture: Contemporary clinical views (Part A). *Culture Diversity and Mental Health, 1,* 3–17.

Al-Issa, I. (1995). The illusion of reality or the reality of illusion: Hallucinations and culture. *British Journal of Psychiatry, 166,* 368–373.

Al-Issa, I. & Oudji, S. (1998). Culture and anxiety disorders. In S. S. Kazarian & D. R. Evans (Eds.) *Cultural clinical psychology. Theory, research, and practice* (pp. 127–151), New York: Oxford University Press.

American Psychiatric Association. (1994). *Diagnostic and statistical manual of mental disorders* (4th ed.). Washington, DC: American Psychiatric Association.

Araneta, E. G. (1993). Psychiatric care of Filipino Americans. In A. C. Gaw (Ed.), *Culture, ethnicity, and mental health* (pp. 377–412), Washington, DC: American Psychiatric Press.

Berry, J. W. (1998). Acculturation and health: Theory and research. In S. S. Kazarian & D. R. Evans (Eds.), *Cultural clinical psychology: Theory, research, and practice* (pp. 39–57), New York: Oxford University Press.

Blazer, D. G., Kessler, R. C., McGonagle, K. A., & Swartz, M. S. (1994). The prevalence and distribution of major depression in a national community sample: The National Comorbidity Survey. *American Journal of Psychiatry, 151,* 979–986.

Boehnlein, J. K., & Kinzie, J. D. (1995). Refugee trauma. *Transcultural Psychiatric Research Review, 32,* 223–252.

Bourne, P. (1973). Suicide among Chinese in San Francisco. *American Journal of Public Health, 63,* 744–750.

Brown, D. R., Eaton, W. W., & Sussman, L. (1990). Race differences in prevalence of phobic disorders. *Journal of Nervous and Mental Disorders, 178,* 434–441.

Buffenstein, A. (1997). Personality disorders. In W.-S. Tseng & J. Streltzer (Eds.). *Culture and psychopathology: A guide to clinical assessment* (pp. 190–205), New York: Brunner/Mazel.

Canino, G. J., Bird, H. R. & Shrout, P. E. (1987). The prevalence of specific psychiatric disorders in Puerto Rico. *Archives of General Psychiatry, 44,* 727–735.

Canino, I. A., & Canino, G. J. (1993). Psychiatric care of Puerto Ricans. In A. C. Gaw (Ed.), *Culture, ethnicity, and mental health* (pp. 467–500). Washington, DC: American Psychiatric Press.

Carter, M. M., Sbrocco, T., & Carter, C. (1996). African Americans and anxiety disorders research: Development of a testable theoretical framework. *Psychotherapy, 33,* 449–463.

Cohen, G. H. (1997). Posttraumatic stress disorder. In W. T. Tseng & G. H. Streltzer (Eds.), *Culture and psychopathology: A guide to clinical assessment* (pp. 137–156). New York: Brunner/Mazel.

De Hoyos, A., & De Hoyos, G. (1965). Symptomatology differentials between negro and white schizophrenics. *International Journal of Social Psychiatry, 11,* 245–255.

Dinges, N. G., & Cherry, D. (1995). Symptom expression and the use of mental health services among American ethnic minorities. In J. F. Aponte, R. Young Rivers, & J. Wohl (Eds.), *Psychological interventions and cultural diversity* (pp. 40–56). Boston: Allyn and Bacon.

Dinges, N. G., & Duong-Tran, Q. (1993). Stressful life events and comorbidity of depression, suicidality, and substance abuse among American Indian and Alaska Native adolescents. *Culture, Medicine and Psychiatry, 16,* 487–502.

Draguns, J. G. (1973). Comparisons of psychopathology across cultures: Issues, findings, directions. *Journal of Cross-Cultural Psychology, 4,* 9–47.

Draguns, J. G. (1982). Methodology in cross-cultural psychopathology. In I. Al-Issa (Ed.), *Culture and psychopathology* (pp. 33–70). Baltimore: University Park Press.

Draguns, J. G. (1996a). Humanly university and culturally distinctive: Charting the course of cultural counseling. In P. B. Pedersen, J. G. Draguns, W. J. Lonner, & J. E. Trimble (Eds.), *Counseling across cultures* (4th ed., pp. 1–20). Thousand Oaks, CA: Sage.

Draguns, J. G. (1996b). Multicultural and cross-cultural assessment of psychological disorder: Dilemmas and decisions. In G. R. Sodowsky & J. Impara (Eds.), *Multicultural assessment in counseling and clinical psychology (Buros-Nebraska Symposium on Measurement and Testing Volume 9)* (pp. 37–76). Lincoln, NE: Buros Institute of Mental Measurements.

Draguns, J. G. (1997). Abnormal behavior patterns across cultures: Implications for counseling and psychotherapy. *International Journal of Intercultural Relations, 21,* 213–248.

Eaton, W. W., Dryman, A., & Weissman, M. M. (1990). Panic and phobia. In L. N. Robins and D. A. Regier (Eds.). *Psychiatric disorders in America: The Epidemiologic Catchment Area Study* (pp. 155–179), New York: Free Press.

Egeland, J. A., Hostetter, A. M., & Eshleman, S. K. (1983). Amish Study: III. The impact of cultural factors on diagnosis of bipolar illness. *American Journal of Psychiatry, 140,* 67–71.

Enright, J. & Jaeckle, W. (1963). Psychiatric symptoms an diagnoses in two subcultures. *International Journal of Social Psychiatry, 9,* 12–17.

Escobar, J. I. (1993). Psychiatric epidemiology. In A. C. Gaw (Ed.), *Culture, ethnicity, and mental illness* (pp. 43–73). Washington, DC: American Psychiatric Press.

Escobar, J. E., Randolph, E. T., & Hill, M. (1986). Symptoms of schizophrenia in Hispanic and Anglo veterans. *Culture, Medicine and Psychiatry, 10,* 259–276.

Fabrega, H. J., Swartz, J. D., & Wallace, C. A. (1968). Ethnic differences in psychopathology: Clinical correlates under varying conditions. *Archives of General Psychiatry, 19,* 218–226.

Flaskerud, J., & Soldevilla, E. (1986). Filipino and Vietnamese clients: Utilizing an Asian mental health center. *Journal of Psychosocial Nursing and Mental Health Services, 24,* 32–36 (cited in Araneta, 1993).

Frerichs, R. R., Aneshensel, C. S., & Clark, V. A. (1981). Prevalence of depression in Los Angeles County. *American Journal of Epidemiology, 113,* 691–699.

Fujii, J. S., Fukushima, S. N., & Yamamoto, J. (1993). Psychiatric care of Indochinese Americans. In A. C. Gaw (Ed.), *Culture, ethnicity, and mental health* (pp. 305–346). Washington, DC: American Psychiatric Press.

Gaw, A. (Ed.), (1993a). *Culture, ethnicity, and mental illness.* Washington, DC: American Psychiatric Press.

Gaw. A. C. (1993b). Psychiatric care of Chinese Americans. In A. C. Gaw (Ed.), *Culture, ethnicity, and mental health* (pp. 245–280). Washingto, DC: American Psychiatric Press.

Gergen, K. (1982). *Toward transformation in social knowledge.* New York: Springer.

Gibbs, J. T. (1990). Mental health issues of Black adolescents: Implications for policy and practice. In A. R. Stiffman & L. E. Davis (Eds.), *Ethnic issues in adolescent mental health* (pp. 21–52). Thousand Oaks, CA: Sage.

Good, B. (1993). Culture, diagnosis, and comorbidity. *Culture, Medicine and Psychiatry, 16,* 427–446.

Good, B. J., & Kleinman, A. M. (1985). Culture and anxiety: Cross-cultural evidence for the patterning of anxiety disorders. In A. H. Tuma & J. Maser (Eds.), *Anxiety and the anxiety disorders* (pp. 297–324). Hillsdale, NJ: Lawrence Erlbaum.

Griffith, E. E. H., & Bell, C. C. (1989). Recent trends in suicide and homicide among Blacks. *Journal of the American Medical Association, 262,* 2265–2269.

Helzer, J. E., Burnham, M. A., & McEvoy, L. T. (1991). Alcohol abuse and dependance. In L. N. Robins & D. A. Regier (Eds.), *Psychiatric disorders in America* (pp. 81–116). New York: Free Press.

Higginbotham, H. N. (1987). The culture accommodation of mental health services for Native Hawaiians. In A. B. Robillard & A. J. Marsella (Eds.), *Contemporary issues in mental health research in the Pacific Islands* (pp. 94–126). Honolulu: Social Science Research Institute.

Higginbotham, H. N., West, S., & Forsyth, D. (1988). *Psychotherapy, and behavior change: Social, cultural and methodological perspectives.* New York: Pergamon Press.

Hippler, A. E. (1975). Transcultural psychiatric and related research in the North American Arctic and Subarctic. *Transcultural Psychiatric Research Review, 12,* 103–115.

Hoppe, S. K., & Martin, H. W. (1986). Patterns of suicide among Mexican Americans and Anglos, 1960–1980. *Social Psychiatry, 21,* 83–88.

Horwath, E., Jonson, J., & Horing, C. D. (1993). Epidemiology of panic disorder in African-Americans. *American Journal of Psychiatry, 150,* 465–469.

Karno, M., Golding, J. M., Sorenson, S. B., & Burnham, M. A. (1988). The epidemiology of obsessive-compulsive disorder in five U.S. communities. *Archives of General Psychiatry, 45,* 1094–1099.

Karno, M., Hough, R. L., Burnham, A., Escobar, J. I., Timbers, D. M., Santana, F., & Boyd, J. H. (1987). Lifetime prevalence of specific psychiatric disorders among Mexican Americans and non-Hispanic whites in Los Angeles. *Archives of General Psychiatry, 44,* 695–701.

Karno, M., Jenkins, J. H., de la Selva, A., Santana, F., Telles C., Lopez, S., & Mintz, J. (1987). Expressed emotion and schizophrenic outcome among Mexican-American families. *Journal of Nervous and Mental Disease, 175,* 143–151.

Katz, M. M., Sanborn, K. O., Lowery, H. A., & Ching, J. (1978). Ethnic studies in Hawaii: On psychopathology and social deviance. In L. Wynne, R. Cromwell, & S. Methysse (Eds.), *The nature of schizophrenia: New approaches to research and treatment* (pp. 572–585). New York.

Kazarian, S. S. (1992). The measurement of expressed emotion: A review. *Canadian Journal of Psychiatry, 37,* 51–56.

Kessler, R. C., McGonagle, K. A., Zhao, S., Nelson, C. B., Hughes, M., Eshelman, S., Wittchen, H., & Kendler, K. S. (1994). Lifetime and 12 month prevalence of DSM-III-R psychiatric disorders in the United States. *Archives in General Psychiatry, 51,* 8–19.

Kim, L. I. C. (193). Psychiatric care of Korean Americans. In A. C. Gaw (Ed.), *Culture, ethnicity, and mental health* (pp. 347–376). Washington, DC: American Psychiatric Press.

Kinzie, J. D., & Leung, P. K. (1993). Psychiatric care of Indochinese Americans. In A. C. Gaw (Ed.), *Culture, ethnicity, and mental health* (pp. 281–304). Washington, DC: American Psychiatric Press.

Kirmayer, L. J., Young, A., & Hayton, B. C. (1995). The cultural context of anxiety disorders. *Psychiatric Clinics of North America, 18,* 503–521.

Klein, D. (1994). Concluding remarks. In S. Friedman (Ed.), *Anxiety disorders in African Americans* (pp. 227–231). New York: Springer Publishing company.

Kleinman, A. (1988). *Social origins of distress and disease.* New Haven: Yale University Press.

Koss, J. D. (1990). Somatization and somatic compliant syndromes among Hispanics: Overview and ethnopsychological perspectives. *Transcultural Psychiatric Research Review, 27,* 5–29.

Kuo, W. H. (1984). Prevalence of depression among Asian Americans. *Journal of Nervous and Mental Disease, 172,* 449–457.

Lin, M. C., & Endler, N. S. (1993). *State and trait anxiety: A cross-cultural comparison of Chinese and Canadian students in a Canadian sample* (Research report No. 210). North York, Ontario: York University, Department of Psychology (cited by Al-Issa & Oudji, 1998).

Lin, T. Y., Tardiff, K., Donetz, G., & Goresky, Y. (1978). Ethnicity and patterns of help-seeking. *Culture, Medicine and Psychiatry, 2,* 3–13.

MacAndrew, C., & Edgerton, R. B. (1969). *Drunken comportment: A social explanation.* Chicago: Aldine.

Madsen, W. (1964). The alcoholic agringado. *American Anthropologist, 66,* 355–361.

Manson, S. M., Shore, J. H., & Bloom, J. D. (1985). The depressive experience in American Indian communities: A challenge for psychiatric theory and diagnosis. In B. Good & A. Kleinman (Eds.), *Culture and depression* (pp. 331–368). Berkeley: University of California Press.

Marsella, A., Sanborn, K., Kameoka, V., Shizuru, L., & Brennan, J. (1975). Cross-validation of self-report measures of depression among normal populations of Japanese, Chinese, and Caucasian ancestry. *Journal of Clinical Psychology, 31,* 281–287.

Martinez, C. (1993). Psychiatric care of Mexican Americans. In A. C. Gaw (Ed.), *Culture, ethnicity, and mental health* (pp. 431–466). Washington, DC: American Psychiatric Press.

May, P. A., & Smith, M. B. (1988). Some Navajo Indian opinions about alcohol and prohibitions: A survey and recommendations for policy. *Journal of the Study of Alcohol, 49,* 324–334.

Murphy, H. B. M. (1982). *Comparative psychiatry.* Berlin: Springer-Verlag.

Neal, A. M., Lilly, R. S., & Zakis, S. (1993). What are African American children afraid of? *Journal of Anxiety Disorders, 7,* 129–139.

Neal, A. M., & Turner, S. M. (1991). Anxiety disorders research with African Americans: Current status. *Psychological Bulletin, 109,* 400–410.

Paris, J. (1991). Personality disorders, parasuicide, and culture. *Transcultural Psychiatric Research Review, 28,* 25–39.

Prange, A. J., & Vitols, M. M. (1962). Cultural aspects of the relatively low incidence of depression in Southern Negros. *International Journal of Social Psychiatry, 8,* 104–112.

Rader, K. K., Krampen, G., & Sultan, A. S. (1990). Kontrolluberzeugungen Depressiver im transkulturellen Vergleich (Beliefs about control by depressive patients in a transcultural comparison). *Fortschritte der Neurologie und Psychiatrie, 58,* 207–214.

Radford, M. H. B. (1989). *Culture, depression, and decision-making behaviour: A study with Japanese and Australian clinical and non-clinical populations.* Unpublished Doctoral Dissertation, Flinders University of South Australia.

Rivera Ramos, A. N. (1984). *Hacia una psicoterapia para el puertorriqueno* (Toward psychotherapy for Puerto Ricans). San Juan: Centro para el Estudia y Desarollo de la Personalidad *Puertorriquena.*

Roberts, R. E. (1980). Prevalence of psychological distress among Mexican Americans. *Journal of Health and Social Behavior, 21,* 134–145.

Robins, L. N., & Regier, D. A. (Eds.). (1991). *Psychiatric disorders in America. The Epidemiologic Catchment Area Study.* Washington, DC: American Psychiatric Press.

Robins, L. N., Tipp, J., & Przybeck, T. (1991). In. L. N. Robins & D. A. Regier (Eds.), *Psychiatric disorders in America. The Epidemiologic Catchment Area Study* (pp. 258–290). Washington, DC: American Psychiatric Press.

Rogers, T. A., & Izutsu, S. (1980). The Japanese. In J. F. McDermott, W. S. Tseng, & T. W. Maretzky (Eds.), *People and cultures of Hawaii: A psychocultural profile* (pp. 73–99). Honolulu: University Press of Hawaii.

Schlenger, W., & Fairbank, J. (1996). Ethnocultural considerations in understanding PTSD and related disorders among military veterans. In A. J. Marsella, M. J. Friedman, E. T. Gerrity, & R. M. Scurfield (Eds.), *Ethnocultural aspects of posttraumatic stress disorder: Issues, research, and clinical applications* (pp. 415–438). Washington, DC: American Psychological Association.

Simon, R. J., Fleiss, J. L., Gurland, B., & Sharpe, L. (1973). Depression and schizophrenia in black and white mental patients. *Archives of General Psychiatry, 28,* 509–512.

Simons, R. C., & Hughes, C. C. (1993). Culture-bound syndromes. In A. C. Gaw (Ed.), *Culture, ethnicity, and mental illness* (pp. 75–93). Washington, DC: American Psychiatric Press.

Singer, B. D. (1967). Some implications of differential psychiatric treatment of Negro and white patients. *Social Science and Medicine, 1,* 77–83.

Sorenson, S. B., & Golding, J. M. (1988). Prevalence of suicide attempts in a Mexican-American population: Prevention implications of immigration and cultural issues. *Suicide and Life Threatening Behavior, 18* (4), 322–333.

Srole, L., Langner, R. S., Michael, S. T., Opler, M. K., & Rennie, T. A. C. (1962). *Mental health in the metropolis.* New York: McGraw-Hill.

Sue, S. (1996). Measurement, testing, and ethnic bias: Can solutions be found? In G. R. Sodowsky & J. C. Impara (Eds.), *Multicultural assessment in counseling and clinical psychology* (pp. 7–36). Lincoln, NE: Buros Institute of Mental Measurements.

Sue, S., & Morishima, J. (1982). *The mental health of Asian Americans.* San Francisco: Jossey Bass.

Tanaka-Matsumi, J., & Draguns, J. G. (1996). Culture and psychopathology. In J. W. Berry, M. H. Segall, & C. Kagitcibasi (Eds.), *Handbook of cross cultural psychology. Volume 3: Social behavior and applications* (2nd ed., pp. 449–491). Boston: Allyn & Bacon.

Thompson, J. W., Walker, R. D., & Silk-Walker, P. (1993). Psychiatric care of American Indians and Alaska Natives. In A. C. Gaw (Ed.), *Culture, ethnicity, and mental illness* (pp. 189–244). Washington, DC: American Psychiatric Press.

Tseng, W. S. (1975). The prevalence of somatic complaints among psychiatric patients: The Chinese case. *Comprehensive Psychiatry, 16,* 237–245.

Tseng, W. S., Asai, M., Jieqiu, L., Wibulswasd, P., Suryani, L. K., Wen, J. K., Brennan, J., & Heiby, E. (1990). Multi-cultural study of minor psychiatric disorders in Asia: Symptom manifestations. *International Journal of Social Psychiatry, 36,* 252–264.

Tseng, W.-S., & Streltzer, J. (Eds.). (1997). *Culture and psychopathology: A guide to clinical assessment.* New York: Brunner/Mazel.

Vitols, M. M., Waters, H. G., & Keeler, M. H. (1963). Hallucinations and delusions in white and Negro schizophrenics. *American Journal of Psychiatry, 120,* 472–476.

Walker, D. B., & La Due, R. (1986). An integrative approach to American Indian mental health. In C. B. Wilkinson (Ed.), *Ethnic psychiatry* (pp. 143–194). New York: Plenum.

Weissman, M. M., Bruce, M. L., Leaf, P. J., Florio, L. P., & Holzer, C. (1991). Affective disorders. In L. N. Robins & D. A. Regier (Eds.), *Psychiatric disorders in America: the Epidemiologic Catchment Area Study* (pp. 53–80). New York: Free Press.

Yamamoto, J. (1976). Japanese-American suicides in Los Angeles. In J. Westermeyer (Ed.), *Anthropology and mental health* (pp. 29–36). Chicago: Mouton.

Young, D. M. (1997). Depression. In W. S. Tseng & J. Streltzer (Eds.), *Culture and psychopathology: A guide to clinical assessment* (pp. 28–45). New York: Brunner/Mazel.

4 Psychological Assessment in the Diagnosis and Treatment of Ethnic Group Members

RICHARD H. DANA

This chapter has several purposes: (1) to provide a rationale for the seven tests currently used in standard psychological assessment in the United States; (2) to describe a technology using moderator variables to distinguish among assimilated, traditional, bicultural, and marginal cultural orientations as a necessary precursor to standard psychological assessment; (3) to examine some deficits in standard psychological assessment in construction, administration, and interpretation for those individuals within each ethnic minority group who do not have an assimilated cultural orientation; (4) to discuss the usefulness of the standard psychological tests for psychodiagnosis, personality, and intelligence with ethnic minority populations; and (5) to present a format for culturally competent psychological assessment services using an assessment-intervention model.

Standard Psychological Assessment

Standard psychological assessment refers to the small number of tests used since 1960 for clinical diagnosis, personality description, and measurement of intelligence. Piotrowski and Keller (1989) found that only seven tests were used in 80 percent of their surveyed outpatient mental health facilities. These tests were the Wechsler Adult Intelligence Test (WAIS), the Wechsler Intelligence Tests for Children and Infants (WISC-R/WPPSI), Figure Drawings, Sentence Completions, the Rorschach, the Bender-Gestalt and the Minnesota Multiphasic Personality Inventory (MMPI). When recommendations from APA-approved doctoral programs are included (Craig & Horowitz, 1990; O'Donohue, Plaud, Mowatt, & Fearon, 1989), the Thematic Apperception Test (TAT) is added to this list. Neither scientist-practitioner nor practitioner-scholar models of training have differed in their assessment curricula (Dana, 1992).

Students in the majority of doctoral programs are still not trained to administer these tests using culturally acceptable styles of service delivery, or a social etiquette for interpersonal transactions that is acceptable to ethnic minority clients. In addition, students are only infrequently provided with experiences in examining culture-specific perspectives that would be relevant for interpretation of test protocols (as in López et al., 1989). As a result, training in standard psychological assessment is deficient for practice with ethnic minority populations. The failure to incorporate culture-specific tests into the assessment curriculum has further reduced the likelihood of providing acceptable services for these populations. In the absence of cultural competence, the practice of standard psychological assessment has unforeseen consequences. These may include not only faulty diagnosis, but also caricature and dehumanization in personality description by minimizing differences and stereotyping client behaviors. A majority of Anglo-American professional psychologists and counselors surveyed did not feel competent to provide services for clients from diverse cultural/racial populations in spite of training experiences and exposure to these persons in their practices (Allison, Crawford, Echemendia, Robinson, & Kemp 1994; Allison, Echemendia, Crawford, & Robinson, 1996). For example, only 8 percent, 21 percent, and 26 percent of these clinicians felt competent with American Indian/Alaska Native, Asian American, and Hispanic clients, respectively.

Within each ethnic minority group, standard psychological assessment will be suitable for some members but inappropriate for others because of their varying degrees of assimilation. Moreover, the percentages of persons who are assimilated differ greatly among ethnic minority groups and by generation of residence in the United States. As a result, it is always mandatory to distinguish those individuals within each minority population who are assimilated and for whom standard psychological assessment is appropriate. This may be done by assessment of cultural orientation using moderator variables (Dana, 1993, 1998e).

Cultural Orientation and Moderator Variables

Four possible cultural orientations are usually distinguished. A *traditional orientation* is defined as retention of an original culture, whereas *nontraditional* refers to assimilation into the majority Anglo-American culture. *Bicultural* individuals have retained many aspects of their original culture while simultaneously functioning in a manner acceptable to and understood within the majority culture. *Marginality* implies rejection of substantial segments of both the original and the dominant society cultures. A fifth cultural orientation, *transitional,* has been used to describe American Indians/Alaska Natives who are bilingual but who question their traditional religion and values (LaFromboise, Trimble, & Mohatt, 1990).

Although complete information on the number of persons fitting each cultural orientation category is not known at this time, there is some consensus on cultural orientation base rates for the major cultural/racial populations in the United States (see Dana, 1998e). Immigrants, refugees, non-English speakers, and foreign nationals are typically traditional in cultural orientation status. However, large segments of each cultural/racial population who are classified as marginal also have to be considered during assessment as potential recipients subsequently of combined standard and culture-specific intervention services.

Moderator variables are now available to measure cultural orientation for some of the major ethnic minority populations in the United States (Dana, 1993, 1996b), although there are few assessment examples using these instruments (e.g., Chang, Dana, & Yan, in press). For ethical reasons, cultural competence in assessment practice requires information on client cultural orientation that is obtained prior to the onset of assessment services (Dana, 1994). This information will suggest not only the specific tests to use but also the likelihood of bias using standard psychological tests and interventions (Dana, 1998e, in press b). Most of these measures are bilevel; they provide information not only on traditional culture but also on the acquisition of dominant society values.

For examples, some of these moderators for different groups will be briefly described. The ARSMA and ARSMA-II (Cuéllar, Arnold, & Maldonado, 1995; Cuéllar, Harris, & Jasso, 1980) are the most widely used measures in acculturation research (Cuéllar, in press). These measures have been used to identify significant elevations on MMPI/ MMPI-2 clinical scales that incorrectly pathologize not only Hispanics but traditional persons from all ethnic groups as well by confounding cultural values and behavior with psychopathology. The ARSMA instruments have also been used to provide acculturation status norms for some standard tests (e.g., Arnold, Montgomery, Castaneda, & Longoria, 1994) and to prepare detailed descriptions of cultural identity for use in preparation of DSM-IV cultural formulations. In addition to ARSMA/ARSMA-II, a variety of other acculturation measures for Hispanic populations are available (Dana, 1996b).

Measures for African Americans describe cultural identity (Landrine & Klonoff, 1996), stages in the process of becoming racially identified (Helms, 1990), and an Africentric personality outcome of racial identification (Baldwin & Bell, 1985). For Asian Americans, there are a variety of group-specific measures, none of which is ready for clinical application at the present time. However, the Suinn-Lew measure, an adaptation of the Acculturation Scale for Mexican Americans for persons of Chinese, Japanese, and Korean ethnic origin, is acceptable for cautious assessment applications (Suinn, Rickard-Figueroa, Lew & Vigil, 1987). For Southeast Asian refugees and other Asian immigrants, it is often preferable to infer cultural orientation from information collected in an interview. This information should include willingness to acculturate, current phase of acculturation process, current group sociocultural data, and individual psychological characteristics. This information is available in checklist format (Dana, 1993, p. 114).

Assessment of American Indians/Alaska Natives cultural orientation in reservation settings should use tribe-specific measures whenever feasible. For urban residents, however, the Brown interview technique is recommended regardless of tribal origin. This technique provides a descriptive chart for acculturation in terms of family relationships, social-recreational activities, spiritual-religious practices, and training-education preferences (Brown, 1982). For college-educated persons, the Allen and French (1996) measure should be used. Finally, whenever an application of group-specific measures is unavailable or unfeasible, more general measures of world view, or world view components, may be used. These measures, however, usually will not be as appropriate for American Indians/Alaska Natives as tribe-specific tests or the Brown Pan-Indian interview technique.

Deficiencies in Standard Psychological Assessment for Cross-Cultural Practice

Test Construction

The standard psychological assessment instruments were constructed on the basis of unquestioning acceptance and use of a psychometric paradigm that has been applied in the United States and Western Europe primarily by White male psychologists. As a result, these tests are culture-specific and usable only in a European-American cultural context with English-speaking persons who have a Eurocentric worldview, as a result of either early childhood socialization or assimilation as an adult. *Worldview* embraces shared group and individual identity components, consensual values and beliefs, and common language.

Contemporary psychometric practices have developed in a context of Western science. To be sure, the underlying model of science is now in the throes of change in the direction of a social constructionism (Dana, 1987). Assessment practice is being informed indirectly by this paradigm shift toward an emphasis on persons in social contexts with specific and interactive causes of behavior, and using modified methods to achieve these purposes. This new assessment perspective expands the concept of individual differences by adding dimensions based on culture and gender.

In a radical conceptual attempt to mitigate the damage to all cultural/racial groups by research on group differences using the Null Hypothesis, a Euro-American emic formulation, Malgady (1996, in press) has proposed a statement of bias rather than no bias as the Null Hypothesis. In using the Null Hypothesis historically, the effects of client-centered or Type II errors are more serious than service system or Type I errors because Type II errors substantiate and reinforce minimization of group differences by White professional psychologists. Helms (1992) has also indicated that some assumptions underlying conventional statistics may be invalidated by cultural factors.

The details of culture-specific assessment technology and service delivery style have not yet been applied with all ethnic minority groups. However, there are now recent state-of-the-practice reviews of assessment issues with African Americans (Lindsey, 1998), American Indians/Alaska Natives (Allen, 1998), Asian Americans (Okazaki, 1998), and Hispanics (Cuéllar, 1998; Geisinger, 1992). Two major edited books provide broad gauge review of multicultural assessment across clinical, psychological, and educational domains (Suzuki, Meller, & Ponterotto, 1996), and an advanced multicultural assessment textbook (Sodowsky & Impara, 1996) evidences "a proper marriage between cross-cultural psychology and applied research areas of counseling and clinical psychology..." (Dana, 1996a, p. 482). Assessment of Asians and Asian Americans will be advanced as a result of a national conference and subsequent publication of proceedings sponsored by the National Research Center on Asian American Mental Health at the University of California-Davis in November 1998.

Matarazzo (1992) predicted that assessment during the next century will emphasize individual differences, using new types of tests to measure mental abilities and personality in the form of "specific psychological styles and predispositions" (p. 1014) within the general nonpathological population. Some of these new tests for personality and psychopathology are already available (see Holden, in press), but they require additional validation before being routinely used with multicultural populations (Dana, 1998a).

Test Administration

The assessment process in Western practice is a professional relationship with established rules for acceptable client behavior that were derived from the medical model of service delivery for physical health problems. This model emphasizes patient compliance in the face of provider expertise and credibility based on formal credentials provided by educational experience and professional licensing—what Naisbitt (1982) calls "high technology and low touch." As a consequence, the interaction between health service providers and consumers in this society has been somewhat impersonal, structured, and formal, with minimal give-and-take questioning and relevant discussion.

This model is no longer comfortable or acceptable even for many White consumers of health and/or mental health services who may accept a medical model conception of their psychological distress (Dana, 1985). Nonetheless, to the extent that this service delivery model has been institutionalized and has system characteristics, change has not occurred rapidly. Although mainstream clients may be restive and somewhat put off or dissatisfied with this relatively impersonal service delivery style, they do have lifelong familiarity with this style and have learned to adapt in an effort to receive the best service possible. Clients with traditional orientations representing non-Anglo-American cultures may not accept services preferred in an impersonal manner, especially when their conceptions of mental illness and legitimate remediations differ from the standard nomenclature and interventions.

Distinct culture-specific styles of assessment service delivery can increase rapport and willingness to participate in an assessment process. These styles for all groups have been described in detail elsewhere (Dana, 1993, 1998a) and only the major references are noted here (Gibbs, 1985; Hornby 1993; Sue & Zane, 1987; Triandis, Marin, Lisansky, & Betancourt, 1984). The practice of a credible social etiquette during the entire assessment process is essential for rapport and sufficient task orientation to permit responsible interpretation of test data.

Test Interpretation

Test interpretation for multicultural clients includes low- and high-frequency inference data processing, the use of test data for clinical diagnosis, and a continuing danger of dehumanizing clients. Test interpretation is informed by a variety of unverbalized expectations for client responsivity to the standard assessment process and particular tests. It can require either high- or low-inference processing from data. Nonetheless, there is preference for low-inference interpretation whenever feasible, although this preference may be a function of assessor personality (Handler, 1996). This distinction is useful because it identifies the Rorschach Comprehensive System (RCS) and the TEMAS as low-inference measures while the TAT has been criticized for remaining a high-inference measure, a "projective interview" (Rossini & Moretti, 1997) in dire need of a scoring system and normative data to attain the status of a test. In Spain, Avila-Espada (in press) has developed low-inference objective TAT scoring with national normative data. This system merits exportation to the United States for initial research use with Hispanics and subsequent development of norms.

Unfortunately, there is a dearth of empirical and conceptual cultural knowledge to inform assessors who use high-inference interpretation. One compilation of information resources is available for use in training psychologist assessors to use projective assessment with cultural/racial populations (Dana, 1998c). In addition, there remains some prejudice against use of the Rorschach among psychologists who believe that the RCS is not an adequate psychometric instrument. As a consequence, a rationale has been developed for projective testing with Hispanics that includes use of low-inference RCS interpretation and guidelines for improving the reliability and subsequent validity of high-inference interpretation with other projective methods (Dana, 1998d).

Pathologization.   Pathologization refers to interpretation that characterizes assessees as more disturbed than in fact they are. The danger of stigma from erroneous pathologization has been somewhat reduced in the Diagnostic and Statistical Manual of Mental Disorders, fourth edition (DSM-IV) (American Psychiatric Association, 1994) by use of cultural formulations and a glossary of culture-bound disorders. Cultural formulations are now essential for accurate diagnoses of many persons from various cultural/racial groups, particularly foreign nationals, refugees or immigrants, as well as traditional persons, non-English speakers, and some marginal persons. It is now imperative that all assessors learn to prepare cultural formulations to increase the reliability and accuracy of their clinical diagnoses with these populations. For a review of the cultural formulation literature and procedures for preparation, see Cuéllar and González (in press).

Dehumanization.   *Dehumanization* is a strong word, but the application of personality theory developed in one culture to persons in another culture can have exactly this effect. Psychoanalysis provides a convenient example because this personality theory of European-American origin was espoused by many anthropologists and psychologists of an earlier generation and was used as a basis for cross-cultural personality research, often with projective techniques. Psychoanalysis as a personality theory or a method of psychotherapy can be applied to persons who are not of European origins. Whenever this occurs, however, this theory should be used with caution because it may not constitute a universal framework for understanding human beings.

To my knowledge, the most egregious example of dehumanization by application of psychoanalytic theory to an assessee occurred using the Rorschach with a Mescalero Apache shaman. This shaman was diagnosed as a "character disorder with oral and phallic fixations…with occasional hysterical dissociations" (Klopfer & Boyer, 1961, p. 178). Such a diagnosis on the basis of the Rorschach alone needs to be placed in a frame of reference that includes the reservation community and peer judgment, since there is culturally relevant personality information that may be invoked to account for the Rorschach protocol (Dana, 1993, p. 156). My intent in using this example is to argue that culture-specific personality theories are a necessary component of cultural competence in assessment. Unfortunately, there is scant literature on differences in self-construal between American Indians/Alaska Natives and Euro-Americans as it affects assessment by White psychologists or indigenous healers, although it has been suggested that these differences are immense (Dana, submitted).

The Current Status of Cross-Cultural Validity in Standard Tests

This description will include the tests used in standard psychological assessment and some other tests that have had cross-cultural usage (for detail see Dana, in press b). The Minnesota Multiphasic Personality Inventory will be examined separately because it is now the most widely used test for psychopathology and personality. Two projective techniques for personality assessment—the Rorschach and the TAT—will be discussed in a context of other inkblot and picture-story techniques. The Sentence Completions, Bender Gestalt, and Figure Drawings will be considered together under the heading "Other Projective Techniques." In addition, the standard intelligence tests for adults and children as well as other intelligence tests with cross-cultural applications will be described. Additional tests that tap limited assessment domains will also be included. Finally, there will be consideration of the kinds of measures that have been largely omitted in psychological assessment, particularly culture-specific or *emic* methods.

Minnesota Multiphasic Personality Inventory (MMPI, MMPI-2)

The MMPI has been translated into 150 languages for use in diagnosis and personality description in more than 50 countries. Translations of standard tests are required for those persons in the United States whose first or primary language is not English. Nonetheless, there has been relatively little interest in the development and use of translations for cultural minority groups in the United States, with the exception of Hispanics. For Spanish-speaking persons, several translations of varying quality now exist, and many bicultural, bilingual Hispanics should have a choice of English or Spanish test versions.

Many of the MMPI translations used in other parts of the world have not controlled for accuracy or linguistic equivalence (Williams, 1986) and are of questionable cross-cultural validity. Cross-culturally valid translations should be carried out according to acceptable criteria for linguistic and construct equivalence. In addition to the translations, the formats for item presentation, the item contents (including contexts), and cultural restrictions for self-disclosure are relevant for cross-cultural validity.

An exception is a Castilian version in which both linguistic issues and inadequacies of t-tables led to comparisons between this translation and Chilean, Argentinian, and Mexican translations for use of local idioms and consistency of norms (Avila-Espada & Jiminez-Gomez, 1996). When completed, a principal components factor analysis strongly suggested that a proper translation coupled with national/local norms can lead to satisfactory cross-cultural construct equivalence.

There are significant differences between the MMPI-1 profiles of ethnic minority groups and Anglo-American normative groups. For example, African Americans may have high scores on scales F, 6, 8, and 9 as a result of Nigrescence, a process of becoming Afrocentric, while Hispanic Americans exhibit elevated scores on these scales on the basis of being traditional in cultural orientation (see Chapter 7 in Dana, 1993). However, American Indian/Alaska Native psychiatric patients, regardless of diagnosis, cultural orientation, or tribal affiliation, show similar profiles with elevations on F, 4, and 8 (Pollack & Shore,

1980). These issues are further compounded by a large group comparison literature containing inappropriate statistics, inadequate socioeconomic criteria, and inconsistent definitions of ethnicity (Greene, 1987).

Some caveats for MMPI usage with ethnic minority populations in this country have been abbreviated from a more complete description of these issues for presentation here (Dana, 1993). The MMPI-1 should be used only when the assessee has been demonstrated to be comparable to the standardization population on demographic variables, including worldview as measured by moderator variables, and speaks English as a first language. Even the MMPI-2 has only small and unrepresentative samples from several ethnic minority groups, and the cultural orientations of these individuals are unknown. For example, "corrections" or adaptations with Hispanic populations may be used for acculturation status, in translations for first or preferred language, and modification of standard interpretation procedures to increase reliability (Dana, 1995, 1998a). The use of the MMPI with American Indians/Alaska Natives is more problematic than for other ethnic minority populations (Hoffmann, Dana, & Bolton, 1985). Even with use of moderator variables, tribe-specific norms may be necessary for some isolated reservation residents.

Projective Techniques for Personality Assessment

Inkblot Measures: Rorschach, Rorschach Comprehensive System (RCS), and Holtzman Inkblot Test (HIT).   There has been skepticism among assessors concerning the use of high-inference projective techniques with cultural/racial populations in the United States, particularly Hispanics. This issue has been explicitly addressed for Hispanics, employing a rationale for use of projective methods indicating that their psychometric status is comparable with objective tests and reviewing the status of the major projective methods discussed in this chapter to provide guidelines for increasing reliability and accuracy of high-inference interpretation (Dana, 1998d).

The original Rorschach was used for anthropological studies of many cultures, usually with a psychoanalytic interpretative stance or attention to modal personality, although the cross-cultural validity has been questioned (Lindzey, 1961). The RCS relies on diagnostic indices and normative data for interpretation, although there are no special norms for ethnic minority groups in this country and in Iberoamerican countries the use of the RCS has consistently pathologized normal children and adolescents (e.g., Vinet, in press). As a consequence, the development of national norms has become a mandatory first step prior to cross-cultural construct validation of the RCS (e.g., Pires, in press). The HIT was constructed to provide an inkblot test that had psychometric properties acceptable to most psychologists and has been applied in many different cultural settings, with factor analysis used to establish cross-cultural validity (Holtzman, in press). The HIT, despite the fact that it is not among the tests included in the frequency definition of standard psychological tests, is the only inkblot test that can be recommended for cross-cultural assessment at this time.

Picture-Story Techniques.   The picture-story techniques described here include the TAT (See Dana, in press a), the TEMAS (an acronym for "tell me a story") (see Costantino & Malgady, in press), and a variety of other culture-specific sets of pictures. The culture-specific picture-story techniques used by anthropologists also have been criticized for their use of psychoanalytic theory and reliance on findings that were not verified by direct observation (Mensh & Henry, 1953). In addition, the only consensual TAT scoring system that accounts for all protocol data is in Spain (Avila-Espada, in press), and there is no personality theory that claims universality.

Picture-story TAT variants developed for African Americans include the Thompson Modification (T-TAT) with redrawn Murray pictures (Thompson, 1949) and the Themes Concerning Blacks Test (TCB) (Williams, 1972). The TCB test may be used provisionally in preference to the T-TAT because of the culture-specific nature of the TCB cards, although more research on the scoring categories is needed. It should also be noted that an Anglo-American assessor who is a stranger to the assessee may encounter what Snowden and Todman (1982) have called "reticence," a characteristic caution, vagueness, and inhibition of storytelling.

For Hispanic Americans, TEMAS, a culture-specific set of picture-story cards, is available (Costantino, Malgady, & Rogler, 1988). The TEMAS was developed for bilingual administration to children from 5 to 18 years of age. Everyday interpersonal relationships involving conflict are presented in culturally relevant and gender-balanced chromatic pictures of moderate ambiguity. A variety of personality and cognitive functions are scored and low-inference interpretation is used. There are limited norms for Anglo-Americans, African Americans, Puerto Ricans, and other Hispanic groups. Parallel versions for Anglo-American children and Asian American children have been developed. Validation studies suggest that personality constructs are being measured and that TEMAS can be used for diagnostic screening and prediction of therapy outcome.

For American Indians/Alaska Natives, many sets of tribe-specific pictures have been developed. Tribe-specific pictures are available for Blood, Eskimo, Hopi, Menomini, Northern Cheyenne, Navajo, and Sioux. For reservation residents, tribe-specific pictures are preferred, and it is recommended that pictures be drawn on the basis of Sherwood (1957) design criteria. However, there are no scoring systems that can be recommended for interpretation of the picture-story protocols of American Indians/Alaska Natives. Instead, assessors should be familiar with the history, customs, ethnography, fiction, and published life histories of individuals for any tribe whose members are assessed using picture story techniques. Inservice training for assessors is available in language, healing practices, spirituality, and tribal law in many tribal colleges. In addition, there is a set of guidelines for interpretation of stories provided by acculturated and traditional American Indians/Alaska Natives to the Murray TAT cards (Dana, 1993, pp. 152–155; Monopoli, 1984).

Other Projective Techniques: Sentence Completions and Figure Drawings. These techniques all provide a stimulus situation that offers considerable promise for their use in multicultural assessment settings. An early review (Holtzman, 1980) indicated problems in translation of item stems for use in completion techniques. These techniques also have to demonstrate psychological equivalence of meanings across cultures (Manaster & Havighurst, 1972). Completion techniques developed in the language of a particular culture have merit as *emic* measures.

Human figure drawings have a long history of cross-cultural use as measures of intelligence and personality, especially for values and cognitions (Barnouw, 1963, pp. 347–348)

(Handler, 1996). Any cross-cultural application of existing scoring systems for intelligence for personality is probably unwise in the absence of cultural validity for the constructs used in the scoring systems.

Intelligence Tests.   Standard intelligence tests are used routinely with all ethnic minority populations in this country. These tests have minimized cultural bias by careful matching on some demographic variables, although factor invariance has not been demonstrated for American Indians/Alaska Natives and Hispanics. English versions of these tests usually have been administered. A Spanish translation of the WAIS-R, the Escalade Inteligencia Wechsler para Adultos (EIWA), is available; but this translation is not comparable, especially in conversions of raw scores to scaled scores, and should be limited in use to clients who are rural, language-impaired, and have limited education (López & Romero, 1988). Moreover, users of test data are seldom informed of the normative data used for comparison of the performances of ethnic Minority individuals. Assessors who examine the intelligence of ethnic minority individuals should inform themselves of the cross-cultural validity literature for that group. For example, Verbal Scale scores for American Indians/Alaska Natives may suggest academic expectations in Anglo-American classrooms; Performance Scale measures will provide more reliable estimates of intellectual functioning in other settings. Moreover, the numbers of factors and factorial structure are also culturally distinct for them (e.g., Dana, 1984; Dauphinais & King, 1992).

Consideration should be given to the use of alternative tests of intelligence for ethnic minority populations. The System of Multicultural Pluralistic Assessment (Mercer & Lewis, 1978), the Kaufman Assessment Battery for Children, and the McCarthy Scales of Children's Abilities are all preferable to Wechsler tests for children. Although each of these tests also presents some problems for assessors of non-Anglo-American children, the Kaufman battery is the preferred alternative (Dana, 1993, pp. 188–190).

Limited Domain Measures.   Although the purpose of this chapter is to provide information on the usefulness of standard psychological assessment with ethnic minority populations in the United States, it would be unfair not to indicate that there are a variety of tests with more limited measurement purposes that do have acceptable cross-cultural validity. For example, the State-Trait Anxiety Inventory (STAI) provides brief, self-report measures of state, or general nervousness, and trait, or chronic anxiety (Spielberger, 1976). This inventory and a companion measure for children were factorially derived and have been translated into more than 40 languages using acceptable procedures to maximize idiomatic equivalency. Research on a Spanish-language version including confirmatory factor analysis has suggested cross-cultural validity and the desirability of use in this country with Spanish-speaking individuals.

The Inventory to Diagnose Depression (IDS) was developed to include criteria for major depressive disorders and an ongoing summary of symptom severity not included in other measures. The IDS has been used with American Indian adolescents (Zimmerman, Coryell, & Wilson, 1986). The Vietnamese Depression Scale (VDS) represents careful and systematic translation procedures that included opportunity to provide a culturally consistent array of symptoms including somatization, depressed mood, and symptoms unrelated to lowered mood or Western depression (Kinsie et al., 1982).

Culture-Specific Measures. These measures include behavior observations/ethnographies, life history/case studies, the accounts method, and methods for studying life events (Dana, 1993, pp. 142–146). They become culture-specific on the basis of the development of narratives or categories within a cultural setting, with major assistance from local residents, a collection of local normative data, and an intent to include the context and meaning of behaviors. The accounts method is useful to identify problems, specify adaptive/maladaptive coping styles, and recommend culturally appropriate interventions with community input at each stage of the process (Jones & Thorne, 1987).

Methods for studying life events provide a life span approach to the delineation of culture-specific problems-in-living. The Social Readjustment Rating Scale (Holmes & Rahe, 1967) has been adapted for ethnic minority groups by the addition of stressors related to cultural practices and discrimination. Checklists of stressors are available for urban minority youth (Mosley & Lex, 1990), Hispanic immigrants and Hispanic Americans (Cervantes, Padilla, & deSnyder, 1991), and Native Americans (Dana, Hornby, & Hoffmann, 1984).

Only a small number of tests have been developed exclusively for a single cultural/racial population in the United States, with the exception of African Americans. A two-volume landmark handbook, edited by Jones (1996) has described more than 100 measures of acculturation, coping, life experiences including discrimination, physiology-neuropsychology, racial identity, service delivery, spirituality, stress, racism, values, and worldview. Thirteen of these measures were designed for children and six for adolescents. The racial and cultural identity measures should be routinely used with African American assessees. However, few of these tests are currently used in assessment practice.

Bridging the Gap between Knowledge and Culturally Competent Psychological Assessment and Intervention Services

Malgady's suggestion to reverse the Null Hypothesis has been embodied in a model of the assessment-intervention process (Dana, 1997, 1998b). This model contains steps at which relevant questions can be asked to increase the reliability and accuracy of the assessment process and the efficacy of any subsequent interventions, and it was designed to counter what Hall (1997) has described as cultural malpractice.

The initial step begins with a premise question pertaining to the availability of etic assessment instruments that could lead to universal diagnostic formulations and subsequent culture-universal interventions. However, such instruments for clinical practice do not exist at present, although their development is a primary objective of cross-cultural psychologists.

The second step raises questions concerning cultural orientation status, or the extent to which assimilation has occurred as described by the outcome of acculturation. Information from interview and/or tests is used to label cultural orientation status and subsequently to describe the cultural self and cultural/racial identity.

This information permits an informed decision on selection of assessment instruments during Step 3, instrumentation. The question posed here is whether to use standard instruments, with or without adjustments, or to apply available culture-specific tests. There are few culture-specific tests at present. Nonetheless, these emic tests need to be applied either to describe the cultural self for persons who have limited or no English, problems with cultural identification, or who may require cultural formulations at Step 4 to facilitate clinical diagnosis. In a climate of strong preference for standard tests among mainstream, Western assessors, additional questions concerning possible adjustments of standard tests are raised. These questions include the use of translations, local or cultural orientation norms for standard tests, as well as culturally credible social etiquette.

Questions concerning the presence of culture-specific issues resulting from interaction stressors are pertinent during Step 4, when a subsequent diagnostic formulation may or may not be required. If these issues are not present in assessment data that suggest psychopathology, then a standard diagnostic formulation can be used. However, if such issues have been identified in context with psychopathology in clients who are traditional, immigrants, or do not speak English fluently, then a culture-specific conceptualization leading to a cultural formulation will be required for DSM-IV diagnosis.

The purpose of these first four general steps and specific questions is to increase the probability that clinical diagnosis or an absence of clinical diagnosis leads to an appropriate, acceptable, and potentially beneficial intervention at Step 5. Interventions may be classified as culture-general, combined culture-general and culture-specific, or culture-specific (Dana, 1998e). Culture-specific interventions are further subdivided into identity-specific interventions when the presenting problems are not psychopathological in nature but involve deficit or confusion in cultural/racial identity. In applying these interventions, relevant questions must be asked of the cultural information present in the assessment data to determine the goodness-of-fit between particular clients and recommended cultural components present in all three intervention categories. For example, when psychopathology is not present, the culture-specific conceptualization leads directly to a culture-specific intervention. Moreover, whenever there is no clinical diagnosis, the likelihood is increased that cultural issues will be the focus for either a culture-specific intervention or an identity-specific intervention. The employment of a cultural formulation suggests that an intervention incorporating cultural ingredients will more likely be effective than a standard intervention.

At present, the practice of culturally competent assessment is rare indeed. Despite awareness and formal pressure from program accreditation guidelines and site visitors, there is a paucity of relevant training available to students. In addition, the assessment establishment remains skeptical regarding the necessity of translations, local, group or acculturation status norms, moderator variables, culture-specific service delivery styles, or any need for new *emic* tests for ethnic minority groups in the United States. The solution to these dilemmas lies in greater understanding of the cultural specificity of the Western world view as expressed in our assessment technology. Such understanding requires an ethnorelativism that honors and is responsive to a much wider range of individual differences than occurs at the present time. Implementation of cultural competence in assessment training will require not only a greater ethnic minority faculty presence in training but also political persuasion that will occur only when a larger proportion of the United States population represents various ethnic minorities.

REFERENCES

Allen, J. (1998). Personality assessment with American Indians and Alaska Natives: Instrument considerations and service delivery style. *Journal of Personality Assessment, 70,* 17–42.

Allen, J., & French, C. (1996). *Northern Plains Bicultural Immersion Scale-Preliminary manual and scoring instructions* (Version 5). Vermillion: University of South Dakota.

Allison, K. W., Crawford, I., Echemendia, R., Robinson, L., & Kemp, D. (1994). Human diversity and professional competence: Training in clinical and counseling psychology revisited. *American Psychologist, 49,* 792–796.

Allison, K. W., Echemendia, R., Crawford, I., & Robinson, W. L. (1996). Predicting cultural competence: Implications for practice and training. *Professional Psychology: Research and Practice, 27,* 386–393.

American Psychiatric Association. (1994). *Diagnostic and statistical manual of mental disorders* (DSM-IV) (4th ed.). Washington, DC: Author.

Arnold, B. R., Montgomery, G. T., Castanada, I., & Longoria, R. (1994). Acculturation and performance of Hispanics on selected Halstead-Reitan neuropsychological tests. *Assessment, 1,* 239–248.

Avila-Espada, A. (in press). Objective scoring for the TAT. In R. H. Dana (Ed.), *Handbook of cross-cultural and multicultural personality assessment.* Hillsdale, NJ: Erlbaum.

Avila-Espada, A., & Jimenez-Gomez, F. (1996). The Castilian version of the MMPI-2 in Spain: Development adaptation, and psychometric properties. In J. N. Butcher (Ed.), *International adaptations of the MMPI-2: Research and clinical applications* (pp. 305–325). Minneapolis: University of Minnesota Press.

Baldwin, J. A., & Bell, Y. R. (1985). The African Self-Consciousness Scale: An Africentric personality questionnaire. *Western Journal of Black Studies, 13* (2), 27–41.

Barnouw, V. (1963). *Culture and personality.* Homewood, IL: Dorsey.

Brown, S. (1982, May). *Native generations diagnosis and placement on the conflicts/resolutions chart.* Paper presented at the annual meeting of the School of Addiction Studies, Center for Alcohol and Addiction Studies, University of Alaska, Anchorage.

Cervantes, R. C., Padilla, A. M., & deSnyder, N. S. (1991). The Hispanic Stress Inventory: A culturally relevant approach to psychosocial assessment. *Psychological Assessment: A Journal of Consulting and Clinical Psychology, 3,* 438–447.

Chang, M., Dana, R. H., & Yan, K. (in press). Chinese cultural identity assessment. In R. H. Dana (Ed.), *Handbook of cross-cultural and multicultural personality assessment.* Hillsdale, NJ: Erlbaum.

Costantino, G., & Malgady, R. (in press). Tell-Me-A-Story (TEMAS). In R. H. Dana (Ed.), *Handbook of cross-cultural and multicultural personality assessment.* Hillsdale, NJ: Erlbaum.

Costantino, G., Malgady, R. C., & Rogler, L. H. (1988). *TEMAS (Tell-Me-a-Story) manual.* Los Angeles: Western Psychological Services.

Craig, R. J., & Horowitz, M. (1990). Current utilization of psychological tests at diagnostic practicum sites. *Clinical Psychologist, 43,* 29–36.

Cuéllar, I. (1998). Cross-cultural clinical psychological assessment of Hispanic Americans. *Journal of Personality Assessment, 70,* 71–86.

Cuéllar, I. (in press). Mexican American acculturation: ARSMA/ARSMA-II. In R. H. Dana (Ed.), *Handbook of cross-cultural and multicultural personality assessment.* Hillsdale, NJ: Erlbaum.

Cuéllar, I., Arnold, B., & Maldonado, R. (1995). Acculturation Rating Scale for Mexican American-II: A revision of the original ARSMA scale. *Hispanic Journal of Behavioral Sciences, 17,* 275–304.

Cuéllar, I., & González, G. (in press). Cultural identity description and cultural formulations for Hispanics. In R. H. Dana (Ed.), *Handbook of cross-cultural and multicultural personality assessment.* Hillsdale, NJ: Erlbaum.

Cuéllar, I., Harris, I. C., & Jasso, R. (1980). An acculturation scale for Mexican American normal and clinical populations. *Hispanic Journal of Behavioral Science, 2,* 199–217.

Dana, R. H. (1984). Intelligence testing of American Indian children: Sidesteps in quest of ethical practice. *White Cloud Journal, 3* (3), 35–43.

Dana, R. H. (1985). A service-delivery paradigm for personality assessment. *Journal of Personality Assessment, 49,* 598–604.

Dana, R. H. (1987). Training for professional psychology: Science, practice, and identity. *Professional Psychology: Research and Practice, 18,* 9–16.

Dana, R. H. (1992). A commentary on assessment training in Boulder and Vail Model programs: In praise of differences! *Journal of Training and Practice in Professional Psychology, 6* (2), 19–26.

Dana, R. H. (1993). *Multicultural assessment perspectives for professional psychology.* Boston: Allyn and Bacon.

Dana, R. H. (1994). Training and assessment ethics for all persons: Beginning and agenda. *Professional Psychology: Research and Practice, 25,* 349–354.

Dana, R. H. (1995). Culturally competent MMPI assessment of Hispanic populations. *Hispanic Journal of Behavioral Sciences, 17,* 305–319.

Dana, R. H. (1996a). Culturally competent assessment practice in the United States. *Journal of Personality Assessment, 66,* 472–487.

Dana, R. H. (1996b). Editorial and contributor excellence in multicultural assessment. *World Psychology, 2* (3–4), 480–483.

Dana, R. H. (1996c). Measurement of acculturation in Hispanic populations. *Hispanic Journal of Behavioral Sciences, 17,* 305–319.

Dana, R. H. (1997). Multicultural assessment and cultural identity: An assessment-intervention model. *World Psychology, 3* (1–2), 121–142.

Dana, R. H. (1998a). Cultural identity assessment of culturally diverse groups: 1997. *Journal of Personality Assessment, 70,* 1–16.

Dana, R. H. (1998b). Multicultural assessment in the United States: Still art, not yet science, and controversial. *European Journal of Personality Assessment, 14,* 62–70.

Dana, R. H. (1998c). Personality and the cultural self: Emic and etic contexts as learning resources. In L. Handler & M. Hilsenroth (Eds.), *Teaching and learning personality assessment* (pp. 325–345). Hillsdale, NJ: Erlbaum.

Dana, R. H. (1998d). Projective assessment of Latinos in the United States: Current realities, problems, and prospects. *Cultural Diversity and Mental Health, 4* (3), 1–20.

Dana, R. H. (1998e). *Understanding cultural identity in intervention and assessment.* Thousand Oaks, CA: Sage.

Dana, R. H. (in press a). Cross-cultural and multicultural use of the Thematic Apperception Test. In M. L. Geiser & M. Stein (Eds.), *Celebrating the Thematic Apperception Test.* Washington, DC: American Psychological Association.

Dana, R. H. (in press b). Multicultural assessment of adolescent and child personality and psychopathology. In M. L. Comunian, & U. P. Gielen (Eds.), *Human development in cross-cultural perspective.*

Dana, R. H. (submitted). The cultural self as a locus for assessment and intervention with American Indians/Alaska Natives. *Journal of Multicultural Counseling and Development.*

Dana, R. H., Hornby, R., & Hoffmann, T. (1984). Local norms of personality assessment for Rosebud Sioux. *White Cloud Journal, 3* (2), 17–25.

Dauphinais, P., & King, J. (1992). Psychological assessment with American Indian children. *Applied and Preventive Psychology, 1,* 97–110.

Geisinger, K. (Ed.). (1992). *Psychological testing for Hispanics.* Washington, DC: American Psychological Association.

Gibbs, J. T. (1985). Treatment relationships with Black clients: Interpersonal vs. instrumental strategies. *Advances in clinical social work.* Silver Spring, MD: National Association of Social Workers.

Greene, R. L. (1987). Ethnicity and MMPI performance: A review. *Journal of Consulting and Clinical Psychology, 55,* 497–512.

Hall, C. C. I. (1997). Cultural malpractice: The growing obsolescence of psychology with the changing U.S. population. *American Psychologist, 52,* 642–651.

Handler, L. (1996). The clinical use of drawings: Draw-A-Person, House-Tree-Person, and Kinetic Family Drawings. In C. S. Newmark (Ed.), *Major psychological assessment instruments* (2nd ed., pp. 206–293). Boston: Allyn & Bacon.

Helms, J. (1992). Why is there no study of cultural equivalence in standardized cognitive ability testing? *American Psychologist, 47,* 1083–1101.

Helms, J. E. (Ed.). (1990). *Black and White racial identity: Theory, research, and practice.* New York: Greenwood.

Hoffmann, T., Dana, R. H., & Bolton, B. (1985). Measured acculturation and the MMPI-168. *Journal of Cross-Cultural Psychology, 16,* 243–256.

Holden, R. R. (in press). Are there promising MMPI substitutes for assessing psychopathology and personality? Review and prospects. In R. H. Dana (Ed.), *Handbook of cross-cultural and multicultural personality assessment.* Hillsdale, NJ: Erlbaum.

Holmes, T. H., & Rahe, R. H. (1967). The Social Readjustment Rating Scale. *Journal of Psychosomatic Research, 11,* 213–218.

Holtzman, W. H. (1980). Projective techniques. In H. C. Triandis & J. W. Berry (Eds.), *Handbook of cross-cultural psychology: Vol 2. Methodology* (pp. 245–278). Boston: Allyn and Bacon.

Holtzman, W. H. (in press). Application of the Holtzman Inkblot Technique in different countries. In R. H. Dana (Ed.), *Handbook of cross-cultural and multicultural personality assessment.* Hillsdale, NJ: Erlbaum.

Hornby, R. (1993). *Competency training for human service providers.* Mission, SD: St. Gleska University Press.

Jones, E. E., & Thorne, A. (1987). Rediscovery of the subject: Intercultural approaches to clinical assessment. *Journal of Consulting and Clinical Psychology, 55,* 488–495.

Jones, R. L. (Ed.). (1996). Handbook of tests and measurements for Black populations. Hampton, VA: Cobb & Henry.

Kinsie, J. D., Manson, S. M., Vinh, D. T., Tolan, N. T, Anh, B., & Pho, T. N. (1982). Development and validation of a Vietnamese-language depression rating scale. *American Journal of Psychiatry, 139,* 1276–1281.

Klopfer, B., & Boyer, L. B. (1961). Notes on the personality structure of a North American Indian shaman: Rorschach interpretation. *Journal of Personality Assessment, 25,* 170–178.

LaFromboise, T. D., Trimble, J. E., & Mohatt, G. V. (1990). Counseling intervention and American Indian traditions: An integrative approach. *The Counseling Psychologist, 18,* 628–654.

Landrine, H., & Klonoff, E. A. (1996). *African-American acculturation: Deconstructing race and reviving culture.* Thousand Oaks, CA: Sage.

Lindsey, M. L. (1998). Culturally competent assessment of African American clients. *Journal of Personality Assessment, 70,* 43–53.

Lindzey, G. (1961). *Projective techniques and cross-cultural research.* New York: Appleton-Century-Crofts.

López, S. R., Grover, K. P., Holland, D., Johnson, M. J., Kain, C. D., Kanel, K., & Mellins, S. A. (1989). Development of culturally sensitive psychotherapists. *Professional Psychology: Research and Practice, 20,* 369–376.

López, S. R., & Romero, A. (1988). Assessing the intellectual functioning of Spanish-speaking adults: Comparison of the EIWA and the WAIS. *Professional Psychology: Research and Practice, 19,* 263–270.

Malgady, R. G. (1996). The question of cultural bias in assessment and diagnosis of ethnic minority clients: Let's reject the Null Hypothesis. *Professional Psychology: Research and Practice, 27,* 73–77.

Malgady, R. G. (in press). Myths about the Null Hypothesis and the path to reform. In R. H. Dana (Ed.), *Handbook of cross-cultural and multicultural personality assessment.* Hillsdale, NJ: Erlbaum.

Manaster, G. J., & Havighurst, R. J. (1972). *Cross-national research: Socio-psychological methods and problems.* Boston: Houghton-Mifflin.

Matarazzo, J. D. (1992). Psychological testing and assessment in the 21st century. *American Psychologist, 47,* 1007–1118.

Mensh, I. N., & Henry, J. (1953). Direct observation and psychological tests in anthropological studies. *American Anthropologist, 55,* 461–480.

Mercer, J., & Lewis, J. (1978). *System of Multicultural Pluralistic Assessment.* New York: Psychological Corporation.

Monopoli, J. (1984). *A culture-specific interpretation of thematic test protocols for American Indians.* Unpublished master's thesis, University of Arkansas, Fayetteville, AR.

Mosley J. C., & Lex, A. (1990). Identification of potentially stressful life events experienced by a population of urban minority youth. *Journal of Multicultural Counseling and Development, 18.*

Naisbitt, J. (1982). *Megatrends.* New York: Warner.

NIMH-Sponsored Group on Culture and Diagnosis, Steering Committee. (1993, January). *Cultural Proposals and Supporting Papers for DSM-IV (3rd Rev.).* Pittsburgh: University of Pittsburgh Medical School.

O'Donohue, W., Plaud, J. J., Mowatt, A. M., & Fearson, J. R. (1989). Current status of curricula of doctoral training programs in clinical psychology. *Professional Psychology: Research and Practice, 20,* 196–197.

Okazaki, S. (1998). Psychological assessment of Asian Americans: Research agenda for cultural competency. *Journal of Personality Assessment, 70,* 54–70.

Piotrowski, C., & Keller, J. W. (1989). Psychological testing in outpatient mental health facilities: A national study. *Professional Psychology: Research and Practice, 20,* 423–425.

Pires, A. (in press). National norms for the Rorschach Comprehensive System in Portugal. In R. H. Dana (Ed.), *Handbook of cross-cultural and multicultural personality assessment.* Hillsdale, NJ: Erlbaum.

Pollack, D., & Shore, J. H. (1980). Validity of the MMPI with Native Americans. *American Journal of Psychiatry, 137,* 946–950.

Rossini, E. D., & Moretti, R. J. (1997). Thematic Apperception Test (TAT) interpretation: Practice recommendations from a survey of clinical psychology doctoral programs accredited by the American Psychological Association. *Professional Psychology: Research and Practice, 28,* 393–398.

Sherwood, E. T. (1957). On the designing of TAT pictures, with special reference to a set for an African people assimilating Western culture. *Journal of Social Psychology, 45,* 161–190.

Snowden, L., & Todman, P. (1982). The psychological assessment of Blacks: new and needed developments. In E. E. Jones & S. J. Korchin (Eds.), *Minority mental health* (pp. 193–226). New York: Praeger.

Sodowsky, G. R., & Impara, J. C. (Eds.). (1996). *Multicultural assessment in counseling and clinical psychology.* Lincoln, NE: Buros Institute of Mental Measurements.

Spielberger, C. D. (1976). The nature and measurement of anxiety. In C. D. Spielberger & R. Diaz-Guerrero (Eds.), *The nature and measurement of anxiety* (Vol. 1, pp. 1–11). Washington, DC: Hemisphere.

Sue, S., & Zane, N. (1987). The role of culture and cultural techniques in psychotherapy: A critique and reformulation. *American Psychologist, 42,* 37–45.

Suinn, R. M., Rickard-Figueroa, K., Lew, S., & Vigil, S. (1987). The Suinn-Lew Asian Self-Identity

Acculturation Scale: An initial report. *Educational and Psychological Measurement, 47,* 401–407.

Suzuki, L. A., Meller, P. J., & Ponterotto, J. G. (Eds.). (1996). *Handbook of multicultural assessment: Clinical, psychological, and educational applications.* San Francisco: Jossey-Bass.

Thompson, C. E. (1949). The Thompson modification of the Thematic Apperception Text. *Rorschach Research Exchange and Journal of Projective Techniques, 13,* 469–478.

Triandis, H. C., Mirín, G., Lisansky, J., & Betancourt, H. (1984). Simpatía as a cultural script of Hispanics. *Journal of Personality and Social Psychology, 47,* 1363–1375.

Vinet, E. (in press). Use of the Rorschach Comprehensive System in Iberoamerica. In R. H. Dana (Ed.), *Handbook of cross-cultural and multicultural personality assessment.* Hillsdale, NJ: Erlbaum.

Williams, C. L. (1986). Mental health assessment of refugees. In C. L. Williams & J. Westermeyer (Eds.), *Refugee mental health in resettlement countries* (pp. 175–188). New York: Hemisphere.

Williams, R. L. (1972). *Themes concerning Blacks.* St. Louis, MO: Williams & Associates.

Zimmerman, M., Coryell, C., & Wilson, S. (1986). A self-report scale to diagnose major depressive disorder. *Archives of General Psychiatry, 43,* 1076–1081.

5 Psychotherapy and Cultural Diversity

JULIAN WOHL

The primary audience envisioned for this chapter is composed of White, mainstream counselors and psychotherapists whose clients[1] will include members from among the four ethnic groups with which this book is concerned. Despite efforts to develop a culturally and ethnically diverse pool of service providers, these providers represent only a small portion of those who deliver such services. The normative situation in providing service to ethnic minority group members remains one in which a White, mainstream clinician renders the service (Mays & Albee, 1992).

This chapter concentrates on the applicability of some basic psychotherapeutic principles and practices to a population of clients who are ethnically and culturally different from White, middle- and upper-class European-Americans ("mainstream"), the source and usual target of traditional individual psychotherapy. In contrast to the majority of the chapters in this book, the focus is less on individual ethnic groups and the treatment problems specific to them, and more on the application of general principles of psychotherapy to ethnic groups that differ culturally from those to whom psychotherapy has traditionally been applied.

Early in the history of modern psychotherapy, Freud (1919/1953) said that it would be necessary to modify his psychoanalytic method in order to treat people who might be in need but might not be suitable candidates for psychoanalysis. He suggested, for example, that psychoanalysis could be supplemented with direct suggestion. The approach taken in this chapter is consistent with that idea of adapting established approaches to make them functional with a different kind of patient. The intent is to help a practitioner trained in basic psychotherapeutic theory and practice to make use of that knowledge in work with nontraditional clients. These clients might not fit the conventional criteria for traditional individual psychotherapy but nevertheless might benefit from it.

Cultural Embeddedness and Adaptation

Any system of psychotherapy is embedded within a particular cultural-historical context, which shaped and conditioned the thought processes and values of both its practitioners and the clientele for which it was designed. Psychoanalysis with its variants and derivatives, behaviorism and its cognitive modifications, and the humanistic-experiential approaches make up the three major categories of contemporary psychotherapy. In addition to these major categories are movements aimed at integrating various theories and methods (Arkowitz, 1992; Ivey, Ivey, & Simek-Morgan, 1997; Norcross & Goldfried, 1992).

Despite the differences among and within these categories, they comprise methods created largely by White, middle-class practitioners, intended to be applied to people presumed to share with the European and North American creators of these methods cultural content such as value orientations, cause–effect relationships, and cognitive modes ("worldviews"). This broad framework of psychotherapy developed gradually through the latter half of the nineteenth century and the first half of the twentieth. In the last half of the twentieth century, however, and accelerating dramatically in the last third, the claim that this framework was universally valid and suitable for all comers has been forcefully challenged as the ethnic and cultural character of the target population changed (see Chapter 1, and Draguns, 1996).

These changes shattered the comfortable assumption that everyone was more or less alike and more or less equally susceptible to the application of basic methods of psychotherapy. It became clear that for many of this new class of patients, the structure, framework, "contract," or "ground rules" of psychotherapy were not automatically comprehended, and the procedures therapists wished to employ were not immediately acceptable. Two conclusions emerged from these perceptions. The first of these is the positive, healthy rediscovery of the principle that cultural variation among patients and cultural differences between patients and therapists always exist to varying degrees in psychotherapy and require the attention of therapists (Lee, 1997; Wohl, 1989a). No pairing of patient and psychotherapist will be without its cultural variety in some way, however minute, and the wise therapist should make no assumption about cultural commonality with patients that is not left open to question. Appreciating the ubiquity of cultural variation and the importance of cultural issues in psychotherapy can do much to heighten the consciousness of therapists and foster a sharpening of skill and an enhancement of their therapeutic efforts.

Such appreciation, however, does not automatically require that a whole new brand of psychotherapy be manufactured for each cultural, subcultural, or ethnic variant of client. Yet a second but erroneous conclusion sometimes drawn with regard to acknowledging the multicultural nature of United States society and therefore the ethnic diversity of clinical clientele, is the therapeutically nihilistic one that so-called traditional therapies cannot be used effectively with cultural minorities and should be replaced by some new "culturally specific" techniques. Culturally specific approaches are psychotherapeutic methods designed to be congruent with the cultural characteristics of a particular ethnic clientele, or for problems believed to be especially prominent in a particular ethnic group or to ethnic groups in general.

An extensive literature on this subject continues to appear. One example of the approach is provided by Ramirez (1991). Sue (1990) presents a conceptual discussion. Rogler, Malgady, Costantino, and Blumenthal (1987/1998) and Atkinson and Lowe (1995) contribute thoughtful and dispassionate reviews. Sue, Zane, and Young (1994) include an exhaustive and critical analysis in their comprehensive review of research literature on treatment and cultural diversity. Considering how much attention is devoted to the desirability of culture-specific methods, surprisingly little support for their efficacy can be garnered from the research literature. Sue, Zane, and Young (1994) found no studies that actually examined the relative merits of their effectiveness with Asian Americans, although culturally relevant modifications of treatment methods for them appear frequently in the literature. They note that many recommendations for treatment designed explicitly for Black Americans exist, but very little by way of assessment of results can be seen. Neither is there much evidence for the effectiveness of particular methods dedicated to treating American Indians, although programs are continually appearing. For Latino populations, a variety of culturally sensitive or specific treatment procedures have been developed. And only with this group does empirical research provide encouragement regarding the effectiveness of treatment (Sue et al., 1994).

Although experimentation to develop more efficacious means of treating ethnic minorities using culturally specific techniques is desirable, these efforts should not be taken to rule out the use of traditional psychotherapies. Weiner (1975) notes that race and socioeconomic class differences between patient and therapist do not automatically make basic psychotherapy an inappropriate choice. "What is needed," he says, "is for the therapist to know *how to conduct psychotherapy* with groups of people who differ from him, and *not* to conclude that it is inapplicable" (p. 21, emphasis in original).

To decide simply on the basis of ethnicity, race, religion, socioeconomic class, age, or sex that a particular client will be unsuitable for a "talking therapy" or a therapy involving some degree of self-scrutiny constitutes by itself an ethnic slur (Wohl, 1989b). Such a conclusion is violative of ethical and clinical rules of practice. Psychotherapists and psychological counselors are not supposed to prejudge and make treatment decisions about clients prior to having the opportunity to assess them. Any reasonable review of the literature shows no justification for the sweeping conclusion that would dismiss traditional psychotherapies out of hand (Atkinson, 1985; Atkinson & Lowe, 1995; Parloff, Waskow, & Wolfe, 1978; Ponterotto, 1984; Sue, 1988; Sue et al., 1994). To the contrary, evidence exists to support the opposite notion, that basic psychotherapeutic approaches can work effectively with United States subcultures and minority groups (Jones, 1987; Jones & Matsumoto, 1982; Lerner, 1972; Meadow, 1982; Wilkinson & Spurlock, 1986).

The fundamental notion is that traditional psychotherapies can be used, but they must be adapted and flexibly applied by taking into account social, economic, cultural, ethnic, and political determinants of the patient's situation (Atkinson, Morten, & Sue, 1998; Draguns, 1996). This approach is consistent with what Jackson (1990) in her discussion of frameworks for "ethnocultural psychotherapy" characterizes as a model that combines a traditional treatment approach with an appreciation of cultural factors. *There is no escape in psychotherapy from the requirement that the therapist become conscious of factors that might affect or condition the patient's reactions within the therapeutic situation or bear upon the patient's life outside that situation.*

When faced with ethnic minority (or other) clients who seem not to fit their conventional criteria for psychotherapy, therapists may well be tempted to discard or forgo what they have learned are useful approaches to engaging people in psychotherapy. In working with these clients, therapists must walk one of the several fine lines that are found in psychotherapy. A balance must be struck between the impulse on the one hand to discard as inappropriate or useless basic psychotherapeutic methods, and, on the other, to insist that a particular construction of psychotherapy be maintained when it obviously presents profound difficulties for patients or provokes their rejection. Avoidance of the pitfall requires a careful attention to the path. To change metaphors, while the bathwater drains, one wants to preserve the baby.

Beginning Psychotherapy

The most crucial point in psychotherapy with people for whom psychotherapy clearly presents a culturally different adaptational experience, and perhaps even for any potential patient, is the very beginning (Brammer, Abrego, & Shostrum, 1993: Griffith & Jones, 1978). Here the effort to engage the client must pass its most serious test, and here the failure of many therapists to draw the client into treatment is rooted. At the point of entry, when patient and therapist first meet, before the structure and procedure are understood by the patient, the two participants stand poised, facing each other across a canyon. To construct the bridge across that space is the first responsibility of the psychotherapist. Failure to do so can signal the onset of a spiral of miscommunication ending in an early termination of unsuccessful psychotherapy. To begin to close the gap is to initiate what just about all theories of psychotherapy insist is vital and basic: the special therapeutic relationship (Frank, 1982; Frank & Frank, 1991; Lambert & Bergin, 1992; Langs, 1973; Root, 1998; Strupp, 1973, 1982; Wohl, 1989a). This relationship has come to be appreciated as the essential ingredient of effective psychotherapy. Its components, most of which are dependent upon the conduct of the therapist, are well known and widely discussed in the literature. Although not all observers use precisely the same terminology, consensus does prevail. These qualities are what all seek in a good (ideal) human relationship, as Greben (1981) asserts. Most often mentioned are empathic concern, respect, realistic hope, reliability, emotional support, strength, genuineness, capacity to build trust, honesty, tolerance of ambiguity, flexibility, caring, open accepting listening attitude, self-awareness, understanding, and tactful communication. Such pan-human desirable characteristics of psychotherapists and counselors provide a base and justification for extending any kind of psychotherapeutic intervention beyond the cultural setting in which it originated.

Culturally different clients may require more introduction to the process than a sentence or two about how talking is useful and that the therapist wants the patient to express thoughts, feelings, and problems and that the patient should feel free to do so. Working with patients for whom our psychotherapy may be foreign, strange, and exotic, psychotherapists must educate or inform patients about how the treatment operates (Nishio & Bilmes, 1987/1998; Root, 1998). Ethnic minority patients, on the basis of past experience, may have no reason to accept and trust what the nonminority, mainstream White therapist says, the more so when the whole idea just presented as a procedure may be inconsistent with prevailing norms about getting help in a particular minority group or subgroup (Fadiman, 1997; Kaplan & Johnson, 1964; Kleinman, 1980; Pedersen, 1982; Root, 1998).

Emerging from psychoanalysis, but applicable to all psychotherapy, is the concept of resistance. One of the oldest concepts in psychotherapy, it has proved very helpful in understanding client conduct in treatment, but it is all too easy to misuse it with ethnically or culturally different patients. In brief, resistance refers to reactions of patients inspired by threat perceived in the psychotherapeutic situation. Ultimately, that threat for the client is that protective illusions may have to be confronted and that significant, valued aspects of the self may have to be changed.

Resistance is an internal process and occurs in all patients. It will, therefore, be a part of the ethnic minority patient's repertoire also. But it would be a serious mistake to lay all confusion, reluctance, hesitation, mistrust, skepticism, or suspicion displayed initially by the patient at the door of an internally rooted resistance and nothing else. Enmeshed in the emotional component may well be a purely cognitive puzzlement that an appropriate introduction to psychotherapy by the therapist can dispel, thus reducing some of what appears to be classical resistance (Wohl, 1989b). Easily confused with internally rooted resistance is the protective garb of reluctance, caution, and wariness worn by members of minority groups as a result of prior discrimination and frustration in their transactions with private and governmental bureaucracies.

Although we focus now on barriers to treatment that might be mistaken for internally based resistance but are a product of external experiences, rarely if ever will such a distinction between an inner barrier and an outer one be complete. The psychotherapist needs always to realize that even the most realistic, culturally based reasons for a patient's reluctance or difficulty in initiating psychotherapy will have also its inner correlate. Procedurally, however, therapists must begin with the external reality aspects, before attacking the more refractory internal resistances. Upon encountering a culturally different client, it is helpful to bear in mind (and perhaps especially comforting to the beginner) that not everyone who enters the office is suitable for psychotherapy or for a particular therapist's way of conducting it. The nature or severity of the disorder on the one side, and the skills, theoretical orientation, or experience of the therapist on the other may argue against a particular patient–therapist combination. This observation, of course, applies across the board and not just to the culturally different patient.

In intercultural psychotherapy situations, many candidates for help can be found whose differences from the therapist and from the therapist's concepts of disorders and remediation are so great that the gap cannot be closed. The most extreme examples of this can be found in reports of the application of Western psychotherapy to patients in non-Western societies. The record of success is not encouraging, and even where it seems successful, substantial modifications in procedure are evident (Wohl, 1989a). Another category of clients unsuitable for traditional psychotherapy would be unacculturated recent immigrants—frequently refugees—from non-Western societies. Fadiman (1997) poignantly portrays the tragic result of treatment failure in such a context.

In this book (Chapter 9), Koss-Chioino discusses the difficult problem of treating minimally acculturated Native Americans with Western psychotherapies. On the other hand, Devereaux (1951; 1953) reported satisfactory psychoanalytic psychotherapy results with well-acculturated Plains Indians. Trained in anthropology as well as in psychoanalysis, Devereaux emphasized that, despite their degree of acculturation, therapy required him to understand the patients' cultural traditions in order to deal appropriately with the therapeutic relationship, dreams, and the goals of therapy. Trimble, Fleming, Beauvais, and Jumper-Thurman (1996) provide a detailed discussion with several illustrative case examples of the importance of variation in acculturation with respect to American Indians. Unquestionably, the degree of acculturation of a patient greatly affects the feasibility of employing mainstream individual psychotherapy (Chapter 2; Atkinson et al., 1998; Garrett & Garrett, 1998; Kitano & Maki, 1996; LaFromboise, Trimble, & Mohatt, 1998; Rogler et al., 1987/1998; Root, 1998).

In responding to cultural (including ethnic, linguistic, religious, and class) diversity in patients that differentiates them from the therapist, a basic psychotherapy framework can be used. Psychotherapists should maintain the psychotherapeutic stance, mode of understanding, and empathic quality consistent with their psychotherapy theories. At the same time, they must take into account issues presented by the client's cultural context. This approach derives from and reaffirms a basic principle in psychotherapy that, although therapists work within a theoretical framework, the framework allows and informs therapists to stand ready to appreciate and respond flexibly to the uniqueness of individual clients.

By way of illustration, the mainstream, highly intelligent, verbally facile patient may or may not be sophisticated about psychotherapy. Such patients tempt therapists to assume that they are knowledgeable. Wiser therapeutic practice recommends that therapists await confirmation from the patient. But regardless of the patients' actual understanding of psychotherapy, therapists will tailor their language and form of presentation to the intellectual level of the patient so that the cognitive element in the therapist's message is delivered while the self-esteem of the patient is protected. At the other extreme, in working with patients with limited formal education and no particular enlightenment regarding psychotherapy, again therapists will utilize language and conduct designed to inform the patient and to avoid damaging the patient's self-esteem.

Making a Relationship

Therapists recognize that they must establish working conditions with their patients and that they need to communicate certain information about the procedure in order to do so. Normally, we would do this more or less automatically without thinking that we are doing something "cross-culturally." The difference is that, in interethnic, intercultural situations, one must pay much more attention to the work of establishing the basis for a communicative relationship than in those where this factor is not evident.

The therapist's appreciation of the patient's social, educational, and intellectual position, and the use of tactful interventions derived from that knowledge, are basic and general psychotherapeutic characteristics in any treatment context and in any and all theories of psychotherapy. We modify or adapt our "method," "procedure," or "technique" to fit the concrete facts of the clinical situation. We finely tune the mode of communication, including vocabulary, language level, and style of relating, so that we effectively communicate what we think we need to get across in order to create a good collaborative working arrangement.

Furthermore, the manner in which we proceed in these initial steps demonstrates for the patient civility, rationality, careful listening, respectful attention, and genuine interest—a syndrome of attitudes, values, and conduct that the therapist takes for granted as part of the universal professional culture of psychotherapy, and therefore characteristic of any kind of psychotherapy. But this design for social interaction is not necessarily as familiar to the patient as to the therapist and thus may itself constitute a significant "cultural difference," which requires adaptation on the patient's part and recognition of the patient's struggle with it on the therapist's. As therapists, we consider our characteristics and conduct as normal, humane, desirable, and appropriate ways of interacting, but they may not necessarily appear so to clients, in whose lives such modes of conduct may be neither commonplace nor even infrequently evident.

A second reason that a therapist's psychotherapeutically correct conduct might surprise a patient lies in quite another direction. Many people who in their everyday lives would hope, enjoy, and expect to be treated in the aforementioned manner by their fellows do not expect such egalitarian conduct from their authorities, among whom are included their "doctors." This group includes people from many countries around the world, some of whom now reside in this country, as well as the descendants of such immigrants who perpetuate at least some of the traditional ways of their predecessors. The literature, for example, tells us that Asians tend to expect a more direct, forceful, authoritative manner and a less personal demeanor in their experts, whereas Hispanics are said to want authoritativeness blended with a greater degree of personal intimacy than the principles prescribe for the patient more familiar to the Euro-American clinician (Atkinson & Lowe, 1995; Leong, 1986; Maduro, 1982; Nishio & Bilmes, 1987/1998; Owan, 1985; Root, 1998). Roll, Millen, and Martinez (1980) present an exceptionally thoughtful discussion of relationship issues along with common errors and suggestions for avoiding them in the treatment of Latinos. Similarly, Tsui and Schultz (1985) describe mistakes and explicate relationship issues in the interethnic treatment of Asians, whereas Garrett and Garrett (1998) and LaFromboise, Trimble, and Mohatt (1998) discuss the issues and provide suggestions for working with American Indians. Block (1981; 1984) E. E. Jones (1987) and N. Jones (1990) contribute similarly useful suggestions for psychotherapy with African Americans.

Confronting Noticeable Differences

When we note unusual characteristics of the kind conveniently labeled as cultural—dialect, accent, skin color, name, religion, or other indicators of ethnic identity—we know that more than normal attention might need to be devoted to clarifying with the patient an array of matters about the psychotherapeutic process and procedure.

To begin to do so, ideally we might want to know the patient's conceptions of the nature and source of the problems being experienced, the patient's expectations about what will happen, and the patient's construction of the ways in which the therapist will help. From the patient, and perhaps from other sources of information about the patient's general cultural background, we might expect, and actually discover, deviations from our normative expectations or conceptions of the cause of the troubles, unusual metaphoric representation of difficulties, and ideas about the role of third parties in treatment that contradict ours.

Kleinman (1980) has provided a comprehensive approach to the question of bridging the gap between patients' views of their troubles and those of the therapists. He uses the concept of "explanatory model" to refer to conceptions that both clients and therapists maintain of etiology, course, appropriate sick role behavior, and treatment. Kleinman also suggests an array of specific questions aimed at eliciting the patient's explanatory model. If the explanatory models of the clinician and the patient are far apart and the distance between them is not negotiated, treatment will flounder. If the therapist sees the patient's abdominal discomfort as a reaction to inner conflict or as a learned way of reacting to stress, and the patient sees it as the revenge of an offended ancestor, little basis for a common approach to the problem exists.

In such extreme situations, therapeutic communication is well nigh impossible because the two parties apply contradictory explanatory principles and conceptual frameworks to the same events. They maintain contrary constructions of their experience and cognitive systems, their ways of comprehending reality (Fadiman, 1997). Such gross disparities exemplify one aspect of the "worldview" problem (Frank & Frank, 1991; Torrey, 1986; see also Chapter 2 for a description of the "worldview" concept.) Another aspect of the cognitive issue shows itself when language differences exist between the two participants in a psychotherapy situation.

A language difference between therapist and patient can provide a truly formidable barrier to their effective collaboration in individual psychotherapy. When one party speaks French and the other Japanese, unless a third common language is available, psychotherapy cannot occur. Interpreters can be used in the assessment and problem definition stage of an inquiry, though not without error (Marcos, 1979), but the therapy itself requires a substantially shared language and the interaction of the participants alone together. The interpreter's presence triangulates, and thus transforms drastically, the intimacy of a two-person situation into a far more complicated one.

In a less extreme and more common situation than a complete absence of a common language, one participant might speak English as a second language or be a native speaker of nonstandard English while the other uses standard English (see Chapter 2 for a discussion of language, or Russell, 1988, and Sue, 1981, who discusses language as a barrier to psychotherapy). Another frequently found situation would include some degree of bilingualism and the need to find a convenient common tongue. Where both parties are relatively fluent in two languages (Spanish and English are the most obvious examples), shifting back and forth might occur.

The issues associated with bilingual communication in psychotherapy have been explored in detailed in a series of papers by Marcos and his associates (Marcos, 1976a, 1976b; Marcos & Alpert, 1976; Marcos & Urcuyo, 1979; Pitta, Marcos, & Alpert, 1978) and by Marrero (1983). Despite the complexity introduced by a bilingual situation, such therapy can be effective. In one experimental study, a well-qualified bilingual psychiatrist, speaking English with one group of six bilingual patients and Spanish with the other group of six bilingual patients, used brief, psychodynamic psychotherapy and achieved equally positive results with both groups (Gomez, Ruiz, & Laval, 1982). Marcos (1988) warns us not to assume a linear relationship between English proficiency and acculturation in Hispanics. Their culturally rooted "worldviews" and explanatory models might differ from those of therapists even though they were competent speakers of English.

Working from our appreciation of the patient's point of departure, we negotiate the distance between that conceptual framework and the one we want to construct. We need to communicate what we are doing, what we expect the patient to be doing, and how we expect to interact. In instances of obvious, blatant cultural differences, we become hypersensitive to these matters, but the point is that in psychotherapy we need always to pay attention to the same issues even when the client is ostensibly a member of the majority culture and presumably understands the ways of helping and being helped with personal difficulties in that culture. Short of the patient's being a member of our encapsulated professional subculture, psychotherapists and counselors ought not to take anything for granted about what a client's conceptions of treatment and its rationale might be.

The literature in psychotherapy and counseling abounds with information, warnings, and advice to therapists on working with cultural minorities and culturally different people in general. It insists repeatedly that therapists embarking on such activities need to acquire knowledge about the culture of the people they will be treating (Abel, Metraux, & Roll, 1987; Atkinson et al., 1998; Marsella & Pedersen, 1981; Pedersen, 1987; Pedersen, Draguns, Lonner, & Trimble, 1996; Sue, 1981). Advice runs the gamut from reading suitable sociological and anthropological works to immersing oneself in the everyday life of the group in question. Psychotherapists who are to devote all or most of their professional time to a particular cultural, subcultural, or ethnic group should learn as much as possible about the folkways, communication styles, traditions, belief systems, mores, and values of the group.

Reading can be very helpful in this educational process. Living closely and informally within the group, participating in its social activities, and developing friendships can obviously enhance and deepen immeasurably any such externally developed knowledge. It can provide a very useful sense of the context of a patient's life. The realities and practicalities of professional life, however, do not allow most practitioners the luxury of such intensive, virtually anthropological, fieldwork immersion. Depending on the nature of the practice, contacts with members of different cultural groups will not absorb a major part of the practice, and therapists will have to content themselves with a less thoroughgoing investment in learning about the culture in question. Finally, although such knowledge can be helpful, it can pose a problem.

Students of ethnic relations and conflicts, as well as many writers in the clinical literature on interracial and interethnic psychotherapy, have warned of the danger of stereotyping (Smith, 1981; Sue, 1981). Usually, concern centers on situations where the therapist, ignorant of both the cultural background and the individual situation of the patient, might impose on the patient and the patient's life situation prejudices and preconceptions based on a stereotypic image within the therapist. From this comes the frequently expressed injunction to learn as much about the culture as possible before initiating therapy with members of the particular group, as well as coming to appreciate one's own prejudices and values. Knowledge about the group in question combined with a substantial degree of self-awareness can do a great deal to overcome that kind of threat.

But another kind of threat exists. Instead of stereotyping based upon ignorance, we can also find it arising from superficial knowledge. A little knowledge, indeed, can be dangerous. The danger here is that, armed with a superficial knowledge of the culture, the therapist will cast the patient into the mold of the generalized member of that particular culture and lose sight of the individual. We need to remember that knowledge gained from studying about a group is generalized and expressive of many truths about members of the group, but that no individual member of the group will be a living representation of all the generalizations. Neither is any group so homogeneous that all generalizations about the group apply to all members of the group (Atkinson & Lowe, 1995; Atkinson et al., 1998; Casas & Vasquez, 1996; Lee, 1997; Suro, 1998).

With any American ethnic or subcultural minority, the therapist must consider the patient's degree of assimilation by the majority group. United States society is pluralistic, but most members of subcultures participate to varying degrees in the larger culture, and the psychotherapist will want to ascertain the degree of acculturation to that larger culture (see Chapter 2). Ethnic identity may be an issue with which both the client and the therapist must grapple (Helms, 1995). In sum, stereotyping can derive from the therapist's personal prejudices and biases, but it can also emerge from the therapist's honest effort to deny those prejudices their power by learning about the culture in question. In either case, the result is the treatment of the individual patient as a member of a class or a category rather than as a real human person who is also a member of a specific social, cultural, racial, or ethnic group.

An alternative to the "anthropological" approach is exemplified nicely in a statement by Dr. Peter Ng, a pediatrician at Asian Health Services, a clinic in Oakland, California's Chinatown, "There are 20 zillion cultures out there and there's no way you can know every quirk. What we can do as providers is be curious. We have to ask, and then ask again.... It's about caring, and out of caring searching out what we need to know" (Gross, 1992, p. 10). Understanding and caring are crucial and universal values in psychotherapy as well as in medicine. Caring is reflected in the clinician's effort to understand the client's meanings, and care is demonstrated in the compassionate and thoughtful fashion in which that understanding is sought. Psychotherapists from outside the patient's ethnic group cannot be expected to know the ins and outs of the client's group, and pretending to do so is quickly detectable by the patient as fraudulent. Such pretense also violates the values of honesty and openness in relationships that are supposed to characterize our psychotherapy systems. The correct position for therapists must be an open, receptive readiness to learn from the client so that the client's world view can be understood.

From both conscious and unconscious revelations, we learn patients' ideas about the nature and origins of their troubles, the personal meaning of "treatment" or "therapy" or "counseling" or whatever terms they use to refer to whatever they expect will take place between the participants. When the "cultural" differences between the participants are greater than the average expectable cultural difference (a phrase adapted from Hartmann, 1958), therapists need to be more conscious of the possibility that they might misread the patient's communications, and they need to be more than usually careful to investigate ambiguities or uncertainties in their understanding of references and terminology. But here once again we see a quantitative difference, not a qualitative one. Any psychotherapist seeks understanding of the patient through the patient's communications; clarification of meaning is a part of that process.

Historically Oppressed Minorities as Clients

Because of our special American agony in race relationships, the term intercultural is too pallid and puny to characterize interracial and interethnic clinical relationships adequately. Every clinical interaction between a White clinician and a Black patient occurs in the historical context of relationships between Black and White people in this country and the psychocultural effects of those relations on both patient and therapist. The heritage of slavery, oppression, brutality, dehumanization, segregation, and discrimination gives a special quality to this particular clinical situation. Given the tradition of racism in the United States, this applies as well to clinical relationships between White therapists and Native Americans, Latinos, and Asian Americans (Jones, 1990; Toupin, 1980). (A summary of this "tradition" for each of the minority groups referred to in this book appears in Chapter 2.)

The White therapist–Black patient interaction perhaps most dramatically demonstrates the problem and is where that much used, even abused term *sensitivity* forces itself into play. Certainly our services need to be "culturally sensitive" (Rogler et al., 1987/ 1998), but they must also be highly responsive to the sensitivities of individual clients. Overwhelmingly, those who address the issue in the literature agree that White psychotherapists need to appreciate the importance of race and the pervasiveness of racial sensitivity in Black patients (Block, 1984; Brantley, 1983: Butts, 1980; Ridley, 1989; Wohl, 1983). This is most crucial in the earliest stage of therapy when trying to establish a collaborative working relationship, and it remains important all through the work. Race and racial identity are omnipresent for the patient, consciously and unconsciously, as well as for the therapist (in whom we hope *conscious* appreciation of it dominates).

Much of the literature notes that therapists' race problems pose as great a difficulty as do those of patients, and argues that therapists must first treat their own racism before that can well serve their patients in interracial psychotherapy. Block (1981), Lorion and Parron (1987), and Griffith (1977) join others who have observed that therapists carry into clinical relationships with poor and minoritv patients preconceptions, assumptions, and stereotypes about them that can blind them to the real potential of these patients to respond favorably to treatment.

The history and prevalence of racial and ethnic prejudice in the United States and the existence of unconscious stereotypes mean that therapists will be peculiarly vulnerable to experiencing inappropriate and distorted reactions to ethnically different clients. Such countertransference reactions that spring more from their own personal backgrounds than from the material communicated by the client impair and interfere with their effective functioning. As Jones (1987) observes, countertransference is "perhaps the most extensively addressed topic in discussions of the Black patient" (p. 178). It may also be the most fundamental and crucial issue in any psychotherapy (Gorkin, 1987; Slakter, 1987).

The possibilities for countertransference distortion are virtually unlimited. Commonly noted manifestations of such effects in interethnic psychotherapy are those stemming from "white guilt." These can include avoidance of dealing with issues that might be seen as distressing to the client, and overidentification with the client's suffering, or that part of it viewed as due to ethnic/racial discrimination. Other typical reactions might be fear of the client's latent "black rage" (Grier & Cobb, 1969) and therefore a tendency to avoid saying things that might be thought to provoke it; patronizing the patient; difficulty with sexual material because of stereotypic images about the "primitive" sexuality of ethnic group members; avoidance of the topic of ethnicity/race and denial of racial awareness; inappropriate injection of race or insistence on exploring racial feelings when the client is concerned with other matters (Ridley, 1995). Interethnic treatment can evoke personal reactions in therapists that are more or less unique to the interethnic situation (Gorkin, 1987; Jones & Seagull, 1977).

In the last analysis, all the warnings and cautions in the literature telling psychotherapists and counselors to beware of stereotyping, forgo prejudice, be "sensitive," hear the client accurately, be empathic, know their own biases, and be tuned in to their own cognitive and emotional processes are dealing with the same issue. The point is that effective psychotherapeutic performance, with any patient, requires that the therapist manage the countertransference. In this context, that management means preventing one's own cognitive and emotional reactions from intruding and interfering with the therapist's proper functioning.

Unconscious racist derogation can be as insidious as it is destructive. (For a review of the early literature, see Griffith, 1977; for a later assessment of White therapist–Black patient issues, see Jones, 1990.) One very common example of derogating patients is calling them by their first names without authorizing patients to return the favor. This practice is of course not limited to interethnic work. We all too often observe young male service providers address older female patients this way, and poorly trained receptionists in professional offices frequently assume a first-name relationship with all comers, regardless of race, color, creed, age, sex, or national origin.

Sometimes we do not know what it takes to offend, but we can know the result, perhaps in a chilling of the atmosphere, a subtle withdrawal, a sullen smoldering anger, or an open outburst. An American trying to work with a Thai patient might say or do something inappropriate in a Thai context while trying to be useful. The Thai might think the American foolish or ignorant of Thai ways but generally will tolerate the lapse because the poor fool is a foreigner and the Thai does not expect foreigners to understand Thai ways. The Thai will not be so ready to personalize the error as derogation because there has not been a bitter tradition of pain-laden relations between Thais and Americans. By contrast, interethnic therapy in the United States with a Native American, Latino, African American, or Asian American client, an offense, equally innocent and unknown to the therapist, might have much more destructive consequences.

Working with traditionally oppressed minorities threatens the therapist's ability to walk a fine line in several ways. One of these follows from acknowledging that race is a real factor in interracial psychotherapy. Having granted that, then what to do about it becomes the question. Two general alternatives are available. One would have therapists introduce the topic of race and its possible impact on the therapeutic relationship openly at the outset of psychotherapy. Presumably this would lead to an exploration of the patient's attitudes about and difficulties with ethnic conflict and ethnic identity. It would also serve the purpose of communicating the therapist's courageous readiness to deal with this touchy topic, thereby contributing to building the patient's trust and forging the therapeutic alliance, that more or less tacit agreement between the participants to cooperate in an effort to bring the therapy to a successful conclusion.

The other position holds that therapists should be willing to discuss racial issues but provides no specific technical guidance about how they are to be introduced and by which participant. Psychoanalytic psychotherapy theory would instruct the therapist to wait until the patient, either manifestly or in disguised derivative form, introduces the subject of race before commenting on it (Langs, 1973). The fine line in this instance, then, is to balance out readiness to deal with a problem that is believed to be a part of the therapeutic interaction against the sense that generally it is better to wait until one has evidence that the issue exerts sufficient pressure within the patient that would make dealing with it fruitful. Above all, it is important to avoid the comfort of an intellectualized discussion of race and the evils of racism.

Psychotherapy and Reality

Prior to about 1970, at least in the psychodynamically informed literature, White psycho-therapists found themselves instructed in "color blindness" in their work with Black patients (Griffith, 1977). As Adams (1950) expressed it, the patient must be helped "to face the core of his inner problems which are the same kind that haunt, enslave, torture and degrade men of all races" (p. 310). The ideal seemed to be for therapists to work with Black patients as they would with anyone else. This presumptively egalitarian view held sway in the period when psychoanalytic theory, with its concentration on internal dynam-ics and with minimal attention given to "reality" factors such as social, economic, cultural, political, and ethnic influences, dominated psychotherapy. In this framework, therapists would tend to regard patients' references to racial issues such as discrimination or segrega-tion as reflections of an inner resistance to the treatment that exploited plausible external realities. Therapists were warned to beware of confusing inner resistance with external reality, to stick to clinical problems, and to avoid getting caught up in attempts to solve the social problems of the patient that were realities of an unjust society (Heine, 1950).

By the late 1960s, with the civil rights movement in high gear, with psychoanalytic theories competing with and losing popularity to a variety of approaches that emphasized the importance of external forces rather than internal influences and of immediate rather than past experience, with many therapists politicized and committing themselves in their work to social activism, the emphasis shifted. Now many psychotherapists came to view minority patients' difficulties as rational and appropriate responses to intolerable abuse and privation. The tendency to attribute problems to societal oppression and discrimination while minimizing or denying entirely their neurotic, self-maintaining aspects increased (see, for example, Majors & Nikelly, 1983). Here again another fine line is introduced for the psychotherapist. At one extreme, one can be color-blind, deny the significance of race, and see racial references only as serving resistance. At the other, one can ignore the inter-nal conflictual struggles of the patients, avoid the unpleasantness of helping them to con-front their inner truths, and concentrate on the struggle against the social environment as the culprit.

Reality—the reality of the social environment in which many African Americans, Asian Americans, Hispanics, and Native Americans grow up—is cruel and unfair. The neurotic conflicts that beset people, whatever their ethnicity, are to a significant degree the results of developmental experience in their social environments. To the extent that inter-personal struggles and conflicts have been internalized and lie within, the problems do not get solved or changed by attacking the external sources. Nor is psychotherapy a tool for changing the external forces that sustain the patient's suffering. It can only hope to improve and strengthen the patient's ability to feel more comfortable and to operate more effectively upon the environment.

Throughout this book are discussions of a variety of problems and approaches to them that do not depend on individual psychotherapy. Many of these confront directly the familial, social, economic, and political forces that contribute to the miseries of clients. Such external approaches will often have more power and practicality than psychotherapy can claim. There are many ways to attack human difficulties. Individual psychotherapy is only one of them and, measured against the scale of human suffering, not a very power-ful one. Freud (1905/1953) noted that psychotherapy can be practiced in many ways but that the important criterion is whether the patient is helped. We may extend this to say that there are many ways other than psychotherapy to help clients, and any that work are satisfactory.

Psychotherapy is peculiarly designed to cope with those aspects of the client's diffi-culties that are internally based. This is the underlying justification for the admonition not to confuse resistance with reality. That warning holds true for any therapist working with any patient in any kind of psychotherapy. The fact that an event or circumstance is true and real in the patient's life makes it more functional as a vehicle of resistance. All of us do, after all, want to appear reasonable as we struggle to avoid anxiety and evade the pain of the therapeutic process. In these protective efforts we use whatever lies handy. Something factual is always available; fiction is not required. The psychotherapeutic task is to use pro-fessional knowledge and human understanding to help patients to know their own truths, to come to grips with themselves, and to promote their psychological freedom, thereby enabling them to function more effectively.

N O T E

1. Recipients or consumers of individual psychotherapy services are usually referred to either as *cli-ents* or *patients*. The term used depends on various factors, such as whether the treatment context is a med-ical or nonmedical one, and on the provider's personal and theoretically based preferences. In keeping with the eclectic direction of this chapter, both terms are used throughout as equivalents.

R E F E R E N C E S

Abel, T., Metraux, R., & Roll, S. (1987). *Psychotherapy and culture.* Albuquerque: University of New Mexico Press.

Adams, W. A. (1950). The Negro patient in psychiatric treatment. *American Journal of Orthopsychiatry, 20,* 305–310.

Arkowitz, H. (1992). Integrative theories of therapy. In D. K. Freedman (Ed.), *History of psychotherapy: A century of change* (pp. 261–303). Washington, DC: American Psychological Association.

Atkinson, D. R. (1985). Research on cross-cultural coun-seling and psychotherapy: Overview and update of reviews. In P. B. Pedersen (Ed.), *The handbook of cross-cultural counseling and psychotherapy* (pp. 191–197). New York: Praeger.

Atkinson, D. R., & Lowe, S. M. (1995). The role of eth-nicity, cultural knowledge, and conventional tech-niques in counseling and psychotherapy. In J. G. Ponterotto, J. M. Casas, L. A. Suzuki, & C. M. Alex-ander (Eds.), *Handbook of multicultural counseling* (pp. 387–414). Thousand Oaks, CA: Sage.

Atkinson, D. R., Morten, G., & Sue, D. W. (Eds.). (1998). *Counseling American minorities* (5th ed.). New York: McGraw-Hill.

Block, C. B. (1981). Black Americans and the cross-cultural counseling experience. In A. J. Marsella & P. B. Pedersen (Eds.), *Cross-cultural counseling and psychotherapy* (pp. 177–194). New York: Pergamon Press.

Block, C. B. (1984). Diagnostic and treatment issues for Black patients. *The Clinical Psychologist, 37,* 51–54.

Brammer, L. M., Abrego, P. J., & Shostrom, E. L. (1993). *Therapeutic counseling and psychotherapy* (6th ed.). Englewood Cliffs, NJ: Prentice-Hall.

Brantley, T. (1983). Racism and its impact on psychother-apy. *American Journal of Psychiatry, 140,* 1605–1608.

Butts, H. F. (1980). Racial issues in psychotherapy. In T. B. Karasu & L. Bellak (Eds.), *Specialized tech-niques in individual psychotherapy* (pp. 352–381). New York: Bruner/Mazel.

Casas, J. M., & Vasquez, M. J. T. (1996). Counseling the Hispanic: A guiding framework for a diverse population. In P. B. Pedersen, J. G. Draguns, W. J. Lonner, & J. E. Trimble (Eds.), *Counseling across cultures* (4th ed., pp. 146–175). Thousand Oaks, CA: Sage.

Devereaux, G. (1951). Three technical problems in the psychotherapy of a Plains Indian woman. *American Journal of Psychotherapy, 5,* 411–423.

Devereaux, G. (1953). Cultural factors in psychoanalytic therapy. *Journal of the American Psychoanalytic Association, 1,* 629–635.

Draguns, J. G. (1996). Humanly universal and culturally distinctive. In P. B. Pedersen, J. G. Draguns, W. J. Lonner, & J. E. Trimble (Eds.). *Counseling across cultures* (4th ed., pp. 1–20). Thousand Oaks, CA: Sage.

Fadiman, A. (1997). *The spirit catches you and you fall down.* New York: Farrar, Straus & Giroux.

Frank, J. D. (1982). Therapeutic components shared by all psychotherapies. In J. H. Harvey & M. M. Parks (Eds.), *Psychotherapy research and behavior change* (pp. 5–37). Washington, DC: American Psychological Association.

Frank, J. D., & Frank, J. B. (1991). *Persuasion and healing* (3rd ed.). Baltimore: Johns Hopkins University Press.

Freud, S. (1905/1953). On psychotherapy. *Standard edition of the complete psychological works, Vol. 7* (pp. 255–269). London: Hogarth.

Freud, S. (1919/1953). Lines of advance in psychoanalytic therapy. *Standard edition of the complete psychological works, Vol. 17* (pp. 157–168). London: Hogarth.

Garrett, J. T., & Garrett, M. W. (1998). The path of good medicine: Understanding and counseling Native Americans. In D. R. Atkinson, G. Morten, & D. W. Sue (Eds.), *Counseling American minorities* (5th ed.) (pp. 183–192). New York: McGraw-Hill.

Gomez, E., Ruiz, P., & Laval, R. (1982). Psychotherapy and bilingualism: Is acculturation important? *Journal of Operational Psychiatry, 13,* 13–16.

Gorkin, M. (1987). *The uses of countertransference.* New York: Jason Aronson.

Greben, S. E. (1981). The essence of psychotherapy. *British Journal of Psychiatry, 138,* 449–455.

Grier, W., & Cobb, P. M. (1969). *Black rage.* New York: Bantam.

Griffith, M. (1977). The influence of race on the psychotherapeutic relationship. *Psychiatry, 40,* 27–40.

Griffith, M., & Jones, E. E. (1978). Race and psychotherapy: Changing perspectives. In J. H. Masserman (Ed.), *Current psychiatric therapies, Vol. 18.* New York: Grune & Stratton.

Gross, J. (1992, June 28). Clinics help Asian immigrants feel at home. *New York Times,* Section 1, p. 10.

Hartmann, H. (1958). *Ego psychology and the problem of adaptation.* New York: International Universities Press.

Heine, R. (1950). The Negro patient in psychotherapy. *Journal of Clinical Psychology, 6,* 373–376.

Helms, J. E. (1995). An update of Helms' White and people of color racial identity models. In J. C. Ponterotto, J. M. Casas, L. A. Suzuki, & E. M. Alexander (Eds.), *Handbook of multicultural counseling* (pp. 181–198). Thousand Oaks, CA: Sage.

Ivey, A. E., Ivey, M. B., & Simek-Morgan, L. (1997). *Counseling and psychotherapy: A multicultural perspective* (4th ed.). Boston: Allyn and Bacon.

Jackson, A. M. (1990). Evolution of ethnocultural psychotherapy. *Psychotherapy, 27,* 28–35.

Jones, A., & Seagull, A. (1977). Dimensions of the relationship between the Black client and the White therapist. *American Psychologist, 32,* 850–855.

Jones, E. E. (1987). Psychotherapy and counseling with Black clients. In P. B. Pedersen (Ed.), *Handbook of cross-cultural counseling and psychotherapy* (pp. 173–179). Westport, CT: Praeger.

Jones, E. E., & Matsumoto, D. R. (1982). Psychotherapy with the underserved: Recent developments. In L. R. Snowden (Ed.), *Reaching the underserved: Mental health needs of neglected populations* (pp. 207–228). Beverly Hills, CA: Sage.

Jones, N. (1990). Black/White issues in psychotherapy. *Journal of Social Behavior and Personality, 5,* 305–322.

Kaplan, B., & Johnson, D. (1964). The social meaning of Navajo psychopathology and psychotherapy. In A. Kiev (Ed.), *Magic, faith, and healing* (pp. 203–229). New York: Free Press.

Kitano, H. H. L., & Maki, M. T. (1996). Continuity, change, and diversity: Counseling Asian Americans. In P. B. Pedersen, J. G. Draguns, W. J. Lonner, & J. E. Trimble (Eds.), *Counseling across cultures* (4th ed., pp. 124–145). Thousand Oaks, CA: Sage.

Kleinman, A. (1980). *Patients and healers in the context of culture.* Berkeley: University of California Press.

LaFromboise, T. D., Trimble, J. E., & Mohatt, G. V. (1998). Counseling intervention and American Indian tradition: An integrative approach. In D. R. Atkinson, G. Morten, & D. W. Sue (Eds.), *Counseling American minorities* (5th ed., pp. 159–182). New York: McGraw-Hill.

Lambert, M. J., & Bergin, A. E. (1992). Achievements and limitations of psychotherapy research. In D. K. Freedham (Ed.), *History of psychotherapy: A century of change* (pp. 360–390). Washington, DC: American Psychological Association.

Langs, R. (1973). *The technique of psychoanalytic psychotherapy, Vol. 1.* New York: Jason Aronson.

Lee, Courtland C. (Ed.). (1997). *Multicultural issues in counseling: New approaches to diversity* (2nd ed.). Alexandria, VA: American Counseling Association.

Leong, F. T. L. (1986). Counseling and psychotherapy with Asian-Americans. *Journal of Counseling Psychology, 33,* 196–206.

Lerner, B. (1972). *Therapy in the ghetto: Political impotence and personal disintegration.* Baltimore: Johns Hopkins University Press.

Lorion, R. P., & Parron, D. L. (1987). Countering the countertransference: A strategy for treating the untreatable. In P. B. Pedersen (Ed.), *Handbook of cross-cultural counseling and psychotherapy* (pp. 79–86). Westport, CT: Praeger.

Maduro, R. J. (1982). Working with Latinos and the use of dream analysis. *Journal of the American Academy of Psychoanalysis, 10,* 609–628.

Majors, R., & Nikelly, A. (1983). Serving the Black minority: A new direction for psychotherapy. *Journal of Non-White Concerns, 11,* 142–151.

Marcos, L. R. (1976a). Bilinguals in psychotherapy: Language as an emotional barrier. *American Journal of Psychotherapy, 30,* 552–560.

Marcos, L. R. (1976b). Linguistic dimensions in the bilingual patient. *American Journal of Psychoanalysis, 36,* 347–354.

Marcos, L. R. (1979). Effects of interpreters on the evaluation of psychopathology in non-English-speaking patients. *American Journal of Psychiatry, 136,* 171–174.

Marcos, L. R. (1988). Understanding ethnicity in psychotherapy with Hispanic patients. *American Journal of Psychoanalysis, 48,* 35–42.

Marcos, L. R., & Alpert, M. (1976). Strategies and risks in psychotherapy with bilingual patients: The phenomenon of language independence. *American Journal of Psychiatry, 133,* 1275–1278.

Marcos, L. R., & Urcuyo, L. (1979). Dynamic psychotherapy with the bilingual patient. *American Journal of Psychotherapy, 33,* 331–338.

Marrero, R. (1983). Bilingualism and biculturalism: Issues in psychotherapy with Hispanics. *Psychotherapy in Private Practice, 1,* 57–64.

Marsella, A. J., & Pedersen, P. B. (Eds.). (1981). *Cross-cultural counseling and psychotherapy.* New York: Pergamon Press.

Mays, V., & Albee, G. (1992). Psychotherapy and ethnic minorities. In D. K. Freedheim (Ed.), *History of psychotherapy: A century of change* (pp. 552–570). Washington, DC: American Psychological Association.

Meadow, A. (1982). Psychopathology, psychotherapy and the Mexican-American patient. In E. E. Jones & S. J. Korchin (Eds.), *Minority mental health* (pp. 331–361). New York: Praeger.

Nishio, K., & Bilmes, M. (1987/1998). Psychotherapy with Southeast Asian American clients. *Professional Psychology: Research and Practice, 18,* 342–346. Reprinted in D. R. Atkinson, G. Morten, & D. W. Sue (Eds.), *Counseling American minorities* (5th ed., pp. 235–243). New York: McGraw-Hill.

Norcross, J. C., & Goldfried, M. R. (Eds.). (1992). *Handbook of psychotherapy integration.* New York: Basic Books.

Owan, T. C. (Ed.). (1985). *Southeast Asian mental health: treatment, prevention, services, training, and research.* Rockville, MD: National Institute of Mental Health.

Parloff, M. B., Waskow, I. E., & Wolfe, B. S. (1978). Research on therapist variables in relation to process and outcome. In S. L. Garfield & S. A. Bergin (Eds.), *Handbook of psychotherapy and behavior change* (2nd ed., pp. 233–282). New York: Wiley.

Pedersen, P. (1982). The intercultural context of counseling and psychotherapy. In A. J. Marsella & G. M. White (Eds.), *Cultural conceptions of mental health and therapy* (pp. 333–358). Dordrecht, Holland: Reidel.

Pedersen, P. (Ed.). (1987). *Handbook of cross-cultural counseling and psychotherapy.* Westport, CT: Praeger.

Pedersen, P. B., Draguns, J. G., Lonner, W. J., & Trimble, J. E. (Eds.). (1996). *Counseling across cultures* (4th ed.). Thousand Oaks, CA: Sage.

Pitta, P., Marcos, L. R., & Alpert, M. (1978). Language switching as a treatment strategy with bilingual patients. *American Journal of Psychoanalysis, 38,* 255–258.

Ponterotto, J. G. (1984). Racial/ethnic minority research in *The Journal of Counseling Psychology:* A content analysis and methodological critique. *Journal of Counseling Psychology, 35,* 410–418.

Ramirez, M. (1991). *Psychotherapy and counseling with minorities.* New York: Pergamon Press.

Ridley, C. R. (1989). Racism in counseling as an aversive behavioral process. In P. Pedersen, J. Draguns, W. Lonner, & J. Trimble (Eds.), *Counseling across cultures* (3rd ed., pp. 55–77). Honolulu: University of Hawaii Press.

Ridley, C. R. (1995). *Overcoming unintentional racism in counseling and psychotherapy.* Thousand Oaks, CA: Sage.

Rogler, L. H., Malgady, R. G., Costantino, G., & Blumenthal, R. (1987/1998). What do culturally sensitive services mean? The case of Hispanics. *American Psychologist, 42,* 565–570. Reprinted in D. R. Atkinson, G. Morten, & D. W. Sue (Eds.), *Counseling American minorities* (5th ed., pp. 268–279). New York: McGraw-Hill.

Roll, S., Millen, L., & Martinez, R. (1980). Common errors in psychotherapy with Chicanos. *Psychotherapy: Theory, Research and Practice, 17,* 158–168.

Root, M. P. P. (1998). Facilitating psychotherapy with Asian American clients. In. D. R. Atkinson, G.

Morten, & D. W. Sue (Eds.), *Counseling American minorities* (5th ed., pp. 214–234). New York: McGraw-Hill.

Russell, D. M. (1988). Language and psychotherapy: The influence of nonstandard English in clinical practice. In L. Comas-Díaz & E. E. H. Griffith (Eds.), *Clinical guidelines in cross cultural mental health* (pp. 33–68). New York: Wiley.

Slakter, E. (Ed.). (1987). *Countertransference.* Northvale, NJ: Jason Aronson.

Smith, E. (1981). Cultural and historical perspectives in counseling Blacks. In D. W. Sue (Ed.), *Counseling the culturally different* (pp. 141–185). New York: Wiley.

Strupp, H. H. (1973). Toward a reformulation of the psychotherapeutic influence. *International Journal of Psychiatry, 11,* 263–365.

Strupp, H. H. (1982). The outcome problem in psychotherapy: Contemporary perspectives. In J. H. Harvey & M. Parks (Eds.), *Psychotherapy research and behavior change* (pp. 39–71). Washington, DC: American Psychological Association.

Sue, D. W. (1981). *Counseling the culturally different.* New York: Wiley.

Sue, D. W. (1990). Culture-specific strategies in counseling: A conceptual framework. *Professional Psychology: Research and Practice, 21,* 424–433.

Sue, S. (1988). Psychotherapeutic services for ethnic minorities: Two decades of research findings. *American Psychologist, 43,* 301–308.

Sue, S., Zane, N., & Young, K. (1994). Research on psychotherapy with culturally diverse populations. In A. E. Bergin & S. L. Garfield (Eds.), *Handbook of psychotherapy and behavior change* (4th ed., pp. 783–817). New York: Wiley.

Suro, R. (1998). *Strangers among us: How Latino immigration is transforming America.* New York: Random House.

Torrey, E. F. (1986). *The mind game.* New York: Harper & Row.

Toupin, E. S. W. A. (1980). Counseling Asians: Psychotherapy in the context of racism and Asian-American history. *American Journal of Orthopsychiatry, 50,* 76–86.

Trimble, J. E., Fleming, C. M., Beauvais, F., & Jumper-Thurman, P. (1996). Essential cultural and social strategies for counseling Native Americans. In P. B. Pedersen, J. G. Draguns, W. J. Lonner, & J. E. Trimble (Eds.), *Counseling across cultures* (4th ed., pp. 177–209). Thousand Oaks, CA: Sage.

Tsui, P., & Schultz, G. L. (1985). Failure of rapport: Why psychotherapeutic engagement fails in the treatment of Asian clients. *American Journal of Orthopsychiatry, 55,* 561–569.

Weiner, I. B. (1975). *Principles of psychotherapy.* New York: Wiley.

Wilkinson, C. B., & Spurlock, J. (1986). Mental health of Black Americans. In C. B. Wilkinson (Ed.), *Ethnic psychiatry* (pp. 13–60). New York: Plenum Press.

Wohl, J. (1983, October). *White therapists and Black patients: Advice from the experts.* Paper presented at the meetings of the Arkansas Psychological Association.

Wohl, J. (1989a). Cross-cultural psychotherapy. In P. B. Pedersen, J. G. Draguns, W. J. Lonner, & J. E. Trimble (Eds.), *Counseling across cultures* (3rd ed., pp. 79–113). Honolulu: University of Hawaii Press.

Wohl, J. (1989b). Integration of cultural awareness into psychotherapy. *American Journal of Psychotherapy, 43,* 343–355.

6 Cultural Relativistic Approach toward Ethnic Minorities in Family Therapy

MELVIN N. WILSON

LAURA P. KOHN

TRINDA S. LEE

It is important to understand the role of ethnicity in the psychological intervention and treatment of ethnic minority families in this country (Wilkinson, 1987). Problems in living are not only the products of aberrant intrapsychic development and familial dysfunctions, but also a consequence of the specific political, social, economic, and legal histories that ethnic minorities have had in the United States. Past conditions of slavery, legal discrimination and segregation, immigration exclusion and restrictions, internment, and forced removal to reservations have influenced the attitudes, perceptions, and behavioral patterns of ethnic minorities. In effect, the larger society has played a major role in the developmental etiology of certain mental health disturbances and in the way mental health professionals have responded to these groups.

The mental health delivery system has long struggled with understanding the context of one's experiences in the etiology of mental illnesses (Cheung & Snowden, 1990). The system has sought to develop services that reflect acceptance and accommodation of the differences among Americans, rather than reflecting the assimilation of those differences to the cultural majority. Unfortunately, the recognition of contextual influences has not always translated into appropriate services to diverse populations. Because of the small number of ethnic minority professionals, indigenous paraprofessionals have often been employed in the delivery of mental health services to ethnic minority communities. However, paraprofessionals often do not possess the professional sophistication needed to understand the role of ethnicity in the etiology and treatment of mental disturbances.

The definitions and treatment of abnormal behavior endorsed by ethnic minority groups are often very different from those of the majority population (see Chapter 9 of this book). Indeed, it is often important to appreciate indigenous definitions of abnormal behavior and curative procedures in order to gain entry and deliver mental health services effectively to the ethnic minority communities. Service providers need to acquire a clear understanding and appreciation of these cultural differences. Cultural empathy on the part of the service provider instructs minority clients about the mental health professional's understanding of the culture-specific proprieties of their problems and symptoms.

Most important for this chapter is the increase in the number of minority families and children in the general population (Ashburg & DeVita, 1992; O'Hare, 1992). Differences among ethnic groups' traumatic historical relationships with nonminority Americans and experiences with discrimination have led to differences in adaptation experiences. These experiences are related to economic success and the preservation of familial stability. Furthermore, this chapter argues that mental health practitioners must consider differences in adaptation experiences in their intervention and treatment plans with ethnic minority families.

Some cautions are warranted as well. Although we provide information regarding the variation within each of the ethnic groups, we sometimes fall victim to discussing each ethnic group and their families as a homogeneous entity. This is especially troublesome if one is trying to acquire improved clinical interviewing and diagnostic strategies that are culturally sensitive to ethnic minorities. Diversity and variation commonly occur within each ethnic minority group (Hirabayashi & Saram, 1980; O'Hare, 1992). Variation exists in living conditions, in languages, and thus in cultural values and practices. A review of ethnic groups may describe characteristics that are applicable to most of the members but not to all of them. Accordingly, this chapter will not attempt an exhaustive exploration of specific subgroup characteristics. Instead, it will focus primarily on characteristics that are generally applicable to most groups.

Family Life among Ethnic Minority Americans

Until fairly recently, the "normal" family was synonymous with nuclear structure based on immediate family membership (Saba, Karrer, & Hardy, 1990). As a result, all else was labeled aberrant (Moynihan, 1965). However, changing demographic patterns (delayed marriages, higher divorce rates, unemployment, and urban migratory trends) have all influenced and broadened the traditional definition of the "family" (London & Devore, 1988; McGoldrick, Pearce, & Giordano, 1982; Wilson, 1986). While all groups have been affected by these trends to some degree, the greatest impact has been on minority and immigrant groups. Unfortunately, services to the groups most affected by demographic and economic fluctuations are the least adequate in the mental health system.

For cultural and social reasons, family and family life take on special meaning for ethnic minority groups. The extended family is the most important common element shared by ethnic minorities. By *extended family*, we refer to family composition, structure, and interaction that goes beyond the nuclear family unit to include consanguine, in-law, conjugal, and fictive relationships (Foster, 1983). The extended family directly influences the primary values, beliefs, and behaviors of its members. A consistent finding across ethnic groups is the supportive role and mutual-aid function of the extended family. The extended-family network is an alternative structure of support that supplements the nuclear family. In this respect, the extended family is both a tangible family unit of kin and nonkin and an intangible cohesive force in ethnic minority communities. Extended families are the centers of economical activity, decision making, and care for children and other dependents (Wilson, 1989). Moreover, extended families transmit values, including emotional closeness, economic cooperation, child care, and social regulation.

African American Families

Historically, Africans had elaborate support networks and extended family relationships (Franklin, 1988; Nobles, 1988; Sudarkasa, 1988). Before enslavement, Africans were members of a diverse population, with different languages and cultural practices (Karst, 1986). This cultural diversity, combined with the practice of slave masters separating family members, forced African American slaves into situations that disrupted familial ties and/or social support. Nevertheless, the African American family developed and maintained strong ties (Nobles, 1988; Sudarkasa, 1988). African American slaves formed support networks made up of biologically related and nonbiologically related members (Sudarkasa, 1988). The persistence of African familial networks throughout slavery suggests that they are an example of an enduring cultural phenomenon (Denby, 1996; Franklin, 1988; Wilson, 1986; Wilson & Tolson, 1990).

Currently, African American families are characterized by the high prevalence of mother-only households, due primarily to high fertility rates among single African American women and the high rate of unemployment among African American men, rather than to rising divorce rates (Glick, 1988; U.S. Bureau of Census, 1990). In addition, African Americans consistently delay marriage as opposed to other American groups, and there is a rising proportion of African Americans in their twenties and thirties who have never been married. Until recently, most African American families consisted of married couples. Since 1970, however, there has been a decline in the number of married couples with young children, and an increase in the proportion of children being raised in single-parent homes (McAdoo, 1991).

In sum, the current social difficulties facing African American families include high birth rates among single women, the predominance of mother-only households, and large numbers of marital dissolutions (see Chapter 1). African American families also experience poverty more often than do majority families (O'Hare, Pollard, Mann, & Kent, 1991). In addition, African American families are often exposed to violent crime, particularly assaults and homicides directed at males. Such experiences make them vulnerable to economic and social stress, which can have a detrimental impact on their psychological well-being (McCollum, 1997).

American Indian Families

Native Americans often maintain strong tribal identification and high degrees of respect for their heritage (Brown & Shaughnessay, 1981; Lewis, 1970). Native American communities can also be characterized as having an important regard for the land, highly democratic governmental societies, and great respect for their elders (Brown & Shaughnessay, 1981; London & Devore, 1988). Similarly, Native Americans portray a strong sense of communalism, generosity, and harmony. These concepts stem from the prevalence of the extended family, the sense of biological relationship within the clan and/or the tribe, and the belief that Native Americans discover themselves through interpersonal relationships (Anderson, 1989; Brown & Shaughnessay, 1981; Ho, 1987).

Native American cultural tradition is noteworthy for the positive value it places on children (Brown & Shaughnessay, 1981; Garbarino, 1985). Among the Crows of the Plains, children of conquered tribes were adopted into families of the victors. Among the Tlingit of the Northwest coast, children were rarely punished but were socialized instead through shaming and praise (Bergman, 1977; Byler, 1977; Garbarino, 1985). Utmost care was taken to ensure the child's happiness among the Camas because it was believed that if the infant child was not happy, he or she could choose to return to heaven (Bird & Melendy, 1977; Lewis, 1970). While traditional family structure, attitude, and practices toward children provide a healthy form of child-rearing, other experiences, such as those with federal boarding schools, have had a detrimental impact on Native American children (Tafoya, 1989).

Native Americans experience a variety of problems, including social and mental health problems, alcoholism, child abuse and neglect, adolescent delinquency, and violent deaths (LaFromboise, 1988). Although the demand for mental health services by Native Americans has recently increased, contact between Native American families and mental health agencies has often been negatively colored by previous experiences with mainstream social agencies (Ho, 1987). In addition, many Native Americans have been inappropriately and ineffectively served by mental health agencies (LaFromboise, 1988; Westermeyer, 1977a, 1977b).

Latino Families

Although it appears that the nuclear family structure is the most common form of family life in the Latino community, others have observed a great deal of diversity in Latino family organization (Klor de Alva, 1988; Lichter & Landale, 1995; Massey, Zambrana, & Alonzo Bell, 1995). Latino nuclear family tends to be embedded in an extended family network that includes other relatives (Acosta-Belen, 1988; Anderson, 1989; Davis, Haub, & Willette, 1988; Ho, 1987; Vega, 1990). According to Klor de Alva (1988), extended family members tend to live near but not with each other, except during periods of transition. As families become acculturated, they tend not to live in the same household but may still reside in the same neighborhood.

Although a great deal of diversity exists within Latino groups (Gonzalez, 1997; Valdivieso & Davis, 1988), there is an increasing trend toward mother-only households. The proportion of mother-only households has increased by approximately 10 percent whereas the proportion of dual-parent households has decreased by almost 6 percent over the last decade (U.S. Bureau of Census, 1992). This trend has been augmented by high birth and poverty rates among Latino groups (Ashburg & DeVita, 1992). These changes increase the stress on Latino families and can contribute to psychological dysfunction.

Asian American Families

Several authors agree that the family plays a central role in many Asian American individuals' lives (Hong, 1989; Kitano, 1989; Lin & Lin, 1980; Tamura & Lau, 1992). Families tend to be stable and interconnected. Generally, marriage rates are higher and divorce rates are lower among Asian Americans than among other ethnic minority Americans (Schaefer, 1996). Chinese American family composition often includes the husband-wife dyad, families with dependant children, families with adult children and aging parents, and split-household reunification (Hong & Ham, 1992).

The traditional Southeast Asian family tends to be extended (Anderson, 1989; Ruetrakul, 1987). In many Asian families, the father assumes a family leadership role, and sons are sometimes valued more highly than daughters (Ho, 1987). Children are socialized to respect the entire family system, including parents, elders, and ancestors (Lin & Lin, 1980). Importance is placed on family needs over individual needs (Berg & Jaya, 1993). Tamura and Lau (1992) believe the most significant difference between Japanese and European cultural systems is the Japanese preference for connectedness of relationships as opposed to separateness and clear boundaries in relationships.

Differences in affective expression in Asian American families have been documented in the literature. Value may be placed on pragmatic solutions through negotiation and mediation rather than exploration of feelings and head-on confrontation (Berg & Jaya, 1993). Pragmatism is used to describe Chinese families' approach to dealing with life and solving problems (Lin & Lin, 1980). A study comparing Asian American and European American college students' family styles obtained reports of greater emotional restraint in Asian Americans (Kao, Nagata, & Peterson, 1997). Interpersonal harmony is highly regarded; therefore, Asian Americans may choose to conceal their true feelings when harmony is at stake (Anderson, 1989).

Another issue relative to Asian American families that is receiving growing recognition is the prevalence of interethnic relationships. Both intraracial and interracial marriages are increasing in number among Chinese (Wang, 1994) and other Asian groups (Agbayani-Siewert, 1994; del-Carmen, 1990). Families may include biethnic or biracial individuals (Kitano & Maki, 1996). Therefore, questions of identity and degree of cultural affiliation may be central issues for many Asian families (Kitano, 1989).

Family Therapy Approaches with Ethnic Minority Families

Our discussion of family therapy approaches includes an examination of the current models of family therapy described in the literature, including the culturalist, ecological, ecostructural, and family systems models, and the degree to which they are being utilized. The rationale for the use of family therapy with specific ethnic minority groups is also presented. Finally, we discuss the issues and problems that may be faced in working with ethnic minority families, as well as guidelines for engaging in culturally relevant family therapy.

Family therapy successfully coalesced as a treatment method during the late 1960s. This approach began with the recognition of the connection between child disturbances and parental problems. Since then, family interventions have taken many forms, the techniques have been expanded and refined, and family therapy continues to he an effective and widely used model of treatment. A wide range of methods of family assessment are in use, reflecting the numerous conceptual models about how families function. Regardless of the general method or theory preferred, in order to ensure that ethnic minority families have opportunities for appropriate help, it is vital that the therapist be culturally sensitive and competent (Hill & Strozier, 1992).

Not only must we be aware of the culture of the clients, we must also gain perspective on our own culture and how our constructs and paradigms are interpreted in another culture. Similarly, Wilkinson (1987) indicated that professionals should recognize the need for understanding ethnic minorities, particularly how disparate lifestyles, attitudes, and behavior of minority ethnic persons are perceived and/or misperceived by others. It would be incorrect to assume that mental disturbance in the individual results solely from intrapsychic development. Rather, we must also consider how psychological health is influenced by the political, social, economic, and legal histories that ethnic minorities have experienced in the United States.

Theoretical Models of Family Therapy

According to Minuchin (1974), family therapy involves the process of feedback between situations and the individual. Altering the position of a person in relation to the situation changes the experience of that person. Different experiences that are produced in therapy reinforce the new method of relating to the circumstances and are therefore likely to generalize to other situations outside of treatment (Minuchin, 1974). A critical activity of therapy involves the therapist joining with the family to begin to facilitate interventions directed at change. Change occurs at the basic structural level of the family and is organized around changing familial organization and interactions by using alternative modalities of transaction (Minuchin, 1974).

Of the many family therapy models, a few have been consistently cited in the literature. Some of these models include family systems, culturalist, ecological, structural, eco-structural, and Bowenian models. The family systems model posits that family structure and process is primary; therefore, examination of the hierarchies and boundaries through observation of family interaction is the core of family therapy (Inclan, 1990). The culturalist perspective further contends that culture is the primary source of behavior patterns that are both prevalent and condoned by members of the culture (Inclan, 1990).

The culturalist model has been criticized because it tends to view culture as fixed and ahistorical and may result in justifying culturally sanctioned behaviors that are maladaptive (Inclan, 1990; Rogier, Malgady, Costantino, & Blumenthal, 1987). Conversely, a strict family systems approach examines family process while completely ignoring the social reality that creates the context in which these processes are manifested (Inclan, 1990). Ecological therapy seeks to integrate the culturalist and family systems approaches by viewing families and their social context as one integrated process (Aponte, 1991; Boyd-Franklin, 1987; Inclan, 1990). Therefore, it has been asserted that ecological therapy is particularly useful for ethnic minority families who are often undergoing both cultural and intrafamilial transitions.

The structural approach expands the definition of the traditional family in order to accommodate three-generational familial structures and parent-child issues (Boyd-Franklin, 1989a, 1989b). This form of therapy provides a method for assessing family structure (Boyd-Franklin, 1987). In so doing, it allows for the identification of areas of difficulty and facilitates restructuring of the family system in order to produce change (Minuchin, 1974). Strengths of the model include a problem-solving approach that is focused, concrete, and offers direct resolutions (Boyd-Franklin, 1987, 1989a).

Ecostructural therapy is similar to ecological therapy in that it is an elaborated treatment model that emphasizes engagement and problem-solving techniques. Furthermore, ecostructural therapy seeks to include other institutions that impinge on some families in therapy (Aponte, 1991). Thus, the ecostructural model presumes that therapists must always consider a family's environment and community as relevant to the diagnostic process and planning of treatment (Inclan, 1990). In some instances, therapists may find it necessary to restructure or to help the family renegotiate its relationship with a particular agency.

The Bowenian model has been mentioned in the literature as an appropriate approach with ethnic minority clients (Boyd-Franklin, 1989a, 1989b). This approach has two major strengths in that it provides strategies for exploring extended family dynamics and also creates a theoretical framework useful in generating hypotheses regarding familial patterns (Boyd-Franklin, 1987). Genograms are diagrams of family relationships across generations that include significant family members and institutions outside the family. Genograms have been advocated as a primary agent for gathering extended ethnic family information (Boyd-Franklin, 1989a, 1989b; Moore-Hines & Boyd-Franklin, 1982).

Extended Family Structure and Family Therapy

It is important that family therapy approaches accommodate the characteristics of the extended family structure. Within these structures there exist reciprocal obligations, considerable influence on decision-making and membership roles, and reinforcement of traditional values and patterns (Boyd-Franklin, 1989a, 1989b; McGoldrick et al., 1982). Interdependent extended family structures that promote survival within the family are essential to obtaining and maintaining familial health. In other words, because the family relies on extended membership and intergenerational relations, it is logical that this same network would be crucial to ensuring optimal mental health. Incorporating the extended family members into therapy allows many minority groups to work in an environment that most closely mirrors their real-life experience. Creating such an environment facilitates both the therapeutic process and improved familial functioning.

The presence of grandparents as primary caregivers as well as other extended family members in ethnic minority families speaks to the necessary inclusion of these members in therapy (Attneave, 1982; Boyd-Franklin, 1989a, 1989b; Everett, Proctor, & Cartmell, 1983; Harrison, Wilson, Pine, Chan, & Buriel, 1990; LaFromboise, Trimble, & Mohatt, 1990; Moore-Hines & Boyd-Franklin, 1982) and reflects the familial structure. Omission of these members would mean the loss of valuable information regarding familial structure and processes. For example, Wilson (1984) has shown that grandmothers in the home perform a significant amount of the child-rearing tasks, particularly in single-parent households.

Some authors have noted that within the Asian family structure the individual is often considered a part of the whole and is therefore subordinated to the extended family (Chin, 1983; Shon & Ja, 1982). Specific hierarchical family roles are emphasized, with formalized rules of behavior for each member within the group. It is through this clearly hierarchical structure and sanctioned code of conduct that traditional Chinese families control behavior, manage human relationships, and transmit moral, religious, and social values from generation to generation (Lin & Lin, 1980). It has been suggested that family therapy is particularly suitable for these Asian families because the process brings the kin into the treatment naturally, thereby more accurately reflecting the familial environment. Family therapy allows an interactive and contextual perspective of the roles of Asian American family members (Ho, 1987). However, it is crucial for family therapists to maintain proper respect for family hierarchy (Berg & Jaya, 1993; Hong, 1989).

Given the primary influence of intergenerational family members, often the focus of conflict is between generations within the family, each struggling with differing sets of cultural expectations and norms depending on the level of acculturation (Lee, 1989; Shon & Ja, 1982; Vazquez-Nuttal, Avila-Vivas, & Morales-Barreto, 1984). Family therapy can address these intergenerational conflicts and resolve them within the extended familial context that includes all relevant members present. A multigenerational approach to therapy is an efficient and effective method for handling the problems that occur across the generations within one family.

Cultural Characteristics and Family Therapy

Other cultural features of ethnic minority families support the use of family therapy as a particularly effective form of treatment. For example, the therapists' use of self is an important indicator of an intervention's success (Aponte, 1991). Among Latino populations, the term *personalismo* refers to the establishment of relationships through personal and effective bonds (Inclan, 1990). *Personalismo* can enhance the development of trust between therapists and their Latino clients. Given that most models of family therapy require extensive use of the therapist's personality and increased activity level to help direct and guide successful joining with the family, there is a greater chance that *personalismo* will develop at a faster rate than in traditional forms of therapy (Inclan, 1990).

Similar to modern-day multisystems approaches, traditional Native American healing ceremonies have been conducted within an extended family setting. These traditional ceremonies included public disclosure, confession, and storytelling (Everett et al., 1983; LaFromboise et al., 1990; Tafoya, 1989). According to Tafoya (1989), usage of such techniques provided a nonthreatening and indirect way of structuring the problem and served as a "therapeutic metaphor." Stories or case histories of other family members, particularly elders, can be used within family therapy to triangulate the problem, thereby providing a comfortable distance between family members. Furthermore, resolution of these stories provides valuable insight into the way in which the family conceptualizes their current difficulties.

Tharp (1991) has suggested that family therapy rather than individual therapy may be particularly appropriate with ethnic minority groups since the family is a central mechanism for the development of ethnic identity. Furthermore, with family therapy the potential for stereotypes and racial attitudes held by White therapists to hurt treatment is diminished because the therapist must operate within the context of the family's ethnicity. Since immediate problem solving is the primary focus of structural family therapy, therapist biases may be avoided because psychological interpretations are minimal and interventions tend to be specific and direct.

Immediate problem solving, as a feature of structural family therapy, is a particularly attractive feature for ethnic minority families who often face numerous economic and social hardships. Using a multisystems model, the therapist is able to conceptualize interventions with any family at many different levels, and the model builds on problem-solving techniques. Targeting particular problems allows the therapist to keep the family problem focused and empowers him or her to intervene at the appropriate system levels. In particular, Boyd-Franklin (1987) noted that African American families can benefit from concrete, goal-oriented, short-term therapy. Such an approach reduces the presence of threatening outsiders, incorporates the inherent strengths of the family, and addresses the daily stresses often experienced by these families (Moore-Hines & Boyd-Franklin, 1982).

Issues and Problems in Family Therapy

Despite the characteristics that lend themselves to the appropriateness of family interventions with ethnic minority families, several issues may arise around suspiciousness among groups, myths of sameness, treatment expectations, process of acculturation, and language barriers. Traditionally, members of ethnic minority groups have relied on informal support networks such as extended family and the church (Attneave, 1982; Boyd-Franklin, 1987; London & Devore, 1988). Investigators have speculated that reliance on natural support systems results in fewer feelings of guilt, defeat, humiliation, and powerlessness when compared with reliance on outside institutions (McGoldrick et al., 1982). Although more ethnic minorities are starting to utilize family therapy, these issues and problems must be addressed before full integration and trust can be developed.

Suspicion has often led to unusually high attrition rates, with many clients not returning after the first few sessions and in some cases not after the initial session (Everett et al., 1983; London & Devore, 1988). Boyd-Franklin (1987) notes that among African Americans a defensive, guarded reception to intervention might be seen as appropriate, given the historical experience of this group in the United States. Relying on outsiders to solve intimate family problems is often perceived as a violation of family confidentiality. As such, until the therapist can be trusted, the client will maintain his or her distance.

Myths of Sameness

Although ethnicity has begun to be addressed in the family therapy literature, the view of ethnic minority families as being similar to nonminority families continues to dominate the field. Hardy (1989) has referred to this universal approach as a "theoretical myth of sameness," whereby the epistemological assumption for most family therapy training is that all ethnic families are the same. Hardy asserts it would be more appropriate to focus on the ways in which minority and nonminority families are different as well as similar. For instance, the diverse familial structures found in African American, Native American, Latino, and Asian American cultures have yet to be addressed in mainstream family therapy literature.

The universal approach is compounded by insufficient multicultural training, which leads to misunderstanding and misinterpretation of social and cultural mores displayed by members of ethnic groups. For instance, among some Native Americans a firm handshake is perceived as competitive, and therefore a very light grasp is used (Everett et al., 1983). Such an initial greeting or handshake can be misinterpreted as distant, which may disrupt the working relationship between the client and therapist. Such misunderstandings could ultimately result in premature termination by the Native American client. Clinical training programs need to include an emphasis on understanding the sociopsychological and family reality of ethnic minorities from a system sociopsychological perspective.

Treatment Expectations

Another problem that contributes to early attrition of clients is differing expectations of treatment, depending on the families' values and perception of mental health intervention (McMiller & Weisz, 1996). A study of Puerto Rican patients found that they expected their doctor to be active and concrete, either giving advice or prescribing medication. Confronted with a traditional psychological approach in which the therapist role is supposed to be passive while the client is expected to discuss and reflect on the problems, the Puerto Rican client may choose to terminate treatment prematurely (Abad, Ramos, & Boyce, 1974).

Dauphinais, LaFromboise, and Rowe (1980) conducted a similar study to determine the expectations of Native American clients. The researchers concluded that knowledge and appreciation of the client's cultural values and the willingness to participate in community activities were qualities Native Americans sought from an effective counselor. Furthermore, the tendency of some Native American clients neither to ask direct questions nor to challenge treatment may be misperceived as a lack of involvement in the therapy process and thus may maintain distance between the therapist and the client (Everett et al., 1983).

Introspective and insight-oriented therapies utilizing techniques such as reflective listening may also have little or no relevance to many Native American clients or to members of other minority groups (Atkinson, Morton, & Sue, 1989). In contrast, some self-disclosure by the therapist may greatly aid the therapeutic process by enhancing trust and rapport (Everett et al., 1983; Ho, 1987). Many Native American clients become impatient and will terminate therapy that is primarily client-centered or reflective; therefore, strategic and directive interventions may be preferred (LaFromboise et al., 1990; Unger, 1977).

Process of Acculturation

A salient issue for recent immigrants concerns the level of acculturation of each family member and the resulting conflict when generations in the family are acculturating to the host country at differing rates. Baptiste's work with Latino immigrant families showed that several characteristics of the recent migration experiences caused conflict and were consistent across families despite their differing national heritage (Baptiste, 1987). For example, family members were often unaware of the difficulties resulting from migration and acculturation experiences. Thus, parents tended to attribute the cause of conflict to their children having been negatively influenced by American culture (Baptiste, 1987). The task of therapy was often focused on recognizing the stress associated with migration, grieving the loss of the "old country," and reconciling unrealized expectations for their new life. In addition, therapy can help the family adapt old family functioning rules to new ones that are more adaptive in the new country (Baptiste, 1987).

Chin's work with Chinese American families indicates that families' differing rates of acculturation depend on several variables, such as number of years in the United States, age at the time of migration, amount of exposure to Western culture, and amount of contact with American peers (Chin, 1983). Hong (1989) describes problems for immigrant Chinese American families as related to social isolation and adjustment difficulties due to relocation, as well as cultural and language barriers between parents and children. Similarly, Southeastern Asian refugee families have many difficulties that stem from intergenerational tension and differing values as a result of acculturation differences among the family members (Lee, 1989). Such differences and their ensuing consequences need to be acknowledged and addressed in the therapeutic process. Kitano and Maki (1996) describe a model for therapists to use to help determine where various Asian American groups are in terms of assimilation and ethnic identity.

Native Americans have been found to vary regarding their degree of commitment to preserving their cultural and tribal legacy (LaFromboise et al., 1990; Unger, 1977). At least five levels of acculturation have been identified by LaFromboise and her colleagues among Native Americans: traditional, transitional, marginal, assimilated, and bicultural. Prior to any intervention, a thorough assessment must be made in order to determine where the family is along the acculturation continuum and the degree to which they identify with their culture (see Chapter 2). By being cognizant of these diverse levels of acculturation, therapists will be better able to help Native American clients cope with their concerns.

Language Barriers

Language is one of the most salient barriers to treatment, particularly among first- and second-generation migrant families (see Chapter 2). Working with Spanish-speaking families can be a complex process because members often vary in their command of English and Spanish (Fillmore, 1991; Sciarra & Ponterotto, 1991). A classification of bilingual status has been developed and may be helpful in determining how the process of bilingual family therapy proceeds (Marcos, 1976). For example, the degree of proficiency in either language has implications for language preference in therapy, ability to convey affective experiences, and the amount of language switching that takes place within a session (Sciarra & Ponterotto, 1991).

Despite the limited information addressing bilingualism in therapy, several recommendations are offered. The therapist should be aware of the dynamics of bilingualism and the communication patterns among family members, and should have some knowledge of the level of language proficiency of the family members (Sciarra & Ponterotto, 1991). In addition, evidence suggests that the presence of bilingual staff and trained translators from the community increases treatment utilization (see Chapter 8; Rogler et al., 1987). When translators are used, care needs to be taken to ensure understanding of mental health terms and accuracy of the translations.

Recommendations and Guidelines for Treatment

Guidelines for treatment of ethnic minority families include assessment prior to treatment, with particular emphasis on ecostructural or contextual factors. Also avoidance of universal models of family functioning is important. Many of the issues such as level of acculturation, linguistic proficiency, expectations of treatment, definition of family, and familial roles must be explored when assessing ethnic minority families. Other areas should be examined, such as the ecological context, socioeconomic level, employment history, and involvement and experiences with outside institutions and agencies.

For families that are relatively recent migrants, it is necessary to assess premigratory family life and experiences, the actual migration experience, and the impact of migration on the individual family members (see Chapter 12). In some instances, information regarding physical health, medication history, and reliance on indigenous healers may be salient. Indigenous healers are frequently used by Native Americans and various Latinos and Asian subgroups and may need to be incorporated into the treatment process (see Chapter 9).

Although it is also important to determine the nature and the degree of support provided by the extended family and the community to which the person belongs, overreliance on cultural conceptualizations and interpretations can lead to misguided expectations that the therapeutic process should precisely reflect cultural principles and standards. However, obtaining optimal functioning may require adjusting these cultural characteristics (Padilla, Ruiz, & Alvarez, 1975; Rogler et al., 1987). The difficulty arises in deciding what constitutes "optimal functioning," and ways in which the therapeutic goals and cultural characteristics interact and are processed with family members in treatment.

With ethnic minority families as with nonminority families, it is important to communicate acceptance of the family and approach the problem in a manner similar to the way the family chooses to frame it (Baptiste, 1987; Ho, 1987; Sciarra & Ponterotto, 1991). It is imperative that therapists be aware of their own attitudes toward the ethnic group and the culture with which they are working. In addition, therapists must educate themselves about differences within groups, to avoid subscribing to the convenient and prevailing "cookbook" approach, which divides minority groups into four broad categories (i.e., Americans of Asian, Latino, African, or Native descent). Self-exploration of feelings helps therapists resist ethnocentric bias and avoid pseudoinsight. Attempting to learn about the family's culture from the family rather than operating under prior assumptions will prevent stereotyping and misunderstanding.

In order to be effective, then, therapists of minority clients must understand cultural issues of the client's specific ethnic group. This notion has lead many to assert that therapy is most effectively conducted within a same-culture context. That is, the best therapist for a minority client is one from the same ethnic background as the client. While such matching may provide some benefits in the therapy process, it is unlikely that this characteristic is essential for effective counseling (see Chapter 14). Rather, it is possible that similar therapy benefits can be achieved by a culturally sensitive clinician who makes a strong effort to understand the client within the client's own cultural context (Dana, 1998)

Although the ethnic identity of family members will often be addressed in therapy, it is particularly important not to limit therapy to the issues that revolve exclusively around this topic (see Chapter 2; Sciarra & Ponterotto, 1991). Therapy generally works best when it is direct, active, and highly focused on a limited number of issues that are salient to the client (Sciarra & Ponterotto, 1991). Many times intervention must be altered to incorporate education and information about the process of therapy itself (McGoldrick et al., 1982). The process of therapy may need to be further modified to extend beyond the family to include nontraditional members and organizations that affect the family.

Therapy with families who have recently migrated must address the issues of loss of community and support networks (Sciarra & Ponterotto, 1991; see Chapter 12). Often it is necessary to give the family permission to mourn the loss of country of origin, while they deal with the issues of discrepant expectations and the actual reality of the new country (Baptiste, 1987). Also, differential rates of assimilation may occur across generations in the family, resulting in stress and conflict (Szapocznik et al., 1986). Older family members may be less inclined to be assimilated into the majority culture or may have more difficulty than younger ones in doing so.

It is useful to form social and cultural alliances with families that include an initial focus on highly structured informative sessions. Early sessions should provide information about the therapeutic process, including the expectations and limitations of therapy. Additionally, alliances with influential family members serve to acknowledge the therapist's appreciation of the culture. With many Asian families, it is important to show respect for traditional roles—for example, by initially reinforcing the fathers' role as head of family. It is also important to avoid interpreting the mother–child relationship as overdependent and to recognize the family's expectations of each sibling.

Other specific recommendations can be made for providing family therapy to particular ethnic minority families. Ho (1989) describes the Fundamental Interpersonal Relations Orientations theory and model as an applicable framework for working with Asian/Pacific American families due to the focus on structural and communicative interaction. It has been suggested that structural family therapy is the preferred approach in providing treatment for Asian Americans because of the indirect communication style, patterns of expression, and process of disagreement that exist in some Asian American families (Kim, 1985; Lee, 1989; Wang, 1994). Structural approaches are preferred because of the indirect communication style, patterns of expression, and process of disagreement that exists in some Asian American families. Structural family therapy emphasizes the active restructuring of family interactions to create change without relying heavily on direct and open expression in families (Shon & Ja, 1982). Since many Asian families delay help-seeking from mental health providers due to a reluctance to call upon outside help, contact tends to be crisis-oriented (Lin & Lin, 1980). Therefore, brief and solution-oriented approaches may be more helpful than insight and growth-oriented approaches or experiential models of family therapy (Berg & Jaya, 1993; Wang, 1994). An authoritative therapist style, the use of individual sessions, and silence and other nonverbal techniques may be helpful to use with Japanese families with whom the desired change is toward better integration of the individuals within the family system as opposed to reinforcing differentiation of members (Tamura & Lau, 1992).

Furthermore, the use of family therapy with Chinese American immigrant families should focus on a holistic view that includes a psychoeducational approach while reinforcing culturally sanctioned coping mechanisms and cultural strengths (Shon & Ja, 1982). Trust in closely guarded traditional Chinese American families can be gained when the family is convinced that therapist has an understanding of the cultural roles governing familial roles and relationships (Lin & Lin, 1980).

When addressing the needs of African American families, a multisystems approach has been consistently advocated as the optimal means of intervention (Boyd-Franklin, 1987; 1989b; Moore-Hines & Boyd-Franklin, 1982; Willis, 1988). This model directly empowers the family by incorporating strengths such as the extended family, role flexibility, and religion into treatment (Boyd-Franklin, 1989b; Wilson & Stith, 1998). Moreover, with regard to African American clients, it has been suggested that they should be approached in an egalitarian manner that reduces status differences. Since family therapy focuses on the broader community and social context, rather than on the individual, these goals are best facilitated by the family and multisystems models (Moore-Hines & Boyd-Franklin, 1982).

In many African American families, role flexibility is a commonly utilized coping strategy, particularly in single-parent homes. Role flexibility often results in children assuming adult roles and responsibilities at an earlier age than would be expected. Such patterns must be interpreted in the context of the specific familial situation. A complete and thorough assessment of these roles must be made before the arrangement is deemed dysfunctional, leading to the prescription of inappropriate interventions that may in fact lead to family disequilibrium. It may be appropriate and therapeutic for the therapist to be supportive of role flexibility in the African American family.

Network therapy has been consistently cited as the treatment of choice when working with Native Americans (LaFromboise et al., 1990). This form of intervention has been noted to be most compatible with traditional Native American healing approaches, and, although it has been primarily utilized with individual clients, it has many broad and valuable implications for use with families (Attneave, 1977, 1982). The network approach utilizes the extended family and community system as an integral part of the treatment plan and as a "social force" or network that can provide social support. Broadening treatment beyond the immediate family provides greater likelihood that support and improvements made during therapy will continue after termination.

Concluding Remarks

It is apparent that the basic premise of family therapy is potentially consistent with the life beliefs and lifestyles of many ethnic minority Americans. To use this approach with ethnic minority families, practitioners will need to possess sensible and sensitive appreciations of cultural differences. Although the appreciation of cultural differences as a therapeutic objective is easier than its implementation in practice, it is reasonable to assume that clinical training programs could address many of the issues raised in this chapter. Our point is that familial problems of ethnic minority Americans are influenced by social, ecological, and cultural contexts. Put another way, when things go wrong, it is important that we understand the family's problem within a unique cultural and ethnic framework. In doing less, we are ineptly applying universal solutions that could do more harm than good.

Finally, the objective of the various phases of family therapy is to obtain two fundamental kinds of information. First, the nature of the problem must be determined. Second, the problem's context must be understood. Both types of information require the ability to comprehend the cultural and ethnic background of the families being helped. Appreciating the contribution of culture and ethnicity will improve service to this significantly under-served portion of the United States. A better understanding and recognition of cultural differences will make training relevant to ethnic minority families. Clients who are culturally different understand the nature of their differences. It is time that professional training and services do the same.

R E F E R E N C E S

Abad, V., Ramos, J., & Boyce, E. (1974). A model for delivery of mental health services to Spanish-speaking minorities. *American Journal of Orthopsychiatry, 44,* 584–595.

Acosta-Belen, E. (1988). From settlers to newcomers: The Hispanic legacy in the United States. In E. Acosta-Belen & B. R. Sjostrom (Eds.), *The Hispanic experience in the United States: Contemporary issues and perspectives* (pp. 1–33). New York: Praeger.

Agbayani-Siewert, P. (1994). Filipino American culture and family: Guidelines for practitioners. *Families in Society, 75,* 429–438.

Anderson, P. P. (1989). Issues in serving culturally diverse families of young children with disabilities. *Early Child Development and Care, 50,* 167–188.

Aponte, H. J. (1991). Training on the person of the therapist for work with the poor and minorities. *Journal of Independent Social Work, 5,* 23–39.

Ashburg, D. A., & DeVita, C. J. (1992). New realities of the American family. *Population Bulletin, 47*(2), 1–44.

Atkinson, D. R., Morton, G., & Sue, D. W. (1989). *Counseling American minorities* (3rd ed.). Dubuque, IA: Brown.

Attneave, C. (1977). The wasted strengths of Indian families. In S. Unger (Ed.), *The destruction of American Indian families* (pp. 29–33). New York: Association on American Indian Affairs.

Attneave, C. (1982). American Indians and Alaska Native families: Emigrants in their own homeland. In M. McGoldrick, J. K. Pearce, & J. Giordano (Eds.), *Ethnicity and family therapy* (pp. 55–83). New York: Gardner.

Baptiste, D. A. (1987). Family therapy with Spanish-heritage immigrant families in cultural transition. *Contemporary Family Therapy, 9,* 229–250.

Berg, I.-K., & Jaya, A. (1993). Different and same: Family therapy with Asian-American families. *Journal of Marital and Family Therapy, 19,* 31–38.

Bergman, R. (1977). The human cost of removing Indian children from their families. In S. Unger (Ed.), *The destruction of American Indian families* (pp. 34–36). New York: Association on American Indian Affairs.

Bird, A. R., & Melendy, P. (1977). Indian child welfare in Oregon. In S. Unger (Ed.), *The destruction of American Indian families* (pp. 43–46). New York: Association on American Indian Affairs.

Boyd-Franklin, N. (1987). The contribution of family therapy models to the treatment of Black families. *Psychotherapy, 24,* 621–629.

Boyd-Franklin, N. (1989a). *Black families in therapy.* New York: Guilford Press.

Boyd-Franklin, N. (1989b). Five key factors in the treatment of Black families. *Journal of Psychotherapy and the Family, 6,* 53–69.

Brown, E. F., & Shaughnessay, T. F. (1981). *Education for social work practice with American Indian families: Introductory text. Child Welfare Training* (DHHS Report No. OHDS 81–30298). Washington, DC: Children's Bureau.

Byler, W. (1977). The destruction of American Indian families. In S. Unger (Ed.), *The destruction of American Indian families* (pp. 1–11). New York: Association on American Indian Affairs.

Cheung, F. K., & Snowden, L. R. (1990). Community mental health and ethnic populations. *Community Mental Health Journal, 26,* 277–291.

Chin, J. L. (1983). Diagnostic considerations in working with Asian-Americans. *American Journal of Orthopsychiatry, 53,* 100–109.

Dana, R. H. (1998). *Understanding cultural identity in intervention and assessment.* Thousand Oaks, CA: Sage.

Dauphinais, P., LaFromboise, T., & Rowe, W. (1980). Perceived problems and sources of help for American Indian students. *Counselor Education and Supervision, 21,* 37–46.

Davis, C., Haub, C., & Willette, L. (1988). U.S. Hispanics: Changing the face of America. In E. Acosta-Belen & B. Sjostrom (Eds.), *The Hispanic experience in the United States: Contemporary issues and perspectives* (pp. 3–56). New York: Praeger.

del-Carmen, R. (1990). Assessment of Asian-Americans for family therapy. In F. Serafica & A. I. Schwebel (Eds.), *Mental health of ethnic minorities* (p. 98–117). New York: Praeger.

Denby, R. W. (1996). Resiliency and the African American family: A model of family preservation. In S. L. Logam (Ed.), *The Black family: Strengths, self-help, and positive change* (pp. 144–163). Boulder, CO: Westview Press.

Everett, F., Proctor, N., & Cartmell, B. (1983). Providing psychological services to American Indian children and families. *Professional Psychology: Research and Practice, 14,* 588–601.

Fillmore, L. W. (1991). When learning a second language means losing the first. *Early Childhood Research Quarterly, 6,* 323–346.

Foster, H. J. (1983). African patterns in Afro-American family. *Journal of Black Studies, 14,* 201–232.

Franklin, J. H. (1988). A historical note on Black families. In H. P. McAdoo (Ed.), *Black families* (2nd ed., pp. 23–26). Newbury Park, CA: Sage.

Garbarino, M. (1985). *Native American heritage* (2nd ed.). Prospect Heights, IL: Waveland.

Glick, P. C. (1988). Demographic pictures of Black families. In H. P. McAdoo (Ed.), *Black families* (2nd ed., pp. 111–132). Newbury Park, CA: Sage.

Gonzalez, G. M. (1997). The emergence of Chicanos in the twenty-first century: Implications for counseling, research, and policy. *Journal of Multicultural Counseling & Development, 25*(2), 94–106.

Hardy, K. V. (1989). The theoretical myth of sameness: A critical issue in family therapy training and treatment. *Journal of Psychotherapy and the Family, 6,* 17–33.

Harrison, A. O., Wilson, M. N., Pine, C. J., Chan, S. Q., & Buriel, R. (1990). Family ecologies of ethnic minority children. *Child Development, 61,* 347–362.

Hill, H. I., & Strozier, A. L. (1992). Multicultural training in APA-approved counseling psychological program: A survey. *Professional Psychology, 23,* 43–51.

Hirabayashi, G., & Saram, P. A. (1980). Some issues regarding ethnic relations research. In K. V. Ujimoto & G. Hirabayshi (Eds.), *Visible minorities and multiculturalism: Asians in Canada* (pp. 379–388). Toronto: Butterworth.

Ho, M. K. (1987). *Family therapy with ethnic minorities.* Newbury Park, CA: Sage.

Ho, M. K. (1989). Applying family therapy theories to Asian/Pacific Americans. *Contemporary Family Therapy: An International Journal, 11,* 61–70.

Hong, G. K. (1989). Application of cultural and environmental issues in family therapy with immigrant Chinese Americans. *Journal of Strategic and Systemic Therapies, 8,* 14–21.

Hong, G. K., & Ham, M. D. (1992). The impact of immigration on the family life cycle: Clinical implications for Chinese Americans. *Journal of Family Psychotherapy, 3,* 27–40.

Inclan, J. (1990). Understanding Hispanic families: A curriculum outline. *Journal of Strategic and Systemic Therapies, 9,* 64–82.

Kao, E. M., Nagata, D. K., & Peterson, C. (1997). Explanatory style, family expressiveness, and self-esteem among Asian American and European American college students. *Journal of Social Psychology, 137,* 435–444.

Karst, K. L. (1986). Paths to belonging: The Constitution and cultural identity. *North Carolina Law Review, 64,* 303–377.

Kim, S. C. (1985). Family therapy for Asian-Americans: A strategic structural framework. *Psychotherapy, 22,* 343–348.

Kitano, H. L. (1989). A model for counseling Asian Americans. In P. B. Pedersen, J. G. Draguns, W. J. Lonner, & J. E. Trimble (Eds.), *Counseling across cultures* (pp. 139–151). Honolulu: University of Hawaii.

Kitano, H. L., & Maki, M. T. (1996). Continuity, change and diversity: Counseling Asian Americans. In P. B. Pedersen, J. G. Draguns, W. J. Lonner, & J. E. Trimble (Eds.), *Counseling across cultures* (pp. 139–151). Honolulu: University of Hawaii.

Klor de Alva, J. J. (1988). Telling Hispanics apart: Latino sociocultural diversity. In E. Acosta-Belen & B. R. Sjostrom (Eds.), *The Hispanic experience in the United States* (pp. 107–136). New York: Praeger.

LaFromboise, T. D. (1988). American Indian mental health policy. *American Psychologist, 43,* 388–397.

LaFromboise, T. D., Trimble, J. E., & Mohatt, G. V. (1990). Counseling intervention and American Indian tradition: An integrative approach. *The Counseling Psychologist, 18,* 628–654.

Lee, E. (1989). Assessment and treatment of Chinese-American immigrant families. *Journal of Psychotherapy and the Family, 6,* 99–122.

Lewis, C. (1970). *Indian families of the Northwest coast: The impact of change.* Chicago: University of Chicago Press.

Lichter, D. T., & Landale, N. S. (1995). Parental work, family structure, and poverty among Latino children. *Journal of Marriage & the Family, 57*(2), 346–354.

Lin, T. Y., & Lin, M. C. (1980). Love, denial and rejection: Responses of Chinese families to mental illness. In A. Kleinman & T. Y. Lin (Eds.), *Normal and abnormal behavior in Chinese culture* (pp. 86–108). Boston: Reidel.

London, H., & Devore, W. (1988). Layers of understanding: Counseling ethnic minority families. *Family Relations, 37,* 310–314.

Marcos, L. R. (1976). Linguistic dimensions in the bilingual patient. *American Journal of Psychoanalysis, 36,* 347–354.

Massey, D. S., Zambrana, R. E., & Alonzo Bell, S. (1995). Contemporary issues in Latino families: Future directions for research, policy, and practice. In R. E. Zambrana (Ed.), *Understanding Latino families: Scholarship, policy, and practice,* Vol. 2 (pp. 190–204). Thousand Oaks, CA: Sage.

McAdoo, H. P. (1991). Family values and outcomes for children. *Journal of Negro Education, 60,* 361–365.

McCollum, V. J. C. (1997). Evolution of the African American family personality: Considerations for family therapy. *Journal of Multicultural Counseling & Development, 25*(3), 219–229.

McGoldrick, M., Pearce, J., & Giordano, J. (Eds.). (1982). *Ethnicity and family therapy.* New York: Gardner.

McMiller, W. P., & Weisz, J. R. (1996). Help-seeking preceding mental health clinic intake among African-American, Latino, and Caucasian youths. *Journal of the American Academy of Child & Adolescent Psychiatry, 35*(8), 1086–1094.

Minuchin, S. (1974). *Families and family therapy.* Cambridge, MA: Harvard University Press.

Moore-Hines, P., & Boyd-Franklin, N. (1982). Black families. In M. McGoldrick, J. K. Pearce, & J. Giordano (Eds.), *Ethnicity and family therapy* (pp. 84–107). New York: Gardner.

Moynihan, D. P. (1965). *The Negro family, the case for national action: Moynihan report.* Washington, DC: U.S. Government Printing Office.

Nobles, W. W. (1988). African-American family life: An instrument of culture. In H. P. McAdoo (Ed.), *Black families* (2nd ed., pp. 44–53). Newbury Park, CA: Sage.

O'Hare, W. P. (1992). America's minorities—The demographics of diversity. *Population Bulletin, 47*(4), 1–47.

O'Hare, W. P., Pollard, K. M., Mann, T. L., & Kent, K. M. (1991). African Americans in the 1990s. *Population Bulletin, 46,* 1–40.

Padilla, A. M., Ruiz, R. A., & Alvarez, R. (1975). Community mental health services for the Spanish-speaking/surnamed population. *American Psychologist, 30,* 892–905.

Rogler, L. H., Malgady, R. G., Costantino, G., & Blumenthal, R. (1987). What do culturally sensitive mental health services mean? *American Psychologist, 42,* 565–570.

Ruetrakul, P. (1987). *A study of problems and stress of Southeast Asian students with accompanying families at the University of Pittsburgh.* Paper presented at the annual meeting of the Comparative and International Education Society, Washington, DC.

Saba, G. W., Karrer, B. M., & Hardy, K. Y. (Eds.). (1990). *Minorities and family therapy.* New York: Haworth.

Schaefer, R. T. (1996). *Racial and ethnic groups.* New York: HarperCollins.

Sciarra, D. T., & Ponterotto, J. G. (1991). Counseling the Hispanic bilingual family: Challenges to the therapeutic process. *Psychotherapy, 28,* 473–479.

Shon, S. P., & Ja, D. Y. (1982). Asian families. In M. McGoldrick, J. K. Pearce, & J. Giordano (Eds.), *Ethnicity and family therapy* (pp. 208–228). New York: Gardner.

Sudarkasa, N. (1988). Interpreting the African heritage in Afro-American family organization. In H. P. McAdoo (Ed.), *Black families* (2nd ed., pp. 27–43). Newbury Park, CA: Sage.

Szapocznik, J., Rio, A., Perez-Vidal, A., Kurtines, W., Hervis, O., & Santiste-Ban, D. (1986). Bicultural Effectiveness Training (BET): An experimental test of an intervention modality for families experiencing intergenerational/intercultural conflict. *Hispanic Journal of Behavioral Sciences, 8,* 303–330.

Tafoya, T. (1989). Circles and cedar: Native Americans and family therapy. *Journal of Psychotherapy and the Family, 6,* 71–98.

Tamura, T., & Lau, A. (1992). Connectedness versus separateness: Applicability of family therapy to Japanese families. *Family Process, 31,* 319–340.

Tharp, R. G. (1991). Cultural diversity and treatment of children. *Journal of Consulting and Clinical Psychology, 59,* 799–812.

Unger, S. (Ed.). (1977). *The destruction of American Indian families.* New York: Association on American Indian Affairs.

U.S. Bureau of Census (1990). *Fertility of American women: June 1990, Current Population Reports, Series P-20, No. 454.* Washington, DC: U.S. Government Printing Office.

U.S. Bureau of Census (1992). *Statistical abstract of the United States: 1992.* Washington, DC: U.S. Government Printing Office.

Vazquez-Nuttal, E., Avila-Vivas, Z., & Morales-Barreto, G. (1984). Working with Latin American families. *Family Therapy Collections, 9,* 75–90.

Valdivieso, R., & Davis, C. (1988). *U.S. Hispanics: Challenging issues for the 1990s.* Washington, DC: Population Reference Bureau.

Vega, W. A. (1990). Hispanic families in the 1980's: A decade of research. *Journal of Marriage and the Family, 52,* 1015–1024.

Wang, L. (1994). Marriage and family therapy with people from China. *Contemporary Family Therapy: An International Journal, 16,* 25–37.

Westermeyer, J. (1977a). The drunken Indian: Myths and realities. In S. Unger (Ed.), *The destruction of Amer-*

ican Indian families (pp. 22–28). New York: Association on American Indian Affairs.

Westermeyer, J. (1977b). The ravage of Indian families in crisis. In S. Unger (Ed.), *The destruction of American Indian families* (pp. 47–56). New York: Association on American Indian Affairs.

Wilkinson, C. B. (1987). Introduction. In C. B. Wilkinson (Ed.), *Ethnic psychiatry* (pp. 1–11). New York: Plenum Press.

Willis, J. T. (1988). An effective counseling model for treating the Black family. *Family Therapy, 15,* 185–194.

Wilson, L. L., & Stith, S. M. (1998). Culturally sensitive therapy with Black clients. In D. R. Atkinson (Ed.).

Counseling American minorities (5th ed., pp. 116–126). Boston: McGraw-Hill.

Wilson, M. N. (1984). Mother's and grandmothers' perceptions of parental behavior in three generational Black families. *Child Development, 55,* 1333–1339.

Wilson, M. N. (1986). The Black extended family: An analytical review. *Developmental Psychology, 22,* 246–258.

Wilson, M. N. (1989). Child development in the context of the Black extended family. *American Psychologist, 44,* 380–385.

Wilson, M. N., & Tolson, T. F. J. (1990). Familial support in the Black community. *Journal of Clinical Child Psychology, 19,* 347–355.

7 Group Intervention and Treatment with Ethnic Minorities

AY LING HAN

MELBA J. T. VASQUEZ

Group interventions have long been considered the treatment of choice for various kinds of problems and difficulties (Kaplan & Sadock, 1993; Kaul & Bednar, 1986). The approach is seen as relevant for populations whose concerns focus on feelings of social isolation, stresses in interpersonal relationships, and the need for support (Boyd-Franklin, 1987; Ettin, 1988; Talley & Rockwell, 1985; Yalom, 1985). Group therapy has particular value for ethnic and racial minorities who struggle with issues of confidence, self-esteem, empowerment, and identity (Boyd-Franklin, 1991; Ho, 1984; Mays, 1986; Nayman, 1983), within a sociocultural context that is characterized by stereotypes, prejudice, and discrimination.

In preparing and providing group treatment for ethnic and racial minorities, two sociocultural realities must be assessed and addressed: one, their unique cultural needs and variations (Boyd-Franklin, 1991; Comas-Díaz, 1984; Nayman, 1983); and, two, their experiences and functioning as members of an underrepresented group that is devalued in America's predominantly White society. More recent writings on multicultural/multiracial group therapy have focused on factors pertaining to the role of culture (Arcaya, 1996; Leong, Wagner, & Kim, 1995; Sue, 1996), as well as the role of oppression and unequal power in the lives of racial/ethnic minorities in general and in the dynamics of multiracial groups in particular (Fenster, 1996; Merta, 1995; White, 1994), or both (Sutton, 1996). However, they do not provide a more systematic philosophical and treatment approach that incorporates both.

Philosophy of Group Treatment with Ethnic Minority Clients

To incorporate these dual sociocultural realities into contemporary practice of group therapy, our treatment philosophy and work with members of underrepresented ethnic/racial groups are informed by three perspectives: the process, multicultural perspective, and feminist-relational perspective. We believe that these three are interrelated and mutually reinforcing, each informing and complementing the other.

Process Perspective

Our process-oriented perspective is largely informed by Yalom (1985, 1995). A "keystone" concept is that groups will, in time, develop into a "social microcosm" of the members' lives outside the group (Yalom, 1985, 1995); that is, members' ways of relating outside the group will be manifested in the ways that they relate with one another in the group. Through "here-and-now" interpersonal learning involving feedback and experimentation, the group provides its members with opportunities to explore both maladaptive and more adaptive ways of functioning in the group and, ultimately, outside the group (Yalom, 1985, 1995). Importantly, leaders move out of the expert role and instead facilitate members' involvement with and responsiveness to each other (Yalom, 1985). Leaders make observations and comments about the process, themes, and dynamics underlying the content of the group, and teach members to do the same (Yalom, 1985). This approach to leadership facilitates the empowerment of minority members who have not necessarily experienced the validation of their perceptions and the value of their contributions in group settings.

Yalom (1985) categorized therapeutic experiences in group work into 11 primary factors, including universality, socializing techniques and skills, imitative behavior, catharsis, existential factors, and interpersonal learning. While these are valuable factors, we believe they are grounded in Eurocentric assumptions about the primacy of individualism in group treatment. Indeed, some of these factors may be problematic for group members whose ethnic heritage and cultural values are more collective. For example, direct expressions of assertiveness and disagreement may be unthinkable for some group members: These may be considered impolite, presumptuous, and unacceptable in the member's personal life; their expression may even precipitate or exacerbate intrapsychic and/or familial cultural conflicts. Yalom, in his later edition of *The Theory and Practice of Group Psychotherapy,* seemed to suggest that the therapeutic factor of "universality" may be culture-bound, and that "cultural minorities may feel excluded because of different attitudes toward disclosure, interaction, and affective expression" (1995, p. 7). Thus, while the process approach informs us about important group dynamics, it does not adequately deal with group work involving cultural diversity or majority-minority racial dynamics.

Multicultural Perspective

The multicultural approach expands on Yalom's process approach to group therapy. Here, we propose three goals for treatment involving ethnic/racial minorities.

Valuing Diversity. First, group work must value diversity. Leaders have a responsibility to be (a) cognizant of the individualistic cultural bases of prevailing group approaches and interventions; (b) inclusive of the collectivistic bases of minority members' needs, values, and realities; and (c) understanding of the reality that many ethnic minorities are socialized and develop within at least three cultural contexts. Those include their own ethnocultural context, the mainstream cultural context, and the oppressive context of living in a society

(Boykin, 1986) in which minorities have a history of suffering stereotyping, prejudice, and discrimination (Fiske, 1998). Valuing diversity involves facilitating an exploration of ethnic minority members' multiple ethnic and racial heritages and experiences, their attitudes about them, and how they impact functioning. It involves ascertaining whether they overvalue one cultural heritage and undervalue another, and helping them reclaim disavowed but adaptive cultural values. It also involves leaders actively "generating a set of group norms which is by and large consonant with the varying cultural" values and perspectives of the group members (Tsui & Schultz, 1988, p. 141).

Developing Multicultural Competence.   Second, group therapy must facilitate the development of bicultural competence or multicultural competence (Cross, 1987; Ramirez, 1984, 1998; Rotheram-Borus, 1993; Szapocnik, Kurtines, & Fernandez, 1980). Here, group leaders adopt a treatment approach that includes (a) encouraging ethnic minority group members to view their interpersonal issues within the multicultural contexts of their lives, (b) promoting the development or widening of their repertoire of multiculturally based interpersonal competence, (c) contextualizing the cultural bases of such learning, and (d) reinforcing the adaptive value of adeptly "switching" (Padilla, 1993) back and forth between culturally contexed interpersonal skills. For example, a member from a traditional ethnic background may be encouraged to experiment with both mainstream direct and ethnically more indirect ways of saying "No," rather than automatically labeling and pathologizing his or her indirect communication as passive aggressive, manipulative, or maladaptive.

Incorporating a Multicultural Identity.   Third, group work must facilitate the internalization of a more accurate, positive, and affirming sense of racial identity (Pack-Brown, Whittington-Clark, & Parker, 1998; Tatum, 1993; White, 1994), and a clear and integrated sense of self (Comas-Díaz, 1988). This task is particularly complex and challenging for biracial/multiracial group members with multiple heritages and also for adoptees who may have little or no information about their origins. It is important to discern that while some ethnic/racial minorities may have internalized oppressive messages into shame and self-hatred, others have not; and some may develop adaptive distrust toward the groups that oppress them, while cultivating a strong and clear pride in their sense of ethnic/racial identity and belongingness (Fenster, 1996).

Feminist Perspective

Fedele and Harrington (1990) describe four healing processes operative in group treatment with women that we believe are particularly relevant for ethnic and racial minorities. These healing factors are based on a relational approach (Miller, 1986) in which groups that foster particular kinds of interactions and connections between people promote psychological growth and the healing of emotional wounds. The four healing processes are (a) validation of one's experience, (b) empowerment to act in one's relationships, (c) development of self-empathy, and (d) mutuality in one's relationships. We believe that they are potent antidotes for dealing with the wounds of oppression while also addressing the three multicultural goals delineated in the previous section.

Validation as a Healing Process. Validation refers to processes of hearing, seeing, acknowledging, and affirming perceptions, needs, values, and experiences. Racial and ethnic minorities receive numerous messages and undergo experiences in society that invalidate their reality (Atkinson, Morten, & Sue, 1989; Comas-Díaz, 1988). Pervasive invalidation may result in discouragement, feeling devalued, hesitation in voicing a personal perspective, and reduced group participation, to name just a few of the costs. Healing for ethnic or racial minorities can occur when group work involves acknowledgment and validation of the following in both current and historical settings: unrecognized or devalued relationships; pathologization, undue criticism, or punishments of otherwise normative difficulties or mistakes; and denigrations or idealizations of successes.

Empowerment as a Healing Process. Empowerment involves processes of effecting desired changes in one's life. A feminist view of mutual power differs from the traditional norm of power over another person in that it emphasizes the capacity to both be moved by, and to move, another person (Fedele & Harrington, 1990; Surrey, 1987). Pervasive stereotypes, prejudice, and discrimination may contribute to ethnic and racial minorities' difficulties in effecting desired changes in their lives, and can result in resignation, learned helplessness, and/or compromised functioning, especially in cross-racial situations. These may manifest themselves in the academic, occupational, and social arenas; inside the group, they may be revealed in nonadaptive participation and/or premature termination.

A group approach that emphasizes the empowering effects of connectedness involves encouraging members to be effective on their own behalf with one another, and to share how they impact each another. In a multiracial therapy group where personal, internal problems may be displaced onto race (White, 1994), this may involve acknowledgment of members' stereotyping of one another or projection of disavowed characteristics; may result in a reexamination and letting-go of stereotypes, internalized oppression, and projections; and may pave the way for the internalization of more reality-based and affirming multicultural experiences and images of self and others. It is important that the group provide a context in which both minorities' struggles and their abilities to be effective and resourceful are validated, so that group members may feel empowered about themselves and with others.

Self-Empathy as a Healing Process. Self-empathy involves having informed understanding and compassion for one's struggles and concerns, and accepting that which is human in oneself (Fedele & Harrington, 1990; Jordan, 1989). Some ethnic or racial minorities who have experienced harsh or judgmental relationships with significant persons in their lives may internalize long-standing and pervasive oppressive messages into harsh attitudes toward themselves. They may define themselves as "failures" when making mistakes or having difficulties, instead of accepting that errors, mistakes, or difficulties are natural parts of life, living, and learning. The relative lack of minority role models in key power positions in society contributes significantly to this misinformed self-perception. If one views one's primary reference group (i.e., ethnic, racial, gender, socioeconomic, religious, and other groups with which one most identifies) as being unentitled or a failure in society, then the tendency is to either see oneself as a failure or to disengage from the primary reference group, both of which increase the potential for self-harshness and marginalization.

When group members learn to hear each other's deepest fears, insecurities, shame, and mistakes in the context of informed, nonjudgmental, and caring relationships, they learn to develop self-empathy and compassion for their own vulnerabilities, imperfections, and mistakes. In so doing, members let go of internalized oppression in their attributions of their difficulties, gain a sense of "universality" in their acceptance of shared fallibility, and develop positive perceptions of their primary reference groups.

Mutuality as a Healing Process.   Mutuality is two-or-more persons' attunement into each other's subjective experiences at cognitive and affective levels (Fedele & Harrington, 1990; Jordan, 1989). It involves the ability to understand fully and convey respect for the other person's experience and uniqueness, the willingness to allow others to have an impact on oneself, and an openness to understanding and appreciating one's impact on others.

Racial minorities often experience imbalances in mutuality. Tatum (1993) has described failures of empathy and the challenges of mutuality for Black and White women. Minor imbalances in relationships are challenging and painful, but pervasive and traumatic disconnections can lead to psychological wounds such as an inhibition of the ability to act. Lack of mutuality in relationships often results in a loss of self-understanding, a diminished sense of self-worth, a decrease in energy, and a confusing sense of isolation (Miller, 1988). Long-term effects may include a seriously distorted view of self and others, an inability to express feelings, overreliance on maladaptive coping mechanisms, and isolation and/or unfulfilling attachments (Miller, 1988).

Mutuality as a healing factor for ethnic/racial minority group members involves other members being able to respect their pain and to value their growth without feeling threatened. For example, an American Indian group member shared her experience of isolation in her current community, and other members focused on giving her advice to join social organizations. When the group leaders commented on these quick-fix responses, one insightful member shared her realization of how her advice-giving must have contributed to the group's apparent lack of interest in the American Indian woman's life, and wondered whether she felt isolated in the group as well. In doing so, this member conveyed her abilities to validate, empathize with, and be attuned to the American Indian member who, in response, felt validated and empowered to explore her deeper concerns of isolation. Mutuality in relationships results in more energy and ability to act, deepened awareness and understanding of others, increased sense of worth, and a heightened experience of closeness and connection with others (Miller, 1986).

Group Composition

Therapy groups may be racially or ethnically homogeneous or heterogeneous. Members in homogeneous groups share similar ethnic or racial characteristics—for example, a group for Latinas, a group for African Americans and so forth. It is important to be mindful of heterogeneity within any one homogeneous group. For example, a group of Asian Americans could be all college-aged and female. However, this same group could be diverse in terms of the members' sociocultural histories. That is, it may include a second-generation

Japanese American who is Christian and has a middle-class background; a South Asian Indian who is Hindi and wealthy; a Vietnamese refugee who is Buddhist and Catholic and has a low-paying part-time job; and so on. Thus, leaders must look for both commonalties and differences among members of a seemingly homogeneous group.

Racially or ethnically heterogeneous groups consists of members from both the dominant culture and subcultures in the U.S. Such mixed compositions parallel society at large and often mirror attitudes, behavior, and dynamics found outside the group. Homogeneous and heterogeneous group compositions present different advantages and risks.

Homogeneous Groups

Ethnically homogeneous groups provide opportunities for more immediate trust and cultural understanding, which can foster and enhance group cohesion and more in-depth self-disclosure (Davis, 1984). Compared to heterogeneous groups, homogenous groups may have less conflict, more mutual support, and better attendance; they may also bring more immediate symptom relief (Johnson & Johnson, 1994; Merta, 1995; Unger, 1989). The enhancement of ethnic identity is a typical goal for ethnically homogeneous groups. Thus, additional advantages include greater ease in sharing unique cultural experiences and more in-depth exploration of questions of identity. A clinical focus in these areas may help members "resolve identity conflicts and move to a more secure and positive grounding in their own group and hence healthier self-esteem" (White, 1994, p. 98).

However, in homogeneous groups, both leaders and members may assume or exaggerate similarities, and deemphasize or even devalue differences. Stereotypes based on general group differences may be inadvertently reinforced (Sue, 1996). Thus, homogenous groups run the risk of being more superficial and less productive (Johnson & Johnson, 1994; Merta, 1995; Unger, 1989). Due to projections of personal vulnerability or stereotyped perceptions of minority members as helpless or fragile, they may also be overly protective or supportive and underchallenging of minority members.

The opportunity exists to acknowledge differences in ethnic identity among group members, and to explore different experiences with acculturation and oppression, and the significance of these differences on their views of themselves, their views of their own and other groups, their views of majority groups, and their functioning in various sociocultural contexts. Thus, group leaders need to facilitate a balanced validation of both commonalties and differences, universality and uniqueness, and strengths and vulnerabilities; and help members clarify relevant issues of identity and role expectations.

Heterogeneous Groups

Ethnically and racially mixed groups serve as a social microcosm of our society's race relations. They run the risks of reenacting oppressive dynamics of invalidation, disempowerment, and lack of empathy and mutuality. Conversely, important advantages of heterogeneous groups include built-in opportunities to provide and receive diverse feedback (Merta, 1995), develop more knowledge and understanding of oneself and others (Avila & Avila, 1988; Merta, 1995), develop skills in relating across differences (Fenster, 1996), and resolve long-standing misunderstandings about racial and ethnic differences. Mixed group therapy may be more effective than individual therapy (Fenster, 1996; Yalom, 1995) or homogenous group compositions in resolving transferential distortions (Merta, 1995).

Racially mixed group compositions present challenges for group leaders and members alike. First, "[f]or many, if not all,...parataxic distortions [of perceptions of other group members] are likely to take the forms of racial biases and stereotypes, ethnocentrism, and ignorance of various multicultural issues and perspectives" (Merta, 1995, p. 571). For example, the group may endorse only certain communication styles, ways of handling emotions, and conflict resolution styles that are culturally inappropriate or dystonic in a minority member's particular ethnocultural community. Moreover, leaders and majority members, as well as minority members, may accept stereotypes and prejudices (White, 1994).

Second, in groups where minority members are significantly underrepresented, conscious and unconscious group dynamics of mainstreaming and devaluation of differences undermine needed therapeutic work by ethnic minority group members. Being "one of a kind" in a group—for example, being the only ethnic/racial minority, gay man, or physically disabled—can be isolating, and may make it difficult for that member to relate to others in the group. Such members may question their own judgment, feel inferior, wish to agree with the majority, experience significant anxiety, and derive least benefit, even when they have the courage and ability to disagree with the majority (Fenster, 1996). "The group norms comprising the so-called therapeutic milieu are actually Caucasian group norms that, in themselves, resist intrusion and disruption from minority cultures" (Tsui & Schultz, 1988, p. 137).

Third, as the interpersonal distortions and intensity of "multiple transferences" (a concept developed for group applications by Wolf & Schwartz, 1962) are exacerbated by racial/ethnic differences (White, 1994), the process of bringing to awareness feelings and thoughts about race and ethnicity tends to activate resistance (Akamatsu, 1998; White, 1994) and defenses, including denial, intellectualization, projection or scapegoating, and between-member polarization (Fenster, 1996; Tsui & Schultz, 1988). Minorities may be the recipients of underidentifications or negative identifications from other members (White, 1994). Majority group members may project their own unacceptable impulses and characteristics onto a member whose race or ethnicity is devalued; similarly, a minority member may focus on issues of discrimination to avoid dealing with generalized difficulties in interpersonal relationships. Thus, members may shift focus onto race (White, 1994; also Fenster, 1996) to avoid acknowledging responsibility for their own thoughts, feelings, actions, reactions, and difficulties.

Fourth, inherent in racial majority-minority dynamics are very different awarenesses and experiences of power among group members; while people of color are very aware of White privilege and of their own relative powerlessness, Whites are often unaware and even tend to feel very threatened when these experiences are brought to consciousness (Akamatsu, 1998), thus, further complicating the processing of group dynamics that involve mainstreaming and devaluation of differences. Last but not least, leaders and members may overprotect or underprotect and overly confront ethnic/racial minority group members (Tsui & Schultz, 1988), and may underchallenge or overchallenge White group members.

Thus, race and ethnicity of the group members and leader are always of importance, even when race or ethnicity as such is unrelated to the goals of the members (Davis, 1984; Fenster, 1996; Merta, 1995; Tsui & Schultz, 1988). Mutual empathy among members must involve the facilitation of trust and safety among minority members to share experiences they do not usually discuss in mixed groups and for White members to hear these experiences without undue defensiveness. When issues of racial and ethnic oppression come up, White members may struggle with feelings of fear, shame, guilt, remorse, sadness, or resentment.

Self-empathy must also be a clear goal for White members in the group. Self-empathy is facilitated when coleaders are able to model empathy for White members of the group—communicating understanding without condoning oppression—so that White members are able to reach a paradoxical stance toward themselves, one that depersonalizes yet also assumes responsibility for the oppressor in them, where they are able to see that they are recipients of an oppressive cultural heritage and that they have a choice over their attitudes and behaviors with respect to diversity. In short, it is important that group leaders be informed about, attuned to, and adept in processing the following: the roles of culture/ethnicity (Arcaya, 1996; Fenster, 1996; Leong et al., 1995; Sutton, 1996; Tsui & Schultz, 1988), the majority-minority dynamics of racism and ethnocentrism (Fenster, 1996; Sutton, 1996; Tsui & Schultz, 1988), and relevant personal issues that may underlie racial issues (Sutton, 1996; White, 1994).

Other Considerations in Group Composition

Associated with the importance of knowing the possible advantages and challenges of various ethnic/racial groupings, three other factors are also important to consider: verbal participation, acculturation status, and gender composition. First, verbal participation has seemed to be an important factor in ethnically homogeneous and heterogeneous groups (Shen, Sanchez, & Huang, 1984). Shen et al. (1984) examined the verbal participation of Anglos, Mexican Americans, and Native Americans with comparable educational backgrounds in group therapy for alcoholic patients, and found that Anglo patients had significantly higher verbal participation than either of the two other groups. Chu and Sue (1984) suggested that Asians in heterogeneous groups may tend toward lower verbal participation for fear of interrupting others, grounded in the cultural value of politeness. In addition, White (1994) believes that members' freedom in discussing feelings about their own and other racial groups and their freedom in expressing aggressive and loving feelings toward one another reflect a measure of cohesiveness in a multiracial/ethnic group. Because higher verbal participation seems to yield greater positive change in members' views of themselves (Corey, 1990; Yalom, 1985), degree of verbal participation by all members should be addressed. Group leaders should make careful differential assessment regarding verbal and nonverbal behaviors: For example, silence may reflect cultural values of respect or nonintrusiveness, and/or it may reflect a minority member's feeling silenced and marginalized in a racially mixed group.

Second, acculturation is an important factor influencing receptiveness to group counseling (Leong et al., 1995). Specifically, in a study of Asian American students,

Leong et al. (1995) found that being active in both the heritage culture and mainstream society significantly predicted positive orientations toward group counseling. In contrast, some African Americans (Sutton, 1996), Asian Americans (Baruth & Manning, 1991; Gladding, 1991), and Native Americans (Baruth & Manning, 1991) may be less receptive to racially mixed or even homogeneous groups, in part due to traditional cultural values against self-disclosure (Merta, 1995). Acculturation may be a significant moderator of cultural values that influences receptiveness to therapy in general and group therapy in particular.

Third, gender composition also influences dynamics in racially homogeneous and heterogeneous groups. Proponents of same-sex groups describe the advantages of such a composition. Bernardez (1983) considers women's groups the treatment of choice for most women. She believes that single-sex groups allow women to focus on their unique experiences as women, to practice assertiveness, and to redefine goals and notions of womanly behavior.

Likewise, there are advantages to organizing an all-men's group. While recruiting for such a group may be a challenge, Andronico (1996) argues that group modalities are "ideal forums [for raising]...issues pertinent to men in the twenty-first century," with benefits that include reduced sexual tension, competitiveness, and feelings of shame, and increased bonding, supportiveness, and cooperation (p. xviii). All-men's groups may provide greater freedom to express feelings without being bound by the traditional gender role restrictions men may experience with women present, to focus on their unique issues and experiences as men, and to explore new ways of expressing needs and feelings with one another (Kaufman & Timmers, 1986; McLeod & Pemberton, 1984; Van Wormer, 1989). Moreover, a group of ethnically homogenous but less acculturated men may be more beneficial than a mixed-gender group because the men may feel freer to share their views without the presence of relatively more verbal women (Sue, 1996). Nonetheless, recruitment of minority men into group therapy may not be easy due to a combination of factors such as economic constraints, racism, gender socialization that discourages men from showing their vulnerability in the presence of others, and distrust of the helping profession (Sutton, 1996).

Alonso (1987) advocates mixed-sex groups, in the belief that mixed groups offer more options for working through sex role issues. Fedele and Harrington (1990) suggest that both same- and mixed-sex group perspectives have merit. At certain developmental points an individual may need a same-sex group to focus on gender identity issues. At other times, a mixed group can help both sexes get to know one another (Abell, 1959; Fenster, 1996), integrate women's and men's experiences into a "coherent and dynamic understanding of the human experience" (Fedele & Harrington, 1990, p. 3), and offer skills to resolve long-standing differences and misunderstandings.

In conclusion, homogeneous groups may provide members with unique opportunities to explore and work through racial/ethnic identity and sex role issues. Heterogeneous groups may optimize opportunities for both a deepened understanding of self and others as well as increased skills in relating across differences relative to race/ethnicity and gender. Both compositions present equally challenging dynamics and valuable therapeutic opportunities for group members and leaders alike.

Group Leadership

The role of the group leader will vary according to the goals and focus of the group and the theoretical orientation of the leaders (Corey, 1990; Lakin, 1985). Group leaders may be called upon to engage in various roles and tasks, such as seeking and giving information, responding to feelings, summarizing, confronting, and modeling (Bertcher, 1979). This section of the chapter will deal with the ethnicity of the group leader and the specific tasks of group leaders working with ethnic groups.

Ethnicity of the Group Leader

There are mixed findings with regard to ethnic minorities' preferences for the ethnicity of their psychotherapist (Atkinson & Wampold, 1993; López & López, 1993; López, López, & Fong, 1991). Ethnic match was related to length of treatment for Asian, African, Mexican, and White Americans; it was significantly related to fewer dropouts after one session, a greater number of treatment sessions, and markedly improved outcomes on a global evaluation measure. For minorities whose primary language is not English, ethnic and language match was a predictor of treatment length and outcome (Sue, Fujino, Hu, Takeuchi, & Zane, 1991). However, other studies suggest that ethnic match may be a weak preference in relation to other counselor characteristics, such as counselor effectiveness (Sue, 1998).

Davis (1984) described how White leaders of minority group members may be subject to challenges of their leadership for philosophical, political, or personal reasons, as well as subject to the perception that they are not credible in their knowledge of minority culture. Indeed, leaders may enhance their effectiveness and credibility if they learn more about their group members' ethnocultural heritages (Arcaya, 1996; Sue, 1996; Sutton, 1996; Tsui & Schultz, 1988), and how they impact group dynamics (Merta, 1995). White leaders may also gain credibility in acquiring understanding of and ability to facilitate majority-minority dynamics. Leaders must develop ongoing awareness of their vulnerability to "cultural encapsulation," where they may unwittingly impose their own cultural perspectives and values on minority members (Wrenn, 1985), and their own biases and stereotypes about certain racial or ethnic groups (Tsui & Schultz, 1988).

Challenges to racial or ethnic minority group leaders may come from both White and ethnic minority group members. Because a position of leadership is inconsistent with "ascribed lower status" of minorities in society, and because both White and minority group members may have internalized that oppressive perception, minority group leaders are likely to experience more aggression or other consequences of lack of credibility from participants. Minority leaders are also more likely to be targeted for members' projections of their own personal sense of inadequacy. Leaders' processing and discussion of the significance of their race and ethnicity relative to each other and the group can empower them to attend to related dynamics in the group. Thus, it is important for leaders—between themselves and with the group—to use self-awareness to sort out the personal, cultural, and racial meanings of group members' various ways of challenging their authority and/or credibility.

Tasks for Group Leaders

Provide Psychoeducation and Promote Trust and Safety.   A primary task in providing group therapy to ethnic minorities is to promote trust and safety within the bicultural context of their lives. Although most clients enter group treatment with anxieties about confidentiality and about being understood, accepted, and respected, these concerns may be intensified for ethnic/racial minorities. Reasons for ethnic minorities' hesitancy to utilize mental health services include lack of familiarity with counseling as a helping resource, cultural imperatives against talking about personal problems with strangers, linguistic and cultural differences in encoding and decoding verbal and nonverbal communication, lack of minority mental health professionals, and lack of culturally relevant and culturally sensitive services (Sue, 1981). Given these numerous barriers, promotion of trust and safety are particularly important goals. A potential minority member should be informed about group treatment to alleviate anxieties about being "mainstreamed" and/or stereotyped.

During the screening interview and throughout group treatment, leaders should assess a minority's extent of identification with and acculturation to both ethnic background and the dominant culture (see Chapter 2). Leaders can do much to promote safety and trust by using this information to discuss ground rules about confidentiality, expectations of the member- and leader-involvement, cancellation policy, fees, and so on. Generally, the greater a potential member's identification with his or her ethnic background, the greater the effort that should be made by the leaders to frame expectations related to group work in bicultural terms. Issues of power and intimacy are common in every group (Corey, 1990; Lakin, 1985) and are particularly important for minority group members who have experienced discrimination, second-class citizenship, and relative lack of power in society. A group leader can promote trust and safety issues by modeling openness, respect, caring, genuineness, and honesty through making inquiries about experiences of diversity and oppression, and incorporating them into explorations of group dynamics.

Promote Empowerment.   Empowering group members means that the therapist implements interventions to help members trust their own observations and feelings. As such, leaders must themselves ask "if we are prepared to hear, see, and understand [minorities'] authentically told experiences. Unless the answer is 'yes,' we will not be able to help facilitate the empowerment of [ethnic minority clients]" (Tatum, 1993, p. 6). Group leaders can support and challenge members to develop awareness of themselves and their needs, and to learn ways of responding on the basis of personal meaning rather than relying exclusively on meanings as defined by others. Ethnic minority group participants, particularly women of color, have often been denied validation of their perceptions, experiences, and sense of the world. Group leaders can help members learn to listen, respect, and feel entitled to their experiences, perceptions, and needs, and to express them in the open interactions that characterize groups.

Focus on Group Members' Strengths.   Psychotherapy in general tends to focus on client behavior and attitudes that contribute to difficulties in living. While such exploration and challenge is helpful, it is especially important to facilitate exploration of minority member's strengths, abilities, and resiliency. In so doing, the therapist and the group validate and mirror aspects of the client's personality and functioning that are typically undervalued in society, thereby enhancing rather than undermining self-esteem.

Promote Skills of Communication and Assertiveness. Group leaders may help members develop communication and assertiveness skills (Bertcher, 1979). When group members realize that they can assert their needs and influence the group or individual members directly and powerfully, they will begin to develop trust and confidence in themselves, thereby validating their needs and empowering their capacities to effect changes. Leaders may promote interpersonal skills in ways that build mutual connection and enhance personal power. Sensitivity to and incorporation of cultural concerns in such promotion may minimize mainstreaming and enhance contextually adaptive learning (Wood & Mallinckrodt, 1990). Leaders can frame such learning in terms of repertoire expansion of bicultural competence and increased ability to negotiate different social interactions and cultural contexts.

Facilitate Expression of Difficult Feelings. Most ethnic minority group members value connectedness, cooperation, interpersonal relationships, and family (Atkinson et al., 1989; Comas-Díaz & Griffith, 1988). Because of this, it is sometimes difficult for minority participants, particularly women, to address feelings and behaviors related to anger, conflict, and competition. Group leaders can create norms that facilitate the exploration of these and associated issues. For example, leaders may teach that expressing anger may be vital to recognizing and challenging the restrictiveness of role expectations, and to deepening authenticity in relationships; leaders may also model hearing, receiving, and validating others' anger while remaining connected. It is important for the leader to acknowledge that direct verbal expressions of feelings such as anger may be counterproductive in certain cultural contexts. In such cases, leaders may encourage minority members to explore more culturally acceptable yet personally productive ways of dealing with these feelings.

Promote "Here-and-Now" Focus. Because people tend to recapitulate their interpersonal problems in group therapy, progress can occur when members express "here-and-now" emotional experiences and examine them to understand their defensiveness or resistance to dealing with interpersonal difficulties (Yalom, 1985). The group therapist explores patterns that may have been useful in the past, but which are no longer functional in the individual's current life and relationships. Healing comes partly from helping members understand the connection between past experiences and current behavior; and for ethnic minorities, from helping integrate historically unvoiced or devalued multicultural concerns with related current psychological issues.

Focus on Sociocultural Issues. The group leader can support change at individual and systems levels. A basic tenet of multicultural and feminist therapy is that environmental, societal, and political forces influence the development of the individual. Racial/ethnic minority groups of all backgrounds face particular social, economic, and political pressures. Despite advances in the past few decades, minority Americans find themselves greatly behind the larger society in education, occupational status, income, housing, political representation, and professional roles (see Chapter 1). Thus, primary goals include not only helping clients deconstruct internalized oppression through an understanding of how these influences have had impact, but also promoting the empowerment of their ability to effect desired changes in their lives.

Basic Group Processes

Developmental Nature of the Group

Groups tend to be developmental in nature, and a number of writers have described the phases through which groups progress (Bennis & Shepard, 1974; Corey, 1990). These phases tend to be consistent aspects of group development and do not necessarily occur in a predictable order. Long-term groups may revisit aspects of these phases several times. Among them are trust and cohesion, conflict and struggle, cohesion, mature working group, and termination (Bennis & Shepard, 1974). Different issues emerge for ethnic persons in each of these phases.

Trust and Cohesion.   Group members who are open to trust will tend to be involved in this phase; those with difficulties will tend to hold back. Initially, members may search for commonalties and focus on problems external to the group. Members tend to search for a role in the group paralleling the role they take in other group situations and their families. Unfortunately, the sociopolitical history of many racial and ethnic minorities is riddled with betrayal. Thus, minority members may initially distrust the sponsoring agency, the leader, and other group members. Knowing their sociocultural and familial history may inform leaders about possible dynamics, including lack of in-depth disclosure, low member participation, and, ultimately, attrition (Davis, 1984). To promote an atmosphere of trust and safety, interventions must incorporate members' sociocultural experiences and concerns.

Conflict and Struggle.   The next phase of group development typically involves issues of conflict and struggle, with power and interpersonal dominance taking the form of anger, disagreement, or disappointment. For some ethnic minority members, especially women of color, such feelings may be difficult to acknowledge and express, and it is often easier to focus anger on the injustices of the external world. Validating feelings about unjust social realities is as important as facilitating exploration of unacknowledged anger within the group. However, minority members risk being scapegoated or punished. If they are fearful of conflict, they may flee by participating less, not going deeper into their feelings, and/or terminating prematurely. For example, an activist African American group member who is generally angry at conservative Blacks who disengage from ethnic identity may also be resentful of a group member who is biracial (part Black and part White), and may avoid meaningful contact with this member.

In this phase, group members may also experience disappointment with the leaders for what is or is not happening in the group. This process must be acknowledged as meaningful and constructive; leaders should be able to draw anger to themselves, and to separate personal attacks from attacks on the role of leader. This phase also presents an opportunity for group members to learn effective ways of experiencing hurts, disappointments, and admission of wrongdoing. Group leaders should model nondestructive ways of expressing anger. Appropriate boundary-setting—for example, that members talk constructively about their anger, not talk or act from it in a destructive way—may serve to promote safety in this phase.

Cohesion. After a period of conflict, the group gradually develops into a cohesive unit, with increased morale, mutual trust, and self-disclosure (Corey, 1990; Lakin, 1985). More in-depth communication, including "painful secrets" or "real" reasons for coming to the group are shared, and intimacy and closeness are chief concerns. While emotional support and validation from leaders and members are important, the usual therapeutic proscription against providing more concrete help or advice does not necessarily apply to some ethnic minority members. Group therapists in this context must often provide advocacy, advice, and general cultural information. For example, leaders may provide an immigrant member who is being harassed or abused by an unscrupulous employer with information or referral to resources about immigrant worker rights. Here, the sharing of relevant cultural information validates unique multicultural reality and needs, promotes empowerment, informs mutuality, and ultimately, reinforces cohesion of the group.

Mature Working Group. During this phase, group members take on many leadership roles and tasks (Corey, 1990). There is a clear sense of purpose and direction to the group, and the atmosphere is relatively comfortable, genuine, and focused. The group also has resources to resolve internal conflicts and mobilize its resourcefulness. Members are more comfortable with differences and able to tolerate a wide range of diversity. For example, a usually cynical group member is open to hearing about herbs to help depression and lack of energy; an angry separatist is considerate of interpreting for the minimally Spanish-speaking member when the need arises. Issues affecting members both within and outside the group are addressed openly and effectively.

Termination. If the group is time limited, there is a tendency among members to want to continue. If the group is one in which individual members end their participation based on their own needs and timing, the group will clearly feel the loss of a departing member. During this phase, leaders must help the group with endings, and should facilitate good-byes, expression of disappointments or regrets, consolidations of learning, and exploration of future needs. It can be damaging to the trust in the group if a member simply drops out without acknowledgment, and it is valuable to both communicate concern about a premature departure as well as to celebrate the accomplishment of a group member who feels ready to terminate. Endings can stir up feelings of abandonment or rejection, especially for those whose histories of endings have been problematic. In a multiracial group, the meaning of endings may be complicated by historical and current intragroup racial or majority-minority issues. Ideally, all members should process endings by clarifying any transferential distortions. For a time-limited group, when the entire group terminates at once, it is important to reserve at least two full group sessions for this process.

Central Issues in Groups

Power.   Power is a central issue in any relationship, particularly for groups with ethnic and racial minority members. As members of oppressed groups, minorities and women are often uncomfortable with the notion of power as domination, control, mastery, competition, or winning over others. Psychological empowerment, on the other hand, is defined by Surrey (1987) as "the motivation, freedom, and capacity to act purposefully, with mobilization of the energy, resources, strengths, or power of each person through a mutual relational process" (p. 3). This approach to empowerment is very valuable in working with clients whose ethnic heritages value dignity and respect, and favor collaboration and interdependence over confrontation and competition. Group leaders can help members learn healthy awareness and contextually adaptive expressions of feelings, reactions, and needs.

Self-esteem, Identity, and Intimacy.   For many racial and ethnic minorities, self-esteem, identity, and intimacy are central to and are interwoven with being a minority in American society, where stereotypic and prejudicial messages are pervasive. Low self-esteem may be partly related to an internalization of societal rejection of one's reference group. Within an oppressive context, self-identity issues may include self-estrangement and maladaptive psychological behavior, confusion (e.g., "Who am I?"), conflicts (e.g., "Am I Chinese? American? Chinese American?"), self-rejections (e.g., hating one's ethnic facial features), and foreclosure (e.g., "I am American, not Hispanic") relative to one's multiethnic identity. These issues can be further complicated by differing perceptions from others (e.g., a Korean being derided as "Jap" by White Americans, and "traitor" by relatively more traditional Korean counterparts).

Various writers have elaborated on ways of thinking about minority identity development (e.g., Atkinson et al., 1989; Rowe, Behrens, & Leach, 1995), as well as African American (Cross, 1991, 1995), American Indian (Choney, Berryhill-Paapke, & Robbins, 1995), Asian American (Sodowsky, Kwan, & Pannu, 1995), Hispanic (Casas & Pytluk, 1995), White (Helms, 1990, 1995), and biracial identity (Kerwin & Ponterotto, 1995). Some investigators found that exploration of identity issues was significantly higher among minority group subjects than among a comparison White group, and that self-esteem was related to the extent that minority subjects had thought about and resolved issues of ethnicity (Phinney & Alipura, 1990). In addition, subjects who reported a strong single-ethnic identification (rather than a bicultural identification) were significantly more "separatist," engaged in less cross-ethnic contact out of school, and reported more cross-ethnic conflict (Rotheram-Borus, 1990). Moreover, higher ratings of moratorium or unclear identity status were associated with significantly more behavioral problems, less social competence, and lower self-esteem (Rotheram-Borus, 1989).

Thus, group interventions with minorities should address issues of self-esteem and identity. Comaz-Díaz and Jacobsen (1987) suggest three major therapeutic functions for helping clients deal with issues of identity: (1) reflection of the pieces of a client's identity and societal/environmental sources of his or her identity that contribute to the client's issues with identity, (2) examination of his or her inconsistencies in self-identity, and (3) mediation between the client's ethnocultural identity and personal identity to achieve a more integrated and consolidated sense of self. Leaders need to attend to the ways in which only parts of ethnic identity may be shared or validated and other parts unvoiced or invalidated, and to facilitate explorations that encourage an examination and integration of all sources of minority members' ethnic and racial identities. The more complete and cohesive one's identity, the more meaningful the connections and intimacy one is capable of forging.

Group Applications to Ethnic Minorities

The focus of group intervention may be largely psychotherapeutic, developmental, or preventive (Drum & Lawler, 1988). A psychotherapeutic group is designed primarily to help members repair or reconstruct the self, overcome recurring crises, and resolve lifelong traumas. A developmental group is designed "to facilitate normal development by assisting people in adding new skills or dimensions to their lives, or by providing strategies to help in the resolution of critical issues" (Drum & Lawler, 1988, p. 17). A preventive group is one designed to "prevent or forestall the onset of a problem or need through anticipation of the consequences of non-action" (Drum & Lawler, 1988, p. 17). Each of these types of group interventions may be helpful in working with ethnic minority populations.

The literature suggests success in utilizing group services for ethnic and culturally diverse populations, especially when issues of diversity are incorporated. Levine and Padilla (1980) reported positive results in their review of a number of studies that examined group therapy with Hispanic children, adolescents, and young adults. Comas-Díaz (1981) found that low-income Puerto Rican women who participated in either cognitive or behavioral group therapy showed significant reductions in depression compared to control group patients who received no immediate treatment. Kinzie et al. (1988) found that South Asian refugees' acceptance of group therapy was enhanced when the group maintained a bicultural focus, provided practical information, met concrete needs, and was flexible in its periodic facilitation of formal group psychotherapy. Boulette (1976), who compared assertiveness training with nondirective psychotherapy, found that Mexican American women showed greater gains in self-esteem and in assertiveness through the assertiveness training group. Sutton (1996), who discussed the tremendous challenges of engaging African American men in group therapy, argued that among the advantages for including low-income African American men in mixed groups are that they may confront their fears and biases toward Whites, forge open and honest connections with them, and learn to function more effectively in a mixed environment.

Psychotherapy Groups

The primary purpose of moderate to long-term psychotherapy groups (i.e., months to years) is to repair entrenched, dysfunctional life patterns as well as to provide support with major recurring crises (Drum & Lawler, 1988). Psychotherapy for ethnic minorities offers the opportunity to deal with unique issues. For example, Wyatt (1990) reviewed the literature on sexual abuse of ethnic minority children. While she did not find differences in prevalence of child sexual abuse among different ethnic groups, she suggested that other forms of victimization experienced by minorities (negative sexual stereotypes, racism and discrimination, stigmatization, being considered "less than good," powerlessness, etc.) may complicate the sequelae associated with child sexual abuse and professionals' interpretation of those events.

Another issue that ethnic minorities may face pertains to bicultural conflicts. The extended family is an integral part of numerous American ethnic minority groups, including American Indian (LaFromboise, Berman, & Sohi, 1994), African American (Martin & Martin, 1978), Hispanic (Atkinson et al., 1989; Levine & Padilla, 1980; Martinez, 1993; Romos-McKay, Comas-Díaz, & Rivera, 1988; Sabogal, Marin, Otero-Sabogal, Martin, & Perez-Stable, 1987), and Asian American (Root, 1985). A child who grows up in an ethnic community learns the existence of many sources of love and support. However, when normal family structure and function are disrupted—as with substance abuse, domestic violence, or incest—psychological loyalty and secrecy are reinforced by culture-bound proscriptions against self-disclosure of family secrets, complicating damage to psychological development and intensifying isolation in resultant trauma. Group psychotherapy may be a treatment of choice, sequential to or concurrent with individual psychotherapy (Briere, 1989; Courtois, 1988), for those survivors whose combination of psychological resources and vulnerabilities allows them to benefit from advantages commonly associated with group work (Briere, 1989). Group leaders should become knowledgeable about minority clients' cultural perspectives and realities as well as be able to provide broader alternative intercultural perspectives that encourage the development of sexual norms and values as they relate to child sexual abuse (Courtois, 1988).

Developmental Groups

Developmental group interventions empower participants by promoting the acquisition or enhancement of critical life skills after the need for help arises (Drum & Lawler, 1988). Assertiveness training groups are an example of developmental interventions. Comas-Díaz and Duncan (1985) and Wood and Mallinckrodt (1990) have described the importance of sensitivity to cultural context in assertiveness training, particularly with regard to value differences regarding assertiveness, including the importance of teaching the client about values held in the majority society. The client must be empowered to make choices as she or he implements assertive skills, but the choice of how to behave must always remain with the client.

Groups for college students that focus on the challenges and milestone opportunities accompanying leaving home are another example of developmental interventions. Moving into adulthood brings with it many developmental tasks. One of those tasks involves redefining one's relationship with parents, from being a dependent child to an independent adult. Ethnic minorities have the same developmental task as other young adults; however, some minority group members may experience complications in that process, especially if their cultural values prioritize family over the individual (Sung, 1985; Szapocznik et al., 1980). A person from an Hispanic or Asian family may experience confusion and perhaps even conflict in the process of changing his or her relationships with parents, especially if White peers are used as models for that process. A goal of a developmental group intervention would thus be to support and strengthen the relationship of ethnic minority group members with their parents in terms of relational differentiation, as opposed to separation individuation (Surrey, 1987), in a context that integrates their bicultural or multicultural realities, values, and needs.

Preventative Groups

Preventative group interventions are similar to developmental group interventions in that both are highly preplanned, focused on a single issue, and attempt to raise consciousness and educate. However, preventative interventions are intended to occur before the need for help arises (Drum & Lawler, 1988). Learning theories usually form the foundation of preventative and developmental group interventions, but behavioral, experiential, and in-depth psychodynamic explorations can be effective in all group interventions at times. A time-limited structured psychoeducational group is generally the format of a preventive group intervention. Some examples include workshops on date rape prevention, safe sex, the dangers of alcohol, interracial dating, and so on.

Summary

In this chapter, we presented our threefold philosophy and approaches for providing group interventions with ethnic minorities; they are the process, multicultural perspective, and feminist perspective. We elaborated on the latter two approaches to address the importance of incorporating relevant issues of diversity and oppression in the facilitation of process observations, feedback, and experimentation in both homogeneous and heterogeneous groups. We discussed advantages and challenges of ethnically/racially homogeneous and heterogeneous group compositions, challenges and tasks for group leaders, and basic group processes. Finally, we described the use of psychotherapeutic, developmental, and preventative group interventions.

REFERENCES

Abell, R. G. (1959). Personality development during group psychotherapy: Its relation to the etiology and treatment of neurosis. *American Journal of Psychoanalysis, 19,* 53–70.

Akamatsu, N. N. (1998). The talking oppression blues: Including the experience of power/powerlessness in the teaching of "cultural sensitivity." In M. McGoldrick (Ed.), *Re-visioning family therapy: Race, culture, and gender in clinical practice* (pp. 129–143). New York: The Guilford Press.

Alonso, A. (1987). Discussion of women's groups led by women. *International Journal of Group Psychotherapy, 37,* 155–162.

Andronico, M. P. (Ed.). (1996). *Men in groups: Insights, interventions, and psychoeducational work.* Washington, DC: American Psychological Association.

Arcaya, J. M. (1996). The Hispanic male in group psychotherapy. In M. P. Andronico, *Men in groups: Insights, interventions, and psychoeducational work* (pp. 163–179). Washington, DC: American Psychological Association.

Atkinson, D. R., Morten, G., & Sue, D. W. (1989). *Counseling American minorities.* Dubuque, IA: Wm. C. Brown Company Publishers.

Atkinson, D. R., & Wampold, B. E. (1993). Mexican Americans' initial preferences for counselors: Simple choice can be misleading—Comment on Lopez, Lopez, and Fong (1991). *Journal of Counseling Psychology, 40,* 245–248.

Avila, D. L., & Avila, A. L. (1988). Mexican Americans. In N. A. Vacc, J. Wittmer, & S. DeVaney (Eds.), *Experiencing and counseling multicultural and diverse populations* (2nd ed., pp. 289–316). Muncie, IN: Accelerated Development.

Baruth, L. G., & Manning, M. L. (1991). *Multicultural counseling and psychotherapy: A lifetime perspective.* New York: Merrill.

Bennis, W. G., & Shepard, H. A. (1974). A theory of group development. In G. S. Gibbard, J. H. Hartman, & R. Mann (Eds.). *Analysis of groups, contributions to theory, research and practice* (pp. 127–153). San Francisco: Jossey-Bass.

Bernardez, T. (1983). Women's groups. In M. Rosenbaum (Ed.). *Handbook of short-term therapy groups* (pp. 119–138). New York: McGraw-Hill.

Bertcher, J. J. (1979). *Group participation: Techniques for leaders and members.* Beverly Hills, CA: Sage.

Boulette, R. T. (1976). Assertive training with low-income Mexican American women. In M. R. Miranda (Ed.), *Psychotherapy with the Spanish-speaking: Issues in research and service delivery. Monograph 3* (pp. 73–84). Los Angeles: Spanish Speaking Mental Health Research Center, University of California.

Boyd-Franklin, N. (1987). Group therapy for Black women: A therapeutic support model. *American Journal of Orthopsychiatry, 57,* 394–401.

Boyd-Franklin, N. (1991). Recurrent themes in the treatment of African-American women in group psychotherapy. *Women and Therapy, 11,* 25–40.

Boykin, A. W. (1986). The triple quandary and the schooling of Afro-American children. In U. Neisser (Ed.), *The school achievement of minority children* (pp. 57–92). Hillsdale, NJ: Erlbaum.

Briere, J. (1989). *Therapy for adults molested as children: Beyond survival.* New York: Springer Publishing Company.

Casas, J. M., & Pytluk, S. D. (1995). Hispanic identity development: Implications for research and practice. In J. G. Ponterotto, J. M. Casas, L. A. Suzuki, & C. M. Alexander (Eds.), *Handbook of multicultural counseling* (pp. 155–180). Thousand Oaks, CA: Sage.

Choney, S. K., Berryhill-Paapke, E., & Robbins, R. R. (1995). In J. G. Ponterotto, J. M. Casas, L. A. Suzuki, & C. M. Alexander (Eds.), *Handbook of multicultural counseling* (pp. 73–92). Thousand Oaks, CA: Sage.

Chu, J., & Sue, S. (1984). Asian/Pacific Americans and group practice. *Social Work with Groups, 7,* 23–36.

Comas-Díaz, L. (1981). Effects of cognitive and behavioral group treatment on the depressive symptomatology of Puerto Rican women. *Journal of Consulting and Clinical Psychological, 49,* 627–632.

Comas-Díaz, L. (1984). Content themes in group treatment with Puerto Rican women. *Social Work with Groups, 7*(3), 75–84.

Comas-Díaz, L. (1988). Cross cultural mental health treatment. In L. Comas-Díaz, & E. E. H. Griffith (Eds.), *Clinical guidelines in cross-cultural mental health* (pp. 337–361). New York: John Wiley.

Comas-Díaz, L., & Duncan, J. W. (1985). The cultural context: A factor in the assertiveness training with mainland Puerto Rican women. *Psychology of Women Quarterly, 9*(4), 463–475.

Comas-Díaz, L., & Griffith, E. E. H. (Eds.). (1988). *Clinical guidelines in cross-cultural mental health.* New York: John Wiley.

Comas-Díaz, L., & Jacobsen, F. M. (1987). Ethnocultural identification in psychotherapy. *Psychiatry, 50,* 232–241.

Corey, G. (1990). *Theory and practice of group counseling* (3rd ed.). Pacific Grove, CA: Brooks/Cole.

Courtois, C. A. (1988). *Healing the incest wound: Adult survivors in therapy.* New York: W. W. Norton & Company, Inc.

Cross, W. E., Jr. (1987). A two-factor theory of Black identity: Implications for the study of identity development in minority children. In L. Phinney & M. Rotheram (Eds.), *Children's ethnic socialization: Pluralism and development* (pp. 117–133). Beverly Hills, CA: Sage.

Cross, W. E., Jr. (1991). *Shades of Black: Diversity in African-American identity.* Philadelphia: Temple University Press.

Cross, W. E., Jr. (1995). The psychology of Nigrescence: Revising the Cross model. In J. G. Ponterotto, J. M. Casas, L. A. Suzuki, & C. M. Alexander (Eds.), *Handbook of multicultural counseling* (pp. 93–122). Thousand Oaks, CA: Sage.

Davis, L. E. (1984). Essential components of group work with Black Americans. *Ethnicity in Group Work Practice, 7,* 97–109.

Drum, D. J., & Lawler, A. C. (1988). *Developmental interventions: Theories, principles, and practice.* Columbus, OH: Merrill Publishing Company.

Ettin, M. (1988). The advent of group psychotherapy. *International Journal of Group Psychology, 38,* 139–167.

Fedele, N. M., & Harrington, E. A. (1990). Women's groups: How connections heal. *Work in Progress, No. 47.* Wellesley, MA: Stone Center Working Paper Series.

Fenster, A. (1996). Group therapy as an effective treatment modality for people of color. *International Journal of Group Psychotherapy, 46*(3), 399–416.

Fiske, S. T. (1998). Stereotyping, prejudice, and discrimination. In D. T. Gilbert, S. T. Fiske, & G. Lindsey (Eds.), *The handbook of social psychology* (4th ed.), volume 11, 357–414.

Gladding, S. T. (1991). *Group work: A counseling specialty.* New York: Merrill.

Helms, J. E. (Ed.). (1990). *Black and White racial identity: Theory, research and practice.* Westport, CT: Greenwood Press.

Helms, J. E. (1995). An update of Helms' White and people of color racial identity models. In J. G. Ponterotto, J. M. Casas, L. A. Suzuki, & C. M. Alexander (Eds.), *Handbook of multicultural counseling* (pp. 181–198). Thousand Oaks, CA: Sage.

Ho, M. K. (1984). Social group work with Asian/Pacific-Americans. In L. E. Davis (Ed.), *Ethnicity in social work practice* (pp. 49–61). New York: Haworth Press.

Johnson, D. W., & Johnson, F. P. (1994). *Joining together: Group theory and group skills* (5th ed.). Boston: Allyn and Bacon.

Jordan, J. (1989). Relational development: Therapeutic implications of empathy and shame. *Work in Progress, No. 23.* Wellesley, MA: Stone Center Working Paper Series.

Kaplan, H. I., & Sadock, B. J. (Eds.). (1993). *Comprehensive group psychotherapy* (3rd ed.). Baltimore: Williams & Wilkins.

Kaufman, J., & Timmers, R. L. (1986). Searching for the hairy man. *Women and Therapy, 4,* 45–57.

Kaul, J. J., & Bednar, R. L. (1986). Experiential group research: Results, questions, and suggestions. In S. L. Garfield & A. E. Bergin (Eds.), *Handbook of psychotherapy and behavior change* (3rd ed., pp. 671–714). New York: John Wiley & Sons.

Kerwin, C., & Ponterotto, J. G. (1995). Biracial identity development: Theory and research. In J. G. Ponterotto, J. M. Casas, L. A. Suzuki, & C. M. Alexander (Eds.), *Handbook of multicultural counseling* (pp. 199–217). Thousand Oaks, CA: Sage.

Kinzie, J. D., Leung, P., Bui, A., Ben, R., et al. (1988). Group therapy with Southeast Asian refugees. *Community Mental Health Journal, 24*(2), 157–166.

LaFromboise, T. D., Berman, J. S., & Sohi, B. K. (1994). American Indian women. In L. Comas-Díaz & B. Greene (Eds.), *Women of color: Integrating ethnic and gender identities in psyhotherapy* (pp. 30–71). New York: Guilford Press.

Lakin, M. (1985). *The helping group: Therapeutic principles and issues.* Reading, MA: Addison-Wesley.

Leong, F. T. L., Wagner, N. S., & Kim, H. H. (1995). Group counseling expectations among Asian American students: The role of culture-specific factors. *Journal of Counseling Psychology, 42(2),* 217–222.

Levine, E. S., & Padilla, A. M. (1980). *Crossing cultures in therapy: Pluralistic counseling for the Hispanic.* Monterey, CA: Brooks/Cole.

López, S. R., & López, A. A. (1993). Mexican Americans' initial preferences for counselors: Research methodologies or researchers' values? *Journal of Counseling Psychology, 40,* 249–251.

López, S. R., & López, A. A., & Fong, K. T. (1991). Mexican Americans' initial preferences for counselors: The role of ethnic factors. *Journal of Counseling Psychology, 38,* 487–496.

Martin, E. P., & Martin, J. M. (1978). *The Black extended family.* Chicago: University of Chicago Press.

Martinez, C. Jr. (1993). Psychiatric care of Mexican Americans. In A. C. Gaw (Ed.), *Culture, ethnicity, and mental illness* (pp. 431–466). Washington, DC: American Psychiatric Press.

Mays, V. M. (1986). Black women and stress: Utilization of self-help groups for stress reduction. *Women and Therapy, 4,* 67–79.

McLeod, L. W., & Pemberton, B. K. (1984). Men together in group therapy. *Voices: Art and Science of Psychotherapy, 20,* 63–69.

Merta, R. J. (1995). Group work: Multicultural perspectives. In J. G. Ponterotto, J. M. Casas., L. A. Suzuki, & C. A. Alexander (Eds.), *Handbook of multicultural counseling* (pp. 567–585). Thousand Oaks, CA: Sage.

Miller, J. B. (1986). *Toward a new psychology of women* (2nd ed.). Boston: Beacon Press.

Miller, J. B. (1988). Connections, disconnections and violations. *Work in Progress, No. 33.* Wellesley, MA: Stone Center Working Paper Series.

Nayman, R. L. (1983). Group work with Black women: Some issues and guidelines. *Journal for Specialists in Group Work, 8,* 31–38.

Pack-Brown, S. P., Whittington-Clark, L. E., & Parker, W. M. (1998). *Images of me: A guide to group work with African American women.* Boston: Allyn and Bacon, Inc.

Padilla, A. M. (1993, February). Growing up in two cultures. Keynote speech presented at The Tenth Annual Teachers College Winter Roundtable on Cross-Cultural Counseling and Psychotherapy, New York City.

Phinney, J. S., & Alipura, L. L. (1990). Ethnic identity in college students from four ethnic groups. *Journal of Adolescence, 13,* 171–183.

Ramirez, M. III (1984). Assessing and understanding biculturalism-multiculturalism. In J. L. Martinez & R. H. Mendoza (Eds.), *Chicano psychology* (2nd ed., pp. 77–94). New York: Academic Press.

Ramirez, M. III (1998). *Multicultural/multiracial psychology: Mestiso perspectives in personality and mental health.* Northvale, NJ: Jason Aronson.

Romos-McKay, J. M., Comas-Díaz, L., & Rivera, L. A. (1988). Puerto Ricans. In L. Comas-Díaz & E. E. H. Griffith (Eds.), *Clinical guidelines in cross-cultural mental health* (pp. 204–232). New York: John Wiley.

Root, M. (1985). Guidelines for facilitating therapy with Asian American clients. *Psychotherapy, 22,* 349–357.

Rotheram-Borus, M. J. (1989). Ethnic differences in adolescents' identity status and associated behavioral problems. Special issue: Adolescent identity: An appraisal of health and intervention. *Journal of Adolescence, 12,* 361–374.

Rotheram-Borus, M. J. (1990). Adolescents' reference-group choices, self-esteem, and adjustment. *Journal of Personality & Social Psychology, 59,* 1075–1081.

Rotheram-Borus, M. J. (1993). Biculturalism among adolescents. In M. E. Bernal & G. P. Knight (Eds.), *Ethnic identity: Formation and transmission among Hispanic and other minorities* (pp. 81–102). Albany, NY: SUNY Press.

Rowe, W., Behrens, J., & Leach, M. M. (1995). Racial/ethnic identity and racial consciousness: Looking back and looking forward. In J. G. Ponterotto, J. M. Casas, L. A. Suzuki, & C. M. Alexander (Eds.), *Handbook of multicultural counseling* (pp. 218–235). Thousand Oaks, CA: Sage.

Sabogal, F., Marin, G., Otero-Sabogal, R., Martin, B. V., & Perez-Stable, E. J. (1987). Hispanic familism and acculturation: What changes and what doesn't? *Hispanic Journal of Behavioral Sciences, 9,* 397–412.

Shen W. W., Sanchez, A. M., & Huang, T. (1984). Verbal participation in group therapy: A comparative study on New Mexico ethnic groups. *Hispanic Journal of Behavior Sciences, 6,* 277–284.

Sodowski, G. R., Kwan, K. K., & Pannu, R. (1995). Ethnic identity of Asians in the United States. In J. G. Ponterotto, J. M. Casas, L. A. Suzuki, & C. M. Alexander (Eds.), *Handbook of multicultural counseling* (pp. 123–154). Thousand Oaks, CA: Sage.

Sue, D. (1996). Asian men in groups. In M. P. Andronico (Ed.), *Men in groups: Insights, interventions, and psychoeducational work* (pp. 69–80). Washington, DC: American Psychological Association.

Sue, D. W. (1981). *Counseling the culturally different: Theory and practice.* New York: John Wiley.

Sue, S. (1998). In search of cultural competence in psychotherapy and counseling. *American Psychologist, 53*(4), 440–448.

Sue, S., Fujino, D. C., Hu, L., Takeuchi, D. T., & Zane, N. W. S. (1991). Community mental health services for ethnic minority groups: A test of the cultural responsiveness hypothesis. *Journal of Consulting and Clinical Psychology, 59,* 533–540.

Sung, B. L. (1985). Bicultural conflicts in Chinese immigrant children. Special Issue: Family, kinship, and ethnic identity among the Overseas Chinese. *Journal of Comparative Family Studies, 16,* 255–269.

Surrey, J. L. (1987). Relationship and empowerment. *Work in Progress, No. 30.* Wellesley, MA: Stone Center Working Paper Series.

Sutton, A. (1996). African American men in group therapy. In M. P. Andronico (Ed.), *Men in groups: Insights, interventions, and psychoeducational work* (pp. 131–149). Washington, DC: American Psychological Association.

Szapocznik, J., Kurtines, W., & Fernandez, A. (1980). Bicultural involvement and adjustment in Hispanic-American youth. *International Journal of Intercultural Relations, 4,* 353–365.

Talley, J. E. & Rockwell, W. J. (1985). *Counseling and psychotherapy services for university students.* Springfield, IL: Thomas.

Tatum, B. D. (1993). Racial identity development and relational theory: The case of Black women in White communities. *Work in Progress No. 63.* Wellesley, MA: Stone Center Working Paper Series.

Tsui, P., & Schultz, G. L. (1988). Ethnic factors in group process: Cultural dynamics in multi-ethnic therapy groups. *American Journal of Orthopsychiatry, 58*(1), 136–142.

Unger, R. (1989). Selection and composition criteria in group psychotherapy. *Journal for Specialists in Group Work, 14*(3), 151–157.

Van Wormer, K. (1989). The male-specific group in alcoholism treatment. *Small Group Behavior, 20,* 228–242.

White, J. G. (1994). The impact of race and ethnicity on transference and countertransference in combined individual/group therapy. *Group, 18*(2), 89–99.

Wolf, A., & Schwartz, E. K. (1962). *Psychoanalysis in groups.* New York: Grune & Stratton.

Wood, P. S., & Mallinckrodt, B. (1990). Culturally sensitive assertiveness training for ethnic minority clients. *Professional Psychology: Research and Practice, 21,* 5–11.

Wrenn, C. G. (1985). Afterward: The culturally encapsulated counselor revisited. In P. Pederson (Ed.), *Handbook of cross-cultural counseling and therapy* (pp. 323–329). Westport, CT: Greenwood Press.

Wyatt, G. E. (1990). Sexual abuse of ethnic minority children: Identifying dimensions of victimization. *Professional Psychology: Research and Practice, 21,* 338–343.

Yalom, I. (1985). *The theory and practice of group psychotherapy* (3rd ed.). New York: Basic Books.

Yalom, I. (1995). *The theory and practice of group psychotherapy* (4th ed.). New York: Basic Books.

8 Community Approaches with Ethnic Populations

JOSEPH F. APONTE

HOWARD F. BRACCO

Goodstein and Sandler (1978) identified several approaches by which the field of psychology can be used to enhance human welfare. These approaches included *clinical psychology, community mental health, community psychology,* and *public policy psychology.* This chapter will focus on the *community mental health* and *community psychology* models and the strategies inherent in them. Both of these approaches extend their interventions beyond "troubled individuals" to the community as reflected in the *community mental health* model, and to social systems that are of importance in socializing, supporting, and managing people (e.g., school system, churches, prisons, judicial system) as exemplified in the *community psychology* model.

These approaches focus on the environmental, social, community, and institutional forces that lead to the development of problems or that prevent people from developing as effective human beings. Such a framework is particularly important for ethnic persons who are often blamed for their plight, while, oftentimes being the victims of oppression, racism, prejudice, and discrimination (Aponte & Barnes, 1995; Shapiro, 1975). An approach that focuses on the community will begin to address these experiences and their consequences.

This chapter will focus on community-based approaches. A discussion of *community mental health* approaches and their effectiveness with ethnic clientele is followed by a description of *community psychology* and alternative service delivery models and their common elements. Particular emphasis is placed on prevention and consultation efforts, elements that cut across these models. Several illustrative programs created for ethnic populations that exemplify these common elements are discussed. Finally, guidelines for providing community-based services and intervention strategies are presented.

Community Mental Health Approaches

The community mental health revolution had its roots in the early work of such pioneers as Dorothea Dix, Samuel Tuke, Clifford Beers, Adolph Meyer, Eric Lindemann, and Maxwell Jones (Bloom, 1984; Cutler, 1992), eventually culminating in the formation of the Joint

Commission on Mental Illness and Mental Health and the subsequent publication, in 1961, of the commission report entitled *Action for Mental Health* (Appel & Bartemier, 1961). This report was the basis for President John F. Kennedy's historical proposal for a new national mental health program and the appropriation of funds for planning grants for the program (Kennedy, 1963).

After the death of President Kennedy, Public Law 88–164 (the Community Mental Health Centers Act of 1963) was passed by the United States Congress. This and subsequent legislation provided funding for the construction and staffing of a network of community mental health centers (CMHCs) to be located in 1500 designated catchment areas in the United States. The act required that the centers provide five essential services: inpatient, outpatient, emergency, partial hospitalization, and consultation and education. These basic services were viewed as the vehicles for addressing the mental health needs of the country.

Bloom (1984) has noted a number of characteristics of the community mental health movement that were embedded in CMHCs, several of which have direct relevance to ethnic groups. These include an emphasis on: (1) the delivery of services or practice in the community, (2) comprehensiveness and continuity of services, (3) disease-prevention and health-promotion services, (4) innovative clinical strategies designed to meet the needs of community residents, (5) tapping new sources of personnel, including paraprofessionals and indigenous mental health workers, (6) community control, and (7) identifying and eliminating sources of stress within the community.

The early years of the community mental health movement were characterized by great enthusiasm, high expectations, much optimism, and rapid development of CMHCs (Cutler, 1992). Many amendments to the original CMHC legislation provided additional funding for the centers, either for categorical services (e.g., substance abuse) or for specific populations (e.g., children, chronically mentally ill, elderly). Ethnic minorities were also recognized as an underserved population in the 1960s and 1970s (Vega & Murphy, 1990). However, efforts to increase funding for this group, as well as other high-risk groups, were scuttled by the Omnibus Budget Reconciliation Act (OBRA) of President Reagan, which deeply cut funding for all mental health programs (Foley & Sharfstein, 1983).

In addition to the direct consequences of reduction in funds, the OBRA had a number of far-reaching effects. The Act introduced the concept of "block grants," which clearly shifted responsibility for funding and designing community mental health services from federal agencies to state mental health authorities (Wilkinson, 1984). Given that state priorities tend to focus on severe mental illness, emphasis on prevention, consultation, and education services, including outreach to ethnic minorities, was reduced (Drolen, 1990; Hargrove & Melton, 1987). OBRA also began a shift from concern about the delivery of health services to a concern about health costs (Rabiner, 1986).

Despite the Reagan administration budget cuts, the majority of the CMHCs remained open (Hadley & Culhane, 1993). During the 1990s, however, in an effort to contain health care costs, a variety of "managed care systems" were developed, including Utilization Review Organizations (UROs), Health Maintenance Organizations (HMOs), and Preferred Provider Organizations (PPOs). These systems are basically designed to reduce either the rates at which services are used or the average cost per unit of service (DeLeon, Vandenbos, & Bulatao, 1991; Frank & Vandenbos, 1994; Hersch, 1995). A number of CMHCs are already operating as managed care systems, perhaps because of the opportunity this approach affords to generate revenues for programs—particularly in light of escalating health care costs and dwindling financial resources (Broskowski & Marks, 1992).

Another strategy being employed by community mental health centers is the development of joint ventures with private, for-profit managed care companies to form provider-owned networks. Partnerships have been formed in Oregon, Tennessee, and Vermont. These organizations range from $2 million to $40 million in size (Ray, 1995). Over 40 states have converted, or are currently in the process of converting, their Medicaid programs to managed care. In most of these states, private managed care companies and community mental health centers are joining together to secure state contracts to deliver mental health services.

Although ethnic groups were clearly an underserved targeted population in the *community mental health* movement, the efforts of planners, service providers, and practitioners have met with mixed results. Some studies have found that African Americans and American Indians overutilized services in comparison to their proportion of the general population, whereas Hispanics and Asian Americans underutilized services (Sue, 1977; Sue, Chun, & Gee, 1995). More recent data reveal greater utilization rates for these populations (O'Sullivan, Peterson, Cox, & Kirkeby, 1989), while others have found trends similar to the older data (Bui & Takeuchi, 1992; Snowden & Cheung, 1990; Sue, Fujino, Hu, Takeuchi, & Zane, 1991).

Early research consistently found that ethnic clients had more premature terminations and stayed in treatment for fewer sessions than Whites (Sue, 1977). More recent research showed that these differences have diminished (O'Sullivan et al., 1989; Sue et al., 1995); however, it has been noted that large differences among ethnic groups still remain (Hu, Snowden, Jerrell, & Nguyen, 1991; Sue et al., 1991). Sue and his colleagues (1991) found that African Americans had a significantly higher proportion of dropouts than all other groups, whereas Asian Americans, once in treatment, had a lower proportion of dropouts than Whites. Asian Americans tended to stay longer in treatment, and African Americans tended to stay in treatment for shorter periods than Whites (Bui & Takeuchi, 1992; Sue et al., 1991).

Little research has been published on treatment outcomes for mental health services received by ethnic clients (see Chapter 14 for an extensive discussion of this topic). The data available indicate that ethnic clients, in general, do not experience outcomes as successful as those of White clients. Closer scrutiny of studies reveals differential outcomes among ethnic groups: African Americans do not have treatment outcomes as successful as Whites, Hispanics, or Asian American clients, even when socioeconomic status is controlled (Sue et al., 1991; 1995). These findings, coupled with disproportionately high dropout rates and shorter lengths of stay in treatment, put African Americans, particularly, at high risk in the mental health system.

Many of the studies available have not controlled for differences in socioeconomic status (SES) and diagnosis (Cheung & Snowden, 1990; Snowden, Storey, & Clancy, 1989). When such variables are controlled statistically, differences in utilization rates, premature termination, length of stay in treatment, and treatment outcomes tend to diminish. Despite these attenuation effects, however, many barriers to service utilization by ethnic populations still exist, including lack of familiarity with mental health services, lack of availability of services, cost of services, organizational barriers, and culturally unresponsive services (Aponte, 1997; Atkinson, Morten, & Sue, 1998; Cheung & Snowden, 1990; LaFromboise, 1988; Loo, Tong, & True, 1989; Taube & Rupp, 1986).

The progression of managed care, the blurring of public and private sector boundaries, and the integration of traditional nonprofit with for-profit values create an uncertain impact on the community mental movement and the mental health care of ethnic populations. Will privatization in combination with managed care reduce help-seeking on the part of these populations, or will the high risk of hospitalization create incentives for outreach and early intervention to prevent expensive hospitalizations? There is concern that managed care will pose increased barriers to access, particularly when combined with a profit motive (Davis, 1997). In 1998, concerns regarding managed care abuses in the private sector led to a proliferation of patient rights bills before the U.S. Congress and a multitude of state legislatures. Others optimistically have noted that many of the leaders in the private managed care industry came from the public sector and have "deep roots in the community mental health movement." They have argued that social and business missions can be balanced permitting "profit with honor."

Cost-effective ways of delivering mental health services to ethnic populations have been developed. Jerrell (1995) found that ethnic matching between clients and therapists resulted in annual cost savings of about $1,000 per matched client. Outcomes of this nature provide incentives to provide culturally appropriate and competent services. The merging of public and private systems can also further the elimination of a "two-tiered" system of health care (Shaffer et al., 1995). These factors in combination with the direct involvement of consumers in the design and delivery of services can promote a behavioral health care system that is accessible, available, appropriate, and acceptable to a diverse population—fulfilling the original mission of the community mental health movement.

Community Psychology Approaches

The previous discussion of traditional *community mental health* services offered to ethnic clients through the local CMHC described the underutilization of existing services, high dropout rates, premature termination, and general dissatisfaction with these services. The overall effectiveness of the model and its implementation with all groups has also been challenged (Bloom, 1984; Chu, 1974). Many psychologists argued that rather than correcting those shortcomings of the *community mental health* movement it was necessary to turn to another approach that had a different theoretical, practice, and research base. Such an approach was that of *community psychology,* which developed in part because of dissatisfaction with more traditional approaches to helping people (Anderson et al., 1966).

Psychologists adhering to a *community psychology* approach focus their attention on identifying and helping to eliminate deleterious environmental, social, and institutional conditions that affect all members of a population (Iscoe, Bloom, & Spielberger, 1977; Rappaport, 1977). Community psychologists do not restrict the scope of their concern to those with established disorders (Heller et al., 1984). Instead, they tend to focus on situational or contextual contributors to an individual's problems and argue that, whereas individual change can promote a better person-environment fit, efforts to change the environment and social context are often more appropriate targets for intervention.

A *community psychology* approach to mental health service delivery is decidedly different in its assumptions, goals, research, and practices than those of traditional clinical and *community mental health* approaches (Iscoe et al., 1977). *Community psychology* has an organizational-community, nondeficit, competence-building, and primary-prevention focus (Bloom, 1984; McClure et al., 1980). Differentiation from *community mental health,* however, according to McClure et al., (1980) has been realized only in its theoretical underpinnings—not in its practice. One key ingredient to the *community psychology* approach is the construct of empowerment (Florin & Wandersman, 1990; Heller et al., 1984; Zimmerman, 1990).

Rappaport (1984) suggests that empowerment can best be understood in the context of what it is not—by seeing it as the absence of alienation, powerlessness, and helplessness. These feelings are often experienced and endured by ethnic group members who are subjected to oppression, racism, discrimination, and limited economic opportunities. Parsons (1989) speaks of empowerment as a process that enables people to master their environment and achieve self-determination. Galan (1988) defines empowerment as self-accountability, a developmental process by which individuals first come to believe in their own competencies for self-mastery, and second, become willing to act on behalf of their own best interests. Gutiérrez and Ortega (1991) describe three levels of empowerment: the personal level, the interpersonal level, and political empowerment. The last level emphasizes the goals of social action and social change.

Common Elements of Alternative Community Service Delivery Models

Alternative community service delivery models seek to incorporate approaches that can have, or have had, demonstrated effectiveness with ethnic populations and clientele. Such approaches, subsumed under the heading of alternative community service delivery models, have been used in different settings (e.g., urban, rural) and with different ethnic groups. Borrowing from the *community mental health model,* there is a focus on the "catchment area" or community being served, coupled with a strong emphasis on active community board involvement. From the *community psychology model,* alternative programs also focus on efforts to remediate negative environmental, social, and institutional forces.

Alternative community service delivery models emphasize a number of common elements, including: (1) ecological validity, (2) a multiproblem approach, (3) a commitment to interagency collaboration and coordination, (4) employment of bilingual and bicultural staff, (5) use of paraprofessionals, (6) development of cultural competency with helping networks, (7) strengthening social support networks, (8) use of prevention and consultation strategies, and (9) use of culturally compatible service delivery models. Each of these elements is particularly relevant to ethnic persons and will be discussed in the following sections.

Emphasis on Ecological Validity

To achieve ecological validity, the delivery of mental health services must be designed to be consonant with, and less disruptive of, the ongoing relationships, strengths, and resources within the "ecosystem" or community. Rather than relying on the traditional office-based model, nearly all alternative models advocate and deliver treatment in the community. Many programs offer services through local churches, housing projects, beauty and barber shops, malls, and other community facilities frequented by ethnic persons. Such increased availability of services enhances their utilization by low-income groups, especially those who may have had difficulty accessing traditional office-based services due to transportation problems.

Going to where clients are, especially ethnic clients whose cultural environment may be quite different from that of the mental health professional, lessens client defenses and encourages the development of empathy, understanding, and rapport on the part of the mental health professional by providing him or her with a realistic and practical understanding of that client's daily demands and stressors. Furthermore, community-based service produces more accurate pictures of needs, consequent goal setting, and outcome evaluation. Due to a more accurate needs assessment, the duration, type, and intensity of services can be tailored to meet the specific needs of the individual client. Given the heterogeneity of ethnic groups, such individualization of service delivery is by far more appropriate than the often traditional reliance on "prepackaged" services (Vega & Murphy, 1990).

Emphasis on a Multiproblem Approach

Most traditional human service delivery systems are organized and financed around targeted categories of problems—for example, income needs, housing, delinquency, substance abuse, and mental health. The ever-increasing caseloads for human service workers may also contribute to a narrowing of focus in that they rarely consult with each other and may even develop treatment goals that run counter to each other. For ethnic people in need of many services, such decentralization requires clients to establish several effective working relationships with White middle-class agency staff, successfully negotiate each agency's procedures, organize their appointments, and work toward diverse goals.

Alternative community service delivery models assume a systemic perspective in which adaptive individual and family functioning has, most likely, been impaired by many different and interacting problems. Service providers in these models are deliberately charged with the responsibility to recognize and respond to a range of presenting needs, a tenet requiring that services offered must be comprehensive (Vega & Murphy, 1990). Effective service delivery to those with multiple problems requires the mental health worker to slip in and out of many various roles—teacher, therapist, advocate, organizer, and case manager, to name a few. A broader, more comprehensive focus must be maintained if ethnic clients are to be empowered to act more effectively on their own behalf.

Commitment to Interagency Collaboration and Coordination

Because of the array and complexity of problems with which ethnic clients tend to present to service agencies (Acosta, Yamamoto, & Evans, 1982), particularly if they come from low socioeconomic status or immigrant backgrounds, it is imperative that community agencies collaborate with each other. Such efforts would avoid duplication of services and maintain continuity of care, while also ensuring that community needs are being met. To achieve this latter goal, the value of maintaining an open dialogue with community representatives cannot be overemphasized.

Gordon (1991) illustrates how conflicting attitudes and inaccurate beliefs regarding agency practices on the part of other community agencies, as well as indigenous leaders, can result in both a drop in referral rates and negative expectations regarding the likelihood of receiving effective treatment. In instances where formal and informal linkages were achieved with community groups (e.g., churches), ethnic persons were more aware of services and were also more likely to use them in times of need (Starrett, Todd, Decker, & Walters, 1989). Eng and Hatch (1991) describe an effective lay health advisory model for networking between Black churches and agencies.

Marburg (1983) suggested several mechanisms by which better relations among community organizations could be formed. These included monthly, reciprocal in-service training presentations to provide detailed descriptions of available services, community forums to discuss gaps in service delivery with suggestions for remediation, and attempts to open avenues of communication for the purposes of reducing atmospheres conducive to "turf wars." Such efforts would be beneficial to all service recipients, but would be particularly useful for working with ethnic clients due to the lack of cultural knowledge and practical experience in such relationships.

Employment of Bilingual and Bicultural Staff

High visibility of bilingual, and preferably bicultural, staff not only encourages ethnic members to seek out services initially, but also aids in establishing rapport and helps to build trust among the client, the service provider, and the agency in general (Reeves, 1986). The mental health provider who can converse in the particular language or dialect spoken in the community is in a much better position to understand the symbolism, idiosyncrasies, and life experiences of his or her clients and is therefore in a much better position to provide appropriate services (Preciado & Henry, 1997; see Chapter 2). An additional benefit of employing ethnically similar personnel is the opportunity for these professionals to serve as role models for the ethnic client (Curtis, 1990).

Use of Paraprofessionals

It is recognized in well-organized alternative programs that one of the best ways to establish effective working relationships with ethnic communities is to utilize indigenous resources and paraprofessionals (Granski & Carrillo, 1997; Lefley & Bestman, 1991; Snowden, 1987). Gordon (1991) reported that the most important resource for identification and intervention with Hispanic alcohol abusers is not the treatment professional, but rather, the Hispanic female paraprofessional from the neighborhood with whom the client may already be acquainted. Hispanic women, especially, tended to disclose information regarding alcohol-abusing spouses to Hispanic workers but not to the physician or counselor. Consequently, Gordon suggests that ethnic paraprofessionals should receive special training in problem identification and motivating clients to commit to treatment.

Development of Cultural Competency with Helping Networks

Ethnic persons must continuously grapple with issues of ethnic identity (see Chapter 2). Through this process, many members of ethnic groups adaptively struggle to develop cultural competencies with both their culture and the majority culture, thereby filtering advantages from both as best they can. Whereas some are remarkably successful in their endeavors, others experience rejection, ridicule, and lack a sense of true belonging to either group. Given the fact that they often come into mental health treatment via other community agencies such as the court, social services, or school, some ethnic clients may lack sophistication regarding the different responsibilities of the many agencies to which they are referred. Such experiences, coupled with the insensitivity sometimes exhibited by White middle-class professionals, can lead to problems for the ethnic person in the mental health system.

Many alternative models recognize the need to teach ethnic clients how to network with formal supports available in the community (e.g., job training, public school personnel, medical care professionals, mental health professionals, civic organizations). Workers from programs may accompany ethnic clients on appointments with other service workers to provide support and to model appropriate ways of gathering information, enlisting services, and clearly detailing contractual responsibilities so that the service provider and the client walk away with mutual understandings. In the same way that service providers need to be culturally competent with ethnic cultures, clients need the requisite skills to better represent their needs, abilities, and expectations to the majority culture.

Strengthening Social Support Networks

Social support networks are used extensively by African Americans, Hispanics, Asian Americans, and American Indians (see Chapter 2). When African Americans receive informal support from family, friends, and other respected individuals in their community, they tend to utilize formal service networks to a greater degree than those with less social support (Eng & Hatch, 1991; Mindel & Wright, 1982; Spence & Atherton, 1991). Building social support networks into treatment interventions through the involvement of family members can lead to enhanced levels of mutual support among family members, more effective dealings with community agencies, and the development of advocacy groups to deal with common social issues (Aponte, Zarski, Bixenstine, & Cibik, 1991; Keefe & Casas, 1980).

Instead of traditional strategies that focus on the community agency as the sole deliverer of services, alternative models suggest that ethnic minorities who may be hesitant to seek formal services may best be helped by utilizing agency resources to organize and strengthen natural helping networks in the community (Mays, 1986). Such self-help groups serve many purposes; they provide mutual support (Gottlieb, 1982), reduce isolation and alienation (Mays, 1986; Parsons, 1989), afford a sense of community and in-group membership (Katz, 1981), encourage the development of personal empowerment to better manage one's own life, and provide opportunities for people to form social action groups for political empowerment (Gutiérrez & Ortega, 1991).

Prevention and Consultation Strategies

Prevention and consultation strategies are often used with alternative community service delivery models. Prevention has traditionally been divided into three categories: *primary, secondary,* and *tertiary* prevention. Heller et al. (1984) suggest the following definitions: *primary prevention* refers to efforts aimed at keeping mental disorders from occurring at all; *secondary prevention* refers to reducing the duration and severity of disorders that do occur; and *tertiary prevention* attempts to minimize the extent of disability or impairment that may result from disorders. Forgays (1991) argues that *secondary* and *tertiary* prevention are not prevention, and it is the focus on *primary prevention* where community-based programs can have a significant impact on the population.

Heller et al. (1984) define *consultation* as "an approach to social change through improvement of existing community organizations and institutions" (p. 231). Consultation efforts are often included in primary prevention programs (Bell, 1987; Mann, 1987), but are more commonly included within secondary prevention programs (DeBruyn, Hymbaugh, & Valdez, 1988; Tolan, Perry, & Jones, 1987; Tyler, Cohen, & Clark, 1982). Consultation efforts target existing networks of primary caregivers and agents of social control, such as teachers, police, ministers, physicians, and welfare workers. Implicit in the operating principles of consultation is that the community has the strengths and expertise to solve its own problems; consultants merely act as catalysts and assistants to motivate and mobilize indigenous community leaders to take action.

Culturally Compatible Service Delivery Models

The organization and delivery of mental health services require them to be culturally compatible with the ethnic populations that they serve. Flaskerud (1986) noted that culturally compatible approaches resulted in improved utilization of mental health services. Locating services in ethnic communities rather than in institutional settings, in combination with increased similarity between the ethnic population by matching language, race, and ethnic culture, lead to the building of trust and rapport (Gottesfeld, 1995). Snowden, Hu, and Jerrell (1995) also found that ethnic and language matching led to improved coping and decreased use of emergency mental health services in mainstream programs.

Different program structures can be developed in CMHCs in order to increase compatibility with the ethnic populations they serve (Uba, 1982; Zane, Hatanaka, Park, & Akutsu, 1994). Services can take the form of (1) training personnel from existing programs to be culturally sensitive; (2) developing independent but parallel services that mirror the mainstream services; and (3) establishing new, nonparallel service programs that are different than the mainstream services (Sue, 1977; Uba, 1982; Zane et al., 1994). Regardless of the program structure the programs need to employ professional and paraprofessional staff who are indigenous to the population being served or who are bicultural and bilingual.

When the surrounding community contains small numbers of ethnic persons, the ethnic staff may be included in teams that serve populations that are heterogeneous in terms of ethnicity, presenting problems, or a combination of the two. In larger communities where there is a diversity of ethnic persons in sufficient number, services may be organized around ethnic teams. Asian American Mental Health Services in New York specializes in services to severely mentally ill adults. It is organized into a Chinese unit, a Japanese Unit, a Korean unit, and a Southeast Asian unit (Sue, 1997). Similarly, many programs in Miami are organized into Cuban, Dominican, and Haitian teams. When the surrounding community is homogeneous, the entire program may be ethnic specific. Ethnic clients in these types of programs are more often self-referred or referred by natural support systems such as family and friends, as compared to ethnic clients who use mainstream programs, indicating higher levels of acceptability (Akutsu, Snowden, & Organista, 1996).

Examples of Community-Based Programs

To illustrate the aforementioned elements of alternative community approaches, several programs will be described in this section. These include: (1) the Black on Black Violence Program developed by Bell (1987); (2) the Little Havana Parent Leadership Program (Szapocznik et al., 1997); (3) the South Cove Community Health Center, which targeted Chinese elderly (Lee & Yee, 1988); and (4) the Target Community Partnership Program, which involved American Indians (Rowe, 1997). Although sometimes targeting specific groups, each of these programs has relevance to all ethnic populations.

Black on Black Violence

Bell (1987) reports that Black males have a 1 in 21 chance of being murdered, whereas White males have a 1 in 121 chance. Similarly, Black females have a 1 in 194 chance, and White females, a 1 in 369 chance. Homicide is the leading cause of death among young Black males; they are 7.6 times more likely to be killed by homicide than their White counterparts (O'Hare, Pollard, Mann, & Kent, 1991). Furthermore, two-thirds to three-fourths of Black homicide victims will know the murderer as family, friend, or acquaintance. Thus, a majority of Black-on-Black murders occur in the context of familiar interpersonal relationships.

To address the devastating effects of such violence on the African American community, Bell's initial efforts were aimed at consciousness raising and support building from both community agencies and the community at large. Toward that end, the following strategies were employed: A series of question-and-answer sessions staffed by experts in interpersonal violence were broadcast on call-in radio programs; an advisory board to the local CMHC was formed; and a citywide, multimedia blitz billed as "No Crime Day" was held. Such efforts had the impact of making the community more aware of the seriousness and nature of the problem.

Surveys of several CMHC's catchment area schools resulted in alarming statistics: Thirty-one percent of second, fourth, sixth, and eighth graders had seen someone shot, 34 percent had seen a person stabbed, and 84 percent had witnessed someone being beaten. Armed with these data, the local CMHC sponsored a retreat for concerned families in order to develop strategies to reduce family violence. Out of this retreat grew a women's support group for battered and abused women and an Elderly Respite Care Service. Other primary prevention strategies included vocational programs to assist clients in starting their own businesses, as well as programs that provided recreational activities to community youth as an alternative to gang membership.

Secondary prevention efforts included the development of a screening instrument used at the CMHC to identify victims of violence. Once identified, clients were referred to the CMHC's Victim Assistance Service for information regarding legal aid. CMHC staff also developed liaison relationships with a community women's shelter in order to safely harbor women and children, and with community ministers to raise their sensitivity to issues of family violence. Thus, both primary and secondary prevention components of the program were comprehensive and involved continuity of services through an array of networks.

Little Havana Parent Leadership Program

Szapocznik and his colleagues (1997) describe the evolution of a structural ecosystems theory for working with Latino families. This approach evolved from the two decades of programmatic theory development, research, and intervention application efforts with Latino families at the Spanish Family Guidance Center at the University of Miami. The ecosystemic approach builds upon the work of Bronfenbrenner (1979, 1986), who identified four contextual systems within which families are embedded: (1) *microsystems,* including family, school, and peers; (2) *mesosystems,* or systems resulting from interactions of microsystems; (3) *exosystems,* or external systems affecting family members; and (4) *macrosystems,* or structures affecting families through regulations and policies.

The Little Havana Parent Leadership Project (Szapocznik et al., 1997) is an experimental program that targets Latino immigrant families with high-risk adolescents between 12 and 15 years of age who are experiencing behavioral problems. Included in these problems are academic failure, chronic truancy, multiple suspensions, and aggressive behavior, all of which place them at risk for becoming involved in gangs. These high-risk adolescents are referred for services by school counselors and are assigned either to a control condition, "treatment as usual," or to the experimental program which was a community-based, multifamily, and parent-focused prevention approach (Szapocznik et al., 1997).

Using concepts derived from structural ecosystems theory, Szapocznik et al. (1997) designed their experimental program and interventions to target the families' *mesosystems* and *exosystems.* A strong social network made up of multiple neighborhood families was created, and parents were instructed in leadership and resource-seeking skills. Parents became involved in their adolescents' peer groups through the organization of field trips and youth team sports. Parents also collaborated with the City of Miami police in crime prevention and in promoting a better understanding of their culture. Through these efforts, Szapocznik and his associates have been able to successfully bridge theory, research, and services.

The South Cove Community Health Center (SCCHC)

Lee and Yee (1988) suggest that the tendency for Asian immigrant populations to live in and depend on closely knit ethnic enclaves (e.g., Chinatowns) may serve to maintain barriers when they interact in Western society. Of particular concern to these authors is the process by which traditional Chinese beliefs about health and illness, language, and the lack of continuity of care act as cultural barriers to adequate health care services for Asian elderly. For example, in traditional Chinese thought, blood is considered a vital entity that cannot be replaced. As a result, many elderly persons actively avoid Western health practitioners who order blood tests for diagnostic purposes.

To improve the accessibility and quality of health care for Chinese elderly in their community, these authors initiated a three-pronged intervention. First, they developed home health care services for debilitated elderly. Staffed by bilingual nurse practitioners, the program provided primary care services in the patient's home. Second, health care services were centralized by establishing satellite medical clinics, also staffed by bilingual personnel, in several elderly housing complexes in and around Chinatown. Third, a health education program, presented to regular meetings of elderly people, provided instruction on various health-related topics as well as a forum in which elderly persons could discuss cultural barriers, learn about the Western system, and learn how better to obtain services for themselves.

Despite these efforts, however, inadequate interagency communication created a lack of effectively coordinated services. To address this lack of coordination, the SCCHC initiated a new project to introduce the role and concept of case management to the elderly Chinese community, to help elderly patients and their families coordinate post-hospital care, and to respond to the loneliness and isolation experienced by many homebound elderly. To address this latter issue, a volunteer program of primarily bilingual high school and college students was developed to regularly visit homebound elderly for companionship.

Target Community Partnership Project

Operating on a culturally consistent model, Rowe (1997) describes a community-based prevention program designed to address American Indian substance abuse problems as well as other related health and social conditions. This prevention project was supported by the Center for Substance Abuse Prevention (SAP) and was designed to change attitudes and behaviors among community members. Enclosed in this comprehensive program were community collaboration between tribal agencies, community empowerment and education, cultural enhancement, and development of support services and networks of tribal members engaged in substance abuse recovery.

An integral part of the project was the creation of the *Chi-e-chees* (a Target Community word for "the workers") from the Tribal Council and church members. This group was highly regarded in the community and involved in all project planning and final decision making around goals, objectives, and programmatic activities. Other key project elements were the establishment of a Youth Council to coordinate and support alcohol and drug-free activities, formation of a tribal Project Steering Committee, establishment of an informal network of tribal staff members, and the training and eventual assumption of Project Coordinator by a tribal member.

The program successfully sponsored 215 cultural and educational events. A comprehensive process and outcome evaluation involving baseline and multiple post-program assessments was implemented based on the Customized Framework for Evaluating Community Partnership Projects (Yin, Kaftarian, & Jacobs, 1996). Programmatic efforts led to a community-wide change in wellness and substance abuse norms, the creation of new communication and collaborative networks, new tribal policies and enforcement practices to curtail drug and alcohol abuse, and the commitment of a significant number of community members to remain sober.

Each of these community-based programs described in this section has elements of the alternative community service delivery models. The programs were particularly consistent with the values, beliefs, and practices within the community, involved a multiproblem approach, included interagency collaboration and coordination, focused on the ethnic individual's developing personal competency in dealing with helping networks, and encouraged the development of social support networks. Some of the programs utilized bilingual staff and paraprofessionals to deliver their services. It was evident from the published reports that all the programs were sensitive and responsive to those community residents they served.

Guidelines for Using Community-Based Approaches with Ethnic Groups

Effective delivery of alternative community services and programs requires effective planning. Such planning needs to be based on detailed information about the community and its residents (Humm-Delgado & Delgado, 1986; Vega & Murphy, 1990). Ethnic community leaders and residents should be invited and warmly welcomed to the needs assessment planning in order to ensure that program goals are consistent with community-held values and to customize services, thereby enhancing a sense of community ownership of the program (Bell, 1987; Heller, 1992; Tyler et al., 1982). The needs assessment can take the form of using key informant, community survey, and social area analysis strategies (Aponte, 1983; Aponte & Young, 1981).

Those services and programs directed at ethnic populations need to be conceptualized, developed, and implemented at multiple levels within society and the community. The impact of environmental and social forces such as poverty, racism, oppression, and limited economic opportunities on individuals from ethnic groups cannot be overlooked. *Community psychology,* and its subareas such as *social ecology,* need to continue moving beyond merely classifying social environments and forces to developing and implementing interventions that clearly achieve environmental changes for the improved psychological well-being of people (Insel, 1980).

Developers of alternative community service models directed at ethnic populations may find it helpful to use unorthodox methods of marketing, such as advertisements on ethnic radio stations, TV commercials, billboards, and fliers in ethnic grocery stores and restaurants to provide outreach efforts in disseminating service and program information (Spence & Atherton, 1991). Other useful techniques are to make bilingual staff highly visible in the ethnic community via speaking engagements at church and civic organizations. Such efforts should clarify how the service model operates and how it may be different from the traditional services that may have been received in the community in the past.

Service delivery must be flexible in order to meet the needs of individual communities (Applewhite, Wong, & Daley, 1991). After a careful needs assessment for the targeted population, services should be organized and designed to achieve an appropriate balance between direct and indirect service provision. Those services that are provided through CMHCs should be culturally sensitive, compatible, and relevant (Campinha-Bacote, 1991; Flaskerud, 1986; Rogler, Malgady, & Costantino, 1987) and may require the use of different service delivery models (Campinha-Bacote, 1991; Uba, 1982; Zane et al., 1994) that allow services to be delivered more directly and effectively to ethnic groups in the community.

Services should be organized in such a way that ethnic clients are asked to disclose personal information to as few program representatives as possible. For example, many traditional CMHCs operate in a hierarchical fashion so that a client may be interviewed by one person for the intake, another for assessment, then finally the therapist. Because many ethnic clients present with an understandably suspicious demeanor, such organizational hierarchies may simply add to feelings of frustration and pessimism about the likelihood of benefit. By contrast, interacting with few, preferably bilingual, staff members seems much more "user-friendly" and is likely to develop trust and positive expectations from clients.

Outside community agencies must accurately understand the goals of the alternative programs, their intended target population, and what they are *not* intended to do. If other community agencies do not have accurate perceptions of new programs, inappropriate referrals may occur. All links in the community chain must work together to provide integrated services. Those agencies that should be targeted in any community include, but are not limited to, the following: vocational rehabilitation services, hospital emergency rooms and walk-in medical clinics, state psychiatric facilities, local CMCHs, local substance abuse centers, public school personnel, the housing authority, rape crisis centers, homeless shelters, and social service agencies.

Thus far, several guidelines by which alternative models can be implemented have been discussed. Careful needs assessment, multilevel intervention, creative marketing, flexibility of direct and indirect service provision, a streamlined "intake" process, and ongoing efforts to maintain interagency collaboration are all necessary, but not sufficient, elements for community change. No matter how well organized the program or how skilled the staff, the ethnic community itself remains the most powerful resource for improving the quality of life for its ethnic citizens. The sense of community involvement and ability to effect change is essential to combating helplessness, lack of power, and pessimism in ethnic persons.

Community-based approaches may begin by sending empowering messages to the community via ongoing community education, outreach advertisement, and recruitment of volunteer help in order to create an awareness of the community's needs, resources, and strengths. Efforts need to be directed toward strengthening informal social networks of community members and encouraging strong indigenous leadership. Education programs designed to emphasize shared cultural history, values, practices, and accomplishments can be used to develop cohesion and team building. Encouraging pride and the development of positive aspects of racial/ethnic identity can reduce feelings of powerlessness, helplessness, and lack of involvement. In the final analysis, empowerment remains the key for initiating and maintaining effective community-wide change.

REFERENCES

Acosta, F. X., Yamamoto, J., & Evans, L. A. (1982). *Effective psychotherapy for low-income and minority patients.* New York: Plenum Press.

Akutsu, P. D., Snowden, L. R., & Organista, K. C. (1996). Referral patterns in ethnic-specific and mainstream programs for ethnic minorities and Whites. *Journal of Counseling Psychology, 43,* 56–64.

Anderson, L. S., Cooper, S., Hassol, L., Klein, D. C., Rosenblum, G., & Bennett, C. C. (1966). *Community psychology: A report of the Boston Conference on the Education of Psychologists for Community Mental Health.* Boston: Boston University.

Aponte, J. F. (1983). Need assessment: The state of the art and future directions. In R. A. Bell, M. Sundel, J. F. Aponte, S. A. Murrell, & E. Lin (Eds.), *Assessing human service needs: Concepts, methods, and applications* (pp. 285–302). New York: Human Sciences Press.

Aponte, J. F. (1997). *The role of culture in the treatment of culturally diverse populations.* Presented at the Workshop on Culture, Therapy, and Healing, New York Academy of Sciences.

Aponte, J. F., & Barnes, J. M. (1995). Impact of acculturation and moderator variables on the intervention and treatment of ethnic groups. In J. F. Aponte, R. Young Rivers, & J. Wohl (Eds.), *Psychological interventions and cultural diversity* (pp. 19–39). Boston: Allyn and Bacon.

Aponte, J. F., & Young, R. (1981). *Need assessments with minority groups: Conceptual, methodological, and utilization issues.* Paper presented at the Third National Conference on Needs Assessment in Health and Human Service Systems, Louisville, KY.

Aponte, H. J., Zarski, J. J., Bixenstine, C., & Cibik, P. (1991). Home/community-based services: A two-tier approach. *American Journal of Orthopsychiatry, 61,* 403–408.

Appel, K. E., & Bartemeier, L. H. (1961). *Action for mental health: Final report of the Joint Commission on Mental Illness and Health.* New York: Basic Books.

Applewhite, S. R., Wong, P., & Daley, J. M. (1991). Service approaches and issues in Hispanic agencies. *Administration and Policy in Mental Health, 19,* 27–37.

Atkinson, D. R., Morton, G., & Sue, D. W. (1998). *Counseling American minorities: A cross-cultural perspective* (5th ed.). Boston: McGraw-Hill.

Bell, C. C. (1987). Preventive strategies for dealing with violence among Blacks. *Community Mental Health Journal, 23,* 217–228.

Bloom, B. L. (1984). *Community mental health: A general introduction* (2nd. ed.). Monterey, CA: Brooks/Cole.

Bronfenbrenner, U. (1979). *The ecology of human development.* Cambridge, MA: Harvard University Press.

Bronfenbrenner, U. (1986). Ecology of the family as a context for human development: Research perspectives. *Developmental Psychology, 22,* 723–742.

Broskowski, A., & Marks, E. (1992). Managed mental health care. In S. Cooper & T. H. Lentner (Eds.). *Innovations in community mental health* (pp. 23–49). Sarasota, FL: Professional Resource Press.

Bui, K. T., & Takeuchi, D. T. (1992). Ethnic minority adolescents and the use of community mental health care services. *American Journal of Community Psychology, 20,* 403–417.

Campinha-Bacote, J. (1991). Community mental health services for the underserved: A culturally specific model. *Archives of Psychiatry Nursing, 5,* 229–235.

Cheung, F. K., & Snowden, L. R. (1990). Community mental health and ethnic minority populations. *Community Mental Health Journal, 26,* 277–291.

Chu, F. D. (1974). The Nader report: One author's perspective. *American Journal of Psychiatry, 131,* 775–779.

Curtis, P. A. (1990). The consequences of acculturation to service delivery and research with Hispanic families. *Child and Adolescent Social Work, 7,* 147–160.

Cutler, D. L. (1992). A historical overview of community mental health centers in the United States. In S. Cooper & T. H. Lentner (Eds.), *Innovations in community mental health* (pp. 1–22). Sarasota, FL: Professional Resource Press.

Davis, K. (1997). Managed care, mental illness and African Americans: A prospective analysis of managed care policy in the United States. *Smith College Studies in Social Work, 67,* 623–641.

De Bruyn, L. M., Hymbaugh, K., & Valdez, N. (1988). Helping communities address suicide and violence: The Special Initiatives Team of the Indian Health Service. *American Indian and Alaska Native Mental Health Research, 1,* 56–65.

DeLeon, P. H., VandenBos, G. R., & Bulatao, E. Q. (1991). Managed mental health care: A history of the federal policy initiative. *Professional Psychology: Research and Practice, 22,* 15–25.

Drolen, C. S. (1990). Community Mental Health: Who is being served? What is being offered? *The Journal of Mental Health Administration, 17,* 191–199.

Eng, E., & Hatch, J. W. (1991). Networking between agencies and Black churches: The lay adviser model. *Prevention in Human Services, 10,* 123–146.

Flaskerud, J. H. (1986). The effects of culture-compatible intervention on the utilization of mental health services by minority clients. *Community Mental Health Journal, 22,* 127–141.

Florin, P., & Wandersman, A. (1990). An introduction to citizen participation, voluntary organizations, and community development. Insights for empowerment through research. *American Journal of Community Psychology, 18,* 41–54.

Foley, H. A., & Sharfstein, S. S. (1983). *Madness in government: Who cares for the mentally ill?* Washington, DC: American Psychiatric Press.

Forgays, D. G. (1991). Primary prevention of psychopathology. In M. Hersen, A. E. Kazdin, & A. S. Bellack (Eds.), *The clinical psychology handbook* (2nd ed., pp. 743–761). New York: Pergamon.

Frank, R. G., & VandenBos, G. R. (1994). Health care reform: The 1993–1994 evolution. *American Psychologist, 49,* 851–854.

Galan, F. J. (1988). Alcoholism prevention and Hispanic youth. *Journal of Drug Issues, 18,* 49–58.

Goodstein, L. D., & Sandler, I. (1978). Using psychology to promote human welfare: A conceptual analysis of the role of community psychology. *American Psychologist, 33,* 882–892.

Gordon, A. J. (1991). Alcoholism treatment services to Hispanics: An ethnographic examination of a community's services. *Family and Community Health, 13,* 12–24.

Gottesfeld, H. (1995). Community context and the underutilization of mental health services by minority patients. *Psychological Reports, 76,* 207–210.

Gottlieb, B. H. (1982). Mutual help groups: Members' views of their benefits and of roles for professionals. *Prevention in Human Services, 1,* 55–67.

Granski, G., & Carrillo, D. I. (1997). The use of bilingual, bicultural paraprofessionals in mental health services: Issues for hiring, training, and supervision. *Community Mental Health Journal, 33,* 51–60.

Gutiérrez, L. M., & Ortega, R. (1991). Developing methods to empower Latinos: The importance of groups. *Social Work with Groups, 14,* 23–43.

Hadley, T. R., & Culhane, D. P. (1993). The status of community mental health centers ten years into block grant financing. *Community Mental Health Journal, 29,* 95–102.

Hargrove, D. S., & Melton, B. (1987). Block grants and rural mental health services. *Journal of Rural Community Psychology, 8,* 4–11.

Heller, K. (1992). Ingredients for effective community change: Some field observations. *American Journal of Community Psychology, 20,* 143–160.

Heller, K., Price, R. H., Reinharz, S., Riger, S., Wandersman, A., & D'Aunno, T. A. (1984). *Psychology and community change: Challenges of the future* (2nd ed.). Pacific Grove, CA: Brooks/Cole.

Hersch, L. (1995). Adapting to health care reform and managed care: Three strategies for survival and growth. *Professional Psychology: Research and Practice, 26,* 16–26.

Hu, T., Snowden, L. R., Jerrell, J. M., & Nguyen, T. D. (1991). Ethnic populations in public mental health: Services choice and level of use. *American Journal of Public Health, 81,* 1429–1434.

Humm-Delgado, D., & Delgado, M. (1986). Gaining community entree to assess service needs of Hispanics. *Social Casework, 67,* 80–89.

Insel, P. M. (1980). Task force report: The social climate of mental health. *Community Mental Health Journal, 16,* 62–78.

Iscoe, I., Bloom, B. L., & Spielberger, C. D. (Eds.). (1977). *Community psychology in transition: Proceedings of the National Conference on Training in Community Psychology.* New York: Hemisphere.

Jerrell, J. M. (1995). The effects of client-therapist match on service use and costs. *Administration and Policy in Mental Health, 23,* 119–126.

Katz, A. H. (1981). Self-help and mutual aid: An emerging social movement. *Annual Review of Sociology, 7,* 129–155.

Keefe, S. E., & Casas, J. M. (1980). Mexican Americans and mental health: A selected review and recommendations for mental health service delivery. *American Journal of Community Psychology, 8,* 303–326.

Kennedy, J. F. (1963). *Message from the President of the United States Relative to Mental Illness and Mental Retardation* (88th Congress, 1st Session, Document 58). Washington, DC: U.S. Government Printing Office.

LaFromboise, T. D. (1988). American Indian mental health policy. *American Psychologist, 43,* 388–397.

Lee, S. S., & Yee, A. K. (1988). The development of community-based health services for minority elderly in Boston's Chinatown. *Pride Institute Journal of Long-Term Home Health Care, 7,* 3–9.

Lefley, H. P., & Bestman, E. W. (1991). Public-academic linkages for culturally sensitive community mental health. *Community Mental Health Journal, 27,* 473–488.

Loo, C., Tong, B., & True, R. (1989). A bitter bean: Mental health status and attitudes in Chinatown. *Journal of Community Psychology, 17,* 283–296.

Mann, P. A. (1987). Prevention of child abuse: Two contrasting social support services. *Prevention in Human Services, 4,* 73–111.

Marburg, G. S. (1983). Mental health and Native Americans: Responding to the challenge of the biopsychosocial model. *White Cloud Journal, 3,* 43–51.

Mays, V. (1986). Black women and stress utilization of self-help groups for stress reduction. *Women & Therapy, 4,* 67–79.

McClure, L., Cannon, D., Belton, E., D'Ascoli, C., Sullivan, B., Allen, S., Connor, P., Stone, P., & McClure, G. (1980). Community psychology concepts and research base: Promise and product. *American Psychologist, 35,* 1000–1011.

Mindel, C. H., & Wright, R., Jr. (1982). The use of social services by Black and White elderly: The role of social support systems. *Journal of Gerontological Social Work, 4,* 107–120.

O'Hare, W. P., Pollard, K. M., Mann, T. L., & Kent, K. M. (1991). African Americans in the 1990s. *Population Bulletin, 46,* 1–40.

O'Sullivan, M. J., Peterson, P. D., Cox, G. B., & Kirkeby, J. (1989). Ethnic populations: Community mental health services ten years later. *American Journal of Community Psychology, 17,* 17–30.

Parsons, R. J. (1989). Empowerment for role alternatives for low income minority girls: A group work approach. *Social Work With Groups, 11,* 27–45.

Preciado, J., & Henry, M. (1997). Linguistic barriers in health education and services. In J. G. Garcia & M. C. Zea (Eds.), *Psychological interventions and research with Latino populations* (pp. 235–254). Boston: Allyn and Bacon.

Rabiner, J. (1986). Changes in hospital psychiatry: Implications for the future: or Whatever happened to the concept of asylum? *Hillside Journal of Clinical Psychiatry, 8,* 89–98.

Rappaport, J. (1977) *Community psychology: Values, research, and action.* New York: Holt, Rinehart, & Winston.

Rappaport, J. (1984). Studies in empowerment: Introduction to the issue. *Prevention in Human Services, 3,* 1–7.

Ray, G. (1995). Why CMHCs belong in networks. *Behavioral Health Management, 15,* 15–16.

Reeves, K. (1986). Hispanic utilization of an ethnic mental health clinic. *Journal of Psychosocial Nursing and Mental Health Services, 24,* 23–26.

Rogler, L. H., Malgady, R. G., & Costantino, G. (1987). What do culturally sensitive mental health services mean? The case of Hispanics. *American Psychologist, 42,* 565–570.

Rowe, W. E. (1997). Changing ATOD norms and behaviors: A Native American community commitment to wellness. *Evaluation and Program Planning, 20,* 323–333.

Shaffer, I., Croze, C., Flynn, L., Pattullo, E., Ray, C., Surles, R. C., Penney, D., & Keller, J. (1995). How can privatized plans and delivery systems preserve the spirit of community? *Behavioral Healthcare Tomorrow, 4,* 40–47.

Shapiro, R. (1975). Discrimination and community mental health. *Civil Rights Digest, 8,* 19–23.

Snowden, L. R. (1987). The peculiar successes of community psychology: Service delivery to ethnic minorities and the poor. *American Journal of Community Psychology, 15,* 575–586.

Snowden, L. R., & Cheung, F. K. (1990). Use of inpatient mental health services by members of ethnic minority groups. *American Psychologist, 45,* 347–355.

Snowden, L. R., Hu, T., & Jerrell, J. (1995). Emergency care avoidance: Ethnic matching and participation in minority-serving programs. *Community Mental Health Journal, 31,* 463–473.

Snowden, L. R., Storey, C., & Clancy, T. (1989). Ethnicity and continuation in treatment at a Black community mental health center. *Journal of Community Psychology, 17,* 111–118.

Spence, S. A., & Atherton, C. R. (1991). The Black elderly and the social service delivery system: A study of factors influencing the use of community based services. *Journal of Gerontological Social Work, 16,* 19–35.

Starrett, R. A., Todd, A. M., Decker, J. T., & Walters, G. (1989). The use of formal helping networks to meet the psychological needs of the Hispanic elderly. *Hispanic Journal of Behavioral Sciences, 11,* 259–273.

Sue, S. (1977). Community mental health services to minority groups: Some optimism, some pessimism. *American Psychologist, 32,* 616–624.

Sue, S. (1997). Cultural considerations in treating Asians. *Closing the Gap: A Newsletter from The Office of Minority Health,* Sept. 1–2.

Sue, S., Chun, C. A., & Gee, K. (1995). Ethnic minority intervention and treatment research. In J. F. Aponte, R. Young Rivers, & J. Wohl (Eds.), *Psychological interventions and cultural diversity* (pp. 266–282). Boston: Allyn and Bacon.

Sue, S., Fujino, D.C., Hu, L. T., Takeuchi, D. T., & Zane, N. W. S. (1991). Community mental health services for ethnic minority groups: A test of the cultural responsiveness hypothesis. *Journal of Consulting and Clinical Psychology, 59,* 533–540.

Szapocznik, J., Kurtines, W., Santisteban, D. A., Pantin, H., Scopetta, M., Mancilla, Y., Aisenberg, S., McIntosh, Pérez-Vidal, & Coatsworth, J. D. (1997). The evolution of structural ecosystemic theory for working with Latino families. In J. G. Garcia & M. C. Zea (Eds.), *Psychological interventions and research with Latino populations* (pp. 166–190). Boston: Allyn and Bacon.

Taube, C., & Rupp, A. (1986). The effect of Medicaid on access to ambulatory mental health care for the poor and near-poor under 65. *Medical Care, 24,* 677–686.

Tolan, P. H., Perry, M. S., & Jones, T. (1987). Delinquency prevention: An example of consultation in rural community mental health. *Journal of Community Psychology, 15,* 43–50.

Tyler, J. D., Cohen, K. N., & Clark, J. S. (1982). Providing community consultation in a reservation setting. *Journal of Rural Community Psychology, 3,* 49–58.

Uba, L. (1982). Meeting the mental health needs of Asian Americans: Mainstream or segregated services. *Professional Psychology, 13,* 215–221.

Vega, W. A., & Murphy, J. W. (1990). *Culture and the restructuring of community mental health.* New York: Greenwood.

Wilkinson, G. (1984). Psychotherapy in the market place. *Psychological Medicine, 14,* 23–26.

Yin, R. K., Kaftarian, S. J., & Jacobs, N. (1996). Empowerment evaluation at federal and local levels. In D. M. Fetterman, S. J. Kaftarian, & A. Wandersman (Eds.), *Empowerment evaluation* (pp. 188–207). Thousand Oaks, CA: Sage.

Zane, N., Hatanaka, H., Park, S. S., & Akutsu, P. (1994). Ethnic-specific mental health services: Evaluation of the parallel approach for Asian-American clients. *Journal of Community Psychology, 22,* 68–81.

Zimmerman, M. A. (1990). Taking aim on empowerment research: On the distinction between individual and psychological conceptions. *American Journal of Community Psychology, 18,* 169–177.

9 Traditional and Folk Approaches among Ethnic Minorities

JOAN D. KOSS-CHIOINO

Although anthropologists have had a long-standing interest in traditional and folk healing (referred to in this chapter as "ethnomedical systems"), psychologists and other behavioral scientists have only recently begun to consider the importance of these practices to ethnic minority peoples. All ethnic groups have transferred to the United States many or all of their main beliefs and practices connected to healing. There is evidence that these practices have undergone significant changes, and in some cases have even intensified as a result of the difficult adaptations faced by ethnic minority persons in a societal environment that can be economically and psychologically stressful, even hostile, for newcomers. These difficult conditions become even more salient for ethnomedical practice when we consider that healing beliefs and practices are multivocal in terms of what they symbolize for both practitioners and clients. In addition, contact with other healing systems, including biomedicine, enhances the eclecticism common to noncodified healing practices.

Symbols integral to ethnomedical practices connote and represent concerns about ethnic identity, selfhood, worldview, expressions of family and community values, and reaffirmations of cultural cohesiveness and tradition. Additionally, traditional and folk healing systems are commonly interrelated with, or encompassed by, religious and political goals. Unlike what is often described for biomedicine—that it serves only to prevent or cure disease—or for psychotherapy—that it is aimed mainly at treating emotional disorders (although these perspectives are more ideal than actual, since both marginally serve many other goals)—alternative healing systems in ethnic communities are formally multidimensional, in part because they are often embedded in the processes by which ethnic individuals and their communities adapt to their adopted environments. It must also be noted that alternative healing practices can also be found in White-majority, middle-class, suburban communities (McGuire, 1988), implying fulfillment of needs that go beyond those served by biomedicine or psychotherapy.

Scope of the Chapter

This chapter first presents an overview of ethnomedical systems in the larger ethnic minority populations in the United States (Hispanic, African American, Asian American, and American Indian), beginning with a relatively detailed description of Hispanic ethnomedical systems as models of traditional perspectives on etiology, diagnosis, healing process, healer initiation and training, beliefs, ritual practices, and patterns of utilization. Finally, the nature of the interface between psychotherapeutic treatment and ethnomedicine in ethnic minority groups as well as the possibilities of integrating ethnomedical approaches into standard treatment modalities are explored. Since there are many ethnic groups, as well as variations within both the groups and their healing systems, only highlights of these phenomena can be described here. The intent is to illustrate variability in types and modes of traditional healing found in the United States. Each ethnic category includes very different cultural traditions, such as Puerto Rican, Cuban, and Mexican in the Hispanic cultural tradition, and these will be examined separately.

Individual cultural differences are reflected in indigenous traditional healing practices; however, extensive borrowing and some cross-utilization also take place. Despite variations associated with different Hispanic cultures, the reader will appreciate that there are also a number of broad similarities, such as these:

1. There is a widespread belief that the cause of illness and misfortune has a locus external to the individual, and is mostly spiritual (or spiritual combined with physical aspects).

2. Frequent group participation in healing ritual is often preferred to individual sessions.

3. The individual as sufferer is most often treated within a family or community perspective.

4. Morality, as both cause of illness and condition for recovery, is integral to healing.

5. The healing process depends largely upon nonverbal and symbolic interactions, together with the common use of herbal pharmacopeias (Koss, 1986; Koss-Chioino, 1992).

In these and other ways, traditional healing in Hispanic populations (as well as in other ethnic groups) is different from the psychology-based, largely individual-centered concepts and practices found in standard psychotherapeutic treatments. Interpretations can be made (many are found in the literature) that describe parallel psychological processes and effects (such as catharsis). Some of these parallels will be included in the descriptions below. However, similarities can best be thought of as part-analogies since, if considered in their entirety as a system of concepts and practices, traditional healing systems are very different from contemporary psychological therapies.

Before we proceed, a number of background assumptions must be explained. Basic to understanding traditional healing systems is that they are conceptually constructed and organized on their own terms. They often ignore (simply do not consider) the mind-body distinction and are not based upon the logicodeductive scientific paradigm of biomedicine that focuses, first, on the body as most relevant to diagnosis and treatment, and secondarily on "mind" or psyche, both of which are assumed to have a physical structure and locus

(Koss-Chioino, 1992). Salient differences in paradigms underlying diverse healing systems will be discussed. The main contrasting paradigms are what have been labeled in the literature as *etic* (scientific, universal) versus *emic* (the insider, relativistic view), and may be associated with biomedical and ethnomedical (traditional, folk) systems, respectively. It can be argued, however that all medical/healing systems are shaped by the values, worldviews, and self-views of the cultures in which they develop and are utilized; therefore all healing systems are "ethnomedical." The far-reaching implication is that not every healing system or practice can be assessed by the same (standard, universal) measures. Each is constructed of its own set of meanings and views of self and world. Each has its own set of rules and a particular logic within a paradigm and structure made up of interrelated (however loosely) parts.

These perspectives will be illustrated in the following descriptions of healing systems in each of the ethnic subcultures discussed below. It is also important to note that the terms *traditional* and *folk* do not represent hard and fast categories that are easily differentiated. Generally, these terms allude to the history of the healing system. Chinese medicine, for example, is widespread throughout Asia and has a long, written tradition permitting a high degree of codification. In contrast, shamanic healing systems in tribes of North American Indians are local in their provenance and in their clientele. They are generally not codified in written form nor formally regulated by societal bodies, but are passed on as oral traditions and informally regulated through custom and patronage. Both categories could be dubbed "popular" medicine in the sense that they are most often informally regulated by healers and clients, as opposed to professional biomedicine regulated by government-based licensing boards. However, these distinctions are not definitive since the rules and principles guiding ethnomedical—as opposed to biomedical—systems are usually of a different genre altogether. It is therefore very difficult to compare types of medical systems systematically.

Hispanic Healing Systems

Three popular ethnomedical systems are found in the United States among Hispanics—*Espiritismo* (Spiritism), *Santería*, and *Curanderismo*—associated with the three major ethnic communities of Puerto Ricans, Cubans, and Mexican Americans. (See Garrison, 1977; Gonzalez-Wippler, 1973; Harwood, 1977; Kay, 1977; Koss-Chioino, 1992; Sandoval, 1977, for more detailed descriptions.) Each is a synthesis of beliefs and practices derived from separate colonial histories: Spiritism from the conjunction of European (French) and Afro-Caribbean traditions; *Santería,* from a conjunction of folk Catholicism and West African traditions; and *Curanderismo,* a synthesis of folk Catholicism and Mexican Indian traditions. Spiritualism (a variation of Spiritism with a similar European and folk Catholicism background) is also found in Mexico and on the U.S. Mexico border (Finkler, 1985; Trotter & Chavira, 1981).

Illness Etiologies

The major causal paradigm for all of these systems is that malicious or unaware other-than-human beings or forces are the final causes of physical suffering, emotional distress, or personal problems. Spirits in Spiritism or saints/gods in *Santería* are the direct cause of suffering in those systems. In *Curanderismo,* the will of God is invoked as causal in many cases, but there are also a number of provoking agents in Mexican American belief: spoiled food; environmental factors (*aires*); contact with persons wishing harm, consciously or inadvertently (*mal de ojo, el ojo*—the evil eye); immoral excesses of sex or money acquisition; deviant behavior; congenital or hereditary characteristics; and witchcraft (Kay, 1977; Koss-Chioino & Cañive, 1993; Trotter & Chavira, 1981). Age and general weakness, as well as a "weak character," add to the effect of the agents listed above. Vestiges of these etiological beliefs are also found in Spiritism and *Santería;* probably the most important is bewitchment (Koss-Chioino, 1992).

The unifying theme for all of these systems is that of harmony and balance. To heal (*sanar* or *curar*) also means "to restore to health," the latter interpreted as harmony within individuals, between them and within the cosmos. What are referred to in orthodox Western thought as the physical, social, and existential dimensions of health, are inexorably bound up together in Hispanic healing. In Spiritism, the spiritual (the Holy Spirit and his realm) encompasses all of these dimensions; in *Santería,* the rule of the Gods/saints is similar to concepts of the spirit world in Spiritist belief and practice. However, practitioners believe that although goodness exists it is easily overbalanced by evil, and the gods who interfere with worldly affairs must be amoral. Much of the work of the *santero* (healer) involves protection and freedom from the anxiety of uncertainty. One phrasing of "harmony/balance," much described in the literature among less acculturated Mexican Americans and Mexicans and Puerto Ricans in New York in the past, is the theory of balance between hot and cold. For example, foods that are too "hot" cause "hot" illness, and "cold" herbal remedies are prescribed by *curandero/as* (healers). Although extremes in change of climate or contact with heat or cold are believed to cause illness, temperature per se is not what is at risk; rather, hot–cold is a metaphoric symbology that expresses excesses and an ever present awareness of the danger of imbalance. However, this symbolic paradigm may be dropping out of the belief systems of Mexican Americans and Puerto Ricans in the United States (Kay, 1977; Koss, 1987). In all Hispanic healing systems imbalance is a moral issue; thus, in Spiritism, illness-causing (*causa*) spirits are attracted to persons who behave immorally. In *Curanderismo* or *Espiritismo,* those who "break the rules" (including "uncleanliness" in the moral sense) often become ill because they threaten the integrity of social fabric. Transgressions are sinful both because they unbalance the "good" within an individual and because they generate conflict among persons. *Santería* belief differs in its assumption that, like people, the saints/gods can do both good and evil, and the only way to cope is to ally with and manipulate these powerful beings for your own ends.

Diagnosis: Identifying the Illness

Hispanic healers make few significant distinctions among physical illness, emotional disorder, and social problems, such as being criminally charged or failing in business. There is an informal practice of referring complaints assessed as "*material*" (somatic) to medical doctors while simultaneously apportioning spiritual aspects of the distress to traditional treatments. All complaints are interpreted as having similar etiologies, and diagnosis proceeds in much the same way regardless of the type of complaint. As we shall later see, remedies may differ according to type of complaint (but not systematically); the cause of the distress, such as "bewitchment" or "nervousness," often becomes the label for the distressing condition. Distinctions between somatic and other types of complaints (i.e., psychological or spiritual) are also unsystematic; for example, some of the Spiritist healers in Puerto Rico asserted that "nerves are almost always physical," but also maintained that a particular *causa* spirit (sent by a women who desired the client's husband) could cause her "pain and nerve sickness," or that nerves run in the family (see Koss-Chioino, 1992). However, the common ground in a condition labeled "nerves" is that of conflict in interpersonal, usually intimate, relationships that generates extreme emotions, particularly anger.

The process of "diagnosis" in traditional healing is quite different from the method in biomedicine or psychotherapy. Clients rarely describe their complaints as the main step in an intake process; rather, the healer is expected to "know" what the client's complaints are without verbal input from the client. In *Santería* the diagnostic process is divinatory and is called a "*registro*." The *santero* who specializes in reading the shells (*los cara-coles*—modeled after the West African cowrie shells) or palm nuts—is known as an *italero* (Gonzalez-Wippler, 1973). The sixteen shells, called the "mouthpieces of the Gods," are for sale in any botanica (shops that sell remedies, prayers, herbs, candles and other prescriptions and ritual objects). Sixteen or twelve (if the diviner is not yet a priest) are thrown four times onto a straw mat and the patterns interpreted according to the position of the shells. Each letter or pattern "speaks" for one or more *orishas* and is interpreted according to a legend or proverb associated with it; this is standardized in the "Table of *Ifá*" used by the high priests (*babalaos*). The diviner then particularizes the interpretation for a specific client and his or her problem. Not only do healers and priests (*babalawos*) deal with problems and disordered emotions, but they also prescribe herbal remedies and amulets (*res-guardos*) to protect against future harm or to bring about a desired event. It is these latter services, actual manipulations of the future, that appear most sought after.

A different type of "diagnostic" divination is found among Spiritist mediums. First, their personal spirit guides assist them to "see" into the spirit world to identify the spirit causing a client's problems. Then a process of probing takes place in which the healer describes the client's complaints (somatic distress, bad feelings, persistent interpersonal or social problems) and the client confirms (most frequently) or denies them. The *causa* spirit is then called down to possess the body of one of the healers and enjoined to explain its actions. Spirit and client carry on a spirit-dominated discourse in which the social context (usually interpersonal relations) of the client's problems/complaints, including the circumstances and relationships in past lives, is revealed. Much of the remedy (intervention or solution) is symbolically or metaphorically contained within this spirit-client interchange. Medium-healers at the healing table, who are not possessed, dialogue, cajole and exhort the *causa* spirit to leave the suffering client. The spirit usually expresses the recognition of his or her wrongdoing in molesting the client, and agrees to leave once the client forgives it for causing distress. Other remedies, to be carried out at home (prayers, candle lighting, herbs, aromatic baths, ritual cleansing of various kinds), may also be prescribed by the healers, who "receive" this knowledge from their spirit guides.

There are many variations on these two patterns: In *Santería,* a god (*orisha*) possessing a priest will give an oracle. In Spiritualism among Mexican Americans in the border area, the guardian-guide spirit may be a folk saint, such as *El Niño Fidencio,* who speaks through a medium-healer to advert a disaster or, at times, to recommend that the illness be treated by a physician (Trotter & Chavira, 1981). In *Curanderismo,* cards (Spanish deck or tarot) may be read to diagnose or prognosticate, or an egg will be broken after the client is "swept" or "cleansed" with it.

Healing Process

Both one-on-one consultations and group ritual sessions are contexts for healing; individuals as clients are most frequent, but couples or two to four relatives, and even places (i.e., one's home or shop), may be "treated," the last with a purification process employing incense or other aromatic materials. Again, it might be noted that some aspect of balance is central to healing, whether the etiological belief is in spirits, saints/gods, the devil versus God, natural forces, energies, or vibrations. This focus on other-than-natural forces beyond visible reality and daily life events results in a number of significant differences in the ways healing is carried out and experienced.

In Spiritism among Puerto Ricans and other Latinos in the United States, the medium-healer is not the agent of intervention but only a vehicle, an instrument to bring about change in the sufferer's condition. Briefly described, the group healing ritual consists of the mediums (mostly adepts but also some novices) sitting behind a table. The session is opened by the recitation of prayers to the Holy Spirit, Jesus (often the "Our Father" and other items of Catholic liturgy). Then the mediums exhort the audience of potential clients to relax by directing them to meditate, and to enter the spirit world by seeking visual experience of it. The mediums commonly follow suit and become possessed for a brief moment by their main protector-guide spirit who then stands behind each medium-healer and presides over the session. The group of mediums then concentrate on the spirit world and certain *videncias* (visions) that indicate the relationship of a certain spirit to someone in the audience. That client is then singled out according to a visual description given by the spirit to the medium, summoned to the table (on which sits a vessel of blessed water in which the spirit fluids are encapsulated). The "diagnostic" process described above takes place.

The central feature of Spiritist healing is the use of image and metaphor in these spirit-produced explanations. Much of what takes place can only be described as the manipulation of symbolic material that somehow gets "inside" of the sufferer. How this happens can be explained in part by belief in, and experience of, *plasmación,* that is, that the healer feels the client's complaint within his or her own body. The feelings of clients are literally "shaped" or "formed" inside the healer through the action of the particular spirit causing the distressing feelings in the suffering client. Symbols, in spirit communication, are not representational, indexical, or referential, but instead cue feelings and emotions. Spiritist healer-mediums model these feelings and emotions—through messages (visions from the spirits) or direct bodily transfer of feelings from the spirits that they mirror for clients. A cycle of resonating feelings is set up, including not only the medium-healers and often other mediums working at a table (at a group session), but also the audience of participants. The Spiritist ritual healing session in its group form has been compared with psychodrama and likened to an imaginal theatrical performance (Koss, 1979; Seda Bonilla, 1964).

The implication of this kind of healing process is the power it conveys to the suffering client in terms of concern and caring, as well as shared experience and intimacy among persons who know about suffering (see also McClain, 1989). The facts of the healers' former suffering, as central to the initiation into the healer role (to be described), are not usually known to clients, but the feelings are readily available upon contact with a healer, most especially during the ritual process. The altered states phenomena (ritual trance and possession-trance) illustrate the healer's contact with suffering as well as her or his ability to control distressing feelings and emotions.

This same interpretation can also be applied to Spiritualist and *Santería* healing practices among Mexican Americans and Cubans, both of which utilize altered states of consciousness in their ritual healing. In the latter, *santeros* and *babalawo* undergo elaborate initiations and are usually self-selected during bouts of problems or illness. In *Curanderismo,* healers receive their healing avocations both as a gift from God (*el don*) and through apprenticeship to an elderly relative. Often, however, they are selected for the healer role because they are recognized to possess high sensitivity and interest in the suffering of other persons, for whose benefit they renew connection with God and the saints. In this way, their relationships with clients appear to have similar features to those of spiritists and *santeros;* they are open to sharing their clients' pain as a route to facilitating their healing, and the incorporation of other-than-human forces in the healing process.

Patterns of Utilization

Very little epidemiological data are available for utilization of ethnomedical treatments by Hispanics in the United States. In California, *Curanderismo* is variously reported to be used by 5 to 8 percent of Mexican American parents for their children in Santa Barbara (Gilbert, 1980); Keefe (1981) found that 7 percent of her sample in Los Angeles had been to a *curandero;* and Chavez (1984) reported 23 percent of Mexican immigrants to San Diego said they would use a *curandero,* but only 1 percent actually reported using such services. In urban barrios in Colorado and South Texas, reported utilization was found to be much higher, 32 percent in the former and 54 percent in the latter (Rivera, 1988; Trotter & Chavira, 1981; see especially Mayers, 1989). There is little objective evidence for the extent of utilization of Spiritism (and its variations) or *Santería,* but older studies of the New York City area (Garrison, 1977; Harwood, 1977) describe the widespread use of Spiritism in the seventies, and subsequent studies in small eastern cities such as Hartford, Connecticut (Singer & Borrero, 1984), show this to be the case wherever there is a large concentration of Puerto Ricans. Similarly, various studies (Brandon, 1991; Sandoval, 1977) indicate that *Santería* is a flourishing health and mental health alternative in Miami, Florida, as well as other areas of concentrated Cuban population. Some studies separate the belief in traditional healing practices from records of actual use. This suggests both use as a potential resource, and the common use of home remedies and rituals, which has not been well documented but has been frequently observed (Harwood, 1977; Mayers, 1989; Trotter, 1981).

Healers in each of the Hispanic ethnomedical systems described here commonly describe themselves as generalists. But in *Curanderismo,* various investigators (Kay, 1977; Rivera & Wanderer, 1986) point out that these healers are most widely used by women, frequently for their childrens' illness problems, but also for their own problems. The mental health aspects of *Curanderismo* among Mexican Americans in the United States have not been well studied (but see Koss-Chioino & Cañive, 1993 and Newton, 1978). Conditions generally perceived as physical illnesses—*susto, empacho, bilis, caida de la mollera,* and *mal de ojo*—have emotional concomitants, while bewitchment and *nervios* are directly related to emotional distress, as well as to somatic distress. Because these popular illnesses are culturally constructed as syntheses of somatic and psychological factors, and this paradigm differs from that of biomedicine where soma and psyche are most often separated in diagnostic schemata, popular illnesses are presented to folk healers who understand them in culturally responsive ways. The treatments for the illnesses are usually also synthetic, integrating soma and psyche.

African American Ethnomedicine

Snow (1977) characterizes the underlying belief system of African American ethnomedicine as "a composite of the classical medicine of an earlier day, European folklore regarding the natural world, rare African traits, and selected beliefs derived from modern scientific medicine" (p. 83). All of this is blended with fundamentalist Christianity, and elements from West Indian Voodoo (including basically similar "magical" practices of rootwork, hoodoo, "crossing-up," hexing, and witchcraft). There is so much diversity in the description of beliefs, practices, and types of healers that one gets the impression of several overlapping healing systems, in part distributed according to locale, with differences in the northern and southern states, as well as in places of special tradition such as Louisiana and the Sea Islands of South Carolina (Baer, 1985; Blake, 1984; Hall & Bourne, 1973; Watson, 1984b). As pointed out by Baer (1985) however, there are limited systematic or representative data to clarify the types of healers, systems, or their distribution.

Baer (1985) suggests a typology based upon two main types of African American healers, "independent" and "cultic." (The same division could be made for Hispanic healers since *Curanderos* generally work independently and *Santeros* within cult groups; spiritists are almost always members of healing cults but also may hold private consultations.) Within this division he classifies healers according to whether they are generalists or specialists. This then neatly accounts for an amazing variety: Independent generalists (conjurers, spiritualists) deal with illnesses and problems of "unnatural cause" (Snow, 1978); specialized independents (midwives, herbalists, "magic" vendors, neighborhood "prophets") are local healers, supplying herbs or occult articles (perfumed oils, candles), or counseling, prayer, and prophecy for common problems. In this category also are found healers in the rural South (bone-setters, blood-stoppers) who still, though in lesser number, treat physical ailments. Cultic generalists work within groups, and are identified as Spiritualists, some few as Voodoo (or "hoodoo") priests or priestesses, and some as Black Muslim or Black Hebrew healers (the latter are sectarian organizations with religio-political tenets and goals). Finally, cultic specialists function within religious organizations as "divine" or "faith" healers in evangelistic congregations such as the Holiness, Pentecostal, or Baptist churches. These healers are well known but their ways of healing have not been well studied.

Etiology and Diagnosis of Illness

Snow (1978, 1993) points to the prevalent belief that good health is an instance of good fortune that includes a good job, faithful spouse, and loving children. "The cure for one, therefore, might cure them all" (Snow, 1978). Here again there is no real separation between illness and other types of distress; nor is there a significant difference between psyche and soma in folk theory. Moreover, diagnosis focuses not on symptoms but on causes. The most prevalent of causes is that conceived as failure to avoid dangerous situations that bring on illness or misfortune. Appropriate and timely action can neutralize danger from attack by other humans, natural events, or nonhuman beings such as ghosts, ancestors, or evil spirits. While symptoms are fluid and may change easily or be shifted to another causal category (i.e., natural to unnatural), knowing the cause of the illness is essential to finding the right healer and treatment even when shifts may be made between types of healers.

Etiological notions divide into natural and unnatural categories—the former having to do with beliefs in proper action according to God's plan for people aimed at maintaining both harmony and well-being. Unhealthy lifestyles and excesses will lead to illness, or God may take punitive action for failure in one's duty to serve him. While physicians or herbalists can cure the former, the latter demands a contract with God or the intercession of a religious healer.

With regard to unnatural illness (i.e., listed by Snow, 1978), as caused by excessive, nonproductive worry, evil influence, or sorcery/magic). This type of distress is probably closest to the problems treated by psychotherapists. It is often caused by "fixes" or "hexes" (also referred to as voodoo, hoodoo, rootwork, crossing-up) carried out by human agents, usually intimate others who are envious or angry with the victim and therefore require the help of a specialist with unusual powers. This healer should have a special bond with God for a successful intervention that counteracts the beyond-human quality of the causal factors, such as Satan or magical attack. Folk diagnosis of magical illness includes poisoning to account for gastrointestinal symptoms or weight loss, a hex worked on clothes or items worn next to the body to explain behavior that feels out of personal control, and any unusual symptoms such as the feelings that an animal (spider, lizard, snake) has intruded itself into one's body.

Patterns of Utilization

Decisions of African Americans regarding utilization of professional health care services are reported as unrelated to income; however, a national survey showed that the problems experienced by those with lower income were more serious (Neighbors, 1984). A general pattern signifying underutilization of mental health care is that somewhat more than half of those who reported a serious problem (phrased as a "nervous breakdown") did not seek professional assistance. Neighbors's (1984) conclusion was that African Americans widely utilize a "lay network" as a source of assistance, which confirms the descriptive studies cited above. A systematic survey in Detroit, Michigan, found that even for hypertension, defined as a "natural" illness in the folk system, 24 percent of African American women and about 10 percent of men reported using folk or "personal" care treatments; 41

percent of the women said they were likely to use a traditional/folk therapy as compared to 14 percent of the Anglo-American women (Bailey, 1991). Although various authors (Blake, 1984; Watson, 1984a) describe the widespread use of home remedies and ethnomedical healing in isolated rural populations due to the lack of professional medical services or conservation of tradition, it seems clear that there are other important factors in decisions to utilize ethnomedicine such as explanations of the cause of an illness that are different from the etiologies of biomedicine.

Ethnomedicine among Asian Americans

As in the Hispanic community there is substantial variation between ethnomedical systems among Chinese, Japanese, Vietnamese, Koreans, and tribal peoples such as the Hmong or Lao. The basic tenets of Chinese medicine were set out in written documents dating to the 13th and 14th centuries B.C. and may be over 5000 years old. In these writings, health and disease were recognized as subject to the principles of the natural world (Xiu, 1988). Shamanic healing probably diminished in importance by the third century B.C., as indicated by the publication of *The Canon of Internal Medicine,* the first Chinese medical textbook. However, shamanic healers are still working in Taiwan and China, although they have not been reported in the United States (Kleinman, 1980). A complex system of herbal remedies is of great antiquity as part of both types of ethnomedical systems (Xiu, 1988), but the religious ideas and ritual practices associated with the beginnings of Chinese medicine have largely dropped out. Physical/bodily manipulation or exercises are central, such as acupuncture, moxibustion, massage, and breathing exercises (i.e., *Tai Chi, Qigong*).

Although current diagnosis and treatment appear focused on the somatic, a psychological approach is an integral aspect; in particular, there is a stipulated relationship between a person's mind and his or her state of health (Wu, 1984). A balanced and disciplined life maintains health; this includes regulations of emotions and desires, a balanced diet, and adjustment when physical changes occur. The central tenet of the Chinese conception of health is balance, both inner and outer (with nature and the world), particularly between *yin* (dark, heavy, inner, female) and *yang* (bright, light, outer, male). Good health depends upon the equilibrium of the basic emotions and organs. Body physiology is made up of five *yin* viscera and five *yang* organs, each responsible for a bodily function and associated to an external part of the body. The heart presides over all the organ systems and governs all mental activities. If the heart malfunctions (i.e., symbolic imbalance), palpitations, memory loss, insomnia, or mental disorders can occur. Illness etiology differentiates between inner and outer causes: External causes include the six evils: wind, cold, heat, wetness, dryness, and fire; internal causes are the seven emotions, excesses of which can cause imbalance, blockage of *ch'i* (life force, energy) and malfunction of the organs. Irregularity of food and drink and fatigue can also lead to illness. Moreover, imbalances can occur because transitions over time are inevitable and cause instabilities. External, cosmic imbalances should be avoided; astrological almanacs are consulted for mating as well as for important times of transition such as weddings and funerals.

Currently, Chinese medicine has given up treating external imbalances that have moral dimensions; these are handled by Buddhist or Taoist priests, or by spirit healers.

Chinese medicine takes as its focus internal imbalances within the human being, while ritual experts deal with the external. The Taoist system metaphorically relates immoral actions to five demons conjured up by antisocial human behavior. Buddhist concepts of rebirth account for imbalances such as antipathies between a parent and child because of a relationship in a past life or label a child's irritability as "fright" due to an imbalance among animating forces, including the Buddhist soul (Topley, 1976). Traditionally, these healing systems were used in an alternative or complementary way—dependent on the course of events (particularly the illness), recommendations by family elders, or diagnoses of the problem.

With regard to mental health, traditional Chinese medicine took the position that the human mind was unable to remain normal if distracted by extreme emotions such as worry, fear, anger, or fixed desires (Li, 1984). Various investigators, such as Kleinman and Kleinman (1985), analyze the ways in which emotions are "somatized" and expressed as physical illness when mood disorders are present. Since the biomedical categories of illnesses of the mind and of the body are not found in Chinese ethnomedical nosology, which instead has categories best characterized as "psychosomatic" (for want of a better term to connote their synthesis), some dispute the validity of "somatization" as an explanatory psychological process that accounts for the ample expression of somatic symptoms and few affective ones (Kawanishi, 1992). It has been further suggested that somatization among Asians leads to high levels of "errors" in mental health professionals' diagnosing mood or anxiety disorders based upon somatic symptomatology; instead, somatic symptom expression may be related to overcoming obstacles to legitimate entry into the sick role, or to ways that patients relate to non-Asian therapists.

here about ethnomedicine among Japanese traditional medicine and in part on itions (Otsuka, 1976). However, there s the Salvation Cult (Gedatsukai), and tan, specifically focused on Japanese fer, 1977). Murase (1984) shows how both of these innovative therapies are based upon the Japanese concept of *sunao,* which refers to a pristine state of mind, like that of a baby, an unconditional state of trust in others. *Sunao* is closely linked with Shintoism; other aspects of these therapies are linked to Buddhist and Confucian traditions.

Among Southeast Asians, the hill tribes (Hmong and Mien) in the United States see shamans when they are available and generally continue their traditional beliefs and practices regarding herbal remedies (Muecke, 1983; see also Westermeyer, 1988 for descriptions of Hmong and Lao ethnomedicine). Central concepts of their traditional medical systems include the notion that continued health depends on the continued residence of many souls; absence of one or more causes illness or death. These beliefs are vividly illustrated in a recent work that describes the difficult interaction of medical doctors and a Hmong family in the treatment of an infant with a "wandering soul" (Fadiman, 1998). In addition, spirits (*phii*) are omnipresent throughout nature and associated with special places; they can cause or heal illness and must be respected. Magic and sorcery can be employed to cause illness, but illness can also result from inherited defects in "blood" or "wind" (akin to the elements in Chinese medicine). As with the Chinese, too much think-ing or worrying can cause illness and disturb balance. Among the Lao, as compared to the hill tribes (Hmong), Buddhist concepts have been more influential and prayer and bodily cleanliness are more important. Several investigators have documented the presence of Laotian ethnomedical practices in the United States (D. Kinzie, E. Foulks, personal communication).

Traditional Healing among American Indians

Extensive diversity in ethnomedical practices is found in this population, since traditional healing systems vary along tribal lines (there are 451 federally recognized tribes), and are largely, though not entirely, shamanic (that is, made up of independent practitioners and culture-specific beliefs and practices). An ample literature can be consulted for descrip-tions of traditional healing in each tribe or area. (See, especially, the Smithsonian Institu-tion's *Handbook of North American Indians,* 1978-; also Vogel, 1977, who presents a descriptive overview of therapeutic techniques and healing plants among American Indi-ans; and individual studies such as Bahr, Gregorio, Lopez, & Alvarez, 1974 [Pima]; Jilek, 1982 [Pacific Northwest]; Kunitz, 1983; Levy, Neutra, & Parker, 1987; [Navaho], among many others.)

Two popular, religious healing traditions transcend tribal boundaries: The Native American Church and the Pentecostal Church. I will briefly discuss the former, from the perspective of how its activities and healing ideology radically differ from psychotherapy, making attempts at cooperation or linking extremely difficult. This discussion is a preface to the final section of this chapter, which will deal with perspectives on interfacing or inte-grating traditional healing systems and psychotherapy.

The Native American Church is a pan-Indian religion based upon a ritual that facili-tates direct contact with the Great Spirit (also God) through peyote, pipe and cigarette smoking, drumming, songs, and prayer (Bergman, 1974). Imported from Mexico in the last decades of the nineteenth century, it incorporates many elements of traditional Native American Indian cultures, especially those of the Plains tribes, integrated with Christianity (Aberle, 1966; Anderson, 1980). Predominantly revivalistic and oriented toward an Amer-ican Indian identity (rather than tribal identity) it meets the needs of some, especially younger persons who undergo intensive conversion experiences. Therapeutic effects are engendered in two ways: first, through a curing ceremony in which members of the church are treated for specific problems, often physical but also psychosocial (i.e., alcoholism) or emotional in nature. One traditional technique used is that of sucking out the evil spirit that is in the patient, while other members sing and pray. Confession of sins at the ceremony is also employed. Second, the ceremony itself includes a number of therapeutic aspects: Con-version occurs by taking peyote, a powerful psychoactive drug, and experiencing new insights or a revelation, then being purged of sins through the physical purging brought on by the drug and the associated cathartic process. Strong emotions in all participants are facilitated by the ceremony, accompanied by clear moral injunctions regarding abstinence from alcohol, marital fidelity, restraint from vengeance and fighting, and so on. As in many types of small-group religious ceremonies, a high degree of communality is fostered when food, cigarettes or pipe, and emotions and problems are all shared without distinction.

The Native American Church is one of many examples of widespread, new, cultic religions, based upon goals of cultural reaffirmation and nationalistic ideals, that have particular as well as general healing aspects (some were identified as "revitalization movements" by Wallace, 1961). They are formed through individual need arising out of far-reaching cultural change, and are typified by emphases on a traditional ethos synthesized with newer symbols. They return people to a quasitraditional community to replace one that had become fragmented and chaotic, providing the opportunity for a new type of personal commitment to social goals (Jones & Korchin, 1982).

The cultic religions offer group experiences intending resocialization as well as validating personal change within a reconstructed social arena and fit with Native American world and self views. As Topper (1987) points out, the traditional Navaho healing ceremony, led by the medicine man as a community leader, is a group phenomenon, attended by family and close neighbors. Moreover, it symbolically recreates the cosmos for the sufferer with the intent of restoring harmony. These basic attributes are extremely difficult to reproduce within behavioral or psychodynamic psychotherapies (even group and family modalities), given their individualistic (rather than communal or cosmic) orientation (Jones & Korchin, 1982; Topper, 1987).

Interface or Integration?

The question of how to interface with traditional healing among ethnic minority patients can be discussed at four levels: (1) therapist–client interaction; (2) consultation with, or referrals to, traditional healers on behalf of clients; (3) institutional attempts to work with traditional healers; and (4) innovation of synthesized therapies combining standard and ethnomedical approaches. All of these approaches are complex and full of difficulties—theoretical, practical, and ethical. Each level will be briefly discussed with examples from the literature and the author's experience.

Therapist–Client Interaction

Some authors suggest that attributes of the healer-client relationship, and the conceptual bases of ethnomedical healing systems, are so different as to make many psychotherapies invalid or inappropriate for culturally diverse clients. Topper (1987) makes a strong case that therapies that promote self-exploration or restructuring of the personality (and often bring up emotional conflicts) are negative and divisive within the context of traditional Navaho culture. They conflict with the Navaho healing goal of restoration of harmony in all life (and nonhuman) spheres. However, because ethnic minority persons do utilize mental health services, inevitably, considerations of content of the therapies, prior expectations about healer-client relationships, and the benefit of revealing certain types of personal information or other individual-centered processes need to be introduced into the therapeutic situation.

At the simplest level in the therapy process, the therapist needs to inform himself or herself about the client's experiences with traditional healing. Secondary sources can be consulted, but an attitude of ethnographic inquiry, in which the client becomes the teacher of his or her experience, is probably most productive in eliciting the content and importance of the client's ethnomedical beliefs and practices. The therapist as "clinical" ethnographer must be open, accepting, and humble at this juncture in the relationship. The most important aspect is the willingness of the client to bring this content into therapy. Therapists of similar ethnic background seem to find that clients bring this material into therapy if an opening is made (Vargas & Koss-Chioino, 1992). Though not well documented, there are indications that the therapist's attitude toward this material as well as his or her interest and prior experience may be the salient factors (Maduro, 1975).

Snow (1978) discusses cases where physicians or psychotherapists claimed success in treating symptoms and illnesses defined ethnomedically by patients. Pharmacological remedies were called or likened to ethnomedical preparations, or folk remedies were used as placebos. Not only the ethical issues but also the possibility of disruption of the therapeutic relationship make such approaches highly undesirable for use with ethnic minority clients (Koss-Chioino & Cañive, 1993).

Cooperation with Healers

In my experiences in Puerto Rico and New Mexico, consultations with healers about general matters were easy to obtain; dealing with a specific patient led directly into ethical issues as well as to questions involving the entire structure and organization of the healing professions (both ethnomedical and biomedical); see Dinges, Trimble, Manson, and Pasquale (1981) for a discussion of these issues for American Indians and Alaskan natives. With regard to ethical issues, a client must request such services, as either consultation or treatment. Issues of credibility of the traditional healer must be defined and defended; fees for service must be negotiated (which is particularly difficult when traditional healers do not charge or accept gifts); the form and content of reporting must be agreed on (including confidentiality requirements); and some way of synthesizing the two very different approaches to the disorder must be negotiated to the satisfaction of all concerned. As illustrated for Puerto Rico (Koss-Chioino, 1992), even where there is a pattern of dual use of alternative treatments for the same episode of illness, it may be difficult(but not impossible) to establish areas of complementarity. An example of this type of difficulty occurs when a healer insists that antipsychotic medication interferes with spiritual treatment of a diagnosed schizophrenic patient with a prescribed regimen of halperidol or stelazine.

Institutional Arrangements for Linking

A number of experimental projects have been attempted, such as the School for Medicine Men (Bergman, 1973), the Therapist-Spiritist Training Project in Puerto Rico (Koss, 1980; Koss-Chioino, 1992), and the employment of Spiritists at Lincoln Hospital in New York (Ruiz & Langrod, 1976). Additionally, a number of informal efforts to bring traditional healers into a clinic setting are anecdotally reported, especially for the southwestern United States. Most of these projects publicize these efforts as educational, a way to make clinicians aware of ethnomedical beliefs and practices. This tactic, though a step toward understanding and tolerance, creates the problem of recognizing the true value of the healers to their clients. The healers are often perceived as either foreign or marginal to the clinic and its mandates, and they are considered both socially inferior to physicians and mental health professionals and outside of professional boundaries.

In efforts to incorporate ethnomedicine into its services, the Indian Health Service has installed hoganlike rooms in some of its newer hospitals in New Mexico and Arizona to encourage Navaho medicine men to come into the hospitals to work with patients. Navaho staff report that these internal hogans are not really used as intended, even though medicine men regularly visit their clients in the hospitals. The issue is one of possible cooptation, in which healers working within biomedical institutional settings might change their techniques or be compromised by monetary reimbursements otherwise unavailable to them. On this point, I observed the reactions of over fifty Spiritist healers in Puerto Rico, who steadfastly maintained that they could not accept payment or carry out their usual healing work in a clinical setting. However, the healers did act as willing consultants and also worked directly with patients in hospitals or clinics who requested them. My experience has led to the conclusion that referral to alternative or traditional healers is the best policy, if the aforementioned issues can be worked out. In Puerto Rico, a successful referral unit was organized with cooperation between mental health professionals and spiritist healers, but it was never fully integrated into the structure of the community mental health system (Koss, 1980).

New Therapeutic Syntheses

There are a number of examples of innovative therapies that incorporate ethnomedical beliefs or practices in combination with standard psychotherapeutic techniques of Western, biomedical origin. The Japanese therapies Naikan and Morita have been mentioned; they are considered quite successful with persons suffering particular syndromes, such as anxiety disorders. At one extreme of a synthetic approach, there is the incorporation of specific techniques, such as acupuncture, outside of its context of Chinese medicine. Or, for example, where direct parallels have been drawn in treating depression, such as between mainstream psychotherapy and Spiritism as suggested by Comas-Díaz (1981) a synthesis might emerge. At the other extreme, there has been wholesale adoption of an entire segment of ritual healing practice where it has been deemed effective for a particular disorder or problem. For example, Wilson (1993) analyzes in detail how the sweat lodge ritual works in treating alcoholism among Native Americans, including its psychological and psychobiological dimensions, and then suggests that it could function as an efficacious form of treatment for anxiety, depression, and stress-related disorders. However, it is not clear if Wilson perceives the sweat lodge as being efficacious for other than American Indians sufferers, nor does it appear that he has attempted to actually measure its effects.

The potential of synthesizing diverse healing systems is illustrated by the Indian Shaker Church, found in California and the Northwest (Slagle & Weibel-Orlando, 1986). Although the biomedical approach is not included, since this "curing cult" is a reaction to the failure of conventional alcoholism treatment, the healing traditions of the Indian Shaker Church are comprised of ritual elements and beliefs of fundamentalist Christianity framed by indigenous models of illness and spirituality. In an approach that is in some ways like AA (but lacking the medical model of alcoholism), individuals undergo initiation and conversion experiences in a setting in which their group identity is affirmed and new roles and statuses are acquired. They also can acquire shamanic power: Those healed become healers. "The Indian Shaker Church is, at once, syncretic, nativistic and vitalistic" (Slagle & Weibel-Orlando, 1986 p. 317).

It is clearly extremely difficult to evaluate the efficacy of ethnomedical healing since measures utilized in studies of psychotherapy make very little sense when concepts, beliefs, and practices so widely differ (Pillsbury, 1982). Guidelines for both the development of new, culturally responsive therapies and their evaluation are presented in Vargas and Koss-Chioino (1992). The main thrust is to synthesize form and process with culture, defined as both context and content. The content of the therapy could be drawn from ethnomedical beliefs or a set of practices incorporated into process or structure. This and other similar formulations need to be operationalized and the resulting manualized therapies carefully assessed using quasi-experimental methodologies. This task could occupy a complete generation of researchers. It appears that ethnicity and ethnomedicine in the United States will not disappear, but will continue to provide opportunities and challenges for practice and research.

REFERENCES

Aberle, D. (1966). *The peyote religion among the Navaho.* Chicago: Aldine.

Anderson, E. F. (1980). *Peyote: The divine cactus.* Tucson: University of Arizona Press.

Baer, H. A. (1985). Toward a systematic typology of Black folk healers. *Phylon, 43,* 327–343.

Bahr, D. M., Gregorio, J., Lopez, D. I., & Alvarez, A. (1974). *Piman shamanism and staying sickness.* Tucson: University of Arizona Press.

Bailey, E. J. (1991). Hypertension: An analysis of Detroit African American health care treatment patterns. *Human Organization, 50,* 287–296.

Bergman, R. L. (1973). A school for medicine men. *American Journal of Psychiatry, 130,* 663–666.

Bergman, R. L. (1974). The peyote religion and healing. In R. H. Cox (Ed.), *Religion and psychotherapy* (pp. 296–306). Springfield, IL: Charles C. Thomas.

Blake, J. H. (1984). "Doctor can't do me no good": Social concomitants of health care attitudes and practices among elderly Blacks in isolated rural populations. In W. H. Watson (Ed.), *Black folk medicine* (pp. 33–40). New Brunswick, NJ: Transaction, Inc.

Brandon, G. (1991). The uses of plants in healing in an Afro-Cuban religion, Santería. Special issue: African aesthetics in Nigeria and the diaspora. *Journal of Black Studies, 22,* 55–76.

Chavez, L. R. (1984). Doctors, curanderos, and brujas: Health care delivery and Mexican immigrants in San Diego. *Medical Anthropology Quarterly 15,* 31–37.

Comas-Díaz, L. (1981). Puerto Rican espiritismo and psychotherapy. *American Journal of Orthopsychiatry, 51,* 636–645.

Dinges, N. G., Trimble, J. E., Manson, S. M., & Pasquale, F. L. (1981). The social ecology of counseling and psychotherapy with American Indians and Alaskan Natives. In A. J. Marsella & P. Pedersen (Eds.), *Cross-cultural counseling and psychotherapy: Foundations, evaluation, cultural considerations* (pp. 243–276). Elmsford, NY: Pergamon Press.

Fadiman, A. (1998). *The spirit catches you and you fall down: A Hmong child, her American doctors and the collision of two cultures.* New York: Farrar, Straus and Giroux.

Finkler, K. (1985). *Spiritualist healing in Mexico: Successes and failures of alternative therapies.* Hadley, MA: Bergin & Garvey.

Garrison, V. (1977). The Puerto Rican syndrome in espiritismo. In V. Crapanzano & V. Garrison (Eds.), *Case studies in spirit possession* (pp. 383–450). New York: Wiley.

Gilbert, M. J. (1980). *Mexican-Americans parents' perceptions of folk childhood disease: Little evidence of a strong folk tradition.* Paper presented at the Annual Meeting of the American Anthropological Association, Los Angeles.

Gonzalez-Wippler, M. (1973). *Santería: African magic in Latin America.* New York: Julian Press.

Hall, A. L., & Bourne, P. G. (1973). Indigenous therapists in a southern Black urban community. *Archives of General Psychiatry, 28,* 137–142.

Harwood, A. (1977). *Rx: Spiritist as needed.* New York: Wiley.

Jilek, W. G. (1982). *Indian healing: Shamanic ceremonialism in the Pacific Northwest today.* Blaine, WA: Hancock House.

Jones, E. E., & Korchin, S. J. (1982). Minority mental health perspectives. In E. E. Jones & S. J. Korchin (Eds.), *Minority mental health* (pp. 3–36). New York: Praeger.

Kawanishi, Y. (1992). Somatization of Asians: An artifact of Western medicalization? *Transcultural Psychiatric Research Review, 29,* 5–36.

Kay, M. (1977). Health and illness in a Mexican-American barrio. In E. H. Spicer (Ed.), *Ethnic medicine in the Southwest* (pp. 99–166). Tucson: University of Arizona Press.

Keefe, S. M. (1981). Folk medicine among urban Mexican-Americans: Cultural persistence, change and displacement. *Hispanic Journal of Behavioral Sciences, 3,* 41–58.

Kleinman, A. (1980). *Patients and healers in the context of culture.* Berkeley: University of California Press.

Kleinman, A., & Kleinman, J. (1985). Somatization: The interconnectedness in Chinese society among culture depressive experience and the meaning of pain. In A. Kleinman & B. Good (Eds.), *Culture & Depression* (pp.429–490). Berkeley: University of California Press.

Koss, J. (1979). On the normal and abnormal from a contemporary viewpoint: Commentary. *Journal of Operational Psychiatry, 10,* 113–118.

Koss, J. D. (1980). The Therapist-Spiritist Training Project in Puerto Rico: An experiment to relate the traditional healing system to the public health system. *Social Science and Medicine, 14,* 373–410.

Koss, J. D. (1986). Symbolic transformations in traditional healing rituals: A perspective from analytical psychology. *Journal of Analytical Psychology, 31,* 341–355.

Koss, J. D. (1987). Expectations and outcomes for patients given mental health care or spiritist healing in Puerto Rico. *American Journal of Psychiatry, 144,* 56–61.

Koss-Chioino, J. D. (1992). *Women as healers, women as patients: Mental health care and traditional healing in Puerto Rico.* San Francisco: Westview Press.

Koss-Chioino, J., & Cañive, J. (1993). The interaction of cultural and clinical diagnostic labeling: The case of embrujado. *Medical Anthropology, 15 ,* 171–188.

Kunitz, S. J. (1983). *Disease change and the role of medicine: The Navajo experience.* Berkeley: University of California Press.

Lebra, T. S. (1984). Self-reconstruction in Japanese religious psychotherapy. In A. J. Marsella & G. M. White (Eds.), *Cultural conceptions of mental health and therapy* (pp. 269–283). Boston: Reidel.

Levy, J. E., Neutra, R., & Parker, D. (1987). *Hand trembling, frenzy witchcraft and moth madness: A study of Navaho seizure disorder.* Tucson: University of Arizona Press.

Li, Z. Z. (1984). Traditional Chinese concepts of mental health. *Journal of the American Medical Association, 252,* 3169–3171.

Maduro, R. (1975). Hoodoo possession in San Francisco. *Ethos, 3,* 424–447.

Mayers, R. S. (1989). Use of folk medicine by elderly Mexican-American women. *Journal of Drug Issues, 19,* 283–295.

McClain, C. S. (1989). Reinterpreting women in healing roles. In C. S. McClain (Ed.), *Women as healers: Cross-cultural perspectives* (pp. 1–19). New Brunswick, NJ: Rutgers University Press.

McGuire, M. B. (1988). Ritual healing in suburban America. *Culture, Medicine and Psychiatry, 14,* 133–138.

Muecke, M. A. (1983). In search of healers: Southeast Asian refugees in the American health care system. *The Western Journal of Medicine, 139,* 835–840.

Murase, T. (1984). Sunao: A central value in Japanese psychotherapy. In A. J. Marsella & G. M. White (Eds.), *Cultural conceptions of mental health and therapy* (pp. 317–329). Boston: Reidel.

Neighbors, H. W. (1984). Professional help use among Black Americans: Implications for unmet need. *American Journal of Community Psychology, 12,* 551–566.

Newton, F. (1978). The Mexican American emic system of mental illness: An exploratory study. In J. M. Casas & S. E. Keefe (Eds.), *Family and mental health in the Mexican-American community* (pp. 69–89). Los Angeles: Spanish Speaking Mental Health Research Center.

Otsuka, Y. (1976). Chinese traditional medicine in Japan. In C. Leslie (Ed.), *Asian medical systems* (pp. 322–340). Berkeley: University of California Press.

Pillsbury, B. L. K. (1982). Policy and evaluation perspectives on traditional health practitioners in national health care systems. *Social Science and Medicine, 16,* 1825–1834.

Reynolds, D. K., & Kiefer, C. W. (1977). Cultural adaptability as an attribute of therapies: The case of Morita psychotherapy. *Culture, Medicine and Psychiatry, 1,* 395–412.

Rivera, G., Jr., (1988). Hispanic folk medicine utilization in urban Colorado. *Social Science Review, 72,* 237–241.

Rivera, G., Jr., & Wanderer, J. J. (1986). Curanderismo and childhood illnesses. *The Social Science Journal, 23,* 361–372.

Ruiz, P., & Langrod, J. (1976). Psychiatry and folk healing: A dichotomy? *American Journal of Psychiatry, 133,* 95–97.

Sandoval, M. C. (1977). Afro-Cuban concepts of disease and its treatment in Miami. *Journal of Operational Psychiatry, 8,* 52–63.

Seda Bonilla, E. (1964). *Interacción social y personalidad en una comunidad en Puerto Rico.* San Juan: Ediciones Edil.

Singer, M., & Borrero, M. (1984). Indigenous treatment for alcoholism: The case of Puerto Rican spiritism. *Medical Anthropology, 8,* 246–273.

Slagle, A. L., & Weibel-Orlando, J. (1986). The Indian Shaker Church and Alcoholics Anonymous: Revitalistic Curing Cults. *Human Organization,* 45(4), 310–319.

Smithsonian Institution. (1978–). *Handbook of North American Indians* (W. C. Sturtevant, General Ed.). Washington, DC: Smithsonian Institution Press.

Snow, L. (1977). Popular medicine in a Black neighborhood. In E. H. Spicer (Ed.), *Ethnic medicine in the Southwest* (pp. 19–95). Tucson: University of Arizona Press.

Snow, L. (1978). Sorcerers, saints and charlatans: Black folk healers in urban America. *Culture, Medicine and Psychiatry, 2,* 69–106.

Snow, L. (1993). *Walkin' on medicine.* Boulder, CO: Westview Press.

Topley, M. (1976). Chinese traditional etiology and methods of cure in Hong Kong. In C. Leslie (Ed.), *Asian medical systems* (pp. 243–265). Berkeley: University of California Press.

Topper, M. D. (1987). The traditional Navajo medicine man: Therapist, counselor, and community leader. *Journal of Psychoanalytic Anthropology, 10,* 217–249.

Trotter, R. T. (1981). Folk remedies as indicators of common illnesses: Examples from the United States–Mexico border. *Journal of Ethnopharmacology, 4,* 207–221.

Trotter R., & Chavira, J. (1981). *Curanderismo: Mexican folk healing.* Athens: University of Georgia Press.

Vargas, L. A., & Koss-Chioino, J. D. (1992). *Working with culture: Psychotherapeutic interventions with ethnic minority children and adolescents.* San Francisco: Jossey-Bass.

Vogel, V. J. (1977). *American Indian medicine.* Norman: University of Oklahoma Press.

Wallace, A. (1961). *Religion: An anthropological view.* New York: Random House.

Watson, W. H. (1984a). Folk medicine and older Blacks in southern United States. In W. H. Watson (Ed.), *Black folk medicine* (pp. 53–66). New Brunswick, NJ: Transaction.

Watson, W. H. (1984b). Central tendencies in the practice of folk medicine. In W. H. Watson (Ed.), *Black folk medicine* (pp. 87–97). New Brunswick, NJ: Transaction.

Westermeyer, J. (1988). Folk medicine in Laos: A comparison between two ethnic groups. *Social Science & Medicine, 27,* 769–778.

Wilson, J. P. (1993). Culture and trauma: The sacred pipe revisited. In J. P. Wilson (Ed.), *Trauma, transformation, and healing: An integrative approach to theory, research, and post-traumatic therapy* (pp. 38–71). New York: Brunner/Mazel.

Wu, D. Y. H. (1984). Psychotherapy and emotion in traditional Chinese medicine. In A. J. Marsella & G. M. White (Eds.), *Cultural conceptions of mental health and therapy* (pp. 285–301). Boston: Reidel.

Xiu, R. J. (1988). Microcirculation and traditional Chinese medicine. *Journal of the American Medical Association, 260,* 1755–1757.

10 Understanding and Treating Ethnic Minority Youth

ROBIN YOUNG PORTER

Ethnic minority children and adolescents are the largest growing segment of the United States population. By the year 2000, ethnic minority youth will make up approximately 30 percent of the population. This change will be due primarily to increased birth rates among Hispanics and rising immigration rates among Asians (Gibbs & Huang, 1989; see Chapter 1 of this book). Although the rate of growth of Black youth has been stable over the last decade, they still constitute 34 percent of the African American population (U.S. Bureau of Census, 1992). The Native American population has the largest percentage of children and adolescents (Berlin, 1987), with 37.4 percent under 18 years of age (U.S. Bureau of Census, 1992).

Ethnic minority youth present unique mental health issues because of their developmental status and membership in their ethnic culture. Some of the issues are related to sociocultural conditions (e.g., poverty, prejudice, racism), whereas others are developmental issues faced by all youth. Developmental tasks, however, are also influenced by cultural factors (Berlin, 1982). All children grow up within the context of a family, whose members bear primary responsibility for the socialization of the children. When working therapeutically with ethnic minority youth, it is important to understand the culture's concept of family so that effective interventions can be developed and implemented.

This chapter will explore issues related to the treatment of ethnic minority children and adolescents. The focus of the chapter will be on African American, Native American, Asian American, and Latin American (Hispanic) youth. Although comparisons will be made across these groups, variations within groups also need to be recognized. Sociocultural conditions and mental health problems experienced by ethnic minority children and adolescents, the types of interventions directed toward these children and adolescents, and some of the issues involved in treating them will be discussed.

Sociocultural Factors

Sociocultural factors often interfere with the ethnic minority youth's mastery of developmental tasks. Poverty, language barriers, and negative stereotypes restrict perceived as well as real access to environmental resources. As a result, the effective clinician must assess the youth's environment. Such practical issues may include helping caretakers develop transportation options to sessions, arranging tutorial services for youth and educational resources for parents, and openly discussing with youth the impact of daily exposure to discrimination, conflicting values, and racial stereotypes. Clinicians who directly observe the ethnic minority youth in their classrooms and home environment gain more accurate knowledge of their peer relationship skills, attitudes toward authority, study habits, and degree to which primary needs such as safety, shelter, hygiene, and nutrition are being met. In summary, the effective clinician must address practical sociocultural issues in addition to intrapsychic concerns.

Poverty and Low Socioeconomic Status (SES)

The high rates of poverty in Black, Hispanic, Asian American, and Native American families has been well established in the census data and in the literature (U.S. Bureau of Census, 1990; see Chapter 1). However, variations in poverty rates within each of these groups need to be recognized (Liu, Yu, Chang, & Fernandez, 1990; Ramirez, 1989). Perhaps the most direct effect of poverty is restricted access to environmental resources with which to combat substandard housing, lack of comprehensive health care, and inadequate nutrition. Several studies lend strong support to the relationship of low SES, its concomitant stressors, and high rates of psychological maladjustment among ethnic minority youth (Canino & Spurlock, 1994; Gibbs, 1984; Myers, 1989; Tolmach, 1985; Wissow, Gittelsohn, Szklo, Starfield, & Mussman, 1988).

Language Issues

Children generally learn second languages more easily and more quickly than adults. As a result, the language skills of bilingual children may threaten the traditionally strict hierarchical role of monolingual parents and children, particularly for first-generation Asian and Hispanic families (Curtis, 1990; Ho, 1992; Huang, 1994). Language issues may also interfere with academic achievement for ethnic minority youth (Canino & Spurlock, 1994). Traditional learning styles for Native American children, for example, rely heavily on nonverbal communication, observation, and enactment, as well as linguistic structures that are entirely different from those of English. As a result, the English skills of Native American children are among the poorest of any group in the United States, which partially explains their historical academic underachievement (Ho, 1992).

Although African American children may experience the least difficulty in learning standard English, many develop two forms, a "Black English" and the more standard English (Russell, 1988). In fact, many African American youth may intentionally oscillate between them ("code switching") in an attempt to regulate distance and emotional intimacy (see Chapter 2). Such language facility on the African American youth's part requires an astute clinician to understand the function of code switching and to ask for feedback to ensure accurate understanding and communication between the clinician and the client.

Stereotypes

Stereotypes are transmitted through overtly negative images and attitudes as well as in covert omissions of the positive aspects of minority cultures (Hopson & Hopson, 1990). These pervasive messages can become internalized if not countered by evidence to the contrary. When they are internalized, identity exploration may be restricted and a dichotomous mode of thinking can result (e.g., White is "good," ethnic minority is "bad"). One must choose between identifying with dominant White values in order to "achieve" or to "hang ethnic," thereby fulfilling the prophecy and acting out the negative stereotype. Such dichotomies are represented in the derogatory slurs that ethnic minority adolescents sometimes use to refer to one who has "sold out" to the dominant culture: "Oreo" refers to an African American who is considered "Black on the outside but White on the inside." Similarly, the terms "banana," "coconut," and "apple" are used for Asian Americans, Latin Americans, and Native Americans, respectively.

Academic Underachievement and School Dropout

The frequency of school dropout for the general population ranges from 5 to 30 percent. Comparable rates for dropout among Puerto Rican youth in New York City range from 42 to 80 percent (Fitzpatrick, 1987); for Native American students on reservations and in boarding schools, 50 percent drop out (Coladarci, 1983); for Black inner-city youth, 40 to 60 percent drop out (Gibbs, 1990). Fewer than half of all Hispanics complete high school (Malone, 1985). In contrast, Liu et al. (1990) report lower dropout rates for Asian American adolescents than for Whites.

Major Psychological and Social Issues

Identity Conflicts

Ethnic identity is conceptually separate from one's personal identity and from one's ethnicity, or sense of group membership. Ethnic identity is thought to be achieved through a process of crisis (exploration of alternatives) followed by commitment (decisions that reflect personal investment) (Phinney & Alipuria, 1990). Marcia (1966) provides a stage model of ethnic identity. *Idetitity achievement* is characterized by exploration of relevant issues and commitment to an identity; *moratorium* status exists when one is engaged in ongoing exploration without commitment; a *foreclosed* identity refers to commitment after little or no exploration; and identity *diffusion* refers to the absence of both exploration and commitment.

Research with Marcia's model has fairly consistently reported that minority adolescents tend to score higher in *foreclosure* than do White adolescents (Abraham, 1986; Hauser, 1972; Streitmatter, 1988). As Spencer and Markstrom-Adams (1990) point out, a viable explanation for these results may lie in the lifestyle preferences, migration patterns, and acculturation rates of the ethnic group that serve to encourage premature *foreclosure*. For example, Native American youth living on reservations may, adaptively, foreclose

identity explorations under pressure from parents and community leaders to adhere to traditional cultural norms. However, consistent failure to explore ethnic issues critically can
leave minority youth at risk for long-term psychological maladjustment (Parham & Helms,
1985; Phinney, 1989).

Although most of the research regarding ethnic identity has focused on ethnic minority adolescents, this developmental process undoubtedly has its roots in childhood, particularly with the precursor constructs of self-concept and self-esteem. Ethnic minority
children are exposed at an early age to negative messages about ethnic groups. As they
develop more cognitive maturity (e.g., inference making, self-other comparisons), they
begin to take an increasingly sophisticated approach to the self-concept. As a result of
societal experiences, however, ethnic minority children may begin to feel they have more
limited options than majority children, which can lead to a sense of inferiority, resentment,
and frustration.

Everett, Proctor, and Cartmell (1983) refer to an old Iroquois saying that one cannot
for long have one's feet in two canoes. This has relevance for ethnic minority youth who
are confronted with daily conflicts between the values of the larger dominant culture and
those of their own reference group. Adherence to the rules of one group is usually regarded
as rejection of the other group. For example, respectful love of one's parents (*oya-koko*)
requires Japanese youth to show unquestionable loyalty to lineage and parents; they are
expected to comply with familial authority even to the point of sacrificing their personal
desires and ambitions (Ho, 1992). Such clashes may foster or contribute to identity diffusion or an inability to develop bicultural competencies (i.e., successful adaptations to both
cultures).

Phinney, Lochner, and Murphy (1990) discuss four coping strategies frequently used
by ethnic youth as they struggle with identity conflicts: (1) *alienation/marginalization*—
accepting a negative self-image, which leads to alienation from one's own culture and an
inability to adapt to the majority culture; (2) *assimilation*—attempting to become part of
the dominant culture without maintaining ties to the ethnic culture; (3) *withdrawal or
separation*—seeking insulation within one's own culture and avoiding contact with the
dominant group; and (4) *integration/biculturalism*—retaining ethnic culture and learning
the necessary skills to maneuver or adapt to the dominant culture. Biculturally competent
adolescents are able to assert their own ethnic values without rejecting those of the majority and can demonstrate ethnic pride without disparaging other ethnic groups.

Substance Abuse

Although substance experimentation is relatively common among the general population
of adolescents, unique characteristics emerge among ethnic minority adolescents (see
Chapter 13). Many researchers using school populations report that alcohol and other drug
use is lower among Black and Hispanic teenagers than among White youth (Barnes &
Welte, 1986; Harford, 1985; Harper, 1988). Because of the positive association between
school dropout and substance abuse (Schinke, Moncher, Palleja, Zayas, & Schilling,
1988), however, such results may be confounded with the sampling methodology. If those
students who drop out are considered, substance abuse rates among ethnic adolescents
would appear to be much higher.

Researchers have documented the early, habitual, and widespread use of alcohol among Hispanic males, who frequently begin drinking regularly before the teen years (Caetano, 1986; Comas-Diaz, 1986; Malone, 1986a). Research has also found that Native American adolescents use drugs and alcohol earlier, more heavily, and with more dire consequences than any other ethnic/racial population in the United States (Beauvais & LaBoueff, 1985; Okwumabua & Duryea, 1987; Welte & Barnes, 1987). Native Americans lead the nation in rates of alcohol-related cirrhoses, diabetes, fetal abnormalities, accident fatalities, and homicide (Moncher, Holden, & Trimble, 1990).

Teenage Pregnancy

Whereas teenage mothers account for 12 percent of all births among White Americans, comparable proportions among Hispanics, Blacks, and Native Americans are 18 percent, 25 percent, and 22 percent, respectively (Malone, 1986b). Approximately 4 out of 10 Whites and 6 out of 10 Blacks become pregnant at least once by age 20 (McGowan & Kohn, 1990). In addition, the Black infant mortality rate is almost twice the rate for White infants (U.S. Department of Health and Human Services, 1984). As Schinke, Schilling, Palleja, and Zayas (1987) report, teenage pregnancy and parenthood are associated with educational setbacks, unemployment, family and marital problems, welfare dependency, and increased infant morbidity and mortality.

Given the relatively high rate of teenage pregnancy among ethnic minorities, Scott, Shifman, Orr, Owen, and Fawcett (1988) measured the popular beliefs and level of knowledge regarding sexuality and contraception among Black and Hispanic inner-city adolescents. The results indicated that males of both groups outscored females in accurate knowledge; Hispanic males were by far the most knowledgeable and Hispanic females the least knowledgeable. The authors suggest that these differences in sexual knowledge between Hispanic men and women can be understood within the context of two core values: *machismo* (values relating to virility) and *marianismo* (values related to virginity). Traditional Hispanic sex roles dictate that the male is assertive and deals with the outside world, whereas the female is submissive, sexually naive, and concerned only with home life.

Other reasons have been proposed for the lack of effective contraceptive use to prevent adolescent pregnancy. In the Black community, Allen-Meares (1989) suggests that one barrier is the suspicion that birth control methods and programs are a form of Black genocide imposed by the dominant White society. Other researchers suggest that many adolescents have accurate information about preventing pregnancy but may choose to have a baby as a way of assuming the adult female role (Falk, Gispert, & Baucom, 1981; Ladner, 1972). Given the lack of role models, skills, and self-confidence necessary to pursue alternative life paths, many ethnic minority girls, especially those from low-SES families, may actively seek the traditional role of mother as the only rite of passage by which to enter into adult womanhood.

Suicide and Homicide

Native Americans have the highest rate of completed suicide of any ethnic group. Suicide is the second leading cause of death for Native American adolescents, with 23.6 deaths per

100,000 in the 15–19-year cohort (U.S. Congress, 1986). Rates vary, however, from tribe to tribe (Berlin, 1985). Among those factors found to be related to Native American adolescent suicide attempts are boarding school attendance prior to ninth grade, family disruption, and marked residential mobility even when families stayed together (Dizmang, Watson, May, & Bopp, 1974; May & Dizmang, 1974; Teicher, 1979). Young (1988) suggests that alcohol abuse is a critical risk factor for suicidal behavior on the basis of the finding that 80 percent of Native American adolescent suicide attempters also abuse alcohol.

Liu et al. (1990) report minimal change in the suicide rate for Asian American youth from 1970 to 1980 after adjusting for population increases. Proportional mortality rates for suicide during this time, however, showed that suicide accounts for a much larger proportion of deaths among Asian American youth than among White American cohorts. For both Japanese and Chinese American adolescents, the suicide death rate has been reported to be consistently higher for foreign-born than for American-born adolescents. Such differences can be attributed either to cultural beliefs and practices and/or to the stress associated with acculturation to United States society.

Although suicidal behavior for Black adolescents is increasing, suicide rates for this group are much lower than for White adolescents (Gibbs, 1990). Gibbs (1990) warns, however, that the incidence of suicide for Black youth may be underestimated given that actual suicidal behavior may be masked by acting out and high-risk behaviors, thereby making suicidal intent more difficult to assess. Little consistent data are available regarding recent suicide rates for Hispanic adolescents (Heacock, 1990; Wyche & Rotheram-Borus, 1990). The general consensus is that the Mexican American rate is approximately half that of Whites (Hope & Martin, 1986).

In 1986, the leading cause of death for Black males aged 15–19 was homicide, perhaps because of the rapid rise of drug-related activity and violent crime. Black-on-Black homicide is the leading cause of death among young Black males (Bell, 1987). Hispanic homicide, often substance related, has a rate of 88 per 100,000 as compared to 19 per 100,000 for non-Hispanic young males (Centers for Disease Control, 1988; Loya et al., 1986). In New York City, for example, Hispanics disproportionately account for 42 percent of all drug-related deaths, a figure far in excess of their representation in the city's population (Schinke et al., 1988).

Delinquency

Research has found that male and female ethnic minority adolescents have higher incarceration rates than White adolescents (Krisberg et al., 1987). Several studies also report that Black juvenile delinquents have higher rates of depression and of other psychological and neurological symptoms than their White counterparts and that these disorders are frequently undetected, undiagnosed, and untreated (Dembo, 1988; Gibbs, 1982). These authors point out that whereas White youth with similar behaviors are more likely to be referred to the mental health system, Black offenders are channeled into the juvenile justice system.

Chavez, Oetting, and Swaim (1994) investigated delinquent behavior among a large sample of Mexican American and White adolescents and found a consistent relationship between academic status and every type of delinquent behavior studied for both groups. These results suggest that Mexican American dropouts are no more delinquent than White dropouts. Proportionally, however, there are more of them. Given the strong relationship between delinquency and achievement, the remediation of social and learning conditions that prevent Mexican American children from succeeding academically should be targeted in prevention programs. Such efforts would not only reduce dropout but also contribute to reducing delinquency.

Violence and Gangs

A growing body of literature has begun to address the recent rise in violence and gang behavior among ethnic minority youth. Some of the rise in violence and gangs has been attributed to the growing popularity and distribution of "crack" cocaine. Gang affiliation or membership is often associated with substance abuse (Clark, 1992). Gangs provide emotional support and a sense of belonging (Clark, 1992; Lyon, Henggeler, & Hall, 1992), which is often lacking in the families of gang members. In addition, the influence of deviant peers is often associated with gang membership (Frauenglass, Routh, Pantin, & Mason, 1997; Lyon et al., 1992). Lyon, Henggeler, and Hall (1992) found that incarcerated gang members reported engaging in more criminal offenses than incarcerated juvenile offenders who were not gang members. In addition, they found higher rates of delinquency among 13- to 18-year-old Caucasian offenders than among Hispanic American offenders. For Hispanic youth, family factors often mediate the influence of deviant peers and gang involvement (Frauenglass et al., 1997; Lyon et al., 1992). Some of the symptoms experienced by adolescent gang members include depression, social withdrawal, hopelessness about the future, alienation, and substance abuse (Clark, 1992). Hritz and Gabow (1997) describe a gang intervention program conducted in Denver, Colorado. This approach has many similarities to the Alcoholics Anonymous (AA) model. In addition, a number of school-based and community-based violence prevention programs have been developed for youth (Ward, 1995). Some authors advocate incorporating culture into violence-prevention programs (Ward, 1995). African American youth are witnessing an ever-increasing influence of violent incidents, and the emotional effects of this exposure to violence is just beginning to be studied (Farrell & Bruce, 1997).

Impact of Psychological and Social Issues

In summary, it is important to understand how the sociocultural and ethnic group contexts influence the development of mental health problems in ethnic minority youth. Some researchers (Phinney et al., 1990) postulate that the common element among ethnic youth at risk for future psychological maladjustment is the maintenance of a foreclosed or diffuse identity status. In addition, cultural marginality and the stress associated with acculturation results in heightened anxiety, lowered self-esteem, and aggressive acting-out or withdrawal behavior, which can contribute to such problems as substance abuse, academic underachievement or dropout, teenage pregnancy, delinquency, violence, gang involvement, and suicide and homicide among ethnic minority youth.

Treatment Issues

Trust is a major issue in the therapeutic relationship, for it enhances rapport and contributes to change in the client. With ethnic minority clients and White therapists, however, there is often a lack of trust based on the client's personal and historical experiences with Whites and helping professionals (Everett et al., 1983; Gibbs & Huang, 1989). Even with ethnically similar therapists and clients, there may be a lack of trust arising from the perception that the therapist has sold out and supports the values of the White middle class. Trust is usually a major issue with ethnic minority adolescents, who are typically coming to therapy involuntarily (Gibbs & Huang, 1989; Sykes, 1987). Like most adolescents, they often do not perceive they have a problem, nor do they trust that talking about issues with an adult will help.

One way to enhance trust with ethnic minority youth is for the therapist to be self-disclosing and to share limited personal information. This accomplishes three things:

1. It provides a model for self-disclosure to the adolescent who may feel uncomfortable discussing intimate feelings.
2. It enhances rapport with the adolescent.
3. It facilitates open communication (Gibbs & Huang, 1989).

Other important aids to developing trust are educating the client about the therapist's role, the client's role, and the process of therapy; reinforcing the parents as the authority; emphasizing confidentiality; discussing racial differences; and displaying ethnic material in the office.

A second important issue is transference. Some ethnic minority cultures (e.g., Asian Americans) tend to view professionals as experts and authority figures. Therefore, there may be a tendency for the ethnic minority child or adolescent to view the therapist as an authority or parental figure (Sykes, 1987). Consequently, the child or adolescent may not feel free to express his or her feelings without some fear of "parental" reprisal or sanction. Anger is also frequently part of the transference, particularly from ethnic minority adolescent males. It is important for the therapist to be aware of and understand the sociocultural, historical, and immediate source of the anger rather than ascribing it to the narrow transference context.

Countertransference can also hinder the effectiveness of therapy with ethnic minority children and adolescents (Hobbs, 1985). Countertransferential reactions or feelings can be a problem with ethnically dissimilar as well as similar therapists. There may be misunderstandings between ethnically similar therapists and clients when the therapist fails to explore unique client issues because of assumptions of shared meaning based on a common cultural background. Maki (1990) has identified several obstacles to therapy related to the countertransference between ethnically similar clients and therapists: (1) an assumption of cultural themes, (2) a denial of identification or overidentification, (3) manifestations of aggression, and (4) avoidance of envy.

White therapists may experience countertransferential feelings of fear, intimidation, hatred, aggression, patronization, or denial, which can inhibit exploration of significant issues and themes with the client (Spurlock, 1985). For example, the White therapist may attempt to deny racial differences with the ethnic minority child or adolescent by trying to appear "color-blind." Such a position invalidates the client's ethnic and/or racial identity and denies his or her daily experiences. In addition, the therapist may fail to set and/or enforce limits, particularly with African American male adolescents, who often express anger at the external controls placed on their behavior by the larger society as well as by the therapist (Hobbs, 1985). In working with ethnic minority youth, it is important for the therapist to be aware of and understand his or her own feelings of ethnicity, racism, stereotypes, and oppression (Hull, 1982; Spurlock, 1985; Sykes, 1987; and see Chapter 5).

Treatment Approaches

Therapeutic intervention with ethnic minority children and adolescents requires a culturally sensitive, well-organized, and theoretically sound framework (Canino & Spurlock, 1994; Ho, 1992; Malgady, Rogler, & Costantino, 1990). As with ethnic minority adults, many contextual factors must be considered, such as the client's culture, level of acculturation and bicultural competency skills, English verbal ability, developmental levels, family traditions and structure, and attitudes toward help-seeking behaviors. In the following sections, three modes of intervention will be discussed: (1) individual therapy for the ethnic minority child or adolescent, (2) family therapy, and (3) group therapy. Within each approach, specific examples will be offered to illustrate ways in which these can be modified to demonstrate cultural sensitivity to ethnic minority youth.

Individual Therapy

Perhaps the first task of the therapist who hopes to engage an ethnic minority child or adolescent in individual therapy is to enlist parental cooperation and collaboration for the child's treatment. Failure to do so is perhaps the primary cause of premature termination among ethnic minority children and adolescents (Ho, 1992). An integral part of this invitation process is the therapist's ability to demonstrate awareness of and sensitivity toward cultural norms and social mores. For example, more traditional Native American children and adults consider direct eye contact to be disrespectful (Everett et al., 1983). Therapists from the White majority culture, on the other hand, may interpret the lack of eye contact to imply lack of interest, resistance, or even rudeness.

Behavior that is adaptive in one culture may be considered maladaptive in another culture (Spurlock, 1985). African American parents, for example, tend to discipline their children more harshly than White parents, but this discipline is not always seen as abusive (Spurlock, 1985). In addition, a Native American cultural value is the shared responsibility for raising children. However, to an individual outside of this culture, it may appear that parents are neglecting children who have been sent to live with nonrelatives (Hull, 1982). In Hispanic culture, traditional norms regarding sex roles that are strictly defined clash with middle-class American norms that allow for more flexibility (Hardy-Fanta & Montana, 1982).

In addition to careful monitoring of nonverbal cues, the therapist should also remain mindful of the ethnic client's perception of the interpersonal dynamics during the sessions.

During intake procedures, for example, many mental health providers attempt to gather as much information as early as possible in the form of a series of detailed personal questions. Such an interviewing style may be perceived by many ethnic group members as an overly intrusive interrogation. Consequently, stylistic modifications are advised. For Native Americans, such modifications may include moderate amounts of personal self-disclosure on the part of the professional in order to create an atmosphere of reciprocity (Everett et al. 1983; Katz, 1981; LaFromboise & Rowe, 1983). With Hispanic and Asian clients, therapists (especially young female therapists) may need to inform parents of their credentials in order to foster a heightened sense of ascribed status (Ho, 1992; Sue & Zane, 1987).

Individual Therapy with Children.   Because of its problem-solving focus, time-limited nature, and emphasis on strengthening coping skills, Ho recommends short-term ego-supportive psychotherapy for most ethnic minority children with nonpsychotic disorders (Ho, 1992). Because the main goal of this therapy is solution-focused (i.e., getting needs met adoptively through identification of alternatives and decision making), a trusting relationship between the child and the therapist is crucial to foster motivation for change, strengthen self-esteem, permit role modeling, and promote corrective emotional experiences. Neal-Barnett and Smith (1996) describe the use of an Afrocentric approach to behavior therapy with African American children.

Some ethnic minority children, especially those whose cultures do not sanction open expression of feelings, or those with limited English skills, may not be able to participate verbally to the degree required by the approaches advocated here. In these situations, play therapy may be the only avenue by which a child can communicate conflicts, fantasies, and emotional issues. As Ho (1992) points out, traditional cultures may view therapeutic play as frivolous, a view commonly held by some Asian cultures. As a result, play therapists may first need to educate parents about the value of therapeutic play.

Individual Therapy with Adolescents.   Ethnic minority adolescents most often come to the attention of mental health providers as a result of transgressions against societal norms and laws. By the time a referral is initiated, many ethnic minority adolescents have already internalized negative images of themselves. As a result, many adolescents approach therapists with hostility or apathy, both of which are manifestations of the adolescent's struggle to defend against overwhelming powerlessness and hopelessness (Hobbs, 1985). Thus, an initial goal of therapy is to acknowledge these feelings and help the adolescent recognize the value of treatment and take advantage of the opportunity to learn about and change one's self through therapy.

As previously noted, ethnic minority adolescents often experience identity conflicts, particularly in their attempts to develop "bicultural competence." Not exploring ethnic issues during the identity process makes the adolescent vulnerable to a poor self-concept and low self-esteem. Helping the adolescent develop a positive integrated identity will empower him or her and enhance his or her self-concept. Academic intervention efforts should target remediation of social and learning conditions that prevent ethnic minority youth from succeeding academically. Such efforts would not only reduce dropout, but also contribute to reducing delinquency. In addition, for adolescent pregnancy prevention, the focus should be on economic, educational, and social opportunities that make delaying pregnancy a desirable goal. One implication for treatment with teen mothers is that social isolation must be a target for intervention.

Because of the tendency for many poor ethnic minority adolescents to be involved with multiple agencies in addition to the mental health professional, therapists are cautioned to balance carefully the pull for case management services with the need for in-depth psychotherapy (Hobbs, 1985; Spurlock, 1985). Although the early stages of therapy can be strengthened when therapists demonstrate awareness of and assistance with practical issues, this role should be limited in order to focus on issues such as perceptions of personal power, responsibility, autonomy, and appropriate outlets for the expression of anger and frustration (Hobbs, 1985; Katz, 1981; LaFromboise & Bigfoot, 1988). Social skills training can be a valuable component of therapy in the areas of conflict resolution, anger management, and assertiveness.

Family Therapy

Family therapy offers many unique advantages for serving ethnic children and adolescents that are not easily afforded by individual and group formats (see Chapter 6). Reliance on the extended family as the primary support resource has traditionally characterized ethnic minority families and may represent a more familiar approach to problem solving than other modes of therapy. Family therapy seeks to enhance an individual's interactions with others who can provide support and nurturance, which increases the likelihood that changes can be maintained outside the context of the therapeutic relationship. Any successful attempts to strengthen familial functioning are likely to benefit a child. Particularly salient situations in which family treatment is recommended occur when the child is scapegoated as a result of parental frustrations or feelings of victimization, and when the child and the parents are experiencing generational, acculturation, or cultural conflicts (Ho, 1992).

To demonstrate cultural sensitivity to families, therapists should express personal interest in the family and search for strengths, perhaps by praising the family for its willingness to seek assistance in solving the identified problem. Issues of race should be raised early, especially when the therapist is of a different ethnic or racial background from the family. Conveying to the family that the therapist is not "color-blind" facilitates more open and honest discussion (Grevious, 1985; Ho, 1992; Sykes, 1987). Boyd-Franklin (1989) cautions against attempting extensive data collection and using a genogram with African American families in the initial interview because many are suspicious of therapists "prying" into their lives. She advises waiting until some degree of trust has been established, which increases the likelihood of getting more detailed and constructive information.

Sykes (1987) advocates using structural family therapy with African American adolescents. He postulates that this form of therapy is helpful because it focuses less on pathology within the individual and more on alterations in family structure that have resulted from stressful life situations. In addition, this approach is short-term and goal-oriented, and it accounts for the impact of external sources on the family. Cultural sensitivity is also demonstrated by exploring the family's kinship network and inviting relevant individuals to participate in sessions (Boyd-Franklin, 1989). Therapists should bear in mind that many ethnic families include non–blood relatives within the family network, such as friends, neighbors, ministers and deacons, Hispanic godparents, tribal leaders, and elderly members of Asian communities.

Frequently, therapeutic efforts that focus on helping parents to become reestablished into natural helping networks within their communities are the best means by which to help a child or adolescent. These efforts not only can stabilize home life but also can empower the family to solve its own problems (Edwards & Egbert-Edwards, 1990; McGowan & Kohn, 1990; Rodriguez & Zayas, 1990). The therapist may suggest or the family may already be involved with indigenous support systems, such as *curanderos, espiritistas,* and medicine men (see Chapter 9). It may also be helpful to integrate indigenous healers into the therapy or to consult with them with the family's permission.

It is important for the therapist to understand that the roles of family members in ethnic minority cultures may vary. In African American families, for example, the roles of husband and wife tend to be relatively egalitarian (see Chapter 11), whereas Asian American and Latin American husbands tend to be ascribed a more dominant role than their wives. It is also important that the therapist be sensitive to family structure issues (Nagata, 1989). In Asian American culture, for example, the structure tends to be hierarchical and male-dominated. This can have implications in treatment regarding whom the therapist should address. All communication should be addressed to the father, who is considered the head of the household (Nagata, 1989). In addition, any use of a child as an interpreter during the session should be avoided, as this unbalances the hierarchy of the family by providing the child with more power than the parents, particularly the father (see Chapter 11).

Group Therapy

Having experienced discrimination and oppression within the larger dominant culture, ethnic groups historically have found refuge and survival value in their group (see Chapter 7). In a cohesive group atmosphere, ethnic minority children and adolescents may benefit greatly from the power of collective feedback (Canino & Spurlock, 1994). In heterogeneous groups composed of people from diverse ethnic and racial backgrounds and varying levels of acculturation, members may learn new communication styles and alternative coping skills, and may experiment with new ways to solve problems through peer modeling and social reinforcement. Ho (1992) suggests that group therapy can be an especially effective modality for the following problems: (1) difficulties with acculturation processes, (2) exploration of ethnic awareness and identity issues, (3) strengthening of bicultural socialization skills, and (4) feelings of isolation and loneliness.

For group therapy with ethnic minority children and adolescents, group composition deserves careful forethought. Generally, groups developed with the goal of ethnic identity exploration should be homogeneous in membership, whereas groups established to lessen racial prejudice and stereotypes should consist of members with different ethnic and racial backgrounds in order to provide an opportunity for positive interracial interaction. An additional group composition parameter is the verbal communication styles of the members. Whereas Asian, Native American, and Hispanic children are generally discouraged from interrupting and are less likely to push to be heard, African American and White children are typically more aggressive and verbose in a group (Bilides, 1991; Ho, 1992). Similarly, Asian and Latin American minority youth may feel less comfortable making personal disclosures in the group setting. Given different communication styles and levels of comfort regarding self-disclosure, the group therapist must provide a structure that allows verbally active ethnic minority youth to express themselves and also enables less vocal youth to participate.

Conclusion

As the ethnic minority youth population continues to increase into the next century, it is incumbent upon mental health practitioners to learn effective ways of working with these youth and their families. In order to provide culturally sensitive treatment to ethnic minority children and adolescents, the therapist should be knowledgeable about communication style differences (verbal and nonverbal), family structure and role differences, language and acculturation issues, stereotypes, sociocultural influences, ethnic minority identity development, and how racism and oppression affect the psychological development of ethnic minority youth. The issues of trust, transference, and countertransference are especially crucial in the treatment process of ethnic minority youth.

Further research would be helpful in the area of how ethnic identity status may influence psychopathology in ethnic minority adolescents. All the modalities of treatment discussed in this chapter share a focus on the need to help ethnic minority youth integrate ethnic identity with personal identity and the importance of exploring the perception of limited alternatives. This process can be vital in increasing the youth's self-esteem and self-concept. The therapist can accomplish this by helping ethnic minority youth become educated about their culture, helping them to learn how to counteract negative stereotypes, and empowering them to confront and deal with racism effectively.

REFERENCES

Abraham, K. G. (1986). Ego-identity differences among Anglo-American and Mexican American adolescents. *Journal of Adolescence, 9,* 151–166.

Allen-Meares, P. (1989). Adolescent sexuality and premature parenthood: Role of the Black Church in prevention. *Journal of Social Work and Human Sexuality, 8,* 133–142.

Barnes, G. M., & Welte, J. W. (1986). Alcohol consumption of Black youth. *Journal of Studies on Alcohol, 47,* 53–61.

Beauvais, F. B., & LaBoueff, S. (1985). Drug and alcohol abuse intervention in American Indian communities. *International Journal of the Addictions, 20,* 139–171.

Bell, C. C. (1987). Preventive strategies for dealing with violence among Blacks. *Community Mental Health Journal, 23,* 217–228.

Berlin, I. N. (1982). Prevention of emotional problems among Native American children: Overview of developmental issues. *Journal of Preventive Psychiatry, 1,* 319–330.

Berlin, I. N. (1985). Prevention of adolescent suicide among some Native American tribes. *Adolescent Psychiatry, 12,* 77–93.

Berlin, I. N. (1987). Suicide among American Indian adolescents. *Suicide and Life-Threatening Behavior, 17* 218–232.

Bilides, D. (1991). Race, color, ethnicity, and class: Issues of biculturalism in school-based adolescent counseling groups. *Social Work with Groups, 13,* 43–58.

Boyd-Franklin, N. (1989). Five key factors in the treatment of Black families. *Journal of Psychotherapy and the Family, 6,* 53–69.

Caetano, R. (1986). Patterns and problems of drinking among U.S. Hispanics. In T. E. Malone (Ed.), *Report of the Secretary's Task Force on Black and Minority Health: Volume VII: Chemical dependency and diabetes* (pp. 141–186). GPO Publication No.

491-313/4409. Washington, DC: U.S. Government Printing Office.

Canino, I. A., & Spurlock, J. (1994). *Culturally diverse children and adolescents.* New York: Guilford Press.

Centers for Disease Control. (1988). *High-risk racial and ethnic groups—Blacks and Hispanics, 1970–1983.* Atlanta, GA: Author.

Chavez, E. L., Oetting, E. R., & Swaim, R. C. (1994). Dropout and delinquency: Mexican American and Caucasian non-Hispanic youth. *Journal of Clinical Child Psychology, 23,* 47–55.

Clark, C. (1992). Deviant adolescent subcultures: Assessment strategies and clinical interventions. *Adolescence, 27*(106), 283–293.

Coladarci, T. (1983). High school dropout among Native Americans. *Journal of American Indian Education, 23,* 15–23.

Comas-Díaz, L. (1986). Puerto Rican alcoholic women: Treatment considerations. *Alcohol Treatment Quarterly, 3,* 47–56.

Curtis, P. A. (1990). The consequences of acculturation to service delivery and research with Hispanic families. *Child and Adolescent Social Work, 7,* 147–159.

Dembo, R. (1988). Delinquency among Black male youth. In J. T. Gibbs (Ed.), *Young, Black and male in America: An endangered species* (pp. 174–189). Dover, MA: Auburn House.

Dizmang, L., Watson, J., May P., & Bopp, J. (1974). Adolescent suicide at an Indian reservation. *American Journal of Orthopsychiatry, 44,* 43–50.

Edwards, E. D., & Egbert-Edwards, M. (1990). American Indian adolescents: Combating problems of substance use and abuse through a community model. In A. R. Stiffman & L. E. Davis (Eds.), *Ethnic issues in adolescent mental health* (pp. 285–302). Newbury Park, CA: Sage.

Everett, F., Proctor, N., & Cartmell, B. (1983). Providing psychological services to American Indian children and families. *Professional Psychology: Research and Practice, 14,* 588–603.

Falk, R., Gispert, M., & Baucom, D. H. (1981). Personality factors related to Black teenage pregnancy and abortion. *Psychology of Women Quarterly, 5,* 737–746.

Farrell, A. D., & Bruce, S.E. (1997). Impact of exposure to community violence on violent behavior and emotional distress among urban adolescents. *Journal of Clinical Child Psychology, 26*(1), 2–14.

Fitzpatrick, J. P. (1987). *Puerto Rican Americans.* Englewood Cliffs, NJ: Prentice-Hall.

Frauenglass, S., Routh, D. K., Pantin, H. M., & Mason, C. A. (1997). Family support decreases influence of deviant peers on Hispanic adolescents' substance use. *Journal of Clinical Child Psychology, 26*(1), 15–23.

Gibbs, J. T. (1982). Personality patterns of delinquent females: Ethnic and sociocultural variations. *Journal of Clinical Psychology, 38,* 198–206.

Gibbs, J. T. (1984). Black adolescents and youth: An endangered species. *American Journal of Orthopsychiatry, 54,* 6–21.

Gibbs, J. T. (1990). Mental health issues of Black adolescents: Implications for policy and practice. In A. R. Stiffman & L. E. Davis (Eds.), *Ethnic issues in adolescent mental health* (pp. 21–52). Newbury Park, CA: Sage.

Gibbs, J. T., & Huang, L. N. (1989). A conceptual framework for assessing and treating minority youth. In J. T. Gibbs, L. N. Huang, & Associates (Eds.), *Children of color: Psychological interventions with minority youth* (pp. 1–29). San Francisco: Jossey-Bass.

Grevious, C. (1985). The role of the family therapist with low-income Black families. *Family Therapy, 12,* 115–122.

Hardy-Fanta, C., & Montana, P. (1982). The Hispanic female adolescent: A group therapy model. *International Journal of Group Psychotherapy, 32,* 351–366.

Harford, T. C. (1985). Drinking patterns among Black and non-Black adolescents: Results of a national survey. In E. M. Freeman (Ed.), *Social work practice with clients who have alcohol problems* (pp. 276–291). Springfield, IL: Thomas.

Harper, F. D. (1988). Alcohol and Black youth: An overview. *Journal of Drug Issues, 18,* 7–14.

Hauser, S. T. (1972). Adolescent self-image development. *Archives of General Psychiatry, 27,* 537–541.

Heacock, D. R. (1990). Suicidal behavior in Black and Hispanic youth. *Psychiatric Annals, 20,* 134–142.

Ho, M. K. (1992). *Minority children and adolescents in therapy.* Newbury Park, CA: Sage.

Hobbs, S. R. (1985). Issues in psychotherapy with Black male adolescents in the inner city: A Black clinician's perspective. *Journal of Non-White Concerns, 13,* 79–87.

Hope, S. K., & Martin, H. W. (1986). Patterns of suicide among Mexican-Americans and Anglos, 1960–1980. *Social Psychiatry, 21,* 83–88.

Hopson, D. W., & Hopson, D. S. (1990). *Different and wonderful.* New York: Simon & Schuster.

Hritz, S. A., & Gabow, P. A. (1997). A peer approach to high risk youth. *Journal of Adolescent Health, 20,* 259–260.

Huang, L. N. (1994). An integrative approach to clinical assessment and intervention with Asian-American adolescents. *Journal of Clinical Child Psychology, 23,* 21–31.

Hull, G. H., Jr. (1982). Child welfare services to Native Americans. *Social Casework: The Journal of Contemporary Social Work, 63,* 340–347.

Katz, P. (1981). Psychotherapy with Native adolescents. *Canadian Journal of Psychiatry, 26,* 455–459.

Krisberg, B., Schwartz, I., Fishman, G., Eisikovits, Z., Guttman, E., & Joe, K. (1987). The incarceration of minority youth. *Crime and Delinquency, 33,* 173–205.

Ladner, J. (1972). *Tomorrow's tomorrow: The Black woman.* Garden City, NY: Doubleday.

LaFromboise, T. D., & Bigfoot, D. S. (1988). Cultural and cognitive considerations in the prevention of American Indian adolescent suicide. *Journal of Adolescence, 11,* 139–153.

LaFromboise, T. D., & Rowe, W. (1983). Skills training for bicultural competence: Rationale and application. *Journal of Counseling Psychology, 30,* 389–595.

Liu, W. T., Yu, E. S. H., Chang, C. F., & Fernandez, M. (1990). The mental health of Asian American teenagers: A research challenge. In A. R. Stiffman & L. E. Davis (Eds.), *Ethnic issues in adolescent mental health* (pp. 92–112). Newbury Park, CA: Sage.

Loya, F., Garcia, P., Sullivan, J. D., Vargas, L. A., Allen, N. H., & Mercy, A. (1986). Conditional risks of types of homicide among Anglo, Hispanic, Black, and Asian victims in Los Angeles, 1970–1979. In T. E. Malone (Ed.), *Report of the Secretary's Task Force on Black and Minority Health: Volume V: Homicide, suicide, and unintentional injuries* (pp. 117–133). GPO Publication No. 491-313/44710. Washington, DC: U.S. Government Printing Office.

Lyon, J. M., Henggeler, S., & Hall, J. A. (1992). The family relations, peer relations, and criminal activities of Caucasian and Hispanic-American gang members. *Journal of Abnormal Child Psychology, 20*(5), 439–449.

Maki, M. (1990). Countertransference with adolescent clients of the same ethnicity. *Child and Adolescent Social Work, 7,* 135–145.

Malgady, R. G., Rogler, L. H., & Costantino, G. (1990). Culturally sensitive psychotherapy for Puerto Rican children and adolescents: A program of treatment outcome research. *Journal of Consulting and Clinical Psychology, 58,* 704–712.

Malone, T. E. (1985). *Report of the Secretary's Task Force on Black and Minority Health: Volume 1: Executive summary.* GPO Publication No. 487-637/QL3. Washington, DC: U.S. Government Printing Office.

Malone, T. E. (1986a). *Report of the Secretary's Task Force on Black and Minority Health: Volume V: Homicide, Suicide, and Unintentional Injuries.* GPO Publication No. 491-313/44710. Washington, DC: U.S. Government Printing Office.

Malone, T. E. (1986b). *Report of the Secretary's Task Force on Black and Minority Health: Volume VI:*

Infant mortality and low birth weight. GPO No. 491-313/44711. Washington, DC: U.S. Government Printing Office.

Marcia, J. E. (1966). Development and validation of ego identity status. *Journal of Youth and Adolescence, 13,* 419–438.

May, P., & Dizmang, L. (1974). Suicide and the American Indian. *Psychiatric Annals, 4,* 22–28.

McGowan, B. G., & Kohn, A. (1990). Social support and teen pregnancy in the for policy and practice. In A. R. Stiffman & L. E. Davis (Eds.), *Ethnic issues in adolescent mental health* (pp. 189–207). Newbury Park, CA: Sage.

Moncher, M. S., Holden, G. W., & Trimble, J. E. (1990). Substance abuse among Native American youth. *Journal of Consulting and Clinical Psychology, 58,* 408–415.

Myers, H. F. (1989). Urban stress and mental health of Afro-American youth: An epidemiologic and conceptual update. In R. L. Jones (Ed.), *Black adolescents* (pp. 123–152). Berkeley, CA: Cobbs & Henry.

Nagata, D. K. (1989). Japanese American children and adolescents. In J. T. Gibbs, L. N. Huang, & Associates (Eds.), *Children of color: Psychological interventions with minority youth* (pp. 67–113). San Francisco: Jossey-Bass.

Neal-Barnett, A.M., & Smith Sr., J.M. (1996). African American children and behavior therapy: Considering the Afrocentric approach. *Cognitive Behavioral Research and Practice, 2,* 351–369.

Okwumabua, J. O., & Duryea, E. J. (1987). Age of onset, periods of risk, and patterns of progression in drug use among American Indian high school students. *International Journal of the Addictions, 22,* 1269–1276.

Parham, T., & Helms, J. (1985). Attitudes of racial identity and self-esteem of Black students: An exploratory investigation. *Journal of College Students Personnel, 26,* 143–147.

Phinney, J. S. (1989). Stages of ethnic identity development in minority group adolescents. *Journal of Early Adolescence, 9,* 34–49.

Phinney, J. S., & Alipuria, L. L. (1990). Ethnic identity in college students from four ethnic groups. *Journal of Adolescence, 13,* 171–183.

Phinney, J. S., Lochner, B. T., & Murphy, R. (1990). Ethnic identity development and psychological adjustment in adolescence. In A. R. Stiffman & L. E. Davis (Eds.), *Ethnic issues in adolescent mental health* (pp. 53–72). Newbury Park, CA: Sage.

Ramirez, O. (1989). Mexican American children and adolescents. In J. T. Gibbs, L. N. Huang, & Associates (Eds.), *Children of color: Psychological interven-*

tions with minority youth (pp. 224–250). San Francisco: Jossey-Bass.

Rodriguez, O., & Zayas, L. H. (1990). Hispanic adolescents and antisocial behavior: Sociocultural factors and treatment implications. In A. R. Stiffman & L. E. Davis (Eds.), *Ethnic issues in adolescent mental health* (pp. 147–171). Newbury Park, CA: Sage.

Russell, D. M. (1988). Language and psychotherapy: The influence of nonstandard English in clinical practice. In L. Comas-Díaz & E. E. H. Griffith (Eds.), *Clinical guidelines in cross-cultural mental health* (pp. 33–68). New York: Wiley.

Schinke, S. P., Moncher, M. S., Palleja, J., Zayas, L. H., & Schilling, R. F. (1988). Hispanic youth, substance abuse, and stress: Implications for prevention research. *International Journal of the Addictions, 23,* 809–826.

Schinke, S. P., Schilling, R. F., Palleja, J., & Zayas, L. H. (1987). Prevention research among ethnic-racial minority group adolescents. *The Behavior Therapist, 10,* 151–155.

Scott, C. S., Shifman, L., Orr, L., Owen, R. G., & Fawcett, N. (1988). Hispanic and Black American adolescents' beliefs relating to sexuality and contraception. *Adolescence, 23,* 667–688.

Spencer, M. B., & Markstrom-Adams, C. (1990). Identity processes among racial and ethnic minority children in America. *Child Development, 61,* 290–310.

Spurlock, J. (1985). Assessment and therapeutic intervention of Black children. *Journal of the American Academy of Child Psychiatry, 24,* 168–174.

Streitmatter, J. L. (1988). Ethnicity as a mediating variable of early adolescent identity development. *Journal of Adolescence, 11,* 335–346.

Sue, S., &. Zane, N. (1987). The role of culture and cultural techniques in psychotherapy: A critique and reformulation. *American Psychologist, 42,* 37–45.

Sykes, D. K., Jr. (1987). An approach to working with Black youth in cross cultural therapy. *Clinical Social Work Journal, 15,* 260–270.

Teicher, J. D. (1979). Suicide and suicide attempters. In J. D. Noshpitz (Ed.), *Basic handbook of child psychiatry: Disturbances of development* (Vol. 2, pp. 685–697). New York: Basic Books.

Tolmach, J. (1985). "There ain't nobody on my side": A new day treatment program for Black urban youth. *Journal of Clinical Child Psychology, 14,* 214–219.

U.S. Bureau of the Census. (1990). *1990 census of population and housing—Summary tape file 1. Summary population and housing characteristics.* Washington, DC: U.S. Government Printing Office.

U.S. Bureau of the Census. (1992). *1990 census of population, 1990 CP-1-4, General population characteristics.* Washington, DC: U.S. Government Printing Office.

U.S. Congress. (1986). *Indian health care* (OTA-H-290). Washington, DC: U.S. Government Printing Office.

U.S. Department of Health and Human Services. (1984). National Center for Health Statistics. *Monthly Vital Statistics Report* (Vol. 33, No. 3). Washington, DC: Author.

Ward, J. V. (1995). Cultivating a morality of care in African American adolescents: A culture-based model of violence prevention. *Harvard Educational Review, 65* (2), 175–191.

Welte, J. W., & Bames G. M. (1987). Alcohol use among adolescent minority groups. *Journal of Studies on Alcohol, 48,* 329–336.

Wissow, L. S., Gittelsohn, A. M., Szklo, M., Starfield, B., & Mussman, M. (1988). Poverty, race, and hospitalization for childhood asthma. *American Journal of Public Health, 78,* 777–781.

Wyche, K. F., & Rotheram-Borus, M. J. (1990). Suicidal behavior among minority youth in the United States. In A. R. Stiffman & L. E. Davis (Eds.), *Ethnic issues in adolescent mental health* (pp. 323–338). Newbury Park, CA: Sage.

Young, T. J. (1988). Substance use and abuse among native Americans. *Clinical Psychology Review, 8,* 125–138.

11 Clinical Issues and Intervention with Ethnic Minority Women

ROBIN YOUNG PORTER

Of the 262,820,000 persons identified in the mid-decade census data, 134,509,000 or 51.2 percent are female (U.S. Bureau of Census, 1997a). Over 27 percent of these females are members of ethnic minority groups. More specifically, there are 17,427,000 Black, 13,297,000 Hispanic, 4,836,000 Asian/Pacific Islander, and 1,333,000 Native American/ Eskimo/Aleutian females (U.S. Bureau of Census, 1997a). A closer inspection of the demographic profiles reveals a number of variations within these ethnic groups. Sex ratios, for example, vary: There are more Black females than Black males and more Hispanic males than Hispanic females. Such patterns reflect different immigration, fertility, and mortality rates among the groups (O'Hare, 1992).

Ethnic minority populations and ethnic minority women, in particular, continue to be underserved and ineffectively served by mental health providers (see Chapters 2, 8, 15 of this book; LaFromboise, Heyle, & Ozer, 1990; Palacios & Franco, 1986; Russo, 1985). Ethnic minority women also bring unique issues and concerns to treatment. Although some of the presenting problems may be similar to those of White women (e.g., depression, anxiety), often the contributing factors are different (e.g., poverty, oppression, acculturation stress). Ethnic minority women, in contrast to White women, experience the unique effects of the interaction of racism and sexism (Greene, 1994a, b, c). The psychological well-being of ethnic minority women is affected not only by racism and sexism but oftentimes by the experiences of low socioeconomic status, immigration, acculturation, assimilation, discrimination, and stereotyping.

This chapter will explore the sociocultural history of women in four major racial/ ethnic groups: African American, Native American, Asian American, and Latin American. The heterogeneity among and between ethnic minority women in these groups must be recognized. Differences in history as well as commonalities in experience with oppression, racism, and discrimination in this country will be discussed. The impact of sociocultural factors (e.g., economic, acculturation, culture conflict/role strain, stereotypes) on the psychological well-being of ethnic minority women will be delineated, as well as the barriers to treatment. Guidelines for conducting effective psychotherapy with this population will be presented.

Historical Issues

The psychological development and functioning of ethnic minority women has been influenced by their history prior to arrival in the United States, by their history in this country, and by their efforts at acculturation. Each ethnic group has a unique social and cultural history. However, differences exist in the treatment each ethnic group has received during its existence in this country. There continue to be differences in how the majority culture of this country perceives and treats ethnic minority people. However, these differences are better illustrated within a historical context.

Historically, the indigenous peoples of the Americas were conquered by the Europeans, Africans were captured and brought to this country by slave traders, and Asians came as immigrants to the United States. In America, each group was expected to adopt the values of the dominant group (European Americans). Some of these values, through time, became incorporated into the minority groups' own value system. Although some native cultural patterns were retained, disruptions in familial and sex roles were caused by the pressures created by the majority culture for assimilation.

Smith, Burlew, Mosley, and Whitney (1978), describe the ancient African tribal family as characterized by customs and rituals where sex roles were clearly defined. The male was dominant, and the female and children occupied subordinate roles. Although the roles were clearly defined, they appeared to be flexible as husband and wife often shared the daily tasks. This role flexibility was carried over into slavery in America, where both spouses often worked alongside each other in the cotton fields. With the termination of legal slavery, African Americans were then expected to fulfill the roles practiced by the dominant society; that is, African American males were expected to provide for their families, but they were denied access to educational and occupational opportunities.

Traditionally, in the family, African American women have had at least equal status with African American men (Davenport & Yurich, 1991). African American women have always worked outside the home and been strong, independent figures within the African American family. They have not been "traditionally feminine" women who stayed home with their children (Greene, 1994a, b). However, as African Americans "began to fight for their rights and to participate more fully in this society, they began to take on its values—and these values included male dominance and the traditional role of women" (Rohrbaugh, 1979, p. 250).

It is questionable whether African American women have ever accepted the "traditional" role of women. While White women tend to evaluate themselves on the basis of the roles of wife and mother, Myers (1980) found from her study of 400 African American women in Michigan and Mississippi that African American women do not necessarily evaluate themselves on the basis of any one role. They appear to use several roles as measures of success in order to think well of themselves. She notes that these roles are most often occupational and family maintenance. African American women tend to value some roles more than others, and some roles are viewed as more important than others for developing and maintaining a positive self-image (Myers, 1980).

For Mexican American women the situation was different; they have always been ascribed an inferior status to men. With the arrival of the Spanish in Mexico in the sixteenth century came an imperialistic and patriarchal value system with a history of subjugating people of color. Nieto-Gomez (1976) states, "Traditionally, sex through marriage or rape, which are the tools of conquest, have been a means of taking possession of women and land" (p. 227). Women in this culture had long been viewed as property and now came to belong to the man or men who had sexually penetrated them. Both the economic system and the church sanctioned the continued dominance and sexual abuse by the men. The church was used as an ideological force "to maintain social control and subjugation of the Indian woman to her oppression" (p. 728). Women were expected to embrace the concept of *marianisma,* the veneration of the Virgin Mary as the ultimate role model. "Church tradition has directed the women to identify with the emotional suffering of the pure, passive, bystander, the Virgin Mary" (Nieto-Gomez, 1976, p. 228).

From the concept of *marianisma* grew the notion that the woman was to blame for her husband's problems, and *marianisma* convinced the woman to endure injustices committed against her. In addition, this concept inculcated the submission and passivity of women while facilitating and encouraging *machismo* in men. Because the concept has been fostered that the Mexican woman is inferior to the man, it has been reported that the patriarchal structure of Mexican culture works so as to "to instill serious neurosis in the women" (Levine & Padilla, 1980, p. 10). The effect of the patriarchal structure on the Mexican woman is highlighted in the United States today as Chicanas are often torn between the patriarchal values of their Mexican American culture and the more liberal White/American norms.

This patriarchal structure is also found in Puerto Rican society, where there was a similar history of Spanish conquest. Puerto Rican women tend to experience the same type of conflicts as Chicanas. For Latin American women, in addition to culture conflict, there is significant role strain. Levine and Padilla (1980) note that Hispanic women may use various strategies in an effort to minimize such role strain. Some establish successful compromise in their roles and values. Others reject traditional Hispanic culture completely. In addition, there are those women who never fully resolve the conflict and often exhibit psychological or psychosomatic symptoms.

Confucius had a deleterious effect on the status of Asian women (Bradshaw, 1994). The philosophy of Confucius subordinated women and ascribed to them an inferior status within the family (Bradshaw, 1994; Chu & Sue, 1984; Ho, 1990; Yamamoto & Acosta, 1982). Prior to this time, Asian women had been scholars, warriors, and leaders, "but the emergence of his [Confucius'] teachings as the principles of social relationships for all of Asia ensured for women several centuries of status inferiority and imposed incapability" (Fujitomi & Wong, 1976, p. 237). Asian society was patriarchal, patrilineal, and patrilocal, and prearranged marriages were the rule (Homma-True, 1990). Through marriage, the woman became the possession of her husband's family, where she was expected to cater to the demands of all the family members and to attend to menial household tasks. Asian women were socialized to behave submissively as preparation for marriage, and were often denied formal education. The woman worked in both the home and the field and was a servant to her husband, father, and brothers.

Very few women were a part of the large influx of Chinese into the United States in the 1850s because of the constraints of cultural attitudes and the belief that the woman was not to leave her husband's family home for any reason. The passage of the Chinese Exclusion Act in 1882 further precluded the entry of Chinese women to join their husbands. Because the sexual needs of the married or single Chinese male in America were going unsatisfied as a result of laws prohibiting racial integration, Chinese prostitutes were transported to fulfill these needs. In coming to the United States, Chinese men also had transported the traditional Chinese values of female inferiority, and thus Chinese women in the United States "were severely oppressed, reduced to mere slaves and sexual commodities" (Fujitomi & Wong, 1976, p. 242).

The experience of Japanese women was similar to that of the Chinese. Japanese women were also ascribed an inferior status, and marriages tended to be prearranged. For the Japanese woman, her role as a good wife was to sacrifice and be dutiful to her husband first, her children second, and herself last. Asian women who came to the United States found that "American customs permitted greater flexibility and opportunity than did those in their native land" (Rohrbaugh, 1979, p. 251). Today, many Asian American women are beginning to reject the traditional role, but they are still struggling to achieve equal status and to overcome the inferiority complex inculcated by traditional Asian thinking.

Native American society provides a contrast to the other ethnic minority groups. Historically, African, Latin, and Asian cultures have exhibited a patriarchal/patrilineal structure. However, Native American society has traditionally been matriarchal/matrilineal. In earlier years, Native American women held great political and economic power. According to Rohrbaugh (1979), Native American women had considerable power and status in their tribes at the times Europeans arrived in this country. For example, among the Senecas, women owned and cultivated the land, which they had inherited through their mothers. After marriage, the husband moved into the wife's household, where he lived with the wife's female relatives, their spouses, and their children. The men were responsible for hunting and being warriors. Witt (1976) notes that because of the matrilineal, matriarchal, and matrilocal structure of the Navajos, Navajo women performed a number of roles that were necessary for the survival of the extended family. With the European arrival, a paternalistic and patriarchal value system was imposed upon the Native Americans and the women were stripped of their power and economic function. Many of the women's roles began to be taken over by men. The White man sought to "civilize the Indians" by imposing White/European cultural values and customs on the Native Americans.

Sociocultural Issues

The mental health status of ethnic minority women is often related to sociocultural factors such as economic/financial stress, educational and occupational discrimination, acculturation issues, culture conflict/sex-role conflict, and stereotyping. In addition, ethnic minority women are often subjected to racism, sexism, and oppression, which continue to keep them at the bottom of income, educational, and occupational levels (Greene, 1992; Pyant & Yanico, 1991). All these factors can have a negative impact on women's view of themselves and can produce stress, which may affect their physical health, mental health, and emotional well-being (Watts-Jones, 1990).

Economic/Financial Stress

Minority women tend to suffer from a double stigma in that they are both women and members of a specific racial/ethnic group in a society that devalues both of these characteristics. Minority women may experience a "triple" stigma, for they are also often poor.

When ethnic minority women are employed, they are often found in low-wage positions, with limited opportunities for advancement (Helms, 1979). Therefore, as a result of either underemployment or unemployment, ethnic minority women and their families are disproportionately represented among the poverty ranks (O'Hare, 1992; 1996). Decreased earnings coupled with high unemployment contribute to the poverty of many minority women.

Poverty, in today's society, has many stressful consequences: lowered social status, inadequate or nonexistent health care, substandard housing, inadequate nutrition, and a generally reduced quality of life (Kemer, Dusenbury, & Mandelblatt 1993; Ruiz & Padilla, 1977; Watts-Jones, 1990). In addition, stress may be experienced directly as the result of frustration about racism and discrimination in employment. Although the stress of being low income can apply to all poor people, economic and occupational discrimination exacerbates the stress for minority women. Whereas traditionally many majority women have worked out of choice, ethnic minority women have worked because of necessity; for a minority woman, her salary has been needed to supplement that of her mate's as his earnings were less than his White counterpart's (Greene, 1994a, b; Malson, 1983).

This situation is highlighted by Myers's (1980) assertion that most African American women cannot afford to stay home, although many would like to, because of the need to supplement the family income. Research has, in fact, indicated that most African American women expect to work throughout their adult lives (Harrison, 1989; Malson, 1983). The financial stress experienced by other ethnic minority women, as well as African American women, has also increased as a result of the rise in female-headed households (Ahlburg & De Vita, 1992; O'Hare, 1992; O'Hare, Pollard, Mann, & Kent, 1991). These increases in female-headed households have been due to increased rates of birth to unmarried mothers and increased divorce rates.

As previously mentioned, ethnic minority women tend to receive the lowest wages. Because these women are likely to have earnings that fall below the poverty level, trying to raise and maintain a family is a major source of tension. According to the 1990 census data, Black, Hispanic, Asian/Pacific Islander, and American Indian women had significantly higher poverty rates than White women (Young Rivers, 1995). Such findings are similar to earlier ones from the 1980 census (Amaro & Russo, 1987; Levine & Padilla, 1980). This bleak economic picture continues to be reflected in recent family poverty rates for Black, Hispanic, and Asian/Pacific Islander families which were 28.4, 29.4, and 14.5 percent, respectively, according to 1996 census data (U.S. Bureau of Census, 1997b).

Educational and Occupational Discrimination

Often as a result of racial discrimination in employment, ethnic minority women are relegated to menial and low-paying jobs (more so than White females and African American males) (Harrison, 1989; Helms, 1979). Discrimination has also prevented ethnic minority women from obtaining the education they need for better paying jobs. For example, the government-sponsored educational system has offered vocational choices to Native American women that are extremely narrow and sexist, often channeling them into secretarial and domestic roles (LaFromboise, Heyle, & Ozer, 1990). As Witt (1976) states, "Native American females cannot put to use their skills neither off nor on the reservation because reservation life is not conducive to the life of the average Native American homemaker"

(p. 252). Essentially, Native American women have been inappropriately educated by the U.S. government, and the failure of the educational system to assimilate these females adequately often leads to depression among them.

Acculturation

It has been proposed that the degree of acculturation to United States society produces stress for ethnic minority women (LaFromboise, Berman, & Sohi, 1994). Olmedo and Parron (1981) state, "For Hispanic, Native American, and Asian women, problems related to acculturation to a society that appears prejudicial, hostile, and rejecting place them in a high-risk category for personality disintegration and subsequent need for mental health intervention" (p. 106). Migration and acculturation stress can lead to feelings of depression, loneliness, isolation, and alienation (Curtis, 1990; Sodowsky, Lai, & Plake, 1991; see Ch. 12), particularly when the extended family (which is a primary source of support) has been disrupted. There may also be spousal or intergenerational conflicts resulting from the faster acculturation of some family members than others. Children tend to acculturate faster than adults. It has been noted that Latin American and Native American women tend to be less assimilated by American society, whereas Chinese American women are assimilated faster than Chinese American men (Leong, 1986).

Culture Conflict and Role Strain

There are other problems related to acculturation, such as value conflict emanating from trying to accommodate to two different cultures, particularly as United States values are often incongruent with the values of minority cultures (Bradshaw, 1994). Sue and Sue (1972) note that culture conflict appears to be an intimate part of the Asian American experience. One of the major conflicts for ethnic minority women in the United States is dealing with the significant role strain produced by "culture conflict." Culture conflict causes a great deal of stress for these women as they are expected to acculturate and accommodate to United States society. Culture conflict can lead to sex-role conflict; an identity crisis; and/or feelings of isolation, alienation, or depression. Another problem related to acculturation that produces value conflict for minority women is the acceptance of the American female standard of beauty. Inability to attain this standard because of skin color, facial features, hair texture, and the like produces stress, which can lead to a lowered self-concept, low self-esteem, a poor self-image, and even self-hatred (Bradshaw, 1994; Neal & Wilson, 1989; Ramseur, 1989).

Stereotypes

Dealing with stereotypes is also a problem for minority women, as stereotypes are often used to justify discrimination (Greene, 1994a). African American women have variously been labeled "Mammy," "Aunt Jemina," "Sapphire," and "Whore" (Greene, 1992; Helms, 1979; Young, 1989). The predominant image, however, is that of a Superwoman who can handle extraordinary responsibility (Harrison, 1989). This image perpetuates the notion that the African American woman's lot in life can be ignored because she is able to cope with all of life's difficulties. African American women also appear to have accepted and internalized this image, and it is constantly promoted as a positive model within the African American community (Harrison, 1989). Unfortunately, perpetuating and internalizing this image means failing to acknowledge and recognize the stress it engenders resulting from the tremendous amount of energy required to live up to such standards (Harrison, 1989; Lewis, 1989).

Native American women have also been depicted stereotypically. However, Native American women have been plagued by "invisibility." Often, people have difficulty conjuring up an image of her at all. The most predominant image is that of the squaw:

> The term "Squaw" began as a perfectly acceptable Algonkian term meaning "Woman." In time, it became synonymous with "Drudge" and, in some areas, "Prostitute." The squaw is regarded as a brown lump of a drudge, chewing buffalo hide, putting that tipi up and down again and again, carrying heavy burdens along with the dogs while the tribe moves ever onward, away from the pursuing cavalry. (Witt, 1976, p. 249)

The stereotype of the Native American woman often depicted by Hollywood is that of Pocahontas, a Native American princess. Witt (1976) notes that "the drunken indian, the cadillac indian, lonesome polecat-facelessness—still characterizes Native-American women" (p. 249) as they remain largely invisible.

For the Asian woman, the predominant stereotypic image is one of passivity, sexual attractiveness, and reserve (Chan, 1987). Fujitomi and Wong (1976) note that the pervasiveness of this image creates a continuous struggle for Asian women to develop a more assertive persona and a positive self-image. Asian women are viewed as deferring to males, elders, and authority figures. This image is even accepted among Asian people themselves and is used to subjugate women and prevent them from developing high self-esteem (Bradshaw, 1994).

The stereotypes for Latin American women include the passive, submissive, male-dominated, all-suffering woman. Additionally, Puerto Rican women have been stereotyped as hysterical, loud, and hot-tempered (Davenport & Yurich, 1991; Gibson, 1983; Palacios & Franco, 1986; Zavala-Martinez, 1987). Most ethnic minority people come to accept the existing stereotypes about their women. Ethnic minority women's attempts to overcome such stereotypes can lead to stress. As previously mentioned, they must deal not only with the images applied to them by the larger society but even with those images held by their own people.

In conclusion, the stressful experiences of immigration, acculturation, assimilation, and stereotyping, compounded by both racial and sexual discrimination in obtaining education and employment, influence the psychological functioning of ethnic minority women (Homma-True, 1990; Soto, 1983; Torres-Matrullo, 1976). Although there may also be intrapsychic causes such as anxiety or poor coping skills, mental health problems of ethnic minority women tend to be related to extrapsychic factors—racism, sexism, poverty, and discrimination (Yamamoto & Acosta, 1982). Particularly for African American women, racism usually has more of an impact than sexism (Harrison, 1989; Pyant & Yanico, 1991).

Mental Health Issues

Several researchers have identified sources of stress that pertain to ethnic minority groups: migration, poverty, acculturation, culture conflict, language barriers, and minority group status (Comas-Díaz, 1984; Gibson, 1983; Leong, 1986; Salgado de Snyder, 1987). For many ethnic minority women, stress emanates from the culture conflict experienced as they try to adapt to United States culture, where sex roles are more liberal (Salgado de Snyder, Cervantes, & Padilla, 1990). Ethnic minority women can be considered "at risk" for mental health problems because of the stresses they experience (del Portillo, 1987; Homma-True, 1990; Pyant & Yanico, 1991). Some of the mental health problems they experience include lowered self-concept/self-esteem, depression and anxiety, alcohol and substance abuse, anger and hostility, psychosomatic symptoms, and psychosis (Fleming, 1996; LaFromboise et al., 1990). To discuss all these problems is beyond the scope of this chapter. Therefore, two issues frequently experienced by ethnic minority women will be examined in more depth.

Self-Concept/Self-Esteem

A significant problem experienced by ethnic minority women is poor self-concept. As Olmedo and Parron (1981) note, "the self-concept of minority women has been greatly affected by racial and ethnic stereotyping, making them feel unacceptable according to White standards of beauty" (p. 106). For this reason, ethnic minority women may develop low self-esteem that leads to racial self-hatred and intense conflicts (Gray & Jones, 1987; Ramseur, 1989). Certain racial/cultural traits are denigrated, and some women may even deny their own ethnicity. This tendency to deny one's ethnicity appears to stem from the pressures of acculturation. Ethnic minority women sometimes use various cosmetics to bleach their skin and hair—that is, to become more White in appearance. However, this practice appears to have declined as a result of the social movement that began in the 1960s. In addition, the stereotypes of some ethnic minority women as passive and submissive, in conjunction with a patriarchal family structure, have contributed to a poor self-concept and low self-esteem in these women.

Myers (1980) posits that better coping leads to increased feelings of self-esteem and asserts that one way African American women cope is by judging themselves against other African American women. In addition, she notes that strong family ties and the church have always been a source of support and strength for African Americans. The church and extended family network have generally been supports for all minority groups in America (Ho, 1992). Smith et al. (1978) note that in addition to an inner strength, pride in herself and her race is another quality that contributes to the Black woman's ability to cope successfully. They note that there are at least four characteristics that help the African American woman "cope with a world that creates much stress for her—inner strength, race- (and self-) pride, concern over femininity, and creativity in problem-solving" (p. 38).

However, Olmedo and Parron (1981) assert that the inner strength of minority women, used as a successful coping strategy, serves to mask the degree of stress they experience. These authors state, "evidence of the severe stress they [minority women] undergo is suggested by studies that show an intimate link between behavior and stress-related life-threatening diseases. Minority women are twice as likely to die from diabetes and three times more likely to die from hypertension than White women" (p. 106). Not much other data have been reported regarding the coping abilities of other specific ethnic minority women—Latin American, Native American, and Asian American. Although Levine and Padilla (1980) note that several studies indicate that maintenance of Hispanic values is associated with strong coping abilities. In addition, the authors report that Hispanic females may interact less with the dominant culture than males do, thus reducing some of the stress.

Depression and Anxiety

Most of the research, with the exception of the Epidemiologic Catchment Area (ECA) studies, has found a strong relationship between mental disorders and degree of acculturation of ethnic minorities (Burnam, Hough, Karno, Escobar, & Telles, 1987; Escobar, 1993). Ethnic minority women, in particular, have been found to experience high levels of depression and anxiety as a result of the stress of acculturation (Salgado de Snyder, 1987). In addition, several researchers note that African American women are at high risk for depression due to the chronic environmental stressors they experience (Pyant & Yanico, 1991; Taylor, Henderson, & Jackson, 1991; Watts-Jones, 1990). High rates of depression have also been noted for immigrant Asian women (Franks & Faux, 1990; Kuo, 1984). In particular, Kuo (1984) found that immigrant Chinese and Filipino women had higher rates of depression than men. LaFromboise et al. (1990) reported high prevalence rates of depression in Native American women due to the intensity of life stressors. Their findings indicated that the prevalence of depression for Native American women within certain communities may be four to six times greater than previous estimates. Internalized feelings of anger related to racism also contribute to depression in some minority women.

For Puerto Rican women, depression appears related to sex-role issues and a patriarchal value system. Studies of Puerto Rican women have found higher rates of depression among island than mainland Puerto Ricans (Comas-Díaz, 1984). An epidemiological study of island Puerto Rican women (Canino et al., 1987) found a significantly higher rate of depressive symptomatology in the women than the men. The prevalence rate was twice as high for depressive disorders and four times greater for dysthymia. The authors offered a sex-role explanation for the gender differences in this study. In Puerto Rican culture, it is culturally expected that the men will have a dominant role while the women will assume a more passive and submissive stance, which appears to contribute to depression.

Levine and Padilla (1980) note that when dealing with Hispanic clients, what are perceived to be psychological symptoms may actually be stress manifested in various ways. Olmedo and Parron (1981) suggest that although depressed ethnic minority women may experience symptoms similar to those of depressed White women, their experience is described differently by clinicians. Ethnic minority women are described as having "poor work habits, being apathetic, driving their husbands away, or lacking in mothering skills" (p. 107). Such attributes are demeaning and could contribute to diminished self-esteem in these women. These authors also note that depression in ethnic minority women is often manifested through drug and alcohol abuse.

In addition to depression, African American and Latin American women have been found to experience high levels of anxiety (Gray & Jones, 1987; Palacios & Franco, 1986;

Zavala-Martinez, 1987). For Puerto Rican women, anxiety is often manifested by psycho-somatic symptomatology such as, *nervios* ("nerves") or through an *ataque.* Both of these are stress reactions arising from feelings of anger and powerlessness (Comas-Díaz, 1987; Torres-Matrullo, 1976; Zavala-Martinez, 1987). An *ataque* is a neurotic reaction character-ized by psychomotor seizures, often as a result of the stress experienced from attempting to cope in two cultures (Soto, 1983). An *ataque* can last from five to ten minutes, during which time the individual cries or screams, falls to the floor, and swings her arms and/or legs.

Barriers to Treatment

Ethnic minority women tend to have more positive attitudes toward mental health services and use them more frequently than ethnic minority men (Gary, 1987; Neighbors & Howard, 1987). However, a number of barriers may interfere with the effective treatment of ethnic minority women. One barrier for minority women in seeking therapy arises from stereotypical attitudes and sex-role bias. Olmedo and Parron (1981) state that the

> issues of sex role bias are in many cases compounded for minority women. For example, Asian American and Mexican-American women are often stereotyped as devoted mothers and wives whose lives revolve entirely around the family. On the other hand, the attributed "inner strength" of Black women is often exaggerated into a "matriarchal dominance ste-reotype" which distorts their perceived family roles. (p. 108)

Therefore, ethnic minority women may be reluctant to enter therapy because they see psy-chology and psychiatry as fields dominated by White males, where stereotypes are perpet-uated and the status quo is upheld.

Another cultural barrier pertains to language differences between the ethnic minority female client and the therapist. Language differences can hinder the effectiveness of ther-apy with ethnic minority clients (see Chapter 2; Martinez, 1988; Russell, 1988) and can take the form of the use of non-Standard English by African Americans or the use of another language by the client (Gibson, 1983; Russell, 1988). Bilingual clients sometimes "maintain independence between the two language systems which can serve to compart-mentalize their feelings" (Espin, 1987, p. 497). Several authors note that some bilinguals, when making the translation to English, may exhibit flat affect or appear withdrawn (Espin, 1987; Gibson, 1983; Russell, 1988). In addition, the therapist may have difficulty under-standing the English translation from another language (Yamamoto & Acosta, 1982), and it may take the client some time to make the translation so that the therapist understands it clearly. Latin American clients tend to encode experiences with affective meaning in Span-ish, so that accurate understanding when translated to English can be problematic (Espin, 1987; Gibson, 1983; Russell, 1988). It has also been suggested that language may be a bar-rier when working with Native Americans, as their language structure is different (Ho, 1992), making the expression of certain feelings and ideas difficult. In addition, each tribe has its own language, which contributes to the complexity of verbal communication. With Spanish and some Native American and Asian languages, there is not always a direct trans-lation or correspondence with English words (Edwards & Edwards, 1989; Gibson, 1983).

In addition to the language differences between the client and the therapist, some cultures place great emphasis on nonverbal communication. In some cultures, direct eye contact is seen as a form of disrespect (Brower, 1989; Everett, Proctor, & Cartmell, 1989). Other nonverbal behaviors that may have different meanings for ethnic minority and nonminority clients include personal space, body movements, and touching. Differences between the client and the therapist in understanding nonverbal behavior may create a barrier in therapy because they can result in misinterpretation and miscommunication. As a result, the client may feel that she has not been heard or may feel misunderstood and rejected by the therapist.

Guidelines for Effective Therapy

It is important to be aware of the cultural issues discussed in this chapter when providing psychotherapeutic services to ethnic minority women. The awareness of these issues and their impact on the emotional and behavioral functioning of ethnic minority women should help the therapist render more effective services. In working effectively with ethnic minority women, it is important to understand how culture conflict, poverty, low educational and occupational levels, sex bias, race discrimination, and stereotyping contribute to stress and to the psychological functioning of ethnic minority women. In working with ethnic minority clients in general, and ethnic minority women in particular, the therapist must distinguish intrapsychic difficulties (low self-esteem, anxiety, poor coping skills) from extrapsychic conflict (distress caused by social factors such as racism, poverty, and discrimination) (Greene, 1993). Errors in treatment can occur by focusing exclusively on either intrapsychic or extrapsychic problems. It should not be assumed, for example, that all problems emanate from racism. However, the therapist must be aware of the effect of racism on the client. Ethnic minority women will in all likelihood present with a combination of both intra- and extrapsychic issues to be addressed in treatment (see Chapter 5).

One overall goal of treatment with ethnic minority women is to empower them to handle the stresses of their daily lives (Greene 1994a; Lewis, 1994; Mays, 1986; Vasquez, 1994; Zavala-Martinez, 1987). In that process, the therapist should recognize racism and sexism when and where they exist and acknowledge their deleterious effects. The therapist should help the client overcome feelings of powerlessness and helplessness inculcated by racism. It is also important for the therapist to focus on the effects of stereotyping and to discuss ways to counteract stereotypes and negative images of ethnic minority women. This can lead to feelings of empowerment and help the client develop a more positive identity and increased self-esteem. The therapist also should seek to examine his or her own biases regarding women and race and to counter her or his own stereotypes and negative perceptions of ethnic minority women clients. Ethnic minority therapists may have difficulties with racial and sexual bias because they themselves can be as susceptible to these stereotypes as nonminority therapists.

The therapist needs to listen sensitively to the client and not assume that pathology is due exclusively to intrapsychic causes. In general, the therapist should focus on the client's strengths and help the client look at options and choices available to her (del Portillo, 1987). In cross-cultural therapeutic encounters (White therapist and ethnic minority client), the therapist should broach the difference in race in one of the initial sessions (Fujino,

Okazaki, & Young, 1994; Green, 1994b; Jones & Seagull, 1989). This lets the client know that racial issues can be discussed in the therapy setting since this can be a salient issue for some ethnic minority women (Greene, 1992).

In working with ethnic minority women, it would also be helpful for the therapist to discuss spirituality issues. As spirituality tends to be a pervasive aspect of minority cultural life and has a great influence on attitudes and beliefs (Gibson, 1983; Lewis, 1994; Yamamoto & Acosta, 1982). It is important for the therapist to understand how spirituality and religious issues may affect the therapy (Yamamoto & Acosta, 1982) and contribute to conflicts experienced by ethnic minority women. Ethnic minority women may experience conflicts related to religion or spirituality especially regarding the role of women, the concept of fatalism, and so on (Boyd-Franklin, 1987; 1991). In Latin American cultures, Catholicism has had a major influence on the role of women and sex-role attitudes.

In African American culture as in Latin American culture, the church is typically seen as a major source of support, and spirituality tends to play an important role in the lives of these ethnic minority women (Boyd-Franklin, 1987; 1991; Lewis, 1994). However, some African American women may experience conflicts regarding their spirituality and being in therapy due to their minister's nonsupport of therapy, a view of therapy as antireligious, the promotion of the concept of a punitive God, or personal issues of shame related to sexuality and morality (Boyd-Franklin, 1991). In addition, it may be helpful at times to involve religious leaders in the client's treatment (Yamamoto & Acosta, 1982) or to refer the client to spiritual guides (see Chapter 9).

It is also important for the therapist to understand extended family issues and their impact on the client (Ho, 1987). Because of the interdependence that tends to characterize ethnic minority families, it may be that the client needs help resolving the interdependent-independent conflict. An attempt should be made to involve the family in treatment so that interventions can be formulated with the family's support and within their cultural framework (see Chapter 6). Interventions should be designed that are consonant with the family's culture, as these are more likely to be carried out. In addition, working with the family provides an opportunity to address issues of culture and sex-role conflict. The therapist may have to facilitate the client's becoming "bicultural"—that is, learning behaviors that are adaptive in both the minority and majority cultures. This may also help to ease conflicts around sex-role and acculturation issues.

It is also important that the therapist assess the availability and quality of the client's support systems. Involving the client with mutually satisfying support systems can lead to an increase in self-esteem for ethnic minority women. Social supports can also serve as effective buffers and mediators of stress (see Chapter 2). In addition, participating with others in organized groups and mutual aid self-help groups, particularly around the issues of racism, social/civic activity, civil rights, and/or sexism, can lead to social change and contribute to the empowerment of the client (Mays, 1986).

For some ethnic minority women, particularly African Americans, it is important to discuss skin color differences, which are sometimes a salient issue within families and ethnic communities (Boyd-Franklin, 1991; Greene, 1992; Neal & Wilson, 1989). Sometimes, within the immediate and extended family, there are wide variations in skin color. Skin color differences within families may create conflicts for the ethnic minority woman because some family members may have been afforded differential treatment within the

CHAPTER 11 / Clinical Issues and Intervention with Ethnic Minority Women **195**

family based on their skin color. Historically, lighter skinned African Americans also have enjoyed more societal advantages and opportunities than darker skinned African Americans (Neal & Wilson, 1989). In addition, skin color often affects the individual's feelings of attractiveness, which contribute to self-esteem. Therefore, the therapist should assess the significance and impact of skin color in the client's life. Although this is an important issue, it is not always problematic for ethnic minority women.

In working with Latin American women, the therapist must be aware that some experiences will be interpreted differently in Spanish than in English. The therapist should be sensitive to these language differences. It might greatly facilitate communication if the therapist is bilingual (Homma-True, 1990). Other possibilities with Asian American, Native American, and Latin American cultures include the use of a translator, if necessary, or of bilingual paraprofessionals. In using translators from the family, however, the therapist should be cognizant of family structure issues. Using a child as translator displaces the adult male from the power position in the family, which has a high value in patriarchal family systems (Gibson, 1983). In working with African American women, it also would be helpful for the therapist to be aware of African American dialects and certain regional idioms (see Chapter 2; Russell, 1988).

The therapist should be especially attuned to nonverbal cues, such as eye contact, personal space, body movements, and touching, which tend to differ between minority and nonminority clients. Differences in nonverbal cues between ethnic minority men and women will also need to be noted. For some clients, differences in nonverbal cues would depend not only on the client's ethnic background but also on the degree to which she has been assimilated into the majority culture. The awareness of the meanings of nonverbal behavior can help to avoid misunderstanding and misinterpretation.

On a broader level, the therapist should consider interventions that help ethnic minority women seek the education and training needed to increase their standard of living and quality of life. That is, the therapist should be familiar with available programs and opportunities in the local community and should use a multiservice approach (Homma-True, 1990). In addition, the therapist at times may have to be an advocate for the client with social service agencies, government agencies, and private-sector businesses (see Chapter 8; Grevious, 1989). The therapist's efforts on the client's behalf should help to increase and enhance rapport with ethnic minority female clients.

Although this chapter has focused on issues in individual therapy, group therapy has also been found to be a useful therapeutic modality for ethnic minority women (see Chapter 7; Azocar, Miranda, & Dwyer, 1996; Boyd-Franklin, 1987, 1991; Chu & Sue, 1984; Comas-Díaz, 1984; Gibson, 1983; Ho, 1984; LaFromboise, Berman, & Sohi, 1994; Nayman, 1983; Vasquez, 1994). Ho (1984) and Chu and Sue (1984) discuss group therapy with Asian Americans. Boyd-Franklin (1991) lists some recurrent themes in group psychotherapy with African American women, while Comas-Díaz (1984) has identified themes in group therapy with Puerto Rican women. The principles of the Nguzo Saba have also been applied to groupwork with African American women (Pack-Brown, Whittington-Clark, & Parker, 1998). Groups can serve therapeutic, supportive, preventive, and educational purposes (see Chapter 7). The communal, collective, and interdependent nature of ethnic minority cultures tends to lend support to the use of groups. Self-help groups have been reported to be effective for dealing with stress for African American women (Mays, 1986).

Conclusion

The mental health issues of ethnic minority women tend to be closely tied to societal issues such as acculturation (culture and sex-role conflict), stereotyping, poverty, discrimination, racism, and sexism. Indeed, a salient issue for ethnic minority women is the interaction between racial and sexual discrimination. Another major issue for ethnic minority women is low socioeconomic status, which can contribute to psychological problems. Because of educational and economic discrimination, most minority women continue to have low-paying, low-status jobs and receive menial salaries, often while trying to raise a family. For these women, the tremendous stress emanating from poverty is coupled with the stress generated by trying to overcome stereotypes and the role strain produced by culture conflict, as ethnic minority women attempt to function in two different cultures. However, despite all this, ethnic minority women are coping, and more of their strengths and successes need to be investigated and disseminated. Once therapists have a better understanding of the issues that ethnic minority women bring to therapy as well as an awareness and understanding of their own biases in regard to women and race, they should be able to serve this population more effectively.

R E F E R E N C E S

Ahlburg, D. A., & De Vita, C. J. (1992). New realities of the American family. *Population Bulletin, 47,* 1–44.

Amaro, H., & Russo, N. F. (1987). Hispanic women and mental health: An overview of contemporary issues in research and practice. *Psychology of Women Quarterly, 11,* 393–407.

Azocar, F., Miranda, J., & Dwyer, E. V. (1996). Treatment of depression in disadvantaged women. *Women and Therapy, 18*(3-4), 91–105.

Boyd-Franklin, N. (1987). Group therapy for Black women: A therapeutic support model. *American Journal of Orthopsychiatry, 57,* 394–401.

Boyd-Franklin, N. (1991). Recurrent themes in the treatment of African-American women in group psychotherapy. *Women & Therapy, 11,* 25–40.

Bradshaw, C. K. (1994). Asian and Asian American women: Historical and political considerations in psychotherapy. In L. Comas-Díaz & B. Greene (Eds.), *Women of color: Integrating ethnic and gender identities in psychotherapy* (pp. 72–113). New York: Guilford Press.

Brower, I. C. (1989). Counseling Vietnamese. In D. R. Atkinson, G. Morten, & D. W. Sue (Eds.), *Counseling American minorities: A cross-cultural perspective* (3rd ed., pp. 129–143). Dubuque, IA: Brown.

Burnam, M. A., Hough, R. L., & Karno, M., Escobar, J. T., & Telles, C. A. (1987). Acculturation lifetime prevalence of psychiatric disorders among Mexican-Americans in Los Angeles. *Journal of Health and Social Behavior, 28,* 89–102.

Canino, G. J., Rubio-Stipec, M., Shrout, P., Bravo, M., Stolberg, R., & Bird, H. R. (1987). Sex differences and depression in Puerto Rico. *Psychology of Women Quarterly, 11,* 443–459.

Chan, C. S. (1987). Asian American women: Psychological responses to sexual exploitation and cultural stereotypes. *Women & Therapy, 6,* 33–38.

Chu, J., & Sue, S. (1984). Asian/Pacific Americans and group practice. *Ethnicity in Group Work Practice, 7,* 23–36.

Comas-Díaz, L. (1984). Content themes in group treatment with Puerto Rican women. *Ethnicity in Group Work Practice, 7,* 75–84.

Comas-Díaz, L. (1987). Feminist therapy with mainland Puerto Rican women. *Psychology of Women Quarterly, 11,* 461–474.

Comas-Díaz, L., & Greene, B. (Eds.). (1994). *Women of color: Integrating ethnic and gender identities in psychotherapy.* New York: Guilford Press.

Curtis, P. A. (1990). The consequences of acculturation to service delivery and research with Hispanic families. *Child and Adolescent Social Work, 7,* 147–160.

Davenport, D. S., & Yurich, J. M. (1991). Multicultural gender issues. *Journal of Counseling & Development, 70,* 64–71.

del Portillo, C. T. (1987). Poverty, self-concept, and health: Experience of Latinas. *Women & Health, 12,* 229–242.

Edwards, E. D., & Edwards, M. E. (1989), American Indians: Working with individuals and groups. In D. R.

Atkinson, G. Morten, & D. W. Sue (Eds), *Counseling American minorities: A cross-cultural perspective* (3rd ed., pp. 72–84). Dubuque, IA: Brown.

Escobar, J. I. (1993). Psychiatric epidemiology. In A. C. Gaw (Ed.), *Culture, ethnicity, and mental illness* (pp. 43–73). Washington, DC: American Psychiatric Press.

Espin, O. M. (1987). Psychological impact of migration on Latinas: Implications for psychotherapeutic practice. *Psychology of Women Quarterly, 11,* 489–503.

Everett, F., Proctor, N., & Cartmell, B. (1989). Providing psychological services to American Indian children and families. In D. R. Atkinson, G. Morten, & D. W. Sue (Eds), *Counseling American minorities: A cross-cultural perspective* (3rd ed., pp. 53–71). Dubuque, IA: Brown.

Fleming, C. M. (1996). Cultural formulation of psychiatric diagnosis: Case No. 01. An American Indian women suffering from depression, alcoholism, and childhood trauma. *Culture, Medicine, and Psychiatry, 20*(2), 145–154.

Franks, F., & Faux, S. A. (1990). Depression, stress, mastery and social resources in four ethnocultural women's groups. *Research in Nursing & Health, 13,* 283–292.

Fujino, D. C., Okazaki, S., & Young, K. (1994). Asian-American women in the mental health system: An examination of ethnic and gender match between therapist and client. *Journal of Community Psychology, 22*(2), 164–176.

Fujitomi, S., & Wong, D. (1976). The new Asian-American woman. In S. Cox (Ed.), *Female psychology: The emerging self* (pp. 236–248). Chicago: Science Research Associates.

Gary, L. E. (1987). Attitudes of Black adults toward community mental health centers. *Hospital and Community Psychiatry, 38,* 1100–1105.

Gibson, G. (1983). Hispanic women: Stress and mental health issues. *Women & Therapy, 2,* 113-133.

Gray, B. A., & Jones, B. E. (1987). Psychotherapy and Black women: A survey. *Journal of the National Medical Association, 79,* 177–181.

Greene, B. (1992). Still here: A perspective on psychotherapy with African-American women. In J. C. Chrisler & D. Howard (Eds.), *New directions in feminist psychology* (pp. 13–25). New York: Springer.

Greene, B. (1993). Psychotherapy with African-American women: Integrating feminist and psychodynamic models. *Journal of Training and Practice in Professional Psychology, 7*(1), 49–66.

Greene, B. (1994a). African-American women: Derivatives of racism and sexism in psychotherapy. In E. Tobach & B. Rosoff (Eds.), *Challenging racism and sexism: Alternatives to genetic explanations. Genes and gender. 7.* New York: Feminist Press at the City University of New York.

Greene, B. (1994b). African American women. In L. Comas-Díaz & B. Greene (Eds.), *Women of color: Integrating ethnic and gender identities in psychotherapy* (pp. 10–29). New York: Guilford Press.

Greene, B. (1994c). Lesbian women of color: Triple jeopardy. In L. Comas-Díaz & B. Greene (Eds.), *Women of color: Integrating ethnic and gender identities in psychotherapy* (pp. 389–427). New York: Guilford Press.

Grevious, C. (1989). The role of the family therapist with low-income Black families. In D. R. Atkinson, G. Morten, & D. W. Sue (Eds.), *Counseling American minorities: A cross-cultural perspective* (3rd ed., pp. 192–199). Dubuque, IA: Brown.

Harrison, A. O. (1989). Mental health issues of African-American women and adults. In R. L. Jones (Ed.), *Black adult development and aging* (pp. 91–115). Berkeley, CA: Cobb & Henry.

Helms, J. E. (1979). Black women. *The Counseling Psychologist, 8,* 40–41.

Ho, C. K. (1990). An analysis of domestic violence in Asian American communities: A multicultural approach to counseling. *Women & Therapy, 8,* 129–150.

Ho, M. K. (1984). Social group work with Asian/Pacific Americans. *Ethnicity in Group Work Practice, 7,* 49–61.

Ho, M. K. (1987). *Family therapy with ethnic minorities.* Newbury Park, CA: Sage.

Ho, M. K. (1992). *Minority children and adolescents in therapy.* Newbury Park, CA: Sage.

Homma-True, R. (1990). Psychotherapeutic issues with Asian American women. *Sex Roles, 22,* 477–486.

Jones, A., & Seagull, A. A. (1989). Dimensions of the relationship between the Black client and the White therapist. In D. R. Atkinson, G. Morten, & D. W. Sue (Eds.), *Counseling American minorities: A cross-cultural perspective* (3rd ed., pp. 200–210). Dubuque, IA: Brown.

Kerner, J. F., Dusenbury, L., & Mandelblatt, J. S. (1993). Poverty and cultural diversity: Challenges for health promotion among the medically underserved. *Annual Review of Public Health, 14,* 355–377.

Kuo, W. H. (1984). Prevalence of depression among Asian-Americans. *The Journal of Nervous and Mental Disease, 172,* 449–457.

LaFromboise, T. D., Berman, J. S., & Sohi, B. K. (1994). American Indian women. In L. Comas-Díaz & B. Greene (Eds.), *Women of color: Integrating ethnic and gender identities in psychotherapy* (pp. 30–71). New York: Guilford Press.

LaFromboise, T. D., Heyle, A. M., & Ozer, E. J. (1990). Changing and diverse roles of women in American Indian cultures. *Sex Roles, 22,* 455–476.

Leong, F. T. L. (1986). Counseling and psychotherapy with Asian-Americans: Review of the literature. *Journal of Counseling Psychology, 33,* 196–206.

Levine, E. S., & Padilla, A. M. (1980). *Crossing cultures in therapy: Pluralistic counseling for the Hispanic.* Monterey, CA: Brooks-Cole.

Lewis, E. A. (1989). Role strain in African-American women: The efficacy of support networks. *Journal of Black Studies, 20,* 155–169.

Lewis, S. Y. (1994). Cognitive-Behavioral therapy. In L. Comas-Díaz & B. Greene (Eds.), *Women of color: Integrating ethnic and gender identities in psychotherapy* (pp. 223–238). New York: Guilford Press.

Malson, M. R. (1983). Black women's sex roles: The social context for a new ideology. *Journal of Social Issues, 39,* 101–113.

Martinez, C. (1988). Mexican-Americans. In L. Comas-Díaz & E. E. H. Griffith (Eds.), *Clinical guidelines in cross-cultural mental health* (pp. 182–203). New York: Wiley.

Mays, V. M. (1986). Black women and stress: Utilization of self-help groups for stress reduction. *Women & Therapy, 4,* 67–79.

Myers, L. W. (1980). *Black women: Do they cope better?* Englewood Cliffs, NJ: Prentice-Hall.

Nayman, R. L. (1983). Group work with Black women: Some issues and guidelines. *Journal for Specialists in Group Work, 8,* 31–38.

Neal, A. M., & Wilson, M. L. (1989). The role of skin color and features in the Black community: Implications for Black women and therapy. *Clinical Psychology Review, 9,* 323–333.

Neighbors, H. W., & Howard, C. S. (1987). Sex differences in help seeking among adult Black Americans. *American Journal of Community Psychology, 15,* 403–415.

Nieto-Gomez, A. (1976). A heritage of LaHembra. In S. Cox (Ed.), *Female psychology: The emerging self* (pp. 226–235). Chicago: Science Research Associates.

O'Hare, W. P. (1992). America's minorities—The demographics of diversity. *Population Bulletin, 47*(4), 1–47.

O'Hare, W. P. (1996). A new look at poverty in America. *Population Bulletin, 51*(2), 1–48.

O'Hare, W. P., Pollard, K. M., Mann, T. L., & Kent, K. M. (1991). African Americans in the 1990s. *Population Bulletin, 46,* 1–40.

Olmedo, E. L., & Parron, D. L. (1981). Mental health of minority women: Some special issues. *Professional Psychology, 12,* 103–111.

Pack-Brown, S. P., Whittington-Clark, L. E., & Parker, W. (1998). *Images of me: A guide to group work with African-American women.* Boston: Allyn and Bacon.

Palacios, M., & Franco, J. N. (1986). Counseling Mexican-American women. *Journal of Multicultural Counseling and Development, 14,* 124–131.

Pyant, C. T., & Yanico, B. J. (1991). Relationship of racial identity and gender-role attitudes to black women's psychological well-being. *Journal of Counseling Psychology, 38,* 315–322.

Ramseur, H. P. (1989). Psychologically healthy Black adults: A review of theory and research. In R. L. Jones (Ed.), *Black adult development and aging* (pp. 215–241). Berkeley, CA: Cobb & Henry.

Rohrbaugh, J. B. (1979). *Women: Psychology's puzzle.* New York: Basic Books.

Ruiz, R., & Padilla, A. M. (1977). Counseling Latinos. *Personnel and Guidance Journal, 32,* 401–408.

Russell, D. M. (1988). Language and psychotherapy: The influence of Nonstandard English in clinical practice. In L. Comas-Díaz & E. E. H. Griffith (Eds.), *Clinical guidelines in cross-cultural mental health* (pp. 33–68). New York: Wiley.

Russo, N. F. (Ed.). (1985). *A women's mental health agenda.* Washington, DC: American Psychological Association.

Salgado de Snyder, V. N. (1987). Factors associated with acculturative stress and depressive symptomatology among married Mexican immigrant women. *Psychology of Women Quarterly, 11,* 475–488.

Salgado de Snyder, V. N., Cervantes, R. C., & Padilla, A. M. (1990). Gender and ethnic differences in psychosocial stress and generalized distress among Hispanics. *Sex Roles, 22,* 441–453.

Smith, W. D., Burlew, A. K., Mosley, M. H., & Whitney, W. M. (1978). *Minority issues in mental health.* MA: Addison-Wesley.

Sodowsky, G. R., Lai, E. W. M., & Plake, B. S. (1991). Moderating effects of sociocultural variables on acculturation attitudes of Hispanics and Asian Americans. *Journal of Counseling & Development, 70,* 194–204.

Soto, E. (1983). Sex-role traditionalism and assertiveness in Puerto Rican women living in the United States. *Journal of Community Psychology, 11,* 346–354.

Sue, D. W., & Sue, S. (1972). Counseling Chinese-Americans. *Personnel and Guidance Journal, 50,* 637–644.

Taylor, J., Henderson, D., & Jackson, B. B. (1991). A holistic model for understanding and predicting depressive symptoms in African-American women. *Journal of Community Psychology, 19,* 306–320.

Torres-Matrullo, C. (1976). Acculturation and psychopathology among Puerto Rican women in mainland United States. *American Journal of Orthopsychiatry, 46,* 710–719.

U.S. Bureau of Census. (1997a). *Current Population Reports: Special Studies* (pp. 23–123). Washington, DC: U.S. Government Printing Office.

U.S. Bureau of Census. (1997b). *Consumer Income,* (pp. 60–198). Washington, DC: U.S. Government Printing Office.

Vasquez, M. J. T. (1994). Latinas. In L. Comas-Díaz & B. Greene (Eds.), *Women of color: Integrating ethnic and gender identities in psychotherapy* (pp. 114–138). New York: Guilford Press.

Watts-Jones, D. (1990). Toward a stress scale for African-American women. *Psychology of Women Quarterly, 14,* 271–275.

Witt, S. H. (1976). Native women today: Sexism and the Indian woman. In S. Cox (Ed.), *Female psychology: The emerging self* (pp. 249–259). Chicago: Science Research Associates.

Yamamoto, J., & Acosta, F. X. (1982). Treatment of Asian Americans and Hispanic Americans: Similarities and differences. *Journal of the American Academy of Psychoanalysis, 10,* 585–607.

Young, C. (1989). Psychodynamics of coping and survival of the African-American female in a changing world. *Journal of Black Studies, 20,* 208–223.

Young Rivers, R. (1995). Clinical issues and intervention with ethnic minority women. In J. F. Aponte, R. Young Rivers, & J. Wohl (Eds.), *Psychological interventions and cultural diversity* (pp. 181–198). Boston: Allyn and Bacon.

Zavala-Martinez, I. (1987). En la lucha: The economic and socioemotional struggles of Puerto Rican women. *Women & Therapy, 6,* 3–24.

12 Psychological Intervention with Immigrants and Refugees

FRED BEMAK

RITA CHI-YING CHUNG

Migration trends have shown that, since the late twentieth century, the pattern of migration has been from developing to more developed countries (Bemak, in press). This is consistent with international problems such as political instability, economic and social pressures, natural disasters, and local, state, and civil wars that occur frequently throughout the world, especially in developing countries. Accordingly, the immigrant and refugee populations have been steadily increasing, causing migration to be a global issue. The trends have shown that immigrants and refugees have been moving and will continue to move from developing to more developed countries including the United States (Coleman, 1995).

The unique experiences of this population may place migrants at a higher risk for developing serious mental health problems. It is therefore critical that mental health professionals in resettlement countries clearly understand the issues and implications associated with migration and be equipped to deal effectively with this globally diverse and complex group. This chapter will describe the status of migration and explore the similarities and differences between immigrant and refugee populations. There will be a focus on the unique premigration experiences of refugees and the similarities and dissimilarities of the postmigration process for each of the two groups, followed by a discussion on acculturation and the influence of culture on mental health, help-seeking behavior, and utilization of mental health services. The chapter will conclude with a model for effective and culturally responsive psychotherapy for both refugees and immigrants.

The Status of Migration

It has been estimated that there are seventy to a hundred million immigrants and refugees in the world today (United Nations, 1995). Although immigrants and refugees may have similar experiences, there is a major difference between the two groups. This distinction is in the migration process—regarding whether individuals experienced a "forced" or "free" migration (Murphy, 1977). Refugees who are subjected to forced or "involuntary" migration are oftentimes fleeing from political, religious, or ethnic persecution, war, and repression with little or no planning, preparation, or choice in the sudden decision to flee their homeland. Immigrants, on the other hand, are voluntarily migrating to another country in search of a better quality of life, due mainly to economic hardship in their home country. Furthermore, the two groups may also differ in their countries of origin, as well as in level of education, skills, and resources.

With the growing numbers of immigrants and refugees, governments are reconsidering their immigration policies as well as the legal definition of refugee status. For example, Japan, which has less than one percent of a foreign population, has avoided debates by maintaining a closed door policy (Watanabe, 1994). The current controversy in Australia is another example, with national disagreements about the numbers of immigrants and refugees who should be allowed to enter the country. This is a reaction to a previous policy, whereby Australia had an acceptance rate of two to three times the number of immigrants in proportion to it's population as compared to Europe (Coleman, 1995). These examples represent major global tensions between immigrants and refugees and resettlement countries, sometimes escalating into reactionary dialogue, platforms, and policies by conservative governments advocating to reinstate an "all White immigration" policy. Other issues also generate discussions about refugee status, such as the current situation in the United Kingdom. The controversy there now is centered on government policy that has recently defined refugees as victims of war, excluding those suffering from economic hardship due to war and natural disasters, which is the plight of many refugees. This narrow definition excludes victims of other war atrocities such as women and girls who were subjected to rape and sexual abuse during the war. Despite debates such as the one in the United Kingdom over immigrant and refugee policies, governments in developed countries cannot ignore the growing numbers of immigrants and refugees. Given the expected increasing numbers of immigrants and refugees, governments will be forced to continue to reexamine policies related to this population.

The United States has continued to accept large numbers of immigrants. Currently it is estimated that approximately 10 percent of the U.S. population is from a migrant background (Balian, 1997), with nearly one of eleven Americans being foreign-born (U.S. Bureau of Census, 1997). Estimates indicate that approximately 3,000 immigrants and refugees arrive daily to the United States, which combined with illegal immigrants increases the annual U.S. population by about one million (Martin & Midgley, 1994). The majority of U.S. immigrants (78%) entered as immediate relatives of current citizens, through the sponsorship of a U.S. family, or to accept employment (U.S. Immigration and Naturalization Service, 1996). Most went to five major urban areas including Los Angeles-Long Beach, New York, Miami, Chicago, and the Washington, D.C., area (U.S. Immigration and Naturalization Service, 1996), with the majority of legal immigrants (37%) coming from North America (primarily Mexico), followed by Asia (34%) and Europe (16%) (see Chapter 1). The median age for immigrants was 28, with most being female (54%). Forty-seven percent of those admitted to the United States between the ages of 16 and 64 reported having an occupation, with approximately 49 percent of those having a professional or technical specialty (U.S. Immigration and Naturalization Services, 1996).

Refugees' Premigration Experiences

Studies on the premigration experiences of refugees are extensive (e.g., Ajdukovic & Ajdukovic, 1993; Bottinelli, 1990; Dadfar, 1994; El-Sarraj, Tawahina, & Heine, 1994; Farias, 1991; Karadaghi, 1994; Kinzie et al., 1990; Kozaric-Korvacic et al., 1995; Mollica, Wyshak, & Lavelle, 1987; O'Brien, 1994; Westermeyer, 1988). The studies have found that many refugees have been subjected to the atrocities of war, such as experiencing and witnessing torture and killing, being forced to commit atrocities, being incarcerated and placed in reeducation camps, starvation, rape and sexual abuse, and physical beatings and injury. These events occur during the actual war or conflict, in the subsequent escape, as well as in the refugee camps. It is therefore not surprising that studies have found that refugees are at risk for developing serious mental health problems including depression, anxiety, posttraumatic stress disorder (PTSD), and generalized psychological difficulties. Refugees therefore exhibit a higher incidence of psychopathology and other psychological problems compared to the general population of the resettlement country (e.g., Kinzie, 1993; Marsella, Friedman, & Spain, 1993; Mollica & Lavelle, 1988; Weisaeth & Eitinger, 1993; Williams & Berry, 1991). For example, PTSD among the clinical refugee population is estimated to be 50 percent or higher, and depressive disorders range from 42 percent to 89 percent (e.g., Hauff & Vaglum, 1995; Mollica et al., 1987; Ramsay, Gorst-Unsworth, & Turner, 1993; Van Velsen, Gorst-Unsworth, & Turner, 1996). Different studies have found depression ranging from 15 to 80 percent in the refugee community (e.g., Carlson & Rosser-Hogan, 1991; Pernice & Brook, 1994; Westermeyer, 1988). Premigration trauma therefore contributes to the psychosocial maladjustment, along with problems related to resettlement and adjustment.

Specific subgroups within the refugee population have been identified as particularly at risk for developing serious mental health disorders. Older refugees have been identified as one such group, who due to their age and deeply ingrained behavior patterns may have more difficulties in adjustment and learning new skills and language (Bemak & Chung, in press). In contrast, single men below age 21 also have been found to be highly distressed because of the lack of familial and social support (Lin, Tazuma, & Masuda, 1979). Refugee women and girls are also at risk due to their experiences of multiple rape and sexual abuse (Refugee Women in Development, 1990). In addition, a large percentage of refugee women are widowed due to their husbands being killed or lost during the war, as well as having lost their children (Mollica et al., 1987). This group also experienced extreme difficulties in postmigration adjustment due to low or no levels of education, English proficiency, family and emotional support, and community resources. Unaccompanied minors—that is, children and adolescents who were not accompanied by adult family members during the resettlement process—are another at-risk group. For any of these at-risk groups, certain events such as holidays or reports from the media may trigger increased anxiety, loneliness, homesickness, depression, or feelings of guilt (Chung & Okazaki, 1991).

Postmigration Adjustment Issues

There are similarities between immigrants and refugees with regard to postmigration adjustment. Both groups experience similar formidable tasks during postmigration. One major challenge encountered by both groups is culture shock. Although immigrants may be willing and psychologically prepared to leave their home country, arrival to a new country may still have a strong effect. The country of resettlement for both groups is often different from their home countries, especially if one moves from a developing to a developed country. Oftentimes, individuals are confronted with a new culture as well as geographic and climate differences that influence such things as food, clothing, housing, and employment opportunities. For example, immigrants and refugees who may have earned incomes fishing or farming in their home countries may have difficulty finding similar work in the resettlement countries. To compound the situation there is the loss of family and community support and networks.

The movement from a developing country to a developed country also highlights the differences between the two countries in terms of worldviews, differentiating individualistic and collectivistic value and belief systems. Many of the Western resettlement countries are individualistic in nature, where social behavior is motivated by personal needs, self-development, individual achievement, and individual goals. Collectivistic cultures, in contrast, value family, friends, community, collective goals and accomplishments, and interdependence rather than independence (Triandis, 1990). Therefore many immigrants and refugees face a new culture in which there is a focus on self rather than on family or the group, while simultaneously having to contend with the loss of their family, community, social network, and reference group (Bemak, Chung, & Bornemann, 1996). The change may cause culture shock, which precipitates feelings of helplessness, disorientation, and doubt about whether the choice to relocate was the right decision.

Language

Another area where both refugees and immigrants experience difficulties in the resettlement country is language. In the United States, for example, the lack of English language proficiency is potentially a major barrier to successful adaptation and mental health. Proficiency in English not only provides employment opportunities and career mobility, but also is the key to many important aspects of mastering a new culture. Without English it is difficult to access community resources, utilize available supports such as social service agencies, understand and discuss children's progress and performance in school, utilize transportation systems, shop, use telephones, or go to the bank. What had once been a routine in the home country may become a major ordeal.

Although ESL (English as a second language) classes may be available in the community, there may be some barriers that inhibit attendance. Financial concerns may cause some immigrants and refugees to focus on economic self-sufficiency and thus regard English classes as an intrusion on their efforts to attain economic independence. This may be particularly true if they are solely responsible for supporting their families and view language study as time-consuming and less important than the immediate goal of earning money to provide food and shelter for their family. It may also be that studying English, in addition to attempting to survive financially and emotionally in a new culture, is highly taxing. If family members are already working long hours, to also participate in English classes is wearisome.

Education

The lack of formal education may also include having little or no experience as a student and may therefore be an obstruction. Not only must the immigrant or refugee learn new content areas such as English, but also simultaneously he or she must "learn how to learn" (Chung & Bemak, 1998). Individuals who are literate in their native language achieve English literacy much faster (Raccine, 1984). In addition, the location of classes may create difficulties, if public transportation access is difficult, if the cost of getting to the classes prohibitive, or if the classes are held in areas where the migrants feel unsafe. Finally, some refugees may have impaired memory and concentration as a result of injuries caused by beatings to the head, which is a form of torture (Allden, 1997). This may not only result in problems learning English, but also interfere with routine daily functioning, socialization skills, memory, general intelligence, and/or problem-solving abilities (Chung & Bemak, 1998).

Employment

Finding employment is also challenging to immigrants and refugees. Educational qualifications attained from the home country do not always transfer to the resettlement countries. Therefore, many immigrants and refugees find themselves either unemployed or underemployed (Chung & Okazaki, 1991). The socioeconomic status of immigrants and refugees who are more educated lessens considerably in the resettlement country. Some of the initial decrease in status and employment levels can be recovered over time, with increased acculturation, language improvement, retraining programs, and persistence, although most remain underemployed (Lin, Masuda, & Tazuma, 1982; Lin et al., 1979; Masuda, Lin, & Tazuma, 1980).

The result of the underemployment and unemployment of immigrant and refugee men has forced women to work. This is contrary to the established norms in many of the home countries where oftentimes women are in traditional roles of caring for the children and attending to the home. However, in the resettlement country, it may be important to contribute financially to the household, so that, ironically, the socioeconomic status for men declines while the status for women moves up (Chung, 1991). The changes in the gender roles may present a serious conflict between the values of the home culture and those of the resettlement country. Furthermore, to compound the situation, as a result of women working they are exposed to the mainstream culture and values. This may lead them to question their traditional values and seek greater independence and freedom, similar to women in the resettlement country. This has the potential to disrupt the balance and established roles within families.

Children

Children in migrant families tend to acculturate much more rapidly than their parents. The fact that they are in school—exposed on a daily basis to nonmigrant peers, forced to speak

English, and spend significant time in a structured educational environment—accelerates acculturation. As the children better adjust to the new culture, they may challenge the traditional family values such as dating, religious practices and beliefs, gender roles, peer relations, traditional norms, and social activities. In many cases the children become cultural and language translators for their parents and other adults. This creates profound shifts in roles within the family. The men who were once the head of the household become reliant on their children to assist them in understanding and accessing community resources, and women who are caretakers of the home, in turn, become dependent on the children to understand the new world. These changing family dynamics for the parents, children, and other adults in the family may create frustration and family tensions as the roles change, and can lead to an increase in domestic violence that may not have occurred in the home country (Chung & Okazaki, 1991).

Acculturation to the Resettlement Country

Immigrants and refugees must adapt to the resettlement country while dealing with many psychosocial issues. Bemak (1989) developed a three-phase bicultural model of acculturation. In this model, migrants initially utilize former skills from their country of origin in an attempt to adjust to the new culture. Although the old skills may assist partially in their adjustment, individuals fall short in mastering the new culture so that, in the second stage, there is the learning and testing of new skills as they attempt to adjust in the resettlement country. In the third and final stage, there is an integration of new and old skills with a perspective on the future. As migrants become more acculturated and gain an understanding of the new culture, there is a process of integrating past, present, and future, whereby the traditional culture merges with the new culture to form a newly fashioned perspective on the world. This model is consistent with findings that bicultural cultural integration facilitates the healthiest adaptation to a new culture (Berry, 1986; Wong-Reiger & Quintana, 1987).

During the acculturation process there may be an initial period of euphoria as one is resettling, appreciating the safety associated with resettlement and the psychological relief of having finally arrived in the country of resettlement. However, as the reality of resettlement emerges, the euphoric feelings may transform into a sense of emotional and psychological discomfort and frustration as the newcomers begin to confront the loss of their culture, identity, relationships, and practices, while simultaneously coping with major resettlement issues such as housing, employment, and language. Relatively simple tasks that are embedded in the culture, such as using modern household kitchen or bathroom facilities, using checking accounts, or understanding public transportation, may become complex and overwhelming. This, when combined with changing family dynamics, confusion about norms, lack of a social support network, and economic hardship, may create psychological difficulties for some migrants. In addition, for refugees, premigration trauma or emotional turmoil may interfere with successful daily functioning, psychosocial adjustment, and acculturation (Bemak & Chung, 1998).

Adaptation to a new country requires learning new ways of coping as well as different behavioral and communication patterns (Bemak et al., 1996). Many refugees have learned to survive by employing skills and behavior that may appear antisocial, or even psychopathological, in the resettlement country (Stein, 1986). For example, in order for

Cambodian refugees to avoid further torture or being killed, they acted "dumb." To survive, individuals acted as if they were deaf, stupid, foolish, or confused and learned to obey orders without asking questions or complaining because they knew that if they appeared "smart" they would be tortured or executed in Cambodia. They have maintained the fear of this happening and therefore have continued to "act dumb" and afraid to express feelings in the resettlement country. This behavior may be inappropriate for effective functioning in the host country (Bemak et al., 1996).

Survivor's Guilt

Furthermore, for refugees, survivor's guilt can also compound the situation (Brown, 1982; Lin et al., 1982). Many are haunted by the guilt of successfully escaping from their home country, while leaving family, relatives, and friends behind in a potentially dangerous situation in their country of origin. Refugees oftentimes have little or no information about those who have been left behind, which adds to the already existing guilt. Some may experience nostalgia, depression, anxiety, and frustration as a result of the experienced loss and separation. Survivor's guilt may therefore interfere with learning new skills and personal development and may create difficulties in successful adjustment.

The Role of Culture in Mental Health

Culture influences immigrants' and refugees' conceptualizations and manifestations of mental health and mental disorder, as well as help-seeking behavior and expectations for treatment (see Chapter 2). Their worldviews oftentimes differ from those that prevail in the resettlement countries, especially developed countries that typically subscribe to Western models of mental health. To provide effective psychotherapy, Kleinman and Good (1985) emphasized the need for mental health professionals to understand, accept, and confirm the client's cultural conceptualization of his or her problem. The dominant medical model of Western mental health focuses upon the *individual* and the *individual's* pathology with a goal of treating the *individual* in order to promote optimum *individual* functioning and personal growth and development. The emphasis on individuality and independence may conflict with the collectivistic cultural backgrounds of many migrants, where one's identity is defined by family, community, and social networks, with an emphasis on interdependence rather than independence. In the migrant's conceptual world, mental health and physical health may be an integration of mind, body, and spirit as one entity, in contrast to Western views where there is a dichotomy between mind and body, physical and mental. It is crucial that mental health professionals understand and accept the migrant client's conceptualization of mental health and mental disorder before effective treatment can be provided.

Furthermore, culture shapes how mental illness is manifested. Despite the influence of culture on symptom expression, similar complaints and symptoms are found across different cultures. However, they may appear in different patterns and be attributed to a different causation (e.g., Fabrega, 1989; Kirmayer, 1989; Kleinman, 1982; Phillips & Draguns, 1969; Tseng & Hsu, 1969; and see Chapter 3). The meaning and symbolic value of similar symptoms may be culture specific and not interchangeable across cultures. For example, it has been found that, for Asian immigrants and Southeast Asian refugees, neurasthenia is a culturally sanctioned method of expressing mental illness (Chung & Kagawa-Singer, 1995). The expressed pattern of symptoms, which combines both the somatic and psychological manifestations of distress, is consistent with Asian nosology, and therefore does not fit precisely into a framework for Western mental illness. Effective diagnosis without considering the migrant client's conceptualization and expression of mental illness and the attainment of conceptual equivalence between clinician and client will be difficult if not impossible, and it may lead to inappropriate treatment and perhaps to high dropout rates from mainstream mental health services (Chung & Kagawa-Singer, 1995). Generally, identification and characterization of mental illness for this population have been conducted primarily using Western measures or diagnostic criteria (as currently embodied in DSM-IV or ICD-10). Accurate assessment with conceptual equivalence is essential before a cluster of symptoms is labeled with a diagnosis (Good & Good, 1981). Furthermore, prescribing medication that is common for mainstream populations for symptom relief without consideration of ethnic and biological differences may also be problematic (Lin, Inui, Kleinman, & Womack, 1982). Previous research has found that misclassification of mental health disorders of ethnic clients (e.g., African American, Latino American, and Asian American) have been due to the clinician's lack of understanding of cultural and/or linguistic differences (e.g., Huertin-Roberts & Snowden, 1993).

As stated previously, the conceptualization of mental health and mental disorders influences not only the conceptualization and manifestation of symptoms, but also help-seeking behavior and in turn the treatment outcome. Although there is a disproportionate number of immigrants and refugees who have mental health problems (Stuwe, 1994), there is an unwillingness to access mainstream mental health services (Higginbotham, Trevino, & Ray, 1990; Chung & Lin, 1994). One reason for the low utilization of mainstream mental health services is the immigrant's and refugee's lack of understanding and familiarity with the kinds of services available. A second reason is cultural insensitivity of the service provided. The fact that these services are not culturally responsive may account for their low utilization (Sue, Fujino, Hu, Takeuchi, & Zane, 1991). One aspect of this is found in the problems that immigrants and refugees have in communicating with mental health professionals. In addition to a language barrier between psychotherapist and client there may also be cultural differences in both verbal (e.g., tone and volume of the speaking) and nonverbal (e.g., eye contact and personal space) behavior (Bemak et al., 1996). It should be noted that this communication problem is not only a language barrier, but also, more broadly, a cultural barrier where worldviews and relationships of oneself to the world may differ dramatically—and interfere even when trained bilingual and bicultural interpreters are available.

A third reason for nonuse of services by many migrants may be a preference for indigenous treatment models, such as traditional healing (see Chapter 9). Research has found that immigrants and refugees tend to rely on traditional medicine and healing methods and to underutilize mainstream mental health services (e.g., Chung & Lin, 1994; Lin et al., 1982). For example, studies of Mexican immigrants have found that a large percentage of this group frequently utilize *curanderismo* (folk medicine) (e.g., Higginbotham et al., 1990). For immigrant and refugee family members, community elders and traditional healers might well be the first choice for mental health treatment. Many in this population search for indigenous healing methods (herbs, spiritualists, healers). This is more probable with older immigrants and refugees, the uneducated, and more recent migrants (Chung & Lin, 1994). It is only when the indigenous methods of treatment are unsuccessful and the traditional resources are exhausted that there will be a utilization of mainstream mental health providers. At this point, if the problem remains unresolved, the immigrant or refugee client may well be in an acute stage (Sue, 1993). Even with the contact and attempts at treatment with Western mental health providers, there is still a continued search and belief in healing as it is understood in a non-Western cultural context. Clients may not only be seeing the Western trained practitioner for treatment, but simultaneously be utilizing traditional methods of healing that are culturally comfortable for them (Chung & Lin, 1994). This challenges Western-trained mental health professionals to accept the two approaches to treatment utilized by immigrant and refugee clients, one of which is alien to their belief system.

Intervention and Psychotherapy

For mental health professionals to be effective, not only must they have the required skills, but it is essential that they be aware of and accept the immigrant and refugee clients' cultural background and life experiences. Psychotherapy with immigrants and refugees requires unique skills, understanding, and sensitivity. Given the number of immigrants and refugees entering into the United States, it is unfortunate that training and supervision of mental health professionals rarely address specific issues relevant to this population (Bemak et al., 1996).

Given the complexity of immigrant and refugee experience, numerous issues must be carefully and simultaneously considered in psychotherapy. The Multilevel Model Approach (MLM) to psychotherapy was designed to address the specific needs of refugees, but may also be applied to immigrants (Bemak et al., 1996). To understand the intricacy that immigrant and refugee clients bring with them to the psychotherapy sessions, the model takes into account the group's historical, sociopolitical, and cultural background, reasons for migration, the migration process, past and present stressors, and psychosocial adjustment and adaptation issues, as well as the interplay among these variables. Given the complexity of these issues, the psychotherapist must possess unique skills as well as an acute sense of cultural and political sensitivity to the client's life and history. The MLM is a psychoeducational model that comprises cognitive, affective, and behavioral interventions inclusive of cultural foundations and their relation to community and social processes (Bemak et al., 1996), while simultaneously reconceptualizing and diversifying the psychotherapist's role. The MLM consists of four phases: *Level I:* mental health education; *Level II:* individual, group, and/or family psychotherapy; *Level III:* cultural empowerment; and *Level IV:* integration of Western and indigenous healing methodologies. The four levels in the MLM are interrelated and may be implemented concurrently. Although the levels may be considered separately, their interrelationships are essential for attaining the goals of psychotherapy. The emphasis or utilization of one level or combination of levels is based upon an assessment by the psychotherapist.

Level I: Mental health education addresses the fact that most migrant populations will not be familiar with Western mental health practices and processes. Refugees and immigrants may come to psychotherapy with uninformed and unrealistic expectations. Therefore, it is essential that the psychotherapist educate clients about the psychotherapeutic process, including fundamental procedures such as intake, assessment, the role of the professional, interpersonal dynamics in the psychotherapeutic process, the role of an interpreter, time boundaries, usage or nonusage of medication, and the course of treatment. This alleviates the discomfort and awkwardness many immigrant and refugee clients may experience in the therapeutic relationship while setting the course of events. Therefore during Level I, information for the individual, family, or group about the process of psychotherapy and the mental health encounter is presented and discussed to instill a clear understanding in clients. Although Level I is addressed at the beginning of psychotherapy, the psychotherapist may need to revisit this level at various stages of the therapeutic process for clarification.

Level II: Individual, group, and/or family psychotherapy is based upon the traditional Western individual, group, and family psychotherapy (see Chapter 5). It is important during this stage to maintain awareness that when working with immigrants and refugees the traditional skills may not be effective if the interventions are not culturally sensitive and responsive. This requires that interventions incorporate an understanding of cultural norms and practices in healing. For example, psychotherapists working with Southeast Asian refugees must be more directive and active (Kinzie, 1985), since this is consistent with expectations and healing within the cultural context of Southeast Asia. It also necessitates theoretical flexibility in order to meet the needs of particular clients who present specific histories and problems within a cultural context, as well as creativity and innovation in the usage of techniques. For different migrant groups, various strategies and theories have been used such as cognitive-behavioral approaches (Bemak & Greenberg, 1994; Egli, Shiota, Ben-Porath, & Butcher, 1991; Stumphauser & Davis, 1983); storytelling (Pynoos & Eth, 1984); dreamwork (Bemak & Timm, 1994); group therapy (Friedman & Jaranson, 1994; Kinzie et al., 1988) and family therapy (Bemak, 1989; Szapocznik & Cohen, 1986).

Regardless of the theoretical approach or strategies employed, it is essential for the therapist to be perceived as credible. Sue and Zane (1987) differentiated between ascribed and achieved credibility. Ascribed credibility is associated with the psychotherapist's status (e.g., age, education, gender, or professional status), while achieved credibility is gained only after earning the trust and confidence of the client based on the demonstration of cultural sensitivity, understanding, and competency. An achieved credibility will be earned as one adapts theory and practice to the refugee and immigrant experience.

Level III: Cultural empowerment is the stage during the therapeutic encounter when the focus is on achieving mastery over the new environment. Cultural empowerment is critical to the refugee's or immigrant's acculturation and mental health and parallels the deeper psychological issues that the psychotherapist may be addressing in Level II. This stage not only includes effectively accessing resources, such as housing, employment, and language, but also assisting the client in developing effective coping strategies in dealing with everyday life challenges, such as racism and discrimination. Another aspect to this level is the therapeutic focus on biculturalism or the integration of two cultures. This is crucial for the development of a healthy and positive cultural identity of self, which in turn, impacts on all other facets of one's life.

Level IV: Integration of Western and indigenous healing methods for immigrants and refugees tends to rely on traditional methods of healing. Because clients who have migrated tend to use both traditional and Western methods of treatment concurrently, psychotherapists must acknowledge, understand, and accept that their clients will use both methods of healing. This connotes respect for the client's worldview and provides a better chance of attaining achieved credibility with the client. The World Health Organization (1992) describes how an integration of indigenous healing with Western healing practices resulted in more effective outcomes. Thus it is important for mental health professionals to be receptive to non-Western, culturally bound forms of healing, and display acceptance, understanding, and support of their clients' cultural beliefs.

Conclusion

It is important for mental health professionals to understand the distinct differences between refugee and immigrant populations and native-born citizens who have not experienced relocation. Furthermore, although immigrants and refugees have many similar premigration and postmigration experiences, the two groups also differ dramatically in their premigration history and the migration process. It is essential that mental health professionals recognize these similarities and differences. In addition, mental health professionals must have a clear understanding of the context and conceptualization of the mental health of the refugee or immigrant client.

The MLM is a four-level intervention approach that emphasizes that for psychotherapists to be effective they must first be aware of, acknowledge, understand, accept, and be sensitive to this population's cultural, historical, and sociopolitical backgrounds, as well as the postmigration adjustment difficulties it encounters. The four levels incorporate the integration of traditional Western psychotherapy with indigenous healing methods, cultural empowerment, and psychoeducational training. The MLM provides a holistic framework that conceptualizes an integrated strategy to meet the multiple needs of the immigrant and refugee population.

R E F E R E N C E S

Ajdukovic, M., & Ajdukovic, D. (1993). Psychological well-being of refugee children. *Child Abuse Neglect, 17,* 843–854.

Allden, K. (1997). *Treatment programs for survivors of torture: What do they tell us?* Paper presented at the meeting on Survivors of Torture: Improving Our Understanding Conference. Washington, DC.

Balian, K. (1997). *Overview of issues and the United Nations role.* Paper presented at the meeting on Survivors of Torture: Improving Our Understanding Conference, Washington, DC.

Bemak, F. (1989). Cross-cultural family therapy with Southeast Asian refugees. *Journal of Strategic and Systemic Therapies, 8,* 22–27.

Bemak, F. (in press). Migrants. *Encyclopedia of psychology.* London: Oxford University Press.

Bemak, F., & Chung, R. C-Y. (1998). Refugee psychotherapy. In U. Gielen, J. Draguns, & J. Fish (Ed.), *Culture, therapy and healing.* Unpublished manuscript.

Bemak, F., & Chung, R. C-Y., & Bornemann, T. (1996). Counseling and psychotherapy with refugees. In P. Pedersen, J. Draguns, W. Lonner, & J. Trimble

(Eds.), *Counseling across cultures* (4th ed., pp. 243–265). Thousands Oaks, CA: Sage.

Bemak, F., & Greenberg, B. (1994). Southeast Asian refugee adolescents: Implications for counselling. *Journal for Multicultural Counseling and Development, 22* (4), 115–124.

Bemak, F., & Timm, J. (1994). Case study of an adolescent Cambodian refugee: A clinical, developmental and cultural perspective. *International Journal of the Advancement of Counseling, 17,* 47–58.

Berry, J. W. (1986). The acculturation process and refugee behavior. In C. L. Williams & J. Westermeyer (Eds.), *Refugee mental health in resettlement countries* (pp. 25–37). Washington, DC: Hemisphere.

Bottinelli, M. (1990). *Psychological impact of exile: Salvadoran and Guatemalan families in Mexico.* Washington, DC: Center for Immigration Policy and Refugee Assistance.

Brown, G. (1982). Issues in the resettlement of Indochinese refugees. *Social Casework, 63,* 155–159.

Carlson, E. B., & Rosser-Hogan, R. (1991). Trauma experiences, posttraumatic stress, dissociation, and depression in Cambodian refugees. *American Journal of Psychiatry, 148,* 1548–1551.

Chung, R. C-Y. (1991, August). *Predictors of distress among Southeast Asian refugees: Gender and group differences.* Paper presented at the Asian American Psychological Association Convention, San Francisco.

Chung, R. C-Y., & Bemak, F. (1998). Gender differences in psychological distress among Southeast Asian refugees. *Journal of Nervous and Mental Disease, 186* (2), 112–119.

Chung, R. C-Y., & Kagawa-Singer, M. (1995). Interpretation of symptom presentation and distress: A Southeast Asian refugee example. *The Journal of Nervous and Mental Disease, 183* (10), 639–648.

Chung, R. C-Y., & Lin, K. M. (1994). Helpseeking behavior among Southeast Asian refugees. *Journal of Community Psychology, 22,* 109–120.

Chung, R. C-Y., & Okazaki, S. (1991). Counseling Americans of Southeast Asian descent: The impact of the refugee experience. In C. C. Lee & B. L. Richardson (Eds.), *Multicultural issues in counseling: New approaches to diversity* (pp. 107–124). Alexandria, VA: American Counseling Association.

Coleman, D. A. (1995). International migration: Demographics and socioeconomic consequences in the United Kingdom and Europe. *International Migration Review, 29* (1), 155–180.

Dadfar, A. (1994). The Afghans: Bearing the scars of a forgotten war. In A. J. Marsella, T. Bornemann, S. Ekblad, & J. Orley (Eds.), *Amidst peril and pain: The mental health and well-being of the world's refugees* (pp. 125–140). Washington, DC: American Psychological Association.

Egli, A., Shiota, N., Ben-Porath, Y., & Butcher, J. (1991). Psychological interventions. In J. Westermeyer, C. Williams, & A. Nguyen (Eds.), *Mental health services for refugees* (pp. 157–188). Washington, DC: Government Printing Office.

El-Sarraj, E. R., Tawahina, A. A., & Heine, F. A. (1994). The Palestinians: An uprooted people. In A. J. Marsella, T. Bornemann, S. Ekblad, & J. Orley (Eds.), *Amidst peril and pain: The mental health and well-being of the world's refugees* (pp. 141–152). Washington, DC: American Psychological Association.

Fabrega, H. (1989). Cultural relativism and psychiatric illness. *Journal of Nervous and Mental Disease, 177* (7), 415–425.

Farias, P. (1991). Central and South American refugees: Some mental health challenges. In A. J. Marsella, T. Bornemann, S. Ekblad, & J. Orley (Eds.), *Amidst peril and pain: The mental health and well-being of the world's refugees* (pp. 101–113). Washington, DC: American Psychological Association.

Friedman, M., & Jaranson, J. (1994). The applicability of the posttraumatic stress disorder concepts to refugees. In A. J. Marsella, T. Bornemann, S. Ekblad, & J. Orley (Eds.), *Amidst peril and pain: The mental health and well-being of the world's refugees* (pp. 207–228). Washington, DC: American Psychological Association.

Good, B. J., & Good, M. J. D. (1981). The meaning of symptoms: A cultural hermeneutic model for clinical practice. In L. Eisenberg & A. Kleinman (Eds.), *The relevance of social science for medicine* (pp. 165–196). Dordrecht, Holland: Reidel.

Hauff, E., & Vaglum, P. (1995). Organized violence and the stress of exile: Predictors of mental health in a community cohort of Vietnamese refugees three years after resettlement. *British Journal of Psychiatry, 166,* 360–367.

Higginbotham, J. C., Trevino, F. M., & Ray, L. A. (1990). Utilization of Curanderos by Mexican Americans: Prevalence and predictors findings from HHANES 1982–1984. *American Journal of Public Health, 80* Supplement, 32–35.

Huertin-Roberts, S., & Snowden, L. (1993). *Comparison of ethnographic descriptors of depression and epidemiological catchment area data for African-Americans.* Paper presented at the 18th Annual American Anthropology Association Meeting, Washington, DC.

Karadaghi, P. (1994). The Kurds: Refugees in their own land. In A. J. Marsella, T. Bornemann, S. Ekblad, & J. Orley (Eds.), *Amidst peril and pain: The mental health and well-being of the world's refugees* (pp. 115–124). Washington, DC: American Psychological Association.

Kinzie, D. (1985). Overview of clinical issues in the treatment of Southeast Asian refugees. In T. C. Owan (Ed.), *Southeast Asian mental health: Treatment, prevention, services, training, and research* (pp. 113–135). Washington, DC: National Institute of Mental Health.

Kinzie, D. (1993). Posttraumatic effects and their treatment among Southeast Asian refugees. In J. Wilson & B. Raphael (Eds.), *International handbook of traumatic stress syndromes* (pp. 311–320). New York: Plenum.

Kinzie, D., Boehnlein, J., Leung, P., Moore, L., Riley, C., & Smith, D. (1990). The prevalence of PTSD and its clinical significance among Southeast Asian refugees. *American Journal of Psychiatry, 147,* 913–917.

Kinzie, D., Leung, P., Bui, A., Ben, R., Keopraseuth, K. O., Riley, C., Flectk, J., & Ades, M. (1988). Group therapy with Southeast Asian refugees. *Community Mental Health Journal, 23,* 157–166.

Kirmayer, L. J. (1989). Cultural variation in the response to psychiatric disorders and emotional distress. *Social Science & Medicine, 28* (3), 327–339.

Kleinman, A. (1982). Neurasthenia and depression: A study of somatization and culture in China. *Culture, Medicine & Psychiatry, 6,* 117–190.

Kleinman, A., & Good, B. (1985). *Culture and depression: Studies in the anthropology and cross-cultural psychiatry of affect and disorder.* Berkeley: University of California Press.

Kozaric-Kovacic, D., Folnegovic-Smalc, V., Skrinjaric, J., Szajnberg, N., & Marusic, A. (1995). Rape, torture, and traumatization of Bosnian and Croatian women: Psychological sequelae. *American Journal of Orthopsychiatry, 65,* 428–433.

Lin, K. M., Inui, T. S., Kleinman, A. M., & Womack, W. (1982). Sociocultural determinants of the help-seeking behavior of patients with mental illness. *Journal of Nervous and Mental Disease, 170* (2), 78–85.

Lin, K. M., Masuda, M., & Tazuma, L. (1982). Adaptational problems of Vietnamese refugees: Part III. Case studies in clinic and field: Adaptive and maladaptive. *Psychiatric Journal of University of Ottawa, 7* (3), 173–183.

Lin, K. M., Tazuma, L., & Masuda, M. (1979). Adaptational problems of Vietnamese refugees. *Archives of General Psychiatry, 36,* 955–961.

Marsella, A. J., Friedman, M., & Spain, H. (1993). Ethnocultural aspects of PTSD. *Review of Psychiatry, 12,* 157–181.

Martin, P., & Midgley, E. (1994). Immigrants to the United States: Journey to an uncertain destination. *Population Bulletin, 49* (2), 1–47.

Masuda, M., Lin, K. M., & Tazuma, L. (1980). Adaptation problems of Vietnamese refugees. Part II: Life

changes and perception of life events. *Archives of General Psychiatry, 37,* 447–450.

Mollica, R. F., & Lavelle, J. (1988). Southeast Asian refugees. In L. Comas-Díaz & E. H. Griffith (Eds.), *Clinical guidelines in cross-cultural mental health* (pp. 262–303). New York: Wiley.

Mollica, R. F., Wyshak, G., & Lavelle, J. (1987). The psychosocial impact of war trauma and torture on Southeast Asian refugees. *American Journal of Psychiatry, 144,* 1567–1572.

Murphy, H. B. (1977). Migration, culture and mental health. *Psychological Medicine, 7,* 677–684.

O'Brien, L. S. (1994). What will be the psychiatric consequences of the war in Bosnia? *British Journal of Psychiatry, 164,* 443–447.

Pernice, R., & Brook, J. (1994). Relationship of migrant status (refugee or immigrant) to mental health. *International Journal of Social Psychiatry, 40,* 177–188.

Phillips, L., & Draguns, J. (1969). Some issues in intercultural research on psychopathology. In W. Caudill & T. Y. Lin (Eds.), *Mental health research in Asia and the Pacific* (pp. 21–32). Honolulu: East West Center Press.

Pynoos, R., & Eth, S. (1984). Children traumatized by witnessing acts of personal violence: Homicide, rape or suicide behavior. In S. Eth & R. Pynoos (Eds.), *Posttraumatic stress disorder in children* (pp. 17–44). Washington, DC: American Psychiatric Press.

Raccine, M. (1984). Why literacy in the native language: The case of adult Haitian illiterates. *Paper of Social Sciences, 4,* 61–77.

Ramsay, R., Gorst-Unsworth, C., & Turner, S. (1993). Psychiatric morbidity in survivors of organized state violence including torture: A retrospective series. *British Journal of Psychiatry, 162,* 55–59.

Refugee Women in Development. (1990). *What Is refugee?* (Available from RefWID, Washington, DC.)

Stein, B. N. (1986). The experience of being a refugee: Insights from the research literature. In C. L. Williams & J. Westermeyer (Eds.), *Refugee mental health in resettlement countries* (pp. 5–23). Washington, DC: Hemisphere.

Stumphauser, J., & Davis, J. (1983). Training Mexican-American mental health personnel in behavior therapy. *Journal of Behavior Therapy and Experimental Psychiatry, 14,* 215–217.

Stuwe, G. (1994). Training health and medical professionals to care for refugees: Issues and methods. In A. J. Marsella, T., Bornemann, S. Ekblad, & J. Orley (Eds.), *Amidst peril and pain: The mental health and well-being of the world's refugees* (pp. 311–324). Washington, DC: American Psychological Association.

Sue, S. (1993). The changing Asian American population: Mental health policy. In LEAP Asian Pacific American Public Policy Institute and UCLA Asian American Studies Center (Eds.), *The state of Asian Pacific*

America (pp. 79–94). Los Angeles: LEAP Asian Pacific American Public Policy Institute and UCLA Asian American Studies Center.

Sue, S., Fujino, D, Hu, L., Takeuchi, D., & Zane, N. (1991). Community mental health services for ethnic minority groups: A test of cultural responsive hypothesis. *Journal of Consulting and Clinical Psychology, 59* (4), 533–540.

Sue, S., & Zane, N. (1987). The role of culture and cultural techniques in psychotherapy: A critique and reformulation. *American Psychologist, 42* (1), 37–45.

Szapocznik, J., & Cohen, R. E. (1986). Mental health care for rapidly changing environments: Emergency relief to unaccompanied youths of the 1980 Cuba refugee wave. In C. L. Williams & J. Westermeyer (Eds.), *Refugee mental health in resettlement countries* (pp. 141–156). New York: Hemisphere.

Triandis, H. (1990). Cross cultural studies of individualism and collectivism. In J. Berman (Ed.), *Cross-cultural perspectives* (pp. 41–134). Lincoln: University of Nebraska Press.

Tseng, W., & Hsu, J. (1969). Chinese culture, personality formation, and mental illness. *International Journal of Social Psychiatry, 16,* 5–14.

United Nations. (1995). *Notes for speakers: Social development.* New York: Department of Public Information, United Nations.

U.S. Bureau of Census. (1997). *Current population reports: Special studies* (pp. 23–193). Washington DC: U.S. Government Printing Office.

U.S. Immigration & Naturalization Services. (1996). *Immigration in fiscal year 1996 and characteristics of legal immigrants.* Washington, DC: U.S. Immigration & Naturalization Services.

Van Velsen, C., Gorst-Unsworth, C., & Turner, S. (1996). Survivors of torture and organized violence: Demography and diagnosis. *Journal of Traumatic Stress, 9,* 181–193.

Watanabe, S. (1994). The Lewisian turning point and international migration: The case of Japan. *Asian and Pacific Migration Journal, 3* (1), 134–143.

Weisaeth, L., & Eitinger, L. (1993). Posttraumatic stress phenomena: Common themes across wars, disasters, and traumatic events. In J. Wilson & B. Raphael (Eds.). *International handbook of traumatic stress syndromes* (pp. 69–78). New York: Plenum Press.

Westermeyer, J. (1988). DSM-III psychiatric disorders among Hmong refugees in the United States: A point prevalence study. *American Journal of Psychiatry, 145,* 197–202.

Williams C. L., & Berry, J. W. (1991). Primary problems among adolescent Southeast Asian refugees. *Journal of Nervous and Mental Disease, 171* (2), 79–85.

Wong-Reiger, D., & Quintana, D. (1987). Comparative acculturation of Southeast Asian and Hispanic immigrants and sojourners. *Journal of Cross-Cultural Psychology, 18* (3), 345–362.

World Health Organization. (1992). *Refugee mental health: Draft manual for field testing.* Geneva, Switzerland: Author.

13 Intervention and Treatment with Ethnic Minority Substance Abusers

PAMELA JUMPER THURMAN

BARBARA PLESTED

RUTH W. EDWARDS

JULIE CHEN

RANDALL SWAIM

The problem of alcohol and other drug abuse in the United States has been firmly established as a matter of great concern (Bratter & Forrest, 1985; Helzer, 1987). Three factors need to be considered in a discussion of alcohol and other drug abuse: physiological, sociological, and psychological (Lawson & Lawson, 1989). Physiological studies have indicated a genetic factor for some forms of substance abuse (Cotton, 1979), sociological research has demonstrated the influence of family and peers on abuse of alcohol and other drugs (Cahalan, 1970; Glynn, 1981; Oetting & Beauvais, 1987), and psychological factors have been found to play a role in alcohol abuse (Lawson, Peterson, & Lawson, 1983) and in the chronic abuse of drugs such as cocaine, barbiturates, and heroin (Craig, 1982; Spotts & Shontz, 1982).

It is clear that there are multiple pathways leading to substance abuse (Bry, McKeon, & Pandina, 1982; Maddahian, Newcomb, & Bentler, 1988; Newcomb, Maddahian, & Bentler, 1986). Early childhood traits such as the "difficult child syndrome" and hyperactivity have been associated with alcohol and substance abuse as well as later-appearing antisocial behaviors. Social factors such as family dysfunction, parental modeling of use, and use by peers have been identified as risk factors for the development of substance use. The combined and additive nature of these risk factors may be responsible for the development and emergence of substance abuse (Swaim, 1991). The interaction of these risk factors with genetic, psychological, and sociological factors may help explain variations in substance use as well as patterns of protective factors that may prevent others from initiating use or developing abusive patterns of substance use.

Just as the etiology of this problem may vary greatly across individuals, treatment strategies need to be individualized as well so that they address those risk factors that are unique to specific clients. To some degree, this uniqueness should be considered across larger groups such as ethnic minorities who vary in their history, experiences, socioeconomic characteristics, values, beliefs and behaviors (see Chapters 1 and 2). However, the treatment needs of the individual, whether a member of an ethnic minority or not, must always be assessed and taken into account.

In the last decade, health risk behavior in various ethnic groups has gained the active attention of researchers, treatment providers, and policymakers (Orlandi, Weston, & Epstein, 1992). Some results indicate that minority populations are at higher risk for alcohol and other drug abuse than the general population (U.S. Department of Health and Human Services, 1985). However, it is important to note that many earlier studies on substance abuse in ethnic communities focused on negative aspects rather than resiliency factors, and data were often obtained from sources where minorities were likely to be overrepresented (e.g., emergency room facilities, public treatment programs). Most studies have compared ethnic minorities to Whites, often using one sample or the study of one group to generalize to the entire ethnic population. This has unfortunately led to stereotypes and negative assumptions regarding the nature and extent of alcohol and other drug abuse among minority groups.

Current research indicates that Whites generally tend to use alcohol and most drugs at higher rates than African Americans, Hispanics, or Asians, whereas studies on youth have found that Whites and Native Americans have the highest rates of lifetime and annual prevalence and the highest rates of heavy use of alcohol (Bachman et al., 1991; Rebach, 1992). Results from four years of survey data conducted on over 200,000 eighth- and twelfth-grade students indicated that Native American, Mexican American, and White youth had higher lifetime prevalence rates for a number of substances compared to Black and Asian youth.

May (1986) indicates that 50 to 90 percent of Native American youth, depending on the tribe, have experimented with alcohol. One in every seven Indian eighth graders is currently using inhalants (Beauvais, 1992). Rates of frequent heavier drinking seem to be highest among Whites, followed by Hispanics, then African Americans (Caetano, 1984). Asian Americans generally demonstrate lower rates of alcohol use than Whites, Native Americans, or Hispanics (Kitano, Lubben, & Chi, 1988).

Diversity within Native American, Latino, African American, and Asian American groups makes it hazardous to generalize from a particular subgroup to the larger group. For example, differences exist between rural, reservation, and urban Indians; among tribes; and even within tribes. The same is true for Asian Americans, Latinos, and African Americans (see Chapter 1). The terms *Native American* and *Alaska Native, African American, Latino, and Asian American* vary in usage and reflect the richness of hundreds of various subcultures and perspectives.

This chapter will focus on the nature and extent of alcohol and other drug abuse among the aforementioned ethnic groups. The historical factors, epidemiology, and correlates of substance abuse for these groups will be presented briefly. (For a more extensive survey, see Austin & Gilbert, 1989; Beauvais, 1992; Brown & Tooley, 1989; De La Rosa, Khalsa, & Rouse, 1990; Herd, 1985; Sue, 1987; Watts & Wright, 1983.) The chapter will also discuss interventions and culturally specific treatment modalities, as well as recommendations and suggestions for the treatment provider working with specific ethnic groups.

Nature and Extent of Alcohol and Other Drug Abuse

African Americans

Historical Factors.   According to the 1996 U.S. Bureau of Census, African Americans make up the largest ethnic minority group in the United States, with 33.9 million people or 12.6 percent of the total population (U.S. Bureau of Census, 1996). It would appear likely that research in the area of alcohol and other drug use, patterns, problems, and treatment within this population would be plentiful due to the number of African Americans. However, only minimal information is available on this group. Few African Americans were included in the drug and alcohol surveys of the 1960s and 1970s.

At the time of the Civil War, the temperance movement was closely associated with the antislavery movement. This may have had a major influence on Blacks, who, at that time, demonstrated very low rates of alcohol-related problems (Herd, 1985). After the Civil War, however, many changes occurred. With their new-found freedom, Blacks began to migrate more and to build small communities. Fewer Blacks associated with the temperance movement as it became more racist. This may have had the effect of increasing their drinking behavior. As free men and women, Blacks also had greater opportunity to purchase and use alcohol. Although clearly these were not the only contributing factors, drinking among Blacks did begin to increase. More recent studies indicate that African Americans do experience problems with alcohol and other drug abuse (King, 1982).

Epidemiology.   National surveys indicate that African American adolescents use drugs and alcohol to a lesser degree than their White counterparts and have fewer alcohol-related consequences (Albrecht, Amey, & Miller, 1996; Brown & Tooley, 1989; Group for Advancement of Psychiatry, 1996; Johnston, O'Malley, & Bachman, 1996). For example, the National Household Survey on Drugs (National Institute on Drug Abuse, 1988) found African American youth aged 12 to 17 reported use of alcohol at least once in 38.8 percent of the sample compared to 60.7 percent of Whites and 44.1 percent of Latinos. Similar responses were found in use during the past year and the past month. For African American females in high school, they reflected a strong abstinence tradition. For example, Globetti, Alsikafi, and Morse (1980) found that 65 percent of the girls indicated that they were nondrinkers. Among the drinkers, only 24 percent drank frequently, 35 percent drank seldom, and 32 percent occasionally.

The research on the drinking patterns of African American adult males, however, is less clear. One report shows that for those over 30 years of age, the heavy drinking rate within this group is approximately 32 percent, compared to 20 percent for White males (Freeman, 1992). Another report indicates that heavy drinking peaked in the 50- to 59-year age group and then steadily declined (Group for Advancement of Psychiatry, 1996). For African American males over 30, however, the picture begins to change. The heavy drinking rate within this group is approximately 32 percent, compared to 20 percent for White males (Freeman, 1992). Likewise, there were substantial differences between Black men and White men with regard to binge drinking (4 percent versus 1.6 percent), symptoms of physical dependence (29.5 percent versus 9.9 percent), and symptoms of loss of control (17.2 percent versus 11.2 percent) (Herd, 1985). African American women report fewer alcohol-related problems than their White counterparts, and they report higher abstinence rates (46 percent versus 34 percent of White women).

There are few alcohol and other drug abuse studies on African American youth. One study (Globetti et al., 1980) on African American high school females reflected a strong abstinence tradition, with 65 percent of the girls indicating that they were nondrinkers. Among the drinkers, only 24 percent drank frequently, 35 percent drank seldom, and 32 percent occasionally. The National Household Survey on Drug Abuse also found differences in drinking behavior between African American and White youth (National Institute on Drug Abuse, 1988). African American youth age 12 to 17 reported use of alcohol at least once in 38.8 percent of the sample compared to 60.7 percent of Whites and 44.1 percent of Latinos. Similar responses were found in use during the past year and the past month. African American females reported lower use rates (17.9 percent) than did African American males (23.8 percent). These data may reflect underreporting due to higher dropout rates and unrepresentative samples. It is possible to conclude tentatively, however, that alcohol use among African American youth is less than that of White youth, but that, after the age of 30, drinking-related problems increase for males. Overall, these data should be viewed with reservations. Brown (1993) argued that the epidemiological studies may be hampered by underrepresentation of African Americans by not including dropouts. The actual drug and alcohol use may be significantly higher than what is found.

Correlates.   Too often, African Americans, even more so than other ethnic populations, are treated as a monolithic group, with important regional and demographic differences overlooked or ignored. Of particular note are the differences in socioeconomic status that exist among African Americans (see Chapters 1 and 2). Socioeconomic status has been a focus of several studies (Clifford & Jones, 1988; Watts & Wright, 1983). Alcohol use has been related to factors such as unemployment and poverty across all ethnicities (Beauvais & LaBoueff, 1985; Harvey, 1985; Yee & Thu, 1987). Such studies make a strong case that the stress of coping with poverty, unemployment, discrimination, and inadequate housing could contribute to substance abuse. Certainly, living in these communities and knowing that there is such limited opportunity for economic and social advancement could have significant impact on the decision to use. It is imperative that additional correlate studies be undertaken in an effort to explain and prevent substance abuse among African Americans.

Native Americans and Alaska Natives

Historical Factors.   According to figures released by the U.S. Census Bureau, there are approximately 2 million Native Americans and Alaska Natives in the United States. Census data also indicate a very youthful population—a median age of 26.3 years compared to 34.0 years for Whites (U.S. Bureau of Census, 1992). There are approximately 300 federal reservations and 500 federally recognized tribes in the United States, including some 200 Alaska Native village groups (Klein, 1993). Although most reservations and tribes are concentrated in a few states, Native Americans can be found in every state (see Chapter 1).

Frequently there is the tendency to view Native Americans and Alaska Natives as a homogeneous group—as "Indians" whose customs, beliefs, and traditions are very similar. Native Americans and Alaska Natives, however, are a highly diverse group of people, not only with individual and family differences, but with tribal differences that vary greatly from location to location and often even within the same general areas. Differences exist in appearance, clothing, customs and ceremonies, practices, family roles, child-rearing practices, beliefs, and attitudes. Each tribe, band, or village maintains an unique perception of the world both inside and outside its particular area. Even within the same geographic locality, differences exist. Some Native Americans or Alaska Natives are very traditional in their beliefs, maintaining tribal languages, ceremonies, and customs. Others may be more contemporary, retaining some Native American traditions while maintaining a successful orientation to non-Native American society as well.

One striking similarity shared by all Native Americans and Alaska Natives is federal or governmental control over tribal/Native issues as well as control over many individual decisions. There have been major federal attempts at assimilation, removal of Native Americans and Alaska Natives from homelands, sterilization, and relocation programs. Pamela Kalar (1991) states: "Cultural insensitivity, voracious greed, paternalism and the bitter fruits of inept lawmaking have compounded the inequities suffered by Native peoples on and off the reservation (p. 10). Often it is forgotten or overlooked that these "First Americans" were not given voting citizenship until 1924 in most states and until 1946 in Arizona and New Mexico.

Another encounter with the White majority culture shared by most Native groups is the boarding school experience. From the late 1800s to the 1960s, church-affiliated boarding schools literally terrorized many Native children. They were punished, often severely, for speaking their own language; were humiliated in front of their peers; and received extreme haircuts in an effort to assimilate them to the White Christian culture. Such experiences, as well as those mentioned previously, have had a profound impact on the ethnic identity of Native groups and their view of majority culture.

Recent legislative actions have returned some power to Native American and Alaska Native nations through measures such as the Self-Determination Act, the Indian Education Act, and the Indian Child Welfare Act. It is believed that such events have finally begun to empower Indian people to the extent that many Native American and Alaska Natives have involved themselves politically in major decision-making issues. It is significant to note, however, that although there have been some political successes, sadly, few economic successes have occurred. Many Native families still experience poor nutrition, live in substandard housing, and lack the resources necessary to give their children choices for positive opportunities. Their experiences with assimilation, their lack if access to many of society's benefits, and the prejudice they experience place Natives at high risk for substance abuse.

Epidemiology.   Given the tribal and village differences that exist, it is not surprising that alcohol and drug use among Natives varies tremendously from one group to the next (May,

1982). May (1986) cites some tribes as having fewer drinking adults (30 percent) than the United States population (67 percent), whereas other tribal groups have more (69–80 percent). Some believe the rates may be underestimated as a result of deaths occurring for reasons such as alcohol-related injury, suicide, or homicide in which the use of alcohol goes unreported.

A large proportion of the Native American and Alaska Native population, as previously mentioned, is young. It has been established that Native American youth use almost every type of drug with greater frequency than non-Native American youth and that the age of first involvement with alcohol is younger for Native American children. The rates of drug use and involvement can be two to three times higher for Native American youth than for Anglo youth (Beauvais, 1992). Inhalants are also problematic for Native American and Alaska Native youth. They are often the first drugs used, and prevalence rates for reservation Native Americans are almost three times those of their White counterparts, although later data are showing slight decreases in inhalant use (Beauvais & Jumper-Thurman 1998).

Oetting and Beauvais (1983) have developed a classification system of drug use that ranks youth in three categories, from essentially no use to continued heavy use. Group one consists of low-risk nonusers, young people who have tried a drug but are not currently using any drug. The second group is made up of moderate-risk users, youth who get drunk once a month or more and who may use some marijuana. The third group includes high-risk users, youth who use marijuana more than once or twice a week or who use other drugs at least once a month. High-risk users are those who are currently using drugs and/or alcohol in such a way they may incur some physical or emotional harm from that use. Using this system, since 1977 the high-risk users' group has not changed substantially. Between 17 and 20 percent of reservation youth continue to use drugs at a rate sufficient to place them at high risk (Beauvais, 1992).

Correlates. Recent research in the area of risk factors for substance-abusing Native American youth has cited use by peers, weak family bonding, poor school adjustment, weak family sanctions against drugs, positive attitudes toward alcohol use, and risk of school dropout (Swaim, Oetting, Thurman, Beauvais, & Edwards, 1993; Swaim, Thurman, Beauvais, Oetting, & Wayman, 1993). Other studies have reported that substance abuse behavior among Native Americans may be influenced by cultural values and norms (May, 1986). Yet another risk factor that accounts for high use rates among Native American youth is low educational achievement and employment opportunity. School dropouts report rates of substance use far in excess of those of students who remain in school (Chavez, Edwards, & Oetting, 1989).

When Native American youth begin to reach adulthood, they find few chances of securing decent jobs, limited educational opportunities, and scant resources for improving their situation. Even though the abuse of substances may be well established by dropouts by the time they leave school, the lack of opportunity they will face in obtaining adequate employment may contribute to the maintenance or exacerbation of their use of alcohol and/or drugs (Oetting, 1992; Oetting & Beauvais, 1990). Unfortunately, limited economic opportunity and other negative community factors such as prejudice and violence are prevalent in disadvantaged minority neighborhoods (Oetting, 1992).

Latinos

History.   Morales (1984) traces some of the historical factors that form the background for use and abuse of substances among Hispanics. The abuse of alcohol can be traced back to the Aztecs of the fifteenth century, ancestors of present-day Mexican Americans. To control excessive drinking, they established elaborate mechanisms of social control that prescribed those conditions when drinking was sanctioned, primarily ceremonial and religious occasions. No more than five gourds of alcohol were to be consumed on these occasions, and there were severe penalties for breaking these societal rules (Paredes, 1975).

Prejudice and stereotypes regarding Hispanic substance use have historically resulted in arrests and imprisonment of this group at rates that exceed their relative population within the country. For example, in 1914 it was reported that "the excessive use of liquor is the Mexican's greatest moral problem. With few exceptions both men and women use liquor to excess" (McEuen, 1914, p. 13). Examination of Los Angeles police records in 1913 revealed the effect of such prejudicial thinking. A total of 24.3 percent of all arrests for drunkenness were of Mexicans, compared to their share of the population in Los Angeles of only 5 percent. Overrepresentation of Mexicans within the California state prison system from 1918 to 1930 was primarily the result of arrests for violation of the "State Poison Act," mostly for marijuana use. In 1931 the California State Narcotics Committee stated that marijuana use was widespread among Mexicans. During this period, however, there were only sixty-three arrests of Mexicans for narcotics violations.

Epidemiology

Recent census statistics indicate a rapid projected growth rate for Latinos. The population will increase at a rate 3 to 5 times faster than the general population (U.S. Bureau of the Census, 1992 and see Chapter 1). This means that Latinos will be the largest minority group in United States (Garcia & Marotta, 1997). Much of this growth rate can be attributed to a larger proportion of young people of childbearing age and to the flow of immigrants across the U.S. border (Amaro & Russo, 1987). The rapidly expanding population underscores the need to address the problem of alcohol and substance use within this ethnic group. Several recent empirical studies and reviews of the literature have reported that drug and alcohol use and abuse are substantial problems within the Latino population (Austin & Gilbert, 1989; Bachman et al., 1991; De La Rosa et al., 1990; National Institute on Drug Abuse, 1987).

Most studies of alcohol use indicate that rates of use are either similar to or slightly below those of White non-Hispanics, but higher than rates for Blacks or Asians (Gilbert, 1989). Bachman et al. (1991) found a similar pattern for illicit drug use among Hispanic high school seniors, with the exception of high rates of cocaine use among Hispanic males. Data from the 1995 NHSDA survey indicate that among adults (age 18 and older), 5.1 percent Latinos reported recent illicit drug use, compared to 6.0 percent of Whites, and 7.9 percent of Blacks (SAMHSA, 1997). Chavez and Swaim (1992a) conducted a national probability study of eighth- and twelfth-grade Mexican American students and found that rates of use for a number of substances was higher for Mexican Americans at the eighth-grade level. This pattern was reversed, however, among twelfth-grade students, with White non-Hispanic seniors reporting higher rates than their Mexican American counterparts. The reversal in rates of use between the two racial groups is likely due to the higher rate of drug use among school dropouts and the higher rate of school dropout among Mexican Americans (Swaim, Oetting, Chavez, & Beauvais, 1993). An alarming result from The 1996 Monitoring the Future study (MTF) found that eighth graders have the highest rates of use for nearly all drugs, including a number of dangerous ones: marijuana, hallucinogens, cocaine, crack, and heroin (Johnston et al., 1996).

One key factor that needs to be taken into account when considering Latino substance use is the gender disparity in rates of use. Differences in rates of use between males and females is often larger than differences observed in other ethnic groups. Among Mexican Americans, substantial differences in alcohol use have been noted, a disparity that tends to increase with age. There is some evidence, however, that these gender differences, especially for alcohol, may be decreasing as a result of higher levels of use among young Hispanic females (Austin & Gilbert, 1989; Chavez & Swaim, 1992b; Gilbert, 1987). The greater gender disparity in rates of use among Hispanics suggests the need for gender-focused interventions (Gilbert & Alcocer, 1988).

Another factor to consider in understanding drug use patterns is the level of acculturation. Epidemiologic research on Mexican and U.S. Hispanics indicates a positive relationship between U.S. cultural exposure and substance use (Farabee, Wallisch, & Maxwell, 1995; Gilbert, 1991; Swanson, Linskey, Quintero-Salinas, Pumariega, & Holzer, 1992). Farabee and colleagues (1995) compared substance use rates of Texas Hispanics who represented three different levels of acculturation and non-Hispanics. They found that Mexican-born Hispanics (i.e., low level of acculturation) had the lowest prevalence rates and the U.S.-born Hispanics (i.e., highly acculturated) had prevalence rates similar to non-Hispanics.

Correlates. Risk and protective factors for alcohol and drug use for Latinos are similar to those found among other adolescents (Gilbert, 1989). However, the relative strength of different factors and their interactive effects may vary when Latino and White non-Hispanic adolescents are compared (Felix-Ortiz & Newcomb, 1992). Important family variables predictive of substance use among Latinos include quality of the family relationship and parental drinking. Frauenglass, Routh, Pantin, and Mason (1997) found family social support reduced the influence of deviant peers on some problem behavior such as tobacco and marijuana use. Use of alcohol by peers is a strong predictor of Latino adolescent alcohol use. Coombs, Paulson, and Richardson (1991) found that peer variables were the most influential in predicting drug and alcohol abuse for both Hispanic and Anglo children and adolescents. However, such findings may be spurious because of differences in the predictor variables used in the Hispanic and Anglo groups.

Asian Americans

Historical Factors. Asian Americans and Pacific Islanders currently make up 3.6 percent of the United States population and number approximately 10 million (U.S. Bureau of Census, 1996). They, too, are a diverse and fast-growing group of people, primarily because of their high immigration rates. In fact, since the 1980 census, the number of

Asian Americans and Pacific Islanders has more than doubled (see Chapter 1 for a more detailed description of the ethnic subgroups).

The Asian culture places a strong emphasis on values such as a sense of duty and obligation to family and work, respect and reverence for elders. Children are taught at a very young age to focus on education, personal discipline, importance of family name, and family unity. These concepts are reinforced throughout one's life (Hsu, 1971; Sung, 1967). Elders, especially the father and the eldest son in the family, control resources in the Asian homeland and therefore are better able to control the behavior of younger family members (Johnson & Nagoshi, 1990). However, the influence of Western cultural values of individuality, independence, and assertiveness may weaken the power of these elders, and may be a significant influence in alcohol use among some Asian American groups.

Despite the recent increase in the number of Asians in the United States, minimal literature exists discussing the drinking and substance use behavior of Asian Americans in the United States. It is generally assumed that alcoholism, or at least heavy drinking, is not a problem for Asians. Some researchers hypothesize that a strong foundation of Confucianist and Taoist beliefs, which emphasize moderation, may account for the low drinking rates. In the late 1970s, research focused on the physiological effects (i.e., flushing response) of alcohol on Asians and Asian Americans. The flushing response that occurs following alcohol consumption causes uncomfortable vasodilation and reddening of the skin, beginning on the face and spreading to the trunk and limbs. The physical symptoms include tachycardia, headache, nausea, dizziness, and drowsiness. These effects are assumed to influence persons of Asian ancestry to drink less (Group for the Advancement of Psychiatry, 1996). The research findings indicate that biological/physiological influences are not absolute (Nakawatase, Yamamoto, & Sasao, 1993). Drinking patterns are influenced not only by physiological effects but also by a combination of sociocultural factors.

Epidemiology.   As with other ethnic groups, discussions of substance use among Asian Americans is difficult because of the diversity involved. Like American Indians and Alaska Natives and Hispanics, Asian Americans cannot be aggregated into a single population. In fact, more than 20 Asian American groups have been identified by the U.S. Bureau of the Census (Zane & Sasao, 1992). Variations occur in the drinking patterns of Chinese, Japanese, Koreans, and Filipinos (Kitano & Chi, 1985). These authors report that there exists a relatively high proportion of heavy drinkers among Japanese and Filipino men. Those men most likely to drink are under the age of 45, with higher social status. Chi, Lubben, and Kitano (1989) compared drinking patterns among Chinese Americans, Korean Americans, and Japanese Americans. They found heavy drinking in each of the Asian groups, but the greatest proportion of drinking was among Japanese Americans and the lowest was among the Chinese Americans. The pattern was similar for women.

In a telephone survey of a Japanese community, results indicated that there were reported frequencies of 73 percent for lifetime alcohol use and 61 percent for thirty-day prevalence use (Sasao, 1989). These figures reflect greater usage than levels found for the United States general public. Important differences were found between American-born and Japan-born Japanese. For example, Japan-born Japanese exhibited higher rates of refusal to participate and demonstrated less knowledge and social concern about substance abuse. They were also less likely to view alcohol use as a substance abuse problem.

Research on Southeast Asians (e.g., Laotians, Cambodians, and Vietnamese) resettled in the United States reveals significant problems with alcohol and other drug abuse (Berry et al., 1992; D'Avanzo & Frye, 1992; Jenkin, McPhee, Bird, & Bonilla, 1990). Many Southeast Asian refugees experienced years of political turmoil and war in their homeland. Therefore, the acculturation level will vary depending on their political background, educational level, and age. Many report higher levels of depression and posttraumatic stress disorder. Morgan, Wingard, and Felice (1984) found that 60 percent of the Southeast Asian youth who drank did so to forget their past. This response differs from other groups that drink for social reasons. Besides the potential use of alcohol as a coping mechanism, drinking is accepted in most cultures. For Cambodian and Vietnamese men, peer pressure to drink is strong and not to join in is considered rude (Amodeo, Robb, Peou, & Tran, 1997).

Use of the general term *Asian American* to describe this heterogeneous group is misleading. It is necessary to examine carefully the Asian American differences in substance use patterns and to be cautious with generalizations. The amount of research on Asians and Asian Americans is small compared to other ethnic groups. Current research is limited by the lack of national sampling strategies, heterogeneity among Asian American groups, and lack of cross-culturally valid instruments. More epidemiological studies are needed to address these issues, given the diversity and the rapid growth of this population.

Correlates. Johnson and Nagoshi (1990) give a very thorough account of the sociocultural influences affecting Asian Americans and alcohol consumption. They argue that the social-psychological variables that vary across Asian American groups have not been fully assessed and probably have important sociocultural/environmental bases. This is likely very true, as there are documented substantial differences in alcohol consumption across these groups that may not be adequately explained through some of the discrepant findings in existing physiological models (Sue, 1987). A number of factors are associated with the drinking patterns among Asians: male gender, a tolerant and permissive attitude toward alcohol, having male friends who drink, nonflushing, and lack of embarrassment about flushing (Group for the Advancement of Psychiatry, 1996).

Treatment Utilization

Most research indicates that minorities are less likely to seek treatment and also less likely to complete a treatment regimen (Sue, 1987), yet some ethnic groups are often overrepresented in federally funded treatment facilities (Atkinson, Morton, & Sue, 1998). Asians in particular as well as African Americans are reported as very unlikely to enter treatment (Sue, 1987). Much of this reluctance may be attributed to a mistrust of the mental health system (Sue, 1981). Such distrust is also found in the use of substance abuse programs; in fact, rather than using traditional forms of treatment, some Blacks have turned to spirituality in an effort to abstain from alcohol. African Americans have reported that they stopped drinking prior to entering the treatment program and reported the reason for this abstinence as their return to spirituality (Brisbane, 1987). In a 1995 SAMHSA (Rouse, 1995) report, African Americans comprised about 12 percent of the U.S. population but 21 percent of the substance abuse clients. Gibbs (1984) found that African Americans made up 27 percent of the clients admitted to federally funded drug abuse treatment centers in 1980. Of these, 12 percent were under the age of 18 (Gibbs, 1984). It was not clear, however, whether these admissions were for alcohol, cocaine, or heroin treatment. Less information is available regarding treatment utilization for American Indians, although an early study reported a significant relationship between societal involvement and treatment outcomes for Navajo Indians. Those with a stake in primarily traditional Indian society had a 72 percent treatment success rate. Those with no stake in either traditional Indian society or White society evidenced only a 23 percent success rate. Those with the highest treatment success rate (74 percent) had a stake in both traditional and White society (Ferguson, 1976).

Hispanics also tend to use health and mental health services at lower rates than other ethnic groups (Angel, 1985). However, they are overrepresented in their use of alcohol services (Butynski, Record, & Yates, 1985), and the majority of these clients are male adults (Santiestevan & Santiestevan, 1984). Data primarily on Mexican Americn alcohol treatment clients indicate that they are also more likely to be married, to be less well educated, to be employed, and to have higher incomes than other clients (Engmann, 1976). But they are similar in age to other clients (Butynski et al., 1985), with most falling between ages 25 and 44. There is also some evidence that Mexican Americans are more likely than White non-Hispanics to self-refer or be referred by a close relative, factors that are predictive of good treatment outcomes (Schuckit, Schwei, & Gold, 1986).

Hispanics are less likely to use detoxification services (Butynski et al., 1985). Gilbert and Cervantes (1986) suggest that this may be due to lower levels of severe dependency, lower rates of withdrawal, or more attempts at withdrawal without medical supervision. Mexican Americans are also less likely to use residential services. Gilbert and Cervantes (1986) propose that this is likely due to the different profile of the residential client, who usually has a longer history of high-level abuse and is more likely to have had multiple admissions, to be separated or divorced, to be living alone, and to be unemployed. Mexican American clients are more likely to remain within stable family systems. Another contributing factor, however, may be the limited number of culturally focused residential programs for Hispanics.

Based on the 1995 SAMHSA (Rouse, 1995) report, Hispanics accounted for 9.0 percent of the total United States population and for 14.4 percent of drug treatment admissions based on client treatment surveys. Although Hispanics are overrepresented in these settings, Moore and Mata (1981) report that Hispanics are likely to perceive drug treatment programs as inaccessible because the settings are perceived as being oriented toward White and Black clients. Data from the 1985 National Drug and Alcoholism Treatment Utilization Survey (National Institute on Drug Abuse, 1988) indicate that only 10.5 percent of all drug treatment units provided specialized programs for Hispanics.

As mentioned above, Asian Americans are unlikely to enter substance abuse treatment centers. Rouse (1995) says that they represent 2.8 percent of the U.S. population but only 0.7 percent are in substance abuse programs. This low rate of admission in programs may be indicative of their help-seeking behavior. In the Asian culture, a strong emphasis is placed on the avoidance of shame and protection of family name and integrity values (Min, 1997). Treatment programs may represent shaming the family. There is a general perception that family problems should be kept and handled within the family and that help outside of the family (e.g., service providers) is not needed.

Treatment Strategies

Although treatment is believed to be effective in the reduction of substance abuse, disagreement is the usual state of affairs when the recommended intervention strategy for a specific case is discussed. There is considerable agreement, however, that a multidisciplinary approach is most effective and that family, variables are a major key to the treatment of all populations, including African American, Latino, American Indian/Alaska Native, and Asian American substance abusers. Such an approach begins to address the multiple pathways leading to substance abuse.

The other critical variable that is most often mentioned is the alteration of substance-focused peer relationships. Unfortunately, very few empirical studies have tested alcohol or drug treatment, incorporating peers into the intervention. In research studies of adolescent substance use, however, use of illicit drugs or alcohol by peers has been the most consistently reported risk factor. A study by Dinges and Oetting (1993) illustrated this point. Among those adolescents who reported no use of drugs, very few of their friends reported use. Among those who reported use of specific drugs, however, over 90 percent of their friends used those same drugs. The results of this study highlight the importance of designing treatment interventions that take into account the strong effects peers can have on the treatment outcome.

Rogler, Malgady, Costantino, and Blumenthal (1987) identified three means of providing culturally sensitive mental health services to Hispanics, which also have application to substance abuse populations. These included increasing the accessibility of services through such means as use of bilingual/bicultural staff participation and development of treatment environments in which ethnic/cultural values and norms were honored. Another component of culturally sensitive treatment included matching ethnic clients with treatment modalities that are consonant with their perceived values, such as providing more behaviorally oriented or crisis intervention services rather than traditional insight-oriented therapy, particularly for less acculturated clients (Ruiz, 1981). A final approach directly incorporates cultural values into the therapeutic modality (e.g., utilizing cultural concepts such as *machismo, respeto,* or *familism,* which are either restructured or used to therapeutic advantage).

Delgado (1988) stresses the importance of both a culture-specific intake and culture-specific intervention in the treatment of alcohol abuse. The intake should consist of five guiding principles: (1) development of an understanding of the role of alcohol and drugs within the family, (2) assessment of the degree of ethnic identity or acculturation, (3) language preference, (4) assessment of the adolescent's social network, and (5) previous treatment experience. Assessment of all of these dimensions should guide the intervention strategies and techniques used with the client (see Chapters 2 and 4).

Retention is one key problem in adolescent treatment services. Many who initially present for treatment drop out after only one or a few sessions. Retention is likely to be improved during the intake process if the client's experience is one in which their cultural experience is valued and understood. Szapocznik et al. (1988) reported on a strategic, structural family systems approach in which the technique of joining was utilized and those interactions that were likely to prevent retention were restructured. The effects of these interventions were dramatic, resulting in a 77 percent completion rate compared to a 25 percent completion rate for a control condition.

Among various intervention strategies, family therapy is one form of treatment that has been emphasized in a number of studies of ethnic minority substance use. Panitz, McConchie, Sauber, and Fonseca (1983) emphasize the crucial element of family variables in both the etiology and the treatment of Latino alcoholism. Included in their recommendation is the important component of distinguishing between pathological and ideal *machismo.* This concept is defined as maleness or virility. The positive aspects of *machismo* are encouraged, in contrast to pathological *machismo* in which peer groups of males exert pressure on others to consume increasing amounts of alcohol to demonstrate one's masculinity.

Moncher, Holden, Schinke, and Palleja (1990) also suggest that the concept of *familism,* the complex interaction among Hispanic family members wherein identity and esteem are established, may be more applicable to Hispanic than to non-Hispanic families. They describe a complex and difficult case in which a Puerto Rican adolescent male was treated for substance abuse using multiple methods of structural family therapy, functional family therapy, cognitive-behavioral therapy, and case management. They indicate that use of *compadrazgo,* the extended kinship ties between godparents or *padrinos* and godchildren or *ahijados* can be utilized in which both family and extended family members can learn to provide reinforcement for positive behaviors such as the avoidance of substance abuse.

Gilbert and Cervantes (1986) also emphasize the importance of the extended family in treating Hispanic alcoholism and note that disintegration of the family begins with distal relationships and then works toward the nuclear family. One of the primary goals of family therapy, then, may be to reestablish extended family ties that have been broken during the course of the alcoholism. Inclusion of supportive treatment or referral to Al-Anon for spouses may be indicated because of the high proportion of Hispanic clients who remain in intact families.

Szapocznik et al. (1989) have developed a comprehensive prevention and intervention approach to Hispanic adolescent substance use and other problem behaviors, utilizing a strategic structural family systems approach. They identify three familial risk factors that are likely to lead to later problem behavior in adolescents: (1) current family maladaptive interactions (i.e., enmeshed or overinvolved maternal relationships combined with distant, excluded paternal relationships, as well as poor conflict resolution skills); (2) intergenerational conflict (i.e., the conflict that occurs developmentally as children move into adolescence); and (3) intercultural conflict (i.e., a problem that may be unique to migrating families in which youth acculturate more rapidly than adults, setting the stage for conflict to emerge over cultural values and behaviors). Family Effectiveness Training is aimed at correcting maladaptive family interactions and strengthening the family by increasing its flexibility in dealing with both developmental and cultural conflicts. Its psychoeducational format, which includes both didactic and experiential components, has been demonstrated to be superior to control conditions in improving family functioning and reducing problem behaviors in adolescents on the basis of both parental and self-report (Szapocznik et al., 1989).

Moore (1992) also supports the use of family therapy with African Americans. She noted that one cause for resistance in therapy may be familial. In the families' attempts to protect their children from treatment programs under the jurisdiction of Whites, Black parents sometimes participate in the maintenance of the problem. Family therapy is also congruent with the Native American community, in that many people have clan systems that are still active today. Extended family systems are important to this population, and inclusion of family in the therapeutic process is paramount to treatment success.

The family system is also of primary importance to the psychosocial functioning of Pacific Islanders (Sue & Morishima, 1982). This group of families and their extended kinship have been recognized as an important protective factor against many health and mental health problems (Hsu, 1973). For some Asian groups, however, family therapy may not be the best therapeutic strategy due their cultural background of not discussing shameful personal experiences with strangers, especially if the situation would cast family members in an unfavorable light (Sue & Sue, 1990). They may feel that they have dishonored their family name by losing face. Until the counselor gains the trust of the client, he or she may refuse to consider bringing family members into treatment. This situation highlights the importance of incorporating client's culture within any treatment strategies.

One culturally based method, originally used in treatment of behavioral problems of Puerto Rican children and adolescents, can be adapted to use in treatment of substance abuse. This method involves the use of *cuentos* (Puerto Rican folktales) in which adult hero and heroine role characters served as therapeutic models (Malgady, Rogler, & Costantino, 1990). According to these authors this has been effective in reducing anxiety and increasing social judgment in participants. Freeman (1992) also utilizes storytelling with young African American males. She uses family and cultural storytelling techniques to gain insight into engaging children and youth for prevention and treatment of substance abuse problems.

Spirituality is also a recognized tool in the treatment of ethnic minorities. In fact, a strong multidisciplinary team might include a spiritual leader reflective of the community culture. Elders and youth might also be included recognizing the special roles that both play in the community. Likewise, medicine wheels, sweat lodges, talking circles, sundance preparation, and other traditional activities are used in some treatment centers to facilitate the healing process. Spiritual leaders, shamans, and medicine men or women are consulted by family members as well as by treatment professionals for inclusion in the therapeutic curriculum (see Chapter 9).

Knox (1985) argues that spirituality is a tool that can be used effectively in the treatment of the Black alcoholic and the family and should be explored in the assessment process. The sources of hope and strength should be examined, as well as the meaning of spirituality and the diversity of beliefs and practices of the family. Trotter and Chavira (1978) describe the role of *curanderos*, traditional folk healers, who have historically been consulted for the treatment of substance abuse problems, particularly alcohol abuse, among Latino families. *Curanderos* identify specific etiologies, and cures for alcohol abuse and make distinctions between problem drinking and alcohol addiction. Cures may consist of counseling, herbal cures, or administration of *Haba de San Ignacio*, a preparation similar to disulfiram, both of which produce nausea and vomiting when mixed with alcohol. Less acculturated Latinos, particularly older females, may be likely to consult traditional folk healers but often use traditional methods to supplement, rather than replace, medical approaches.

Guidelines for Working in Ethnic Communities

Development of culturally sensitive and appropriate treatment interventions requires a careful and thorough scrutiny of the specific population. A solid first step would be the recruitment of staff who are members of the targeted population or are familiar with the culture. At a minimum, recruited staff must be culturally sensitive—able to consider age, gender, socioeconomic status, access to opportunities, degree of acculturation, availability of social supports, cultural values and norms, spirituality, and family system. It is often beneficial to look within oneself and examine one's own values before confronting someone whose cultural values, traditions, and customs may be quite different.

Because of the diversity between and within ethnic populations, it is also necessary to develop an understanding of the target group that resides in the service delivery area (Orlandi et al., 1992). Although it is difficult to generalize across groups, it is often helpful to review the literature. More important, local statistics related to substance abuse behaviors should be examined. Often this type of examination requires both an emotional and an intellectual commitment on the part of the service provider. It is important not to be caught in stereotypes, positive or negative. For example, all Native Americans are not noble warriors, nor are they all "drunken Indians."

There are some client-specific approaches to increase cultural responsiveness that a substance abuse counselor can adopt (see Finn, 1994, for a more detailed discussion). For example, the counselor may have to accommodate the family value of a client who seeks the opinions of a certain family member when he or she has to make a major decision. Another way a counselor can be more culturally responsive in therapy is to match the client's style of communication. For example, a confrontational style of counseling may be incongruent with cultures that communicate in a nonconfrontational way. Also, some cultures encourage different forms of physical expressions such as lack of eye contact, which is a sign of respect. A clinician needs to be careful not to misinterpret or wrongly judge behavior that differs from what one might expect in one's own culture.

The need for multicultural consideration can extend to inclusion of diverse community members on advisory boards and task forces (see Chapter 8). These experts can help plan inservice training, service delivery, and policy format. They also have the opportunity to serve as role models for other community members while building a mutual understanding of the cultural issues between the participants. Such efforts also empower local ethnic communities to deal with the risk factors that can contribute to alcoholism and drug abuse.

Finally, we know that most communities are unique in nature. The various types of local resources vary from community to community as do strengths, challenges, and political climates. It is not really surprising that interventions implemented with one community may not be even minimally effective in another. In order to effect long-lasting community change, it is essential that a community pull together in the development of interventions appropriate to its unique situation and culture. The Community Readiness Model is an emerging and innovative method for assessing the level of readiness of a community to develop and implement interventions that are community specific and culturally appropriate (Plested, Jumper-Thurman, Edwards, & Oetting, 1998; Oetting et al., 1995). The model has nine stages of readiness that are based in community theory and that identify specific characteristics related to different levels of problem awareness and readiness for change. In order to stand a chance of success, interventions introduced in a community must be consistent with the awareness of the problem and the level of readiness for change present among residents of that community. The stages direct the community to interventions that are appropriate at each stage, resulting in more cost-effective and time-focused use of resources and thus a greater potential for success.

Historically, the focus has been on assimilation—integrating the various ethnic populations into the "American" way of life. Current thinking, however, focuses on efforts to help the dominant society understand the values and needs of the minority community. It is no longer acceptable to look upon the traditions of the various ethnic communities as dysfunctional. Instead, one is asked to seek out the strengths and resiliency that these traditions contribute to the ethnic groups. Finally, despite the many challenges that nearly all cultures have experienced at one time or another, they have survived. Many have maintained their cultural traditions even though the losses have been devastating, and they continue to demonstrate the extraordinary capacity to heal and grow.

REFERENCES

Albrech, S. L., Amey, C., & Miller, M. K. (1996). Patterns of substance abuse among rural black adolescents. *Journal of Drug Issues, 26*(4), 751–781.

Amaro, H., & Russo, N. F. (1987). Hispanic women and mental health: An overview of contemporary issues in research and practice. *Psychology of Women Quarterly, 11,* 393–407.

Amodeo, M., Robb, N., Peou, S., & Tran, H. (1997). Alcohol and other drug problems among Southeast Asians: Patterns of use and approaches to assessment and intervention, *Alcoholism Treatment Quarterly, 15*(3), 63–77.

Angel, R. (1985). The health of the Mexican-American population. In R. O. de la Garza, F. D. Bean, C. M. Bonjean, R. Romo, & R. Alvarez (Eds.), *The Mexican-American experience: An interdisciplinary anthology* (pp. 410–426). Austin: University of Texas Press.

Atkinson, D. R., Morton, G., & Sue, D. W. (Eds.) (1998). *Counseling American Minorities* (5th ed.). Boston: McGraw-Hill.

Austin, G., & Gilbert, M. J. (1989). Substance abuse among Latino youth. *Prevention Research Update, 3,* 1–26. Los Alamitos, CA: Southwest Regional Educational Laboratory.

Bachman, J. G., Wallace, J. M., O'Malley, P. M., Johnston, L. D., Kurth, C. C., & Neighbors, H. W. (1991). Racial/ethnic differences in smoking, drinking, and illicit drug use among American high school seniors, 1976–89. *American Journal of Public Health, 81,* 372–377.

Beauvais, F. (1992). Trends in Indian adolescent drug and alcohol use. *American Indian and Alaska Native Mental Health Research Journal, 5,* 1–12.

Beauvais, F., & Jumper-Thurman, P. (1998). [American Indian Epidemiology Data] Unpublished Raw Data.

Beauvais, F., & LaBoueff, W. (1985). Drug and alcohol abuse intervention in American Indian Communities. *International Journal of the Addictions, 20,* 139–171.

Berry, L., Nil, S., Locke, N. McCracken, S., Seth, K. & Koch, V. (1992). *Cambodian oral history research: Preliminary findings on alcohol and other drugs in Cambodia and in the United States.* Chicago: Refugee Substance Abuse Prevention Project, Travelers and Immigrants Aid.

Bratter, T. E., & Forrest, G. G. (Eds.). (1985). *Alcoholism and substance abuse: Strategies for clinical intervention.* New York: Free Press.

Brisbane, F. L. (1987). Divided feeling of Black alcoholic daughters. *Alcohol Health and Research World, 11,* 48–50.

Brown, F., & Tooley, J. (1989). Alcoholism in the Black Community. In G. W. Lawson & A. W. Lawson (Eds.), *Alcoholism and substance abuse in special populations* (pp. 115–128). Rockville, MD: Aspen.

Brown, L. S., Jr. (1993). Alcohol abuse prevention in African-American communities. *Journal of National Medical Association, 85,* 665–673.

Bry, B. H., McKeon, P., & Pandina, R. J. (1982). Extent of drug use as a function of number of risk factors. *Journal of Abnormal Psychology, 91,* 273–279.

Butynski, W., Record, N., & Yates, L. (1985). *State resources and services for alcohol and drug abuse problems.* Fiscal year 1984. DHHS 461 357 20444. Washington, DC: U.S. Government Printing Office.

Caetano, R. (1984). Ethnicity and drinking in Northern California: A comparison among Whites, Blacks, and Hispanics. *Alcohol and Alcoholism, 19,* 31–44.

Cahalan, D. (1970). *Problem drinkers: A national survey.* San Francisco: Jossey-Bass.

Chavez, E. L., Edwards, R. W., & Oetting, E. R. (1989). Mexican-American and White American dropouts' drug use, health status, and involvement in violence. *Public Health Reports, 104,* 594–604.

Chavez, E. L., & Swaim, R. C. (1992a). An epidemiological comparison of Mexican-American and White non-Hispanic eighth- and twelfth-grade students' substance use. *American Journal of Public Health, 82,* 445–447.

Chavez, E. L., & Swaim, R. C. (1992b). Hispanic substance use: Problems in epidemiology. In J. Trimble, C. Bolek, & S. Niemcryk (Eds.), *Ethnic and multicultural drug abuse: Perspectives on current research* (pp. 211–230). New York: Haworth

Chi, I., Lubben, J. E., & Kitano, H. H. (1989). Differences in drinking behavior among three Asian-American groups. *Journal of Studies on Alcohol, 50*(1), 15–23.

Clifford, P. R., & Jones, W., Jr. (1988). Alcohol abuse, prevention issues, and the Black community. *Evaluation and the Health Professions, 11,* 272–277.

Coombs, R. H., Paulson, M. J., & Richardson, M. A. (1991). Peer vs. parental influence in substance use among Hispanic and Anglo children and adolescents. *Journal of Youth and Adolescence, 20,* 73–88.

Cotton, N. S. (1979). The familial incidence of alcoholism: A review. *Journal of Studies on Alcohol, 46,* 98–116.

Craig, R. J. (1982). Personality characteristics of heroin addicts: Review of empirical research 1976–1979. *International Journal of the Addictions, 17,* 227–248.

D'Avanzo, C. E., & Frye, B. (1992). Stress and self-medication in Cambodian refugee women. *Addictions Nursing Network, 4*(2), 59–60.

De La Rosa, M. R., Khalsa, J. H., & Rouse, B. A. (1990). Hispanics and illicit drug use: A review of recent findings. *International Journal of the Addictions, 25,* 665–691.

Delgado, M. (1988). Alcoholism treatment and Hispanic youth. *Journal of Drug Issues, 18,* 59–68.

Dinges, N. M., & Oetting, E. R. (1993). Similarity in drug use patterns between adolescents and their friends. *Adolescence, 28,* 253–266.

Engmann, D. J. (1976). *Alcoholism and alcohol abuse among the Spanish-speaking population in California: A needs and services assessment.* Sacramento: California Commission on Alcoholism for the Spanish-speaking.

Farabee, D., Wallisch, L., & Maxwell, J. C. (1995). Substance use among Texas Hispanics and non-Hispanics: Who's using, who's not, and why. *Hispanic Journal of Behavioral Sciences, 17*(4), 523–536.

Felix-Ortiz, M., & Newcomb, M. D. (1992). Risk and protective factors for drug use among Latino and White adolescents. *Hispanic Journal of Behavioral Sciences, 14,* 291–309.

Ferguson, F. N. (1976). Stake theory as an explanatory device in Navajo alcoholism treatment response. *Human Organization, 35,* 65–78.

Finn, P. (1994). Addressing the needs of cultural minorities in drug treatment. *Journal of Substance Abuse Treatment, 11,* 425–337.

Frauenglass, S., Routh, D. K., Pantin, H. M., & Mason, C. A. (1997). Family support decreases influence of deviant peers on Hispanic adolescents' substance use. *Journal of Clinical Child Psychology, 26*(1), 15–23.

Freeman, E. (1992). The use of storytelling techniques with young African American males: Implications for substance abuse prevention. *Journal of Intergroup Relations, 19,* 53–72.

Garcia, J. G., & Marotta, S. (1997). Characterization of Latino population. In J. G. Garcia, & M. C. Zea (Eds.), *Psychological interventions and research with Latino populations* (pp. 1–14). Boston: Allyn and Bacon.

Gibbs, J. T. (1984). Black adolescents and youth: An endangered species. *American Journal of Orthopsychiatry, 54,* 6–20.

Gilbert, M. J. (1987). Alcohol consumption patterns in immigrant and later generation Mexican-American women. *Hispanic Journal of Behavioral Sciences, 9,* 299–314.

Gilbert, M. J. (1989). Alcohol use among Latino adolescents: What we know and what we need to know. *Drugs and Society, 3,* 39–57.

Gilbert, M. J. (1991). Acculturation and changes in drinking patterns among Mexican-American women: Implications for prevention. *Alcohol Health and Research World, 15,* 234–238.

Gilbert, M. J., & Alcocer, A. M. (1988). Alcohol use and Hispanic youth: An overview. *Journal of Drug Issues, 18,* 33–48.

Gilbert, M. J., & Cervantes, R. C. (1986). Alcohol services for Mexican-Americans: A review of utilization patterns, treatment considerations, and prevention activities. *Hispanic Journal of Behavioral Sciences, 8,* 191–223.

Globetti, G., Alsikafi, M., & Morse, R. (1980). Black female high school students and the use of beverage alcohol. *International Journal of Addictions, 15,* 189–200.

Glynn, T. J. (1981). From family to peer: A review of transitions of influence among drug-using youth. *Journal of Youth and Adolescence, 10,* 363–383.

Group for the Advancement of Psychiatry. (1996). *Alcoholism in the United States: Racial and ethnic consideration.* Report No. 141. Washington, DC: American Psychiatric Press.

Harvey, W. B. (1985). Alcohol abuse and the Black community: A contemporary analysis. *Journal of Drug Issues, 15,* 81–91.

Helzer, J. E. (1987). Epidemiology of alcoholism. *Journal of Consulting and Clinical Psychology, 55,* 284–292.

Herd, D. (1985). The epidemiology of drinking patterns and alcohol-related problems among U.S. Blacks. In *Alcohol use among U.S. Ethnic Minorities.* NIAAA Research Monograph No. 18. DHHS Publication No. (ADM)89-1435 pp. 3–50). Rockville, MD: National Institute on Alcohol Abuse and Alcoholism.

Hsu, F. L. K. (1971). *The challenge of the American dream: The Chinese in the United States.* Belmont, CA: Wadsworth.

Hsu, F. L. K. (1973). Kinship is the key. *Center Magazine, 6,* 4–14.

Jenkin, C. N. H., McPhee, S., Bird, J. A., & Bonilla, N. H. (1990). Cancer risk and prevention practices among Vietnamese refugees. *The Western Journal of Medicine, 153*(1), 34–39.

Johnson, R. C., & Nagoshi, C. T. (1990). Asians, Asian-Americans, and alcohol. *Journal of Psychoactive Drugs, 22,* 45–52.

Johnston, L. D., O'Malley, P. M., & Bachman, J. G. (1996). *National survey results on drug use from the Monitoring the Future Survey study,* 1975–1995 (Vol. 1: Secondary school students). Rockville, MD: National Institute on Drug Abuse.

Kalar, P. (1991). *Issues to consider: The American Indian and the media.* New York: National Conference of Christians and Jews.

King, L. M. (1982). Alcoholism: Studies regarding Black Americans, 1977–1980. In *Special Populations Issues. Alcohol and Health Monograph 4,* DHHS Pub. No. (ADM) 82-1193, 385–410. Rockville, MD: National Institute on Alcohol Abuse and Alcoholism.

Kitano, H. L., & Chi, I. (1985). Asian Americans and alcohol: The Chinese, Japanese, Koreans, and Filipinos in Los Angeles. In D. Spiegier, D. Tate, S. Aitken, & C. Christian (Eds.), *Alcohol use among U.S. ethnic minorities* (pp. 373–382). Rockville, MD: National Institute on Alcoholism and Alcohol Abuse.

Kitano, H. L., Lubben, J. E., & Chi, I. (1988). Predicting Japanese American drinking behavior. *The International Journal of the Addictions, 23,* 417–428.

Klein, B. T. (Ed.) (1993). *Reference encyclopedia of the American Indian* (6th ed., pp. 35–39). West Nyack, NY: Todd Publications.

Knox, D. H. (1985). Spirituality: A tool in the assessment and treatment of Black alcoholics and their families. *Alcoholism Treatment Quarterly, 2,* 31–44.

Lawson, G. W., & Lawson, A. W. (1989). *Alcoholism and substance abuse in special populations.* Rockville, MD: Aspen.

Lawson, G., Peterson, J., & Lawson, A. (1983). *Alcoholism and the family: A guide to treatment and prevention.* Rockville, MD: Aspen.

Maddahian, E., Newcomb, M. D., & Bentler, P. M. (1988). Risk factors for substance use: Ethnic differences among adolescents. *Journal of Substance Abuse, 1,* 11–23.

Malgady, R. G., Rogler, L. H., & Costantino, G. (1990). Culturally sensitive psychotherapy for Puerto Rican children and adolescents: A program of treatment outcome research. *Journal of Consulting and Clinical Psychology, 58,* 704–712.

May, P. A. (1982). Substance abuse and American Indians: Prevalence and susceptibility. *International Journal of the Addictions, 17,* 1185–1209.

May, P. A. (1986). Alcohol and drug misuse prevention programs for American Indians: Needs and opportunities. *Journal of Studies on Alcohol, 47,* 187–195.

McEuen, W. W. (1914). *Survey of the Mexican in Los Angeles.* Los Angeles: University of Southern California, Department of Economics and Sociology.

Min, P. G. (1997). An overview of Asian Americans. In Pyong Gap Min (Ed.), *Asian Americans: Contemporary trends and issues.* Thousand Oaks, CA: Sage.

Moncher, M. S., Holden, G. W., Schinke, S. P., & Palleja, J. (1990). Behavioral family treatment of the substance abusing Hispanic adolescent. In E. L. Feindler & G. R. Kalfus (Eds.), *Adolescent behavior therapy handbook* (pp. 329–349). New York: Springer.

Moore, S. E. (1992). Cultural sensitivity treatment and research issues with Black adolescent drug users. *Child and Adolescent Social Work Journal, 9,* 249–260.

Moore, J., & Mata, A. (1981). *Women and heroin in Chicano communities.* Unpublished manuscript.

Morales, A. (1984). Substance abuse and Mexican-American youth: An overview. *Journal of Drug Issues, 14,* 297–311.

Morgan, M. C., Wingard, D. L., & Felice, M. E. (1984). Subcultural differences in Alcohol use among youth. *Journal of Adolescent Health Care, 5,* 191–195.

Nakawatase, T., Yamamoto, J., & Sasao, T. (1993). The association between fast flushing response and alcohol use among Japanese Americans. *Journal of Studies in Alcohol,* 54:48–53.

National Institute on Drug Abuse. (1987). *Use of selected drugs among Hispanics: Mexican-Americans, Puerto Ricans, and Cuban-Americans, Findings from the Hispanic Health and Nutrition Examination Survey.* DHHS Pub. No. (ADM) 87-1527. Washington, DC: U.S. Government Printing Office.

National Institute on Drug Abuse. (1988). *National household survey on drug abuse: Main findings 1985.* DHHS Publication No. (ADM)88-1565. Washington, DC: U.S. Government Printing Office.

Newcomb, M. D., Maddahian, E., & Bentler, P. M. (1986). Risk factors for drug use among adolescents: Concurrent and longitudinal analyses. *American Journal of Public Health, 76,* 525–531.

Oetting, E. R. (1992). Planning programs for prevention of deviant behavior: A psychosocial model. In J. Trimble, C. Bolek, & S. Niemcryk (Eds.), *Ethnic and multicultural drug abuse: Perspectives on current research* (pp. 313–344). Binghamton, NY: Harrington Park.

Oetting, E. R., & Beauvais, F. (1983). A typology of adolescent drug use: A practical classification system for describing drug use patterns. *Academic Psychology Bulletin, 5,* 55–69.

Oetting, E. R., & Beauvais, F. (1987). Peer cluster theory, socialization characteristics and adolescent drug use: A path analysis. *Journal of Counseling Psychology, 34,* 205–213.

Oetting, E. R., & Beauvais, F. (1990). Orthogonal cultural identification theory: The cultural identification of minority adolescents. *International Journal of the Addictions, 25,* 655–685.

Oetting, E. R., Donnermeyer, J. F., Plested, B. A., Edwards, R. W., Kelly, K., & Beauvais, F. (1995). Assessing community readiness for prevention. *The International Journal of the Addictions, 30*(6), 659–683.

Orlandi, M. A., Weston, R., & Epstein, L. G. (1992). (Eds.), *Cultural competence for evaluators: A guide for alcohol and other drug abuse prevention practitioners working with ethnic/racial communities.* Rockville, MD: U.S. Department of Health and Human Services.

Panitz, D. R., McConchie, R. D., Sauber, S. R., & Fonseca, J. A. (1983). The role of *machismo* and the Hispanic family in the etiology and treatment of alcoholism in Hispanic American males. *American Journal of Family Therapy, 11,* 31–42.

Paredes, A. (1975). Social control of drinking among the Aztec Indians of Mesoamerica. *Journal of Studies on Alcohol, 36,* 1139–1153.

Plested, B. A., Jumper-Thurman, P., Edwards, R., & Oetting, E. R. (1998). Community readiness: A tool for community empowerment. *Prevention Researcher,* 5–7.

Rebach, H. (1992). Alcohol and drug use among American minorities. In J. Trimble, C. Bolek, & S. Niemcryk (Eds.), *Ethnic and multicultural drug abuse: Perspectives on current research* (pp. 23–58). Binghamton, NY: Haworth.

Rogler, L. H., Malgady, R. G., Costantino, G., & Blumenthal, R. (1987). What do culturally sensitive mental health services mean? The case of Hispanics. *American Psychologist, 42,* 565–570.

Rouse, B. A. (Ed.). (1995). Substance abuse and mental health statistics Sourcebook. DHHS Publication No. (SMA) 95-3064. Washington, DC: Superintendent of Documents, U.S. Government Printing Office.

Ruiz, R. (1981). Cultural and historical perspectives in counseling Hispanics. In D. W. Sue (Ed.), *Counseling the culturally different: Theory and practice* (pp. 186–215). New York: Wiley.

Santiestevan, H., & Santiestevan, S. (Eds.). (1984). *The Hispanic almanac.* Washington, DC: Hispanic Policy Development Project.

Sasao, T. (1989). *Patterns of substance use and health practices among Japanese Americans in southern California.* Paper presented at the third annual conference of the Asian American Psychological Association, New Orleans, LA.

Schuckit, M. A., Schwei, M. G., & Gold, E. (1986). Prediction outcome in outpatient alcoholics. *Journal of Studies on Alcohol, 2,* 151–155.

Spotts, J. V., & Shontz, F. C. (1982). Ego development, dragon fights, and chronic drug abusers. *International Journal of the Addictions, 17,* 945–976.

Substance Abuse and Mental Health Services Administration. (1997). *National Household Survey on Drug Abuse: Main Findings, 1995.* Research Triangle Park, NC: National Opinion Research Center.

Sue, D. W. (1981). *Counseling the culturally different: Theory and practice.* New York: Wiley.

Sue, D. W. (1987). Use and abuse of alcohol by Asian Americans. *Journal of Psychoactive Drugs, 19,* 57–66.

Sue, D. W., & Sue, D. (1990). *Counseling the culturally different.* New York: Wiley.

Sue, S., & Morishima, J. K. (1982). *The mental health of Asian Americans.* San Francisco: Jossey-Bass.

Sung, B. L. (1967). *Mountain of gold.* New York: Macmillan.

Swaim, R. C. (1991). Childhood risk factors and adolescent drug and alcohol abuse. *Educational Psychology Review, 3,* 363–398.

Swaim, R. C., Oetting, E. R., Chavez, E. L., & Beauvais, F. (1993). *The effect of dropout status on estimates of adolescent substance use among ethnic groups.* Unpublished manuscript.

Swaim, R. C., Oetting, E. R., Thurman, P. J., Beauvais, F., & Edwards, R. W. (1993). American Indian adolescent drug use and socialization characteristics: A cross-cultural comparison. *Journal of Cross Cultural Psychology, 24,* 53–70.

Swaim, R. C., Thurman, P. J., Beauvais, F., Oetting, E. R., & Wayman, J. (1993). *Indian adolescent substance use as a function of number of risk factors.* Manuscript submitted for publication.

Swanson, J. W., Linskey, A. O., Quintero-Salinas, R., Pumariega, A. J., & Holzer, C. E. (1992). A binational school survey of depressive symptoms, drug use, and suicidal ideation. *Journal of the American Academy of Child and Adolescent Psychiatry, 31,* 669–678.

Szapocznik, J., Perez-Vidal, A., Brickman, A. L., Foote, F. H., Santiseban, D., & Hervis, 0. (1988). Engaging adolescent drug abusers and their families in treatment: A strategic structural systems approach. *Journal of Consulting and Clinical Psychology, 56,* 552–557.

Szapocznik, J., Santisteban, D., Rio, A., Perez-Vidal, A., Santisteban, D., & Kurtines, W. M. (1989). Family effectiveness training: An intervention to prevent drug abuse and problem behaviors in Hispanic adolescents. *Hispanic Journal of Behavioral Sciences, 11,* 4–27.

Trotter, R. C., & Chavira, J. A. (1978). Discovering new models for alcohol. Counseling in minority groups. In B. Velimirov (Ed.), *Modern medicine and medical anthropology in the United States–Mexico border*

population (pp. 164–171). Washington, DC: Pan American Health Organization.

U.S. Bureau of the Census. (1990). *Statistical abstract of the United States: 1990* (110th Ed.). Washington, DC: U.S. Government Printing Office.

U.S. Bureau of the Census. (1992). *1990 census of population, 1990 CP-1-4, General population characteristics.* Washington, DC: U.S. Government Printing Office.

U.S. Bureau of the Census. (1996). *Current population reports: population profections of the United States by age, race, and Hispanics origin: 1995–2050, pp. 25–1130,* Washington, DC: U.S. Government Printing Office.

U.S. Department of Health and Human Services. (1985). *Report of the Secretary's Task Force on Black and Minority Health.* DHHS Pub. No. (ADM) 85-487. Washington, DC: U.S. Government Printing Office.

Watts, T. D., & Wright, R. Jr. (Eds.). (1983). *Black alcoholism: Toward a comprehensive understanding.* Springfield, IL: Thomas.

Yee, B. W. K., & Thu, N. D. (1987). Correlates of drug use and abuse among Indochinese refugees: Mental health implications. *Journal of Psychoactive Drugs, 19,* 77–83.

Zane, N., & Sasao, T. (1992). Research on drug abuse among Asian Pacific Americans. In J. Trimble, C. Bolek, & S. Niemcryk (Eds.), *Ethnic and multicultural drug abuse* (pp. 181–209). Binghamton, NY: Harrington Park.

CHAPTER

14 Ethnic Minority Intervention and Treatment Research

KAREN S. KURASAKI

STANLEY SUE

CHI-AH CHUN

KENNETH GEE

This chapter deals with research issues concerning ethnic minority interventions and treatment. It specifically focuses on (1) conceptual and methodological research issues, (2) psychotherapeutic outcome and process findings, and (3) applications of research to treatment and mental health practices. To aid students and practitioners who want to learn more about how to conduct research with ethnic minorities, as well as practitioners interested in using research in their work, we have attempted not only to present issues and research findings but also to suggest how to use these findings. Those who work with ethnic minority populations must be aware of the issues and be able to translate these issues into research and clinical practice.

Ethnic minority research in psychotherapy has had a relatively short history. Most psychotherapy research initiated about half a century ago examined the question of whether psychotherapy was effective. In time, questions were raised concerning what kinds of treatment were effective and what kinds of treatment were appropriate with what kinds of therapists, clients, and situations (for a history of psychotherapy including ethnicity and treatment, see Freedheim, 1992). The client variable of ethnicity was only of peripheral interest, for a variety of reasons: lack of interest in ethnicity on the part of researchers, lack of available funding for ethnic research, the belief among some that psychotherapy was unimportant because massive social and political interventions were needed in order to address race and ethnic relations, and difficulties in conducting ethnic research. Over time, the situation has changed, as reflected in the growing interest in ethnic research, greater availability of funding opportunities, and realization that although massive interventions are needed, so are efforts to help individual clients. Research contributions have increased, and the numbers of researchers who are themselves members of ethnic groups have helped to provide insider perspectives. Despite the fact that ethnic research has been an exciting area and its contributions have been highly important, a number of conceptual and methodological issues continue to confront the field.

Conceptual Considerations

Many conceptual issues arise in the field of ethnic research: What is the definition of ethnicity (or race)? How can we conceptualize observable ethnic differences? Are Western and traditional concepts of human beings really applicable to culturally different groups?

Definition of Ethnicity

In research and practice, ethnicity has been used to convey group membership according to race or ethnic background. Ethnic groups such as African Americans are often compared with Whites on utilization of services and treatment outcomes. Although such comparisons are meaningful in a broad sense, they often violate a more strict sense of the concept of ethnicity. The strict sense of the concept refers to a social-psychological sense of "peoplehood" in which members of a group share a unique social and cultural heritage. Yet we often fail to ascertain whether members of particular ethnic groups really share cultural features. Data are many times based on self-identification: If we want to conduct a study of clients and we combine self-identified Latino Americans into one group, we have no assurance that the clients are "ethnically" Latino. Some may have similar backgrounds, experiences, and attitudes, whereas others may be quite different. For example, Puerto Rican Americans who have recently arrived on the mainland may not share the same sense of ethnicity as fourth-generation Mexican Americans. Yet, in research, they are often conceptualized as all being Latino Americans. This problem also exists when we compare ethnics to "Whites," who are themselves quite diverse.

How can we address this problem? At times, the broad concept of ethnicity is important to use, especially if we want to establish parameters for ethnic comparisons. For example, in the present era of managed care, which means streamlining services to reduce costs, the absence of ethnic comparisons may lead to elimination of needed services for ethnic minorities (Abe-Kim & Takeuchi, 1996). In this case, however, researchers should acknowledge the limitations in aggregating diverse individuals into an ethnic category. Another way of addressing the problem is to begin studying individual differences among members of an ethnic group. For example, Helms (1984) has studied whether African Americans prefer to see a therapist who is racially similar. She has found that African Americans who accept an African American identity and who are skeptical of White values are most likely to want a therapist of the same race. Those at other stages of identity development are less likely to exhibit a racial preference. The value of the research is not solely in its demonstration that African Americans differ from one another. The specification of the individual difference variables that are important in explaining research results is also important.

Conceptualization of Differences

In the past, studies have revealed behavioral differences among ethnic groups. For instance, Malzberg (1959) found differences in utilization rates of mental facilities in New York between African Americans and Whites. The problem with this study was that other demographic differences, such as gender and social class, that could be confounded with ethnicity were not controlled. Problems like this one are obvious. Less obvious is how the very concept of ethnicity is confounded with another important phenomenon—namely, minority group status.

We often attribute differences between ethnic groups to cultural factors. For example, traditional Chinese values are contrasted with Western values in order to explain why Chinese Americans may tend to show certain attitudinal or personality differences from White Americans. In essence, the two cultures are conceptualized as being orthogonal or independent variables, while in reality, the two are interactive and not independent (Sue, 1983). Chinese Americans have had a long history in the United States. Because they are members of a minority group who have experienced prejudice and discrimination, their attitudes and behavior may be a product not only of Chinese culture but also of their history and experiences in this country. In studying ethnic minority groups, researchers should be aware that minority group status is intertwined with the concept of ethnicity and should attempt to study the interactions between culture and minority group status.

Applicability of Western Theories

Disciplines such as psychology, psychiatry, social work, and nursing, are highly developed in Western societies in terms of their empirical, methodological, and theoretical contributions. An issue raised by many cross-cultural and ethnic minority researchers concerns the applicability and validity of theories developed in the West to non-Western societies or cultures. The issue is exemplified in the *etic-emic* distinction. The term *etic* refers to culture-general concepts or theories, whereas *emic* is defined as a culture-specific phenomenon. This important distinction can be illustrated as follows: Let us assume a psychotherapist finds that catharsis (e.g., having clients express pent-up emotions directly) relieves tension and depressive feelings. For the principle of catharsis to be *etic* or universal in nature, it should be applicable to different cultural groups. If it is not, then the principle is *emic*—perhaps specific only to the cultural group from which the client came.

A common error in research and in people's everyday thinking is to believe that one's concepts, practices, or principles are universal in nature (Brislin, 1993). A parent who believes that all children are better off in an atmosphere of parental permissiveness, a teacher who advocates that the best way to learn is through competition among all students, or a psychotherapist who assumes that nondirective techniques are effective with all clients may be confusing *emics* for *etics* to the extent that these truisms are confined to particular cultures. Of course, theory is necessary in any science. Rather than discarding theoretically based research, one may use cross-cultural or ethnic investigations to test whether proposed theories are applicable to different groups.

In clinical practice, some researchers and clinicians believe that current psychotherapeutic practices based on Western modes of treatment may be culturally inappropriate with certain members of ethnic minority groups. They advocate more culturally responsive forms of treatment. It is important to have treatment approaches consistent with clients' cultural lifestyles. However, the concept of "culturally responsive" interventions often consists only of vague notions of being culturally sensitive and knowledgeable about the client's culture. There is a need to specify more carefully what the concept of culturally responsive therapy means and to test the effectiveness of these interventions, as discussed later.

Methodological Considerations

Conducting research on ethnic minority groups is difficult. Researchers often have difficulty finding and selecting an appropriate sample to study, choosing a good research design and controlling for confounding variables, and finding valid measures. It is important to be familiar with these methodological difficulties, not only to improve future research designs but also to understand better the contributions and limitations of past research findings.

Research Participants

Although ethnic minority populations are rapidly increasing, researchers still face difficulties in finding adequate and representative samples to study. These difficulties include the relatively small size of the populations and the unwillingness of some ethnic minorities (e.g., illegal immigrants in the United States) to become research subjects. For example, large-scale epidemiological studies of the prevalence of mental disorders have been conducted among Americans (Myers et al., 1984). Yet, these studies have failed to include sufficient numbers of ethnic groups such as Native Americans and Asian Americans, so that accurate prevalence rates for these groups have not been found. Similarly, it is frequently difficult to study the effectiveness of treatment for Asian Americans at a particular mental health center because Asian Americans tend to avoid such services.

These difficulties in finding adequate samples may have two unfortunate consequences. First, researchers may simply be unable to find a representative sample of ethnic minority populations. Rather than studying the population of Native Americans, they may confine their investigation to urban rather than reservation Native Americans, or to students rather than those in the community at large. Second, investigators may lump diverse groups together in order to achieve adequate sample sizes. In the past, research compared Whites with the broad category of non-Whites. Even today, research on "Latinos" or "Hispanics" combines many diverse groups—Mexican Americans, Puerto Ricans, immigrants from Cuba, El Salvador, and elsewhere. Asian American research includes as subjects Chinese, Japanese, Koreans, Pilipinos (many Asian American researchers now use this term rather than *Filipino*), Vietnamese, and other groups. The problem is that focusing on a particular segment of the ethnic population limits the generalizability of findings. Forming a large aggregate group (e.g., Latino Americans) often fails to reveal the individual differences within the aggregate group. This problem of limited generality and of failure to consider individual differences also exists in studies of the "White" population. However, it is especially true for ethnic minority populations, which are small in numbers and exhibit considerable cultural and experiential variations.

Research that focuses on a particular segment or on an aggregate group can have important value. Researchers need to draw conclusions that are appropriate to the samples under study and to the research questions being addressed. Furthermore, greater efforts and funds should be expended to overcome some of the problems inherent in studying small and culturally diverse populations. For such populations, researchers must often spend a great deal of time and research funds to find adequate numbers of subjects and to achieve a representative sample. For example, conducting a representative survey of urban Native Americans is far more problematic than conducting a similar survey of urban Whites.

Research Designs and Confounding Variables

Psychological research has available a wide range of research designs and strategies. Research emphasizing experimental, correlational, field, longitudinal, analogue, and other approaches have been used in ethnic minority research. In devising research strategies, however, investigators have often had to consider the availability of sample sizes of ethnics. This is apparent in clinical and counseling studies. For example, a researcher who wants to study whether ethnic similarity between therapist and clients affects treatment outcomes may not be able to find sufficient numbers of ethnic clients and therapists. Consequently, the researcher may use an analogue approach in which students, rather than actual clients and therapists, play the roles of clients and therapists. There are obvious limitations in analogue studies. The external validity and generality of findings can be questioned. But such compromises in research ideals must sometimes be made because of practical realities.

Ethnographic techniques and qualitative methods are recommended in ethnic research (Sue, Kurasaki, & Srinivasan, in press). Ethnographic studies involve more descriptive-analytic techniques to study aspects of culture or the effects of culture, especially as viewed by members of that culture. Often used by anthropologists, ethnography is useful for identifying important aspects of culture, categorizing phenomena, and exploring relationships between cultural variables and behavior. In psychology, it is frequently used to establish research parameters for further investigations. For example, before comparing how different cultural groups fare in psychotherapy, we may wish to study ethnographically how these groups generally respond to those healers already in their cultures in order to understand cultural practices in the different groups and their familiarity with and reactions to Western psychotherapists.

In any research design, it is important to be able to control for confounding variables. As mentioned previously, ethnicity is a broad variable, encompassing many features. Because ethnicity is often associated not only with culture but also with variables such as social class, investigators have often argued whether observed differences between, say, African Americans and Whites are really a matter of race or of social class. Research designs must obviously control for social class, as well as other demographic and social variables, before attributing differences to ethnicity or race. It is important to note that the "disadvantaged" status of ethnic minority groups cannot simply be attributed to social class differences. Although we know that certain groups such as African Americans,

Native Americans, and Latino Americans have lower educational and income levels than do Whites, being a member of an ethnic minority group may involve other disadvantages that are important to study.

Valid Measures

Validity refers to whether tests or assessment instruments accurately measure what they purport to measure. Researchers often have difficulty finding valid measures to use with different cultural groups. Take, for example, this item from the MMPI: "I feel blue." For people in U.S. society who are familiar with English idioms, this statement refers to feeling depressed or sad. But recent immigrants or those with limited English proficiency may not understand the meaning of "blue" in this context and may interpret the item as literally referring to the color blue.

Brislin (1993) identifies two major problems that are pertinent to our discussion of measures. First, concepts may not be equivalent across cultures. He notes that the concept of intelligent behavior is not equivalent in the United States and among the Baganda of East Africa. In the United States, one sign of intelligence is quickness in mental tasks, in East Africa, by contrast slow, deliberate thought is considered a part of intelligence. Obviously, tests of intelligence devised in the two cultures would differ, and individuals taking the tests could be considered intelligent on one measure but not the other. As another example, consider the concept of sincerity. In the United States, sincerity refers to being truthful, genuine, and straightforward—not to enacting roles. For Japanese, however, the sincere individual is one who acts in accordance with role expectations, not subjective personal feelings (DeVos, 1978).

Second, scalar or metric equivalence refers to whether scores on assessment instruments are really equivalent in cross-cultural research. For example, many universities use the Scholastic Aptitude Test (SAT), which has a verbal and quantitative component, as a criterion for admission. Many members of ethnic minority groups score lower on the SAT than do Whites. Do the test scores accurately assess academic potential, achievements, and ability to succeed? SAT scores moderately predict subsequent university grades. However, Sue and Abe (1988) found that the ability of the SAT score to predict success varies according to ethnicity and the components of the SAT. Whereas the SAT verbal component was a good predictor of university grades for Whites, the SAT quantitative portion was a good predictor of grades for Asian American students. Thus, Asian American and White students who have the same total SAT score (combining verbal and quantitative subscores) may perform quite differently on grades, depending on the subscores. Researchers must study the conceptual and scalar equivalence of tests when working with ethnic minority groups. The use of multiple measures is also important to see if the measures provide consistent findings.

The conceptual and methodological issues and the short history of ethnic minority research have had several consequences. Research has had to proceed carefully in order to take into consideration the difficulties in ethnic research. Accordingly, much of the research is exploratory because of the lack of baseline information and the uncertain applicability of Western theories. Nevertheless, as we shall see, much of the research has been pioneering and exciting. The work has also provided insight into the applicability of existing theories and methods to use in cross-cultural studies. Keeping in mind the conceptual and method-ological issues that have been raised, we would now like to review the substantive research on psychotherapy with ethnic minority groups.

Psychotherapy Research

Is psychotherapy effective with members of ethnic minority groups? This question is prob-ably better stated as: "Under what conditions is psychotherapy helpful to members of ethnic minority groups?" Critics of psychotherapy with ethnic groups rarely challenge the value of psychotherapy or psychological interventions. What they do often challenge are the outcomes of psychotherapy when traditional psychotherapeutic practices do not con-sider the culture and minority group experiences of ethnic minority clients. Some critics may also advocate for prevention and for social, political, and economic changes rather than psychotherapy. But few would argue that psychotherapy cannot be effective with ethnic minority group clients.

In our review, we examine several issues: (1) Do ethnic minority groups use mental health services? (2) How long do ethnic clients remain in treatment? (3) What are the find-ings of research on psychotherapy outcomes? Although research has provided some insights into the answers to these questions, we need much more research to enable us to draw stronger conclusions. Our analysis is based primarily on a comprehensive review of psychotherapy research by one of the authors (see Sue, Zane, & Young, 1994).

Utilization of Mental Health Services

Investigations on utilization of mental health services by ethnic minorities have repeatedly found that African Americans and Native Americans tend to overutilize, whereas Asian Americans and Latino Americans tend to underutilize mental health services (Beiser & Attneave, 1982; Brown, Stein, Huang, & Harris, 1973; López, 1981; Mollica, Blum, & Redlich, 1980; O'Sullivan, Peterson, Cox, & Kirkeby, 1989; San Francisco Department of Mental Health, 1982; Scheffler & Miller, 1989; Snowden & Cheung, 1990; Sue, 1977). These patterns of utilization of the four major ethnic groups vary little from inpatient to outpatient settings and among various types of service facilities (e.g., community mental health facilities, state and county mental hospitals, Veterans Administration medical cen-ters, general hospitals, and private psychiatric hospitals). In studies that do report different utilization patterns depending on service type, African Americans and Hispanics under-utilize outpatient care and overutilize inpatient care in comparison to Whites (Cheung & Snowden, 1990; Hu, Snowden, Jerrell, & Nguyen, 1991; Scheffler & Miller, 1989). Accord-ing to the findings of a study by O'Sullivan et al. (1989), which was a follow-up to the Sue (1977) study in Seattle, the utilization pattern of some groups appears to be changing. They found that, although African Americans and Native Americans continued to overutilize, Asian Americans and Latino Americans no longer underutilized services. More studies are needed to confirm these findings.

Many different explanations have been offered by investigators for the presence of ethnic differences in service utilization. Unfortunately, few were based on research findings, and most were speculative (Sue et al., 1994). Snowden and Cheung (1990) and others (Akutsu, 1997; Akutsu, Snowden, & Organista, 1996; Alvidrez, Azocar, & Miranda, 1996; Aponte & Barnes, 1995; Bastida & Gonzalez, 1995; Harada & Kim, 1995; Kang & Kang, 1995; Padgett, Patrick, Burns, & Schlesinger, 1995; Rodriguez & O'Donnell, 1995; Takeuchi, Sue, & Yeh, 1995) have attributed the group utilization differences to the group differences in socioeconomic status, rates of psychopathology, help-seeking tendencies, cultural variables, minority status, therapists' diagnostic bias and involuntary hospitalization (especially in the case of African Americans), and structural barriers. It is imperative that more research be conducted because these differences have serious implications for determining the mental health needs of these groups and the effectiveness of the currently available treatments for them.

Some caution should be taken in interpreting these findings. First, there may be some inconsistencies in service utilization patterns between findings from national surveys that include those who have not sought treatment at mental health facilities and findings from treated samples from community, state, or county mental health facilities. Neighbors (1985) found that in his national survey of adult African Americans, only a relatively small number reported that they used mental health services for psychological problems. Yet, the studies cited earlier on utilization patterns demonstrated that African Americans *overutilized* services. Second, in a review article by Rogler et al. (1983), Puerto Ricans in New York had significantly higher rates of psychiatric admissions, use of outpatient psychiatric services, and community mental health facilities than did non-Latino Whites. Only recently have Puerto Ricans shown relatively low rates of admission. This points to the fact that utilization patterns or statistics change and need to be monitored over time. Third, we have used the terms *underutilization* and *overutilization* loosely to refer to whether groups differ in use compared to their relative population figures. A group may have a low percentage of users simply because it has a low prevalence of mental disorders. Similarly, groups that statistically overutilize services may not be overutilizing if the prevalence of disorders in that group is high. In this case, statistically defined under- and over-utilization are discrepant with definitions based on need for services. Because we do not know enough about the prevalence of mental disorders among ethnic minority populations, most studies have employed a statistical definition as indicators of utilization. It should be noted, however, that indirect indicators of well-being suggest that Asian Americans and Latino Americans are not extraordinarily well adjusted. Thus, their underutilization may reflect actual low use rather than low needs for services.

Length of Treatment

Another commonly used method of examining the impact or effectiveness of psychotherapy for ethnic minorities is investigating the length of treatment. The assumption behind this type of research is that an effective therapy can keep clients in treatment, whereas an ineffective therapy will be terminated prematurely by clients. In fact, studies have consistently shown that the longer clients stay in treatment, the more change occurs (Luborsky, Chandler, Auerbach, Cohen, & Bachrach, 1971; Pekarik, 1986).

Findings on length of treatment of ethnic minority clients are inconsistent. Length of treatment has been measured either as the average number of sessions or the dropout rate after the first session of treatment. Sue (1977) investigated the dropout rate of African Americans, Native Americans, Asian Americans, and Latin Americans in Seattle. He found all groups of ethnic minorities to have significantly higher dropout rates after the first session than White Americans. In the follow-up study in Seattle, O'Sullivan et al. (1989) found no consistent differences in dropout rates between ethnic and White groups. In another study of the outpatient facilities in Los Angeles County (Sue, Fujino, Hu, Takeuchi, & Zane, 1991), only African Americans had a higher dropout rate from treatment after the first session than White Americans. Latino Americans did not differ from White Americans and Asian Americans had even a lower dropout rate than White Americans. Therefore, Asian Americans had the highest average number of sessions, followed by White and Latino Americans. African Americans had the lowest average number of treatment sessions. The inconsistency between the findings of the different studies may be due to variations in region, service system, and time period (Sue et al., 1994), or it may be an indication of some recent improvement in our mental health system's cultural responsiveness.

One study of different ethnic groups has provided some insight into factors associated with length of treatment. The Los Angeles County study (Sue et al., 1991) revealed that among African Americans, Asian Americans, Mexican Americans, and Whites, two factors were related to number of sessions across all groups: income and ethnic match between clients and therapists. Being poorer and not having an ethnically similar therapist predicted a lower number of treatment sessions. Having a psychotic diagnosis was also associated with fewer sessions in all groups except Mexican Americans. Thus, in this study, poor clients were more likely to average fewer sessions than were clients with higher incomes. The finding that having a therapist of the same ethnicity results in more sessions is interesting, although the reasons for this finding are unclear. Perhaps ethnic match tends to increase interpersonal attraction or influence of therapists. Finally, in a study that examined utilization of mental health services by older Asian Americans in Los Angeles County, older clients with a combination of financial coverage were nearly five times as likely as their privately insured counterparts to drop out of treatment after just one session (Harada & Kim, 1995).

Treatment Outcome Research

The paucity of treatment outcome studies on ethnic minorities makes it difficult to draw any definitive conclusions about the effectiveness of psychotherapy with ethnic groups. We need many more studies that rigorously examine treatment effects using (1) within– and between–ethnic group comparisons, (2) sufficient sample sizes, (3) different forms of treatment, (4) a variety of cross-culturally valid outcome measures, (5) follow-up strategies that can shed light on the stability of treatment effects over time, and (6) adequate methodological designs so that researchers can control for confounding variables or alternative explanations for findings. The few studies that are available often provide conflicting findings for all major ethnic groups. In none of the studies, however, did ethnic minorities consistently fare better than White Americans. Ethnic minorities tended at best to have similar treatment outcomes to White Americans.

Treatment outcome literature on African Americans seems to indicate that African Americans do not fare better than other ethnic clients, including White Americans, and that they may even have worse outcomes (Sue et al., 1994). Earlier studies on African Americans have revealed no racial differences from White Americans (Lemer, 1972). Jones (1978; 1982) has repeatedly found that African American clients showed similar rates of improvement to those of White Americans regardless of the ethnicity of their therapists. In more recent studies, however, the treatment outcomes of African Americans were poorer than the outcomes of White Americans and sometimes even poorer than the outcomes of other ethnic minority groups in drug treatment programs and in Los Angeles County mental health facilities (Brown, Joe, & Thompson, 1985; Sue et al., 1991). In no study were the outcomes of African Americans superior to those of White Americans and other ethnic minority groups.

Less is known about the effectiveness of psychotherapy for Native Americans (Manson, Walker, & Kivlahan, 1987; Neligh, 1988). Most mental health-related programs intended for Native Americans have focused on treatment and prevention programs for substance abuse. Query (1985) compared the outcomes of White and Native American adolescents in an inpatient chemical dependency treatment program at a North Dakota State Hospital. He found that Native American adolescents were overrepresented in the unit compared to their population figure. Furthermore, during the six months after discharge, significantly more Native American adolescents than White American adolescents had either thought of or attempted suicide. Overall, the treatment was more effective with White American adolescents than Native Americans. Prevention programs for Native Americans have been more successful in producing positive changes, especially in bicultural competence skills (LaFromboise, Trimble, & Mohatt, 1990; Schinke et al., 1988). Given the few findings, discussion of treatment outcome of Native Americans should wait until more research is conducted.

Outcome studies on Asian Americans, compared to other ethnic minority groups, have found more positive results. In Zane's study of the effectiveness of psychotherapy with Asian American clients in a community-based, ethnic-specific mental health clinic in Richmond, California (1983), Asian American clients showed significant improvement on both client self-report and therapist-rated outcome measures. Southeast Asian Americans have also been successfully treated for depression and posttraumatic stress disorder through psychotherapy and psychopharmacotherapy (Kinzie & Leung, 1989; Mollica et al., 1990). Compared to other ethnic groups, Asian Americans did not differ on posttreatment Global Assessment Score (GAS) from White Americans, even after controlling the pretreatment GAS scores (Zane & Hatanaka, 1988). Sue et al. (1991) have also found that Asian and White Americans had similar outcomes (in the same study, African Americans had worse outcomes than White Americans). In terms of clients' satisfaction with the therapy, however, Asian Americans have been found to be much less satisfied with service or progress of the therapy than were White Americans (Lee & Mixon, 1985; Zane, 1983; Zane & Hatanaka, 1988). Asian Americans in Lee and Mixon's study have rated both the counseling experience and the therapists as less effective.

Much of the treatment outcome research on Latino Americans has examined the effects of "culturally sensitive" treatment programs that can effectively meet the mental health needs of Latinos (Rogler, Malgady, Costantino, & Blumenthal, 1987). These culturally sensitive treatments have aimed to improve the accessibility of services to Latinos (e.g., by providing flexible hours or by placing the treatment facility in a Latino community), employing bicultural/bilingual staff, and selecting, modifying, or developing therapies that either utilize or are most appropriate for Latino cultural customs, values, and beliefs (e.g., involving indigeneous healers or religious leaders in the community in treatment, or increasing participation of family members in treatment). Research suggests that these treatments may increase service utilization, length of treatment, and clients' satisfaction with treatment and may decrease premature termination of treatment (Rogler, Malgady, & Rodriguez, 1989; Sue et al., 1994). How do Latinos fare in mainstream mental health services? When compared to other ethnic groups in mainstream treatments, Mexican Americans in one study were most likely to improve with treatment (Sue et al., 1991). However, having ethnic matches between therapist and client (a Mexican American therapist with a Mexican American client) was associated with better treatment outcomes than were mismatches. The research suggests that interventions involving culturally sensitive approaches produce more positive changes than interventions that do not consider cultural factors.

Treatment outcome research with ethnic groups can be characterized as sparse and targeted to many different aspects of psychotherapy. Under such circumstances, there is a need for more systematic research in order to address more fully the issue of effectiveness of both the mainstream and ethnic-specific treatment plans for ethnic minorities (Akutsu, Snowden, & Organista, 1996). Such research can help us identify treatment elements that are universally effective and those that are culture-specific.

Process Research

Our review has emphasized treatment outcome research. However, we would like to mention that a number of investigators have examined treatment process variables. Research has been conducted on client preferences for the ethnicity of therapists. In many cases, studies have shown that ethnic clients tend to prefer or to view more positively ethnically similar therapists (Atkinson, 1983; Dauphinais, Dauphinais, & Rowe, 1981; López, López, & Fong, 1991; Sattler, 1977), although other investigations have questioned these findings or have questioned whether therapist ethnicity is a very important variable relative to other therapist variables (Acosta & Sheehan, 1976; Furlong, Atkinson, & Casas, 1979; LaFromboise & Dixon, 1981). Preferences for an ethnically similar therapist appear to be a function of individual differences, such as a client's ethnic identity, gender, trust of Whites, and level of acculturation (Bennett & BigFoot-Sipes, 1991; Helms & Carter, 1991; Parham & Helms, 1981; Ponce & Atkinson, 1989; Ponterotto, Alexander, & Hinkston, 1988; Watkins & Terrell, 1988). Thus, research suggests that many ethnic clients prefer ethnically similar therapists but that other variables mediate the preferences. Aponte and Barnes (1995) discuss minority status as a variable that impacts the treatment process. Ethnic minorities are likely to bring their mistrust into the therapeutic setting. When they are met with insensitivity or outright racism on the part of the therapist, poorer outcomes are likely to result.

Ratings of therapist competence or preferences for a therapist are also influenced by the nature of psychotherapy. Therapists who intimately self-disclose to African American clients elicit more intimate self-disclosures than do therapists who do not intimately self-disclose (Berg & Wright-Buckley, 1988); those who acknowledge and deal with cultural issues raised by therapists are perceived to be more culturally competent than are therapists who avoid such issues (Pomales, Claiborn, & LaFromboise, 1986). Culturally sensitive therapists or those who are trained to deal with cultural issues (Dauphinais et al., 1981; Gim, Atkinson, & Kim, 1991; LaFromboise et al., 1990; Wade & Bernstein, 1991) are also judged to be more competent or more favorable. Some studies have found that Asian Americans and Latino Americans prefer directive over nondirective therapists (Atkinson, Maruyama, & Matsui, 1978; Pomales & Williams, 1989; Ponce & Atkinson, 1989). However, further studies are needed to examine whether nondirective approaches may still be effective despite their preferences, and how these preferences and the treatment effectiveness of various approaches may vary by other factors such as acculturation (Akutsu, 1997).

Rather than focusing on therapists, some researchers have examined the benefits of culture-specific forms of treatment—that is, therapies or modification of treatment approaches designed especially for certain ethnic groups. Family-network therapy, extended family therapy, or other forms of treatment that integrate traditional cultural healing practices or cultural aspects have been advocated by some (Comas-Díaz, 1981; Costantino, Maigady, & Rogler, 1986; LaFromboise, 1988; Lee, 1982; Manson et al., 1987; Szapocznik et al., 1989). Although systematic studies of the effectiveness of these culturally based forms of treatment are limited, they appear to be valuable, according to practitioners.

Application of Research Findings to Treatment

Some skepticism has been expressed over the value of research in affecting practice. As noted by Beutler (1992), many practitioners and clinicians do not read research reports, do not find reports helpful, or fail to use research findings in their practice. Nevertheless, Beutler also noted that research has had an impact on the practice of psychotherapy over the course of time. Although a single piece of research may have no had direct impact, the cumulative effect of many studies has been important. How can we apply the research findings and writings of different scholars to psychotherapeutic practice? We can apply research findings to practice by way of incorporating them into how we prepare ourselves as therapists, how we train therapists, and how we design services. Some general recommendations follow.

First, ethnicity, culture, and minority group status are important concepts for psychotherapists who work with ethnic minority clients. The available evidence suggests that therapists should be prepared to deal with these concepts and issues with their clients. While cultural issues may not be salient to all ethnic clients in all situations, therapists who are uncomfortable with these issues may not be able to deal with the issues if they do arise. Therapists should become knowledgeable about the cultural background of ethnic clients and should be adept at working in cross-cultural situations.

Second, having available a therapist of the same ethnicity as the client may be advantageous. While ethnic matches are not necessary for positive outcomes, at times certain clients may prefer or work better with an ethnically similar therapist. Having bilingual and bicultural therapists is vital to clients who are recent immigrants and are not fully proficient in English. The problem is that ethnic clients often have little choice, unless we train more ethnic minority, bilingual, and bicultural therapists.

Third, therapists who are unfamiliar with the cultural backgrounds of their clients may want to consult with mental health professionals who are knowledgeable of the clients' culture. Receiving training in working with culturally diverse clients is also recommended.

It is difficult to be fully proficient in working with many diverse groups. Assistance should be sought in the assessment or treatment of any client whose cultural background or lifestyle is unfamiliar to the therapist or markedly different from that of the therapist.

Fourth, culture-specific treatment should be available to ethnic clients, especially those who are unacculturated or who hold very traditional ethnic values that are discrepant from Western values. As mentioned previously, many researchers have argued that such treatment is valuable and beneficial.

Fifth, for clients who are unfamiliar with Western psychotherapy, some sort of pre-therapy intervention may be important. Before therapy, clients should receive some knowledge of what psychotherapy is, what roles clients and therapists adopt, what to expect in treatment, and how treatment can affect mental disorders. Similarly, efforts should be made to educate community groups on how to recognize emotional disturbance, what to do with someone who is disturbed, what mental health services are, and how to use such services. Issues of confidentiality, client rights, and the like should also be presented to the community. These strategies increase the likelihood that ethnic clients will better understand treatment and reduce feelings of strangeness in the client role.

Conclusions

This chapter has reviewed some of the conceptual and methodological issues facing researchers who study ethnic minority groups. Despite the many problems encountered in ethnic research, psychotherapy research has been growing and has provided some preliminary ideas on helpful strategies to use in providing mental health services to these groups. Much more research is needed that go beyond the descriptive level of discovering ethnic differences in therapy outcome and to begin to identify cultural elements that are important in psychotherapy. The existence of a critical need for more and better ethnic minority research does not imply that current ethnic investigators have failed to make important contributions. Indeed, the relatively small number of ethnic and cross-cultural investigators have made many pioneering contributions despite the obstacles encountered in ethnic minority research. These contributions are the basis for the next generation of research.

What directions should future research take? Beyond the recommendations for conducting more research and methodologically stronger research (in terms of adequate sample sizes, representative samples, valid measures, rigorous research designs, etc.), it is meaningful for future research to be targeted to certain issues. First, research should be devoted to uncovering how cultural elements influence treatment processes and outcomes among ethnic minorities. Second, the application of these cultural elements in devising culture-specific treatment programs needs to be investigated. Third, ethnic minority groups show much within-group variation, and effective therapeutic strategies for a highly acculturated ethnic minority client may differ from those for a recent immigrant. Research on individual differences is needed in order to overcome stereotypes that particular treatment tactics are effective with all members of a certain ethnic minority group. Fourth, because of the multicultural nature of our society, therapists will be increasingly exposed to clients from different ethnic groups. An important research direction is to discover those psychotherapeutic skills that enable therapists to work effectively with a diverse clientele and to find means of training therapists to develop effective skills.

REFERENCES

Abe-Kim, J. S., & Takeuchi, D. T. (1996). Cultural competence and quality of care: Issues for mental health service delivery in managed care. *Clinical Psychology: Science and Practice, 3(4),* 273–290.

Acosta, F. X., & Sheehan, J. G. (1976). Preferences toward Mexican American and Anglo American psychotherapists. *Journal of Consulting and Clinical Psychology, 44,* 272–279.

Akutsu, P. D. (1997). Mental health care delivery to Asian Americans: Review of the literature. In E. Lee (Ed.), *Working with Asian Americans: A guide for clinicians* (pp. 464–476). New York: Guilford Press.

Akutsu, P. D., Snowden, L. R., & Organista, K. C. (1996). Referral patterns in ethnic-specific and mainstream programs for ethnic minorities and whites. *Journal of Counseling Psychology, 43(1),* 56–64.

Alvidrez, J., Azocar, F., & Miranda, J. (1996). Demystifying the concept of ethnicity for psychotherapy researchers. *Journal of Consulting and Clinical Psychology, 64(5),* 903–908.

Aponte, J. F., & Barnes, J. M. (1995). Impact of acculturation and moderator variables on the intervention and treatment of ethnic groups. In J. F. Aponte, R. Young Rivers, & J. Wohl (Eds.), *Psychological intervention and cultural diversity* (pp. 19–35). Boston: Allyn and Bacon.

Atkinson, D. R. (1983). Ethnic similarity in counseling psychology: A review of research. *The Counseling Psychologist, 11,* 79–92.

Atkinson, D. R., Maruyama, M., & Matsui, S. (1978). Effects of counselor race and counseling approach on Asian Americans' perceptions of counselor credibility and utility. *Journal of Counseling Psychology, 25,* 76–85.

Bastida, E., & Gonzalez, G. (1995). Mental health status and needs of the Hispanic elderly: A cross-cultural analysis. In D. K. Padgett (Ed.), *Handbook on ethnicity, aging, and mental health* (pp. 100–110). Westport, CT: Greenwood Press.

Beiser, M., & Attneave, C. L. (1982). Mental disorders among Native American children: Rates and risk periods for entering treatment. *American Journal of Psychiatry, 139,* 193–198.

Bennett, S. K., & BigFoot-Sipes, D. S. (1991). American Indian and white college student preferences for counselor characteristics. *Journal of Counseling Psychology, 38,* 440–445.

Berg, J. H., & Wright-Buckley, C. (1988). Effects of racial similarity and interviewer intimacy in a peer counseling analogue. *Journal of Counseling Psychology, 35,* 377–384.

Beutler, L. (1992). Leading clinical practice. *The Scientist Practitioner, 2,* 10–19.

Brislin, R. (1993). *Understanding culture's influence on behavior.* New York: Harcourt Brace Jovanovich.

Brown, B. S., Joe, G. W., & Thompson, P. (1985). Minority group status and treatment retention. *International Journal of the Addictions, 20,* 319–335.

Brown, T. R., Stein, K. M., Huang, K., & Harris, D. E. (1973). Mental illness and the role of mental health facilities in Chinatown. In S. Sue & N. Wagner (Eds.), *Asian-Americans: Psychological perspectives* (pp. 212–231). Palo Alto, CA: Science & Behavior Books.

Cheung, F. K., & Snowden, L. R. (1990). Community mental health and ethnic minority populations. *Community Mental Health Journal, 26(3),* 277–291.

Comas-Díaz, L. (1981). Effects of cognitive and behavioral group treatment on the depressive symptomatology of Puerto Rican women. *Journal of Consulting and Clinical Psychology, 49,* 627–632.

Costantino, G., Malgady, R. G., & Rogler, L. H. (1986), Cuento therapy: A culturally sensitive modality for Puerto Rican children. *Journal of Counseling and Clinical Psychology, 54,* 639–645.

Dauphinais, P., Dauphinais, L., & Rowe, W, (1981). Effects of race and communication style on Indian perceptions of counselor effectiveness. *Counselor Education and Supervision, 21,* 72–80.

DeVos, G. (1978). *Selective permeability and reference group sanctioning: Psychological continuities in role degradation.* Paper presented at the seminar on Comparative Studies in Ethnicity and Nationality, University of Washington, Seattle.

Freedheim, D. K. (1992). *History of psychotherapy.* Washington, DC: American Psychological Association.

Furlong, M. J., Atkinson, D. R., & Casas, J. M. (1979). Effects of counselor ethnicity and attitudinal similarity on Chicano students' perceptions of counselor credibility and attractiveness. *Hispanic Journal of Behavioral Science, 1,* 41–53.

Gim, R. H., Atkinson, D. R., & Kim, S. J. (1991). Asian-American acculturation, counselor ethnicity and cultural sensitivity, and ratings of counselors. *Journal of Counseling Psychology, 38,* 57–62.

Harada, N. D., & Kim, L. S. (1995). Use of mental health services by older Asian and Pacific Islander Americans. In D. K. Padgett (Ed.), *Handbook on ethnicity, aging, and mental health* (pp. 185–201). Westport, CT: Greenwood Press.

Helms, J. E. (1984). Toward a theoretical explanation of the effects of race on counseling: A Black and White model. *Counseling Psychologist, 12,* 153–164.

Helms, J. E., & Carter, R. T. (1991). Relationships of White and Black racial identity attitudes and demographic similarity to counselor preferences. *Journal of Counseling Psychology, 38,* 446–457.

Hu, T., Snowden, L. R., Jerrell, J. M., & Nguyen, T. D. (1991). Ethnic populations in public mental health: Services choice and level of use. *American Journal of Public Health, 81(11),* 1429–1434.

Jones, E. E. (1978). Effects of race on psychotherapy process and outcome: An exploratory investigation. *Psychotherapy: Theory, Research, and Practice, 15,* 226–236.

Jones, E. E. (1982). Psychotherapists' impressions of treatment outcome as a function of race. *Journal of Clinical Psychology, 38,* 722–731.

Kang, T. S., & Kang, G. E. (1995). Mental health status and needs of the Asian American elderly. In D. K. Padgett (Ed.), *Handbook on ethnicity, aging, and mental health* (pp. 113–127). Westport, CT: Greenwood Press.

Kinzie, J. D., & Leung, P. (1989). Clonidine in Cambodian patients with post-traumatic stress disorder. *Journal of Nervous and Mental Disease, 177,* 546–550.

LaFromboise, T. D. (1988). American Indian mental health policy. *American Psychologist, 43,* 388–397.

LaFromboise, T. D., & Dixon, D. N. (1981). American Indian perception of trustworthiness in a counseling interview. *Journal of Counseling Psychology, 28,* 135–139.

LaFromboise, T. D., Trimble, J. E., & Mohatt, G. V. (1990). Counseling intervention and American Indian tradition: An integrative approach. *The Counseling Psychologist, 18,* 628–654.

Lee, E. (1982). A social systems approach to assessment and treatment for Chinese American families. In M. McGoldrick & J. Giordano (Eds.), *Ethnicity and family therapy* (pp. 527–551). New York: Guilford Press.

Lee, W. M. L., & Mixon, R. J. (1985). *An evaluation of counseling services by college students of Asian and Caucasian ethnicity.* Unpublished manuscript.

Lerner, B. (1972). *Therapy in the ghetto: Political impotence and personal disintegration.* Baltimore: Johns Hopkins University Press.

López, S. (1981). Mexican-American usage of mental health facilities: Underutilization reconsidered. In A. Baron, Jr. (Ed.), *Explorations in Chicano psychology* (pp. 139–164). New York: Praeger.

López, S. R., López, A. A., & Fong, K. T. (1991). Mexican Americans' initial preferences for counselors: The role of ethnic factors. *Journal of Counseling Psychology, 38,* 487–496.

Luborsky, L., Chandler, M., Auerbach, A. H., Cohen, J., & Bachrach, H. M. (1971). Factors influencing the outcome of psychotherapy: A review of quantitative research. *Psychological Bulletin, 75,* 145–408.

Malzberg, B. (1959). Mental disease among Negroes: An analysis of the first admissions in New York State, 1949–1951. *Mental Hygiene, 43,* 422–459.

Manson, S. M., Walker, R. D., & Kivlahan, D. R. (1987). Psychiatric assessment and treatment of American Indians and Alaska Natives. *Hospital and Community Psychiatry, 38,* 165–173.

Mollica, R. F., Blum, J. D., & Redlich, F. (1980). Equity and the psychiatric care of the Black patient, 1950–1975. *Journal of Nervous and Mental Disease, 168,* 279–286.

Mollica, R. F., Wyshak, G., Lavelle, J., Truong, T., Tor, S., & Yang, T. (1990). Assessment symptom change in Southeast refugee survivors of mass violence and torture. *American Journal of Psychiatry, 147,* 83–88.

Myers, J. K., Weissman, M. M., Tischler, C. L., Holzer, C. E., Leaf, P. J., Orvaschel, H., Anthony, J. C., Boyd, J. H., Burke, J. D., Kramer, M., & Stoltzman, R. (1984). Six-month prevalence of psychiatric disorder in three communities: 1980 to 1982. *Archives of General Psychiatry, 41,* 959–967.

Neighbors, H. W. (1985). Seeking professional help for personal problems: Black Americans' use of health and mental health services. *Community Mental Health Journal, 21,* 156–166.

Neligh, G. (1988). Major mental disorders and behavior among American Indians and Alaska Natives. In *Behavioral health issues among American Indians and Alaska Natives: Explorations on the frontiers of the biobehavioral sciences.* American Indian and Alaska Native Mental Health Research. Monograph *1,* 116–159.

O'Sullivan, M. J., Peterson, P. D., Cox, G. B., & Kirkeby, J. (1989). Ethnic populations: Community mental health services ten years later. *American Journal of Community Psychology, 17,* 17–30.

Padgett, D. K., Patrick, C., Burns, B. J., & Schlesinger, H. J. (1995). Use of mental health services by black and white elderly. In D. K. Padgett (Ed.), *Handbook on ethnicity, aging, and mental health* (pp. 145–161). Westport, CT: Greenwood Press.

Parham, T. A., & Helms, J. E. (1981). The influence of Black students' racial identity attitudes on preferences for counselor's race. *Journal of Counseling Psychology, 28,* 250–257.

Pekarik, G. (1986). The use of termination status and treatment duration patterns as an indicator of clinical improvement. *Evaluation and Program Planning, 9,* 25–30.

Pomales, J., Claiborn, C. D., & LaFromboise, T. D. (1986). Effects of Black students' racial identity on perceptions of White counselors varying in cultural sensitivity. *Journal of Counseling Psychology, 33,* 57–61.

Pomales, J., & Williams, V. (1989). Effects of level of acculturation and counseling style on Hispanic students' perceptions of counselor. *Journal of Counseling Psychology, 36,* 79–83.

Ponce, F. Q., & Atkinson, D. R. (1989). Mexican-American acculturation, counselor ethnicity, counseling style, and perceived counselor credibility. *Journal of Counseling Psychology, 36,* 203–208.

Ponterotto, J. G., Alexander, C. M., & Hinkston, J. A. (1988). Afro-American preferences for counselor characteristics: A replication and extension. *Journal of Counseling Psychology, 35,* 175–182.

Query, J. M. N. (1985). Comparative admission and follow-up study of American Indians and Whites in a youth chemical dependency unit on the North Central Plains. *International Journal of the Addictions, 20,* 489–502.

Rodriguez, O., & O'Donnell, R. M. (1995). Help-seeking and use of mental health services by the Hispanic elderly. In D. K. Padgett (Ed.), *Handbook on ethnicity, aging, and mental health* (pp. 165–180). Westport, CT: Greenwood Press.

Rogler, L. H., Cooney, R. S. Costantino, G., Earley, B. F., Grossman, B., Gurak, D. T., Malgady, R., & Rodriguez, O. (1983). *A conceptual framework for mental health research on Hispanic populations.* Bronx, NY: Fordham University, Hispanic Research Center.

Rogler, L. H., Malgady, R. G., Costantino, G., & Blumenthal, R. (1987). What do culturally sensitive mental health services mean?: The case of Hispanics. *American Psychologist, 42,* 565–570.

Rogler, L. H., Malgady, R. G., & Rodriguez, O. (1989). *Hispanics and mental health: A framework for research.* Malabar, FL: Krieger.

San Francisco Department of Mental Health. (1982). *Community mental health services report.* San Francisco: Author.

Sattler, J. M. (1977). The effects of therapist–client racial similarity. In A. S. Gurman & A. M. Razin (Eds.), *Effective psychotherapy: A handbook of research* (pp. 252–290). Elmsford, NY: Pergamon Press.

Scheffler, R. M., & Miller, A. B. (1989). Demand analysis of mental health service use among ethnic subpopulations. *Inquiry, 26,* 202–215.

Schinke, S. P., Orlandi, M. A., Botvin, G. J., Gilchrist, L. D., Trimble, J. E., & Locklear, V. B. (1988). Preventing substance abuse among American-Indian adolescents: A bicultural competence skills approach. *Journal of Counseling Psychology, 35,* 87–90.

Snowden, L. R., & Cheung, F. K. (1990). Use of inpatient mental health services by members of ethnic minority groups. *American Psychologist, 45,* 347–355.

Sue, S. (1977). Community mental health services to minority groups: Some optimism, some pessimism. *American Psychologist, 32,* 616–624.

Sue, S. (1983). Ethnic minority issues in psychology: A reexamination. *American Psychologist, 38,* 583–592.

Sue, S., & Abe, J. (1988). *Predictors of academic achievement among Asian American and White students.* New York: The College Board.

Sue, S., Fujino, D. C., Hu, L. T., Takeuchi, D. T., & Zane, N. W. S. (1991). Community mental health services for ethnic minority groups: A test of the cultural responsiveness hypothesis. *Journal of Counseling Psychology, 59,* 533–540.

Sue, S., Kurasaki, K. S., & Srinivasan, S. (in press). Ethnicity, gender, and cross-cultural issues in clinical research. In P. C. Kendell, J. N. Butcher, & G. N. Holmbeck (Eds.), *Handbook of research methods in clinical psychology* (2nd ed.). New York: Wiley.

Sue, S., Zane, N., & Young, K. (1994). Research on psychotherapy with culturally diverse populations. In A. E. Bergin & S. L. Garfield (Eds.), *Handbook of psychotherapy and behavior change* (4th ed., pp. 783–817). New York: Wiley.

Szapocznik, J., Rio, A., Murray, E., Cohen, R., Scopetta, M., Rivas-Vazquez, A., Hervis, O., Posada, V., & Kurtines, W. (1989). Structural family versus psychodynamic child therapy for problematic Hispanic boys. *Journal of Counseling and Clinical Psychology, 57,* 571–578.

Takeuchi, D. T., Sue, S., & Yeh, M. (1995). Return rates outcomes from ethnicity-specific mental health programs in Los Angeles. *American Journal of Public Health, 85(5),* 638–643.

Wade, P., & Bernstein, B. (1991). Culture sensitivity training and counselor's race: Effects on Black female clients' perceptions and attrition. *Journal of Counseling Psychology, 38,* 9–15.

Watkins, C. E.,Jr., & Terrell, F. (1988). Mistrust level and its effects on counseling expectations in Black client–White counselor relationships: An analogue study. *Journal of Counseling Psychology, 35,* 194–197.

Zane, N. (1983, August). *Evaluation of outpatient psychotherapy for Asian and Non-Asian American clients.* Paper presented at the American Psychological Association Conference, Anaheim.

Zane, N., & Hatanaka, H. (1988, October). *Utilization and evaluation of a parallel service delivery model for ethnic minority clients.* Paper presented at the Professional Symposium: Recent Trends and New Approaches to the Treatment of Mental Illness and Substance Abuse, Oklahoma Mental Health Research Institute.

15 Educating and Training Professionals to Work with Ethnic Populations in the Twenty-First Century

JOSEPH F. APONTE

CATHERINE E. APONTE

Over the last several decades there have been significant changes in the number and distribution of ethnic populations, immigration and migration patterns, and ethnic population characteristics. These changes have significant implications for the training of mental health service practitioners (see Chapter 1). It is predicted that members of ethnic groups will constitute one-third of the U.S. population by the turn of the century and almost half of the population by the year 2050 (Aponte & Crouch, 1995; U.S. Bureau of Census, 1996). It is incumbent upon all graduate and professional programs in the mental health disciplines, and psychology in particular, to incorporate ethnically diverse content and training experiences into their programs in order to be responsive to these present and future population changes as we move into the twenty-first century (Iijima Hall, 1997; Myers, 1992; Myers, Wohlford, Guzman, & Echemendia, 1991; Peterson et al., 1992).

Along with these acknowledged increases in ethnic populations, there has been increased attention directed at the education and training of psychologists to work with ethnic groups. A number of national training conferences have underscored the importance of training in this area (American Psychological Association, 1987; Bourg, Bent, McHolland, & Stricker, 1989; Brammer et al., 1988; Dong, Wong, Callao, Nishihara, & Chin, 1978; Gary & Weaver, 1991; McGovern, 1993; Stricker et al., 1990). These conferences have recommended strongly that the curricula devoted to ethnic groups be increased. Such efforts have been supported by the American Psychological Association (APA), as reflected in its accreditation criteria and standards put forth for working with ethnic populations (American Psychological Association, 1993, 1995; Aponte, 1992).

Although the impetus for focusing on ethnic populations has been present over the last three decades, those efforts that have been put forth have led to limited successes

(Aponte & Clifford, 1995; Bernal & Castro, 1994; Bernal & Padilla, 1982; Iijima Hall, 1997; Puente et al., 1993). The purpose of this chapter is to: (1) review the current status of education and training of psychologists to work with ethnic populations; (2) examine education and training issues from the perspective of what the profession might look like in the twenty-first century; (3) present a number of strategies for enhancing the ethnic education and training of students and professionals; and (4) identify guidelines that can be of use to graduate and professional programs in developing ethnic curricula.

Current Status of Education and Training

To have a full understanding of the issues, problems, and barriers to educating and training psychologists to work with ethnic populations, it is important to identify the number of ethnic students and faculty currently in graduate and professional schools and to describe the curriculum, courses, and training experiences in graduate and professional programs. The discussion that follows is based primarily on data provided by the Office of Demographic, Employment, and Educational Research and by the Office of Ethnic Minority Affairs of the American Psychological Association (APA), as well as published surveys of training programs.

Number of Graduate Students and Faculty

The number of ethnic students in graduate programs is often directly related to the number of ethnic faculty in the programs. Wicherski and Kohout (1992) report that ethnic representation on graduate psychology faculties has shown little improvement. White faculty in psychology programs remained at between 93 and 95 percent from 1983 to 1993, and correspondingly the percent of African American psychology faculty held steady at about 3 percent over that 10-year period (see Table 15.1). Hispanics and Asian Americans have

TABLE 15.1   Percentage of Faculty by Race/Ethnicity in U.S. Graduate Departments of Psychology by Academic Year.

Survey Year	1981–82	1983–84	1986–87	1989–90	1992–93
Sample Size	*(N = 351)*	*(N = 348)*	*(N = 378)*	*(N = 427)*	*(N = 402)*
Race					
White	95	94	94	93	93
Black	3	3	2	3	3
Hispanic	1	1	1	1	2
Asian	1	1	1	2	2
American Indian	<1	<1	<1	<1	<1
Not Specified	1	1	<1	1	<1

Source: Surveys of graduate Departments of Psychology, 1981–82 through 1992–93, American Psychological Association and Council of Graduate Departments of Psychology.

each consistently comprised 1 to 2 percent of psychology faculty, and American Indian faculty account for less than 1 percent of all psychology faculty. Recent data from the APA Research Office indicate that the percentage of full-time minority faculty is 9 percent (Sleek, 1998). Ethnic faculty are still underrepresented in psychology departments in comparison to the number of ethnic persons in the general population (see Chapter 1).

The prospect for recruiting new ethnic psychology faculty is guarded at best. Recent APA data indicate that approximately 20 percent of all first-year psychology doctoral graduates were Black, Hispanic, Asian, or American Indian students (American Psychological Association, 1998). This represents a slight increase in the number of doctoral students over the past decade (Aponte & Clifford, 1995; Bernal, 1990; Bernal & Castro, 1994). Although these figures may appear encouraging, they are not representative of actual graduation rates and the fact that the percent of new doctoral graduates in psychology who wish to pursue an academic career has been declining over the last ten years (Wicherski & Kohout, 1992). The percentage of all Ph.D.s who were working in academic settings, until recently, declined for all ethnic groups (Jones, Goertz, & Kuh, 1992).

Changes in the rate of graduate school enrollment across disciplines have varied historically by ethnic group. From 1976 to 1986, graduate school enrollment for Blacks decreased, whereas the enrollments increased for Hispanics and Asian Americans and remained the same for American Indians (Brown, 1988; Jones et al., 1992). Fewer Blacks, in general, are obtaining doctorates in all fields (Jenkins, 1992; Thurgood & Weinman, 1990). Undergraduate enrollments have shown similar patterns to the graduate profiles, indicating that the pipeline from undergraduate to graduate school and to faculty status, while improving for Hispanics and Asian Americans, has decreased for African Americans—thus making the future prospects for more African American faculty rather bleak.

Overall, ethnic representation in psychology as reflected in psychology doctoral enrollments, psychology doctoral recipients, APA members with Ph.D.s, and psychology faculty in graduate departments has changed slightly in the past decade (American Psychological Association, 1997; Aponte & Clifford, 1995; Howard et al., 1986; Iijima Hall, 1997; Pion, Bramblett, & Wicherski, 1987; Pion, Bramblett, Wicherski, & Stapp, 1985; Stapp, Tucker, & VandenBos, 1985; Tomes, 1998). Most of the data suggest, at best, that any increase of ethnic persons in the field of psychology has been at a rate that continues to fall further behind the rate of increase of ethnic groups in the U.S. population (Aponte & Clifford, 1995; Bernal, 1990).

Available Curriculum Courses and Training Experiences

Over the years a number of surveys on multicultural courses and training experiences in doctoral and internship programs have been conducted. Early studies found that the courses and training experiences offered on ethnicity were sparse and typically not required of all students (American Psychological Association, 1982; Bernal & Padilla, 1982; Boxley & Wagner, 1971; Wyatt & Parham, 1985). Results from more recent surveys acknowledge some measurable progress, with approximately 60 percent of APA clinical programs having a course on cross-cultural or multicultural issues; however, only 26 percent required one such course for graduation (Bernal & Castro, 1994).

Significant changes from the earlier Bernal and Padilla (1982) survey are that there are several programs with specialized curricula and training experiences specifically designed to prepare psychologists for working with ethnic populations (Atkinson, Morten, & Sue, 1998; Bernal, 1990), and programs that have made special efforts to recruit and retain ethnic students (Collins, Green, & Chaney, 1992; Myers, Taylor, & Davila, 1992). Among those programs identified and described by Bernal are the California School of Professional Psychology at Los Angeles, Colorado State University, Oklahoma State University, University of Maryland, and New York University Medical Center. The offerings of these programs vary from the imbedding of ethnic content and training experiences throughout the curriculum to specialized tracks within the programs to prepare students to work with ethnic populations.

Although some gains have been made in the curricula, courses, and training experiences directed specifically at working with ethnic group members, 40 percent of the programs have no course offerings in this area, and the vast majority of the programs apparently do not consider such training important enough to require such a course for graduation (Bernal & Castro, 1994). There is as yet no agreement as to the training models, structure, sequence, and content of courses and training experiences for teaching students to work effectively with ethnic populations, nor is there continuity in ethnic training between doctoral training programs and internship settings (LaFromboise & Foster, 1992).

Ridley (1985) has identified five imperatives that speak to the importance of including ethnic and cultural content and training experiences in graduate programs. These imperatives are (1) professional participation, the underrepresentation of ethnic psychologists in the profession; (2) ethical, the need for competent services to be provided to ethnic populations as exemplified by the APA code of ethics; (3) cultural-context, the importance of culture in all treatment interventions; (4) scholarly, the need to correct inadequate or incorrect information about ethnic groups; and (5) legal, having the necessary qualifications to provide services to ethnic populations as exemplified by state licensing laws. Before considering the approaches to training professionals to work with ethnic populations, it is useful to consider the directions that the profession of psychology may be headed toward in the twenty-first century.

The Profession of Psychology in the Twenty-First Century

Eminent psychologists attending the 1987 Conference on Graduate Education and Training in Psychology noted that centrifugal tendencies operating in social, political, and educational contexts during the 1970s and 1980s were also operating in the field of psychology (Altman, 1987; Spence, 1987; Strickland, 1987). In general, centripetal trends are those that have a consolidating or unifying effect, whereas centrifugal trends have diverging and separating effects. Altman (1987) frames these trends as poles of a dialectic that are both operative, although one may predominate during any given epoch. Centrifugal tendencies described by Altman have predominated since the 1960s and have continued to affect the development of the field of psychology into the 1990s (Rice, 1997). Rice

(1997) has projected several scenarios for the field of psychology based on the degree to which such centrifugal tendencies persist.

Influence of Centrifugal Tendencies on the Profession

Altman (1987) discussed several centrifugal trends existing in American higher education from 1960 through 1987, the time the article was written. These include: (1) curriculum shifts from a traditional broad-base structure of required courses to fewer required courses; (2) departments became more focused on internal development with less regard to their role in the institution as a whole; (3) faculties became more mobile, with professors focusing on financial, research, and professional gains rather than on their institutional affiliation; and (4) a less stable student cohort emerged; for example, people attended universities on a part-time or irregular basis and student–faculty relationships become more fragmented.

Along with these centrifugal trends Altman (1987) noted that the financial difficulties encountered by institutions of higher learning in the 1980s and 1990s lead to a new slogan for academia, "economic development." This slogan refers to the principle by which governors and state legislators support those programs in higher educational institutions that have a direct bearing on local and statewide economic development. This entrepreneurial ethic, Altman (1987) argues, is likely to be another divisive or centrifugal trend in higher education.

Altman (1987) reviewed similar centrifugal trends that predominated psychology at that time. These trends included: (1) professionals having a weaker identity with the field of psychology as a whole; (2) the proliferation of specialty areas; (3) an increase in emphasis on student publications, which results in training in a narrow band of research and methodology; (4) an increase in the applied aspects of traditionally academic pursuits; and (5) a widening split between the academic and professional areas of psychology, including the split between clinical and nonclinical groups and between free-standing professional schools and university-based programs.

The centrifugal trend of the scientist–practitioner split prompted Rice (1997) to raise the question of whether there will one day be two psychological professions, one scientific and academic and one specializing in providing services. Rice (1997) used the technique of scenario building, in which one identifies critical variables to project various trajectories for the future. Using this approach, Rice (1997) identified four future scenarios for psychology ranging from the *reunion* of academic and professional psychologist to *dissolution* of the relationship between academic and professional psychologists—with the latter being the result of increased centrifugal forces. Two other midway scenarios are described by Rice (1997) which he identifies as the *science-based-practice* scenario and the *separate-and-equal* scenario.

Rice (1997) described how psychology might look, given each scenario, with regard to general structure and functioning of programs including such things as: (1) type of degree offered (Ph.D. or Psy.D.); (2) number of students enrolled in the program; (3) structure of the curriculum and training experiences; and (4) length of training required to receive a degree. Each scenario also will look different with respect to the professional academic split, future work settings for psychologists, numbers of professionals called psychologists, and the structure and membership of professional organizations relating to the field of psychology.

Increasing centrifugal trends in the field of psychology will result in a greater split between academic and professional psychology. In the resulting professional training programs the Psy.D. will be the predominant degree conferred, more students will be enrolled in professional programs, and these programs will have shorter curriculums with greater specialization and fewer basic core courses. In addition, the intellectual base for the curriculum will be more practice-based. The practice of psychology may include "personal effectiveness" in nontraditional settings, and counseling psychology may evolve into "spiritual counseling" (Rice, 1997). Psychologists may work in mental health settings and private practice but will also be working in schools, military and government settings including the court system, and in commercial firms.

According to the Rice (1997) scenario-building projections, centrifugal trends will see academic psychology as split from professional psychology. Academic programs will be designated as behavioral science departments to differentiate themselves from the practice of psychology. These departments will offer the Ph.D. and will prepare people for careers in research and teaching. There may develop a unified intellectual core for such behavioral science programs that can be characterized as cognitive behaviorism. Increasing centrifugal trends may see such departments of behavioral science disappear into other academic departments such as neuroscience, computer science, and social science departments.

It is interesting to note, exemplifying the centrifugal forces affecting the field, that NIMH has just recently announced the creation of two separate divisions to support behavioral science research (Trubisky, 1999). One will be the Division of Basic and Clinical Neuroscience, which will promote and support research to increase knowledge about links between cognitive and emotional processes as they relate to brain function along with research that examines such basic processes in personality, social, and interpersonal functioning. The second division, identified as the Division of Mental Disorders, Behavioral Research and AIDS, will have three new branches focusing on: health and behavior; development, behavior, and psychopathology in children and adolescents; and behavior and psychopathology in adults.

Educational and Training Issues Created by Changes

In general, the training of graduate students and professionals in multiculturalism has focused on whether the content and training experiences have been represented only in a specialty core course or two in graduate curricula, or whether such information is integrated throughout the entire core curriculum (Reynolds, 1995; Ridley, Espelage, & Rubinstein, 1997). Another approach for presenting multiculturalism in graduate curricula has been to establish a specialty area of the study of multiculturalism, much as child-clinical, neuropsychology, or health psychology are conceived as specialty areas. Multicultural courses have also been offered only by electives. These approaches are schematically represented in Figure 15.1.

How multiculturalism is incorporated into graduate psychology programs will depend upon how such programs are structured in the future. The structure of such programs will vary according to the kind of scenario that Rice (1997) described. That is, graduate clinical psychology training programs will evolve according to the kind of profession psychology becomes in the twenty-first century. And, training in multiculturalism will be

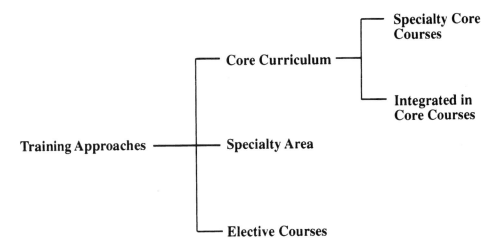

FIGURE 15.1   Mechanisms for offering multicultural courses in training programs.

adapted to fit changes in the graduate training programs that occur as the profession changes.

Brickey (1998) recently described several general trends in the overall availability of entry-level positions in psychology. In general, Brickey (1998) projects declining availability in positions for full-time generalist psychotherapist jobs for doctoral-level psychologists in organizations. Various master's-level professionals will be doing much of the "generic" psychotherapy. Academic positions, clinical positions in government programs and institutions, private practice, and traditional specialty areas will remain stable or decrease slightly. According to Brickey's projections, the specialty area of corrections and geriatrics will be growth areas in positions for doctorally trained psychologists. In addition, he projects that there will be an increase in postdoctoral training programs in specialty areas.

Various suggestions are made by Brickey (1998) as to how to soften the effects of the decrease in growth in certain areas for psychologist. Areas of possible growth in work opportunities for psychologists include: (1) increasing psychology's representation in primary care physician offices; (2) focusing on those problems that managed care organizations do not cover, such as marital therapy, personal development, and ADHD; (3) promoting psychology as a legitimate way in which to improve lifestyle through changing emotional and behavioral patterns detrimental to a positive lifestyle; and (4) consulting, including working with businesses for the purpose of team building, coaching, improving productivity, marketing analysis, and outcomes research.

The centrifugal trends in the field of psychology described by Altman (1987) and Rice (1997) and the specific projections about job opportunities made by Brickey (1998) have a number of implications for training in multiculturalism in graduate psychology training programs. One approach to doing this is to look at how multicultural training might be implemented for the generalist psychologist, for the psychologist whose training is in a specialty area, and for specialty training in multiculturalism. The nature of the content, types of training experiences provided, and emphasis on advocacy would vary according to which training strategy is utilized.

Generalist psychologists ought to be forging connections with primary care physicians, according to Brickey (1998). Such an effort is important in reaching ethnic populations, particularly those who do not seek the services of a mental health professional because of perceived stigma or physical manifestations of psychological dysfunction. In addition, the increasing representation of ethnic populations in the general populations will be reflected in the practices of primary care practitioners. Multicultural issues that are likely to be important in training the generalist psychologist who makes the connections with primary care physicians will include such things as: (1) linkages between psychological and physical conditions; (2) cultural differences between service providers and ethnic patients; and (3) accessing other service agencies and social support systems.

Multicultural training in the generalist model will be represented in both clinical core courses as well as in specialty core courses. The specific content on multiculturalism in the clinical core courses will be determined both by the nature of the core courses and by the ethnic population(s) being covered. Regional differences based on ethnic population concentrations will strongly influence the focus of these courses. A specialty course or courses in multiculturalism will allow content and experiences to be pursued in more depth; however their linkage to core clinical courses may not be realized.

As various specialty areas increase in their representation in psychology training programs, an examination of the role of multiculturalism in such specialty areas needs to be undertaken. It seems likely that how ethnic issues are represented will vary according to the nature of the specialty area. For example, in specialty areas such as child-clinical or geriatrics, the representation of multiculturalism will look similar to that described above in the generalist training approach. In contrast, in a specialty area such as corrections, training programs would be remiss if they did not fully integrate a multicultural perspective that involved a broader systems and advocacy approach given the significant overrepresentation of ethnic populations in the criminal justice system.

As noted in Figure 15.1, multiculturalism training can occur as a specialty area in and of itself on a par with, for example, child-clinical or geriatric psychology. Such a specialty would take as its organizing conceptual framework, ethnicity or multiculturalism. Such a specialty should examine the history and experiences of various ethnic populations, different models of acculturation and racial/ethnic identity development, development of psychopathology and symptom presentation, use of psychological assessment instruments, delivery of mental health services, use of standard and culture-specific treatments, and research with ethnic populations. Such an approach will require the identification of the kinds of positions that psychologists trained in such a specialty area would occupy.

Finally, the importance of training psychologists in alternative roles has been emphasized by Atkinson et al. (1998). These roles include: (1) advocate, (2) change agent, (3) consultant, (4) advisor, (5) facilitator of indigenous support systems, and (6) facilitator of indigenous healing methods. The issue of alternative roles can be addressed as a part of the core curriculum or it can be considered as a separate area in itself. In the former approach, training for alternative roles would arise in attending to such issues as underserved ethnic populations whether in the generalist or specialty area training. In the latter approach, it is likely to be an integral part of a multicultural specialty area.

Enhancing Ethnic Education and Training

As described in the previous section, multicultural training will be significantly affected by the current and projected changes in the field of psychology. It is also the case that whatever structure a training program adopts, given its training orientation, barriers will emerge in incorporating multicultural training. A number of barriers to implementing content and training experiences into graduate and professional programs can be identified in the literature (Aponte & Clifford, 1993, 1995; Hammond & Yung, 1993; Reynolds, 1995). Implicit in the discussion of the above barriers are two ideas: (1) that such training is to be valued; and (2) that there are structural barriers that work against the implementation of such training.

Societal and community-level barriers can include a negative political climate toward ethnic populations and a lack of economic support for training ethnic students (Diaz, 1990; Jones, 1985). Institutional, departmental, and program barriers can take the form of unnecessary admission requirements for ethnic students (Aponte & Clifford, 1995; Astin, 1982; Casas, 1985; Diaz, 1990) and inadequate efforts for recruiting and retaining ethnic students and faculty (Guzman & Messenger, 1991). Individual-level barriers include racist values, attitudes, and behaviors of instructors, supervisors, and trainees (Aponte & Clifford, 1995; Barbarin, 1994; Evans, 1985; Ridley, 1995; Williams & Halgin, 1995). Such individual-level barriers contribute to the failure to understand, appreciate, and respond to the role of culture in working with ethnic populations.

Seen within the framework of centripetal and centrifugal trends in the field of psychology, the concept of barriers refers to those trends in training that are more centripetal in nature. Altman (1987) notes that reactionary trends to centrifugal trends include such things as insisting on traditional patterns of graduate student experiences, strengthening traditional program area boundaries, and rejecting new configurations of program areas. Interest in expanding multicultural training and educational experiences in graduate programs of psychology is predicated on what is fundamental value in diversity in all aspects of experience. It is likely that such value in diversity is in itself a centrifugal trend in the field of psychology.

Programs will be well served to examine various ways in which to decrease the extent to which barriers to multicultural training impede training goals. Addressing such barriers requires an assessment of their nature and extent at the institutional, departmental, program, and individual levels (Aponte & Clifford, 1993; 1995; Hammond & Yung, 1993; Reynolds, 1995). The intercultural sensitivity model developed by M. J. Bennett (1986) provides a useful framework for assessing such barriers. The use of needs assessment approaches that have been developed in the program evaluation field can serve as the tools through which relevant data on these barriers can be collected (Aponte, 1983).

Framework for Assessing Intercultural Sensitivity

M. J. Bennett (1986) has proposed a developmental approach to training for intercultural sensitivity that can be useful in the process of assessing how ethnic populations are viewed. He identified six stages (Denial, Defense, Minimization, Acceptance, Adaptation, and Integration) that vary from ethnocentric to ethnorelativistic positions, as one moves from the Denial to Integration Stages on a developmental continuum. At each of these stages, the person has a particular view on how cultural differences are construed, which subsequently has an impact on sensitivity to diverse groups and how the person communicates with these groups.

At the early stages in the developmental continuum, the person or group assume a parochial position toward the differences between themselves and ethnic persons, evaluate these differences negatively, and at later stages minimize the differences between themselves and ethnic groups (M. J. Bennett, 1986). Later stages on the continuum involve acceptance of differences between Whites and ethnic groups, adaptation to these differences, and an integration of these differences into one's world view of ethnic persons. Though not explicitly stated, it is assumed that the stage in which one finds oneself can be affected by the situational context.

Intercultural sensitivity can be achieved through a variety of mechanisms. At the departmental and programmatic level, for example, the existence of ethnic faculty and graduate students, the existence of structures such as "diversity committees," and specific course offerings on diversity begin to provide clues to the intercultural sensitivity stage. Detailed perusal of course content can reveal how ethnic groups are regarded. At the individual level, identification of administrators, faculty, and students beliefs, attitudes, racial identity (Sabnani, Ponterotto, & Borodovsky, 1991), and behaviors toward different ethnic groups by means of survey, key informant, and nominal group needs assessment procedures (Aponte, 1983) could provide a picture of their stage of development.

The proposed analysis of intercultural sensitivity is directed at multiple levels (e.g., university, department, program, faculty, students). Each of these levels is discrete yet interconnected, and changes directed at each level are assumed to affect all levels. Changes in university and departmental policies and procedures, for example, can have an impact on all faculty and students. Conversely, changes in the values, beliefs, and attitudes of students and faculty can have an impact on the department and university. Such changes can occur through retreats, workshops, and inservice training of administrators, faculty, and staff, and through the use of expert consultants.

Changing the values, attitudes, and beliefs of administrators, staff, faculty, and students is only one step in the process of developing and implementing ethnic content and training experiences into graduate and professional programs. The previously identified barriers, some of which are institutional and organizational, need to be addressed. Recruiting, hiring and promoting ethnic faculty, and recruiting and retaining ethnic graduate students is essential to providing a critical mass that ensures that ethnic issues and content are addressed in training programs. Universities, departments, and programs need to make a commitment and provide the necessary financial support to hire, recruit, and support ethnic faculty and graduate students.

Education and Training Models and Methods

J. M. Bennett (1986) has identified several models for cross-cultural training that provide a framework for organizing courses and training experiences that can be adapted to the previously mentioned projected scenarios. According to Bennett, cross-cultural training can be divided into three broad models: Orientation, Training, and Education, with each model

TABLE 15.2   Strategies for Incorporating Ethnic Content and Experiences into Graduate and Professional Training Programs.

Training Strategies	Description of Strategy	Training Model Emphasized
Culture-specific events approach	Presentations and colloquium	Orientation model
Workshop approach	Extended training experiences	Training model
Interdisciplinary approach	Courses in related disciplines	Orientation model
Separate courses approach	Courses with specific ethnic content	Orientation model
Area of concentration approach	Organized ethnic courses and training experiences	Education model
Integration approach	Ethnic content imbedded in all courses	Orientation model

having a different focus, content, and process. For example, the process for the Orientation model would be intellectual, that of the Training model experiential, and the Education model a combination of intellectual and experiential. Each of the components within the models can be linked to specific education and training strategies.

A number of specific education and training strategies (see Table 15.2) for working with ethnic groups have also been identified by scholars in the field (Copeland, 1982; LaFromboise & Foster, 1992; Peterson et al., 1992). These strategies can be divided into six categories: (1) culture-specific events, such as presentations and colloquium on ethnicity; (2) workshops, involving one- to three-day training experience on ethnicity; (3) interdisciplinary approaches (taking courses in other related disciplines); (4) separate courses, designed to cover ethnicity issues; (5) area of concentration approach, in which a variety of didactic courses and practicum experiences in working with ethnic groups is provided; and (6) integration approach, in which content and experiences on ethnicity are imbedded in all core courses.

Each of these specific education and training strategies can be grouped under the three models previously identified by J. M. Bennett (1986). For example, the culture-specific events can be placed in the Orientation model, the workshop approach in the Training model, and the area of concentration under the Education model. Each strategy varies in its focus, content, and process. Of particular importance is the process component—that is, how much of the process is intellectual, experiential, or a combination of the two. Too often, the emphasis is placed on ethnic content, and this may not even be well presented. Training programs need to have a balance of content and experiential learnings.

Education and Training Components

Education and training components will have to be considered in designing an ethnically relevant curriculum for the projected scenarios. Several different models can be found in the literature for developing curriculum (Carter & Qureshi, 1995; Ridley, 1985). Ridley (1985) has proposed a three-dimensional model that can be used as a framework for such a task. The three dimensions of this model are: (1) population target (e.g., African Americans, Hispanics, Asian/Pacific Islanders, American Indians, Panhuman population); (2) intervention target (e.g., individual, family, group, community); and (3) curriculum (e.g., theory, research, practice). The Panhuman population category refers to those universally applied variables that enhance cross-cultural understanding (Ridley, 1985).

It may not be possible to incorporate all elements of this model into training programs. For some programs it would be best to focus on those ethnic groups that are in close proximity to the training program. Programs in South Florida or Southwest Texas, for example, could specialize in training graduate students to work with Hispanic populations. However, such programs should be designed so that the knowledge and skills acquired in working with these populations could be extrapolated to other ethnic groups. Such a transfer of knowledge and skills is particularly important with the changing demographic profile of this country (see Chapter 1) and the mobility of professionals across the country.

Training all graduate students in a variety of intervention strategies is desirable in general, and it is particularly so for students who eventually will be working with ethnic populations. At times, family and group interventions are called for in working with ethnic groups (see Chapters 6 and 7 of this text). On other occasions, community interventions utilizing prevention and consultation efforts are appropriate (see Chapter 8). Unfortunately, not all of these intervention strategies are equally developed in general—and particularly with ethnic populations, nor are all programs equipped to provide such training. Those programs that have multiculturalism as a specialty area can more readily provide training in a variety of intervention strategies.

Integrating ethnic theory, research, and practice is fundamentally important (Bernal, Bernal, Martinez, Olmedo, & Santisteban, 1983; LaFromboise & Foster, 1992; Ridley, 1985). Programs struggle with integrating these three components, while integrating specific ethnic content and experiences is even more difficult—in part because of the limited empirical psychological research on ethnic populations. There are too few researchers studying ethnic populations and variables. In existing empirical studies, the sample sizes are often too small and unrepresentative, the measures and instruments biased, the research designs inappropriate, and the findings erroneously interpreted.

Specific curriculum, course, and training experiences for preparing students to work with ethnic groups have been described in the literature (Anderson, Bass, Munford, & Wyatt, 1977; Green, 1981; López et al., 1989; McDavis & Parker, 1977; Mio & Morris, 1990; Parker, Bingham, & Fukuyama, 1985; Payne, 1984). Such descriptions typically present a sequence of courses and training experiences that provide a historical and cultural context for ethnic populations, delineate the types of problems and issues encountered by these groups, and train students to provide appropriate and effective interventions to address these problems and issues. The importance of mentorship, particularly for ethnic students, has also been pointed out by a number of scholars (Aponte, 1990; Atkinson, Neville, & Casas, 1991; see Chapter 16).

The need to deal with therapist beliefs and attitudes toward ethnic groups and difficult client–therapist interactions has been noted by a number of writers (Barbarin, 1984; Evans, 1985; Hunt, 1987; see Chapter 16). Such training requires moving beyond "knowing that" to "knowing how" to work with ethnic groups (Johnson, 1987). This type of knowledge requires experiential training that allows for an exploration of one's own beliefs, attitudes, behavior, and interactions with ethnic persons. The Triad Training Model developed by Pedersen (1978), the Multiethnic Counselor Education Curriculum developed by Johnson (1987), the Culture Shock Model of Merta, Stringham, and Ponterotto (1988), and the computer-based client simulation program developed by Lichtenberg, Hummel, and Shaffer (1984) serve such a purpose.

Education and Training Guidelines

The importance of educating and training graduate students and professional psychologists to work with ethnic populations is predicated on two propositions: (1) the changing demographic profile and needs of African American, Hispanics, Asian/Pacific Islanders, and American Indians demand that curriculum, courses, and training experiences be designed and changes so that such populations can be effectively served, and (2) psychologists need to embrace the concept of *affirmative diversity;* that is, the field of psychology needs to value human diversity (Jones, 1990).

The implementation of education and training efforts for serving ethnic populations occurs in the context of the ongoing changes in the field of psychology. Thus, the goals and objectives for implementing such mandates will vary depending on the dominant scenarios in the field. Such issues as whether and how education and training in ethnicity are incorporated in the courses, how they are incorporated into practicum experiences, and ethnic representation among students and faculty will vary according to the kinds of scenarios that are represented in the field of psychology. There are a number of general guidelines for education and training that can be examined within this contextual background of possible scenarios.

The importance of educating and training graduate students and psychologists to work with ethnic populations no longer should be an issue. As has been noted in this chapter, and elsewhere in this text, the changing demographic profile and needs of African Americans, Hispanics, Asian/Pacific Islanders, and American Indians demand that curriculum, courses, and training experiences be designed and changed so as to train all students to work with these groups. For those psychologists who have completed their formal academic education, such training could be achieved through continuing education courses, workshops, and training experiences.

As is evident from this chapter, incorporating ethnic content and training experiences cannot be achieved without addressing the barriers to such efforts at multiple levels, including the societal, community, university, department, program, and individual levels (Aponte & Clifford, 1993; 1995). Such an effort requires a process of rigorous self-examination and evaluation that may require forming committees, task forces, or bringing in outside consultants. From this process a commitment to training in this area needs to emerge. While the training goals, objectives, models, and methods can vary, there are a number of guidelines that should be followed in achieving these goals.

The goals and objectives of such education and training of ethnic students should be clearly articulated and documented in writing (Ridley, 1985). The development of such goals and objectives needs to be as broad based as possible (e.g., community, university, college, department, program). Involvement of individuals from these multiple levels ensures a broad base of commitment to such efforts, allows for a channeling of limited resources and energy into this area, begins to identify individuals who can serve as research and clinical mentors, and identifies training opportunities outside and inside the institution as placements sites for working with ethnic populations (LaFromboise & Foster, 1992).

Efforts to recruit and retain ethnic faculty and graduate students need to continue (American Psychological Association, 1997; Bernal & Castro, 1994; Blount, Frank, & Calhoun, 1992; Iijima Hall, 1997; Jenkins, 1992; Myers, Taylor, & Davila, 1992; Puente et al., 1993; Ricardo & Holden, 1994; Ridley, 1985). Such efforts are required at various levels within the university (Olmedo, 1990). Continued pressure from outside the university through professional organizations such as the APA Committee on Accreditation (Aponte, 1992), through funding sources (such as National Institute of Mental Health), and through state laws and licensing and certification boards also needs to occur. Recruitment of ethnic students needs to assume a long-term perspective with students being encouraged and supported to enter psychology as early as elementary and middle school (Jenkins, 1992; Turnbull, 1986).

Even if the recruitment and promotion of ethnic faculty are reasonably successful, there will not be enough ethnic faculty and service providers to meet the needs of ethnic populations (Aponte & Clifford, 1995; Myers, 1992). The knowledge and skills of all faculty and practitioners will need to be enhanced in order to meet these training and service needs. To accomplish this task it will be necessary to build in "a system of rewards and incentives" in order to encourage faculty to improve their cross-cultural knowledge and skills (Ridley, 1985). Such efforts could take the form of departments paying for continuing education courses and workshops, or bringing in expert consultants to provide inservice training for the faculty.

Departments and training programs need to develop a comprehensive and coherent plan for educating and training students to become "culturally proficient" to work with ethnic populations (Bernal & Castro, 1994). Such training involves a number of elements, including a set of attitudes that value diverse cultures. Programs need to embrace the concept of *affirmative diversity,* i.e., affirming the value of human diversity (Jones, 1990). In addition, training needs to incorporate ethnic content that directly relates to the basic clinical skills taught in all programs, and to the coordination of ethnically relevant didactic and practicum experiences (LaFromboise & Foster, 1992). Mechanisms also need to be established for increasing and incorporating research findings and new knowledge on ethnic groups into programs (Iijima Hall, 1997; Wong, Kim, Lim, & Morishima, 1983).

Training all students to be "culturally proficient" calls for a required series of courses and training experiences. Although there can be a number of ways through which this can be achieved, one effective way is through use of the integration approach (Chunn, Dunston, & Ross-Sheriff, 1983; Copeland, 1982; LaFromboise & Foster, 1992; Ridley, 1985). Such an approach involves integrating cultural content in every course in the department. Another way to train students is to have a multicultural specialty area. Both strategies involve all faculty, bridge theory, research, and practice, and incorporate intellectual and experiential components into the training. Achieving such a goal cannot be realized without educating and training existing faculty and supervisors on ethnic issues.

Departments of psychology need to periodically review their ethnic training goals and objectives (Ridley, 1985). Such a process should include an assessment of barriers impeding progress toward those goals and objectives. The evaluation can be carried out by governance groups or relevant committees (e.g., ethnic committee, curriculum committee) within the department. Once obstacles are identified, action should be taken to change the situation. The evaluation can also be competency based. A number of writers have addressed the specific competencies required to work with ethnic populations (Arrendondo et al., 1996; LaFromboise, Coleman, & Hernandez, 1991; Pope-Davis & Dings, 1995; Pope-Davis & Coleman, 1997; Sue et al., 1998).

The changes that have occurred in the field to date have been limited, and the importance of taking a broad and long-term perspective in educating and training psychologists to work with ethnic populations has been underscored in this chapter. Such a perspective involves changing beliefs, attitudes, and behaviors at multiple levels; increasing the number of ethnic faculty and students; and changing and developing curriculum that allows ethnic content to be embedded in the theoretical, research and practice components of training programs. The task may appear formidable; nevertheless, the profession needs to accelerate its efforts if it is to train culturally competent psychologists to meet the needs of ethnic populations in the twenty-first century.

REFERENCES

Altman, J. (1987). Centripetal and centrifugal trends in psychology, *American Psychologist, 42,* 1058–1069.

American Psychological Association. (1982). *Survey of graduate departments of psychology.* Washington, DC: Author.

American Psychological Association. (1987). Resolutions approved by the National Conference on Graduate Education in Psychology. *American Psychologist, 42,* 1070–1084.

American Psychological Association. (1993). Guidelines for providers of psychological services to ethnic, linguistic, and culturally diverse populations. *American Psychologist, 48,* 45–48.

American Psychological Association. (1995). *Guidelines and principles for accreditation of programs in professional psychology.* Washington, DC: Author.

American Psychological Association. (1997). *The final report: Comission on Ethnic Minority Recruitment, Retention, and Training in Psychology.* Washington, DC: Author.

American Psychological Association. (1998). *APA Research Office draft report of 1998 graduate study in psychology.* Washington, DC. Author.

Anderson, G., Bass, B. A., Munford, P. R., & Wyatt, G. E. (1977). A seminar on the assessment and treatment of Black patients. *Professional Psychology, 8,* 340–348.

Aponte, J. F. (1983). Need assessment: The state of the art and future directions. In R. A. Bell, M. Sundel, J. F.

Aponte, S. A. Murrell, & E. Lin (Eds.), *Assessing human service needs: Concepts, methods, and applications* (pp. 285–302). New York: Human Sciences Press.

Aponte, J. F. (August, 1990). *Mentoring ethnic minority students and faculty: Issues and recommendations.* Paper presented at the Ninety-Eighth Annual Convention of the American Psychological Association, Boston.

Aponte, J. F. (1992). The role of APA accreditation in enhancing cultural diversity in graduate and professional training programs. In S. D. Johnson, Jr., & R. T. Carter (Eds.), *The 1992 Teachers College Winter Roundtable Conference Proceedings: Addressing cultural issues in an organizational context* (pp. 73–90). New York: Columbia University.

Aponte, J. F., & Clifford, J. P. (1993). Incorporating ethnically diverse content and training into predominantly White graduate and professional programs: Dealing with inertia and resistance. In S. D. Johnson, Jr., R. T. Carter, E. I. Sicalides, & T. R. Buckley (Eds.), *The 1993 Teachers College Winter Roundtable Conference Proceedings: Training for cross-cultural competence* (pp. 22–26). New York: Columbia University.

Aponte, J. F., & Clifford, J. (1995). Education and training issues for intervention with ethnic groups. In J. F. Aponte, R. Young Rivers, & J. Wohl (Eds.), *Psychological interventions and cultural diversity* (pp. 283–300). Boston: Allyn and Bacon.

Aponte, J. F., & Crouch, R. T. (1995). The changing ethnic profile of the United States. In J. F. Aponte, R. Young Rivers, & J. Wohl (Eds.), *Psychological interventions and cultural diversity* (pp. 1–18). Boston: Allyn and Bacon.

Arredondo, P., Toporek, R., Brown, S. P., Jones, J., Locke, D.C., Sanchez, J., & Stradler, H. (1996). Operationalization of the multicultural counseling competencies. *Journal of Multicultural Counseling and Development, 24*, 42–78.

Astin, A. (1982). *Minorities in American higher education.* San Francisco: Jossey-Bass.

Atkinson, D. R., Morten, G., & Sue, D. W. (1998). *Counseling American minorities* (5th ed.). Boston: McGraw-Hill.

Atkinson, D. R., Neville, H., & Casas, A. (1991). The mentorship of ethnic minorities in professional psychology. *Professional Psychology: Research and Practice, 22*, 336–338.

Barbarin, O. A. (1984). Racial themes in psychotherapy with Blacks: Effects of training in the attitude of Black and White psychiatrists. *American Journal of Social Psychiatry, 4*, 13–20.

Bennett, J. M. (1986). Models of cross-cultural training. *International Journal of Intercultural Relations, 10*, 117–134.

Bennett, M. J. (1986). A developmental approach to training for intercultural sensitivity. *International Journal of Intercultural Relations, 10*, 179–196.

Bernal, G., Bernal, M. E., Martinez, A. C., Olmedo, E. L., & Santisteban, D. (1983). Hispanic mental health curriculum for psychology. In J. C. Chunn II, P. J. Dunston, & F. Ross-Sheriff (Eds.), *Mental health and people of color: Curriculum development and change* (pp. 65–94). Washington, DC: Howard University Press.

Bernal, M., & Castro, F. (1994). Are clinical psychologists prepared for service and research with ethnic minorities? *American Psychologist, 47*, 797–805.

Bernal, M. E. (1990). Ethnic mental health training: Trends and issues. In F. C. Serafica, A. I. Schwebel, R. K. Russell, P. D. Isaac, & L. B. Meyers (Eds.), *Mental health of ethnic minorities* (pp. 249–274). New York: Praeger.

Bernal, M. E., & Padilla, A. M. (1982). Status of minority curricula and training in clinical psychology. *American Psychologist, 37*, 780–787.

Blount, R. L., Frank, N. C., & Calhoun, K. C. (1992). The recruitment and retention of minority students. *The Clinical Psychologist, 45*, 1–3.

Bourg, E. F., Bent, R. J., McHolland, J., & Strickler, G. (1989). Standards and evaluation in the education and training of professional psychologists: The National Council of Schools of Professional Psychology Mission Bay Conference. *American Psychologist, 44*, 66–72.

Boxley, R., & Wagner, N. (1971). Clinical psychology training programs and minority groups: A survey. *Professional Psychology, 2*, 75–81.

Brammer, L., Alcorn, J., Birk, J., Gazda, G., Hurst, J., LaFromboise, T., Newman, R., Osipow, S., Packard, T., Romero, D., & Scott, N. (1988). Organizational and political issues in counseling psychology: Recommendations for change. *The Counseling Psychologist, 16*, 407–422.

Brickey, M. (1998). Making sure internships are preparing interns for tomorrow's jobs. *The APAGS Newsletter, 10*, (4), 10–12.

Brown, S. V. (1988). *Increasing minority faculty: An elusive goal.* Princeton, NJ: Educational Testing Service.

Carter, R. T., & Qureshi, A. (1995). A typology of philosophical assumptions in multicultural counseling and training. In J. G. Ponterotto, J. M. Casas, L. A. Suzuki, & C. M. Alexander (Eds.), *Handbook of multicultural counseling* (pp. 239–262). Thousand Oaks, CA: Sage.

Casas, J. M. (1985). The status of racial- and ethnic-minority counseling. A training perspective. In P. Pederson (Ed.), *Handbook of cross cultural counseling and therapy* (pp. 267–273). Westport, CT: Greenwood Press.

Chunn, J., Dunston, P., & Ross-Sheriff, F. (1983). *Mental health and people color: Curriculum development and change.* Washington, DC: Howard University Press.

Collins, F. L., Jr., Green, V., & Chaney, J. M. (1992). Clinical psychology training for American Indians. *The Clinical Psychologist, 45*, 35–44.

Copeland, E. J. (1982). Minority populations and traditional counseling programs: Some alternatives. *Counselor Education and Supervision, 21*, 187–193.

Diaz, E. (1990). Barriers to minorities in the field of psychology and strategies for change. In G. Stricker, E. Davis-Russell, E. Bourg, E. Duran, W. R. Hammond, J. McHolland, K. Polite, & B. E. Vaughn (Eds.), *Toward ethnic diversification in psychology education and training* (pp. 77–88). Washington, DC: American Psychological Association.

Dong, T., Wong, H., Callao, M., Nishihara, A., & Chin, R. (1978). National Asian American Psychology Training Conference. *American Psychologist, 33*, 691–692.

Evans, D. A. (1985). Psychotherapy and Black patients: Problems of training, trainees, and trainers. *Psychotherapy: Theory, Research and Practice, 22*, 457–460.

Gary, L. E., & Weaver, G. D. (Eds.). (1991). *A multidisciplinary national conference on clinical training for services to mentally ill ethnic minorities. Proceedings.*

Washington, DC: Howard University, Institute for Urban Affairs and Research.

Green, L. (1981). Training psychologists to work with minority clients: A prototype model with Black clients. *Professional Psychology, 12,* 732–739.

Guzman, L. P., & Messenger, L. C. (1991). *Recruitment and retention of ethnic minority students and faculty: A survey of doctoral programs in psychology.* Washington, DC: American Psychological Association.

Hammond, W. R., & Yung, B. (1993). Minority student recruitment and retention practices among schools of professional psychology: A national survey and analysis. *Professional Psychology: Research and Practice, 24,* 3–12.

Howard, A., Pion, G. M., Gottfredson, G. D., Flattau, P. E., Oskamp, S., Pfaffin, S. M., Bray, D. W., & Burnstein, A. G. (1986). The changing face of American psychology: A report from the Committee on Employment and Human Resources. *American Psychologist, 41,* 1311–1327.

Hunt, P. L. (1987). Black clients: Implications for supervision of trainees. *Psychotherapy, 24,* 114–119.

Iijima Hall, C. C. (1997). Cultural malpractice: The growing obsolescence of psychology with the changing U.S. population. *American Psychologist, 52,* 642–651.

Jenkins, J. O. (1992). The recruitment of Black students at psychology departments of predominantly White institutions of higher education. *The Clinical Psychologist, 45,* 45–49.

Johnson, S. D., Jr. (1987). Knowing that versus knowing how: Toward achieving expertise through multicultural training and counseling. *The Counseling Psychologist, 15,* 320–331.

Jones, J. M. (1985). The sociopolitical context of clinical training in psychology: The ethnic minority case. *Psychotherapy: Theory, Research, and Practice, 22,* 453–456.

Jones, J. M. (1990). Invitational address: Who is training our ethnic minority psychologists, and are they doing it right? In G. Stricker, E. Davis-Russel, E. Bourg, E. Duran, W. R. Hammond, J. McHolland, K. Polite, & B. E. Vaughn (Eds.), *Toward ethnic diversification in psychology education and training* (pp. 17–34). Washington, DC: American Psychological Association.

Jones, J. M., Goertz, M. E., & Kuh, C. V. (Eds.). (1992). *Minorities in graduate education: Pipeline policy and practice.* Princeton, NJ: Education Testing Service.

LaFromboise, T. D., Coleman, H. L. K., & Hernandez, A. (1991). Development and factor structure of the Cross-Cultural Counseling Inventory-Revised. *Professional Psychology Research and Practice, 22,* 380–388.

LaFromboise, T. D., & Foster, S. L. (1992). Cross-cultural training: Scientist-practitioner model and methods. *The Counseling Psychologist, 20,* 472–489.

Lichtenberg, J. W., Hummel, T. J., & Shaffer, W. F. (1984). Client 1: A computer simulation for use in counselor education and research. *Counselor Education and Supervision, 24,* 155–167.

López, S. R., Grover, K. P., Holland, D., Johnson, M. J., Kain, C. D., Kanel, K., Mellins, L. A., & Rhyne, M. C. (1989). Development of culturally sensitive psychotherapists. *Professional Psychology: Research and Practice, 20,* 369–376.

McDavis, R. J., & Parker, M. (1977). A course on counseling ethnic minorities: A model. *Counselor Education and Supervision, 17,* 146–149.

McGovern, T. (Ed.). (1993). *Handbook for enhancing undergraduate education in psychology.* Washington, DC: American Psychological Association.

Merta, R. J., Stringham, E. M., & Ponterotto, J. G. (1988). Simulating cultural shock in counselor trainees: An experiential exercise for cross-cultural training. *Journal of Counseling and Development, 66,* 242–245.

Mio, J. S., & Morris, D. R. (1990). Cross-cultural issues in psychology training programs: An invitation for discussion. *Professional Psychology: Research and Practice, 21,* 434–441.

Myers, H. F. (1992). Overview and historical perspectives on ethnic minority clinical training in psychology. *The Clinical Psychologist, 45,* 5–12.

Myers, H. F., Taylor, S., & Davila, J. (1992). The recruitment and training of ethnic minority clinical psychologists in a multicultural context: The UCLA program. *The Clinical Psychologist, 45,* 23–33.

Myers, H. F., Wohlford, P., Guzman, L. P., & Echemendia, R. J. (Eds.). (1991). *Ethnic minority perspectives on clinical training and services in psychology.* Washington, DC: American Psychological Association.

Olmedo, E. L. (1990). Minority faculty development: Issues in retention and promotion. In G. Stricker, E. Davis-Russell, E. Bourg, E. Duran, E. R. Hammond, J. McHolland, K. Polite, & B. E. Vaughn (Eds.), *Toward ethnic diversification in psychology education and training* (pp. 95–104). Washington, DC: American Psychological Association.

Parker, W. M., Bingham, R. P., & Fukuyama, M. (1985). Improving cross-cultural effectiveness of counselor trainees. *Counselor Education and Supervision, 24,* 349–352.

Payne, C. (1984). Multicultural education and racism in American schools. *Theory into Practice, 23,* 124–131.

Pedersen, P. (1978). Four dimensions of cross cultural skill in counselor training. *The Personnel and Guidance Journal, 56,* 480–484.

Peterson, R. I., McHolland, J. D., Bent, R. J., Davis-Russel, E., Edwall, G. E., Polite, K., Singer, D. L., & Stricker, G. (Eds.). (1992). *The core curriculum in professional psychology.* Washington, DC: American Psychological Association.

Pion, G. M., Bramblett, J. P., Jr., & Wicherski, M. (1987). *Graduate departments of psychology 1986–87: Report of the annual APA/COGDOP department survey.* Washington, DC: American Psychological Association, Office of Demographic, Employment, and Educational Research.

Pion, G., Bramblett, P., Wicherski, M., & Stapp, J. (1985). *Summary report of the 1984–85 survey of graduate departments of Psychology.* Washington, DC: American Psychological Association.

Pope-Davis, D. B., & Coleman, H. L. K. (Eds.) (1997). *Multicultural counseling competencies: Assessment, education and training, and supervision.* Thousand Oaks, CA: Sage.

Pope-Davis, D. B., & Dings, J. G. (1995). The assessment of multicultural counseling competencies. In J. G. Ponterotto, J. M. Casas, L. A. Suzuki, & C. M. Alexander (Eds.), *Handbook of multicultural counseling* (pp. 287–311). Thousand Oaks, CA: Sage.

Puente, A. E., Blanch, E., Canoland, D. K., Denmark, F. L., Laman, C., Lutsky, N., Reid, P. T., & Schiayo, R. S. (1993). Toward a psychology of variance: Increasing the presence and understanding of ethnic minorities in psychology. In T. V. McGovern (Ed.), *Handbook for enhancing undergraduate psychology* (pp. 71–92). Washington, DC: American Psychological Association.

Reynolds, A. L. (1995). Challenges and strategies for teaching multicultural counseling courses. In J. G. Ponterotto, J. M. Casas, L. A. Suzuki, & C. M. Alexander (Eds.), *Handbook of multicultural counseling* (pp. 312–330). Thousand Oaks, CA: Sage.

Ricardo, I. B., & Holden, E. W. (1994). Multicultural training in pediatric and clinical child psychology predoctoral internship programs. *Journal of Clinical Child Psychology, 23,* 32–39.

Rice, C. E. (1997). The scientist-practitioner split and the future of psychology. *American Psychologist, 57,* 1173–1181.

Ridley, C. R. (1985). Imperatives for ethnic and cultural relevance in psychology training programs. *Professional Psychology: Research and Practice, 16,* 611–622.

Ridley, C. R. (1995). *Overcoming unintentional racism in counseling and therapy: A practitioner's guide to intentional intervention.* Thousand Oaks, CA: Sage.

Ridley, C. R., Espelage, D. L., & Rubinstein, K. J. (1997). Course development in multicultural counseling. In D. B. Pope-Davis & H. L. K. Coleman (Eds.), *Multicultural counseling competencies: Assessment, education and training, and supervision* (pp. 131–158). Thousand Oaks, CA: Sage.

Sabnani, H. B., Ponterotto, J. G., & Borodovsky, L. G. (1991). White racial identity development and cross-cultural counselor training: A stage model. *The Counseling Psychologist, 19,* 76–102.

Sleek, S. (1998). Psychology's cultural competence, once "simplistic," now broadening. *APA Monitor, 29,* (12), 1, 27.

Spence, J. T. (1987). Centrifugal versus centripetal tendencies in psychology: Will the center hold? *American Psychologist, 42,* 1052–1054.

Stapp, J., Tucker, A. M., & VandenBos, G. R. (1985). Census of psychological personnel: 1983. *American Psychologist, 40,* 1317–1351.

Stricker, G., Davis-Russell, E., Bourg, E., Duran, E., Hammond, W. R., McHolland, J., Polite, K., & Vaughn, B. E. (Eds.). (1990). *Toward ethnic diversification in psychology and training.* Washington, DC: American Psychological Association.

Strickland, B. R. (1987). On the threshold of the second century of psychology. *American Psychologist, 42,* 1055–1056.

Sue, D. W., Carter, R. T., Casas, J. M., Fovad, N. A., Ivey, A. E., Jensen, M., LaFromboise, T., Manese, J. E., Ponterotto, J. G., & Vazquez-Nutall (1998). *Multicultural counseling competencies: Individual and organizational development.* Thousand Oaks, CA: Sage.

Thurgood, D. H., & Weinman, J. M. (1990). *Summary report, 1989; Doctorate recipients from United States universities.* Washington, DC: National Academy Press.

Tomes, H. (1998). Diversity: Psychology's life depends upon it. *APA Monitor, 29,* (12), 28.

Trubisky, P. (1999). NIMH restructures behavioral research to stimulate new science. *Psychological Science Agenda, 12,* 1–2.

Turnbull, W. W. (1986). Involvement: The key to retention. *Journal of Developmental Education, 10,* 6–11.

U.S. Bureau of Census (1996). *Current population reports, Population projections of the United States by age, sex, race, and Hispanic origin: 1992–2050.* P25-1130. Washington, DC: U.S. Government Printing Office.

Wicherski, M., & Kohout, J. (1992). *1990–91 Characteristics of graduate departments of psychology.* Washington, DC: American Psychological Association.

Williams, S., & Halgin, R. P. (1995). Issues in psychotherapy supervision between the White supervisor and the Black supervisee. *The Clinical supervisor, 13,* 39–61.

Wong, H. Z., Kim, L. T., Lim, D. T., & Morishima, J. K. (1983). The training of psychologists for Asian and Pacific American Communities. In J. C. Chunn II, P. J. Dunston, & F. Ross-Sheriff (Eds.), *Mental health and people of color* (pp. 23–41). Washington, DC: Howard University Press.

Wyatt, G. E., & Parham, W. D. (1985). The inclusion of culturally sensitive course materials in graduate school and training programs. *Psychotherapy: Theory, Research, and Practice, 22,* 461–468.

16 Ethnicity and Supervision: Models, Methods, Processes, and Issues

JOSEPH F. APONTE

LAURA R. JOHNSON

As the number of ethnic persons continues to grow in the United States there will be an increasing need for diversified mental health services (see Chapter 1). Mental health service providers will find themselves working with an increasing number of ethnic clients, and training programs will need to educate and train more practitioners to work with these clients (Aponte & Clifford, 1995; see Chapter 15). Supervisors will find themselves supervising more supervisees who will be working with clients from different cultures. It is imperative that supervisors be equipped to provide competent supervision to these supervisees in order to meet the needs of this growing population.

The importance of ethnicity in supervision is further underscored by recent professional and ethical requirements for providing competent services to diverse clients (American Psychological Association, 1992, 1993; Arredondo et al., 1996; Iijima Hall, 1997, Pope-Davis & Coleman, 1997; Sue et al., 1998; Sue, Arredondo, & McDavis, 1992). In addition, the most recent revision of the criteria for accreditation by the American Psychological Association requires that "the program has made systematic, coherent, and long-term efforts to attract and retain students and faculty from differing ethnic, racial, and personal backgrounds into the program" (American Psychological Association, 1995, p. 9). The role of ethnicity in the supervisory process will thus become more important in the twenty-first century as efforts are made to recruit and retain more culturally diverse students.

In order to understand the nature and role of ethnicity in the supervisory process it is important to recognize that supervision is a complicated, dynamic process, involving simultaneous interactions between the supervisee and supervisor, and between the supervisee and client. Both the experience of being an ethnic person and the context of the supervision are important elements that can influence the content, process, and outcome of supervision (Aponte, 1986; Aponte & Lyons, 1980; Leong & Wagner, 1994). Either the supervisor, supervisee, or client can be an ethnic person. The supervisory process takes place in either an academic setting or clinical setting and can therefore be influenced by the structure, perspectives, and values of those programs and settings (Ruskin, 1996). The quality of psychological services delivered to clients can also be affected by supervision.

This chapter will begin by reviewing a variety of supervisory models that provide structure for and influence the process through which supervision is provided. The potential impact of racial/ethnic identity on the supervisory relationship will next be discussed, since the supervisory relationship is such a critical element in the supervisory process. Variations in racial/ethnic identity among the supervisor, supervisee, and client can affect the supervisory relationship and process. Following that, supervisory interventions, including methods, forms, and techniques through which the supervision is carried out will be reviewed. Finally, guidelines for enhancing the supervisory relationship and for providing more effective cross-cultural supervision will be discussed.

Supervisory Models

Bernard and Goodyear (1998) organize models and theories of supervision into four broad categories: (1) psychotherapy-based theories, (2) developmental models, (3) social role models, and (4) eclectic and integrationist models. Each of these models operates under different assumptions, directs the supervisory process into different paths by emphasizing different psychological processes, and places varying degrees of importance on the supervisor-supervisee and supervisee-client relationships. The nature and degree of focus on these relationships is of particular importance when the supervisor, supervisee, and/or client is an ethnic person.

Psychotherapy-Based Supervision

According to Bernard and Goodyear (1998) these models are a direct extension of psychotherapy theories. Included in these models are psychoanalytic supervision (Dewald, 1997); psychodynamic supervision (Jacobs, David, & Meyer, 1995; Teitelbaum, 1995); person-centered supervision (Patterson, 1997; Rice, 1980); cognitive-behavior supervision (Bradley, 1989; Friedberg & Taylor, 1994; Padesky, 1996; Perris, 1994); and systemic supervision (Liddle, Becker, & Diamond, 1997). Within each of these approaches, the principles and strategies inherent in each theory are brought into the supervisory process. For example, psychodynamic supervision involves extending the *working alliance* model (Bordin, 1979; 1983) and all of its ramifications into the supervisor-supervisee working relationship (Bernard & Goodyear, 1998).

Developmental Models

Chagnon and Russel (1995) note that developmental conceptions of supervision assume that supervisees move through a series of prescribed developmental stages in becoming competent practitioners, and that each stage requires a different supervisor focus in order for the supervisee to have a successful supervisory experience. Developmental models can be found in the literature for supervisors as well as for supervisees. Differences in supervisor roles, activities, domains, supervisor–supervisee dynamics, and learning environments can be found in developmental models (Littrell, Lee-Bordin, & Lorenz, 1979; Loganbill, Hardy, & Delworth, 1982; Stoltenberg, McNeil, & Delworth, 1997).

Social Role Models

A number of social role models are identified by Bernard and Goodyear (1998). Among these are the models of Bernard (1979), Carroll (1996), Holloway (1995), and Williams (1995). These models identify a number of roles that supervisors engage in, including administrator, advisor, counselor, consultant, evaluator, facilitator, and teacher. The roles most common to these models are those of teacher, counselor, and consultant. Within each of these roles the specific tasks required of the supervisor are identified in detail. The particular role utilized by the supervisor during supervision depends upon the needs of the supervisee.

Eclectic and Integrationist Models

Eclectic approaches involve selecting components of other supervisory models and applying them to one's supervisory approach, while integrationist models create a new approach by blending components from other supervisory models (Bernard & Goodyear, 1998). Such efforts usually involve considering the developmental level, cognitive style, and therapeutic skills of the supervisee and customizing the supervision to meet the supervisee's needs. Other components of these approaches include constructing explicit contracts, operating within a coherent framework, and systematically evaluating the outcomes of supervision (Norcross & Halgin, 1997; Skovholt & Ronnestad, 1992).

Psychotherapy treatment models have been criticized by a number of scholars for their Eurocentric perspective (Aponte, Young Rivers, & Wohl, 1995; Atkinson, Morten, & Sue, 1998; Dana, 1998; Ivey, Simek-Morgan, & Ivey, 1997). Among these criticisms has been a focus on: (1) the individual, (2) verbal and emotional openness, (3) employing a linear approach to problem definition and solution, and (4) making a distinction between physical and mental functioning (Aponte & Barnes, 1995). Those supervision models that are direct extensions of psychotherapy models—or as in the social role models—have a therapy or counselor component as part of the supervisory process, are subject to the same criticisms raised in using these models to treat ethnic clients.

The assumptions, values, and approaches of other supervision models also have to be questioned. Developmental, social role, and eclectic and integrationist models have been developed primarily from working with and observing mainstream supervisors, supervisees, and clients and also have Eurocentric perspectives embedded in them. The appropriateness and effectiveness of applying these models to supervisory situations in which the supervisor, supervisee, and/or client is a non-European ethnic person have yet to be demonstrated. There is also a paucity of supervisory models that involve cross-cultural supervision as an integral part of their conceptualizations (Martínez & Holloway, 1997).

Some existing models have been extended to include cultural factors, whereas others have included it as one component of the model. For example, several developmental models can be found in the literature that have been extended to address cultural issues.

Vasquez and McKinley (1982) expanded upon the Loganbill et al. (1982) developmental model to include ethnicity and supervisees' multicultural identity. Carney and Kahn (1984) also identified a developmental supervisory process for acquiring cross-cultural competencies. Holloway (1995), on the other hand, has built into her Systems Approach to Supervision (SAS) "cultural characteristics" as one of the contextual factors to address in the supervisor and supervisee. These "cultural characteristics" are only one of many factors considered in the very complex SAS model.

Supervisory Relationship

The importance of the supervisory relationship has been recognized by a number of scholars and practitioners (Bernard & Goodyear, 1998; Holloway, 1995; Watkins, 1997). The supervisory relationship presents a number of additional challenges when either the supervisor or supervisee is culturally or ethnically different (Fong & Lease, 1997; Martínez & Holloway, 1997; McRae & Johnson, 1991). A number of relationship issues have been noted as being particularly salient in cross-cultural supervision by Fong and Lease (1997), including: (1) unintentional racism, (2) power dynamics, (3) distrust and vulnerability, and (4) miscommunication. Before discussing these issues, it is useful to examine the role of racial/ethnic identity of the supervisor and supervisee.

Nature and Impact of "White" Identity

Social knowledge and self-awareness are considered especially critical for Whites working with ethnic populations. Knowledge of one's own racial/ethnic identity status is a key component in counselor self-awareness and is considered to be a "prerequisite" for cultural competence in counseling (Richardson & Molinaro, 1996). Helms's model of White Racial Identity Development (WRID) is similar to other stage or status racial/ethnic models that have been developed for Blacks and other ethnic groups (see Chapter 2). Helms (1990, 1995) describes the racial identity development of White people as that of recognizing the privileged status of their own racial group, the abandonment of a sense of entitlement, and the development of a new, nonracist identity.

The WRID model (Helms, 1995; Helms & Carter, 1990) includes the following categories: (1) *Contact*—avoidance or denial of the implications of racial group membership; (2) *Disintegration*—strategies for dealing with racial material become inadequate, resulting in confusion and suppression of anxiety-provoking material; (3) *Reintegration*—the struggles at stage two are resolved with "choosing" one's own socioracial group, intolerance for other groups; (4) *Pseudo-Independence*—intellectualized acceptance and tolerance for others; (5) *Immersion/Emersion*—a sincere examination of the benefits of being White and a search for meaning, consideration of one's role in an inequitable system and trying to change it; and (6) *Autonomy*—capacity to relinquish privileges of racism, flexible and internalized standards of conduct.

WRID has been related to self-reported multicultural competency (Ottavi, Pope-Davis, & Dinges, 1994), reactions to interracial situations in the workplace (Block, Roberson, & Neuger, 1995), and racist attitudes (Pope-Davis & Ottavi, 1992). However, some question the stages of Helms's model and argue that it may reflect only one underlying construct, namely racism (Rowe, Behrens, & Leach, 1995). It has also been suggested that WRID may be relevant only when the context includes non-Whites, and that it is not really about White identity per se, but Whites in relation to non-Whites (Rowe, Bennett, & Atkinson, 1994). Rowe and his colleagues (1994, 1995) caution against the blind acceptance of the WRID model and have suggested an alternative paradigm of White racial consciousness that infers neither a developmental sequence nor the existence of a (hypothetical) White identity. Regardless of the problems associated with describing and measuring "White identity," the construct could provide a useful framework for examining majority attitudes regarding culture/race.

People of Color Racial Identity Model (PCRI)

As noted in Chapter 2 of this book, Helms's PCRI model describes five stages that all people of color go through as they come to understand themselves in relation to their own ethnic group, other ethnic groups, and the majority culture. These stages or "statuses" as referred to by Helms (1995) consist of the *Conformity* (Pre-Encounter) status, *Dissonance (Encounter)* status, *Immersion/Emersion* status, *Internalization* status, and *Integrative Awareness* status. People of color are generally viewed as going through these increasing levels of awareness in a linear fashion; however, these statuses are seen as permeable and flexible and a person may simultaneously have attitudes associated with more than one status at any given time (Helms, 1995).

A supervisor, supervisee, or client, for example, at the *Conformity* stage would be characterized as devaluing his or her own ethnic/racial group and aligning with White values, standards, and practices. On the other hand, an individual at the *Immersion/Emersion* stage would have a positive commitment to his or her own racial/ethnic group and have a depreciating view toward Whites. A balance is achieved at the *Integrative Awareness* stage, where the person exhibits flexible and complex thinking and comes to value the many aspects of his or her racial/ethnic identity (Helms, 1990; 1995).

Racial/Ethnic Identity Interactions

Helms (1990, 1995) suggests that it is not racial or ethnic group membership per se, but one's racial/ethnic identity that will influence the tone and quality of interpersonal exchanges. As such, she has proposed a model for examining how different combinations of racial/ethnic identity attitudes will interact to impact interpersonal exchanges, and that these exchanges will be harmonious or disharmonious based on individuals' expressed racial identities (Helms, 1990, 1995). Helms classified different types of relationships based on various combinations of racial/ethnic identity statuses. The hypothesized impact on the relationship is similar whether the pair is ethnically mixed (a person of color and a White) or similar (two persons of color or two Whites).

Four types of relationships between the counselor and client based on racial/ethnic statuses have been identified by Helms (1990; 1995). These include: (1) *Parallel*—individuals are governed by the same or analogous racial identity statuses; (2) *Crossed*—individuals are influenced by directly opposing racial identity statuses; (3) *Regressive*—the person with greater social power (therapist) holds racial identity attitudes at a less sophisticated stage than the person with less social power (client); and (4) *Progressive*—the person with greater social power (therapist) responds from a more sophisticated racial identity status in the interaction pattern (Helms, 1990; 1995). These four types of relationships can exist with White, people of color, and mixed counselor–client dyads.

Helms (1990) systematically reviews the common affective issues, counselor strategies, and counseling outcomes for each of the four types of counseling relationships based on racial identity statuses. For example, *Parallel* interactions for a mixed dyad with the counselor being at the *Preencounter (Conformity)* stage of racial/ethnic identity development and the client being at the *Reintegration* stage would be characterized by mutual anxiety, the client's testing the relationship, and the counselor's being unassertive and task oriented. The relationship would continue with stereotypes being reinforced and little symptom relief occurring (Helms, 1990). So far, Helms's interactional model has not been adequately examined. Only a few empirical studies can be found in the literature.

Racial/Ethnic Identity Interactions in Supervision

Most discussions of Helms's model have focused on the interactions between the counselor and client, although her intent was to apply the model more broadly to other interpersonal interactions. Whether supervisors address racial identity and/or other cultural factors in supervision, how they address them, and to what extent they are addressed are important questions to be answered. According to Helms's interaction model, decisions about the relative importance of racial/ethnic and cultural issues in therapy and supervision will likely reflect the supervisor's own awareness of and attitudes toward these issues.

Cook (1994) extended Helms's interaction model to the supervisory process by describing how racial identity attitudes of the supervisor and supervisees can impact: (1) expectations of supervision; (2) the tone and quality of the supervisory relationship; (3) the content of what is discussed, emphasized, or downplayed in supervision; (4) how cases are conceptualized; (5) treatment planning; and (6) evaluation of supervisees. Cook (1994) describes various racial identity statuses of supervisors and supervisees, and their corresponding potential approaches to racial issues (PARI) in supervision. Table 16.1 provides a summary of the ways that these racial issues may be addressed or avoided in supervision using Helms's People of Color (POC) and White Racial Identity Development (WRID) models (Cook, 1994; Helms, 1990, 1995).

Table 16.1 depicts situations in which there can be a mixed dyad (either the supervisor or supervisee can be a person of color or White) or similar dyads (both the supervisor and supervisee are White or both are people of color). It is possible to examine racial/ethnic identity statuses for supervisors and supervisees that are *Parallel* or *Crossed* (Cook, 1994) just as Helms examined the interaction patterns of counselors and clients (Helms, 1990; 1995). The racial issues and responses to racism in Table 16.1 will be similar for those same supervisor–supervisee dyads at the same stage of racial/ethnic identity development.

As can be seen in Table 16.1 a number of supervisor/supervisee interaction patterns can emerge. When the supervisor and supervisee have similar racial/ethnic identity statuses they are considered to be in a *Parallel* relationship, whereas supervisee/supervisor dyads reflecting opposing racial identity attitudes are considered to be in a *Crossed*

TABLE 16.1   Potential Approaches to Racial Issues in Supervision Based on Helms's Racial/ Ethnic Identity Developmental Models.

People of Color Status	White Racial Identity Development Status	Potential Approaches to Racial Issues
Conformity	Contact	Will likely ignore issues of race and adopt a "color-blind" approach, which is generalized to all individuals.
Dissonance	Disintegration	Acknowledge the race of client only, while ignoring their own race and that of supervisee. Client's race acknowledged superficially (e.g., as a demographic or descriptive characteristic).
Immersion/Emersion	Reintegration	Race is a salient factor. Cultural values and standards of own race are lenses through which behavior of supervisor, therapist, and client is judged to be "normal" or "effective."
	Pseudo-Independence	Discuss racial issues or differences only if they are interacting with POC. Recognize cultural biases of theories or inappropriateness of a particular method, however, they lack a knowledge of how to adapt theories and practices to POC.
	Immersion/Emersion	Acknowledge race, racial attitudes, and cultural assumptions and biases of supervisor, supervisee, and client. Consider implications of race in therapy and supervision.
Internalization	Autonomy	Integrate personal, therapeutic, and supervision values into a cohesive professional identity. Race, cultural, and sociopolitical influences acknowledged and discussed, as are conflicts in the supervisory and/or therapeutic relationships.
Integrative Awareness		Exhibit knowledge of, and appreciation for, various aspects of supervisor, supervisee, and client identity. Cultural biases addressed and culturally sensitive approaches used in both supervision and therapy. Serve as advocates for oppressed people in their interactions with institutions, agencies, and training program.

Source: Cook, D. A. (1994). Racial identity in supervision. *Counselor Education and Supervision, 34,* 132–141.

relationship. *Parallel* relationships, at the earliest stages of racial/ethnic identity, may be characterized by denial and avoidance of racial issues or of negative affect associated with racial issues. Stereotypes are likely to be reinforced and, if racial issues are brought up, they will be abandoned without resolution (Cook, 1994; Helms, 1990).

A *Crossed* relationship consists of directly opposed identity statuses. For example, a person of color with dominant *Immersion/Emersion* attitudes, and a White person with dominant *Reintegration* attitudes would be constantly "at odds" with one another. Because these stages are associated with a high degree of race saliency, it is likely that many conflicts would be interpreted as racial in nature. Both supervisor and supervisee may feel angry and resentful. They could become argumentative or avoid active involvement in the supervisory process. Other relationships with "mixed" levels of identity development could be helpful (*Progressive*) or unhelpful (*Regressive*), depending on whether the person with more power (in this case the supervisor) is drawing from a more sophisticated racial identity status than the person of lesser power (the supervisee).

Ideally, the supervisor will be operating from a racial identity status that is at least as sophisticated as the supervisee's, if not more so. If this is the case, a supervisor can facilitate the incorporation of issues related to race, ethnicity, and culture into supervision and therapy. Additionally, in a *Progressive* relationship, the supervisor can help the supervisee enhance his or her racial identity development in a supportive and nonthreatening atmosphere. If, on the other hand, the supervisor is operating from a less developed racial identity status, then the quality of supervision is likely to suffer and the supervisee will feel frustrated.

Looking at the racial identity attitudes of faculty and students, Pope-Davis, Menefee, and Ottavi (1993) found that faculty had more *Pseudo-Independent* and *Autonomous* attitudes, whereas students had more *Contact, Disintegration* and *Reintegration* attitudes. However, as Fukayama (1994) notes, in some cases, students or interns may in fact have more knowledge and/or experience in relating to culturally different persons generally or to a particular ethnic group than the supervisor. At the same time, they have less general therapeutic knowledge and fewer skills than the supervisor. Such differences between the supervisee and supervisor can be awkward at best, and confusing and conflicting at worst. Without the supervisor's guidance on how to incorporate cultural factors into their conceptualization of a case, a supervisee's efforts to effectively treat an ethnic client will be hampered.

Relationship Issues in Cross-Cultural Supervision

The complexity of the supervisory relationship has been underscored in the previous sections of this chapter. Cross-cultural supervision requires an examination of both White and racial/ethnic identity development (Cook, 1994; D'Andrea & Daniels, 1997; Fong & Lease, 1997; Martínez & Holloway, 1997). The different racial/ethnic identity combinations will strongly influence how race, ethnicity, and cultural differences are acknowledged, discussed, and integrated into the supervisory process and therapeutic work with clients. Different identity combinations should also impact the quality of the supervisor–supervisee working relationship. Ladany, Brittan-Powell, and Pannu (1997) found that the strongest alliances were found for *Parallel* relationships at the higher identity statuses. This was followed by *Progressive* relationships, *Parallel* relationships at lower identity statuses, and finally *Regressive* relationships with the weakest alliance of all.

One of the key issues that Fong and Lease (1997) discuss in cross-cultural supervision is that of "unintentional racism." Ridley (1995) provides an extensive discussion of this topic in his book *Overcoming Unintentional Racism in Counseling and Therapy,* in which he notes that unintentional racism can take the form of color blindness, color consciousness, cultural transference, cultural countertransference, pseudotransference, overidentification, and identification with the oppressor. Such forms of unintentional racism can readily occur in supervision where the supervisor is White and the supervisee is an ethnic person (Fong & Lease, 1997).

As is evident from the previous discussion on racial/ethnic interactions in supervision, the supervisor/supervisee dyad is not always a White supervisor/ethnic supervisee combination. It is possible for the combination to be ethnic supervisor/White supervisee, ethnic supervisor/ethnic supervisee, or White supervisor/White supervisee. All of these combinations can occur with either a White or an ethnic client. Race and ethnicity will be a salient issue in the supervisory process in any of the above combinations, and the level of racial/ethnic identity development, as previously noted, of the supervisor, supervisee, and client will be a driving force in acknowledging and addressing racism in supervision.

Bernard and Goodyear (1998) have noted the difficulty that supervisors have in addressing cultural and racial issues in supervision. According to Fong and Lease (1997), supervisors at less evolved White identity statuses of *Contact, Disintegration, Reintegration,* and *Pseudo-Independence* would in all likelihood avoid and minimize cultural and racial issues. When these issues are brought up or emerge with an ethnic supervisee or an ethnic client, the issues may lead to the supervisor's experiencing feelings of conflict at the *Disintegration* status, unconsciously expressing negative feelings toward ethnic groups at the *Reintegration* status, and the exclusive focus on cognitive analysis of cultural and racial issues at the *Pseudo-Independence* status.

Power dynamics refers to the ability to control ourselves and others (Fong & Lease, 1997; Ridley, 1995). Power differentials between the supervisor/supervisee and between the therapist/client are inherent in the supervisory and therapeutic process (Bernard & Goodyear, 1998). In the supervisory relationship, the supervisor is viewed as having more therapeutic knowledge and skills than the supervisee and has the responsibility for monitoring and evaluating the performance of the supervisee. Both the supervisor and supervisee are accountable for the appropriate, effective, and efficient delivery of psychological services to the client.

Relationships between ethnic populations and Whites in the United States have been characterized by power differentials. These power differentials take the form of White paternalism, oppression of ethnic populations, and overt and covert forms of racism (Fong & Lease, 1997; Ridley, 1995; see Chapter 2). These experiences and the ethnic person's reactions to them can be brought into the supervisory process. The ethnic supervisee and/or the supervisee's ethnic client may be reluctant to disclose information about themselves, be unwilling to incorporate feedback, and be guarded about looking at themselves (Brown & Landrum-Brown, 1995). Supervisors may not recognize their own contribution to these behaviors or the broader historical and social context in which they occur. As a result, ethnic supervisees may be blamed for being uncooperative, overly sensitive, or defensive.

A number of scholars and researchers in the literature point out the importance of trust in supervision (Cook & Helms, 1988; Fong & Lease, 1997; Bernard & Goodyear, 1998; Ladany & Friedlander, 1995). According to Fong and Lease (1997), trust and vulnerability interact with issues of power in cross-cultural supervision. The learning and evaluative components of supervision put supervisees in a vulnerable position of identifying and sharing their inadequacies with the supervisor, and yet they must trust that these disclosures will not adversely affect their working with clients and their academic progress in their training programs.

An extensive body of literature exists that deals with distrust of Whites by ethnic populations (Atkinson et al., 1998; Nickerson, Helms, & Terrell, 1994; Priest, 1991; Ridley, 1995; see Chapter 2). African American clients, for example, carry a "healthy cultural paranoia" into the therapy process (Jones, 1990). This suspicion or distrust of majority institutions and the people who work for them by African Americans, as well as by other ethnic groups, is a consequence of experiences with racism, oppression, and prejudice. It is not unreasonable to expect this distrust to be initially present between an ethnic supervisee and White supervisor.

The few empirical studies that have investigated interaction patterns between White supervisors and ethnic supervisees have tended to support the importance of trust, although this construct was not always measured directly. VanderKolk (1974) found that Black supervisees expected their supervisors to be less empathetic, respectful, and congruent than did White supervisees. Similarly, Cook and Helms (1988) reported that a combination of supervisor's liking and conditional interest contributed to greater supervisee satisfaction. Hilton, Russel, and Salmi (1995) found that level of supervisor support was related to the supervisees' reporting a more positive and effective supervisory relationship.

Another important relationship issue in cross-cultural supervision that Fong and Lease (1997) discuss is that of communication. The focus of the literature in this area has been primarily on language usage and fluency and on communication styles between therapists and clients (Aponte & Barnes, 1995; Russell, 1998; Sue & Sue, 1990). More recently, attention has turned toward the impact of different communication styles in supervision (Bernard & Goodyear, 1998; Fong & Lease, 1997; Ryan & Hendricks, 1989; Williams & Halgin, 1995). Most of the literature in this area has involved transposing observations and findings from the therapist–client interactions literature to supervisor–supervisee interactions.

Differences in expressed affect, speed of speech, amount of eye contact, and non-verbal behaviors have been noted between African Americans, Hispanics, Asian Americans, American Indians, and Whites (Fong & Lease, 1997; Sue & Sue, 1990; Williams & Halgin, 1995). Both African Americans and Hispanics may use nonstandard English as a reflection of their ethnic pride (Aponte & Barnes, 1995; Russell, 1988; Williams & Halgin, 1995). White supervisors who are not familiar with these different verbal and nonverbal communication styles are not likely to fully understand their supervisees and may misinterpret their communications during supervision.

Supervisory Interventions: Methods, Forms, and Techniques

The importance of the supervisory models and the role of the supervisory relationship in supervision have been noted in previous sections of this chapter. The type of supervisory intervention used during supervision will directly affect the supervisory process in cross-cultural supervision. Intervention methods, forms, and techniques will also interact profoundly with the supervisory relationship to affect the process and outcome of cross-cultural supervision. Issues around using different supervisory interventions will next be discussed.

Supervisory intervention refers to how the supervision is conducted (Bernard & Goodyear, 1998). It includes individual and group supervision methods as well as the use of self-report, process notes, audio- and videotaping, and live observation techniques with these methods. The choice of intervention will be guided by a number of factors including the supervisee's learning goals, experience level, developmental stage, and learning style. The supervisor's learning goals for the supervisee, theoretical orientation, and his or her own learning goals for the supervisory experience will dictate the choice of supervision interventions (Bernard & Goodyear, 1998; Borders & Leddick, 1987).

Individual Supervision

Individual supervision is the most frequently used method, although most supervisees will experience some form of group supervision (Bernard & Goodyear, 1998). Audio- and videotaping, bug-in-the-ear, and live observations are some of the techniques that can be used in individual supervision. A key element that shapes the conduct of supervision is the degree of structure. A great deal of structure is usually imposed on beginning supervisees because of the strong training component in supervision at this level, while less structure is typically used with more experienced supervisees as supervision approaches consultation with these individuals.

Culture and race are salient throughout cross-cultural supervision; however, cultural and racial issues typically increase for beginning therapists in individual supervision regardless of the amount of structure used. Trust of the supervisor may not be initially present for supervisees who are insecure and anxious about their clinical knowledge and skills. The power differential that exists between supervisor and ethnic supervisee is typically accentuated in individual supervision, and supervisees may also want to present themselves as competent to White supervisors. These factors may contribute to ethnic supervisees not being completely forthright in supervision.

Individual supervision may accentuate racial/ethnic identity interactions. An open discussion of cultural and racial issues in supervision can be hampered by the racial/ethnic status of either the supervisor, supervisee, or both. For example, as previously noted in earlier parts of this chapter, cultural and racial issues are not typically discussed at the beginning stages of a *Parallel* relationship where the White supervisor is at the *Contact* status of White Racial Identity Development, and the ethnic supervisee is at the *Conformity* status. Similarly, *Crossed* dyadic relationships in which the supervisor is at a less sophisticated stage of racial/ethnic identity development than the supervisee hinder effective discussion of cultural and racial issues.

Group Supervision

Group supervision is a frequently used method of supervision in academic training programs and internship settings (Bernard & Goodyear, 1998; Prieto, 1996; Riva & Cornish, 1995). It involves regular meetings of a group of supervisees with a designated supervisor for the purpose of reviewing their clinical work with clients. According to Bernard and Goodyear (1998) group supervision affords the opportunity for vicarious learning, exposure to a broad range of clients, greater quantity and diversity of feedback, greater quality of feedback, a more comprehensive picture of the supervisee, and the occurrence of risk taking.

There is little literature on the use of groups in cross-cultural supervision; however, some of the observations on ethnic participants in group treatments are applicable to group supervision. Vasquez and Han (1995) argue that the group is a microcosm of the ethnic person's life outside the group and society at large (also see Chapter 7). They go on to note that power, self-esteem, racial/ethnic identity, and intimacy issues readily emerge for ethnic group participants. It can be argued that similar issues would be present for ethnic supervisors and supervisees in group supervision.

The atmosphere, composition, structure, and focus of the group are important elements in cross-cultural supervision. Creating a climate in the group that is sensitive to and supportive of ethnic supervisees is important (Fong & Lease, 1997). Having several ethnic supervisees in the group can facilitate discussion of cultural and racial issues. It is the responsibility of the supervisor to initiate and direct the nature of such discussions in the group. The presence of several ethnic supervisees in the group with varying levels of experience can lead to the more experienced supervisees serving as role models for the less experienced ones.

Vasquez and Han (1995) see the task of group leaders as promoting trust and safety, building self-esteem by focusing on group members' strengths, empowering group members by encouraging them to assume responsibility for their behaviors, acquiring more effective communication skills, and focusing on social-cultural issues. Carrying out such tasks effectively assumes that a White or ethnic supervisor is at a level of racial/ethnic identity development that is more advanced than that of the supervisees in the group. This may not occur unless supervisors are aware of their own racial/ethnic identity and take steps to foster their own cultural competence.

Guidelines for Cross-Cultural Supervision

As previously noted, the extent to which cultural factors are integrated into supervision will depend on the supervisor's awareness and experiences with these issues. To provide quality supervision with ethnic supervisees and/or for ethnic clients, supervisors will need to have a certain level of awareness of cultural issues. They will also need to engage in a self-assessment and in ongoing efforts to foster their own development and ability to provide cross-cultural supervision. The levels of awareness, knowledge, and skills needed by counselors to provide culturally competent mental health services have been identified (Sue et al., 1992), and more recent efforts have been made toward the operationalization of these competencies into stage-appropriate goals, tasks, and activities (Arredondo, Toporek, Brown, Jones, Locke, Sanchez, & Stadler, 1996). Many of these recommendations, aimed at counselors and therapists, can be appropriately extended to supervisors to ensure the provision of culturally competent supervision. The following guidelines have been derived largely in this manner.

Supervisor Awareness, Self-Assessment, and Development

Supervisors must first be aware that both supervisory and therapeutic processes and outcomes are affected by multiple cultural factors such as worldview, racial/ethnic identity, socioeconomic status, and racism (D'Andrea & Daniels, 1997). All supervisors, regardless of their racial/ethnic backgrounds, should have an awareness of their own cultural backgrounds and of themselves as cultural beings. They must understand that this awareness is essential in providing quality supervision and services to supervisees and clients (Arredondo et al., 1996). Supervisors should attempt to understand how their own cultural backgrounds affect their definitions of normality and mental illness (Arredondo et al., 1996) and how they proceed with both therapeutic and supervisory activities, including their supervisory relationships, approach to supervision, and the techniques they use in supervision (Constantine, 1997; D'Andrea & Daniels, 1997).

Supervisors should assess their own ethnic identity development and that of their supervisees. They should have an understanding of the potential dynamics resulting from conflicting or complementary levels of White and racial/ethnic identity development and ensure that the supervisory relationship is not regressive or harmful (Atkinson et al., 1998). Supervisors will need to be aware of issues related to racism such as White privilege, cultural mistrust, power differentials/dynamics, and the potential for miscommunication related to these (Fong & Lease, 1997). White supervisors should be able to assess their own attitudes, biases, and experiences using models of White identity/White racial consciousness (Arredondo et al., 1996). Supervisors should realistically assess their own strengths and limitations in working with culturally or racially different clients and supervisees (Constantine, 1997).

Supervisors should consider their own ethnic identity development as an important facet in their overall development, and they should bolster their own sensitivity and competence in working with ethnic clients and supervisees (Constantine, 1997). D'Andrea and Daniels (1997) forwarded several action strategies in which supervisors may engage to nurture their own development in this area. For example, they suggest that supervisors attend workshops and/or presentations designed to promote an understanding of cultural issues in counseling and supervision. Supervisors should also seek out and learn from various religious leaders, political representatives, or other "cultural ambassadors" available in the local community, as well as consult with professionals from other cultures.

Supervisors can read materials and watch videos regarding identity development and then relate it to themselves and others. They can attend annual conferences and workshops or enroll in an ethnic studies course. Supervisors could engage a mentor from their own culture whom they have identified as someone working toward becoming cross-culturally competent and making significant strides. Supervisors may also engage a mentor from a different culture who can provide them with honest feedback about their behavior. Additional activities for the development of supervisor multicultural competency can be derived from Arredondo et al. (1996).

Facilitating Supervisee Awareness and Development

Supervisors should engage in efforts that promote the professional growth and development of supervisees and increase the quality and accountability of the services provided by supervisees. Models of White and racial/ethnic identity development should, therefore, be included in cross-cultural training and supervisory efforts. Supervisors can use information about their own and their supervisees' level of awareness/identity as a guide for selecting appropriate intervention/supervisory strategies. Individuals at different stages of identity development may be primed for different types of interventions, and supervisors should assess the relative risk of various topics and learning strategies so as not to evoke defensiveness or other negative reactions (Sabnani, Ponterotto, & Borodovsky, 1991).

Supervisors should select activities and tasks for supervision that facilitate movement to more advanced levels of awareness. Furthermore, the selected tasks should be congruent with other, more general therapeutic knowledge and skill building techniques (Sabnani et al., 1991). Stone (1997) suggests that supervisees should be given the opportunity to experience being supervised by a culturally different supervisor. Clarifying communication and incorporating cultural perspectives into supervision activities can create a more sensitive environment and a more productive supervisory relationship with supervisees of color (Fong & Lease, 1997). Finally, supervisors should create an open atmosphere and explore cultural and racial issues with "…an attitude of discovery, exploration, and critical thinking as opposed to political correctness" (Stone, 1997, p. 284).

Facilitating Institutional Awareness and Development

Supervisors should foster the development of cultural competence at institution, group, and individual levels to increase the accountability for the quality of services provided to ethnic clients (D'Andrea & Daniels, 1997). Supervisors should encourage the cultural/racial/ethnic identity development of other faculty, the institutions in which they work, and in their supervisees. Respect for cultural differences should be reflected in faculty recruitment and promotion, student recruitment and evaluation, curriculum, and field training. Graduate programs should evaluate their own successes and/or failures in the integration of multicultural and other diversity concepts into all aspects of the academic curriculum, training, and supervision. Programs should solicit feedback from current students and recent graduates about these efforts and apply the information to improve their ability to provide multicultural training (American Psychological Association, 1997).

REFERENCES

American Psychological Association. (1992). Ethical principles of psychologists and code of conduct. *American Psychologist, 47,* 1597–1611.

American Psychological Association. (1993). Guidelines for providers of psychological services to ethnic, linguistic, and culturally diverse populations. *American Psychologist, 48,* 45–48.

American Psychological Association. (1995). *Guidelines and principles for accreditation of programs in professional psychology.* Washington, DC: Author.

American Psychological Association. (1997). *The final report: Comission on ethnic minority recruitment, retention, and training in psychology.* Washington, DC: Author

Aponte, J. F. (1986). *Supervision of ethnic minority students: Models and issues.* Paper presented at the thirty-third meeting of the Southeastern Psychological Association, Orlando, FL.

Aponte, J. F., & Barnes, J. M. (1995). Impact of acculturation and moderator variables on the intervention and treatment of ethnic groups. In J. F. Aponte, R. Young Rivers, & J. Wohl (Eds.), *Psychological interventions and cultural diversity* (pp. 19–39). Boston: Allyn and Bacon.

Aponte, J. F., & Clifford, J. (1995). Education and training issues for intervention with ethnic groups. In J. F. Aponte, R. Young Rivers, & J. Wohl (Eds.), *Psychological interventions and cultural diversity* (pp. 283–300). Boston: Allyn and Bacon.

Aponte, J. F., & Lyons, M. J. (1980). Supervision in community settings: Concepts, methods, and issues. In A. K. Hess (Ed.), *Psychotherapy supervision: Theory, research, and practice* (pp. 381–406). New York: Wiley.

Aponte, J. F., Young Rivers, R. & Wohl, J. (Eds.). *Psychological interventions and cultural diversity.* Boston: Allyn and Bacon.

Arredondo, P., Toporek, R., Brown, S. P., Jones, J., Locke, D.C., Sanchez, J., & Stadler, H. (1996). Operationalization of the multicultural counseling competencies. *Journal of Multicultural Counseling and Development, 24,* 42–79.

Atkinson, D. R., Morten, G., & Sue, D. W. (1998). *Counseling American minorities* (5th ed.). Boston: McGraw-Hill.

Bernard, J. M. (1979). Supervisor training: A discrimination model. *Counselor Education and Supervision, 19,* 60–68.

Bernard, J. M., & Goodyear, R. K. (1998). *Fundamentals of clinical supervision* (2nd ed.). Boston: Allyn and Bacon.

Block, C. J., Roberson, L., & Neuger, D. A. (1995). White racial identity theory: A framework for understanding reactions toward interracial situations in organizations. *Journal of Vocational Behavior, 46,* 71–88.

Borders, L. D., & Leddick, G. R. (1987). *Handbook of counseling supervision.* Alexandria, VA: Association for Counselor Education and Supervision.

Bordin, E. S. (1979). The generalizability of the psychodynamic concept of the working alliance. *Psychotherapy: Theory, Research, and Practice, 16,* 252–260.

Bordin, E. S. (1983). A working alliance based model of supervision. *The Counseling Psychologist, 11,* 35–41.

Bradley, L. J. (1989). *Counselor supervision: Principles, process, practice.* Muncie, IN: Accelerated Press.

Brown, M. T., & Landrum-Brown, J. (1995). Counselor supervision: Cross-cultural perspectives. In J. G. Ponterotto, J. M. Casas, L. A. Suzuki, & C. M. Alexander (Eds.), *Handbook of multicultural counseling* (pp. 263–286). Thousand Oaks, CA: Sage.

Carney, C. G., & Kahn, K. B. (1984). Building competencies for effective cross-cultural counseling: A developmental view. *The Counseling Psychologist, 12,* 111–119.

Carroll, M. (1996). *Counseling supervision: Theory, skills, and practice.* London: Cassell.

Chagnon, J., & Russell, R. K. (1995). Assessment of supervisee developmental level and supervision environment across supervisor experience. *Journal of Counseling and Development, 73,* 553–558.

Constantine, M. G. (1997). Facilitating multicultural competency in counseling supervision: Operationalizing a practical framework. In D. B. Pope-Davis & H. L. K. Coleman (Eds.), *Multicultural counseling competencies: Assessment, education and training, and supervision* (pp. 310–324). Thousand Oaks, CA: Sage.

Cook, D. A. (1994). Racial identity in supervision. *Counselor Education and Supervision, 34,* 132–141.

Cook, D. A., & Helms, J. E. (1988). Visible racial/ethnic group supervisees satisfaction with cross-cultural supervision as predicted by relationship characteristics. *Journal of Counseling Psychology, 35,* 268–274.

Dana, R. H. (1998). *Understanding cultural identity in intervention and assessment.* Thousand Oaks, CA: Sage.

D'Andrea, M. D., & Daniels, J. (1997). Multicultural counseling supervision: Central issues, theoretical considerations, and practical strategies. In D. B. Pope-Davis & H. L. K. Coleman (Eds.), *Multicultural counseling competencies: Assessment, education and training, and supervision* (pp. 290–309). Thousand Oaks, CA: Sage.

Dewald, P. A. (1997). The process of supervision in psychoanalysis. In C. E. Watkins, Jr. (Ed.), *Handbook of psychotherapy supervision* (pp. 31–43). New York: Wiley.

Fong, M. L., & Lease, S. H. (1997). Cross-cultural supervision: Issues for the White supervisor. In D. B. Pope-Davis & H. L. K. Coleman (Eds.), *Multicultural counseling competencies: Assessment, education and training, and supervision* (pp. 387–405). Thousand Oaks, CA: Sage.

Friedberg, R. D., & Taylor, L. A. (1994). Perspectives on supervision in cognitive therapy. *Journal of Rational-Emotive & Cognitive Behavior Therapy, 12,* 147–161.

Fukuyama, M. A. (1994). Critical incidents in multicultural counseling supervision. A phenomenological approach to supervision research. *Counselor Education and Supervision, 34,* 142–151.

Helms, J. E. (1990). Counseling attitudinal and behavioral predispositions: The Black/White interaction model. In J. H. Helms (Ed.), *Black and White racial identity: Theory, research, and practice* (pp. 135–143). Westport, CT: Greenwood Press.

Helms, J. E. (1995). An update of Helms's White and people of color racial identity models. In J. G. Ponterotto, J. M. Casas, L. A. Suzki, & C. M. Alexander (Eds.), *Handbook of multicultural counseling* (pp. 181–198). Thousand Oaks, CA: Sage.

Helms, J. E., & Carter, R. T. (1990). Development of the White Racial Identity Inventory. In J. E. Helms (Ed.), *Black and White racial identity: Theory, research, and practice* (pp. 67–80). Westport, CT: Greenwood Press.

Hilton, D. B., Russel, R. K., & Salmi, S. W. (1995). The effects of supervisor's race and level of support on perceptions of supervision. *Journal of Counseling & Development, 73,* 559–563.

Holloway, E., & Johnston, R. (1985). Group supervision: Widely practiced but poorly understood. *Counselor Education and Supervision, 24,* 332–340.

Holloway, E. L. (1995). *Clinical supervision: A systems approach.* Thousand Oaks, CA: Sage.

Iijima Hall, C. C. (1997). Cultural malpractice: The growing obsolence of psychology with the changing U.S. population. *American Psychologist, 52,* 642–651.

Ivey, A. E., Ivey, M. B., & Simek-Morgan, L. (1997). *Counseling and Psychotherapy: A Multicultural Perspective* (4th ed.). Boston: Allyn and Bacon.

Jacobs, M. (Ed.) (1996). *In search of supervision,* Buckingham, England: Open University Press.

Jacobs, D., David, P., & Meyer, D. J. (1995). *The supervisor encounter: A guide for teachers of psychodynamic psychotherapy and psychoanalysis.* New Haven, CT: Yale University Press.

Jones, N. S. (1990). Black/White issues in psychotherapy: A framework for clinical practice. *Journal of Social Behavior and Personality, 5,* 305–322.

Ladany, N., Brittan-Powell, C. S., & Pannu, R. K. (1997). The influence of supervisory racial identity interaction and racial matching on the supervisory working alliance and supervisee multicultural competence. *Counselor Education and Supervision, 36,* 384–404.

Ladany, N., & Friedlandtz, M. L. (1995). The relationship between the supervisory working alliance and trainee's experience of role conflict and role ambiguity. *Counselor education and supervision, 34,* 220–231.

Leong, F. T. L., & Wagner, N. S. (1994). Cross-cultural counseling supervision: What do we know? What do we need to know? *Counselor Education and Supervision, 34,* 117–131.

Liddle, H. A., Becker, D., & Diamond, G. M. (1997). Family therapy supervision. In C. E. Watkins, Jr. (Ed.), *Handbook of psychotherapy supervision* (pp. 400–421). New York: Wiley.

Littrell, J. M., Lee-Borden, N., & Lorenz, J. A. (1979). A developmental framework for counseling supervision. *Counselor Education and Supervision, 19,* 119–136.

Loganbill, C., Hardy, E., & Delworth, H. (1982). Supervision: A conceptual model. *The Counseling Psychologist, 10,* 3–42.

López, S. R. (1997). Cultural competencies in psychotherapy: A guide to clinicians and their supervisors. In C. E. Watkins, Jr. (Ed.), *Handbook of psychotherapy supervision* (pp. 570–588). New York: Wiley.

Martínez, R. P., & Holloway, E. L. (1997). The supervision relationship in multicultural training. In D. B. Pope-Davis & H. L. K. Coleman (Eds.), *Multicultural counseling competencies: Assessment, education and training, and supervision* (pp. 325–349). Thousand Oaks, CA: Sage.

McRae, M. B., & Johnson, S. D. (1991). Toward training for competence in multicultural counselor education. *Journal of Counseling and Development, 70,* 131–135.

Midgette, T. E., & Meggert, S. S. (1991). Multicultural counseling instruction: A challenge for faculties in the 21st century. *Journal of Counseling and development, 70,* 136–141.

Nickerson, K. J., Helms, J. E., & Terrell, F. (1994). Cultural mistrust, opinions about mental illness, and Black students' attitudes toward seeking psychological help from White counselors. *Journal of Counseling Psychology, 41,* 378–385.

Norcross, J. C., & Halgin, R. P. (1997). Integrative approaches to psychotherapy supervision. In C. E.

Watkins, Jr. (Ed.), *Handbook of psychotherapy supervision* (pp. 203–222). New York: Wiley.

Ottavi, T. M., Pope-Davis, D. B., & Dinges, J. G. (1994). Relationship between White racial identity attitudes and self-reported multicultural counseling competencies. *Journal of Counseling Psychology, 41,* 149–154.

Padesky, C. A. (1996). Developing cognitive therapist competency: Teaching and supervision models. In P. M. Salkovskis (Ed.), *Frontiers of cognitive therapy* (pp. 266–292). New York: Guilford Press.

Patterson, C. H. (1997). Client-centered supervision. In C. E. Watkins, Jr. (Ed.), *Handbook of psychotherapy supervision* (pp. 134–146). New York: Wiley.

Payton, C. (1994). Implications of the 1992 ethics code for diverse groups. *Professional Psychology: Research and Practice, 25,* 317–320.

Perris, C. (1994). Supervising cognitive psychotherapy and training supervisors. *Journal of Cognitive Psychotherapy, 8,* 83–103.

Pope-Davis, D. B., & Coleman, H. L. K. (Eds.) (1997). *Multicultural counseling competencies: Assessment, education and training, and supervision,* Thousand Oaks, CA: Sage.

Pope-Davis, D. B., Menefee, L. A., & Ottavi, T. M. (1993). The comparison of White racial identity attitudes among faculty and students: Implications for professional psychologists. *Professional Psychology: Research and Practice, 24,* 443–449.

Pope-Davis, D. B., & Ottavi, T. M. (1992). The influence of White racial identity attitudes on racism among faculty members: A preliminary examination. *Journal of College Student Development, 33,* 389–394.

Priest, R. (1991). Racism and prejudice as negative impacts on African American clients in therapy. *Journal of Counseling and Development, 70,* 213–215.

Prieto, L. (1996). Group supervision: Still widely practiced but poorly understood. *Counselor Education and Supervision, 35,* 295–307.

Rice, L. N. (1980). A client-centered approach to the supervision of psychotherapy. In A. K. Hess (Ed.), *Psychotherapy supervision: Theory, research, and practice* (pp. 136–147). New York: Wiley.

Richards, H., & Clements, C. (1993). Critique of APA Accreditation Criterion II. Cultural and individual differences. *Professional Psychology: Research and Practice, 24,* 123–126.

Richardson, T. O., & Helms, J. E. (1994). The relationship of the racial identity attitudes of Black men to perceptions of "parallel" counseling dyads. *Journal of Counseling and Development, 73,* 172–177.

Richardson, T. O., & Molinaro, K. I. (1996). White counselor self awareness! A prerequisite for multicultural competence. *Journal of Counseling and Development, 74,* 238–242.

Ridley, C. R. (1995). *Overcoming unintentional racism in counseling and therapy: A practitioner's guide to intentional intervention.* Thousand Oaks, CA: Sage.

Riva, M. T., & Cornish, J. A. E. (1995). Group supervision practices in psychology predoctoral internship programs: A national survey. *Professional Psychology: Research and Practice, 26,* 523–525.

Rowe, W., Behrens, J. T., & Leach, M. M. (1995). Racial/ethnic identity and racial consciousness: Looking back and looking forward. In J. G. Ponterotto, J. M. Casas, L. A. Suzuki, & C. M. Alexander (Eds.), *Handbook of multicultural counseling* (pp. 218–235). Thousand Oaks, CA: Sage.

Rowe, W., Bennett, S. K., & Atkinson, D. R. (1994). White racial identity models: A critique and alternative proposal. *The Counseling Psychologist, 22,* 129–146.

Ruskin, R. (1996). Issues in psychotherapy supervision when participants are from different cultures. In S. E. Greben & R. Ruskin (Eds.), *Clinical perspectives on psychotherapy supervision* (pp. 53–72). Washington, DC: American Psychiatric Press.

Russell, D. M. (1988). Language and psychotherapy: The influence of nonstandard English in clinical practice. In L. Comas-Díaz & E. E. H. Griffin (Eds.), *Clinical guidelines in cross-cultural mental health* (pp. 33–68). New York: Wiley.

Ryan, A. S., & Hendricks, C. O. (1989). Culture and communication: Supervising the Asian and Hispanic social worker. *The Clinical Supervisor, 7,* 27–40.

Sabnani, H. B., Ponterotto, J. G., & Borodovsky, L. G. (1991). White racial identity development and cross-cultural counselor training: A stage model. *The Counseling Psychologist, 19,* 76–102.

Skovholt, T. M., & Ronnestad, M. H. (1992). *The evolving professional self: Stages and themes in therapist and counselor development.* Chichester, England: Wiley.

Stoltenberg, C. D., McNeil, B. W., & Delworth, U. (1997). *IDM: The Integrated Developmental Model of clinical supervision.* San Francisco: Jossey-Bass.

Stone, G. L. (1997). Multiculturalism as a context for supervision: Perspectives, limitations, and implications. In D. B. Pope-Davis & H. L. K. Coleman (Eds.), *Multicultural counseling competencies: Assessment, education and training, and supervision* (pp. 363–289). Thousand Oaks, CA: Sage.

Sue, D. W., & Sue, D. (1990). *Counseling the culturally different: Theory and practice* (2nd ed.). New York: Wiley.

Sue, D. W., Carter, R. T., Casas, J. M., Fouad, N. A., Ivey, A. E., Jensen, M., LaFromboise, T., Manese, J. E., Ponterotto, J. G., & Vazquez-Nutall, E. (1998). *Multicultural counseling competencies: Individual and organizational development.* Thousand Oaks, CA: Sage.

Sue, S., Arredondo, P., & McDavis, J. (1992). Multicultural counseling competencies and standards: A call to the profession. *Journal of Counseling and Development, 70,* 477–486.

Teitelbaum, S. H. (1995). The changing scene in psychoanalytic supervision. *Psychoanalysis & Psychotherapy, 12,* 183–192.

VanderKolk, C. (1974). The relationship of personality, values, and race to anticipation of the supervisory relationship. *Rehabilitation Counseling Bulletin, 18,* 41–46.

Vasquez, M. J., & McKinley, D. (1982). "Supervision: A conceptual model": Reactions and an extension. *The Counseling Psychologist, 10,* 59–63.

Vasquez, M. J. T., & Han, A. L. (1995). Group interventions and treatment with ethnic minorities. In J. F. Aponte, R. Young Rivers, & J. Wohl (Eds.), *Psychological interventions and cultural diversity* (pp. 109–127). Boston: Allyn and Bacon.

Watkins Jr., C. E. (Ed.). (1997). *Handbook of psychotherapy supervision.* Thousand Oaks, CA: Sage.

Williams, A. (1995). *Visual and active supervision: Roles, focus, technique.* New York: Norton.

Williams, S., & Halgin, R. P. (1995). Issues in psychotherapy supervision between the White supervisor and the Black supervisee. *The Clinical Supervisor, 13,* 39–61.

17 Common Themes and Future Prospects for the Twenty-First Century

JULIAN WOHL

JOSEPH F. APONTE

Great change in the ethnic character and culture of the clientele for psychological services is underway, with the rate of such change promising to accelerate dramatically as we move into the twenty-first century (see Chapter 1). Appreciation of both the problems involved and the skills required to cope with this transformation has made intervention and treatment of ethnic populations a topic in all disciplines conventionally identified as the "mental health" or "helping" professions. As the chapters of this book amply demonstrate, a variety of approaches can be brought to bear in formulating means of defining and solving problems. Virtually every chapter acknowledges that, in addition to psychological causes, the broader context of economic, political, and social forces plays a critical etiological role in the problems of clients.

The need to provide effective mental health services and treatment to ethnic groups has begun to be acknowledged by administrators, service providers, clinicians, and researchers as an ongoing issue (Atkinson, Morten, & Sue, 1998; Cheung & Snowden, 1990; Dana, 1998; Sue, 1988; Tomes, 1998). Ethnic persons have characteristically been underserved in the mental health system, have received inappropriate or inadequate services, and have received ineffective treatment (Acosta, Yamamoto, & Evans, 1982; Atkinson et al., 1998; Iijima Hall, 1997; Jackson, 1983; Leong, 1986; Lorion & Felner, 1986). The twenty-first century will see no reduction in the service requirements of this population, nor in the requirement that people be trained to serve them.

In acknowledging the need to expand and modify training in the mental health fields to respond to cultural and ethnic diversity (see Chapters 15 and 16), psychology links itself to the recognition by the broader American society of changes in the cultural makeup of the United States. We are experiencing and will continue to experience increasing representation of people whose ethnic roots are not European. Moreover, African American, Latino/Latina, and Asian American groups may not accept the traditional expectations to assimilate or Americanize themselves. These groups may reject the earlier idea of integration or accept only a restricted view of it, while emphasizing instead their own culturally unique identities. American Indians, squeezed by their history in an acculturation-identity vise, also struggle to extricate and redefine themselves.

For the larger society, the danger in this revaluing of and adjusting to ethnic diversity is an increase in the animosity and conflict that on a more brutal and violent scale have erupted in many other pluralistic societies around the world—such as the former Soviet Union, the remains of Yugoslavia, and India. In these countries, we see how violence and destruction can develop in societies contending with nationalistic, religious, and ethnic differences. One of the dangers inherent in an uncritical national embrace of "multiculturalism" as an ideology, coupled with the denial of any positive unifying national identity to balance it, might well be a further fragmentation in United States society, and an increase in intergroup tensions and conflict.

The struggle to achieve balance between diversity and assimilation to the larger society is mirrored in the personal struggles of many individual members of ethnic groups. As noted in a number of the chapters, they are caught between the pull of their cultural identity and the force of acculturation. This struggle may take the form of intrapersonal, intergenerational, and intergroup tensions and conflicts. In a small way, clinicians who work with clients to achieve this needed balance are dealing with a critical social problem as well as with the personal agony of clients.

In the mental health field we usually deal not with the larger societal issues directly, but with a narrower multicultural issue: the fact that we must intervene clinically in the lives of people whose ethnic and cultural characteristics differ from those of the traditional clients of mental health professions. This idea constitutes the central point of departure for this book. The authors begin there and move outward in many directions as they struggle with this problem. Despite the differences in theoretical viewpoints, specific subject matter, and modes of intervention presented, many of the same questions and problems repeatedly emerge. In this concluding chapter we will summarize the major themes and issues that are most frequently found in this book. This will be followed by a discussion of the directions in which the field is moving, ideas about where it should be going, and suggestions about how to get there.

Political and Scientific Perspectives

Any student of the literature on intervention with ethnic groups in the United States will observe that most of the contributors (including the editors of and contributors to this book) have more than a dispassionate attitude toward their subject matter. Either they are members of ethnic groups themselves and have directly experienced discrimination and oppression, or their moral outrage at the injustice historically or currently experienced by these groups propelled them toward this work. Exceptions exist of course, but for the most part we believe that mental health professionals bring intense personal commitment to their work on interethnic and intercultural intervention. An unfortunate and dangerous consequence of this can be the replacement of scientific or clinical objectivity with ideological fervor.

This passion is reflected in the oft-stated argument that the problems of ethnic populations require more than just conventional clinical interventions and practices. Because they often result from social and economic discrimination, the real attack on the problems must be at their societal roots. This argument says that inequity and injustice created by the social and political structure can be rectified only by changing that structure. To target individuals—placing the locus of troubles within their psychologies and asking them to change—would be to "blame the victim." This conceptualization expresses the political perspective on the sociopsychological difficulties of ethnic groups mentioned by Jones and Korchin (1982) as one of two contrasting frameworks in the field of ethnic mental health.

The political approach, imbued with moral passion and righteous anger, highlights issues of equity, fairness, and rights. In contrast is what Jones and Korchin refer to as a "cross-cultural" view (1982, pp. 3–4), a scientific framework that declares that differences in attitudes, values, and behavior among different cultural groups need to be studied and understood. Psychological functioning is comprehensible only if we understand the culture in which it is embedded. Designing effective interventions requires an understanding of the cultural context of the clients' difficulties (Segall, Lonner, & Berry, 1998). Both perspectives are reflected in the pages of this book. A passionate desire to improve the social position and a wish for effective political change to achieve fairer societal treatment for the groups in question pervade the text. At the same time, emotional commitment is tempered by the embrace of a scientific-clinical framework that demands a degree of detachment and a thoughtful and critical attitude.

Common Themes

We have found it convenient to divide our treatment of thematic ideas into three categories: (1) *context* or framework, consisting of factors that determine the situation within which the intervention occurs, (2) issues more or less directly tied to the *client,* and (3) issues most directly linked to the *service provider.* The distinctions between categories are not sharp. They overlap generously, and they potentially interact with each other.

Contextual Issues

This broadest of the categories refers to and includes all of the antecedent conditions and circumstances that determine the presentation of the client, as well as those situational factors that influence, define, and control the treatment process itself. They can include political, social, economic and historical forces that have affected a particular client's ethnic group, and thus indirectly the client, along with actual experiences of the client that stem from, and psychologically are linked directly to, membership in that group. A good example is racial/ethnic identity, which is a powerful factor in the client's life and therefore a controlling influence in the presentation of the client (see Chapters 2 and 16). Because of the importance of ethnicity to the client and possibly because of their own sensitivity on the subject, service providers need to be aware of the emotional power of this issue for the client.

Another important contextual factor is the history of racial abuse, discrimination, and oppression experienced by ethnic groups. Such experiences are also often reflected in contacts with community, social, and governmental organizations that lead to frustration with these institutions. These experiences can promote varying degrees of distrust, from skepticism through suspicion, to outright hostility toward mental health agencies and service providers.

Deriving in considerable part from that discrimination history is the fact that ethnic minorities are found disproportionately to be of low socioeconomic status (see Chapters 1 and 2). Ethnic children and adolescents, women, and the elderly are overrepresented at these lower levels. They are frequently poor, have relatively less formal education, suffer employment problems, housing problems, and little hope for improvement of these circumstances. The latter state, hopelessness, represents a specific kind of functioning rooted in this socioeconomic contextual feature that can have a detrimental impact on all ethnic groups.

It must be recognized, however, that not all ethnic group members are impoverished. As noted in Chapter 1, there is variability in socioeconomic status both across and within ethnic groups. Selective migration has accounted for some ethnic group members doing well, and over the last two decades the socioeconomic status of some segments of ethnic groups has improved. Some individuals who have grown up in impoverished circumstances have also exhibited remarkable resiliency in being able to function well psychologically and make contributions to their community and society (McCubbin & McCubbin, 1988).

Frustration at the failure of the majority mainstream institutions and systems to redress grievances or function fairly for them can also breed a sense of powerlessness in ethnic group members. For this reason, empowering people has become a common issue in their treatment at the individual, familial, group, and community levels (see Chapter 8). At all these levels a goal of treatment is (as for all clients regardless of ethnicity) personal empowerment—that is, to develop and nurture those inner resources that enable the client to function and act more effectively. But equally important is the recognition that, for ethnic clients, social and political action may be necessary pathways to overcoming powerlessness and hopelessness.

Starting from their own cultural traditions, and perhaps intensified by the discrimination tradition, ethnic groups have evolved strong, collaborative social support systems. Family (nuclear, extended, and transgenerational) seems to play a more important supportive function than majority service providers might expect on the basis of their own backgrounds (see Chapters 2 and 6). Beyond the family are various religious, social, and community organizations. Such support systems function as effective buffers and mediators of stress. Intervention agents need to appreciate and take into account this important aspect of ethnic culture (see Chapters 8 and 9).

Another contextual feature encompasses a class of cultural differences between the average White, majority, mainstream, North American service providers and clients who are either African American, Latino/Latina, Asian American, or American Indian. These differences involve cognitive styles, values, beliefs, and attitudes. Conceptions of personality functioning, psychopathology, assessment, and treatment are products of our Euro-American cultural tradition embodying its philosophy of science, notions of cause and effect, and values. They will not automatically be comprehended and accepted as legitimate aspects of helping, and they may conflict with conceptions of providing help that stem from substantially different worldviews that are part of ethnic cultural traditions. Worldview differences between client and service provider can be a major barrier to intercultural understanding, communication, and effective service.

Finally, but powerful in their effects, are the institutional arrangements for delivering services, of which politics and economics are the fundamental roots. Most evident in this regard is the managed care movement. In the laudable and necessary struggle to reduce costs and increase efficiency, severe restrictions are imposed upon mental health services, with the most onerous falling upon psychotherapy. Practitioners complain that the amount of money allowed for each patient, whether measured in number of sessions or dollars over a period of time, so restricts treatment that all but very brief or emergency psychotherapy may become the rule. Certainly some patients can be helped in six sessions, but this is the exception not the rule. Even brief psychotherapy is usually planned for 15 or 20 sessions, but more important is that the patient and the therapist are denied the freedom to work out together what they see as a reasonable length for the service. If this trend toward restricting psychotherapy continues as practitioners now experience it, psychotherapy will become available only to those who can finance it themselves, and people dependent upon third-party payers will be left with medication as their only treatment option.

Client Factors

An individual client will undoubtedly share many of the contextual features characterizing ethnic groups in general, and many characteristics associated with a specific ethnic group. In our concern with problems of the large units we refer to as "ethnic minorities," we must not forget that the client (unless it is an institution) is always an individual person, notwithstanding instances when individuals are seen collectively as in group and family therapy. The pithy axiom of Kluckhohn and Murray retains validity more than 50 years after its publication: "Every man is in certain respects: (1) like all other men, (2) like some other men, and (3) like no other man" (1948, p. 35). Diversity flourishes within each ethnic group, and no ethnic clients, anymore than nonethnic clients or practitioners, passively accept that they are identical to all other members of their group.

Although we have noted that economic hardship disproportionately besets ethnic groups in general, socioeconomic variation within groups also is a fact (see Chapter 1). The existence of heterogeneity in employment, income, education, and housing means that intervention agents and practitioners need to treat clients as individuals on those dimensions rather than simply assume that all their ethnic clients are impoverished. Recognizing such variations in socioeconomic status also allows the service provider to seek out and distinguish those issues that are a by-product of discrimination and prejudice from those that are due to economic circumstances.

Ethnic clientele can find their way into the mental health system through a number of complex routes. Economically disadvantaged ethnic groups, particularly immigrants, may not utilize the mental health system because they have access to family, indigenous networks, and other help-giving organizations and structures (Rogler, 1993; Rogler & Cortes, 1993). Some cultural groups also tend to somatize distress (Angel & Guarnaccia, 1989; Rogler, 1989), and therefore may present themselves to physicians, public health officials, and emergency rooms. Utilizing these pathways can block or delay their receiving mental health services (Alegria et al., 1991).

A second major variation within ethnic groups that is vital for their adaptation, and therefore for practitioners to appreciate, is the degree of acculturation to the majority culture around them (see Chapter 2). Acculturation can have sociopolitical complications within an ethnic group that result in the criticism or condemnation of a member who has violated some criterion limit on assimilation by having gone "too far" toward the majority group. But unless the ethnic group member is to function only within the confines of the ethnic group world, some degree of acculturation is unavoidable. Ethnic group members must be able to function in each of two cultures and switch back and forth as circumstances require. For many, striking a balance between assimilation and the maintenance of cultural ethnic identity can be a core psychological issue.

Related to the questions of acculturation, assimilation, and racial/ethnic identity are an array of language issues. For immigrants, learning the language of the new society will enhance their potential ability to function effectively in that society. For the second and third generation, language differences between them and their parents and grandparents can produce generational cultural tensions. Native-born persons whose original English is either nonstandard or a dialect confront the same adaptation issues. To function maximally in the majority culture they are best served by standard English, but to maintain the bond with their own tradition, they will want to remain fluent in the original dialect or nonstandard English. As with immigrant peoples, bicultural adaptation means bilingual competence and the ability to switch appropriately.

Service Provider Issues

The major problems of nonminority clinicians with ethnic clients fall in the realms of personal reactions, cultural sophistication, and professional-technical competence (American Psychological Association, 1992; 1993). Personal prejudices, stereotypes, unconscious or semiconscious derogatory attitudes and irrational ideas about members of an ethnically different group can corrupt, contaminate, and destroy the provider's efforts to be of service. Although it is emphasized most with respect to psychotherapy, clinicians in general are advised throughout this book to scrutinize themselves and excise, or at least understand and control, their own biases (see Chapter 5).

From a purely technical viewpoint, practitioners need to recognize the limits of appropriate application of assessment techniques and the need for normative data on the population represented by their clients (see Chapter 4). Similarly, they must bear in mind that some psychotherapeutic methods may be culturally unsuitable for some ethnic clients. The authors in this book agree that clinicians require the personal flexibility that would permit them to modify their methods and adapt them to the culturally based conceptions of the client. To do so, however, calls for both the professional competence and the cultural sensitivity that would inform them when adjustment is needed.

Perhaps the broadest guidance for clinicians is that they become "cross-cultural" (Segall et al., 1998). They are asked to understand the cultural roots and cultural boundedness of their methods, theories, and concepts of assessment, pathology, personality, intervention, and communicative habits, as well as normative assumptions, values, and beliefs about other people in the world. When they appreciate these different worldviews, their contributions to the majority culture, and the disparity between themselves and their clients, they are equipped to become culturally sensitive practitioners. When appropriate skills are built upon this sensitivity, then competency can be achieved.

Required Changes in the Field of Psychology

The need for changes in the field of psychology that will make practitioners more sensitive, responsive, and effective with ethnic populations has been underscored in this book. Changes in psychology can come about through two main sources. One of these is internal to the discipline, as reflected in professional organizations and national education and training conferences. The second source of change is external and consists of external pressures from entities such as the federal government that have the power to influence psychology and other related mental health fields by controlling funding for research and training (Wohl & Aponte, 1995). A brief review of the forces affecting the discipline of psychology follows.

Professional organizations such as the American Psychological Association (APA) are important in determining the direction of the field. APA has recently begun to address diversity issues by increasing ethnic participation in the organization and in the development of structures (e.g., divisions, committees, and offices) to address ethnic issues (Comas-Díaz, 1990) and by cosponsoring conferences (Sleek, 1998). But while ethnic membership has increased over the last two decades, the percentage of ethnic representation within the association has remained about the same and is not reflective of the general population (Tomes, 1998). The prospects for change are not optimistic, given the limited number of ethnic students enrolled in graduate and professional programs (see Chapter 15).

Historically, national training conferences have been another internal vehicle for instituting change in the field of psychology. Over the last four decades there have been six major conferences in psychology, beginning with the Conference on Training in Clinical Psychology, held in Boulder, Colorado in 1949, during which the basic framework or the scientist–practitioner training model was put forth for psychology. Of these six conferences, the last two have been the most relevant for ethnic groups (Comas-Díaz, 1990). These are the National Conference on Levels and Patterns of Professional Training in Psychology (Vail Conference) held in Vail, Colorado, in 1973 (Korman, 1973; 1976) and the National Conference on Graduate Education (Utah Conference) held in Salt Lake City, in 1987 (Bickman, 1987).

Both the Vail Conference and the Utah Conference passed a number of resolutions that were important to ethnic groups. The importance of training students to work with diverse populations in a pluristic society was particularly emphasized in each conference (Comas-Díaz, 1990). In addition to emphasizing the importance of ethnic student recruitment and retention, the Utah Conference passed a number of resolutions on ethnic faculty recruitment and promotion (American Psychological Association, 1987). These resolutions were clearly aimed at increasing the number of ethnic psychologists in the discipline.

Other forces within the discipline of psychology will have an impact on the training and delivery of mental health services to ethnic populations. As noted in Chapter 15, there were a number of centrifugal forces operating in the 1987 Utah Conference that were reflective of the social, political, economic, and educational climate of the times (Altman, 1987). These centrifugal trends have had diverging and separating effects on the field, and it is projected that these forces will continue in the future (Rice, 1997). The nature of the impact of these forces on the field will depend upon how psychology responds to them.

Rice (1997) projected several scenarios for the field of psychology based on the degree to which these centrifugal forces persist. The four scenarios that Rice (1997) proposed consist of *science-based practice, separate and equal, dissolution, and reunion.* Two of these scenarios have dominated the discipline and will in all likelihood continue to do so in the future. These are the *science-based practice,* in which all practitioners have research training that can be used in a variety of settings; and *separate and equal,* where psychology becomes two separate professions, one a service delivery profession and the other a scientific academic discipline.

Each of these scenarios will have a direct effect on the training and potential delivery of mental health services to ethnic populations. If the centrifugal forces continue to widen the split between academic and professional psychology, it will become more difficult to integrate research into practice. This is particularly problematic for the emerging field of multicultural interventions and treatment whose conceptual and research underpinnings are just beginning to appear. There is also the risk that ethnic students will choose practitioner rather than academic-research training programs and careers, further widening the gap between practice and research.

Future Changes and Prospects

The mental health field, and psychology in particular, have been in a state of flux over the last three decades. APA reorganized (American Psychological Association, 1988), and the American Psychological Society (APS) was created. As noted previously in this chapter, some of these changes have been driven by internal forces, others by external events. Changes are expected to continue over the next decades. For purposes of discussion, these can be categorized under the headings of research, intervention and treatment, and education and training trends. The salient issue is how ethnic populations will be affected by these trends and how they can influence each of these complex arenas.

Research Trends

Although the quantity and quality of research on ethnic populations has been called into question (Graham, 1992; Loo, Fong, & Iwamasa, 1988), researchers are beginning to acknowledge that culture and ethnicity are of central importance to the delivery of mental health services, the assessment of mental health, and the treatment of ethnic clientele. Researchers also are beginning to take a multilevel approach that recognizes the role of culture and societal forces at the individual, group, and community levels. Most of the research to date has focused on only one level at a time, not fully recognizing nor investigating how each level compounds the difficulties of providing effective mental health services to ethnic populations, which has confounded research efforts to grasp more fully the role of culture and societal forces in this complicated treatment process.

Difficulties with the concepts of culture, race, and ethnicity and the importance of making distinctions among them have been underscored by a number of individuals (Betancourt & López, 1993; Yee, Fairchild, Weizmann, & Wyatt, 1993; Zuckerman, 1990). Betancourt and López (1993) argue that mainstream and cross-cultural investigators need to define these concepts more rigorously, measure them effectively, examine specific hypotheses, and incorporate the results within a theoretical framework. These researchers believe that mainstream and cross-cultural psychology can assist each other in the study of culture and ethnicity and thereby advance both fields.

Future research needs to focus on within-group differences among racial/ethnic populations (Atkinson et al., 1998). As noted in Chapter 1 and elsewhere in this book, the major ethnic categories of African American, Hispanic, Asian American, and American Indian include many diverse groups. Comparisons across ethnic groups and with Whites have limited value. Future research needs to examine, in depth, within-group variables such as racial/ethnic development (see Chapters 2 and 14). Racial/ethnic identity development has been increasingly recognized as an important variable in the treatment process and outcome (Atkinson et al., 1998).

An integral part of research efforts also needs to be the investigation and identification of those factors that contribute to psychological dysfunction and healthy psychological functioning in ethnic individuals. Coie et al. (1993) have proposed a conceptual framework for developing a "science of prevention" that focuses on the role of *risk factors* and *protective factors* in the functioning of individuals. Such a focus is particularly relevant to ethnic populations because of the environmental and social stressors in their lives (see Chapters 1 and 2) and the role of community, social networks, and family in their psychological well-being (see Chapters 6, 7, and 8).

According to Coie and his associates (1993) the "science of prevention" involves a systems perspective, emphasizes the transactions between individuals and their environments, focuses on short- and long-term process and outcome variables, and is capable of generating explanatory and predictive models of behavior. Preventive sciences research is designed to yield insights into the causes of psychological disorders and into those factors that can prevent such disorders from occurring or contribute to the recovery from them. A direct-treatment approach is required when preventive efforts are not implemented or are not effective.

At the assessment and diagnosis level, Rogler (1993) has argued that psychiatric diagnosis needs to consider three hierarchical levels including "...the role of culture in symptom assessment, the configuration of symptoms into disorders, and the diagnostic situation" (p. 407). Others within this volume have pointed out succinctly how symptom presentations vary across and within groups (see Chapter 3), how certain syndromes can be found in groups such as Hispanics, Asians, and American Indians (see Chapter 9), and how the assessment process has to be sensitive to and incorporate culturally relevant norms, items, and interpretations (see Chapter 4). Not to take culture into consideration at all levels in the process introduces cumulative errors into the final diagnosis (Rogler, 1993).

At the treatment level, research efforts have focused either on the client, the therapist, or the interaction between the two. Such a focus, as previously pointed out, has been found in this book. According to Helms (1990), the client-as-problem (CAP) or the therapist-as-problem (TAP) research has included several themes. The CAP perspective locates the difficulty of clinical work in the client, which emerges in two general forms in the "cultural scar hypothesis" and the "acting out client phenomena" (Helms, 1990, p. 172). The TAP perspective assumes that the impediments to therapeutic progress are largely due to the therapist's cultural insensitivity or prejudice. Only recently has ethnic research focused on the interaction between the two (Sue, Fujino, Hu, & Takeuchi, 1991).

Future research also needs to focus on identifying those characteristics of traditional approaches (e.g., psychodynamic, behavioral, cognitive behavioral, phenomenological, interpersonal, eclectic) that apply to all cultures (Atkinson et al., 1998). Research also needs to move beyond identifying these conceptual and common factor elements (Frank & Frank, 1991) to identifying conceptual frameworks and specific strategies and techniques that apply to specific ethnic groups (Jenkins & Ramsey, 1983; Sue, Zane, & Young, 1994). The specific strategies and techniques are partially determined by patient-predisposing variables—for example, diagnosis, personality characteristics, and environmental circumstances (Beutler & Clarkin, 1990)—and equally by cultural characteristics of the ethnic group.

Intervention and Treatment Trends

Ethnic communities and clients often require multilevel and multimodal interventions and treatment strategies because of the complexity of needs and issues they face (Atkinson et al., 1998; Ponterotto, 1987; Vega & Murphy, 1990). Such a view has been reflected in a number of chapters in this book, including those on individual psychotherapy (Chapter 5), family approaches (Chapter 6), group methods (Chapter 7), community interventions (Chapter 8), and traditional folk and healing methods (Chapter 9). Within each of these approaches, a continuous theme—as previously pointed out in this chapter—is differentiating between those issues and processes that are internal to the individual and those that require action directed at the group, community, and society (Atkinson et al., 1998).

Several future changes in the delivery of mental health services can have an impact on ethnic populations. As previously noted in this chapter and in Chapter 8, managed health care has become the primary vehicle through which health care in general, and mental health services in particular, are being delivered. It is anticipated that such efforts to reduce both service rates and the amount of service provided will continue even if a universal system of health care is ever created. The types of services provided will continue to be designed to contain costs (DeLeon, VandenBos, & Bulatao, 1991; Frank & VandenBos, 1994; Hersch, 1995) and may still be inappropriate and ineffective as the treatment options diminish or if the services continue to be insensitive to those ethnic persons they serve.

Another change is the development of clinical practice guidelines for delivering mental health services (Clinton, McCormick, & Besteman, 1994). These guidelines have taken a variety of different forms. The Agency for Health Care Policy and Research (AHCPR) within the United States Department of Health and Human Services, for example, has been developing clinical practice guidelines for a variety of physical conditions and has recently been developing guidelines for the diagnosis and treatment of depression (Muñoz, Hollon, McGrath, Rehm, & VandenBos, 1994; Rush, 1993; Rush, Trivedi, Schriger, & Petty, 1992). These guidelines are designed to assist health care providers recognize, diagnose, and treat depression (Schulberg & Rush, 1994). The inherent danger of trying to force culturally different patients into an inappropriate and ineffective framework can be reduced by including working with diverse populations as part of the guidelines training.

Progress has been made in incorporating cultural variables in the diagnosis of psychiatric disorders (Fabrega, 1992). The American Psychiatric Association Diagnostic and Statistical Manual (DSM-IV) includes more culturally sensitive and cross-culturally suitable categories (Mezzich, Fabrega, & Kleinman, 1992; Mezzich et al., 1992). Appendix I in DSM-IV provides information on how clinicians can evaluate and report the impact of the individuals' cultural context (American Psychiatric Association, 1994). The inclusion of cultural variables in psychiatric disorders and the identification of culture-bound syndromes in DSM-IV begins to provide a cultural context for the diagnosis and treatment of a number of disorders. Further work needs to occur to refine and expand upon these categories in future revisions of the Diagnostic and Statistical Manual.

A number of practitioners and researchers have also voiced concern about the competencies and skills needed to work with ethnic populations (American Psychological Association, 1992, 1993; Arredondo et al., 1996; Atkinson et al., 1998; Iijima Hall, 1997; Payton, 1994; Richards & Clements, 1993; Sue, Arredondo, & McDavis, 1992). To assist service providers in delivering psychological services to ethnic and culturally diverse populations, guidelines have been developed by the Board of Ethnic Minority Affairs Task Force on the Delivery of Services to Ethnic Minority Populations (American Psychological Association, 1993). These guidelines provide a framework for recognizing the role of ethnicity and culture in the assessment and treatment process, as well as specific admonitions for appreciating and respecting cultural differences between the client and service provider.

Education and Training Trends

The need to educate and train researchers and practitioners to work with ethnic populations and issues has been recognized over the last three decades (Aponte & Clifford, 1995). The importance of this need has been reflected in the structures within APA created to address ethnic concerns, through the resolutions of the national training conferences (see Chapter 15), and through the Government and NIMH initiatives (Wohlford, 1992). These efforts have been designed either to encourage majority practitioners and researchers to work with and address ethnic and cultural issues, or to increase the number of ethnic graduate students, academicians, practitioners, and researchers. These efforts, as pointed out in this book, have achieved only limited success.

A pressing need still exists to train more ethnic psychologists (Myers, Echemendia, & Trimble, 1991), yet there is a clear realization that many of the services and much of the research focusing on ethnic populations will be carried out by White practitioners and researchers (Bernal & Castro, 1994). Such a realization underscores the importance of all graduate students being trained to work with ethnic and culturally diverse populations. Yet, there has been only limited success in achieving this goal (Bernal, 1990). Most programs do not have required courses and training experiences that focus on ethnic populations. Few programs come close to training students to be "culturally proficient" (Bernal & Castro, 1994; Iijima Hall, 1997). Past and recent graduates may find themselves inadequately prepared to work with culturally diverse populations. Both practitioners and researchers may thus be forced either not to work with these groups at all, or to work with them without proper training and experience.

To address these education and training issues in the future, psychology will need to step forward to ensure that there is an increased pool of students and professionals in the field and that all graduate and professional students are trained to work with ethnic populations (Aponte & Clifford, 1993, 1995; Puente et al., 1993). Graduate and professional programs will also need to ensure that all students are exposed to ethnic content and trained to work with diverse populations (American Psychological Association, 1992; Iijima Hall, 1997). Such efforts will also be required in the other mental health disciplines in order to ensure their competency to work with ethnic populations.

As detailed in Chapters 15 and 16, there are a number of steps that can be taken to train psychologists to work with ethnic populations. These steps are also applicable to other mental health disciplines as well. The ethical, cultural context, legal, demographic, and scholarly imperatives identified by Ridley (1985) require that cross-cultural training be included in professional training programs. Such training can be strongly encouraged through internal program initiatives, as discussed in Chapter 15, and through external initiatives such as strengthening accreditation criteria around cultural diversity (American Psychological Association, 1995; Aponte, 1992).

Concluding Comments

Each and every ethnic person is not in need of mental health services. Many ethnic persons function very well despite the racism, discrimination, and oppression they experience. The issues and difficulties in providing services and treating African Americans, Latinos/Latinas, Asian Americans, and American Indians who are in need of treatment do not reside within these groups. The difficulty inheres in the treatment systems, agencies, and people who manage them and provide the services. This book presents a wide ranging survey of facts about ethnic populations, their increasing size, the concomitant increased need for services, and the interventions and treatment strategies for working with them.

Psychological Intervention and Cultural Diversity also points out the historical failure of the mental health system and service providers to respond adequately to the need of ethnic populations, and the relatively recent, belated efforts to acknowledge these deficiencies and to change. Efforts to change research, practice, and training move in fits and starts, with these changes being driven by internal and external forces. The chapters identify these forces and display the difficulties and highlight gaps in knowledge and skills. Yet, despite incomplete knowledge and barriers to service delivery and treatment, positive suggestions for effective understanding and work with these ethnic populations are offered in each chapter.

Notwithstanding sincere efforts to recruit members of these groups into the professions, it remains clear that for many years to come the main source of service will be mainstream, White service providers and clinicians. This means that an overriding requirement is to build cultural and ethnic training into our educational and training systems and to change the values and practices of these systems so that they embrace the need as a positive necessity and not grudgingly accept it as a necessary evil. Such efforts need to occur in conjunction with addressing the racism, discrimination, and oppression (that all ethnic groups face regardless of their socioeconomic status) in the larger society.

REFERENCES

Acosta, F. X., Yamamoto, J., & Evans, L. A. (1982). *Effective psychotherapy for low-income minority patients.* New York: Plenum.

Alegria, M., Robles, R., Freeman, D. H., Vera, M., Jimenez, A. L., Rios, C., & Rios, R. (1991). Patterns of mental health utilization among island Puerto Rican poor. *American Journal of Public Health, 81,* 875–879.

Altman, I. (1987). Centripetal and centrifugal trends in psychology. *American Psychologist, 42,* 1058–1069.

Angel, R., & Guarnaccia, P. (1989). Mind, body, and culture: Somatization among Hispanics. *Social Science Medicine, 28,* 1229–1238.

American Psychiatric Association. (1994). *Diagnostic and statistical manual of mental disorders—DSM-IV* (4th ed.). Washington, DC: Author.

American Psychological Association. (1987). Resolutions approved by the National Conference on Graduate Education in Psychology. *American Psychologist, 42,* 1070–1084.

American Psychological Association. (1988). *A plan for the reorganization of the American Psychological Association.* Washington, DC: Author.

American Psychological Association. (1992). Ethical principles of psychologists and code of conduct. *American Psychologist, 47,* 1597–1611.

American Psychological Association. (1993). Guidelines for providers of psychological services to ethnic, linguistic, and culturally diverse populations. *American Psychologist, 48,* 45–48.

American Psychological Association (1995). *Guidelines and principles for accreditation of programs in professional psychology.* Washington, DC: Author.

Aponte, J. F. (1992). The role of APA accreditation in enhancing cultural diversity in graduate and professional training programs. In S. D. Johnson, Jr., & R. T. Carter (Eds.), *The 1992 Teachers College Winter Roundtable Conference Proceedings: Addressing cultural issues in an organizational context* (pp. 73–80). New York: Columbia University.

Aponte, J. F., & Clifford, J. P. (1993). Incorporating ethnically diverse content and training into predominately White graduate and professional programs: Dealing with inertia and resistance. In S. D. Johnson, Jr., R. T. Carter, E. I. Sicalides, & T. R. Buckley (Eds.), *The 1993 Teachers College Winter Roundtable Conference Proceedings: Training for cross-cultural competence* (pp. 22–26). New York: Columbia University.

Aponte, J. F., & Clifford, J. (1995). Education and training issues for intervention with ethnic groups. In J. F. Aponte, R. Young Rivers, & J. Wohl (Eds.), *Psychological interventions and cultural diversity* (pp. 283–300). Boston: Allyn and Bacon.

Arrendondo, P., Toporek, R., Brown, S. P., Jones, J., Locke, D.C., Sanchez, J., & Stadler, H. (1996). Operationalization of the multicultural counseling competencies. *Journal of Multicultural Counseling and Development, 24,* 42–78.

Atkinson, D. R., Morten, G., & Sue, D. W. (1998). *Counseling American minorities* (5th ed.). Boston: McGraw-Hill.

Bernal, M. E. (1990). Ethnic mental health training: Trends and issues. In F. C. Serafica, A. I. Schwebel, R. K. Russell, P. D. Isaac, & L. B. Meyers (Eds.), *Mental health of ethnic minorities* (pp. 249–274). New York: Praeger.

Bernal, M., & Castro, F. (1994). Are clinical psychologists prepared for service and research with ethnic minorities? *American Psychologist; 47,* 797–805.

Betancourt, H., & López, S. R. (1993). The study of culture, ethnicity, and race in American psychology. *American Psychologist, 48,* 629–637.

Beutler, L. E., & Clarkin, J. F. (1990). *Systematic treatment selection: Toward targeted therapeutic interventions.* New York: Brunner/Mazel.

Bickman, L. (1987). Graduate education in psychology. *American Psychologist, 42,* 1041–1047.

Cheung, F. K., & Snowden, L. R. (1990). Community mental health and ethnic minority populations. *Community Mental Health Journal, 26,* 277–291.

Clinton, J. J., McCormick, K., & Besteman, J. (1994). Enhancing clinical practice: The role of practice guidelines. *American Psychologists, 49,* 30–33.

Coie, J. D., Watt, N. F., West, S. G., Hawkins, J. D., Asarnow, J. R., Markman, H. J., Ramey, S. L., Shure, M. B., & Long, B. (1993). The science of prevention: A conceptual framework and some directions for a national research program. *American Psychologist, 48,* 1013–1022.

Comas-Díaz, L. (1990). Ethnic minority mental health: Contributions and future directions of the American Psychological Association. In F. C. Serafica, A. T. Schwebel, R. K. Russell, P. D. Isaac, & L. B. Myers (Eds.), *Mental health of ethnic minorities* (pp. 275–301), New York: Praeger.

Dana, R. H. (1998). *Understanding cultural identity in intervention and assessment.* Thousand Oaks, CA: Sage.

DeLeon, P. H., VandenBos, G. R., & Bulatao, E. Q. (1991). Managed mental health care: A history of the federal policy initiative. *Professional Psychology: Research and Practice, 22,* 15–25.

Fabrega, H., Jr. (1992). Diagnosis interminable: Toward a culturally sensitive DSM-IV. *Journal of Nervous and Mental Disease, 180,* 5–7.

Frank, J. D., & Frank, J. B. (1991). *Persuasion and healing: A comparative study of psychotherapy* (3rd ed.). Baltimore: Johns Hopkins University Press.

Frank, R. G., & VandenBos, G. R. (1994). Health care reform: The 1993–1994 evolution. *American Psychologist, 49,* 951–954.

Graham, S. (1992). Most of the subjects were White and middle class: Trends in published research on African Americans. *American Psychologist, 47,* 629–639.

Helms, J. E. (1990). Three perspectives on counseling and psychotherapy with visible racial/ethnic group clients. In F. C. Serafica, A. J. Schwebel, R. K. Russell, P. D. Isaac, & L. B. Myers (Eds.), *Mental health of ethnic minorities* (pp. 171–201). New York: Praeger.

Hersch, L. (1995). Adapting to health care reform and managed care: Three strategies for survival and growth. *Professional Psychology: Research and Practice, 26,* 16–26.

Iijima Hall, C. C. (1997). Cultural malpractice: The growing obsolescence of psychology with the changing U.S. population. *American Psychologist, 52,* 642–651.

Jackson, A. (1983). Treatment issues for Black patients. *Psychotherapy: Theory, Research, and Practice, 20,* 143–151.

Jenkins, T. O., & Ramsey, G. A. (1983). Minorities. In M. Hersen, A. E. Kazdin, & A. S. Bellack (Eds.), *The clinical psychology handbook* (pp. 724–740), New York: Pergamon.

Jones, E. E., & Korchin, S. J. (Eds.). (1982). *Minority mental health.* New York: Praeger.

Kluckhohn, C., & Murray, H. A. (Eds.). (1948). *Personality in nature, society, and culture.* New York: Knopf.

Korman, M. (Ed.) (1973). *Levels and patterns of professional training in psychology. Conference proceedings.* Vail, CO.

Korman, M. (1976). *Levels and patterns of professional training in psychology.* Washington, DC: American Psychological Association.

Leong, F. T. L. (1986). Counseling and psychotherapy with Asian Americans: A review of the literature. *Journal of Counseling Psychology, 33,* 192–206.

Loo, C., Fong, K. T., & Iwamasa, G. (1988). Ethnicity and cultural diversity: An analysis of work published in community psychology journals, 1965–1985. *Journal of Community Psychology, 16,* 332–349.

Lorion, R. P., & Felner, R. D. (1986). Research on psychotherapy with the disadvantaged. In S. L. Garfield & A. E. Bergin (Eds.), *Handbook of psychotherapy and behavior change* (3rd ed.) (pp. 739–775). New York: Wiley.

McCubbin, H. I., & McCubbin, M. A. (1988). Typologies of resilient families: Emerging roles of social class and ethnicity. *Family Relations, 37,* 247–254.

Mezzich, J. E., Fabrega, H., & Kleinman, A. (1992). Cultural validity and DSM-IV. *Journal of Nervous and Mental Disease, 180,* 4.

Mezzich, J. E., Kleinman, A., Fabrega, H., Good, B., Johnson-Powell, G., Lin, K. M., Manson, S., & Parron, D. (1992). *Cultural proposals for DSM-IV.* Submitted to the DSM-IV Task Force by the Steering Committee, NIMH-Sponsored Group on Culture and Diagnosis.

Muñoz, R. F., Hollon, S. D., McGrath, E., Rehm, L. P., & VandenBos, G. R. (1994). On the AHCPR depression in primary care guidelines: Further considerations for practitioners. *American Psychologists, 49,* 42–61.

Myers, H. F., Echemendia, R. J., & Trimble, J. E. (1991). The need for training ethnic minority psychologists. In H. F. Myers, P. Wohlford, L. P. Guzman, & R. J. Echemendia (Eds.), *Ethnic minority perspectives on clinical training and services in psychology* (pp. 3–11), Washington, DC: American Psychological Association.

Payton, C. (1994). Implications of the 1992 ethics code for diverse groups. *Professional Psychology: Research and Practice, 25,* 317–320.

Ponterotto, J. G. (1987). Counseling Mexican Americans: A multimodel approach. *Journal of Counseling and Development, 65,* 308–312.

Puente, A. E., Blanch, E., Candland, D. K., Denmark, F. L., Lawman, C., Lutsky, N., Reid, P. T., & Schiavo, R. S. (1993). Toward a psychology of variance: Increasing the presence and understanding of ethnic minorities in psychology. In T. V. McGovern (Ed.), *Handbook for enhancing undergraduate education in psychology* (pp. 71–92), Washington, DC: American Psychological Association.

Rice, C. E. (1997). The scientist–practitioner split and the future of psychology. *American Psychologist, 57,* 1173–1181.

Richards, H., & Clements, C. (1993). Critique of APA Accreditation Criterion II. Cultural and individual differences. *Professional Psychology: Research and Practice, 24,* 123–126.

Ridley, C. R. (1985). Imperatives for ethnic and cultural relevance in psychology training programs. *Professional Psychology: Research and Practice, 16,* 611–622.

Rogler, L. H. (1989). The meaning of culturally sensitive research in mental health. *American Journal of Psychiatry, 146,* 296–303.

Rogler, L. H. (1993). Culturally sensitizing psychiatric diagnosis: A framework for research. *Journal of Nervous and Mental Disease, 181,* 401–408.

Rogler, L. H., & Cortes, D. E. (1993). Help-seeking pathways: A unifying concept in mental health care. *American Journal of Psychiatry, 150,* 554–561.

Rush, A. J. (1993). Clinical practice guidelines: Good news, bad news, or no news? *Archives of General Psychiatry, 50,* 483–490.

Rush, A. J., Trivedi, M. H., Schriger, D., & Petty, F. (1992). The development of clinical practice guidelines for the diagnosis and treatment of depression. *General Hospital Psychiatry, 230,* 230–236.

Schulberg, H. C., & Rush, A. J. (1994). Clinical practice guidelines for managing major depression in primary care practice: Implications for psychologists. *American Psychologists, 49,* 34–41.

Segall, M. H., Lonner, W. J., & Berry, J. W. (1998). Cross-cultural psychology as a scholarly discipline: On the flowering of culture in behavioral research. *American Psychologist, 53,* 1101–1110.

Sleek, S. (1998). Psychology's cultural competence, once "simplistic," now broadening. *APA Monitor, 29,* (12), 1, 27.

Sue, S. (1988). Psychotherapeutic services for ethnic minorities: Two decades of research findings. *American Psychologist, 43,* 301–308.

Sue, S., Arredondo, P., & McDavis, J. (1992). Multicultural counseling competencies and standards: A call to the profession. *Journal of Counseling and Development, 70,* 477–486.

Sue, S., Fujino, D.C., Hu, Li-tze, & Takeuchi, D. T. (1991). Community mental health services for ethnic minority groups: A test of the cultural responsiveness hypothesis. *Journal of Consulting and Clinical Psychology, 59,* 533–540.

Sue, S., Zane, N., & Young, K. (1994). Research on psychotherapy with culturally diverse populations. In A. Bergin & S. Garfield (Eds.), *Handbook of psychotherapy and behavior change* (4th ed., pp. 783–817). New York: Wiley.

Tomes, H. (1998). Diversity: Psychology's life depends upon it. *APA Monitor, 29,* (12) 28.

Wohl, J., & Aponte, J. F. (1995). Common themes and future prospects. In J. F. Aponte, R. Young Rivers, & J. Wohl (Eds.), *Psychological interventions and cultural diversity* (pp. 301–316). Boston: Allyn and Bacon.

Wohlford, P. (1992). Patterns of NIMH support of clinical training for ethnic minorities. *The Clinical Psychologist, 45,* 13–21.

Vega, W. A., & Murphy, J. W. (1990). *Culture and the restructuring of community mental health.* New York: Greenwood Press.

Yee, A. H., Fairchild, H. H., Weizmann, F., & Wyatt, G. E. (1993). Addressing psychology's problems with race. *American Psychologist, 48,* 1132–1140.

Zuckerman, M. (1990). Some dubious premises in research and theory on racial differences. *American Psychologist, 45,* 1297–1303.

NAME INDEX

SUBJECT INDEX